2001
CHILDREN'S WRITER'S & ILLUSTRATOR'S MARKET

800 EDITORS & ART DIRECTORS WHO BUY YOUR WRITING & ILLUSTRATIONS

EDITED BY
ALICE POPE

WRITER'S DIGEST BOOKS
CINCINNATI, OHIO

Editorial Director, Annuals Department: Barbara Kuroff
Managing Editor, Annuals Department: Douglas Hubbuch
Production Editor: Cindy Duesing
Writer's Digest Books websites: www.writersdigest.com, www.writersmarket.com

International Standard Serial Number 0897-9790
International Standard Book Number 1-58297-010-6

Cover illustration by Jim Starr

Attention Booksellers: This is an annual directory of F&W Publications. Return deadline for this edition is April 30, 2002.

Contents

© 1999 Paul Yalowitz

MARKETS

© Maryann Cocca-Leffler

Page 110

© 2000 Magination Press

Page 80

RESOURCES

© 1999 Travis Foster

Page 75

Key to Symbols & Abbreviations

N Indicates a listing new in this edition.

Indicates a Canadian listing.

Indicates a publisher produces educational material.

Indicates a book packager/producer.

✓ Indicates a company's contact information has changed since the 2000 edition.

A Indicates a publisher accepts agented submissions only.

Indicates an award-winning publisher.

• Indicates a comment from the editor of *Children's Writer's & Illustrator's Market*.

ms or **mss** Stands for manuscript or manuscripts.

SASE Refers to a self-addressed stamped envelope.

SAE Refers to a self-addressed envelope.

IRC Stands for International Reply Coupon. These are required with SAEs sent to markets in countries other than your own.

b&w Stands for black and white.

Important Listing Information

- Listings are based on questionnaires, phone calls and updated copy. They are not advertisements nor are markets reported here necessarily endorsed by the editor of this book.
- Information in the listings comes directly from the companies and is as accurate as possible, but situations may change and needs may fluctuate between the publication of this directory and the time you use it.
- *Children's Writer's & Illustrator's Market* reserves the right to exclude any listing that does not meet its requirements.

Complaint Procedure

If you feel you have not been treated fairly by a listing in *Children's Writer's & Illustrator's Market*, we advise you to take the following steps:

- First try to contact the listing. Sometimes one phone call or a letter can quickly clear up the matter.
- Document all your correspondence with the listing. When you write to us with a complaint, provide the details of your submission, the date of your first contact with the listing and the nature of your subsequent correspondence.
- We will enter your letter into our files and attempt to contact the listing.
- The number and severity of complaints will be considered in our decision whether or not to delete the listing from the next edition.

From the Editor

If you say the word *underpants* to kids, it's pretty much guaranteed they'll die laughing, or at least giggle a lot. *Underpants* might even give adults a little chuckle, if they're lucky.

Dav Pilkey's publisher recently sent me copies of a few of the author's epic novels featuring Captain Underpants, the latest called *Captain Underpants and the Perilous Plot of Professor Poopypants*. I laughed at the cover, delighted in that fact that my job brings me such treasures, and hung up a Captain Underpants poster in my office.

For fun, I decided to visit Amazon.com to see what readers thought of this book, the fourth in the Captain Underpants series. Of the twenty-one reviews posted on Amazon, this one was my favorite, by a reader from Atascadero, California:

I am 7 in 2nd grade and this book is soooooo cool! My new name is Pinky Girtlefanny. I like when Mr. Krupp said, "Lumpy Krupp? I don't want to be called Lumpy Krupp!" and then he noticed that his new name was Lumpy Pottybiscuits. Praise for Gidget Hamsterbrains!

I laughed out loud; I was intrigued. This seven-year-old spoke a strange and wonderful language. While I was still on the Internet, I got an e-mail message from my friend/roommate/co-worker, subject line: *Pinky Livertush*. Hmmmm. She seemed to know this language, too. Coincidentally, she was e-mailing instructions for figuring out your own official *Captain Underpants and the Perilous Plot of Professor Poopypants* name.

It gives me great joy when other adults have fun with children's books as I do. You've heard the expression *get in touch with your inner child*. Often I think my child is definitely outer, and occasionally I must get in touch with my inner grown-up—you know, those times when I have to work, meet deadlines, pay my bills, be responsible. Those things are a distraction from watching cartoons, coloring with crayons, swinging on swingsets, reading picture books. As adults, we can become so distanced from these simple pleasures.

As children's writers and illustrators, you must be more aware of these childlike happinesses. You spend time with kids, at home or in a classroom. Children are your audience and your muse, offering a wealth of story ideas. But as children's writers and illustrators you have an excuse not to just watch kids, but to interact with them—play puzzles on the floor, make goofy faces, watch *The Powerpuff Girls*, hang out at the mall, read, read, read. Maybe walk up to an unsuspecting kid and shout *underpants!* It cracks me up just thinking about it.

Above all, when you're in touch with that inner (or outer) child, use that childlike energy to write, draw, speak to the inner and outer children in all of us, and use this edition of *Children's Writer's & Illustrator's Market* to help get your work published. You may even consider using your Captain Underpants name as a pseudonym. (Be sure to read the interview with Captain Underpants creator Dav Pilkey on page 184.) And remember what the Captain says: *Tra-la-laaaa!*

© 2000 Dav Pilkey

Alice Pope (a.k.a. Stinky Hamstertush)
cwim@fwpubs.com

Just Getting Started? Some Quick Tips

If you're new to the world of children's publishing, buying *Children's Writer's & Illustrator's Market* may have been one of the first steps in your journey to publication. What follows is a list of suggestions and resources that can help make that journey a smooth and swift one:

1. Make the most of *Children's Writer's & Illustrator's Market*. Be sure to read How to Use This Book to Sell Your Work on page 4 for tips on reading the listings and using the indexes. Also be sure to take advantage of the articles and interviews in the book. The insights of the authors, illustrators, editors and agents we've interviewed will inform and inspire you.

2. Join the Society of Children's Books Writers and Illustrators. SCBWI, almost 12,000 members strong, is an organization for those interested in writing and illustrating for children from the beginner to the professional level. They offer members a slew of information and support through publications, a website, and a host of Regional Advisors overseeing chapters in almost every state in the U.S. and in several locations around the globe (including France, Canada, Japan and Australia). SCBWI puts on a number of conferences, workshops and events on the regional and national level (many listed in the Conferences & Workshops section of this book). For more information contact SCBWI, 8271 Beverly Blvd., Los Angeles CA 90048, (323)782-1010, or visit their website: www.scbwi.org.

3. Read newsletters. Newsletters, such as *Children's Book Insider*, *Children's Writer* and the SCBWI *Bulletin*, offer updates and new information about publishers on a timely basis and are relatively inexpensive. Many local chapters of SCBWI offer regional newsletters as well. (See Helpful Books & Publications on page 342 for contact information on the newsletters listed above and others. For information on regional SCBWI newsletters, visit www.scbwi.org and click on "publications.")

4. Read trade and review publications. Magazines like *Publishers Weekly* (which offers two special issues each year devoted to children's publishing available on newsstands), *The Horn Book*, *Riverbank Review* and *Booklinks* offer news, articles, reviews of newly-published titles and ads featuring upcoming and current releases. Referring to them will help you get a feel for what's happening in children's publishing.

5. Read guidelines. Most publishers and magazines offer writer's and artist's guidelines which provide detailed information on needs and submission requirements, and some magazines offer theme lists for upcoming issues. Many publishers and magazines state the availability of guidelines within their listings. Send a self-addressed, stamped envelope (SASE) to publishers who offer guidelines. You'll often find submission information on publishers' and magazines' websites. And while you're on the Web, visit www.writersdigest.com for a searchable database of about 1,500 guidelines.

6. Look at publishers' catalogs. Perusing publishers' catalogs can give you a feel for their line of books and help you decide where your work might fit in. Send for catalogs with a SASE if they are available (often stated within listings). Visit publishers' websites which often contain their full catalogs. You can also ask librarians to look at catalogs they have on hand. You can even search Amazon.com (www.amazon.com) by publisher and year. (Click on "book search" then "publisher, date" and plug in, for example, "Atheneum" under "publisher" and "2000" under year. You'll get a list of all the Atheneum titles published in 2000 which you can peruse.)

7. Visit bookstores. It's not only informative to spend time in bookstores—it's fun, too! Frequently visit the children's section of your local bookstore (whether a chain or an independent) to see the latest from a variety of publishers and the most current issues of children's magazines. Look for books in the genre you're writing or with illustrations similar in style to yours, and spend some time studying them. It's also wise to get to know your local booksellers—they can tell you what's new in the store and provide insight into what kids and adults are buying.

8. Read, read, read! While you're at that bookstore, pick up a few things, or keep a list of which books interest you and check them out of your library. Read and study the latest releases, the award winners and the classics. You'll learn from other writers, get ideas and get a feel for what's being published. Think about what works and doesn't work in a story. Pay attention to how plots are constructed and how characters are developed or the rhythm and pacing of picture book text. It's certainly enjoyable research!

9. Take advantage of Internet resources. There are innumerable sources of information available on the Internet about writing for children (and anything else you could possibly think of). It's also a great resource for getting (and staying) in touch with other writers and illustrators through listservs and e-mail, and can serve as a vehicle for self-promotion. (Visit some authors' and illustators' web pages for ideas. See Useful Online Resources on page 345 for a list of helpful websites.)

10. Consider attending a conference. If time and finances allow, attending a conference is a great way to meet peers and network with professionals in the field of children's publishing. As mentioned above, SCBWI offers conferences in various locations year round (see www.scbwi. org and click on "events" for a full calendar of conferences). General writers' conferences often offer specialized sessions just for those interested in children's writing. Many conferences offer optional manuscript and portfolio critiques as well, giving you a chance for feedback from seasoned professionals. See Great Expectations: Conferences Can Make a Difference, on page 67, for advice on getting the most from conference-going.

11. Network, network, network! Don't work in a vacuum. You can meet other writers and illustrators through a number of the things listed above—SCBWI, conferences, online. Attend local meetings for writers and illustrators whenever you can. Befriend other writers in your area (SCBWI offers members a roster broken down by state)—share guidelines, share subscriptions, be conference buddies and roommates, join a critique group or writing group, exchange information and offer support. Get online—sign on to listservs, post on message boards, visit chatrooms. (America Online offers them. Also, visit author Verla Kay's website for information on weekly workshops. See Helpful Internet Resources for more information.) Exchange addresses, phone numbers and e-mail addresses with writers or illustrators you meet at events. And at conferences don't be afraid to talk to people, ask strangers to join you for lunch, approach speakers and introduce yourself, chat in elevators and hallways. Remember, you're not alone.

12. Perfect your craft and don't submit until your work is its best. It's often been said that a writer should try to write every day. Great manuscripts don't happen overnight—there's time, research and revision involved. As you visit bookstores and study what others have written and illustrated, really step back and look at your own work and ask yourself—honestly—*How does my work measure up? Is it ready for editors or art directors to see?* If it's not, keep working. You may want to ask a writer's group for constructive comments, or get a professional manuscript or portfolio critique.

13. Be patient, learn from rejection and don't give up! Thousands of manuscripts land on editors' desks; thousands of illustration samples line art directors' file drawers. There are so many factors that come into play when evaluating submissions. Keep in mind that you might not hear back from publishers promptly. Persistence and patience are important qualities in writers and illustrators working for publication. Keep at it—it will come. It can take a while, but when you get that first book contract or first assignment, you'll know it was worth the wait. (Read First Books on page 70 for proof.)

How to Use This Book to Sell Your Work

As a writer, illustrator or photographer first picking up *Children's Writer's & Illustrator's Market*, you may not know quite how to start using the book. Your impulse may be to flip through the book and quickly make a mailing list, then submit to everyone in hopes that someone will take interest in your work. Well, there's more to it. Finding the right market takes time and research. The more you know about a company that interests you, the better chance you have of getting work accepted.

We've made your job a little easier by putting a wealth of information at your fingertips. Besides providing listings, this directory includes a number of tools to help you determine which markets are the best ones for your work. By using these tools, as well as researching on your own, you raise your odds of being published.

USING THE INDEXES

This book lists hundreds of potential buyers of freelance material. To learn which companies want the type of material you're interested in submitting, start with the indexes.

The Age-Level Index

Age groups are broken down into these categories in the Age-Level Index:
- **Picture books** or **picture-oriented material** are written and illustrated for preschoolers to 8-year-olds.
- **Young readers** are for 5- to 8-year-olds.
- **Middle readers** are for 9- to 11-year-olds.
- **Young adults** are for ages 12 and up.

Age breakdowns may vary slightly from publisher to publisher, but using them as general guidelines will help you target appropriate markets. For example, if you've written an article about trends in teen fashion, check the Magazines Age-Level Index under the Young Adult subheading. Using this list, you'll quickly find the listings for young adult magazines.

The Subject Index

But let's narrow the search further. Take your list of young adult magazines, turn to the Subject Index, and find the Fashion subheading. Then highlight the names that appear on both lists (Young Adult and Fashion). Now you have a smaller list of all the magazines that would be interested in your teen fashion article. Read through those listings and decide which ones sound best for your work.

Illustrators and photographers can use the Subject Index as well. If you specialize in painting animals, for instance, consider sending samples to book and magazine publishers listed under Animals and, perhaps, Nature/Environment. Illustrators can simply send general examples of their style (in the form of tearsheets or postcards) to art directors to keep on file. The indexes may be more helpful to artists sending manuscripts/illustration packages. Always read the listings for the potential markets to see the type of work art directors prefer and what type of samples they'll keep on file, and send for art or photo guidelines if they're available.

The Poetry Index

This index lists book publishers and magazines interested in submissions from poets. Always send for writer's guidelines from publishers and magazines that interest you.

The Photography Index

You'll find lists of book and magazine publishers, as well as greeting card, puzzle and game manufacturers, that buy photos from freelancers in the Photography Index. Copy the lists and read the listings for specific needs. Send for photo guidelines if they're offered.

USING THE LISTINGS

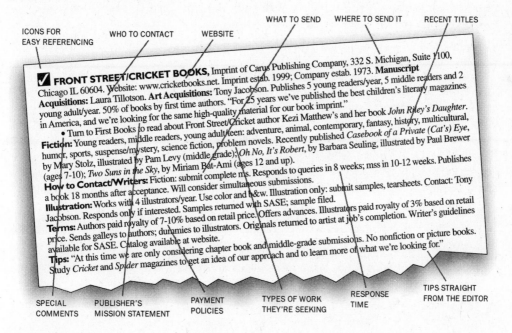

Many listings begin with one or more symbols. (Refer to the inside covers of the book for quick reference.) Here's what each icon stands for:

- **N** indicates a listing is new to this edition.
- ⊞ indicates a listing is a book packager or producer.
- 🗎 indicates a company publishes educational material.
- 🍁 indicates a listing is Canadian.
- ✔ indicates a change in contact information from last year's edition.
- **A** indicates a publisher only accepts submissions through agents.
- 🏆 indicates a company's publications have received awards recently.

In the Book Publishers section, you'll find contact names after **Manuscript Acquisitions** and **Art Acquisitions**. Contact names in Magazines follow boldface titles such as **Fiction Editor**, **Articles Editor** or **Art Director**. Following contact information in many of these listings are mission statements. Read these to get a general idea of the aim of certain publishers and magazines to help you decide whether to explore them further.

The subheadings under each listing contain more specific information about what a company needs. In Book Publishers and Magazines, for example, you'll find such things as age levels and subjects needed under the **Fiction** and **Nonfiction** subheads. Here's an example from a listing in the Book Publishers section:

Fiction: Picture books: adventure, animal, contemporary, fantasy, humor. Young readers: animal, contemporary, humor, sports, suspense/mystery. Middle readers: adventure, humor, sports. Young adults: humor, problem novels.

Also check the listings for information on how to submit your work and response time. In Book Publishers and Magazines, writers will find this information under the How to Contact/ Writers subhead:

How to Contact/Writers: Query with outline/synopsis and 2 sample chapters. Responds to queries in 6 weeks.

For information on submission procedures and formats, turn to Before Your First Sale on page 8.

Also look for information regarding payment and rights purchased. Some markets pay on acceptance, others on publication. Some pay a flat rate for manuscripts and artwork, others pay advances and royalties. Knowing how a market operates will keep you from being shocked when you discover your paycheck won't arrive until your manuscript is published—a year after it was accepted. This information is found under **Terms** in Book Publishers, Magazines and Play Publishers. Here's an example from the Magazines section:

Terms: Pays on acceptance. Buys first North American serial rights or reprint rights. Pays $50-100 for stories/articles. Pays illustrators $75-125 for b&w or color inside; $150-200 for color cover.

Under **Tips** you'll find special advice straight from an editor or art director about what their company wants or doesn't want, or other helpful advice:

Tips: "We are looking for picture books centered on a strong, fully-developed protaganist who grows or changes during the course of the story."

Additional information about specific markets in the form of comments from the editor of this book is set off by bullets (•) within listings:

• This publisher accepts only queries and manuscripts submitted by agents.

Many listings indicate whether submission guidelines are available. If a publisher you're interested in offers guidelines, send for them and read them. The same is true with catalogs. Sending for catalogs and seeing and reading about the books a publisher produces gives you a better idea whether your work would fit in. (You should also look at a few of the books in the catalog at a library or bookstore to get a feel for the publisher's material.) Note that a number of publishers offer guidelines and catalogs on their websites, and a searchable database of more than 1,500 writer's guidelines is available at www.writersdigest.com.

Especially for artists and photographers

Along with information for writers, listings provide information for photographers and illustrators. Illustrators will find numerous markets that maintain files of samples for possible future assignments. If you're both a writer and illustrator, look for markets that accept manuscript/ illustration packages. You'll find sample illustrations from various publishers sprinkled throughout the listings. These illustrations serve as examples of the kind of art these particular companies buy. Read the captions for additional information about the artwork and the market.

If you're a photographer, after consulting the Photography Index, read the information under the Photography subhead within listings to see what format buyers prefer. For example, some want 35mm color transparencies, others want black-and-white prints. Note the type of photos a buyer wants to purchase and the procedures for submitting. It's not uncommon for a market to want a résumé and promotional literature, as well as tearsheets from previous work. Listings also note whether model releases and/or captions are required.

Especially for young writers

If you're a parent, teacher or student, you may be interested in Young Writer's & Illustrator's Markets. The listings in this section encourage submissions from young writers and artists. Some may require a written statement from a teacher or parent noting the work is original. Also watch for age limits.

Young people should also check Contests & Awards for contests that accept work by young writers and artists. Some of the contests listed are especially for students; others accept both student and adult work. These listings contain the phrase **open to students** in bold. Some listings in Clubs & Organizations and Conferences & Workshops may also be of interest to students. Organizations and conferences which are open to or are especially for students also include **open to students.**

COMMON ABBREVIATIONS

Throughout the listings, the following abbreviations are used:
- **ms** or **mss** stands for manuscript or manuscripts.
- **SASE** refers to a self-addressed, stamped envelope.
- **SAE** refers to a self-addressed envelope.
- **IRC** stands for International Reply Coupon. These are required with SAEs sent to markets in countries other than your own.

Before Your First Sale

If you're just beginning to pursue your career as a children's book writer or illustrator, it's important to learn the proper procedures, formats, and protocol for the publishing industry. This article outlines the basics you need to know before you head to the post office with your submissions.

FINDING THE BEST MARKETS FOR YOUR WORK

Researching publishers well is a basic element of submitting your work successfully. Editors and art directors hate to receive inappropriate submissions—handling them wastes a lot of their time, not to mention your time and money, and they are the main reason some publishers have chosen not to accept material over the transom. By randomly sending out material without knowing a company's needs, you're sure to meet with rejection.

If you're interested in submitting to a particular magazine, write to request a sample copy, or see if it's available in your local library or bookstore. For a book publisher, obtain a book catalog and check a library or bookstore for titles produced by that publisher. Many publishers and magazines now have websites that include catalogs or sample articles (websites are given within the listings). Studying such materials carefully will better acquaint you with a publisher's or magazine's writing, illustration and photography styles and formats.

Most of the book publishers and magazines listed in this book (as well as some greeting card and paper product producers) offer some sort of writer's, artist's or photographer's guidelines for a self-addressed, stamped envelope (SASE). Guidelines are also often found on publishers' websites. It's important to read and study guidelines before submitting work. You'll get a better understanding of what a particular publisher wants. You may even decide, after reading the submission guidelines, that your work isn't right for a company you considered. For access to a searchable database of more than 1,500 publishers' guidelines, visit www.writersdigest.com.

SUBMITTING YOUR WORK

Throughout the listings you'll read requests for particular elements to include when contacting markets. Here are explanations of some of these important submission components.

Queries, cover letters and proposals

A query letter is a no-more-than-one-page, well-written piece meant to arouse an editor's interest in your work. Many query letters start with leads similar to those of actual manuscripts. In the rest of the letter, briefly outline the work you're proposing and include facts, anecdotes, interviews or other pertinent information that give the editor a feel for the manuscript's premise—entice her to want to know more. End your letter with a straightforward request to write (or submit) the work, and include information on its approximate length, date it could be completed, and whether accompanying photos or artwork are available.

In a query letter, think about presenting your book as a publisher's catalog would present it. Read through a good catalog and examine how the publishers give enticing summaries of their books in a spare amount of words. It's also important that query letters give editors a taste of your writing style. For more on the topic, and examples of successful queries, see Writing Effective Query Letters on page 22. For good advice and more samples of queries, cover letters and other correspondence, consult *How to Write Attention-Grabbing Query & Cover Letters*, by John Wood (Writer's Digest Books).

- **Query letters for nonfiction.** Queries are usually required when submitting nonfiction material to a publisher. The goal of a nonfiction query is to convince the editor your idea is perfect for her readership and that you're qualified to do the job. Note any previous writing experience and include published samples to prove your credentials, especially samples related to the subject matter you're querying about.

• **Query letters for fiction.** More and more, queries are being requested for fiction manuscripts. For a fiction query, explain the story's plot, main characters, conflict and resolution. Just as in nonfiction queries, make the editor eager to see more.

• **Cover letters for writers.** Some editors prefer to review complete manuscripts, especially for fiction. In such cases, the cover letter (which should be no longer than one page) serves as your introduction, establishes your credentials as a writer, and gives the editor an overview of the manuscript. If the editor asked for the manuscript because of a query, note this in your cover letter.

• **Cover letters for illustrators and photographers.** For an illustrator or photographer the cover letter serves as an introduction to the art director and establishes professional credentials when submitting samples. Explain what services you can provide as well as what type of follow-up contact you plan to make, if any.

• **Résumés.** Often writers, illustrators and photographers are asked to submit résumés with cover letters and samples. They can be created in a variety of formats, from a single page listing information, to color brochures featuring your work. Keep your resume brief, and focus on your achievements, including your clients and the work you've done for them, as well as your educational background and any awards you've received. Do not use the same résumé you'd use for a typical job application.

• **Book proposals.** Throughout the listings in the Book Publishers section, publishers refer to submitting a synopsis, outline and sample chapters. Depending on an editor's preference, some or all of these components, along with a cover letter, make up a book proposal.

A *synopsis* summarizes the book, covering the basic plot (including the ending). It should be easy to read and flow well.

An *outline* covers your book chapter by chapter and provides highlights of each. If you're developing an outline for fiction, include major characters, plots and subplots, and book length.

Sample chapters give a more comprehensive idea of your writing skill. Some editors may request the first two or three chapters to determine if she's interested in seeing the whole book.

Manuscript formats

When submitting a complete manuscript, follow some basic guidelines. In the upper-left corner of your title page, type your legal name (not pseudonym), address and phone number. In the upper-right corner, type the approximate word length. All material in the upper corners should be typed single-spaced. Then type the title (centered) almost halfway down that page, the word "by" two spaces under that, and your name or pseudonym two spaces under "by."

The first page should also include the title (centered) one-third of the way down. Two spaces under that type "by" and your name or pseudonym. To begin the body of your manuscript, drop down two double spaces and indent five spaces for each new paragraph. There should be one-inch margins around all sides of a full typewritten page. (Manuscripts with wide margins are more readable and easier to edit.)

Set your computer or typewriter on double-space for the manuscript body. From page two to the end of the manuscript, include your last name followed by a comma and the title (or key words of the title) in the upper-left corner. The page number should go in the top right corner. Drop down two double spaces to begin the body of each page. If you're submitting a novel, type each chapter title one-third of the way down the page. For more information on manuscript formats, read *Writer's Digest Guide to Manuscript Formats*, by Dian Buchman and Seli Groves, or *Manuscript Submissions*, by Scott Edelstein (both Writer's Digest Books).

Picture book formats

The majority of editors prefer to see complete manuscripts for picture books. When typing the text of a picture book, don't include page breaks and don't type each page of text on a new sheet of paper. And unless you are an illustrator, don't worry about supplying art. Editors will find their own illustrators for picture books. Most of the time, a writer and an illustrator who work on the same book never meet. The editor acts as a go-between and works with the writer and illustrator throughout the publishing process. *How to Write and Sell Children's Picture Books*, by Jean E. Karl (Writer's Digest Books), offers advice on preparing text and marketing your work.

If you're an illustrator who has written your own book, consider creating a dummy or story-board containing both art and text, then submit it along with your complete manuscript and sample pieces of final art (color photocopies or slides—never originals). Publishers interested in picture books specify in their listings what should be submitted. For tips on creating a dummy, refer to *How to Write and Illustrate Children's Books and Get Them Published*, edited by Treld Pelkey Bicknell and Felicity Trotman (North Light Books), or Frieda Gates's book, *How to Write, Illustrate, and Design Children's Books* (Lloyd-Simone Publishing Company).

Writers may also want to learn the art of dummy making to help them through their writing process with things like pacing, rhythm and length. For a great explanation and helpful hints, see *You Can Write Children's Books*, by Tracey E. Dils (Writer's Digest Books).

Mailing submissions

Your main concern when packaging material is to be sure it arrives undamaged. If your manuscript is less than six pages, simply fold it in thirds and send it in a #10 (business-size) envelope. For a SASE, either fold another #10 envelope in thirds or insert a #9 (reply) envelope which fits in a #10 neatly without folding.

Another option is folding your manuscript in half in a 6×9 envelope, with a #9 or #10 SASE enclosed. For larger manuscripts use a 9×12 envelope both for mailing the submission and as a SASE (which can be folded in half). Book manuscripts require sturdy packaging for mailing. Include a self-addressed mailing label and return postage.

If asked to send artwork and photographs, remember they require a bit more care in packaging to guarantee they arrive in good condition. Sandwich illustrations and photos between heavy cardboard that is slightly larger than the work. The cardboard can be secured by rubber bands or with tape. If you tape the cardboard together, check that the artwork doesn't stick to the tape. Be sure your name and address appear on the back of each piece of art or each photo in case the material becomes separated. For the packaging use either a manila envelope, foam-padded envelope, brown paper or a mailer lined with plastic air bubbles. Bind non-joined edges with reinforced mailing tape and affix a typed mailing label or clearly write your address.

Mailing material first class ensures quick delivery. Also, first-class mail is forwarded for one year if the addressee has moved, and can be returned if undeliverable. If you're concerned about your original material safely reaching its destination, consider other mailing options, such as UPS or certified mail. If material needs to reach your editor or art director quickly, use overnight delivery services.

Remember, companies outside your own country can't use your country's postage when returning a manuscript to you. When mailing a submission to another country, include a self-addressed envelope and International Reply Coupons or IRCs. (You'll see this term in many Canadian listings.) Your postmaster can tell you, based on a package's weight, the correct number of IRCs to include to ensure its return.

If it's not necessary for an editor to return your work (such as with photocopies) don't include return postage. You may want to track the status of your submission by enclosing a postage-paid reply postcard with options for the editor to check, such as "Yes, I am interested," "I'll keep the material on file," or "No, the material is not appropriate for my needs at this time."

Some writers, illustrators and photographers simply include a deadline date. If you don't hear from the editor or art director by the specified date, your manuscript, artwork or photos are automatically withdrawn from consideration. Because many publishing houses and companies are overstocked with material, a minimum deadline should be at least three months.

Unless requested, it's never a good idea to use a company's fax number or e-mail address to send manuscript submissions. This can disrupt a company's internal business.

Keeping submission records

It's important to keep track of the material you submit. When recording each submission, include the date it was sent, the business and contact name, and any enclosures (such as samples of writing, artwork or photography). You can create a record-keeping system of your own or look for record-keeping software in your area computer store.

Keep copies of articles or manuscripts you send together with related correspondence to make follow-up easier. When you sell rights to a manuscript, artwork or photos you can "close" your file on a particular submission by noting the date the material was accepted, what rights were purchased, the publication date and payment.

Often writers, illustrators and photographers fail to follow up on overdue responses. If you don't hear from a publisher within their stated response time, wait another month or so and follow up with a note asking about the status of your submission. Include the title or description, date sent, and a SASE for response. Ask the contact person when she anticipates making a decision. You may refresh the memory of a buyer who temporarily forgot about your submission. At the very least you'll receive a definite "no," and free yourself to send the material to another publisher.

Simultaneous submissions

If you opt for simultaneous (also called "multiple") submissions—sending the same material to several editors at the same time—be sure to inform each editor your work is being considered elsewhere. Many editors are reluctant to receive simultaneous submissions but understand that for hopeful freelancers, waiting several months for a response can be frustrating. In some cases, an editor may actually be more inclined to read your manuscript sooner if she knows it's being considered by another publisher. The Society of Children's Book Writers and Illustrators cautions writers against simultaneous submissions. The official recommendation of SCBWI is to submit to one publisher at a time, but wait only three months (note you'll do so in your cover letter). If no response is received, then send a note withdrawing your manuscript from consideration. SCBWI considers simultaneous submissions acceptable only if you have a manuscript dealing with a timely issue.

It's especially important to keep track of simultaneous submissions, so if you get an offer on a manuscript sent to more than one publisher, you can instruct other publishers to withdraw your work from consideration.

AGENTS AND REPS

Most children's writers, illustrators and photographers, especially those just beginning, are confused about whether to enlist the services of an agent or representative. The decision is strictly one that each writer, illustrator or photographer must make for herself. Some are confident with their own negotiation skills and believe acquiring an agent or rep is not in their best interest. Others feel uncomfortable in the business arena or are not willing to sacrifice valuable creative time for marketing.

About half of children's publishers accept unagented work, so it's possible to break into children's publishing without an agent. Some agents avoid working with children's books because traditionally low advances and trickling royalty payments over long periods of time make children's books less lucrative. Writers targeting magazine markets don't need the services of an agent. In fact, it's practically impossible to find an agent interested in marketing articles and short stories—there simply isn't enough financial incentive.

One benefit of having an agent, though, is it may speed up the process of getting your work reviewed, especially by publishers who don't accept unagented submissions. If an agent has a good reputation and submits your manuscript to an editor, that manuscript may actually bypass the first-read stage (which is done by editorial assistants and junior editors) and end up on the editor's desk sooner.

When agreeing to have a reputable agent represent you, remember that she should be familiar with the needs of the current market and evaluate your manuscript/artwork/photos accordingly. She should also determine the quality of your piece and whether it is saleable. When your manuscript sells, your agent should negotiate a favorable contract and clear up any questions you have about payments.

Keep in mind that however reputable the agent or rep is, she has limitations. Representation does not guarantee sale of your work. It just means an agent or rep sees potential in your writing, art or photos. Though an agent or rep may offer criticism or advice on how to improve your work, she cannot make you a better writer, artist or photographer.

Literary agents typically charge a 15 percent commission from the sale of writing; art and photo representatives usually charge a 25 to 30 percent commission. Such fees are taken from advances and royalty earnings. If your agent sells foreign rights to your work, she will deduct a higher percentage because she will most likely be dealing with an overseas agent with whom she must split the fee.

Be advised that not every agent is open to representing a writer, artist or photographer who lacks an established track record. Just as when approaching a publisher, the manuscript, artwork or photos, and query or cover letter you submit to a potential agent must be attractive and professional looking. Your first impression must be as an organized, articulate person.

For listings of agents and reps, turn to the Agents & Art Reps section. Also refer to *Guide to Literary Agents* for listings of agents; for listings of art reps, consult *Artist's & Graphic Designer's Market*; and for photo reps, see *Photographer's Market* (all Writer's Digest Books).

The Business of Writing & Illustrating

A career in children's publishing involves more than just writing skills or artistic talent. Successful authors and illustrators must be able to hold their own in negotiations, keep records, understand contract language, grasp copyright law, pay taxes and take care of a number of other business concerns. Although agents and reps, accountants and lawyers, and writers' organizations offer help in sorting out such business issues, it's wise to have a basic understanding of them going in. This article offers just that—basic information. For a more in-depth look at the subjects covered here, check your library or bookstore for books and magazines to help you, some of which are mentioned. We also tell you how to get information on issues like taxes and copyright from the federal government.

CONTRACTS & NEGOTIATION

Before you see your work in print or begin working with an editor or art director on a project, there is negotiation. And whether negotiating a book contract, a magazine article assignment, or an illustration or photo assignment, there are a few things to keep in mind. First, if you find any clauses vague or confusing in a contract, get legal advice. The time and money invested in counseling up front could protect you from problems later. If you have an agent or rep, she will review any contract.

A contract is an agreement between two or more parties that specifies the fees to be paid, services rendered, deadlines, rights purchased and, for artists and photographers, whether original work is returned. Most companies have standard contracts for writers, illustrators and photographers. The specifics (such as royalty rates, advances, delivery dates, etc.) are typed in after negotiations.

Though it's okay to conduct negotiations over the phone, get a written contract once both parties have agreed on terms. Never depend on oral stipulations; written contracts protect both parties from misunderstandings. Watch for clauses that may not be in your best interest, such as "work-for-hire." When you do work-for-hire, you give up all rights to your creations.

Some reputable children's magazines, such as *Highlights for Children*, buy all rights, and many writers and illustrators believe it's worth the concession in order to break into the field. However, once you become more established in the field, it's in your best interest to keep rights to your work. (Note: magazines such as *Highlights* may return rights after a specified time period, so ask about this possibility when negotiating.)

When negotiating a book deal, find out whether your contract contains an option clause. This clause requires the author to give the publisher a first look at her next work before offering it to other publishers. Though it's editorial etiquette to give the publisher the first chance at publishing your next work, be wary of statements in the contract that could trap you. Don't allow the publisher to consider the next project for more than 30 days and be specific about what type of work should actually be considered "next work." (For example, if the book under contract is a young adult novel, specify that the publisher will receive an exclusive look at only your next young adult novel.)

For more tips on contracts, Society of Children's Book Writers and Illustrators members can find information in *The SCBWI Publications Guide to Writing and Illustrating for Children* (chapter 13: Answers to Some Questions About Contracts). Contact SCBWI at 8271 Beverly Blvd., Los Angeles CA 90048, (323)782-1010, or visit their website: www.scbwi.org. Additional contract tips are available on The Authors Guild website, www.authorsguild.org. (Members of the guild can receive a 75-point contract review from the guild's legal staff.) See the website for membership information and application form, or contact The Authors Guild at 330 W. 42nd St., 29th Floor, New York NY 10036, (212)563-5904. Fax: (212)564-5363. E-mail: staff@author sguild.org. Website: www.authorsguild.org.

Book publishers' payment methods

Book publishers pay authors and artists in royalties, a percentage of either the wholesale or retail price of each book sold. From large publishing houses, the author usually receives an advance issued against future royalties before the book is published. Half of the advance amount is issued upon signing the book contract; the other half is issued when the book is finished. For illustrations, one-third of the advance should be collected upon signing the contract; one-third upon delivery of sketches; and one-third upon delivery of finished art.

After your book has sold enough copies to earn back your advance, you'll start to get royalty checks. Some publishers hold a reserve against returns, which means a percentage of royalties is held back in case books are returned from bookstores. If you have a reserve clause in your contract, find out the exact percentage of total sales that will be withheld and the time period the publisher will hold this money. You should be reimbursed this amount after a reasonable time period, such as a year. Royalty percentages vary with each publisher, but there are standard ranges.

Book publishers' rates

According to the latest figures from the Society of Children's Book Writers and Illustrators, first-time picture book authors can expect advances of $2,000-3,000; first-time picture book illustrators' advances range from $5,000-7,000; text and illustration packages for first-timers can score $6,000-8,000. Rates go up for subsequent books: $3,500-5,000 for picture book text; $7,000-10,000 for picture book illustration; $8,000-10,000 for text and illustration. Experienced authors can expect higher advances. Royalties for picture books are generally about five percent (split between the author and illustrator) but can go as high as ten percent. Those who both write and illustrate a book, of course, receive the full royalty.

Advances for hardcover novels and nonfiction can fetch authors advances of $4,000-6,000 and 10 percent royalties; paperbacks bring in slightly lower advances of $3,000-5,000 and royalties of 6-8 percent.

As you might expect, advance and royalty figures vary from house to house and are affected by the time of year, the state of the economy and other factors. Some smaller houses may not even pay royalties, just flat fees. Educational houses may not offer advances or offer smaller amounts. Religious publishers tend to offer smaller advances than trade publishers. First-time writers and illustrators generally start on the low end of the scale, while established and high-profile writers are paid more.

Pay rates for magazines

For writers, fee structures for magazines are based on a per-word rate or range for a specific article length. Artists and photographers have a few more variables to contend with before contracting their services.

Payment for illustrations and photos can be set by such factors as whether the piece(s) will be black and white or four-color, how many are to be purchased, where the work appears (cover or inside), circulation, and the artist's or photographer's prior experience.

Remaindering

When a book goes out of print, a publisher will sell any existing copies to a wholesaler who, in turn, sells the copies to stores at a discount When the books are "remaindered" to a wholesaler, they are usually sold at a price just above the cost of printing. When negotiating a contract with

Advice on contract issues from an intellectual property attorney

When Ivan Hoffman graduated from UCLA in 1965 with a major in English, he knew he wasn't interested in accounting, and he didn't like blood. That left law school. But law school turned out to be the right choice because afterwards, he had what he calls "a great run for twenty-two years" practicing law in the record business. And although it was called "the record business," he was dealing with copyrights, trademarks, and licensing. Since 1996 he has focused on intellectual property and Internet law for authors, publishers, and website designers and owners.

How does a writer decide whether an agent or an attorney should negotiate a book contract?

Agents make contacts and they know publishers. That's a primary asset of having an agent. And an agent often negotiates the broad strokes of a deal—the advance, the royalties—but the contract is written by publishers to protect publishers' interests. There's esoterica in any contract, and the broad strokes are often illusory because they can't really guarantee how much money you'll put in your pocket. The reserves, for example—the amount held back from each royalty statement to cover potential returns—are often not included in the discussion between the agent and publisher but are as important as the base royalty rate.

So there's a limit to what you can expect an agent to achieve. An agent may strike the deal or improve the deal, but the deal is what's going to be written on paper, and an attorney should look at that piece of paper.

Do you think publishers are antagonistic to writers?

I've been practicing law for twenty-six years, and I wish I could say the buyer sees us as one big family. It simply ain't so. There may be the pretense of that, but when the contract comes through, it is clearly a zero-sum game. If there's a dollar earned on a book and the publisher gets sixty cents, then the author gets forty cents. There's no way to make everything fair. There are only so many pieces of the pie available, and it is almost always going to be "us" versus "them." It has to be us versus them because this is a capitalistic system and it behooves each party to be adequately informed in his or her exercise of personal responsibility. An author should not go into contract negotiation thinking, "We're all one happy family." Especially if you're dealing with public entertainment companies, publishers can't be giving away the store. They have shareholders. An author ought to approach negotiation with the attitude that "this is business, and I as an author need to take care of myself."

Is copyright registration necessary for an unpublished manuscript?

It's not necessary, but I recommend it. A manuscript is copyrighted from the moment of creation and fixation in a tangible medium of expression, but once you have registered a copyright, the rights change dramatically. If someone later infringes on your copyright, you don't have to prove that you've been damaged. You can get a fixed amount per act of infringement and are entitled to attorney's fees in the event of litigation. And if a publisher subsequently accepts your manuscript—and you remain the copyright proprietor—you can re-register the manuscript as a published book when it comes out.

Does a contract have to include an advance in order to be legal?
No. A contract is an offer and acceptance supported by "consideration." Consideration is something, and "something" is the operative word here, that passes from one person to another. Consideration is essential because it's evidence of a change in position of one person or both. One person says, "I will publish your book if you give me the manuscript."

The other person gives the manuscript, and the first person publishes it. The two have changed positions. That's a valid contract.

Is there an ideal electronic rights clause in book contracts?
About four years ago, electronic rights clauses simply said, "Author grants Publisher electronic rights." That's not even remotely sufficient today. For example, there are downloadable rights, e-books rights, CD rights, print-on-demand rights, and unless you intend to transfer each and every one of those rights to the publisher, you ought to define what the term "electronic" means. Does it mean the right to turn the book into an e-book? To put it on a DVD as part of a compilation? To add it to your website but not to my website? What are we talking about?

The law refers to copyright as a "bundle of rights." That bundle grows every day. Before, e-rights were not in the bundle, and now they're in the bundle. You can carve up those rights in any way you like. There's no limit to the imagination and how to structure a deal.

Are some clauses nonnegotiable?
You will hear publishers say, "We don't do that for anybody." But in the one instance where you are in a powerful position, "We don't do that for anyone" becomes: "We don't do that for anyone else." The answer is that everything is negotiable, but you have to have the skills to know what to ask for. And the client has to have the clout. If the client is a first-time author and has a manuscript only of marginal interest, you have no leverage.

But in my experience, authors in general don't want to ask. They're afraid the publisher will pass. You run the risk they will pass, but if what you want isn't outrageous, the answer is often, "This is the deal, take it or leave it." So you decide if you want to take it. I have to tell you that when the publisher says, "This is the deal, it's standard, just accept it," my gut reaction is, "Wait a second. This is not lima beans. My client expects to be treated as an individual. You can pass, but don't tell me it's standard." I feel that if authors had enough dignity, they would make better deals for themselves.

Can an author negotiate a contract over the phone?
If you negotiate over the phone, afterwards you send an e-mail and say, "Confirming our conversation of Tuesday, this is what we agreed to." The e-mail doesn't form a contract, but it does clarify the conversation. This is my training—every time I have a conversation with a publisher, it's an immediate e-mail afterwards: "You said this, I said that. We agreed to this." People often don't hear the same thing. They don't understand things the same way. With

follow-up e-mail, you have a piece of paper that says, "This is what we talked about." If there's a disagreement, then you come back with, "No I didn't say that." We used to see confirming letters. Now it's confirming e-mails.

What's the most frequent question writers ask you?
"Can you get me an agent?"

Can you?
No.

Why did you take five years off from practicing law?
When I retired in 1990 to write my own books, I never thought I would practice law again. But when I discovered the Internet, it re-energized me, and all my creative juices came back. It's the same body of law, but in a brand new world that makes you pay attention every day because it changes minute by minute. Also, it's conceptual law. I'm not selling shoes. These are the products of the mind, and as a result, there are no boundaries to what I do here. There's only so much you can do with shoes, but a book becomes a movie, a website, a school lunch pail—and all that charges me up.
   —*Anna Olswanger*

a publisher you may want to discuss the possibility of purchasing the remaindered copies before they are sold to a wholesaler, then you can market the copies you purchased and still make a profit.

KNOW YOUR RIGHTS

A copyright is a form of protection provided to creators of original works, published or unpublished. In general, copyright protection ensures the writer, illustrator or photographer the power to decide how her work is used and allows her to receive payment for each use.

Essentially, copyright also encourages the creation of new works by guaranteeing the creator power to sell rights to the work in the marketplace. The copyright holder can print, reprint or copy her work; sell or distribute copies of her work; or prepare derivative works such as plays, collages or recordings. The Copyright Law is designed to protect work (created on or after January 1, 1978) for her lifetime plus 50 years.

If you collaborate with someone else on a written or artistic project, the copyright will last for the lifetime of the last survivor plus 50 years. The creators' heirs may hold a copyright for an additional 50 years. After that, the work becomes public domain. Works created anonymously or under a pseudonym are protected for 100 years, or 75 years after publication. Under work-for-hire agreements, you relinquish your copyright to your "employer."

Copyright notice and registration

Some feel a copyright notice should be included on all work, registered or not. Others feel it is not necessary and a copyright notice will only confuse publishers about whether the material is registered (acquiring rights to previously registered material is a more complicated process).

Although it's not necessary to include a copyright notice on unregistered work, if you don't feel your work is safe without the notice, it is your right to include one. Including a copyright notice—© (year of work, your name)—should help safeguard against plagiarism.

Registration is a legal formality intended to make copyright public record, and can help you win more money in a court case. By registering work within three months of publication or before an infringement occurs, you are eligible to collect statutory damages and attorney's fees. If you register later than three months after publication, you will qualify only for actual damages and profits.

Ideas and concepts are not copyrightable, only expressions of those ideas and concepts. A character type or basic plot outline, for example, is not subject to a copyright infringement lawsuit. Also, titles, names, short phrases or slogans, and lists of contents are not subject to copyright protection, though titles and names may be protected through the Trademark Office.

You can register a group of articles, illustrations or photos if it meets these criteria:

- the group is assembled in order, such as in a notebook;
- the works bear a single title, such as "Works by (your name)";
- it is the work of one writer, artist or photographer;
- the material is the subject of a single claim to copyright.

It's a publisher's responsibility to register your book for copyright. If you've previously registered the same material, you must inform your editor and supply the previous copyright information, otherwise, the publisher can't register the book in its published form.

For more information about the proper way to register works, contact the Copyright Office, Public Information Office, (202)707-3000. The forms available are TX for writing (books, articles, etc.); VA for pictures (photographs, illustrations); and PA for plays and music. (To order copyright forms by phone, call (202)707-9100.) For information about how to use the copyright forms, request a copy of Circular I on Copyright Basics. All of the forms and circulars are free. Send the completed registration form along with the stated fee and a copy of the work to the Copyright Office.

For specific answers to questions about copyright (but not legal advice), call the Copyright Public Information Office at (202)707-3000 weekdays between 8:30 a.m. and 5 p.m. EST. Forms can also be downloaded from the Library of Congress website: http://lcweb.loc.gov/copyright. The site also includes a list of frequently asked questions, tips on filling out forms, general copyright information, and links to other sites related to copyright issues. For members of SCBWI, information about copyrights and the law is available in *The SCBWI Publications Guide to Writing and Illustrating for Children* (chapter 6: Copyright Facts for Writers).

The rights publishers buy

The copyright law specifies that a writer, illustrator or photographer generally sells one-time rights to her work unless she and the buyer agree otherwise in writing. Many publications will want more exclusive rights to your work than just one-time usage; some will even require you to sell all rights. Be sure you are monetarily compensated for the additional rights you relinquish. If you must give up all rights to a work, carefully consider the price you're being offered to determine whether you'll be compensated for the loss of other potential sales.

Writers who only give up limited rights to their work can then sell reprint rights to other publications, foreign rights to international publications, or even movie rights, should the opportunity arise. Artists and photographers can sell their work to other markets such as paper product companies who may use an image on a calendar, greeting card or mug. Illustrators and photographers may even sell original work after it has been published. And there are now galleries throughout the U.S. that display and sell the original work of children's illustrators.

Rights acquired through the sale of a book manuscript are explained in each publisher's contract. Take time to read relevant clauses to be sure you understand what rights each contract is specifying before signing. Be sure your contract contains a clause allowing all rights to revert back to you in the event the publisher goes out of business. (You may even want to have the contract reviewed by an agent or an attorney specializing in publishing law.)

The following are the rights you'll most often sell to publishers, periodicals and producers in the marketplace:

First rights. The buyer purchases the rights to use the work for the first time in any medium.

All other rights remain with the creator. When material is excerpted from a soon-to-be-published book for use in a newspaper or periodical, first serial rights are also purchased.

One-time rights. The buyer has no guarantee that she is the first to use a piece. One-time permission to run written work, illustrations or photos is acquired, then the rights revert back to the creator.

First North American serial rights. This is similar to first rights, except that companies who distribute both in the U.S. and Canada will stipulate these rights to ensure that another North American company won't come out with simultaneous usage of the same work.

Second serial (reprint) rights. In this case newspapers and magazines are granted the right to reproduce a work that has already appeared in another publication. These rights are also purchased by a newspaper or magazine editor who wants to publish part of a book after the book has been published. The proceeds from reprint rights for a book are often split evenly between the author and his publishing company.

Simultaneous rights. More than one publication buys one-time rights to the same work at the same time. Use of such rights occurs among magazines with circulations that don't overlap, such as many religious publications.

All rights. Just as it sounds, the writer, illustrator or photographer relinquishes all rights to a piece—she no longer has any say in who acquires rights to use it. All rights are purchased by publishers who pay premium usage fees, have an exclusive format, or have other book or magazine interests from which the purchased work can generate more mileage. If a company insists on acquiring all rights to your work, see if you can negotiate for the rights to revert back to you after a reasonable period of time. If they agree to such a proposal, get it in writing.

Note: Writers, illustrators and photographers should be wary of "work-for-hire" arrangements. If you sign an agreement stipulating that your work will be done as work-for-hire, you will not control the copyrights of the completed work—the company that hired you will be the copyright owner.

Foreign serial rights. Be sure before you market to foreign publications that you have sold only North American—not worldwide—serial rights to previous markets. If so, you are free to market to publications that may be interested in material that's appeared in a North American-based periodical.

Syndication rights. This is a division of serial rights. For example, if a syndicate prints portions of a book in installments in its newspapers, it would be syndicating second serial rights. The syndicate would receive a commission and leave the remainder to be split between the author and publisher.

Subsidiary rights. These include serial rights, dramatic rights, book club rights or translation rights. The contract should specify what percentage of profits from sales of these rights go to the author and publisher.

Dramatic, television and motion picture rights. During a specified time the interested party tries to sell a story to a producer or director. Many times options are renewed because the selling process can be lengthy.

Display rights or electronic publishing rights. They're also known as "Data, Storage and Retrieval." Usually listed under subsidiary rights, the marketing of electronic rights in this era of rapidly expanding capabilities and markets for electronic material can be tricky. Display rights can cover text or images to be used in a CD-ROM or online, or may cover use of material in formats not even fully developed yet. If a display rights clause is listed in your contract, try to negotiate its elimination. Otherwise, be sure to pin down which electronic rights are being purchased. Demand the clause be restricted to things designed to be read only. By doing this, you maintain your rights to use your work for things such as games and interactive software.

RUNNING YOUR BUSINESS

An important part of being a freelance writer, illustrator or photographer is running your freelance business. It's imperative to maintain accurate business records to determine if you're making a profit as a freelancer. Keeping correct, organized records will also make your life easier as you approach tax time.

When setting up your system, begin by keeping a bank account and ledger for your business finances apart from your personal finances. Also, if writing, illustration or photography is secondary to another freelance career, keep separate business records for each.

You will likely accumulate some business expenses before showing any profit when you start out as a freelancer. To substantiate your income and expenses to the IRS, keep all invoices, cash receipts, sales slips, bank statements, canceled checks and receipts related to travel expenses and entertaining clients. For entertainment expenditures, record the date, place and purpose of the business meeting as well as gas mileage. Keep records for all purchases, big and small—don't take the small purchases for granted; they can add up to a substantial amount. File all receipts in chronological order. Maintaining a separate file for each month simplifies retrieving records at the end of the year.

Record keeping

When setting up a single-entry bookkeeping system, record income and expenses separately. Use some of the subheads that appear on Schedule C (the form used for recording income from a business) of the 1040 tax form so you can easily transfer information onto the tax form when filing your return. In your ledger include a description of each transaction—the date, source of income (or debts from business purchases), description of what was purchased or sold, the amount of the transaction, and whether payment was by cash, check or credit card.

Don't wait until January 1 to start keeping records. The moment you first make a business-related purchase or sell an article, book manuscript, illustration or photo, begin tracking your profits and losses. If you keep records from January 1 to December 31, you're using a calendar-year accounting period. Any other accounting period is called a fiscal year.

There are two types of accounting methods you can choose from—the cash method and the accrual method. The cash method is used more often: you record income when it is received and expenses when they're disbursed.

Using the accrual method, you report income at the time you earn it rather than when it's actually received. Similarly, expenses are recorded at the time they're incurred rather than when you actually pay them. If you choose this method, keep separate records for "accounts receivable" and "accounts payable."

Satisfying the IRS

To successfully—and legally—work as a freelancer, you must know what income you should report and what deductions you can claim. But before you can do that, you must prove to the IRS you're in business to make a profit, that your writing, illustration or photography is not merely a hobby.

The Tax Reform Act of 1986 says you should show a profit for three years out of a five-year period to attain professional status. The IRS considers these factors as proof of your professionalism:

- accurate financial records;
- a business bank account separate from your personal account;
- proven time devoted to your profession;
- whether it's your main or secondary source of income;
- your history of profits and losses;
- the amount of training you have invested in your field;
- your expertise.

If your business is unincorporated, you'll fill out tax information on Schedule C of Form 1040. If you're unsure of what deductions you can take, request the IRS publication containing this information. Under the Tax Reform Act, only 30 percent of business meals, entertainment and related tips, and parking charges are deductible. Other deductible expenses allowed on Schedule C include: car expenses for business-related trips; professional courses and seminars; depreciation of office equipment, such as a computer; dues and publications; and miscellaneous expenses, such as postage used for business needs.

If you're working out of a home office, a portion of your mortgage interest (or rent), related utilities, property taxes, repair costs and depreciation may he deducted as business expenses—under special circumstances. To learn more about the possibility of home office deductions, consult IRS Publication 587, Business Use of Your Home

The method of paying taxes on income not subject to withholding is called "estimated tax" for individuals. If you expect to owe more than $500 at year's end and if the total amount of income tax that will be withheld during the year will be less than 90% of the tax shown on the current year's return, you'll generally make estimated tax payments. Estimated tax payments are made in four equal installments due on April 15, June 15, September 15 and January 15 (assuming you're a calendar-year taxpayer). For more information, request Publication 533, Self-Employment Tax.

The Internal Revenue Service's website (www.irs.ustreas.gov/) offers tips and instant access to IRS forms and publications.

Social Security tax

Depending on your net income as a freelancer, you may be liable for a Social Security tax. This is a tax designed for those who don't have Social Security withheld from their paychecks. You're liable if your net income is $400 or more per year. Net income is the difference between your income and allowable business deductions. Request Schedule SE, Computation of Social Security Self-Employment Tax, if you qualify.

If completing your income tax return proves to be too complex, consider hiring an accountant (the fee is a deductible business expense) or contact the IRS for assistance (look in the White Pages under U.S. Government—Internal Revenue Service or check their website, www.irs.ustreas.gov/). In addition to numerous publications to instruct you in various facets of preparing a tax return, the IRS also has walk-in centers in some cities.

Insurance

As a self-employed professional be aware of what health and business insurance coverage is available to you. Unless you're a Canadian who is covered by national health insurance or a full-time freelancer covered by your spouse's policy, health insurance will no doubt be one of your biggest expenses. Under the terms of a 1985 government act (COBRA), if you leave a job with health benefits, you're entitled to continue that coverage for up to 18 months—you pay 100 percent of the premium and sometimes a small administration fee. Eventually, you must search for your own health plan. You may also need disability and life insurance. Disability insurance is offered through many private insurance companies and state governments. This insurance pays a monthly fee that covers living and business expenses during periods of long-term recuperation from a health problem. The amount of money paid is based on the recipient's annual earnings.

Before contacting any insurance representative, talk to other writers, illustrators or photographers to learn which insurance companies they recommend. If you belong to a writers' or artists' organization, ask the organization if it offers insurance coverage for professionals. (SCBWI has a plan available. Look through the Clubs & Organizations section for other groups that may offer coverage.) Group coverage may be more affordable and provide more comprehensive coverage than an individual policy.

Writing Effective Query Letters

BY KARMA WILSON

What can evoke the interest of the world's toughest editor? What can break down the dreaded "no unsolicited manuscripts" barrier? What can leap over staggering slushpiles in a single page? A query letter. But not just any query letter, only . . . The Super Query! Don't feel too intimidated. Writing a super query isn't as hard as you might imagine.

Read on for a step-by-step walk through on writing query letters that includes advice from three of today's leading editors: Emma Dryden, senior editor of Margaret K. McElderry Books; Melanie Cecka, editor at Viking Children's Books; and Barbara Stretchberry, managing editor of *American Girl* magazine.

No matter what genre you write—fiction, nonfiction, magazine articles, or novels, chances are you'll have to write query letters. And if you want your manuscripts requested by editors, you *must* write them well. If you're ready to correspond with an editor, you've already struggled to learn the basic components of a good story. Query letters have many parallels with good stories. They must say much with few words. They must grab your audience (editors!). And they must have a beginning, middle and end. Let's start at the beginning.

THE NAME GAME

The first thing you'll write on your query letter—the editor's name—can make or break it. If you get that wrong, chances are the letter you labored over will be filed under "R," for rejection. The first rule is to never address a query to a vague entity, such as "Dear Editing Department." Always address your letter to a specific editor or the acquisitions editor.

The second rule is to make certain you have the editor's name correct! Cecka, editor at Viking Children's Books, warns, "Never, under any circumstances, put another editor's name on a manuscript mailed to me. It may be an innocent mistake, but it also qualifies for instant rejection."

No problem, right? You have the current edition of *Children's Writer's & Illustrator's Market* in your hot little hands! You'll just look up the editor's name there. Think again. Though *Children's Writer's & Illustrator's Market* works hard to provide readers with the most up-to-date publisher guidelines and information, editors tend to move from house to house faster than you can say "form rejection." A quick call to the publishing house (numbers are listed in *Children's Writer's & Illustrator's Market*) is well worth the small long distance charge. Just ask the receptionist if the editor in question is still on staff, in the same position. While you're on the phone, inquire if the publisher is accepting queries, as policies tend to change as often as editors do—no sense in wasting good postage. A little research goes a long way. Once you've addressed your letter, you can start your first paragraph.

KARMA WILSON *is a freelance writer and children's author. Her first picture book* Bear Snores On, *illustrated by Jane Chapman, will be a fall, 2001 release from Margaret K. McElderry Books. Among her other upcoming titles are* Moose Tracks, Frog in a Log in the Middle of a Bog, Whopper Cake *(all McElderry) and* Sakes Alive! A Cattle Drive *(Little, Brown). Wilson lives in Bonners Ferry, Idaho with her husband and three young children.*

THE HOOK

The first paragraph is generally the most difficult to write. You must sum up your manuscript in one or two sentences—and make it sound not only interesting, but irresistible. This is your "hook" or your "sound-bite."

The best examples of sound-bites are in publishers' catalogs. Publishers try to "hook" book buyers in the same way writers try to hook editors. Studying publishers' catalogs is one way to learn what editors look for in a query. If you're querying a magazine, read current issues. Most have a page devoted to what's coming up in future editions which contains excellent examples of hooks for magazine articles and stories.

If you are connected to the Internet, you have an invaluable resource for studying good "hooks." Go to book sellers' websites like Amazon.com (www.amazon.com) or Barnes & Noble Online (www.bn.com), and look up children's books. (You can search for specific titles or search by publisher name and year.) For each book there is a synopsis provided by the publisher. They are usually no more than a small paragraph and describe the book's theme and story line succinctly. Study these carefully, then consider your own manuscript. Imagine your manuscript has been accepted (this should be second nature to you). What sound-bite would the publishers use to sell your book?

Remember, no matter what publishing house or magazine you are querying, editors appreciate a synopsis that is short and to the point. Dryden, senior editor of McElderry Books, explains, "A query letter should sell me the book in a very brief amount of time and space."

Stretchberry, managing editor of *American Girl* magazine says, "The most important factor in receiving a query is that I want to know quickly what the idea is. Writers who do not present their ideas in a clear, brief way make it harder for me to understand just what I should be getting excited about." So don't meander. Jump into your query with both feet—and be quick about it.

WHYS AND HOWS

Now that you've reeled the editor in with your zingy first paragraph, use your second paragraph to explain why you are qualified to write this story or article. If it is a nonfiction article you're pitching, list your research sources and any interviews you have conducted. If it's a novel or picture book, give some insight into why you think your story needs to be read by today's readers.

Dryden says, "If at all possible, I like a writer to do some market research and explain to me what niche their manuscript can fill." Cecka expresses similar thoughts, "I think it's always important for an author to keep up on market trends, to know what's selling and what's not, and to recognize potentially untapped areas in children's literature and why their writing may work well there."

So ask yourself some tough questions. What niche *does* your book fill? Why should a publisher invest money in you and in your story? How does your book or article stand apart from others already on the market? You'll need firm answers to these questions before writing a query. Study the market to make sure your manuscript is unique and is suited to the publisher or magazine you are targeting.

Stretchberry explains the importance of good market research. "By not reading and understanding the content of *American Girl*, a writer cannot possibly sell me an idea. We have a very specific style, and by reading and studying several back issues, a writer should be able to see why we choose the stories we do. Our writer's guidelines are easily obtainable. By not researching our preferred word length or subject matter, the query will be hard to place in *American Girl*." Do your homework. It's time consuming and can be tedious, but the payoff is worth it.

WRITING CREDITS

In the next paragraph, list any previous writing experience or credits you may have, as well as memberships to children's writing organizations such as the Society of Children's Book Writers and Illustrators (SCBWI).

Submitting to an Agent? Cover Letter Tips

When submitting manuscripts to an agent for consideration, including a good cover letter can make a difference. "A cover letter should tell a little bit about the author and the book," says Steven Malk of Writers House. "I always think it's helpful if an author can pitch her book, because I'm going to turn around and pitch it to publishers. It's going to catch my eye if someone comes up with a hook for her story or if she says, 'This is going to appeal to people who like Peggy Rathmann' or 'This should be very popular with 2- to 4-year-olds.'"

However, just as with querying publishers, the bottom line is the quality of the work. "I really like a good cover letter—it makes an impression on me. But your work's going to speak for itself no matter what." (Turn to page 27 for Malk's comments on a successful query letter and page 83 to read his interview Listen In: An Agent Chats with Richard Jackson.)

Many new writers panic at the thought of having no previous experience. Remember, the story idea, and not a long list of credits, is the deciding factor to most editors.

At *American Girl* magazine, credits will not make or break a sale. Stretchberry explains, "I try to evaluate each idea on its own merit. Previous sales and contest placements will not overcome a weak query letter."

Dryden adds, "Credits are helpful, but I look more at the subject matter and tone of the story that is being described." If you don't have credits, skip this section. But whatever you do, *do not* draw attention to your lack of experience with sentences such as, "Though I've never been published, I have a deep love of children's literature." This will only label you as an amateur.

If you have credits, list two or three that apply to the type of manuscript for which you are querying. Do not list credits for different genres altogether. For instance, don't query a children's book publisher with multiple credits from adult travel magazines. You may write interesting travel articles, but that really has no bearing on your ability to write for children.

Credits, while not essential, can be helpful. Cecka likes to see relevant credits in query letters. "I think it's always worthwhile to know that a writer has prior publishing experience—it suggests that the writer may have familiarity with some of the more artful aspects of the publishing process, such as working with an editor on revisions. Some very good writers just happen to write lousy letters!" So, use any credits you have to your best advantage. If you have none, take comfort in the fact that a good idea can outweigh lack of experience.

THE ENDING

The last paragraph is a no-brainer. You'll want to mention that you've included a self-addressed, stamped envelope (SASE) for the editor's reply. If you are sending sample chapters, according to guidelines, tell the editor if you want them back (be sure your SASE has adequate postage). Also, use this opportunity to display your good manners by thanking the busy editor for taking time to read your query. Make sure your query letter is no longer than one page, and go through it carefully to check grammar and spelling (this will be read by an editor, after all). Now relax. Your query letter is done!

See, writing a Super Query isn't so hard. Of course, editors are individuals and have their own specific needs and tastes, so you won't be able to please them all. But with a little insight into the minds of editors and these basic guidelines, you can avoid the common mistakes that are Kryptonite to queries. (Be sure to look at the example letters that follow for comments from editors on letters that resulted in sales and an example of what *not* to do.) Now, all that's left is to print out your Super Query and mail it off. Up . . . up . . . and away!

Successful Query

Carolyn Zieg Cunningham
Editorial Director
Wild Outdoor World
P.O. Box 1249
Helena, MT 59624

Overall: A friendly informative letter—I have scheduled her pupfish story.

I like this. We're a science-based magazine and often include scientific names of animals and plants.

Immediately grabs my curiosity.

Dear Ms. Cunningham:

What tiny fish lives in hot, salty water and buries itself in the mud when conditions grow too harsh? It can tolerate water up to 115° and breeds so fast that ten generations can mature each year. It's an old and isolated species left behind when ancient seas evaporated. Give up? It's Cyprinodon salinus—the Salt Creek Pupfish—found in Death Valley. There are several species of pupfish scattered across the West, all able to flourish in such extreme habitats.

Good—Our magazine emphasizes "habitat"—sounds like she read our guidelines.

Just right for our publication.

I'd like to do a story about the pupfish for *W.O.W.* My 800-word piece will include an interview with a Death Valley Park Ranger and a photo of the fish. I learned of this unusual creature during a recent trip to Death Valley and was fascinated by its ability to survive. I believe children will find it just as interesting.

Yes! She has personal experience.

Interview with an expert—good! Scientific accuracy is crucial for us.

I've had manuscripts published or accepted for publication by *American Girl, Cricket, Current Health 1 & 2, Highlights,* and *S.I. for Kids.* Recently, I've won the 1998 nature writing contest sponsored by *Children's Writer.* You've had my piece on Sandhill Cranes under consideration for some time now. All of my children's articles have been nonfiction nature topics. How soon can I get my pupfish story swimming your way?

Sincerely,

Obviously, she knows how to write for kids.

Connie Goldsmith
Member SCBWI
990 Hatch St.
Published CA 90029
(818)555-7720

After reading Connie Goldsmith's query about Salt Creek Pupfish, *W.O.W.* editor Carolyn Zieg Cunningham assigned the article, scheduled for the January 2001 issue of *W.O.W.* "I did a lot of research on these fishes," says Goldsmith, who also obtained appropriate slides from the National Park Service. "I'm planning to query an adult outdoors magazine on the topic, too."

Successful Query

Cindy Blobaum
9034 Foxhunter Ln.
New Book IA 50311
515-555-6110

November 19, 1997

Overall: This letter told me we had a match—in subject matter, educational philosophy, target markets, writing style. I couldn't wait to read the sample chapter.

Susan Williamson
Williamson Publishing Company
Church Hill Rd., P.O. Box 185
Charlotte, VT 05445

Dear Ms. Williamson,

Yes, that's what we're all about—understanding through creative activities. Very important because many authors don't really understand this.

Immediatley knew that Cindy had done her homework—most kids' geology books present the same old volcano activity and nothing more.

Do you know how to make a mountain out of a molehill? Kids do. Try to find fun, easy to understand geology activities that go beyond making baking soda and vinegar volcanoes. Imagine constructing your own periodic table while cooking *Igneous Edibles*. Or understanding how fossils form by creating *Sponge Stones*. And it gets really personal when you discover that *You're a Mine Field!*

Her experience field-testing her activities is very important to us once we get the book into development.

For 10 years I have researched, developed and field-tested dozens of hands-on geology activities. Students and teachers have been overwhelmingly enthusiastic about the programs and have requested additional information. I am responding by writing a book—*Geology Rocks!* This manual of interconnected activities addressing conceptual geology:

Title is clever—confirmed for me that this was going to be fun for kids!

- features innovative activities that create the "AHA!" experience
- uses inexpensive, everyday materials like Starburst™ candy and LEGOS™
- provides appropriate background knowledge without burying it in mountains of text
- offers levels of information from beginning to more advanced
- furnishes multiple, flexible ways to learn the same concept
- involves users in simulated geologic processes from cave formation to plate shifting.

A quick take on what her goals are—and they clearly match ours! Better for all of us to know now.

Geology Rocks! emphasizes learning-by-doing fun, similar to your successful *Kids' Nature Book* and *Kids' Science Book*. This single subject book, aimed at children ages 7-12, would fit in well with your *Kaleidoscope Kids®* series. It would be appropriate for kids to use at home, for teachers planning lessons, and for professionals designing enrichment programs. It could easily be marketed through bookstores, scientific supply companies, museum and educational stores and catalogs, and used in workshops, continuing education and pre-service methods classes.

Very perceptive. She cited the appropriate Williamson series for her work, and she knows our market as well as we do.

The enclosed section, *Make Mine Metamorphic*, highlights the type of activities and information included throughout the book. I have also enclosed an outline and SASE. As stipulated in your *Children's Writer's & Illustrator's Market* listing, I am giving you an exclusive six-week period to consider this proposal before sending it to other publishers. I look forward to hearing from you.

Sincerely,

The six weeks exclusivity gives me time to discuss this proposal with my staff, but Cindy also makes it clear she's going to market her proposal aggressively. I like that.

Cindy Blobaum

"Cindy Blobaum was a wonderful author to work with, and her letter is a great example of what to do to get published," says Editor Susan Williamson. "We faithfully read every letter, and there is not doubt, the nature of the letter influences how much further we delve into the proposal." Williamson published Blobaum's first book *Geology Rocks!*

Successful Query

May 5, 2000

Mr. Steven Malk, Agent
Writers House, West Coast Office
3368 Governor Dr., #224F
San Diego, CA 92122

Dear Mr. Malk,

I am writing to ask if you would be interested in reading my historical fiction novel *Trouble Don't Last Always*, written for middle grade readers. The manuscript recently won an Ohio Arts Council Fellowship in Writing.

Trouble Don't Last Always tells the story of two slaves who escape on the Underground Railroad. A young Kentucky slave named Samuel is awakened in the night by Harrison, the oldest slave on Master's farm, who has decided to run away. Although Samuel risks being sold or beaten if he is caught, he begins the dangerous journey to Canada with the old slave who helped to raise him. But, as Samuel says, "Truth is, trouble follows us like a shadow . . . "

Trouble Don't Last Always is written in the first-person voice of Samuel. Other historical fiction books have featured those who helped on the Underground Railroad, but I wanted to give a voice to the runaways themselves. As Samuel and Harrison meet an unusual cast of characters in their attempt to reach freedom, their journey also becomes a story about relationships and trust—between young and old, between "black folks and white folks," between slave and free.

This is my first children's novel. I have written for local publications and for children's theater as a Playwright-in-Residence for Cleveland's Bicentennial. Over the past six years, I have worked with middle grade students as an elementary classroom teacher. I am a member of the Society of Children's Book Writers and Illustrators, and a freelance contributor to Education Center, Inc. publications.

The complete manuscript is available upon request. I've enclosed a SASE for your convenience.

I appreciate your consideration, and I look forward to hearing from you.

Sincerely,

Overall: This is an excellent query letter. The author told me about herself as it related to the book; gave a great, intriguing description; and clearly demonstrated that she put a lot of thought into this query.

Shelley Pearsall
2410 Ashland Ave.
Authorsville OH 44136
(440)555-2951
e-mail: author@aol.com
fax: (440)555-1543

Tells me pertinent information about the book immediately.

This is great. Definitely piques my interest.

Excellent synopsis of story.

Between these two paragraphs, I was very intrigued.

This is all relevant information and establishes her as a real professional.

After reading an Insider Report interview with Agent Steven Malk (2000 *Children's Writer's & Illustrator's Market*), Shelley Pearsall queried the agent. Her letter prompted Malk to request—and soon represent—her manuscript, which is being published by Delacorte in 2002. *Trouble Don't Last Always* (title subject to change) is Pearsall's first book.

Very Bad Query

Don't send them a picturebook! Shows she didn't do her homework.

Don't say this—it simply doesn't matter to and editor.

Editorial Department
Only Nonfiction Publications
6574 Hardcover Street
New York NY 10021

Find a name. (Also note that the majority of children's book editors are female.)

Dear Sir:

Evidence she's not familiar with the genre.

Enclosed is my 5,000-word picture book *Butchie the Big Bad Bully.* I've read it to my grandson's kindergarten class and some kids in my neighborhood and they all think it should be published. It's a rhyming story that's a lot like Dr. Seuss's books. I also sent it to 45 other publishers. *Makes an editor cringe.*

Although it's good to mention submitting multiply, this shows she didn't research publishers.

If you don't have writing credits, it's not necessary to mention it.

I haven't been published anywhere accept my church bulletin, but I've been writing for a year in my spare time. I've been married for 32 years, and I have 3 children and 7 grandchildren, so I've been reading books to kids for years! I also love to garden. Last year I grew a tomato that look an awful lot like Beverly Cleary. Maybe that would make a good book.

Oops! Should be "except." Watch grammar and usage.

Another oops! Be sure to proofread well.

One idea at a time.

Please don't call in the next two weeks because I will be out of town. If I don't hear from you after that, I'll call you.

Bad, bad, bad.

Leave off impertinent personal information.

I know you'll love *Butchie the Big Bad Bully.*

Follow-up with a postcard in a few months if you haven't gotten a response; don't call in two weeks.

Sincerely,

Not a good closing—don't make assumptions. Thank the editor for considering your query and mention that you enclosed an SASE.

Wilma Wannabe-Published
3982 No Way Lane
Slushville KY 46555

Don't forget a phone number (and fax and e-mail if you have them). Make it as easy as possible for the editor to contact you.

This letter is the cliché bad query—it's what *not* to do when submitting. Avoid these pitfalls that scream "unprofessional."

The Basics of Synopsis Writing (With a Hint of Chocolate)

BY VICTORIA J. COE

Writing a synopsis is a lot like eating a Reese's Peanut Butter Cup. In fact, the only difference I can see is there's no wrong way to eat a Reese's.

Maybe nibbling along the outside works for you, or perhaps you're more comfortable diving right into the middle. Some ways just feel right. But if your favorite method has begun to lose its flavor, why not spice it up by trying something new?

Before digging in, I'd like to squash a bit of misinformation. You may have heard that a synopsis is a tantalizing morsel designed to leave the reader salivating for the rest of your story. Not so! Your synopsis is where you tear off the wrapper and highlight your main ingredients, right down to the last tasty crumb.

When an editor or agent reads your synopsis, she wants to get a sense of who your main character is and where you're going with the premise. Your synopsis, along with your query letter and sample chapters, will help her determine whether your story might be a good fit for her. You don't need to include a lot of detail, just what is necessary to understand the protagonist's motivation and the plot.

The first thing I do when writing a synopsis is sum up the whole story in one paragraph.
- Begin by telling the entire plot in one sentence.
- Next, explain the main character's motivation in one or two sentences.
- Then summarize the "middle" of the story and climax in one or two sentences.
- Finally, tell how the main character grows or what he learns as a result of his experiences.
- Of course, if you can combine any of these points, by all means do!Here's an sample of this type of summary using Roald Dahl's *Charlie and the Chocolate Factory* as an example:

Charlie wants to visit Mr. Willy Wonka's top secret candy factory. After he and four other lucky children win a tour of the factory, misfortune befalls the selfish, misbehaving four, while amiable Charlie earns Mr. Wonka's trust and inherits the factory.

This short paragraph not only tells the premise and the plot, but it also shines a light on the theme. Like the unmistakable aroma of chocolate, this story's theme, "good guys finish first," wafts right through the page and stimulates the senses, but doesn't overwhelm the reader. Try this with your own summary. If the theme isn't clear, revise or tweak until it is.

If there is a subplot, next is the place to spell it out. One or two sentences should do it. For example, "Throughout the story, there is a subplot in which . . ."

Skip a line, and dive right in to the plot outline. Think of your story in three major sections:
- Beginning—Main character's motivation is established and basic plot is set up.
- Middle—Main character faces obstacles, which build to a climax.
- End—Climax is resolved.

VICTORIA J. COE, *children's author, writes for WriteJourney.com, VerlaKay.com and other writing websites, as well as newspapers and magazines (when she's not eating or reading about chocolate). Her article about synopsis writing originally appeared on WriteJourney.com.*

The beginning, climax and ending will take up most of the synopsis, with less weight given to the middle:

- Reveal your beginning in two or three paragraphs, leaving off with your plot clearly set.
- For the middle, lead with an introductory sentence, then encapsulate your major plot points as bullets, leading up to the climax. Take two or three paragraphs to describe the climax and twists.
- Finally, tell how the story is resolved in one or two paragraphs.

Here's an example of the rest of the synopsis of *Charlie and the Chocolate Factory.* At 450 words, this synopsis will take up only 2-3 pages. Yet the plot, theme and essence of the main character all come through like the unbeatable combination of peanut butter and chocolate wrapped up neatly in a bright orange wrapper.

Sweet Charlie Bucket loves chocolate. But his family is so poor that he gets it only once a year, on his birthday. Walking past Wonka's Chocolate Factory each day is torture.

Charlie's grandfather tells him that Mr. Willy Wonka is so concerned about guarding his secrets that he has closed off the factory. No one has been seen going in or out for years.

An announcement appears in the newspaper: Five lucky children who find golden tickets inside Wonka bars will win a personal tour of the factory and a lifetime supply of chocolate. Charlie is very excited—his birthday is next week.After the first two tickets are discovered, Charlie opens his birthday chocolate with great anticipation, but his hopes fall when there is no golden ticket inside.Soon the third and fourth tickets are found. Then Charlie's Grandpa Joe shows him a Wonka bar he has kept hidden. The two open it gleefully, but inside is chocolate, nothing more.

One day Charlie finds a dollar in the snow and buys two chocolate bars. He is shocked to find the last golden ticket!

The next day, Charlie, Grandpa Joe and the other winners arrive at the factory, where they are delighted and amazed to meet the wildly eccentric Willy Wonka. While Charlie and his grandfather marvel at the wonders of Wonka's factory, one by one the other children meet with misfortune when they fail to heed their host's admonitions:

- Gluttonous Augustus Gloop drinks from the chocolate river and falls in.
- Gum-chewing Violet Beauregard chews an experimental stick of gum and turns into a gigantic blueberry.
- Spoiled Veruca Salt grabs a squirrel and ends up in a chute for bad nuts.
- Television-obsessed Mike Teavee is shrunk when he tries to become the first human to travel over television waves.

After each mishap, Mr. Wonka tells the dwindling group that the others will all come out in the wash.When at last only Charlie is left, Mr. Wonka tells him that he's giving him

---

A Synopsis or an Outline?

A synopsis is a content-driven summary of a story's plot. Most often a synopsis, along with a query letter and sample chapters, is part of a fiction book proposal. Usually part of a non-fiction book proposal, an outline is structure-driven. As most non-fiction books are not actually written until after the proposal has been accepted, the outline describes the type of material to be covered chapter by chapter. Therefore, the outline is generally not a summary of already-written chapters, but a plan for what the author intends to include.

Sometimes, a publisher's guidelines for fiction request a chapter by chapter outline. This type of outline is really a blend of a synopsis and an outline. A writer might think of an outline of fiction as an expanded synopsis, including each and every chapter in summary.

the whole factory. Wonka explains that he's been looking for his successor—a good, sensible, loving child to entrust with his precious candy-making secrets. Thrilled, Charlie and Grandpa Joe burst through the roof of the factory with Mr. Wonka in the great, glass elevator. They fly to the Buckets' cottage and collect the rest of the family before returning to live at the Wonka Factory.

Sounds easy? It is! Now roll up your sleeves, grab a napkin and dig in!

Quick Tips for a Sensational Synopsis

Content:

- Tell, don't show!
- Use omniscient point of view
- Write in present tense
- Keep it short and sweet

Format:

- Single space your name and contact information in the upper left hand corner of the first page.
- Center your title, all in capital letters.
- Skip a line, then center the word "synopsis," in bold, capital letters.
- Skip two lines, then double space your synopsis.
- Insert a header on subsequent pages, listing "Your Last Name/Manuscript Title, Synopsis" on the top left and listing the page number on the top right.
- The fewer pages, the better.

First Steps for Creating Believable Characters

BY ELAINE MARIE ALPHIN

Story characters can come to life for the child who reads about them.

Remember wanting to go on escapades with Pippi Longstocking? Longing to escape down the river with Huck Finn? Clutching your notebook and yearning to find out everything about the people you saw, like Harriet the Spy? These characters became your friends. And you want your characters to befriend the children who read your book or story.

But where do these characters come from? If you sit down and start to write, who will you write about?

Potential story characters are all around you. You see them walking to school; you see them shopping in the mall; you see them biking or skating down your street. If you close your eyes, you see them in your memory—the child you once were, the friends you remember, the children you've raised or the children you've known. Believable characters are born from real people and revealed to readers through your writer's craft.

When you do this well, your reader will identify with your main character, and she will feel that character's fear and elation as she struggles to succeed in the book. As the characters in your story grow and change, the reader will share that growth. To make this magic happen, you need to believe in the characters whose story you're writing. You need to know them intimately. And you need to show them to your reader.

CHARACTERS DO THINGS

The first step in bringing a character to life is deciding what the character will do in your story. Characters are rarely passive; they take action. And the reader, as well as the other characters in the story, forms an impression of this character based on his actions. When you meet a new kid for the first time, you pay attention to what the newcomer does. If the new boy runs screaming to the teacher when he gets tripped in the school yard, you label him a crybaby. If the new girl shows off her rows of pierced earrings, her spiked hair and her ticket stubs and backstage passes from the hottest rock star (who only played New York and Los Angeles), you know she's a braggart, and you wonder if she's really telling the truth. These actions reveal the personality behind them.

When you write a story, you probably have an idea of how the plot will develop, but you're still getting to know your characters. Suppose you decide to write about a boy sneaking out of a locked house to meet a friend—he'll have to climb out of the window and down the roof. At this stage, you as the writer are moving your character around like a playing piece on the vast

ELAINE MARIE ALPHIN *is author of more than a dozen children's books including her latest YA novel,* Counterfeit Son *(Harcourt), nominated for the YALSA Quick Pick List.* The Ghost Soldier, *the companion book to her title* The Ghost Cadet, *is a spring 2001 release from Henry Holt. Alphin has won numerous awards including the ALA Recommended Book award, the SCBWI Magazine Merit Award for Fiction and Nonfiction and the Virginia Book Award for* The Ghost Cadet. *To learn more about her books, visit www.elai nemariealphin.com. This article was excerpted from* Creating Characters Kids Will Love, © *2000 Elaine Marie Alphin. Used with permission of Writer's Digest Books, an imprint of F&W Publications, Inc.*

gameboard of your plot. You're directing the action. If you leave it at that, however, you'll end up with a cardboard character who's about as believable as a rook in a chess game. To make that boy believable, you need to look inside of him and make him want to take those actions.

After you direct the larger action of the story, plan what specific actions your character will take in order to develop the plot. Now transform your role from director to actor. Ask yourself how your character will perform these actions—with the skill of a third grader tying his shoes, or with the hesitancy of a kindergartner writing his name on the blackboard? If your main character has to climb down a roof, how will he do it? First think about the series of actions needed to climb down a roof, from opening the window to climbing through and across the roof's surface. As you sit at your keyboard, move your arms and legs, stretching them as you imagine you might if you were climbing. Make note of these actions.

Why is your character doing this?

To show your character's actions in the context of his personality, you'll have to know some background about him. Ask yourself questions in order to find out what experience he's had. Has he climbed down a roof before, or is this the first time? Is he scared of heights, or does he revel in them? Then think about his motivation—why is he climbing down this roof? Why is it so important to him to meet that friend? Is he climbing down the roof because he likes the idea of taking a risk? Does he want to see what it will feel like? What's at stake—what will happen if he doesn't succeed? Is his reason compelling? If not, will he decide partway through that he's had enough and he's turning back?

There are many ways you could develop this scene to show the reader something about a character. In *The Ghost Cadet*, I wrote a scene about Benjy, my twelve-year-old main character, like this:

> His sneakers were braced against the roof's shingles. Slowly, Benjy took one hand off the sill and gripped a lower shingle instead. Then he took a deep breath, told himself very firmly not to be afraid, and let go of the sill with his other hand.
>
> There was a bad moment when his free hand couldn't seem to find a shingle, but Benjy made himself stay calm, and finally his damp palm slid down one row of shingles and he hooked his fingers over the next one and held tight. After that, inching his way down row by row didn't seem so terrible.
>
> His sneaker scraped a loose shingle once, and he was afraid everyone had heard. For a second he clung to the roof, waiting for the lights to flash on, but the unexpected noise must have sounded loud only in his own ears, because the house remained dark and silent.
>
> One foot finally brushed the gutter, and Benjy knew he had to look down. He steadied his grip and turned his head, and breathed a sigh of relief. He was positioned directly over the concrete bench. Carefully he lowered himself until he was hanging from the edge of the roof by both hands. His feet dangled just above the bench.
>
> Why couldn't he have been a few inches taller? Benjy cursed his height silently. Even just a couple of inches would have meant his toes might have been able to feel the bench beneath him. But wishing wouldn't make him grow. Benjy looked down one last time and asked himself whether this was really necessary. Flexing his arms, knees, and body, he ordered himself to relax, and took a deep breath, and let go.

You can tell that Benjy is afraid from his slow progress, and that he probably hasn't done this before from his awkward movements. You can see his frustration about being short. You can see the way he talks himself into doing what he doesn't want to do. Determining specific actions and attitudes like this helps you know how your character will be able to do something else in the story. For instance, the next time he has to climb something, he'll probably do it more quickly and use more confident movements. Perhaps his inner voice won't need to talk him into doing something dangerous, but will cheer him on for doing it well. You'll build on the actions your characters take in order to develop these characters for the reader and to show how they grow as people in the course of your story.

CHARACTERS THINK

In the example from *The Ghost Cadet*, Benjy doesn't only act—he also thinks about his actions. He tries to talk himself into courage, and he curses his lack of those last few inches that would make it easier for him to drop down from the roof. Action in a vacuum allows the reader to see the character from the outside. That's fine for secondary characters who are seen through your main character's perspective. But this isn't quite enough to bring your main character to life. The reader identifies with your protagonist and wants to share that character's thoughts. To open your character's mind to the reader, you have to get inside it and express those thoughts.

A character may have fundamental religious or philosophical beliefs in the beginning of the story that will be challenged before the end. For example, middle-grade Jennifer, whose parents have never attended church, may believe she's an atheist. When she makes a friend who goes to church every Sunday, attends Youth Group and prays in the cafeteria before lunch, Jennifer may start to wonder if there really is a God. Or Ryan, a tough adolescent who believes in machismo and likes to wrestle, could discover the other best wrestler in school is gay. Ryan might start out despising gays and slowly change his mind and accept the other boy as a friend. Or these kids may not change. But they will start out with strong thoughts about the matter, thoughts they'll question in the course of your story.

Your characters don't necessarily say what they think. Jennifer's friend may talk about her religious beliefs, but she may have private doubts she doesn't express. She may wonder whether or not God hears her when she prays. She may envy her new friend's freedom on Sunday morning to sleep late. Or her faith may run deeper than she'll admit to her parents or her friend—she may be considering joining a cult. All your characters' thoughts, whether hidden or spoken, will contribute to the tension and drama of your story.

What do they think about each other?

In addition to fundamental beliefs, your characters have opinions about the people around them. A character may like certain classmates based on the sort of clothes or glasses they wear, the sports they play, their hobbies or their shared interests. A youngster has strong opinions about his teachers based on how much homework each teacher assigns, how hard the tests are, how interesting the teacher makes the class or how funny the teacher's jokes are.

Closer to home, a character sees her parents in certain ways. She may judge each of them by whether or not the family does things together, what each of them will let her get away with, what punishments they mete out, or whether or not they listen to her. Some characters will have even more relatives they feel strongly about, starting with siblings. Your characters may also have aunts, uncles, cousins, grandparents or even great-grandparents, and will form opinions about them based on whether or not they're cheek-pinchers, what sorts of presents they give, how their perfume or aftershave smells or what questions they ask when they come to visit.

CHARACTERS FEEL

Thoughts are rational, but real people aren't always rational, especially in tense situations. In addition to thinking with their heads, kids feel with their hearts—or their stomachs, or wherever you want their deepest emotions to come from. They fear, they get angry, they hate, they love and they feel overwhelming delight. Kids feel other emotions, too—they're curious, they may feel guilty, they may be jealous of a friend or an enemy, they get embarrassed, they feel lonely. And they pass through the spectrum of these emotions every day.

Your characters should experience a wide range of natural emotions as they live through the experiences in your story. But expressing believable emotions is more than a matter of opening your thesaurus to look up new words to describe a particular feeling. While you can articulate your character's thoughts with words, emotions are more subtle. You can evoke them in your reader by using physical sensations that the reader will recognize. The catch: You need to find a unique, quirky way to express an emotion believably, and it should spring from the context of your character.

For example, if you write that Kassie felt heat flood into her face in her embarrassment at saying something stupid to Anastasia, the most popular girl in class, the reader will recognize that flush of embarrassment, but won't really feel it. The description is overdone. You need to know a little more about your character and her situation to make the feeling strong and true, so that it will resonate for the reader.

Perhaps Kassie is an artist and knows nothing about volleyball, and Anastasia is the captain of the winning volleyball team. Kassie has said something stupid about the last game and Anastasia has withered her with a scathing reply. Instead of merely wishing the incident had never happened, artist Kassie might wish she could splash turpentine across the last half hour and repaint her life. A different kid might wish she could hit rewind on her life and record a different conversation.

By using specific sensations and reactions to express your character's emotions, you'll bring the scene to life for the reader. And, since each character is unique, the expression of his or her emotions should be unique. If you find yourself writing an emotional cliché, look for a different way to express the same idea. Instead of writing the familiar sensation of a heart "pounding in fear," your football player leaping for the reception could think of the defensive players waiting to tackle him. He doesn't just catch the ball—he crushes it to his chest so that he feels the ball pulsing wildly against his hands as he dreads its being ripped from him.

What is the reason behind the feeling?

Examine why your character feels the emotion. A small child who acts curious may feel a sense of wonder at a butterfly and want to know all about it . . . or he may want to irritate his mother so he plies Mom with questions about the butterfly to get her attention. A third grader who's jealous of a friend's new bike may feel angry at his parents for not buying him one, even if he understands that they can't afford it, and may take out his bitterness on his friend for having this prized possession.

Emotions may not always be clear in your character's mind. When her father doesn't come to kiss her goodnight for the third night in a row, Shona may throw a china nightlight that he gave her across her bedroom. Then, later, she'll creep out to pick up the pieces and use school glue to put them back together. Characters often feel a muddle of emotions or act out in one emotional language (here, Shona uses the emotional language of anger, hurling a breakable item across a room) to mask the real emotion (her fear that he doesn't love her anymore and her desperation to hold on to the security of his love).

Also remember that your character may feel one thing at one point in your story and feel a different emotion at another point. Kids are complex, and they bounce from emotional high to emotional low. Trust your characters enough to let them do this, but constantly ask yourself whether the variety of emotions rings true. Can you remember feeling those mood swings from your own childhood? Have you seen it in your children or in a friend's children? From the jumble of believable emotions, let a pattern emerge that shows a character's progress from the beginning of your story through to the end. If you use specific details to show these emotions in your characters, readers will take the boys and girls of your imagination into their hearts and will care deeply about what happens to them.

CHARACTERS SPEAK

What your character does and thinks and feels only reflects part of her personality. Kids also talk, and what they say (and how they say it) reveals a lot about their character. For readers to believe in your characters, however, you must use language appropriate to that youngster's age and circumstance. That last sentence, for example, is not something a youngster would say, and a conversation in which a child character said it wouldn't ring true to a reader. A kid might say, "If you want kids to believe in your characters, they have to sound like real kids." In other words, you need to use natural kid language.

You can get a feel for natural kid talk by listening to real children. Listen in on kids talking to each other at a fast-food restaurant or at the park. Pay attention to their syntax and vocabulary, and use these in your story dialogue. But fictional conversations shouldn't exactly reproduce the "uhs," "wells," "ums" and repetitions of real speech. These don't bother the listener in real life, but they will irritate an impatient reader who wants the dialogue to move along quickly.

Kids tend to use slang. While you want your dialogue to sound contemporary, avoid using the latest slang on the block, because slang is transitory and geographically based. Since it may take six months to a year for a magazine story to see print and several years for a book to be published, any real slang you try to use will be hopelessly dated by the time kids read the conversation. If you want your characters to use slang, stick to familiar words that have been around long enough that everybody understands them, like "cool," or you can make up your own. Slang evolves from kids arbitrarily changing words or twisting figures of speech into phrases that only the in-crowd can understand. You can create this effect by making up your own words and letting the context make them clear to the reader.

Kids also mispronounce a lot of words. They may be in a hurry and run words together, like "gonna" or "wanna." Or they may drop the final "g" of a word, such as "goin'." Small children may try to use big words they can't quite pronounce yet—adults often find these mispronunciations hilarious, but children know what they mean, and they resent the grown-ups' laughter at their expense. In writing your dialogue, try not to rely too heavily on phonetic misspelling to sound like a child, or you'll alienate your readers by coming across as condescending. It's almost like an insulting dialect, as if you're telling kids that they come from an alien place and speak a strange almost-English. Respect your reader by using this technique carefully. In moderation, it can help differentiate between characters of different ages or who live in different places, but only in moderation.

Personality in dialogue

Each of your characters should sound distinct, since his voice springs from his personality. But that distinct tone should come from a character's thoughts and feelings, not solely from how he speaks. Watch out for placing too much emphasis on your characters' tag lines:

"I didn't do it," he muttered.
"You certainly did," she retorted sharply.
"But it wasn't me," he blurted loudly.
"I saw you running," she insisted firmly.
"I was chasing him!" he cried helplessly.
"Don't make matters worse by blaming someone else," she chided.
"I didn't do it," he repeated.

That scene is full of tension, but you can't tell much about the characters from their argument. Awkward tag lines with inappropriate descriptions of the speech (like 'blurted') or weak adverbs draw the reader's attention away from what's being said to the way the character is saying it. That ends up being distracting. You can show your character more clearly by using simple tags (such as "said" or "told" or "asked") blended with action sentences which show us more about the speaker:

"I didn't do it," the boy said, staring at the school yard ground.
"You certainly did," said the yard teacher.
"But it wasn't me." The boy looked up at her, his eyes intense under tangled hair that needed cutting.

"I saw you running," she told him. But she frowned, as if trying to remember exactly what she had seen.

"I was chasing him!" the boy cried. He flung his arms wide to show he had no lies up his sleeves.

At his gesture, the teacher folded her own arms and glared at him. "Don't make matters worse by blaming someone else."

The boy's arms fell to his sides. He slumped, staring at the cracked concrete again. "I didn't do it," he said in a voice so low the yard teacher leaned forward to make out the words.

Even though you still don't know what the boy is accused of, these two characters begin to come into focus so the reader can care about them. The tension comes from wondering which one to believe.

Nothing but the truth?

Kids (and adults, for that matter) don't always tell the truth, especially when they're speaking to each other. A parent or a teacher may simplify something, thinking the child couldn't possibly understand. The adult might even lie deliberately, not wanting to frighten the child. But kids often sense that sort of untruth. Use the tension between what your characters say and what they know to be true to illuminate their personalities and their thoughts for your reader.

Kids can lie to each other, too. They may be bragging and their imagination just takes over, or they may choose to deliberately mislead a friend or an enemy. Or they may simply fail to say exactly what they mean, and the other kid misunderstands. Some characters may immediately set their friends straight, while others may not realize a misunderstanding has taken root. And some might decide to let the other kid keep the wrong interpretation, justifying it to themselves because it's the other's fault, not their own.

Kids can also lie to their parents or teachers to avoid getting punished or to protect the adult from the truth. In that situation, you can explore the way a character feels about deceiving someone he loves or admires. Whether a youngster tells an adult the truth or not, she'll sound different talking to a teacher or a minister or a parent than she'll sound talking to her friends. Kids won't use the same slang talking to adults, for instance, unless they deliberately want to confuse them. A youngster may be more polite when he's talking to an adult. He may deliberately try to use complete sentences, while he might talk to his friends in phrases. Another kid may become monosyllabic, especially in front of an adult he doesn't know.

PIECES OF THE PUZZLE

As you develop your characters, trust them to let you know how they feel about a situation, and use their dialogue as well as their thoughts and actions to express their feelings. Believable kids act, think, feel and speak. These are pieces of the puzzle that will make up a whole character. Now you need to find ways to think like a youngster and feel like a youngster to breathe life into your child characters.

An editor once told me that a short story I'd sent in was too long, that the vocabulary was too advanced for the age group the story was best suited to and that the cast was too large—but everyone who had read the story loved the main character. They wanted to buy the manuscript and were sure I could fix those other minor problem areas.

Strong, colorful characters will move both readers and editors, and can be your passport to publication. So get out your character journal and start writing—kids out there are waiting impatiently to meet your characters.

Story Sparkers: Exercises for Filling the Blank Page

BY MARCIA THORNTON JONES & DEBBIE DADEY

Great. You grabbed a pen, your journal is open, the computer is up and ready. You've been to the library, read current books, and you liked what you read. You know that, more than anything, you want to write for children.

But what happens now that your screen is blank, that little cursor is teasing you with its blinking-blinking-blinking, and you cry out, "I can't think of anything to write?" Or maybe you've spent three hours scribbling away. You stop to take a breath, glancing over the pages filled with words, and you moan, "These ideas are horrible."

What you need are ideas worthy of your valuable writing time. How do you find them?

At any given time loads of ideas are swirling and tumbling in our brains like clothes being tossed in a dryer. But have you ever noticed that when you sit down, turn on the computer, and press "tab" to start a new paragraph, all those ideas seem to disappear (just like the socks from your laundry)?

Part of the problem may be that the logical portion of your brain is dousing your creativity by focusing on being critical of your creative thinking.

The brain is divided into hemispheres, and each side is responsible for certain activities. The left side of the brain handles logical, linear tasks and processes the world by looking at parts of the whole. This logical hemisphere is responsible for step-by-step, systematic, sequential thinking like classifying, analyzing, ordering, assessing, making literal connections, and drawing cause-and-effect conclusions. All these things are involved in the all-important, rule-governed task of stringing together words to speak and write.

We like to envision the left hemisphere igniting like a string of firecrackers. You light one wick and the firecracker explodes, then another and then another, so you experience a pop-pop-pop series of explosions.

The right hemisphere of the brain isn't sequential. The right hemisphere thinks in random patterns. Rather than trying to make sense of the world by breaking it into recognizable parts, the right side of the brain looks at the whole and uses images instead of words. Since it doesn't rely on systematic methods, the right hemisphere is open to creative imaging, emotions, and metaphorical connections.

We think of the right hemisphere as a Fourth of July sparkler. Once ignited, a beautiful cluster of sparks crackle and pop, reaching out in random patterns.

Effective writing requires cooperation between both hemispheres. Unfortunately, when the right hemisphere sparkles with images and random explosions of thought, the critical left brain

MARCIA THORNTON JONES & DEBBIE DADEY *are the authors of more than seventy-five books for children, including the best-selling series* The Adventures of the Bailey School Kids, Bailey City Monsters, *and* Triplet Trouble. *Learn more about their books at www.baileykids.com. They are contributing editors and columnists for* Writer's Digest *magazine. Jones lives in Lexington, Kentucky. Dadey lives near Chicago, Illinois. The article was excerpted from* Story Sparkers: A Creativity Guide for Children's Writers © 2000 Marcia Thornton Jones and Debbie Dadey. Used with permission of Writer's Digest Books, an imprint of F&W Publications, Inc.*

often kicks into gear saying things like, "What are you thinking? You can't write that! This isn't appropriate! You can't begin until you have a killer first line. Your teachers would never approve. Your parents will be devastated!"

Writers often let the systematic left hemisphere suppress the random images from the right hemisphere. In other words, part of your brain is critical and another part of your brain is inspirational. We think of the hemispheres as our critic and our muse.

The good news is the following strategies help writers encourage both sides of the brain—the creative muse and the logical critic—to work in cooperation to generate unique and exciting ideas.

BRAINSTORMING

Brainstorming . . . the word alone conjures powerful images. It should—brainstorming is a powerful tool for generating ideas and later developing those ideas. This article will introduce specific idea-generating strategies. Each strategy relies on the basic theory behind brainstorming.

Brainstorming is often thought of as a group problem-solving activity during which each member of the group contributes ideas. The rules are simple. Anything goes; no judgments are allowed; all ideas are recorded. Piggybacking, or spinning off of others' ideas, is allowed and encouraged.

Brainstorming is like using the Internet. You start your search with one idea, finding a site that lists a related link. You click on that link and you discover a new site with even more links. The more you click, the more the world of possibilities opens up to you.

At a recent monthly meeting of Marcia's critique group Paul Brett Johnson asked for help generating ideas for a new picture book. "I need help with the ending," he told the group. He had a great cast of animal characters and a terrific conflict centered around a package found at the post office without a delivery address the week before Christmas. But he had not been able to come up with a strong ending. That's when the brainstorming began.

"Maybe the box was empty."

"What if an animal chewed through the paper?"

"How about if the town members sneaked in and peeked at what was inside?"

"What would happen if someone stole what was in the package?"

As a group, we called out possible ideas as Paul furiously scribbled them all down. Some of the ideas were pretty wild, some were clichés, some were downright stupid. It didn't matter because those ideas led to other ideas.

"We've reached a dead end," one writer said. It seemed as though she was right. We all sat there. Silent.

Suddenly, another writer, Becky North, sat up straight. "I've got it," she said. And she did. She had the perfect idea for Paul's ending.

At the end of twenty minutes, Paul had at least three strong ideas for the ending, one of which he was able to use.

People are often frustrated when they reach a lull in a brainstorming session. But Becky did what good creative thinkers must do. She kept her mind open. The truth is, the first ideas during brainstorming are usually not the best—that's why they pop into your head so easily. The best ideas are the ones you have to work for.

Even though brainstorming was first thought of as a group activity, it can help writers who are working alone. That's because each of us always has a group of two with whom to brainstorm—the parts of our brains that act as the critic and the muse.

Now that you know about brainstorming, try sparking your creativity by brainstorming some ideas. Try it with a group of other writers, or just sit down and brainstorm with your personal critic and muse participating. Remember: Write down all your ideas, and no censoring allowed!

WEBBING

Webbing is an activity that goes by many names, including ballooning, clustering, and mind mapping. No matter what you call it, it is one of the most effective ways to ignite idea sparks.

Webbing lets you splatter ideas in a free, nonlinear format so your creative muse is happy, but it also keeps track of connections in a linear fashion so your critic doesn't stress out. Webbing is useful when you're staring at the blank page. It's also helpful as you try to organize ideas for chapters of longer pieces.

Webbing is done by all ages; even kindergartners. That's how easy it is! This is all you need to remember. Start with an idea, word, or phrase and put it in the center of your paper. Put a circle around it as a hint to your brain to remember the "central" idea. Then, free-associate! Jot down on the paper whatever your brain blurts out. Circle the brainstormed ideas and draw lines from the central idea to the ideas you brainstorm. This reminds your creative muse that all these ideas are connected and also satisfies your critic by showing the linear flow of ideas. Keep going until you sense a shift from random association to a more focused cluster around a subtopic. The end result looks something like dandelion seeds ready to be scattered by the wind.

Examine your web. Are there ideas demanding to be connected to other ideas? Are there dense areas of lines and circles where many ideas are clustered? This is the way a web works. It is not only a way to develop ideas, but also a method to focus those ideas in a particular direction.

Now that you know about webbing, try some webbing sparks of your own. Put a topic in the center of the paper, then start free-associating. Remember . . . anything goes!

FREEWRITING

Writing. There is so much to think about—capitals; periods; when to start a new paragraph; spelling; typing errors; creating believable characters; plotting with suspense; chapter hooks; writing with authority; worrying whether the idea is good; wondering if your writing sparkles. Just think about it!

On second thought, *don't think about it*! In fact, thinking is often what keeps writers from writing. Worrying about writing will only send your muse into hiding. After all, why should your muse risk being creative when there are so many things that can go wrong?

Instead of worrying, the best thing to do is to stop thinking and just write. Flow write—typing or writing as fast as you can without stopping for five or ten minutes. Write free, unfettered by worries of technique, style, or content. Just write.

Freewriting allows your muse to speak without risk. In her book *Wild Minds*, Natalie Goldberg states that she used freewriting to help her "learn to cut through first thoughts," and that freewriting helps writers "learn about cutting through resistance."

There are few guidelines, rules, or risks when you freewrite. To freewrite, all you need is a few minutes of your time.

Open your journal or sit down at the computer, and start writing. Don't stop. That's the real trick. Stopping only gives your critic time to butt in with those pesky warnings. Forcing words on the paper keeps the critic at bay and gives your muse a chance to flow through your fingers. So don't stop. If you run out of things to say, list items on your desk, list favorite foods, all the things that bother you, or write about how you don't have anything to write about. Soon, your muse will get motivated again and off you'll go. Freewriting gives you permission—the freedom—to write pages and pages of junk because your critic knows that this isn't "for real." It also lets you get rid of all those bits and pieces of everyday life that might be getting in the way of your muse.

"Junk!" we heard you yell. "We don't want to write junk!"

Don't worry. The more you write the more likely you'll discover bright sparks buried in all that muddy writing. Start with just a few minutes, maybe five. You'll soon find out those five minutes have grown to ten or fifteen.

Freewriting is great for journaling, breaking the evil spell of the blank page, or for getting started on the next section of a longer piece. "How?" you ask. Try this. Pretend you're writing an intermediate chapter book set during the Civil War. The protagonist is hiding in the woods of Virginia when a dog discovers him. What happens? Open your journal and start writing. Don't stop. Just write for a full ten minutes.

LISTING

We all know what a list is. We make lists reminding us what to get at the grocery store, what errands we need to write, to whom we need to send holiday greetings, what presents we hope to receive for our next big birthday. But have you thought about listing to help you generate ideas or to get started on that best-seller you want to write?

Listing is one of the easiest strategies to use. All you need to do is think of a topic and then jot down what comes to mind. But unlike a grocery list, make sure your critic doesn't interfere with playful thought. It's important to make your list fast, free, and fun. Don't worry if you find yourself repeating words, ideas, and phrases. Just keep listing. Try for a list of fifty. Better yet, go for one hundred.

Let's say you're sitting at your desk, staring at a beautiful, white and totally clean piece of paper. You need an idea to help you get started on a new article for a children's magazine story. You know you want to write about ants, but what will be the focus? Start by making a list.

Once a list has been produced, look for patterns of repeated ideas and concepts. Using different-colored highlighting pens can help. You may notice definite categories of ideas such as ant tunnels/hills, ant bites, or the bodies of ants. Once the categories have been determined, you can organize your list into clusters for possible writing.

QUESTIONING

"Why is the grass green?" "Why can't girls pee standing up?" "How did God make the sky?"

Kids are pros at asking questions. So good, in fact, that many of us cringe when we feel that all-too-familiar tug on our shirtsleeves. But we shouldn't dread those questions. We need to listen to them. Questioning is a great way to jerk your brain on to a new path of thinking. It's also a wonderful strategy for producing writing ideas.

Like listing, the goal is to write fast. You can list questions about a specific writing topic, or if you're really stumped for a writing idea, just start listing questions that kids might ask. Here are a few examples.

1. How does grass grow?
2. Do teachers go to the bathroom?
3. Why are most roofs black?
4. How do postal workers plan their routes?
5. Why are stop signs red and yield signs yellow?
6. Who makes computer games?
7. How does a fax machine work?
8. Is it okay to stomp on bugs?
9. What do you do if you find a bat clinging to the basement wall?
10. Do worms sleep?
11. What makes wind?
12. Why do people plant daffodils but pull up dandelions when they're both yellow flowers?
13. How is toilet paper made?
14. Why do kids have to do homework?
15. How many snowflakes does it take to make a snowball?

RESEARCHING

The library is a treasure trove of ideas. If you don't believe us, stop by your closest library and start browsing. Take a notepad to jot down interesting ideas you discover while perusing the shelves. If you have the time, volunteer at a school or public library and help shelve books. Ideas will overwhelm you as you allow yourself to see all the many types of books. Debbie came up with the idea for writing *Shooting Star: Annie Oakley, the Legend* after shelving tall tale after tall tale about male heroes. It seemed only fair that girls should have tall-tale heroes, too.

The library is also the place to dig for ideas. Since many of our books are about folkloric creatures, we use the library to learn about new creatures and to find details that enhance our stories. Invariably we find something that leads us toward a new story idea. Newbery Award–winner Russell Freedman refuses to let anyone do his research for him because he believes in serendipity. There is always that fascinating fact that he comes across while doing research that leads him to explore new ideas for his existing story idea, or perhaps for another. Without library research, the facts would still lie buried, and so would the ideas.

Is there something that has always fascinated you, but somehow you never researched it? Now is the time. Go to the library and discover.

THE FIVE SENSES

Close your eyes. Breathe deep. Can you smell them? Grandma's sugar cookies. Crisp around the edges, but so soft in the center they nearly melt when you bite into them. They're covered with sour-cream icing sprinkled with colorful candies. She baked them just for visitors and kept them in the black cookie jar with fruit painted on the side.

Or maybe your window is open and a spring breeze billows the sheers, causing you to shiver. It reminds you of that night on the beach when you were ten. It was early evening and you put on a sweatshirt because the breeze ruffling the ocean was sending shivers down your arms. It was too cold for bathing suits so your dad bought a Frisbee and tossed it to you over and over. No matter how hard you tried, the ocean breeze caught the disk and sent it twirling in a crazy arch so it landed far from your Dad. Both of you laughed so hard your sides hurt.

Our five senses can be an exciting starting point for story ideas. Because our senses bring back such strong memories, they trigger ideas that have long laid dormant in the backs of our minds. Pay attention to your five senses as you write. Could one be a springboard to a great writing piece?

1. What does Christmas smell like?
2. What are the sounds of a playground?
3. What did your first horseback ride smell like?
4. What are the sounds of an ice-cream shop?
5. What did it sound like at the beach on a windy day?
6. What did the school cafeteria really smell like?
7. What were the sounds in the classroom when your teacher said, "Put your heads down"?
8. What did Santa really look like when you were four years-old?
9. How do your dog's ears really feel?
10. How did it feel when your mother stroked your hair?

Our five senses provide a strong connection to our memories, so don't hesitate to take advantage of them.

OVERHEARD CONVERSATIONS

One of the best ways to get ideas is to be sneaky. Sit on a playground or in a crowded restaurant frequented by kids and open your ears. What are those kids and parents talking about? Try to take notes without being noticed. The longer you sit the more you'll hear and the less obvious you'll be.

Sometimes the conversations may be enough to start a story all by itself. For instance, say you heard a thirteen-year-old girl dressed in dirty jeans say, "I'm not going to invite Kim to my party! She's mean!" Immediately, you wonder if you should feel sorry for Kim or for the party person. Maybe Kim really is mean and will ruin the party for everyone.

Here's another example. You're in a mall and you hear an eight-year-old boy complain, "My dad lied to me." What did he lie about? Did he promise a pony? Did he promise to come to the school open house? Did he promise to never drink again?

You can ask so many questions from one little snippet of conversation, and each question can spark a story idea. All you have to do is clean out our ears, dust off our sleuthing skills, and listen.

PET PEEVES

Let's face it: If everything was hunky-dory all the time, most stories would be pretty boring. As in all works of fiction, children's books have conflicts. Something is wrong and the problem gets worse before the story is resolved. A story may have more than one conflict, although one should be most dominant.

If we look within ourselves, we realize that the things that irritate us most are the things we feel strongly about. Those conflicts are what we can write about with great emotion, and that can turn into our best writing. Think for a moment about the things that bother you most now. Make a list. Perhaps your list is full of simple pet peeves or full-blown conflicts.

Turn the clock back twenty years. What bothered you then? Make a list of ten things. Now, turn the clock back thirty years (of course this depends on your age). What bothered you then? Was it the big girl on the bus who always pulled your hair and made fun of you? Make a list of ten things that bothered you. Pick two of the ones you felt most strongly about. Write a paragraph about those two conflicts. Now, can you put those two conflicts together in a story idea? Try it in one paragraph and see what happens. If you like the result, you have the gold that creates a story.

All of these activities and others can be used over and over again, so redo your favorite activities to see what else you can add to your idea collection.

Here's our most important tip: Write, write, write. Writing is the key. Make yourself write. After that, convince yourself to write even more. It may be hard at first, but the more you write, the easier it becomes. (Don't worry if you hate those first few minutes each day when you get started. That's pretty common.) Soon you will be surprised to find yourself thinking of characters and plots, topics and images, descriptions and dialogues without even trying. You will hunger to find a few precious moments in which to jot down those sparks.

And when you need to write, that is exactly what you should do. Write!

For Illustrators: Super Self-Promotion Strategies

BY MARY COX

Just as an editor is vital to any writer's career, the most important person to a freelance illustrator's career is the art director, the individual who matches a writer's words with an illustrator's images. You have several options for introducing yourself and your work to that all-important person! These guidelines for creating effective direct mail pieces will help you impress the art directors you contact.

Great samples get an art director's attention. There are several options illustrators can choose when creating samples for self-promotion. Here are a few of them:

Postcards & promo sheets

If designed and planned well, a simple postcard is one of the most practical and effective ways to showcase your work to art directors. Art directors like postcards because they are easy to file or tack on cubicle walls or bulletin boards. If the art director likes what she sees, she can always call and ask to see your portfolio or a few more samples. Have your name, address and phone number printed on the front of the postcard beneath the image, or in the return address corner. Somewhere on the card should be printed your name, along with the word "Illustrator."

It is especially effective to send quarterly postcards (with a new image each time) to the same art directors. If you use one or two colors, you can keep the cost below $200 for about 500 postcards. A full-color card will cost a little more.

You can have postcards printed inexpensively at commercial printers like Modern Postcard (see sidebar on page 45 for more information) and Copy Craft (1-800-794-5594, www.copycraft.com). Your printing costs may be lower if you can give the printing company a longer deadline.

If you want to show more of your work on one sample, you can opt for an 8×12 color or black and white photocopy of your work. It is an inexpensive, yet very effective choice for a promotional piece. It's a great way to show many characters at once.

Query or cover letter

A query letter is a nice way to introduce yourself to art directors for the first time. One or two paragraphs stating you are available for freelance work is all you need. Keep your tone friendly and professional, and be sure to include your phone number, samples or tearsheets. If your forte is creative fonts or hand-printing, and you want to show this talent to the art director, it is OK to print your letter, otherwise type your query letter using an easy-to-read font. It's also a nice touch to send a letter on your own professional stationery. Illustrators can design letterhead incorporating a logo or an illustration (of course, be sure to include your name, address, phone, fax, e-mail and website).

MARY COX has been editor of Artist's & Graphic Designer's Market *since the 1995 edition of the book and is a frequent contributor to other Writer's Digest Books titles. In the last few years she's seen thousands of self-promotional pieces from illustrators come across her desk; she often tacks the best ones to her office walls.*

Tearsheets

After you complete assignments, ask the art director if she can arrange to send you copies of any printed pages on which your illustration appears. If the art director agrees and sends you some tearsheets, you can then send those tearsheets to other art directors as samples. Tearsheets impress art directors because they are proof you are experienced and have met deadlines on previous projects.

If you send 8 × 12 photocopies or tearsheets, do not fold them. It is more professional to send them flat, not folded, in a 9 × 12 envelope, along with a typed query letter, preferable on your own professional stationery.

Mailing & following-up

After your first mailing, there will be a period of time—often as long as three or four months—when you say to yourself, "Gee, what's the difference! I've sent out all these samples, but art directors aren't calling me." That is the norm. It will take time for those samples to start working. Look upon those weeks or months as the time it takes for seeds in a garden to start taking root so they can grow. Busy yourself by sending out more samples instead of waiting by the mailbox.

Direct mail is cumulative. You must send follow-up mailings on a regular basis. I recommend quarterly mailing. An art director might really like your style, but she may not have a project requiring that particular style at the moment. But six months from now she might have something that would fit your style perfectly. If she's misplaced or misfiled your sample, she may be waiting for another to get your contact information.

I advise every illustrator to send out holiday promotions. Everyone loves getting holiday cards, and they are more likely to be kept and displayed on bulletin boards than most cards. Use your imagination and come up with seasonal cards that get you remembered!

You don't need to send a portfolio when you first contact a publisher or magazine. But after art directors see your samples, they may want to see more.

These suggestions are the basics. After your first mailing, consider branching out. Think about launching a web page or advertising in an illustration sourcebook or directory such as *Picturebook* (see sidebar below). Before you know it, your self-promotion will have paid off with book and magazine assignments.

Great Self-Promotion Contacts

Here is contact information for *Picturebook*, a sourcebook just for children's illustrators, and Modern Postcard, a highly recommended printer that offers 500 postcards for $95.

Picturebook
2080 Valleydale Rd.
Suite 15
Birmingham, AL 35244
(888)490-0100
Fax: (205)403-9162
E-mail: picturebook@picture-book.com
Website: www.picture-book.com

Modern Postcard
1675 Faraday Ave.
Carlsbad CA 92008
(800)959-8365
Fax: (760)431-1939
FaxBack info system: (760)431-9788
E-mail: modern.cs@irisgroup.com
Website: www.modernpostcard.com

Postcards like the ones above are just one tool in illustrator Phyllis Harris's marketing strategy. "I use Modern Postcard and it cost $107 for 500 regular-sized postcards," she says. Harris designed an identity logo for herself which she uses on her postcards and her website, www.phyllisharris.com. She sends quarterly mailings to a list of a about 75 art directors and editors, including a holiday promotion. She created her website for interested art directors and editors on her mailing list to view more of her portfolio. "But I've recently begun getting jobs through my website from editors who are searching the web to find new talent," Harris says. "It's another great promotional tool and that's the name of the game—promotion, promotion, promotion."

Gianna Marino and Lisa Harkrader have both just begun marketing their work as illustrators. Both chose a single, striking image and had 500 postcards printed. They also designed memorable business cards as part of their promotional packages. "The people looking at these cards can see how you handle design, if you are professional, and what kind of attention you are going to put into a project," says Marino (who also has a website, www.giannamarino.com). Postcards and business cards were first steps for Harkrader, who also put together a portfolio for critique at the L.A. SCBWI conference. "In a few months I'll get a postcard with a new image printed, and send it out as an update to editors and art directors. Promotion is like throwing stones in a pond," she says. "You never know where the ripples will end up."

"It's important to develop a very personal style before anything else," says illustrator Aileen Leijten. To get the attention of art directors and editors, Leijten designs promo pieces on her computer featuring five to eight images like the one above. Using her computer, "I can print out a sample whenever I want, however many I need, and I can always make changes." She includes her promo sheet, a résumé, and her distinctive business card in her mailings. Leijten also created a website (www.aleijten.com) to showcase her work. "I don't need to send a portfolio in the mail that may get lost. People can visit my website and get an immediate broad idea of my work."

Julie Todd created a business card and a simple postcard "with an intriguing and memorable image" as part of her self-promotion arsenal. She gives out her postcard at conferences and uses it for quick hello-reminder notes to editors and art directors. Todd mails a promo package in a folder containing a letter, an 8½ × 11 sheet showcasing 5-8 of her best illustrations, her promo postcard, a reply postcard, and a SASE, and always directs her package to a specific person. "You have to be your best self-promoter," she says. "If someone else can get you work—an agent or an art rep—that's great. But it's your job to stay on top of things and be responsible for yourself."

Don't Fall for These Direct Mail Misconceptions

There's something to be said about plunging into a career head-on with enthusiasm. That enthusiasm is pure gold! But on the other hand, when successful illustrators look back on the beginnings of their careers they invariably wish they could have been a little more prepared for the realities of the market place. "There are some common misconceptions about marketing I know I've fallen for on occasion," says Phyllis Pollema-Cahill, who is featured in the Insider Report on page 233. Here's her list of common traps to avoid as you start your direct mail campaign.

1. The *"I'll change their mind" misconception.* If a publication doesn't use the type of illustration I do they'll see my work, fall in love with it and change their mind. It's very unlikely this will happen.

2. The *"savior" misconception.* A publication would really benefit from my help. I could "save" them from mediocre art. That may be true, but chances are they just don't have the budget to pay for more professional art.

3. The *"shotgun" misconception.* I'll send my samples to everyone and see which ones stick. It's so much better to save your postage and concentrate your efforts on sending samples to those publications for whom your work is really appropriate. When there are huge slush piles it hurts us all.

Historical Fiction: Bringing the Past to Life for Young Readers

BY DEBORAH HOPKINSON

Over the years, I've kept copies of my (many) unpublished stories in binders on my closet shelf. Every so often I pull down a binder and peruse its contents, hoping to discover a forgotten story that somehow, like wine, has improved with age. What I usually find is more like vinegar, or worse. Did I actually write—let alone submit—a story called "The Girl Who Wouldn't Eat Anything Green," about a child who wouldn't eat her peas until they danced on her plate and talked her into it?

Looking back, I think it took about two years of (unpublished) submissions before I found my way to historical fiction, the genre I've come to love best. Along the way I dabbled in silly animal stories, badly retold fairy tales, and, well, vegetable stories.

Now if you're drawn to fantasy, mysteries, or middle grade humor, go ahead and follow your heart. But if you've ever thought about trying your hand at historical fiction, I'd like to offer some hints to get you started. Hopefully you'll end up with many published works—and more closet space than I have.

IS HISTORICAL FICTION FOR YOU?

If you've never considered writing historical fiction because you're not sure if you have the skills, you might want to think again. You don't have to hold a Ph.D. to write good historical fiction. You'll know this genre fits your writing personality if you can answer yes to some of these questions:

Do you love research?
- Are you insanely curious about the details of history?
- Do you ever find yourself rambling on at cocktail receptions and dinner parties about obscure historical personages?
- Do you keep a notepad by your side when you watch *Antiques Roadshow*, in case there might be some tidbit of history you might want to look up later?
- Is Ken Burns one of your heroes?
- Are you willing to spend time reading research books, from scholarly to popular works, to verify one tiny fact?
- Do you search the Internet like a hunting dog on the trail, convinced that what you're looking for just has to be there—somewhere?
- Do you have (or can you get) access to excellent libraries or inter-library loan services?

DEBORAH HOPKINSON *works full-time in educational fundraising for Whitman College in Walla Walla, Washington, where she sometimes teaches children's literature. Her 2001 books are* Fannie in the Kitchen, Bluebird Summer *and* Under the Quilt of Night. *She is the recipient of the 1999 SCBWI Golden Kite Award for picture book text for* A Band of Angels, *which was also an ALA Notable Book for Children. Her other books include* Maria's Comet; Birdie's Lighthouse, *a Parents Choice Honor Book; and* Sweet Clara and the Freedom Quilt, *winner of the 1994 International Reading Association Award.*

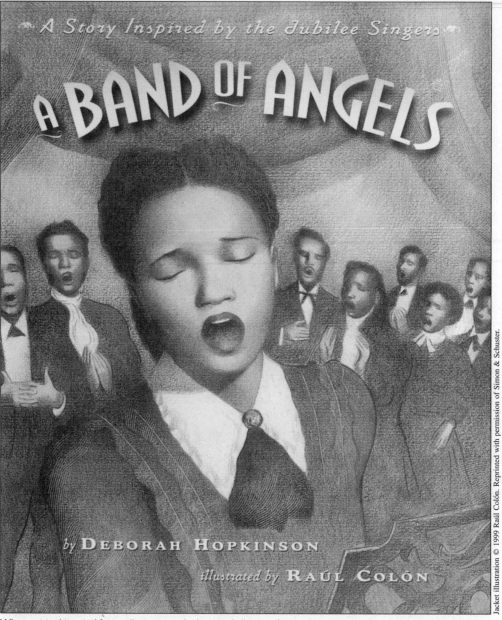

When writing historical fiction, "sometimes the biggest challenge is finding the right voice for your story," says Deborah Hopkinson. In her first draft of *A Band of Angels*, she told the story from Ella Sheppard's point of view, relating her experiences as one of the founding members of the Jubilee Singers of Fisk University. "But my editor felt that it wasn't child-centered enough, and it took several more revisions to create the story-within-a-story format of the final book."

- Are you willing to make phone calls, send e-mails, or go in person to track down facts, check references or simply ask questions?

If you find yourself answering in the affirmative, then you're probably curious and persistent, and willing to work hard for your story. Chances are you'll love historical fiction. The next step is to find something to write about.

FINDING STORIES IN HISTORY

When I visit schools, students always want to know where I get my ideas. I usually lob the question back, "Well, I'm no different from you. Where do you get *yours*?"

In fact, story ideas for historical fiction are all around us: in newspapers, radio, books, museums, roadside markers, the Internet, and of course, in our personal experiences. My first picture book, *Sweet Clara and the Freedom Quilt*, was written after hearing a National Public Radio piece about African-American quilts; *Maria's Comet* grew out of finding Maria Mitchell's name on an Internet calendar of famous women; and *Fannie in the Kitchen* evolved after reading about the real Fannie Farmer in an anthology of women inventors.

But suppose you come across a promising old volume in the town library. How do you determine whether that tantalizing historical footnote you've found will make a good story? How do you decide whether it should be a novel, picture book, easy reader, or a magazine story? Perhaps most important, how do you assess whether something that fascinates you will be equally interesting to an editor and publisher, let alone a young reader?

In general, it's helpful to ask yourself some questions before you start your research. Here are some suggestions to start you off:

- Do the elements of a good story exist? Is there the potential for conflict? Are there characters here whose lives have the power to engage us
- Is there a child in the story? If not, is it possible to tell the story from a child's point of view?
- Is the subject of the story suitable, of interest to young children or teens?
- How complex is this topic? Do you see it as a thirty-two-page picture book, or does it

---

What Do Editors Look For?

Anne Schwartz, Director of Anne Schwartz Books, an imprint of Atheneum Books for Young Readers, looks for "the same spark in historical fiction that I do in any writing—a strong, vivid, unique voice; a compelling story; a subject that hasn't been done to death; and of course, a child-friendly approach that disguises any whiff of educational content the piece might contain!"

Scholastic Press editor Amy Griffin, who edits the Dear America series among others, notes that she "looks mainly for curricular-based stories. We do publish books about smaller areas in history if the author has a strong enough voice and we think the idea is appealing enough to draw readers in. I think good historical fiction, like all fiction, starts with the character. Even if the book is about a terribly gripping time in history, the book will not be appealing without a character with whom our readers can connect. Then there is the task of researching all the wonderful details of the time. What did our character eat? What did she wear? What did he do in the evenings? Basically, what was the daily life like?

"In our books, we try to strike a balance and to make all of that information organic to the plot. The author weaves in certain details from his or her research in a way that the story couldn't exist without it. The reader never feels overwhelmed by the history or by the historical details, but she or he is learning by reading these books and can say, 'Oh, during the Revolutionary War, some families lived like this,' or 'On the Mayflower, some people had to do that.'"

seem to cry out for a longer treatment?
- Is this a story that in your heart you feel *needs* to be told?
- Are you the right person to tell this story?

In addition, I often find myself evaluating whether the topic will be of interest to librarians and educators. Could the subject matter be used in the classroom? Are there obvious curriculum connections? It's difficult to research and write a book and equally hard to sell one. The stronger case you can make for your story, the better the chance that, instead of languishing on a closet shelf, your manuscript will someday get a binder of its very own, complete with a contract, reviews and royalty statements.

But there's another reason to pay attention to the classroom. Since my first picture book was published in 1993, I've come to appreciate the role educators and librarians play as proponents and caretakers of our literary heritage. Teachers and librarians are often the driving force that keeps many historical fiction books alive. They also embrace titles that can be used in multidisciplinary ways. For example, *Sweet Clara and the Freedom Quilt* has been incorporated into social studies units as well as in mathematics activities.

As I've become more aware of the creative ways my books are used in classrooms, I've been careful to include historical notes and background information in my later books. *Maria's Comet* includes both a historical note on Maria Mitchell, as well as a glossary of astronomy definitions. *A Band of Angels* includes a historical note and, on the endpapers, biographical information on the original Jubilee singers whose story inspired the book.

CRAFTING YOUR STORY

You've done your research, your idea has all the elements of a good story, you're ready to write. Where to start? I wish I had one of Fannie Farmer's foolproof recipes to offer, but when I look at my own books and how they came to be, about the only thing I can tell you for sure is to keep trying—and never throw away research or a story idea.

Sometimes the biggest challenge is finding the right voice for your story. In my first draft of *A Band of Angels*, I told the story from Ella Sheppard's point of view, relating her experiences as one of the founding members of the Jubilee Singers of Fisk University. But my editor felt that it wasn't child-centered enough, and it took several more revisions to create the story-within-a-story format of the final book.

Other times it's a matter of finding the right format. Years ago I wrote an (unpublished) Civil War novel. In the course of researching it, I came across a true story of a deserter in the battle of Gettysburg. When it seemed clear the novel was destined to find a permanent home in my closet, I tried re-working the deserter incident into a picture book. That wasn't right either. But when I had the opportunity to write two easy readers recently, I pulled out my research once more. Next year, at long last, *Billy and the Rebel* will be published as a Ready-to-Read by Simon & Schuster. So, never throw that research away.

Sometimes a story simply isn't strong enough for an entire book. I got my start writing stories for *Cricket Magazine*, to which I still contribute. Magazines offer wonderful opportunities for working with editors, compiling a track record, and reaching young readers. If you have a historical fiction idea and think it might work as a magazine story, then you're reading the perfect book to help you decide where to send it!

The best historical fiction helps readers imagine themselves in another time and place. It should also spark critical thinking as well as emotional connections.

In writing about Ella Sheppard or astronomer Maria Mitchell, my aim was not biography. Rather it was to explore through *story* an emotional truth or connection I myself discovered. When I first encountered these women's diaries, I immediately felt the vibrancy of their remarkable spirits across time. I felt connected to these other human beings who preceded me and curious to know more. In crafting my stories for young readers, I tried to share that connection and curiosity.

"*Maria's Comet* grew out of finding Maria Mitchell's name on an Internet Calendar of famous women," says author Deborah Hopkinson. In her author's note, Hopkinson points out, "*Maria's Comet* is a work of fiction, but it was inspired by a real person. Maria Mitchell was America's first woman astronomer. In *Maria's Comet*, I've tried to capture Maria Mitchell's wonderful questioning spirit and dedication to women's education by showing a girl who discovers and stands up for her desire to explore the world of science."

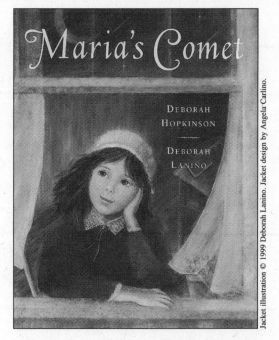

Jacket illustration © 1999 Deborah Lanino. Jacket design by Angela-Carlino.

It's important to remember that once you put words into the mouth of a historical person, you're creating fiction. You may find yourself stepping outside your own time, place and culture, as well as gender, race and class. You'll need to grapple with often difficult questions about accuracy, revisionist history, political correctness. Each writer must come to terms with these on his or her own. It's helpful to consult with experts and others who may know about your story. I was fortunate that Beth Howse, a descendent of Ella Sheppard and a librarian at Fisk, was willing to read the manuscript of *A Band of Angels* in draft form. While working on *Maria's Comet*, illustrator Deborah Lanino faxed the artwork for a small painting of Polaris to me with a question: Was it correct? Dr. Andrea Dobson, a professor of astronomy at Whitman College where I work, consulted a program that showed exactly how Polaris would have looked from a Massachusetts rooftop in January 1828.

Still, errors can happen, and the best you can do is to keep scrupulous notes, take responsibility for accuracy, and, as I'm always telling my seventh grader, "Check your work!"

WHY WRITE HISTORICAL FICTION?

In a 1999 article Professor Sam Wineburg of the University of Washington w
to know others, whether they live on the other side of the tracks or the other s
nium, requires the education of our sensibilities. This is what history, whe
us practice in doing."

Historical fiction books can launch young readers on a lifelong love
tions they make to characters resonate in their own lives, too. After r
one girl wrote me, "I have a connection to Birdie because when n
money. I learned that if you work hard enough, you can do anything."

When I speak to school groups, historical fiction isn't usually the gen
favorite. Scary stories, animal stories and mysteries rank far higher. I

presentation, kids can't wait to touch the replica of Sweet Clara's quilt, pointing out the path she took on the underground railroad.

History is a lifelong study, a search for truth and meaning, not just of the lives of others, but of our own. Discovering stories that have the power to inspire is one of the joys I take in reading about history and in writing historical fiction. I hope you agree.

Historical Fiction Reading List

Reading historical fiction is a great way to learn about the genre. Here are some stellar historical fiction picture books to get you started:

Mary Anning and the Sea Dragon, by Jeannine Atkins, illustrated by Michael Dooling (Farrar Straus & Giroux, 1999). A beautifully illustrated book on Mary Anning focusing on her discovery of the first sea reptile fossil.

Alice Ramsey's Grand Adventure, by Don Brown (Houghton Mifflin, 1997). The amazing story of Alice Ramsey, who drove across America in 1909 in 59 days.

Fly, Bessie, Fly, by Lynn Joseph, illustrated by Yvonne Buchanan (Simon & Schuster, 1998). A picture book inspired by the life of Bessie Coleman, the first black woman aviator.

Molly Bannaky, by Alice McGill, illustrated by Chris K. Soentpiet (Houghton Mifflin, 1999). A historical fiction picture book about Benjamin Banneker's grandmother, who marries Benjamin Bannaky, a man who had been her slave.

Richard Wright and the Library Card, by William Miller, illustrated by Gregory Christie (Lee & Low, 1997). An episode from the autobiography of the writer Richard Wright, who was unable to get a library card in Memphis in the 1920s, retold in this handsome picture book.

Tomas and the Library Lady, by Pat Mora, illustrated by Raúl Colón (Knopf, 1997). A tribute to the life of Tomas Rivera and the librarian who aided him. Rivera began his life as a migrant worker and eventually became a university chancellor.

Dear Benjamin Banneker, by Andrea Davis Pinkney, illustrated by Brian Pinkney (Gulliver Books, 1994). A picture book exploring the life of astronomer Benjamin Banneker.

Minty: A Story of Young Harriet Tubman, by Alan Schroeder, illustrated. by Jerry Pinkney (Dial, 1996). A fictionalized account of the childhood of young Tubman.

Madaket Millie, by Frances Weller, illustrated by Marcia Sewell (Philomel, 1997). The story of a Nantucket girl, Millie Madaket, who trained dogs to patrol beaches and conduct lifesaving rescues.

My Name is Georgia: A Portrait, by Jeannette Winter (Harcourt Silver Whistle, 1998). A portrait of artist Georgia O'Keefe and the development of her distinct artistic style.

Mazes, Dot-to-Dots, Hidden Pictures—Illustrators, Break in with Puzzles!

BY MAURIE J. MANNING

It is difficult and sometimes frustrating to break into the children's illustration market. The field is crowded with talent, much of it well established. For a new illustrator trying to break in, getting an art director to take a serious look at your portfolio and then to actually match you with a story, article or book can take a long time. Puzzles and other fillers can be a quick way to showcase your style and get you that mystical first-published piece.

In general, an editor either buys puzzle ideas from writers, or the puzzles are created in-house and the art director assigns an artist to illustrate. But what busy editor could resist a clever crossword, rebus, secret code or word search with accompanying illustration tailored to their particular magazine's look and feel?

One advantage in sending out puzzles as a first contact is that if you do your research on the markets, you can tailor a piece that an editor may buy on the spot. There is always a need to fill that extra page in a magazine. However, doing your research is critical. Magazines typically specialize in subject matter, audience age and gender and stylistic look, so you'd better not send a haunted house maze to a religious magazine or a hidden picture of a girl playing dress up to a magazine for ten-year-old boys.

Children's magazines often publish several puzzles in each issue. There are entire magazines dedicated to puzzles. Mazes, dot-to-dots, word games, crosswords, hidden pictures, matching games and memory games are some of the traditional favorites, but the list is as long as your imagination. Some time spent looking at the huge variety of published puzzles will leave you amazed and motivated. *Highlights for Children* has a wonderful series of books called Puzzlemania full of diverse, colorful puzzles which I highly recommend as a source of inspiration.

KNOW YOUR MARKET

Go to your local library with a notebook and a ruler and take out a stack of past issues of as many different children's magazines as you can find. Study the puzzles and other fillers. Who publishes line art and who does full color? What is the size of the magazine? In general, do interior illustrations bleed off the page or have a margin or border? Do they typically place text within the illustration or separately above or below the art? Who publishes art styles you feel most comfortable doing? By this time you should be getting that "I can do one of those!" feelings and may even have in your hand a particular magazine you plan to aim at first.

MAURIE J. MANNING, *began her career in the early 1980s by submitting puzzles and hidden pictures to magazines like* Highlights for Children, Children's Digest, Child Life, *and* Humpty Dumpty's. *She's since consistently illustrated stories, too, as well as illustrating and art directing for children's educational software and computer game companies. A full-time freelance illustrator, Manning lives in Costa, California, with her two children and her golden retriever Gisbourne. Visit her website http://members.aol.com/ amjmanning/ to view a sampling of her work, and get more tips on illustrating puzzles.*

Time to Clean Up

Can you find these hidden pictures?

pliers, pear, needle, spoon, candle, mitten, ballpoint pen, feather, flag, banana, artist's brush, screwdriver, pencil, flashlight, heart, fork, toothbrush, kite

Maurie J. Manning's hidden picture drawing, "Time to Clean Up," appeared in *Highlights® Hidden Pictures 1999*. "I have sold countless hidden pictures to *Highlights* and even now, as I am more established in my career, I still do a couple dozen for them a year," says Manning. "I find that besides being a great foot-in-the-door, illustrating puzzles continues to be an excellent 'filler' for that inevitable space between big jobs. It is often the difference between being able to support my family as a freelancer doing what I love, and giving it all up for a steadier paycheck and a cubicle."

By researching and carefully targeting specific magazines, you already have an advantage over the multitude of "blind mailings" publishers get weekly from over-eager artists.

In the mid-1980s, when I was breaking in, I sold mazes and crossword puzzles to *Children's Digest* starring a character I developed specifically to market to them called "Gadgabber the Health Wizard." (Later I even sold them a story I wrote about him—"Gadgabber the Health Wizard and the Mysterious Black Haze," which of course I was also assigned to illustrate.) I knew *Children's Digest* had a health focus. I knew children would like a silly old wizard. And I knew a good puzzle is hard for an editor to resist. I got quite a bit of mileage out of that one idea, primarily because I knew my market.

Note: You can expect to sell your puzzles most often as work-for-hire, which means you give all rights to the publisher. For this reason, I suggest that artists don't create any illustrations that they'll have trouble letting go of emotionally. Don't design any characters you might later like to develop further for your own projects.

But you should use this opportunity to do more than hope for a check for a couple hundred dollars. You should be looking at this as a way to interest an editor and art director in your style and to familiarize them with your name. This is your one-piece portfolio, so this artwork has to be as wonderful as anything you've ever done.

TECHNICALLY SPEAKING

The most obvious statement about puzzles is they are based on logic. For many puzzles, there has to be only one right answer or a child will feel cheated. One way through the maze. One way to put the jigsaw together. One three-letter word for "night bird" starting with the letter *O*. It's okay if a puzzle has several possible correct answers, just take into account that children are clever and creative and hate being told they're wrong for an alternative correct answer. They also love to find errors and then write to scold the editor about them! So be clear of the objective in your puzzle design, and pay attention to details. If you do a puzzle asking "How many smaller words can you find in the word *abracadabra*," make sure you note that the solvers may find more words than the answers listed, because they will.

On the conceptual side, there is no room for ethnic, racial, gender, age or other bias in children's magazines and it's surprising how many artists innocently forget to keep that in mind. They send a sweet scene of five Caucasian Boy Scouts roasting hot dogs and singing campfire songs. In fact, you will find that putting a character in a wheelchair, or a girl sliding into home plate, or a well-researched and accurate depiction of a Cinco De Mayo or Kwanzaa celebration in your puzzle will hook you a quick contract from a magazine. Also, it may sound strange, but remember to put helmets on bicyclers and life jackets on boaters, even if they are polar bears or robots instead of humans. I'm not saying you can't be outrageous and silly; kids love that stuff, but remember that most magazines are subject to scrutiny from special interest groups and PC is the course for most publications nowadays.

NARROWING YOUR FOCUS

How much writing must you do? If you're a puzzle fan yourself and have a knack with words, try tackling a crossword, word search or rebus. If you're a writer as well as an illustrator, there are brain teasers and mini-mysteries where the important clues are in the illustration. If you'd rather not write a word at all, try something like a hidden picture, a maze, or a "what's wrong with this picture."

In addition to puzzles, think about other fillers you might be able to market. Maybe you have a simple recipe kids would enjoy making or a little-known technique for folding super-high-flying paper airplanes. Perhaps you're a trivia buff or keep a collection of the latest jokes the local third graders are cracking up over. You can illustrate a folksong or finger play or a classic nursery rhyme. (Beware, however, of using copyrighted material.)

Remember for these, as is true for word-based puzzles, your text needs to be as professional

DOG DAY AFTERNOON

How many unusual things can you see in this picture?

Dog Shoe

Judges

6 PUZZLEMANIA

Illustrated by Maurie Jo Manning

Illustrator Maurie J. Manning highly recommends *Highlights for Children*'s Puzzlemania series and its diverse, colorful puzzles as a source of inspiration for illustrators interested in creating puzzles themselves. Manning's "what's wrong" drawing "Dog Day Afternoon," (which appeared in Puzzlemania) asks readers to pick out unusual things in the picture. How many can you find?

as your illustration. In including a manuscript, you're giving the editor two directions she must turn her critical eye.

An artist can take virtually any sketch or idea and make it into a puzzle. I often go back through my stacks of sketchbooks to find inspiration. Or I brainstorm, hitting on theme like, "grandparents" or "autumn" or "school," then jot down lists as long as I can of possible scenes to illustrate.

Next I narrow my focus. Say in my "grandparents" list there is a note that says "grandparent jogging with grandchild." I might decide to do a maze. I think, perhaps a maze of jogging paths through a park. Or maybe a hedge maze. Or a maze through the suburban sprawl. (I also think, maybe the child is at the opposite end of the maze and grandparent has to find her—and quickly nix the idea, realizing an editor might not like the idea of a "lost" child for their magazine— so, they jog together.)

Or . . . maybe I'll use that idea for a crossword puzzle instead. I design a simple crossword of fifteen to thirty age-appropriate words having to do with my jogging/grandparent/grandchild theme. Using the longest word as a base, I experiment on a piece of graph paper, branching the shorter words off of the longest one. I'll try to keep the puzzle from sprawling all over the page (though the symmetrical design typical of adult crossword puzzles is not always necessary in children's crosswords.) I type out a simple and clear clue for each word. Now that I know the basic shape of my crossword and can estimate the amount of space that I will need to leave for clues, it's time to design an illustration that will grab an editor.

Give as much care to your design and composition as if this was a lucrative contract from a major publisher. The placement of any title or text is a critical part of your design, just as it will be when you are illustrating your Caldecott-winning picture book.

FROM SKETCH TO SUBMISSION

Your sketch should be drawn at the correct size for the magazine you have targeted. With a ruler, measure the dimensions of the magazine and add a quarter-inch all around if your illustration is intended to bleed off the page.

Once you have your tight sketch, take some cheap photocopies of it and pass them out to children of different ages (as well as some adults). Is the premise clear? Does the text work? Is it hard enough—and not too hard for the audience you intend? Was it fun to solve? Is the illustration appealing? If the answers are all an honest yes, you are ready to go on to finished art.

I usually use bristol board or watercolor paper for my traditional work. My current favorite medium, however, is the computer now that so many publishers accept digital art. You should use your favorite technique to showcase your style. Do NOT include any text on your finished art (though you should leave space for it.) When your final art is finished, get a nice color photocopy of it. You will send the photocopy, with a tracing paper overlay indicating text and/ or puzzle answers taped on top to the editor of the magazine. Never send finished art until you are instructed to do so by an interested editor. If you are doing digital art, your resolution must be at least 300 dpi and you should send a color printout as your sample, indicating in the cover letter that the original is digital art.

If you have a text-based puzzle like a crossword or a puzzle including a setup story you will need to include a separate, double-spaced, typed manuscript in your submission package. For example, a hidden picture of a little girl in her messy bedroom might say:

Lily is Late
by Maurie J. Manning
Oh no, Lily slept too late again! The bus will be here in five minutes to pick her up. Can you help her find these missing objects so she doesn't have to walk? Lily's left shoe, three schoolbooks, an apple, a quarter for milk, her lunchbox, a pencil, an eraser and a box of crayons.

Then, besides your photocopied artwork, you should include a brief cover letter. All you really need to say is that you're an illustrator new to the field, ask if they are interested in publishing the enclosed puzzle, and indicate that you will send them the finished art if they would like. Be polite and businesslike. Keep the cover letter to half a page. Your puzzle should speak for itself.

Lastly, always include a SASE for the return of your work if it is not accepted. Everyone is rejected, even writers and illustrators with many years of experience. It's important not to be discouraged by this and to take great inspiration in any personal notes. My first hidden picture submission to *Highlights* in the early 1980s garnered me a personal rejection letter from the late, great art director, John R. Crane. He spent two typed, single-spaced pages encouraging me on the uniqueness of my style, but pointing out that my children all looked monkeylike and rather "stupid" from an overlarge upper lip I had the habit to draw. Fortunately, I was so thrilled to get a personal note back from a real live art director that I was not discouraged by his criticism and took his comments to heart. Though he didn't buy the next hidden picture I submitted either, he bought the next. And the next.

Over the last seventeen years I have sold countless hidden pictures to *Highlights* and even now, as I am more established in my career, I still do a couple dozen for them a year. I find that besides being a great foot-in-the-door, illustrating puzzles continues to be an excellent "filler" for that inevitable space between big jobs. It is often the difference between being able to support my family as a freelancer doing what I love, and giving it all up for a steadier paycheck and a cubicle.

Puzzle Submission Package

Your submission package should be as professional as possible. You're trying to sell a finished illustration, so your work should speak for itself. Enclose the following in your package:

- A brief cover letter addressed to the proper editor. This should just indicate that you are a new illustrator and that you're hoping they'll be interested in the enclosed puzzle. (Say you have the finished art if they would like you to send it.)
- A good photocopy of your finished puzzle This should be in color if your puzzle is in color and should *not* include any text.
- A tracing paper overlay. Here is where you indicate the puzzle key if necessary, or show where text would go.
- A separate typed manuscript (only if your puzzle includes text.)
- A SASE. Always include a self-addressed, stamped envelope for the return of your materials.

Read illustrator Maurie J. Manning's above recommendations for creating a professional puzzle proposal package including all the elements shown here.

Ghosts, Cheerleaders & Clones: A Series of Series Books

BY LINDA JOY SINGLETON

When I was 14, I mailed off an application to the Famous Writers School. On the form, I wrote: "I hope to be a girl's mystery writer, but mainly to have a series of my own."

My big dream. More than anything, I wanted to write a series like Nancy Drew, Trixie Belden or Judy Bolton. This was the goal I aspired to but never really expected to happen. And yet, decades later, it *did* happen.

Of course, it wasn't an easy journey. In fact, the Famous Writers School turned me down. "Too young," they cited. "Try again when you're 17." Only life interrupted and I didn't seriously pursue a writing career until I was 28.

Then I jumped into the writing world with renewed hopes and high enthusiasm. I joined writing groups and a weekly critique group. I attended conferences, read constantly, and wrote daily. I learned how to write queries, synopses, and how to not take rejections *too* personally.

My first series attempt was a mystery with a 13-year-old sleuth named Penny Candy. Penny made it to the semi-final round of a contest and even garnered a recommendation to a prominent agent. But Penny didn't make the contest's final rounds, and the agent turned me down.

So I tried a different angle. I researched packagers who put together series like Nancy Drew and Sweet Valley. I sent off for writing "auditions," and wrote sample chapters for both Nancy Drew and Sweet Valley Twins. I bombed out with Nancy Drew, but after two tries for Sweet Valley Twins, I was hired to write #59, *Barnyard Battle*.

I read a dozen Sweet Valley books to learn their style. Then I wrote the book per specifications from three editors. Rewrites were challenging and often came with tight deadlines.

Writing for a packager is not for everyone, but if you can write fast and take instruction well, it's a way to earn publishing credits and sharpen skills. Also, it can lead to more series assignments, and in rare cases, your own series.

While I worked for packagers, I continued to submit to publishers and agents. I had sold nine books on my own when I finally got an agent. She liked *My Sister The Ghost*; a completed midgrade novel. Along with this manuscript, I included one page with four short descriptions for additional Ghost books. Months later *My Sister The Ghost* sold to Avon Books as a series.

Finally, I had my own series! I was so thrilled!

This four-book series led to my selling a second series to Avon. The idea for a cheerleading series was editor-generated, and I was invited to submit a series proposal.

Cheer Squad series proposal:

LINDA JOY SINGLETON *is the author of over twenty middle grade and young adult books, including Berkley's mystery series about teen clones, Regeneration (under the name L.J. Singleton). She lives near Sacramento, California and works as a full-time author. Her fifth Regeneration title,* The Killer, *is a January 2001 release. You can read excerpts from this series, view covers, and get writing tips from her website: www.geocities.com/Athens/Acropolis/4815/.*

Tips For Writing Series

- The action in the story should come out of character conflict.
- End chapters with a question/dramatic revelation/ cliffhanger.
- Don't get bogged down with a crowd of characters—you don't have to reintroduce everyone in the opening chapter of each book. Weave in only the important facts.
- Keep the adults few, and make them interesting.
- It's nice to have a pet in the series. In Regeneration, I included a dog who was important to the plot of #2, *The Search*.
- It's also good to have some humor, perhaps one comic character such as nerdy Winston Egbert in Sweet Valley Twins.
- Sometimes it's necessary to kill off characters, but avoid killing off a main character, as readers might feel cheated.
- Have a good setting. Example: Roswell's alien museum.
- Keep a folder with important character information so you don't have to search through the books for small details.
- Give the characters personal growth in each book.
- Don't save the best things—like in #1 Regeneration, Chase's secret is revealed on the last page. I had planned to reveal this in later books, but my editor suggested using it as an ending scene, and it worked great.
- Surprise readers with new writing styles and plot situations. Always strive for improvement.
- Keep current: Read writing magazines like *Publishers Weekly* and newsletters like *Children's Book Insider* and *Children's Writer*. Read teen magazines, watch kid's TV shows, and eavesdrop whenever kids are around.

1. **Opening pages.** I introduced the characters, in an upbeat "cheerful" style to match the series tone: "A big wave for Wendi Holcroft!" "Kick and shout, Krystal Carvell!"
2. **Synopsis.** A three-page synopsis of first book. (See The Basis of Synopsis Writing (With a Hint of Chocolate) on page 29 for more information.)
3. **Additional Books.** One page of descriptions for three additional Cheer Squad books.
4. **First Chapter.** A nine-page first chapter.

My Avon editor liked my proposal, and I wrote six Cheer Squad books. But instead of my career going forward after these series, my career stopped. For three and a half years I was unable to sell another book. Ideas and proposals came and went; rejections poured in. It was like starting over again. I grew very discouraged.

Finally, I came up with the idea for a series about teen clones. This series sold to Berkley books. Regeneration (originally titled Sci-Clones) proposal:

1. **The Series.** Two pages listing ten short book descriptions. Example: Book #3: Missing Persons—Allison helps in the search to find the missing clone, using her physical strength to escape a dire kidnapping. (Note: Title and plot changed later.)
2. **Characters.** A page describing five main characters. Example: Eric Prince—Adopted into a large family, some kids with disabilities. He has enhanced vision, which makes everyday sight awkward, so he wears glasses. He's klutzy, friendly, and brilliant with computers. He was cloned from a computer genius.
3. **Series Premise.** Opening hook—*Party of Five* meets *The X-Files* when five teenagers discover they are the result of a cloning experiment gone wrong. Then nine pages describing the series.

Under the name L.J. Singleton, author Linda Joy Singleton created the Regeneration series for Berkley. In what she describes as "*Party of Five* meets *The X-Files*," Singleton's series follow five teens cloned in an experiment in DNA enhancement, "each created from genes of a different person, each meant to be perfect." The teens band together after fifteen years apart to defeat the madman mastermind behind the experiment who is determined to destroy them. Her fifth Regeneration title, *The Killer*, is a January 2001 release.

4. **Characters.** A more complete breakdown of the five main characters; each two-three pages long.
5. **Chapter 1.** The first chapter; ten pages.

Since I sold Regeneration from a proposal, now the real work began—writing the contracted books. I was given three months to write each book. So I worked five to six mornings a week, pushing myself to produce three to five pages daily. Tip: By working out a writing schedule, even tight deadlines are manageable.

To my pride and joy, my first YA series, Regeneration, began release in January 2000. It's not easy to sell a series, but it can be done. The first thing you need to do is come up with a great series idea.

There are four basic types of juvenile series:

1. *A series based on an activity or skill,* like horseback riding, skating, or babysitting.
2. *A character-based series,* like Sammy Keyes, by Wendelin Van Draanen or Alice by Phyllis Reynolds Naylor.
3. *A situation,* like being an alien or a clone.
4. *A setting,* like a mysterious house, going back in time or finding a fantasy world.

Once you have your series premise, you need to create a compelling proposal. Original series are a challenge to sell. An editor will have to sell the proposal at meetings to other editors as well as the marketing department. The more commercial appeal your series has, the better chance you have of selling it.

Of course, many series don't start out as series. The readers of Caroline B. Cooney's *Face on The Milk Carton* loved this book so much they demanded another story, then another, and even another, until it became a four-book series. Peg Kehret's *Horror At The Haunted House* middle-grade novel was so popular, she wrote several more books with the same brother and sister characters. And Lois Lowry's Anastasia books evolved from a short story.

While setting and a compelling situation are important for a successful series, the characters are the core. Choose your main characters wisely. For my Regeneration series I chose a mixed cast of multi-ethnic boys and girls. Each character has an enhanced clone skill, and each has personal conflicts that will add motivation throughout the series. For instance, Varina, who wants to fit in at a new school, finds out she may be a clone and not fit in with anyone—except other clones.

For me, series books are a good writing fit. I *love* writing series.

Who's Writing Series?

Multi-author/Ghostwritten and/or packaged series (series are written by various authors):

Sweet Valley High/Jr. High	Babysitter Club
Nancy Drew	Love Stories
Hardy Boys	Magic Attic
Boxcar Children	Sweet Sixteen
Thoroughbred	Ghosts of Fear Street
Animorphs	Many licensed TV characters books

These are original series written by a single author:

Sammy Keyes, by Wendelin Van Draanen	Sixth Grade Alien, by Bruce Coville
Alice, by Phyllis Naylor Reynolds	Amber Brown, by Paula Danziger
Clearwater Crossing, by Laura Peyton Roberts	Marvin Redpost, by Louis Sacher
University Hospital, by Cherie Bennett	Polk Street, by Patricia Reilly Giff
Herculeah Jones, by Betsy Byars	Mind Over Matter, by Cheryl Zach
Regeneration, by L.J. Singleton (Couldn't resist including myself!)	Against the Odds, by Todd Strasser

Great Expectations: Conferences Can Make a Difference

BY DARCY PATTISON

"I'm just here to see the editor," said the lady.

I put on my best Conference Director smile. "Everyone comes to see the editor. But you still have to pay for the entire conference. In fact, you'll learn—"

"But the editor only speaks for an hour. Why should I come for anything else? Why should I pay for a whole day?" The lady left the lecture hall in a huff.

This is a true story

This is a sad story. The would-be writer missed a great opportunity.

Conferences are great places to learn more about your craft, to meet other writers and illustrators, and to take the first steps toward furthering your career—no matter what stage that career is in. But expectations make all the difference.

Will you be "discovered" in a conference? Doubtful. (Let's be realistic. Really. It's doubtful.) Then what good is the rest of that long day of meetings?

Attend a conference to learn something

First, expect to learn something. There are four stages of learning: Unconscious Incompetence—you don't know and you don't know that you don't know; Conscious Incompetence—you don't know and you know that you don't know; Conscious Competence—you know and you know you know; Unconscious Competence-you know and you don't know that you know.

When you attend a conference, your expectation should be to move from one level of learning to the next level in a couple areas. This may mean that you find out that you're incompetent in your characterization. This moves you from Unconscious Incompetence to Conscious Incompetence, which means that you now know what you have to work on. It sounds discouraging: "I went to a conference and found out that I can't characterize very well." But I call that a successful conference.

Conferences can not give you competence in a one-hour presentation. Of course, you know that, but sometimes expectations become unreasonable. At most, a conference can help you recognize a deficiency. You'll have to study and practice the skill on your own. Speakers can and do point you in the right direction, give you valuable exercises to practice, and provide examples to follow. However, competence is a hard-won prize that comes only with practice.

Expect serendipity. I usually go to a conference anxious to hear one specific speaker. But more often that not, it's one of the other speakers that surprises me with a new way of looking at something or with a tip that makes all the difference in a story.

Kristin Wolden Nitz, a children's writer who is currently living in Italy, went to the Society

DARCY PATTISON, *www.darcypattison.com, has served as the Conference Director of the Arkansas SCBWI's Writing and Illustrating for Children Conference for the last eight years. She is the author of* The Wayfinder *(Greenwillow, 2000), a middle grade fantasy novel. Her forthcoming picture book,* The Journey of Oliver K. Woodman, *illustrated by Joe Cepeda (Harcourt, 2002) was sold to an editor who first read it for a manuscript critique at the local conference. After revisions, the editor bought the story.*

of Children's Book Writers and Illustrators (SCBWI) conference in France. She says, "I was disappointed that an entire afternoon was dedicated to illustrating, since my primary interest is novels. But author/illustrator Deborah DeSaix demonstrated how every page turn in a picture book is an event and described her process of coming up with a series of images before writing a word of text. I went for information on novels, but instead, I learned about picture books."

I've learned to expect and to look for surprises like this. When you attend a conference, keep an open mind and attend as many sessions as you can.

Attend a conference to be inspired

"Local Illustrator Garners National Attention!" Many conferences include inspirational stories such as this, and for good reason. Writing is a lonely business and we all need to hear stories about successful writers and illustrators. When Plain Jane succeeds, it suddenly seems possible for us to succeed. Plain Jane doesn't have any more charisma than I have, she isn't more intelligent, she isn't even very pretty. In fact, it seems like the only advantage Plain Jane has is that she's too dumb to give up. If she can persevere, so can I!

Attend a conference to meet people

Jane Yolen, author of over 200 children's books, says, "The best thing about conferences is networking, networking, networking." Take a stack of your business cards and be ready to pass them out. Gossip, share the joy of a sale, comfort a discouraged friend, make a new friend—any way you look at it, conferences mean people.

Editors are people. It's one of the best things you'll learn at a conference. Editors have specific likes and dislikes, just like any normal person. You'll learn not to put them on a pedestal, not be scared of them, not to revere them. When you hear an editor speak about their passions, their failures, their children, their bum knees, their frustrating search for a new apartment in the expensive New York housing market—suddenly, the name in a market guide becomes a real person. You begin to understand what they are looking for when they read a manuscript. By the way, an editor is like a snake: she's just as nervous about meeting you as you are about meeting her! But she's a lot nicer than a snake. She doesn't have fangs or a poisonous bite.

Other writers and illustrators are people, too. In your rush to make a good impression on the editor, don't overlook the person sitting next to you. That person may be the next Plain Jane. And she may live in your town and be willing to be your mentor. Or her cousin might be the editor at the publishing house you've wanted to break into. She might even be your next best

---

How to Pick a Conference

Here are some things to take into consideration when choosing a conference:

Location: How close to your home is the conference? How much will it cost to get there and for room and board?

Cost: How does this expense fit into your budget? Local or regional conferences may be as inexpensive as $5 or as expensive as $150. National conference fees can run $350-$1,000.

Speakers: Is there a speaker you particularly want to meet? Have you carried on a correspondence with a particular editor or art director for a while and think that a personal meeting could help?

Program: Are the topics discussed of particular interest to you? Are you interested in a particular genre, a tricky skill, a business matter such as negotiating contracts, or just interested in hearing a particular writer or illustrator talk about their work? Study the program carefully.

Your Goals: How can a conference help you further your career? Do you need to meet a particular person? Do you want your portfolio critiqued by a certain art director?

friend. Take the time to meet other people, not with the idea of using them, but with the goal of making a friend. We all need friends in this difficult business.

Attend a conference to further your career

One of the single most important things you can do at a conference is to have a manuscript or portfolio critique. If the opportunity is offered, I'd advise you to grab it. This typically means that for an extra minimal fee, you may have your work personally evaluated by one of the conference staff. For writers, a typical arrangement is for you to send in your manuscript several weeks before the conference so one of the staff can read and evaluate your writing.

Finally, you say, a chance to be discovered! Sorry, still doubtful.

But where else can you find an editor or an expert writer or illustrator who will focus on your work and give you feedback for a concentrated moment of time? Nowhere. Send your best work for evaluation, or if you are having specific problems, send a manuscript or bring artwork that represents that problem. Leave your easily bruised ego at home, but take with you your student's attitude. Be ready to ask questions, to respond to comments, and to find out where you're going wrong and where you might find help for any deficiencies. If you think of it as a learning experience, it will be positive and will ultimately help you find your way into print.

Attend a conference for the future

Writing and illustrating are not flash-in-the-pan careers. Ten to fifteen years is not an unusual apprenticeship time frame. When you attend a conference, think long term. The editor may be "just" an assistant editor, but she will move up soon to editor, then to senior editor. A friend made nows could be the friend who buys your stories or artwork for the next fifty years.

JoAnne Stewart Wetzel, author of *Onstage/Backstage* (Carolrhoda) and *The Christmas Box* (Knopf), says, "The best thing about a writer's conference is hearing someone who's been coming for five or six years announce that she's just sold her first book."

Attend a conference with great expectations

Expect to learn that you are competent in something. (Move from Unconscious Competence to Conscious Competence!)

Expect to learn that you are incompetent in something. (Move from Unconscious Incompetence to Conscious Incompetence.)

Expect to be inspired. Expect to develop contacts that will last a lifetime. Expect to eat too much. Expect to meet a new friend. Expect to have a great time!

Six Tips for a Successful Conference

1. Request conference information early. If you want to participate in a manuscript or portfolio review, there may be early deadlines.

2. Often speakers are free for breakfast. Ask the conference director if you can take that special speaker to breakfast.

3. Offer to accompany a speaker to lunch. Invite them to sit at your table. They are a stranger in a large crowd and will probably appreciate a friendly word.

4. Volunteer to help. The conference director will be your friend for life. You may be invited to a special pre- or post-conference party at which you can make more friends for life. You'll have a blast!

5. Rest before and after the conference. Take maximum advantage of the limited amount of time that the speakers will be there.

6. Take your business card and give it to everyone.

First Books

BY ALICE POPE

For a writer, working toward publication can be likened to riding a roller coaster. Often, like standing in line at a crowded amusement park, you may have a long wait. After months or years of waiting for an acceptance, finally you get to climb in that shiny red car, put down the safety bar, and head up that hill—more patience, climbing the steep hill from acceptance to published book—revision, more revision, waiting for illustrations to be finished. . . .

And, finally, there you are at the top. You've waited it out, and there you sit. All of a sudden, zoom! It's there in your mailbox—a copy of your first book. Your tummy does flip-flops. You feel a little lightheaded. Wheeeeeeeeeeeeeeeeeeee! The five authors featured in this article have recently experienced the thrill ride of first publication. Read on as they share their stories of publishing ups and down, twists and turns, surprises and excitement, and offer their advice to all those writers still waiting in that long line.

KEZI MATTHEWS
John Riley's Daughter (Front Street/Cricket Books)

Kezi Matthews's first book, *John Riley's Daughter* takes place in 1973 in a Southern town bursting with thick kudzu and complex characters. Her book is a first-person account of three days in the life of Memphis Riley, a thirteen-year-old girl who has lived with her grandmother Naomi four five years, ever since her father, John Riley, dumped her at Naomi's doorstep after Memphis's mother died. Memphis also shares the house with Clover, her 29-year-old, mentally handicapped aunt. After a fight with Memphis, Clover runs off, missing for days, further straining the already precarious relationship between Memphis and her grandmother.

Matthews drew on her Southern roots as she wrote the story, one that sprang forth from her writer's mind. "I didn't choose Memphis Riley, she chose me," says Matthews. "I was working on writing something else when she showed up in the spring of '98. I simply started writing her story and after about six weeks of fourteen-hour days, I had the first draft done. Obviously it had been percolating in my subconscious for a long, long time and finally bubbled to the top."

While many pre-published authors deal with stacks of rejections before that first book contract, the publication of *John Riley's Daughter* came as easily to Matthews as the idea for her story. She did, however, have a working relationship with her editor via magazine writing. She'd written several stories for editor John D. Allen for *Cicada* magazine. Matthews's *Cicada* material is also set in the South, a series of short stories about the same character, Garnette O'Brien. "John liked my stories, and when I told him I'd finished a novel and gave him a brief synopsis over the phone, he told me to send it along."

Allen, an editor for both *Cicada* and Front Street/Cricket Books, read Matthews's manuscript and asked if she'd be willing to delete a scene that he felt was too intense and interrupted the flow of the story. He also asked her to give some thought to stronger closure between Memphis and her grandmother. "I revised, rewrote and re-submitted within two weeks, and signed my contract a few weeks later in December, 1999."

For Matthews, her first book publishing experience "seemed at times almost dreamlike," she

Kezi Matthews first novel, *John Riley's Daughter*, tells of Memphis Riley, a thirteen-year-old living in a small Southern town in 1973 with her grandmother and her handicapped aunt who runs away after a fight with Memphis. Matthews's *Cicada* editor John D. Allen, also an editor with Front Street/Cricket Books, asked to see her novel after she had several stories published in his magazine. "I was completely at ease during the entire editing process because I had the advantage of working with my *Cicada* editor and my trust in his approach and editing style is complete," she says.

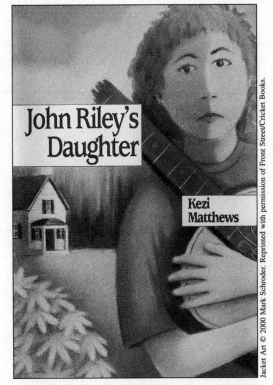

Jacket Art © 2000 Mark Schroder. Reprinted with permission of Front Street/Cricket Books.

says. "I was completely at ease during the entire editing process because I had the advantage of working with my *Cicada* editor and my trust in his approach and editing style is complete. When you look at the list Front Street/Cricket Books is producing, it's easy to see that their thrust is toward publishing enduring literature for young people. To be accepted by them for publication is not only validating, but extremely reassuring to a writer travelling to her own drummer."

Although Matthews's stories are categorized as young adult, she doesn't write with a certain age group in mind. "I just let the story unfold in a natural, unrestricted way," she says. "However, I think YA has extraordinary range, from the younger, less complicated end to the darker, more demanding end, with everything in between. I'm quite happy to find myself there."

A reviewer for *Kirkus Reviews* wrote, "Matthews's strength is that she creates no villains, but sees all her characters, even the most deeply flawed, with a compassionate eye." Matthews says, "That's my natural way of viewing others, though I'm not a Mary Sunshine by any means! I believe that most human beings are heroic in some measure just for getting up and putting one foot in front of the other. I also believe that most people act from a passionate belief in their own acquired truths. It's a writer's basic job to understand and respect that, even if she personally finds those truths detestable."

Matthews advises aspiring authors to remember "writing for young people is incredibly demanding—it's writing you can't fake, and if you try, kids (and editors) will send you packing! Don't worry for an instant who wrote what last year. That's a done deal. Write from your own heart about what matters to you and do it as honestly as you know how. Originality comes from within, and you really do have to trust your inner, intuitive voice in order to grow as a writer and make your way to publication."

JEANIE FRANZ RANSOM
I Don't Want to Talk About It (Magination Press)

I Don't Want to Talk About It, Jeanie Franz Ransom's first published book, was written because the author couldn't find an appropriate book dealing with divorce for her then three-year-old niece. "I wrote my picture book about divorce more than seven years ago." says Ransom. "Off and on over the years, I'd send the manuscript out. Although I received many compliments from editors, no one seemed to want the book on their list. It was a hard topic to sell, which seemed strange to me, given the fact that divorce is so prevalent today."

Ransom continued submitting her manuscript to publishers for years. "The last time I started submitting *I Don't Want to Talk About It* was the winter of 1998. That round of submissions numbered about thirty publishers. In March of 1999, I got a call from Magination wanting to buy my book."

All told, it took Ransom about six years to finally get her book accepted by a publisher. "But I believe in this book so much, I would have kept submitting and submitting if I hadn't sold to Magination Press. Sometimes there's a manuscript you just know in your heart is special and good—it just hasn't found the right home yet."

Two months before Magination accepted *I Don't Want to Talk About It* for publication, however, Peachtree Publishing bought her book *Grandma U.* (sold through an agent who works on a project-by-project basis.) Although *Grandma U.* was accepted first, it won't be released until fall 2001. Originally, both of Ransom's first books were scheduled to be available at the same time, but Peachtree wanted a certain illustrator for *Grandma U.* who wasn't able to work on the book in time for a fall 2000 release. "It was nice to learn that in the children's book publishing world, they wait for the right person to make a book the best it can be, even if it means pushing back a deadline."

So Ransom's first book is really her second, and her second book is really her first. And so it goes in publishing. "I look at it as having two children," she says. "If you have two at once, or close together, you may not be able to devote as much time to each. But by having one 'child' at a time, you have more time and energy to devote and to enjoy!"

Ransom's two first books are very different. *I Don't Want to Talk About It* features a little girl whose parents are telling her they're getting a divorce. Throughout the conversation, the little girl says, "I don't want to talk about it," as she imagines herself a turtle, pulling inside her shell away from the hurtful reality. She imagines herself as animals throughout the book—an elephant to crash through the door and stop her parents from arguing; a wild horse to run away as far as she could go; a prickly porcupine so that "I couldn't be hurt by anything or anybody anymore." Her parents do their best to convince her that they love her and that they'll both still spend time with her like they always have. Magination Press included a Note to Parents on talking to their children about divorce.

Grandma U. is a humorous picture book about an apprehensive grandma-to-be called Molly McCool. "She's a woman who's done it all. She's confident and content, until she learns she's going to be a grandmother—she hasn't held a baby in years, her cookies look like moon rocks." So Ms. McCool enrolls at Grandma University, the school where grandmas learn to be grandmas. "This book is about believing in yourself and trusting yourself—a message I think will resonate with kids as well as adults."

Both of Ransom's first books are with publishers who are not part of gigantic New York-based conglomerates. "It was an accident that both my books are with independent publishers. It may be because my books were a hard-sell to bigger publishers. In the case of *I Don't Want to Talk About It*, it was probably because of the topic. For *Grandma U.*, I think it's because I

Jeanie Franz Ransom's first published book is a tool for parents to initiate a dialogue with their children about divorce. She wrote the story when she couldn't find an appropriate book about divorce for her three-year-old niece. It took Ransom about six years to get her book accepted by a publisher. "But I believe in this book so much, I would have kept submitting and submitting if I hadn't sold to Magination Press. Sometimes there's a manuscript you just know in your heart is special and good—it just hasn't found the right home yet."

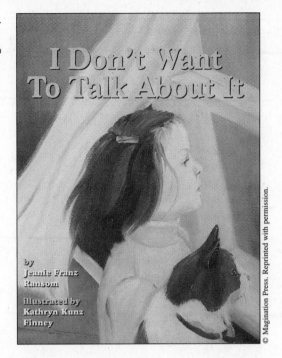

I Don't Want To Talk About It

by
Jeanie Franz
Ransom

illustrated by
Kathryn Kunz
Finney

tend to write humor that's more sophisticated and adult than you usually find in kids' books," Ransom says. "Whatever the case, I believe that my manuscripts ended up where they did for a reason—that the publisher that accepted each one was the best publisher for that book."

On her way to those first sales, Ransom networked with other writers both in a large online listserv and a small online critique group. "A writing friend of mine urged me to join an online list she was part of, and although I was reluctant, I decided to give it a try," she says. "Overall, the list members helped me feel less isolated by encouraging me when I needed a boost and congratulating me when I had a success. I learned just how giving children's writers are of their knowledge and their contacts." Through the list, Ransom "met" people like Jane Yolen and Rick Walton, and found out about publishers and agents open to submission, including Jodi Jill, the agent who sold *Grandma U.*

Ransom, who recently made a career switch from part-time advertising copywriter to full-time elementary school counselor, cautions that online list discussions can swallow up valuable writing time. "As I've gotten busier, I've found that turning a few acquaintances from the list into trusted e-mail writing buddies worked better for me. But I never would have met those friends if I hadn't been on an online list, because of the great exchange of information and the terrific support."

Her online group read both the manuscripts that Ransom sold, and "their comments, encouragement and enthusiasm were priceless," she says. Whether in an in-person or online group, "remember, you also have to spend time giving others feedback on their manuscripts. If you're not willing or able to give back what you receive, you're probably better off finding other ways to get feedback, like exchanging manuscripts with just one writing friend, or reading your work to a group of kids."

However you do it, Ransom strongly suggests writers stay connected with one another. "I recommend online networking as well as getting your face out there by joining local and national children's writers associations and attending workshops and conferences. But don't get caught up in networking or attending functions and neglect the most important thing of all—writing.

Write, write, write. When you're not writing, talk. Talk to kids. Talk to other writers. Talk to anyone and everyone. The more people you know, the more likely you are to hear something that will benefit your writing—and may result in a sale.

TERI DANIELS
The Feet in the Gym (Winslow Press)

When Teri Daniels was growing up, she didn't plan on becoming an author. "I dreamed of being on television," she says. "I used to sing in front of the bathroom mirror. I did TV commercials, too. I remember forever smearing two bars of soap on my cheeks and telling myself, 'On this side I have Dove, and on the other side I have an ordinary brand . . .' I might not have had talent, but I had impeccably clean skin."

Years after her foray into bathroom acting, after earning a B.S. in nursing and having two sons, Daniels finally gets to regularly perform in front of an audience, even if it's not Must See TV. Now she appears at book stores and libraries and schedules about thirty days of school visits yearly to promote her first picture book *The Feet in the Gym*, and her subsequent titles—*G-Rex* (Orchard) and *Just Enough* (Viking).

The Feet in the Gym is a rhyming story about a grade school custodian called Handy Bob. *At Lakeside School, I work each day / to wipe each dab of dirt away. / I search for bits of grit and grime, / specks of mud and drops of slime,* begins Daniels's text. Handy Bob's most important task is mopping the footprints from the school's gymnasium floor. He struggles throughout the story to keep up with the dirt-tromping children as they make their way across the floor.

Writing rhyme well is not easy. It was something that Daniels had to work at. When she first started writing, "I didn't know my assonance from my elbow," she says. "I didn't figure that my writing would be awful. My first attempts at text were syrupy sweet—more like long lists of Kodak moments than stories."

So Daniels hit the library and the bookstore, amassing a stack of instructional books on writing, such as *The Children's Picture Book: How to Write It, How to Sell It*, by Ellen Roberts; *How to Write, Illustrate, and Design Children's Books*, by Frieda Gates; and *What's Your Story*, by Marion Dane Bauer. She read newsletters on children's writing, like *Children's Book Insider*, *Children's Writer* and the SCBWI *Bulletin*.

She also studied piles of picture books. "I read, critiqued and retyped their text on my computer to remove what the artwork had contributed to the whole, then I analyzed openings and closings, sentence structure and page breaks, tension and conflict, and climax and solution. In addition to learning how to develop and pace a story, I got better at editing my own work—a valuable tool."

Daniels also joined a writing group she found through SCBWI. "The meetings still keep me motivated and connected, and the authors are a great bunch. We talk shop, review stories, offer support in this hit-and-miss business, and, always, we eat."

When she began submitting (she's since gotten an agent), Daniels sent one manuscript at a time to one publisher at a time. "As my files grew thick and my patience thin, I multiply circulated two or three manuscripts." She got two bites on *The Feet in the Gym*. "The editor at the first house was very enthusiastic about my rewrites. At the acquisitions meeting, however, her team decided they did not want to publish another school story. Winslow Press was, and remains, enthusiastic about school tales. They were a perfect fit for *Feet*."

Nothing in particular sparked Daniels's idea to write a picture book starring a school custodian. "I commonly type a conversation with my computer. 'What if this?' or 'How about that.'

Then I type everything that crosses my mind," she says. "I brainstormed everything I could think of about an active elementary school setting. Eventually, I zeroed in on the custodian—the unsung hero, central to the doings of school."

The publication process of her first book was definitely a learning experience for Daniels. She wasn't aware that the selection of an illustrator for *The Feet in the Gym* was out of her hands. "I'd been collecting favorite picture book illustrations in a massive binder! Winslow was nice, though. They let me send in samples of my illustration taste and then found someone whose work I adore—Travis Foster."

A few tough hurdles to get over for Daniels were the idea that the author and illustrator don't communicate with one another during the publishing process and the frequent shifts in editorial staff. "I thought I would hook up with one house and work with a single editor. In years to come, we'd finish each other's sentences like an old married couple. In reality, three of my four accepted manuscripts have encountered a change in editor."

Now that she has a few books under her belt (Daniels's fourth picture book *Math Man* is scheduled for a spring 2001 release from Orchard Books), she says she's not as green as she used to be. "I don't have to ask as many questions: 'What's a f&g? Why did the reviewer give away the ending? Can we get on *Reading Rainbow*? *Regis*? *Rosie*? Why not?!' One thing that hasn't changed is my pie-in-the-sky approach to things. If I didn't dream big, I'd be nowhere professionally.

The Feet in the Gym, Teri Daniels's first picture book, stars a conscientious school custodian named Handy Bob. "I brainstormed everything I could think of about an active elementary school setting," says Daniels. "Eventually, I zeroed in on the custodian—the unsung hero, central to the doings of school." Handy Bob's rhyming romp follows him through a day of mopping the gymnasium floor as messy feet tromp over it, ending with a fun surprise for readers.

CATHERINE ATKINS
When Jeff Comes Home (G.P. Putnam's Sons)

When Jeff Comes Home, the debut novel by Catherine Atkins, is compelling, hard to put down, but at the same time often painful to read. Her book tells the story of 16-year-old Jeff Hart who returns to his family after being abducted and abused by a man for four years. His kidnapper finally sets him free, and Jeff must adjust to life with his family and going back to high school and come to terms with what he's been through.

The inspiration for Atkins's story came from a real-life event she remembered from her teen years. "When I was fifteen, a fourteen-year-old boy from a town near mine returned to his family seven years after he had been kidnapped. I was fascinated by his story and wondered how high school life could be for him," she says. "Periodically, the media would check back with the boy as he married, had children and commented on other child abduction cases. In 1989, at the age of twenty-four, he died in a motorcycle accident. It was then I first thought of writing about the boy."

In 1993, Atkins came up with the idea for *When Jeff Comes Home*, using the real-life boy's story as inspiration. "Jeff faces very different circumstances from the boy in the original case. However, the core situation remains the same—how can a teenage boy return to any kind of normal life after such an experience?"

After finishing her first draft of the novel, Atkins began submitting it. "On about the fourth submission, an editor picked *When Jeff Comes Home* out of the slush pile and wrote me a personal response. She offered suggestions on how to improve the manuscript. I wound up rewriting three times for her," Atkins says. "She ultimately did not make an offer, but I am still very grateful for her interest and help."

The next year, Atkins began submitting the book to agents. "That November, Renee Cho of McIntosh and Otis said she wanted to represent me. Renee believed passionately in *When Jeff Comes Home* and submitted it for more than two years until Putnam made an offer on it in February 1998. Overall, it took six years from idea to published novel."

Once Atkins's book was accepted, she had no idea what to expect from the editorial process. She again did revisions on the novel under the direction of Putnam editor Refna Wilkin, changing the narrator from Charlotte, Jeff's younger sister, to Jeff himself. "Refna's style was gentle and inclusive, and I agreed with most of her suggestions. Our only point of disagreement was over the school scenes in *When Jeff Comes Home*. Refna felt the venom of the other students toward Jeff was unrealistic," Atkins says. "She asked that I tone these scenes down and add motivation for the bullying. I don't feel bullies need much motivation for their actions, but as a first-time author, I felt I should compromise. I went ahead and made those changes."

Her editor strongly suggested dropping the school scenes altogether. "This I felt I could not do," says Atkins. "My initial interest in writing the story was based on what would happen to Jeff when he returned to school. I held firm here, though I doubted myself. I'm glad now I didn't cut those scenes. I have heard from many readers that the school scenes are among the most compelling in the book."

Atkins has gotten other positive feedback from both her young adult and adult readers. "I'm thrilled with the reader reaction. A girl wrote me a fan letter that reminded me of the fan letters I wrote to my favorite authors as a young person. I heard from a representative of a District Attorney Victim-Witness program who said she found the book realistic and touching. Through a librarian, I heard of a young victim of abuse who read my book and was moved by it. These responses have been beyond rewarding for me."

During the years before Atkins began writing *When Jeff Comes Home*, she always imagined

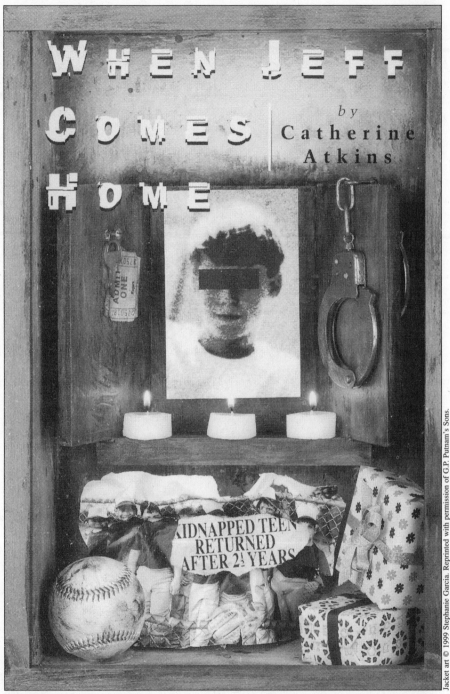

Inspired by a true-life abduction story, *When Jeff Comes Home* is the powerful debut novel by Catherine Atkins telling the story of sixteen-year-old Jeff Hart, who had been kidnapped at knifepoint and held prisoner for four years. Atkins picks up Jeff's story as his kidnapper is finally returning him to his family, exploring Jeff's transition back into "normal" life with his family—and going to high school. "My initial interest in writing the story was based on what would happen to Jeff when he returned to school," says Atkins. "I have heard from many readers that the school scenes are among the most compelling in the book."

Dealing With Reviews—From the Stellar to the So-So.

Being a first-time author can be full of surprises. One thing new authors may not consider is how to approach reading reviews of their own work. A great review can certainly make an author's day and give her confidence in her writing. For some, a bad review can shake that confidence. Here, authors share insights and advice on how they handled reading those first book reviews, even the ones that were less than stellar.

Rhonda Gowler Green: It's kind of scary waiting for reviews of your books to appear. I've been very lucky regarding reviews—getting starred ones in major periodicals. I've only gotten two mixed reviews (and no really bad ones) which point out some good and some negative points about my books. But these same books that got mixed reviews got glowing ones in other major children's review periodicals, so I've learned how subjective reviews can be. You can ignore bad reviews, or you can learn from them sometimes to help make your next work better. There's not much an author or illustrator can do once a review comes out, so my advice is to just accept the mixed or bad ones and celebrate the good ones.

Catherine Atkins: I will never forget the experience of reading my first review. I was checking out my site on Amazon.com one night, and there was a review of *When Jeff Comes Home* from *Kirkus*. I read it line by line, holding my breath, waiting for the zinger. There was none! The reviewer understood exactly what I was trying to do in the book, and she put into words some things I only felt. Every author should have such a first review experience. My second review was positive but mixed; the ones that followed, overwhelmingly positive.

Only one review surprised me. The critic reviewed *When Jeff Comes Home* in terms of its success as a suspense thriller, concluding that I did not maintain the suspense in the second half. But I never considered my book a thriller, more a character study. However, that review was positive overall, so I wasn't bothered by it, just a little confused.

My advice to first-time authors on reading reviews? Savor the good reviews, and try not to take the bad ones too much to heart. Remember, it's one person's opinion. Nurture the belief in yourself that your material is good, and work on other projects so that reviews will occupy only part of your mind.

Kezi Matthews: "Unless you've written an instant classic, chances are that shortly after your reviews begin to appear, you'll begin wondering if all the reviewers read that same book! The reviews for *John Riley's Daughter* ranged from a starred review in children's literature's most distinguished review journal to a review at the other end laced with misinformation about my book's characters and plot. My mind handed me a dandy little metaphor for dealing with this. Picture a shiny red apple. Each person taking a bite of that apple seems to taste something a little different, but the apple doesn't change; it remains the same shiny red apple!

So, I'd say thoroughly enjoy your favorite reviews without letting them lull you into complacency. See if there's anything of value for your writing in the other ones and if not, don't brood. More than one book that's received a pan or two has gone on to win an award. Writing is the most self-revealing of all the arts, so it follows that writers are very easily wounded. But, contrary to mundane advice, don't try to toughen up your hide. Instead, keep your sensitivities on the edge and above all, keep your main focus upon your ongoing work, because what stands in time is always the work.

her future book projects would be young adult novels. "For Jeff's feelings of alienation and fear, I didn't have to look much farther than my own experiences in high school. Those years provide a well of observations to draw upon. I'm very close to those emotions and it's not hard to bring them up. That time informs my writing, and I expect it always will," Atkins says. "Adolescence is such a time of extremes—great tragedy, enormous joy, sweeping changes. It's a fascinating time of life and one I will continue to explore in my work."

Atkins feels the path to publication is as individual as the writer herself. "The business is extremely tough, and I have found that the rule is, there is no rule," she says. "No matter what happens as a writer pursues her dream, she must believe in herself and in the value of her work. As writers, we are looking for that one person in the publishing house or agency who sees something extraordinary in our writing. Once that champion is found, the road becomes smoother. Finding the person takes persistence, patience and endless belief in oneself. Those are three qualities every writer should cultivate.

GLORIA ROTH LOWELL
Elana's Ears (Magination Press)

The inspiration for Gloria Roth Lowell's first book came soon after her daughter, Elana, just shy of two-years-old at the time, was diagnosed with severe hearing impairment. "It was a very big surprise," says Lowell. "The average age for children to be diagnosed with hearing loss in this country is about two or two-and-a-half. By that time, there's so much language missing, they could spend the rest of their lives catching up."

Lowell and her husband had been married for eight years before they had a child. But for those eight years, they had their dog, Lacey. "Lacey was very jealous of Elana from the time we brought her home," says Lowell. "Lacey used to bark incessantly. After her diagnosis, I realized that Elana hadn't been responding to Lacey's barking." So when Lowell began to write her book, she told the story of Elana's hearing loss, using Lacey as the narrator.

"I wrote my story on a yellow legal pad, and I put it away. I'd read it to a few people, and they really liked it, but then again, they were my family and friends," Lowell says. "Then I decided to quit my job, and we moved to Pennsylvania." Lowell also decided to submit her story to publishers. "I bought *Children's Writer's & Illustrator's Market* and picked out three publishers that deal with children's special needs." Two publishers turned her story down. "But I kept getting postcards from Magination Press saying, 'We still have your work. We're merging with the American Psychological Association, and we'll let you know.'"

Finally Lowell got a letter from Magination editor Darcy Johnson, saying they loved her story. "But it really didn't fit their model. It didn't have a strong psychological component," Lowell explains. "But she said if I was open to revision, they would love to publish it. Of course, I was open to revision!" Lowell and Johnson then began revising, eventually choosing to focus on the theme of sibling rivalry, told from the point of view of an "only dog," including Elana's hearing loss as a story element. They added a subtitle to the book: *Elana's Ear, Or How I Became the Best Big Sister in the World.*

Lowell and Johnson worked through e-mail for several weeks, and Lowell got to see some character sketches and possible covers by illustrator Karen Stormer Brooks. "I learned. I didn't know anything about the business before this. It was a wonderful process. I was very lucky."

In *Elana's Ear* Lacey tells the story of Elana coming into the only dog's house, sharing her room, and getting the attention of her parents. Lacey also tells readers about when Elana's parents discovered her hearing loss (after the dog, who loves to bark, did), and how Lacey watches out for Elana at times when she can't wear her hearing aid, like when she swims or

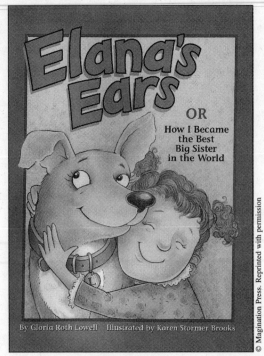

Elana's Ears

OR

How I Became
the Best
Big Sister
in the World

By Gloria Roth Lowell   Illustrated by Karen Stormer Brooks

© Magination Press. Reprinted with permission

The idea for author Gloria Lowell's first book *Elana's Ears* was sparked by her daughter Elana's diagnosis as hearing impaired at the age of twenty-two months. Her book tells the story of how the family dog, Lacey, helped Elana's parents discover her deafness, and also deals with sibling rivalry from the point of view of an "only dog" dealing with the edition of a new baby. When Lowell visits classrooms she discusses both sibling rivalry and hearing loss. "Kids with dogs really relate to Lacey and Elana's relationship," she says.

takes a bath. Lacey finally decides she likes being Elana's big sister. Magination added a "Note to Parents" at the end of the book written by a psychologist discussing how to deal with a child who suddenly has a new sibling in the house.

Now, when Lowell visits classrooms, she discusses both sibling rivalry and hearing loss. "Kids with dogs really relate to Lacey and Elana's relationship. I ask them to write about whether their dogs ever get jealous. I also ask them if they know how deaf people communicate. They all raise their hands and say, 'Through sign language,' unless they know Elana. Elana doesn't sign at all. She's oral deaf, so she's learned to speak and listen. I'm trying to change the perception of deaf people."

Since the publication of *Elana's Ears*, Lowell has had an article published in *Volta Voices*, the publication of the Alexander Graham Bell Association for the Deaf. She's also working on a sequel to her book called *Elana's Goodbyes* dealing with separation anxiety. Magination Press is also pursuing turning Elana and Lacey into cartoon characters in their own animated program. "I watch a lot of cartoons," says Lowell. "There are no main characters with disabilities in children's television today. With the excitement that's going on in the world of hearing loss— cochlear implants, the technology of hearing aids, even the use of hearing eye dogs—I think this would be a good time to address hearing loss on a children's show."

Lowell has also gotten some media attention because of her book, appearing on television, radio and in print. "That's been helpful in selling a book from a small publisher. It's a human-interest story. I appeared in a show called *Take Charge of Your Life* about dealing with difficult situations. People also relate to the story because of their dogs. People love their dogs and consider them part of the family, so my story hits that chord as well."

The real-life Lacey, who was fourteen when Elana was born, has since gone to doggie heaven. Elana got a new puppy named Bingo. "Lacey never got to have any of the glory," says Lowell. "But she's immortalized in *Elana's Ears*."

First Books Follow-up: Rhonda Gowler Greene

Since we last heard from picture book author Rhonda Gowler Greene talking about her first book *When a Line Bends . . . A Shape Begins*, she's gotten an agent and now has eight titles published or upcoming. Her next book due out is *Jamboree Day*, illustrated by Jason Wolff (Orchard, fall 2001), a fun, bouncy piece about all the animals coming to an annual jamboree in the jungle.

Greene also has three picture books coming out in 2002, two with Simon & Schuster/ Atheneum—*Bugbear And Bugaboo*, illustrated by Joseph A. Smith, about two little, scary creatures that frighten kids at night; and *The Very First Thanksgiving Day*, illustrated by Susan Gaber, a companion piece to her book *The Stable Where Jesus Was Born*, which Gaber also illustrated.

Also look for *At Grandma's*, illustrated by Karla Firehammer (Holt, spring 2002); and *The Beautiful World That God Made* (Eerdmans) a cumulative story waiting for an illustrator. Here Greene shares what she's learned as she's worked on her books.

You've gotten eight books accepted. What are you doing differently in the way of marketing your work since your first book, *When a Line Bends . . . A Shape Begins*?
I have an agent now, so I don't market my work myself. I often suggest to my agent, though, where I would like a piece sent.

The reason I started querying agents in the first place was because I sold my first two books (through the slush pile) to two different publishers, then six months later a third story of mine was seriously being considered by a third house. I was very new to all this and wasn't sure whether I should go with a third house or not.

As it ended up, that publisher didn't buy the piece, but one of my other publishers did. But my queries to agents all did receive quick, positive responses. I think this was because I had already sold two pieces and had another manuscript a publisher was ready to buy. I do know unpublished writers who have gotten agents though. Whether you are seeking an editor to take on your work or an agent to represent you, it's your writing that must stand out and get her attention.

What have you learned about the publishing world since you've worked on your first book?
I've learned that just because you're published, it doesn't mean everything you write and submit will get accepted. I've had several manuscripts rejected since I've been published. I've also learned as a picture book author that you have to be patient and wait a very long time, sometimes years, before you actually see your book in print. But, for me, it's always been worth the wait.

Your published and upcoming titles are with several different publishers. How different is the publishing process from one publisher to the next?
Some of my publishers send me all the stages of the book as it is being made—rough sketches, color proofs, etc. I really like it when a publisher does this because I do lots of author visits in schools, and then I can share with students the step-by-step process of how a picture book is made. With one of my books, though, I saw very little of it for two years—only a black and white copy of the cover. Then one day the bound book appeared on my doorstep. I don't have much say with any of my publishers about who illustrates my books. However, I know of publishers or editors who do get the author more involved in helping decide upon

an illustrator. Actually, working with my editors at the different houses has been much the same. I feel very fortunate because I have an excellent editor at each house.

You mentioned you're doing a lot of school visits. Any advice for authors who haven't done them yet?

I speak at a lot of conferences and do a lot of school visits. I really enjoy getting back in the schools since I used to be an elementary schoolteacher. Two books that really helped me when I decided I wanted to start doing school visits were *How to Promote Your Children's Book: A Survival Guide for Published Writers*, by Evelyn Gallardo and *How to Promote Your Children's Book on a Shoestring*, by Nancy Bentley and Donna W. Guthrie.

I would advise writers or illustrators wanting to do visits to decide what kind of program or programs they wish to present, to gear the programs appropriately to certain age groups, and to practice at home and time themselves before going to a school. But once they're at a school doing a visit, they should try to be flexible and accommodate a school's needs as best they can.

Why did you decide to create a website about your books (www.rhondagowlergree ne.com)? How has it been helpful to your career?

I decided to create a website (or have my oldest son, Matt, who attends Michigan State University, create it!), because I felt it could be another way to promote myself. I am an avid user of the Internet, and I think more and more people, including schools, are using the Internet to connect to various resources, and authors are one of those resources. If an author or illustrator wants to get into the schools, a website can be very helpful.

When I send my brochures to schools, my website address, of course, is included on it. The teachers can look at my website to learn more about me and my books, and find activities that go along with my books. I have been contacted through my website a few times, and I foresee being contacted even more through it when my other books are released.

What's your advice for writers striving for that first publication?

My advice would be to keep at it. Read as much as you can, especially within the genre you write. Get feedback, if possible, from other writers. Attend children's writing conferences and send a manuscript ahead to get personal time with an editor or a written critique from an editor. If an editor asks for a revision on an unsold piece, seriously consider revising it, because your writing has caught the attention of that editor.

Were your subsequent acceptances as exciting as your first ones?

It's always exciting to make a sale. I would say on a scale of one to ten, my first sale rated a ten for excitement, and subsequent sales all rated nine-and-a-half.

© 1999 Susan Gaber

Rhonda Gowler Greene's *The Stable Where Jesus Was Born* (Atheneum) tells the story of the nativity in cumulative rhyme. This book is one of the eight books she's had published or are upcoming, including her first book *When a Line Bends . . . A Shape Begins* (Houghton Mifflin).

Listen In: An Agent Chats with Richard Jackson

BY STEVEN MALK

The first time I spoke to Richard Jackson, I was twenty-two, and I had just started to represent books. I was having a very hard time getting any editors to return my phone calls, much less have lengthy conversations with me. This was largely due to the fact that I was young, male, and living in California, which are three things people don't necessarily equate with children's books.

An art director had given Dick the portfolio of an illustrator I represented, and he called me to inquire about the artist. Since I came out of the bookselling world, where I'd developed a wonderful sense of the market but hadn't had occasion to meet many editors, I had no idea who Dick Jackson was. I proceeded to talk to him for the next thirty minutes about children's books, grilling him about what he liked and didn't like and who he worked with, so I could get a sense of what kind of work I might send him in the future. Dick patiently answered all of my questions and asked some of his own. I hung up the phone, satisfied that I had made a new contact.

Richard Jackson

The next day, I spoke to a friend who worked for a publisher in New York and was much more knowledgeable about the who's who of children's publishing than I was. I casually mentioned that I had talked to Dick Jackson, and I heard a gasp on the other end of the line. She told me he was one of the most famous editors in the history of children's publishing, and she wondered why I hadn't been intimidated by him. Indeed, as I soon found out, Dick Jackson has worked with authors such as Judy Blume, Avi, Gary Paulsen, Cynthia Rylant, George Ella Lyon, Chris Raschka, Nancy Farmer, Dav Pilkey and Paula Fox. Needless to say, I was impressed—and amazed that he'd spent so much time with me on the phone.

His books have won numerous awards, including twelve Newbery Medals and Honors, five Caldecott Medals and Honors, and six Boston Globe-Horn Book Awards and Honors. Through the years, he has gained a reputation for not only having a keen editorial eye, but for being a champion for the books he edits, and for pushing authors—and children's literature—in new and innovative directions. People pick up a Richard Jackson book knowing that whether it's a picture book or a novel, the quality of the product will be top-notch.

STEVEN MALK *grew up around children's books. His mother owns the White Rabbit Children's Bookstore, with locations in La Jolla and Costa Mesa, California. After working at the White Rabbit for six years, Malk worked for the Sandra Dijkstra Agency, and, in 1998, he opened a West Coast office for the New York-based Writers House. Among the authors and artists Malk represents are Jon Scieszka, Elise Primavera, Deborah Hopkinson, Franny Billingsley, Marla Frazee, M.T. Anderson, Karen Romano Young, and Sonya Sones.*

Dick ended up using my illustrator on a book he was working on, and that became the first of many projects we would do together. Despite the fact that we're almost forty years apart in age, our sensibilities are remarkably similar, and I've been lucky to have him mentor me through my first years in publishing.

Read on as we discuss Dick's history in publishing, his new imprint with Atheneum, his perspective on the children's publishing industry, and his advice to published and unpublished authors.

Steven Malk: Can you tell me about how you initially got started in publishing and talk about the different companies you have worked for?

Richard Jackson: When I got out of the army in 1960, where I'd been a speechwriter for a general, I went to Harpers, just walked in and said I'd like a job. Someone there directed me to the Graduate Institute of Book Publishing, run by New York University. I took this course for a Master's Degree in Education and was apprenticed at Doubleday, where I started in the manufacturing and subrights departments as a sort of floater. One of my teachers thought I should go into children's books, because I was interested in visual things. I'd never thought of it. I was as a kid, and still am as a grownup, dyslexic and did not do a lot of book reading when I was little. I did know at age 24 that I loved language.

Uncertain but curious, I went to Margaret Lesser, the Children's Editor at Doubleday, and she eventually found me a job as a secretary in her department, where I was making $100 a week. Soon I began writing flap copy and even ghost-writing a couple of books. In 1964 I followed one of my instructors from NYU to Macmillan, where I worked as an editor and "found" Virginia Hamilton and Paula Fox.

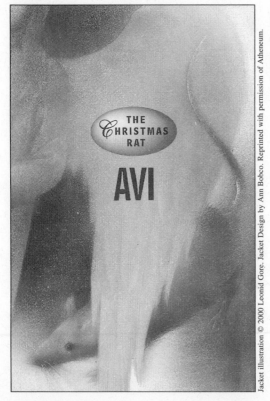

Atheneum launched Richard Jackson Books with two fall 2000 titles. One is *The Christmas Rat*, by Newbery Honor Winner Avi. Says the author, "Simply put, when it comes to the creation of the most vital, entertaining, and significant books for young people, there is no better editor than Richard Jackson."

Jacket illustration © 2000 Leonid Gore. Jacket Design by Ann Bobco. Reprinted with permission of Atheneum.

In 1968, Robert Veronne and I started Bradbury Press, as an imprint of Prentice-Hall. On our first list were Paula Fox and Arnold Lobel. On the second were Stephen Kellog, Rosemary Wells, and newcomer Judy Blume. But it was soon clear that we competed directly with Prentice-Hall's own children's book department; after three seasons they were going to discontinue the line. Panicked, Bob and I borrowed every penny we could from relatives and bought Bradbury ourselves.

We moved the company, which consisted of the two of us and an assistant, to Scarsdale, in the New York suburbs. And we stayed there until 1984. In 1982, we sold the company, ironically, to Macmillan, because Bob was very ill and wanted to be able to leave something to his children. He died in 1984, and I moved into the New York office of Macmillan, where I stayed for 2 years, and didn't love the metropolitan corporate scene.

I was asked to be a founding member of Orchard Books by Sandra Jordan, Bob's widow, in 1986. I stayed there until 1996 and then became a founding editor of DK Ink. In 1999, I moved to Atheneum, which was, of course, part of the old Macmillan and is now part of Simon & Schuster.

SM: So you've come full-circle.

RJ: Yes. Part of the fun is that I can tend the Bradbury backlist, which is still alive and kicking.

SM: Tell me about your imprint now.

RJ: I've been asked to do a small list, 12 books a year, working with some of the people from my past, but also searching for new people to bring to Atheneum. Finding first-time authors has been one of the pleasures of my publishing life.

SM: That's interesting, because I think people have a misconception that you're working with only established successful authors, and you're not looking for new authors. But that's not the case, is it?

RJ: No, in fact it's diametrically opposite. I will work with some of my old pals, but many of them have scattered to other publishing houses. If I can add a new writer or artist to each Atheneum list, I'll be happy. And doing my job.

SM: I think a lot of people think of you for literary fiction, and I know that's an interest of yours, but at the same time, I don't think you're limited to that. One of the books I just sold to you is a young, rhyming, humorous picture book and, ultimately, you're open to almost anything, as long as you're drawn to it, right?

RJ: I'm doing some fantasy, and no one thinks of me for fantasy either. Hard, tough books, yes, but I fancy a lot more than that. I think basically I'm interested in whatever catches my eye, particularly something that I haven't read before.

SM: That's tough to find.

RJ: Very tough, but it can happen.

SM: Do you find that it's hard to define exactly what you're looking for?

RJ: Oh, I know what I'm looking for. Something alive. So much of the stuff out there isn't alive. It's copycat stuff.

SM: I think it comes down to voice.

RJ: Yep. The key to almost everything written.

SM: So what do you think makes a good voice?

RJ: True voice comes from somewhere inside the writer or inside the character. I always ask, Why should I be listening to this person? I want the story and the characters to provide the answer.

SM: It's a hard thing to define, but you know it when you see it.

RJ: Yes, or when you don't. I think because I read with difficulty, I read with my ear. If a manuscript catches my attention at all, I know it's because I'm hearing it.

SM: I've heard you talk about the fact that you're sometimes drawn to subjects that you hate.

RJ: Well, I'm definitely not drawn to writing I hate. But it appeals to me to examine hateful subjects from a social point of view. I don't like guns, but I've published several books in which guns are prominent. Hatred doesn't mean that I can't bear to think about disturbing facts or fantasies of human nature. I am drawn to the challenge of enabling other people to think about them.

Jacket illustration © 2000 Bob Goldstrom. Jacket design by Ann Bobco. Reprinted with permission of Atheneum.

Janet Taylor Lisle's *The Art of Keeping Cool* is one of two debut titles for Atheneum's new imprint Richard Jackson Books. Richard Jackson's "support of his authors is legendary. He's gone to battle for us time and again and is a fierce partisan of every book he brings to press," says Lisle. "As a result, his lists are consistently exciting, and he is dearly loved by every writer he spends time with."

SM: So you like to learn from the books you publish?

RJ: Yes. That's why I edit the books that I publish, as in immerse myself in them. Because I want to learn from them. I want to understand them. I want books to challenge me to think about things in new and different ways.

SM: One of the things that you mention to me a lot as one of your primary concerns is how much you care about the characters, and how much of a connection you feel to the characters. Can you discuss that?

RJ: I really have to feel some kind of curiosity about or sympathy for the characters. Which doesn't mean that every character has to be good. There are some great bad characters. But you have to understand their motivations.

SM: Do you find that a lot of writers try and cater their work to the market and to different trends?

RJ: Writers often ask me about trends. My only answer is: Forget about them! By the time you get your trendy book written, the trend is finished. I understand the compulsion to identify a market, but not at the sacrifice of what you, the writer, have that's personal which you can bring to your book. The only attention I pay to trends is that I try to avoid them.

SM: I find that when people tell me that they wrote their manuscript because the topic is hot, it makes me want to reject it on the spot.

RJ: Absolutely. There is a kind of snobbishness about this, I suppose—another thing people associate me with. It may look like snobbishness, but I consider it interest in personal daring. I want people to do something personal. Reading is very personal; books are personal objects. And I think that whatever's in it should come from somewhere inside the writer, not from the latest low-flying fad.

SM: I agree. What are some other common mistakes that you see writers make?

RJ: I see writers trying to be teacherly through a first-person voice. If you've got an 11-year-old character and suddenly you have a 38-year-old perception popping out of her mouth, that is troublesome and turns me off. Basically, I'm not for little nuggets of truth. Some people can do them, disguise them, but most people come across sounding judgmental and purposeful, and I can just see kids' eyes rolling. Fiction should illuminate, not educate.

SM: Yeah, it seems like there's a lot of preachy and didactic stuff out there.

RJ: Take picture books. Very often people write them as if they're writing longer stories, but in short form. Picture books thrive upon distilled language. "On Friday morning, before Charlie went to school . . . blank." That line might work well enough as part of a longer story, but it absolutely doesn't work in a picture book. There's no resonance there.

SM: When you read something, is it fair to say that you know almost immediately whether it's right for you?

RJ: Yes. I can tell within the first few pages, or, sometimes, within the first few lines.

SM: After you read something, obviously you think about it, but do you ever go out and read similar books and research the market?

RJ: No. I'm not well read in what's being published. Mostly because I don't want to know. It's inhibiting to know too much. Almost every story has been written a thousand times. It does me no good to know that something I love already exists out there in the neighborhood. So, in a sense, I put my head in the sand and focus very intently on what the writer is doing that seems new to me and whether or not it's working. I do read a lot, after all, hundreds of submissions a year—just not a lot of what's published.

SM: When do you know that you're ready to commit to something?

RJ: Instinct. When I take on a book, it's because I want to spend time with it. As I've said, I edit books in order to understand them. I can't just sign up a book and send it off to the copy-editor. That's not my way at all.

SM: I think that's one of the reasons that authors and agents enjoy working with you so much, because you really champion their book and get fully involved in the process and see it all the way through.

RJ: I do. I also like to nudge them in directions they may not have thought of. I try to get them

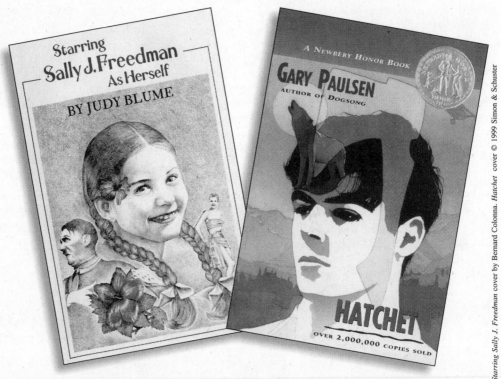

Richard Jackson says part of the fun of being back at Simon & Schuster is that he can mind his Bradbury backlist titles like Gary Paulsen's *Hatchet* and Judy Blume's *Starring Sally J. Freedman As Herself*. Blume says of Jackson, "To this day, when I am writing, it is his voice I hear in my head, asking questions that force me to dig deeper into my characters' lives. After a collaboration of more than thirty years, it is still a thrill to work with him."

to think of characters and scenes in different ways. And most writers I know find that thrilling. Some writers over the years have said to me how surprising it is that I take their characters so seriously. And, why not? They are to be taken seriously. Even funny ones.

I don't question that the characters are real, in some way, and that they have a range of desires and feelings and backstory which make them three-dimensional. So I'm always trying to push the envelope with writers; trying to make stronger whatever it is that they're dreaming. I think that's all part of the process.

SM: Do you also try to push the envelope in terms of the books you choose to publish, and the way you publish them, with, for example, a book like *Making Up Megaboy*?

RJ: Yes. That's a terrific book, and it certainly stirred up some controversy and made people think. I think Chris Raschka was considered a head-turner. His first book, *Charlie Parker Played Be Bop*, was something people hadn't seen before.

SM: How has children's publishing changed since you've been involved in it?

RJ: It's become weirdly competitive, more like adult publishing.

SM: Do you think it's fair to say that adult publishing is becoming more like the movie industry, while children's publishing is becoming more like adult publishing?

RJ: Exactly. A good observation. Things started to change when large corporations got involved and suddenly noticed that their little children's departments have been churning out dollars all these years. Now we're expected to be mega-successful, leading to competition among publishers that disturbs me. A rivalry: it's pirate-time out there! An editor once said wisely, "There isn't anyone who won't leave for more love or for more money."

SM: Do you think that's true?

RJ: Yes, I'm afraid so. And certainly that editor knew what she was talking about. Unfortunately, sometimes more money looks like more love, but isn't.

SM: So, as a result of the way publishing has changed, how has the role of an editor changed and evolved?

RJ: Well my job really hasn't changed. But I hear from writers and agents that nobody edits anymore. And I find that very sad, if it's true.

SM: I don't think it's true that editors don't edit at all, but I think that as publishing has gotten bigger and more corporate, there are more meetings to attend, more books to chase, and more demands on an editor's time in general, don't you think?

RJ: Yes, that's true. Ever since 1986, I've kept myself out of the meeting world. I just do my work. I don't want people grilling me about it.

SM: You mentioned "copycats" earlier. I see a lot of that in publishing these days. It seems like if a book gets published and does well, everyone's dying to copy it, and publishers end up putting out 50 imitations which usually fail. It just seems to me that a truly good book will succeed in any time or place, independent of any trends in the market.

RJ: Imitation may be the sincerest form of flattery, but it can be the sincerest form of laziness. Or, even worse—greed.

SM: Aside from the books you have published, what are some of your favorite children's books?

RJ: Russell Hoban's *A Mouse and His Child*. Barbara Robinson's *The Best Christmas Pageant Ever*. And I love *Julius, Baby of the World*, by Kevin Henkes. He's a wonderful writer.

SM: Let's talk about Judy Blume, someone whose career you launched. What factors do you think contributed to the success of her books?

RJ: For one, she's so adept at telling a story through dialogue. The books "listen" beautifully. With almost no exceptions, her books are very tenderhearted. They're sympathetic to the angst of childhood. They don't make fun of it. So even though they're funny books, they're very serious about what it's like to be a kid. I think she's enormously skillful at what she does. She doesn't try to articulate truth in her own voice. But many truths about growing up and being human do emerge.

SM: What advice would you give to new writers trying to break into children's books?

RJ: Read a lot. Not just from bookstores, but from libraries as well. Go up to the desk at a library or bookstore and ask them what they would recommend for a 10-year-old, for example. If you have children, read to them aloud often, from published books or even from your own unpublished work. Watch what scores and what doesn't. Also, I think that once something is written, a writer should put it away for at least six weeks, then reread it fresh, asking "Does this say what I remember meaning? If it doesn't, or if you can't remember from what you've read, it isn't ready for other readers.

SM: That's such a great point. I think writers need to really work hard on their craft and not just try and rush it out the door. Any good novel is going to take at least a few drafts, and, usually a year or many years, and, while that seems like a very long haul, in the life of a book, that's nothing.

RJ: Yes. Part of a novel is thought. Picture books can come from inspiration, but a novel requires intense thought, and it takes time to think a story through before a writer even sits down to write.

SM: I know you feel that editors sometimes hold back in their rejection letters and don't say what's really on their mind. What would you like to tell writers that most editors don't?

RJ: Often, I would like to say that everyone has a story but not everyone is a writer. And, while I can appreciate the personal investment this manuscript represents, I can't imagine publishing it. As an old friend of mine says, "A lot of people play the violin, but not everyone should give a concert." You don't have to publish to be a writer. Writing is in itself a reward. People write in order to find out what they think. And if they don't, then their work is not of interest to me. If they're writing to sell, merely, I can tell.

SM: Your imprint at Simon & Schuster makes its debut this fall. Can you tell me about the books on your list?

RJ: On the Fall 2000 list are two books, Avi's *The Christmas Rat*, a most unusual, even spooky holiday tale about a boy, a mysterious city exterminator, and the rat they at first seek to eradicate together, which, in the end, the boy does everything he can to save.

And Janet Taylor Lisle's *The Art of Keeping Cool*, set on the Rhode Island coast in 1942, when German submarines were sliding darkly just offshore, when war was moving closer—especially for two boys, cousins, living forcibly in the house of their grandparents and coping with family war just as ominous as the one threatening the sea at their doorstep. This is a book about secrets and the power they gather the longer they are left untold. This is also a book whose story would be changed if any one of its large cast of characters were different. Just my kind of story.

Paula Danziger: Creating Characters with Humor, Truth & Tenderness

BY KELLY MILNER HALLS

Studying the life and works of children's writer Paula Danziger (*The Cat Ate my Gymsuit*, *P.S. Longer Letter Later*, the Amber Brown series), is a little like studying a the weather. With each reging storm, there have been rainbows. With each chilling blizzrd, a spring thaw.

In a recent dramatic twist, Danziger survived a savage, random act of violence. While in Reno, Nevada, in January 2000, a man beat, repeatedly cut and tried to rob her, after following her to her hotel room without invitation. "I fought him," Danziger says, "and I screamed 'Fire.' Watching *Oprah* the day before probably saved my life."

Triumphantly, almost defiantly, Danziger insists she is absolutely fine, now. Her assailant will be behind bars, for many years to come. She is safe and physically healed. Her heart and mind are stronger, braver in the wake of the storm past. But the writing, she says, is the thing. Story is what carried her through.

Danziger's writing story began on a farm in Holidaysburg, Pennsylvania within a family structure she says was

Paula Danziger

less than ideal. Though she admits her parents weren't monsters, life with a loud, sarcastic father and a nervous-natured mother often left her lonely and unsure. "We'd be called dysfunctional today," she says, "but back then we were just the Danzigers."

Humor offered Danziger solace, even as a child. And at the tender age of seven, she caught a glimpse of her destiny. "When my father would yell at me, I'd tell myself, 'Someday I'll use this in a book,' " she says. But it took thirty years, a teaching career and two life threatening car crashes (in two consecutive days) to bring her face-to-face with her ultimate passion—writing top quality literature for kids.

"I had always wanted to write," Danziger says. "But after the second wreck, I decided I better do it before I got hit by a bus."

Though afflicted by trauma-induced dyslexia, Danziger set to work on what would become *The Cat Ate My Gymsuit* in 1970. The story of thirteen-year-old Marcy Lewis and her free-spirited teacher Ms. Finney became Danziger's first published novel in 1974—and the start of a rewarding new career.

A dozen YA books later, Amber Brown was born.

Though the lively little girl was inspired by Carrie, Danziger's niece, the name "Amber Brown" bounced off *Arthur* author Marc Brown. Danziger suggested he name his newborn daughter Amber. When he and wife Laurie opted for Eliza instead ("They were afraid people would call her 'Crayola face' "), Danziger snapped up the moniker for herself.

Amber Brown Is Not a Crayon introduced not only a younger Danziger protagonist, but also her previously untapped ability to touch legions of 9- to 12-year-old elementary aged kids. Each of seven subsequent chapter books proved Amber was much more than a flash in the pan. How

Paula Danziger collaborated with friend Ann M. Martin for *P.S. Longer Letter Later* and it's sequel *Snail Mail No More*. Both are books told in correspondence between best friends Tara★Starr, and Elizabeth, after Tara★Starr moves away. Danziger writes in the voice of Tara★Starr, who "wears glitter and sequins and loves to be the center of attention, and is the only child of young parents who are taking along time to grow up." Danziger and Martin created the books letter by letter and e-mail by e-mail, neither author knowing exactly what would come next.

does Danziger explain the success of Amber Brown? "Amber Brown seems to have struck a chord with so many kids," she says, "and I think that's lovely. I get letters that say Amber's funny or that she helps kids deal with difficult things. But I hope what she does is help kids learn it's okay to take baby steps to get where they need to go."

Ongoing discussions with kids, according to Danziger, is key to her staying in tune. "I speak with children a lot," she says, "and when I speak in schools, I am always observing as well as being part of the interaction. I also spent a week in Austin, Texas observing and hanging out with a second grade class. This was not a speaking visit. It was research."

Tracking trends is another Danziger skill. "I always find things kids would love shopping (Snap Snot) or friends send things to me (Gooey Louie). I look in stores and now, on the net." If glitter skin gel and colored hair dye are hot with kids, Danziger knows it, and passes it on to Amber Brown.

Danziger's latest step forward is actually a giant step back—Amber Brown easy reader prequels. "I was getting on one of the shuttle buses at an International Reading Association conferences and a teacher asked what I was working on," Danziger recalls. "I said, 'A picture book.' And she said, 'Oh great, an Amber Brown picture book?'"

Though she answered, "no," Danziger's creative juices were flowing. "I started to think about it and realized I didn't want to go back to the picture book age," she admits, "but I thought, maybe an easy-to-read. I tried it and I loved being able to write about Justin again. Hooray for teachers who ask questions of writers!"

In May of 2001, Danziger will reveal the fruits of this particular labor in "It's Justin Time," and "What a Trip, Amber Brown"—stories of Amber before the divorce of her parents - before Justin moved away. Was looking back more difficult than looking ahead? Not at all, says Danziger. "I just thought about what the situation was and how Amber would react. I love writing Amber and know her well, although sometimes the final outcome is a bit of a surprise. I also use some acting techniques to figure some things out."

Before you get too nostalgic, take heart. Amber will continue to grow, no matter what direction you look. "The prequels will take Amber from the summer before second grade to the summer before third grade," Danziger says. "The older books will follow Amber's life through sixth grade—and then that's it," she says.

Look for a fresh new character to follow in Amber Brown's footsteps. "I'm working on a book that I love about a character named Skate (Sarah Kate) Tate," says Danziger with visible enthusiasm. "Skate is in sixth grade and is an artist. She has a terrific family. I'm planning on doing several books about her."

And so, the Danziger plan continues. If the radiance of personal strength and regal confidence represent the hard won byproducts of Danziger's successes and struggles, the ring of humor, truth and tenderness are their literary counterparts. But she waves the dramatic suggestion off with impatient finesse. "I only hope that I'm a good writer," she says, "I simply do the best that I can."

Cover illustrations by Jacqueline Rogers. Reprinted with permission of Scholastic.

Paula Danziger followed-up her first book in the beloved Amber Brown series, *Amber Brown Is Not a Crayon*, with several others including *Amber Brown Is Feeling Blue*, *Amber Brown Sees Red* and *Amber Brown Wants Extra Credit*, written for 9- to 12-year-olds. Danziger will speak to a younger audience with the May 2001 release of easy-reader Amber Brown prequels *It's Justin Time* and *What a Trip, Amber Brown*. "The prequels will take Amber from the summer before second grade to the summer before third grade," Danziger says. "The older books will follow Amber's life through sixth grade—and then that's it."

What's So Funny?

From *The Cat Ate My Gymsuit* to her string of Amber Brown young reader chapter books, humor has always added the magic of balance to author Paula Danziger's distinctive work.

What keeps her humor as keen and sharp as her sense of drama? "I think my mind is keen and sharp and so is my warped sense of humor and my sense of play," Danziger says. "Those people—kids and grown-ups—who respond, do so because they, too, are open to looking for the humor in situations."

Can a children's writer go too far in his or her quest for a great laugh? "Most of my humor is the same no matter who is reading/hearing it," says Danziger. "But I suppose the one way I keep from 'going too far' is not talking/joking with kids about sex."

While some frustrated writers complain that what children find funny has shifted, Danziger holds firm. "Funny is funny," she says. "People still laugh at old sitcoms because some of them are ageless. So too, is what's funny."

What is funny? We asked Danziger and a few other famous funny folks to name a few of their "funniest" classics. How does your sense of silly stack up?

Funniest Food
Paula Danziger: Jello
Chris Crutcher: Pop Rocks
Robert Munsch: Beans (guess why!)
Bruce Hale: Broccoli. Close runner-ups are stinkbug pie and cockroach clusters.
Jane Yolen: Ugli fruit (just the name—I've never actually eaten one.)
Lemony Snicket: Beef Wellington.

Funniest Toy
Paula Danziger: Snap Snot
Chris Crutcher: My mind
Robert Munsch: Barbie dolls
Linda Ellerbee: Action figures. Any action figure. What they are, are dolls. But, you see, boys won't play with "dolls," so they call them "action figures."
Bruce Hale: GI Joe with kung-fu grip (also the coolest toy)
Jane Yolen: Hula hoop (because playing with it can put a normal person's back out of alignment for a lifetime.)
Lemony Snicket: Martha, the Little Doll That Talks All By Itself

Funniest Accident
Paula Danziger: I don't think accidents are funny.
Chris Crutcher: Getting my teeth knocked out by a girl with a baseball bat when I was a freshman in high school. I've gotten a lot of mileage out of that one.
Robert Munsch: I leaned over a cliff to look over and my back pack, which was not done up around my waist, flipped over my head and went head first over the cliff. But I was still turning around in midair and I flipped all the way over and landed on my feet on a ledge about a meter below. The cliff was about 20 meters high.
Linda Ellerbee: You see the banana peel. You see the pompous fellow walking down the street. You know he doesn't see the banana peel. He slips and falls. It's funny. If he breaks his leg, it's not funny. If it's a little old lady who falls, it's not funny. If it's you, it's definitely not funny. Such is the nature of humor.
Bruce Hale: One that happens to someone else.
Jane Yolen: I don't find accidents funny.
Lemony Snicket: One in which no one is hurt, thank God.

Funniest Animal

Chris Crutcher: The Dachshund. Man, if that wasn't God's earliest attempt at engineering a dig, I don't know what.

Linda Ellerbee: Tasmanian Devil, Road Runner, Wile E. Coyote. But nobody ever will beat Bugs Bunny for funny.

Robert Munsch: People

Bruce Hale: A tie between wildebeest and warthog.

Jane Yolen: Duck billed platypus (Have you ever seen one? What was God thinking? Or was it Her day off?)

Lemony Snicket: Marmoset

Funniest Relative

Chris Crutcher: My Aunt Fowla. Though her dementia was tragic, it use to crack me up when she put gravy on her icecream. Hey, I was six.

Robert Munsch: Me

Linda Ellerbee: All my relatives are funny. Some are even funny intentionally

Bruce Hale: I don't have any funny relatives. My family is Scottish on one side, Swedish on the other.

Jane Yolen: Glasgow's Govan (when you can understand it!)

Lemony Snicket: Cousin Adrienne.

Funniest Children's Writers

Paula Danziger: Jon Scieszka, Dav Pilkey, Lois Lowry (Anastasia books), Morris Gleitzman

Chris Crutcher: Gotta go with Dr. Seuss.

Robert Munsch: Seuss, Seuss and Seuss.

Linda Ellerbee: Dr. Seuss, Shel Silverstein. By the way, both are also the saddest kids' writers.

Bruce Hale: Jon Scieszka, Dan Greenburg, Dav Piley, Daniel Pinkwater, Bruce Coville.

Jane Yolen: Daniel Pinkwater, Sid Fleischman, Bruce Coville.

Lemony Snicket: Jon Scieszka, Edward Lear, Maira Kalman, J. Otto Seibold, Roz Chast, Lewis Carroll and Henry James.

Markets

Book Publishers

There's no magic formula for getting published. It's a matter of getting the right manuscript on the right editor's desk at the right time. Before you submit it's important to learn publishers' needs, see what kind of books they're producing and decide which publishers your work is best suited for. *Children's Writer's & Illustrator's Market* is but one tool in this process. (Those just starting out, turn to Just Getting Started? Some Quick Tips, on page 2.)

To help you narrow down the list of possible publishers for your work, we've included several indexes at the back of this book. **The Subject Index** lists book and magazine publishers according to their fiction and nonfiction needs or interests. **The Age-Level Index** indicates which age groups publishers cater to. **The Photography Index** indicates which markets buy photography for children's publications. **The Poetry Index** lists publishers accepting poetry.

If you write contemporary fiction for young adults, for example, and you're trying to place a book manuscript, go first to the Subject Index. Locate the fiction categories under Book Publishers and copy the list under Contemporary. Then go to the Age-Level Index and highlight the publishers on the Contemporary list that are included under the Young Adults heading. Read the listings for the highlighted publishers to see if your work matches their needs.

Remember, *Children's Writer's & Illustrator's Market* should not be your only source for researching publishers. Here are a few other sources of information:

- The Society of Children's Book Writers and Illustrators (SCBWI) offers members an annual market survey of children's book publishers. (Members send a SASE with $3 postage. SCBWI membership information can be found at www.scbwi.org.)
- The Children's Book Council website (www.cbcbooks.org) gives information on member publishers.
- If a publisher interests you, send a SASE for submission guidelines *before* submitting. For a searchable database of over 1,150 publishers' guidelines, visit www.writersdigest.com.
- Check publishers' websites. Many include their complete catalogs which you can browse. Web addresses are included in many publishers' listings.
- Spend time at your local bookstore to see who's publishing what. While you're there, browse through *Publishers Weekly*, *The Horn Book* and *Riverbank Review*.

SUBSIDY AND SELF-PUBLISHING

Some determined writers who receive rejections from royalty publishers may look to subsidy and co-op publishers as an option for getting their work into print. These publishers ask writers to pay all or part of the costs of producing a book. We strongly advise writers and illustrators to work only with publishers who pay them. For this reason, we've adopted a policy not to include any subsidy or co-op publishers in *Children's Writer's & Illustrator's Market* (or any other Writer's Digest Books market books).

If you're interested in publishing your book just to share it with friends and relatives, self-publishing is a viable option, but it involves a lot of time, energy and money. You oversee all book production details. Check with a local printer for advice and information on cost.

Whatever path you choose, keep in mind that the market is flooded with submissions, so it's important for you to hone your craft and submit the best work possible. Competition from thousands of other writers and illustrators makes it more important than ever to research publishers before submitting—read their guidelines, look at their catalogs, check out a few of their titles and visit their websites.

ADVICE FROM INSIDERS

For insight and advice on getting published from a variety of perspectives, be sure to read the Insider Reports in this section. Subjects include authors **Kimberly Willis Holt** (page 142) and **Robie Harris** (page 190); illustrators **Tara Calahan King** (page 117) and **Paul Yalowitz** (page 150); author/illustrator **Dav Pilkey** (page 184); and editors **Deborah Brodie** of Viking (page 200), **Stephanie Owens Lurie** of Dutton (page 126) and **Kathy Landwehr** of Peachtree (page 171); and Charlesbridge Publicity Associate **Donna Spurlock** (page 112).

Information on book publishers listed in the previous edition but not included in this edition of Children's Writer's & Illustrator's Market may be found in the General Index.

Electronic Publishing

Even before the exclusively on-line release of Stephen King's novella *Riding the Bullet* (Simon & Schuster), the publishing world was abuzz with speculation about how electronic publishing will impact print publishing. But, more importantly—how will it affect children's book publishing?

Children's Writer's & Illustrator's Market has yet to include electronic publishers among its listings. It seems too soon in the game, too few electronic publishers have track records, and too many charge for their services. And too many questions loom: Will e-publishers edit the material? How will they market electronic children's books? How will authors get paid? How will books with artwork be handled? Will consumers want electronic children's books? Will children?

We asked a couple of editors what they think about the issue of electronic publishing and children's books. Here are their opinions:

Michael Stearns, Senior Editor, Harcourt Children's Books:
I don't see e-publishing affecting children's picture books much at all anytime soon. Novels will most likely be another story, but even that's hard to gauge just yet. But picture books are, I'd bet, safe for a while. You don't introduce children to reading by having them first get used to a computerized reader. At least, that's how I would introduce *my* kid to reading."

Melanie Cecka, Senior Editor, Viking Children's Books:
It's hard for me to say how e-publishing will impact traditional book publishing at the juvenile level. It's particularly difficult to anticipate how e-publishing would effect picture books. Print-on-demand seems a venture more suitable to novels. Picture books strike me as a different beast, however—they're a sacred lap-time commodity, a shared and highly visual experience between reader and child, and I can't imagine that e-publishing could ever replace that—no matter how great the on-screen graphics become.

On the other hand, e-publishing opens up a whole new venue for genres like poetry, essays, and short stories, which can be more difficult to sell to a book publisher. I read hundreds of great submissions every year that are "too slight" to merit a $50,000 investment as a book, but are enjoyable reads nonetheless. Perhaps e-publishing will become that off-shoot new writers need to bridge the chasm between the states of "published" and "unpublished."

☑ **ABINGDON PRESS**, The United Methodist Publishing House, 201 Eighth Ave. S., Nashville TN 37203. (615)749-6384. Fax: (615)749-6512. E-mail: paugustine@umpublishing.org. **Acquisitions:** Peg Augustine, children's book editor. Estab. 1789. "Abingdon Press, America's oldest theological publisher, provides an ecumenical publishing program dedicated to serving the Christian community—clergy, scholars, church leaders, musicians and general readers—with quality resources in the areas of Bible study, the practice of ministry, theology, devotion, spirituality, inspiration, prayer, music and worship, reference, Christian education and church supplies."
Fiction: Picture books, middle readers, young readers, young adults/teens: multicultural, religion, special needs.
Nonfiction: Picture books, middle readers, young readers, young adults/teens: religion.
How to Contact/Writers: Query; submit outline/synopsis and 1 sample chapter. Responds to queries in 3 months; mss in 6 months.
Illustration: Uses color artwork only. Reviews ms/illustration packages from artists. Query with photocopies only. Samples returned with SASE; samples not filed.
Photography: Buys stock images. Wants scenics, landscape, still life and multiracial photos. Model/property release required. Uses color prints. Submit stock photo list.
Terms: Pays authors royalty of 5-10% based on retail price. Work purchased outright from authors ($100-1,000).

N ☐ **ACTION PUBLISHING**, P.O. Box 391, Glendale CA 91209. (323)478-1667. Fax: (323)478-1767. Website: www.actionpublishing.com. Book publisher. Estab. 1996. Publishes rapid learning and values oriented material featuring the Kuekumber Kids and other series by Scott E. Sutton. **Publisher:** Michael Metzler. **Art Acquisitions:** Art Director. Publishes 4 young readers/year; 2 middle readers/year; and 2 young adult titles/year.
Nonfiction: Young readers: arts/crafts, geography, health, how-to, nature/environment, reference, science, sports, textbooks. Middle readers, young adults: arts/crafts, careers, cooking geography, health, history, how-to, reference, science, sports, textbooks.
How to Contact/Writers: Query. Responds to queries/mss in 5 weeks. Publishes a book 16 months after acceptance. Will consider simultaneous submissions and previously published work.
Illustration: Works with 2 illustrators/year. Reviews ms/illustration packages from artists. Query. Contact: Publisher. Send promotional literature. Contact: Art Director. Responds to submissions in 1 week. Samples returned with SASE or kept on file if interested and OK with illustrator.
Photography: Buys stock and assigns work. Contact: Art Director. "We use photos on as-needed basis. Mainly publicity, advertising and copy work." Uses 35mm or 4×5 transparencies. Submit cover letter and promo piece.
Terms: Pays authors royalty based on wholesale price. Offers advances against royalties. Pays illustrators by the project or royalty. Pays photographers by the project or per photo Sends galleys to authors. Original art returned as negotiated depending on project. Book catalog available for #10 SAE and 1 first-class stamp.
Tips: "Many of our projects are originated in-house but we are always interested in new work. Send us a query along with a brief sample allowing fast evaluation. We will respond quickly."

ADVOCACY PRESS, P.O. Box 236, Santa Barbara CA 93102. (805)962-2728. Fax: (805)963-3580. Division of The Girls Incorporated of Greater Santa Barbara. Book publisher. Editorial Contact: Ruth Vitale, curriculum specialist. Publishes 2-4 children's books/year.
Fiction: Picture books, young readers, middle readers: adventure, animal, concepts in self-esteem, contemporary, fantasy, folktales, gender equity, multicultural, nature/environment, poetry. "Illustrated children's stories incorporate self-esteem, gender equity, self-awareness concepts." Published *Nature's Wonderful World in Rhyme* (birth-age 12, collection of poems); *Shadow and the Ready Time* (32-page picture book). "Most publications are 32-48 page picture stories for readers 4-11 years. Most feature adventures of animals in interesting/educational locales."
Nonfiction: Middle readers, young adults: careers, multicultural, self-help, social issues, textbooks.
How to Contact/Writers: "Because of the required focus of our publications, most have been written in-house." Responds to queries/mss in 2 months. Include SASE.
Illustration: "Require intimate integration of art with story. Therefore, almost always use local illustrators." Average about 30 illustrations per story. Reviews ms/illustration packages from artists. Submit ms with dummy. Contact: Ruth Vitale. Responds in 2 months. Samples returned with SASE.
Terms: Authors paid by royalty or outright purchase. Pays illustrators by project or royalty. Book catalog and ms guidelines for SASE.
Tips: "We are not presently looking for new titles."

AFRICA WORLD PRESS, P.O. Box 1892, Trenton NJ 08607. (609)844-9583. Fax: (609)844-0198. E-mail: awprsp@africanworld.com. Website: www.africaworld.com. Book publisher. **Manuscript Acquisitions:** Kassahun Checole. **Art Acquisitions:** Kassahun Checole, editor. Publishes 5 picture books/year; 15 young reader and young adult titles/year; 8 middle readers/year. Books concentrate on African and African-American life.
Fiction: Picture books, young readers: adventure, concept, contemporary, folktales, history, multicultural. Middle readers, young adults: adventure, contemporary, folktales, history, multicultural.

Nonfiction: Picture books, young readers, middle readers, young adults: concept, history, multicultural. Does not want to see self-help, gender or health books.
How to Contact/Writers: Query; submit outline/synopsis and 2 sample chapters. Responds to queries in 30-45 days; mss in 3 months. Will consider previously published work.
Illustration: Works with 10-20 illustrators/year. Reviews ms/illustration packages from artists. Query. Illustrations only: Query with samples. Responds in 3 months.
Terms: Pays authors royalty based on retail price. Pays illustrators by the project or royalty based on retail price. Book catalog available for SAE; ms and art guidelines available for SASE.

☑ **ALADDIN PAPERBACKS,** 1230 Avenue of the Americas, 4th Floor, New York NY 10020. Fax: (212) 698-2796. Website: www.simonsays.com. Paperback imprint of Simon & Schuster Children's Publishing Children's Division. Vice President/Editorial Director: Ellen Krieger. **Manuscript Acquisitions:** Stephen Fraser, executive editor. **Art Acquisitions:** Debra Sfetsios, art director. Publishes 130 titles/year.
   ● Aladdin publishes primarily reprints of successful hardcovers from other Simon & Schuster imprints. They accept query letters with proposals for middle grade and young adult series, beginning readers, middle grade mysteries and commercial nonfiction.

▣ ☐ ☼ **ALL ABOUT KIDS PUBLISHING INC.,** 6280 San Ignacio Ave., Suite C, San Jose CA 95119. (408)578-4026. Fax: (408)578-4029. Website: www.aakp.com. Estab. 1999. Specializes in fiction, educational material, multicultural material, nonfiction. We are an independent book packager/producer. **Manuscript Acquisitions:** Linda L. Guevara. **Art Acquisitions:** Nadine Takvorian, art director.
   ● This new publisher's line was set to debut in the end of 2000 with a website set to go live around the same time. Publishes 20-30 picture books/year. 80% of books by first-time authors.
Fiction: Picture books, young readers: adventure, animal, concept, fantasy, folktales, history, humor, multicultural, nature/environment, poetry, religion, special needs, suspense/mystery. Average word length: picture books—450 words. Recently published *The Where Wolf?*, by Jackie Leigh Ross (picture book); *The Flight of the Sunflower*, by Melissa Bourbon-Ramirez (picture book).
Nonfiction: Picture books, young readers: activity books, animal, biography, concept, history, multicultural, nature/environment, religion, special needs, textbooks. Average word length: picture books—450 words. Recently published *Fishes, Flowers & Fandangles*, by Hua Tao Zhang; *Activity Book to Teach Children Ages 5-12 Art For Teachers & Parents*.
How to Contact/Writers: Fiction: Submit complete ms. Nonfiction: Submit complete ms for picture books; outline synopsis and 2 sample chapters for young readers. Responds to mss in 3 months. Publishes a book 12-18 months after acceptance.
Illustration: Works with 20-30 illustrators/year. Uses both color and b&w artwork. Reviews ms/illustration packages from artists. Submit ms with dummy or ms with 2-3 pieces of final art. Contact: Linda L. Guevara, editor. Illustrations only: Arrange personal portfolio review or send résumé, portfolio and client list. Contact: Nadine Takvorian, art director. Responds in 3 months. Samples returned with SASE; samples filed.
Photography: Works on assignment only. Contact: Linda L. Guevara, editor. Model/property releases required. Uses 35mm transparencies. Submit portfolio, résumé, client list.
Terms: Pays author royalty of 6% based on retail price. Offers advances (Average amount: $2,500). Pays illustrators by the project (range: $3,000 minimum) or royalty of 6% based on retail price. Pays photographers by the project (range: $500 minimum) or royalty of 6%. Sends galleys to authors; dummies to illustrators. Originals returned to artist at job's completion. All imprints included in a single catalog. Writer's, artist's and photographer's guidelines available for SASE.
Tips: "Write from the heart and for the love of children. They are our greatest asset and should be treated with respect. Please submit only one manuscript at a time."

ALYSON PUBLICATIONS, INC., P.O. 4371, Los Angeles CA 90078. (323)860-6065. Fax: (323)467-0173. Book publisher. **Acquisitions:** Editorial Department. Publishes 1 (projected) picture book/year and 3 (projected) young adult titles/year. "Alyson Wonderland is the line of illustrated children's books. We are looking for diverse depictions of family life for children of gay and lesbian parents."
Fiction: All levels: adventure, animal, contemporary, fantasy, history, humor, multicultural, nature/environment, science fiction. Young readers and middle readers: suspense, mystery. Teens: anthology.
Nonfiction: Teens: concept, social issues. "We like books that incorporate all racial, religious and body types, as well as dealing with children with gay and lesbian parents—which all our books must deal with. Our YA books should deal with issues faced by kids growing up gay or lesbian." Published *Heather Has Two Mommies*, by Lesléa Newman; and *Daddy's Wedding*, by Michael Willhoite.
How to Contact/Writers: Submit outline/synopsis and sample chapters (young adults); submit complete ms (picture books/young readers). Responds to queries/mss within 3 months. Include SASE.
Illustration: Works with 2 illustrators/year. Reviews mss/illustration packages from artists. Illustrations only: Submit "representative art that can be *kept on file*. Good quality photocopies are OK." Responds only if interested. Samples returned with SASE; samples kept on file.

Terms: Pays authors royalty of 8-12% based on wholesale price. "We *do* offer advances." Pays illustrators by the project (range: $25-100). Pays photographers per photo (range: $50-100). Book catalog and/or ms guidelines free for SASE.
Tips: "We only publish kids' books aimed at the children of gay or lesbian parents."

AMERICAN BIBLE SOCIETY, 1865 Broadway, New York NY 10023-7505. Fax: (212)408-1305. Website: www.americanbible.org. Book publisher. Estab. 1816. **Manuscript Acquisitions:** Barbara Bernstengel. **Art Acquisitions:** Christina Murphy, assistant director. Publishes 1-2 picture books/year; 1 young reader/year; 1 youth activity/year; and 1 young adult/year. Publishes books with spiritual/religious themes based on the Bible. "The purpose of the American Bible Society is to provide the Holy Scriptures to every man, woman and child in a language and form each can easily understand, and at a price each can easily afford. This purpose is undertaken without doctrinal note or comment." Please do not call. Submit all sample submissions, résumés, etc. for review via mail.
Nonfiction: All levels: activity books, multicultural, religion, self-help, reference, social issues and special needs. Multicultural needs include innercity lifestyle; African-American, Hispanic/Latino, Native American, Asian; mixed groups (such as choirs, classrooms, church events). "Unsolicited manuscripts will be returned unread! We prefer published writing samples with résumés so we can contact copywriters when an appropriate project comes up." Recently published *Experience Jesus Today*, a 248-page Bible storybook with prayers, discussion questions, and background information, full color (ages 7-11).
How to Contact/Writers: All mss developed in-house. Query with résumé and writing samples. Contact: Barbara Bernstengel. Unsolicited mss rejected. No credit lines given.
Illustration: Works with 2-3 illustrators/year. Reviews ms/illustration packages from artists. Contact: Christina Murphy via mail. Illustrations only: Query with samples; if interested, a personal interview will be arranged to see portfolio; send "résumés, tearsheets and promotional literature to keep; slides will be returned promptly." Responds to queries within 1 month. Samples returned; samples sometimes filed. Book catalog free on written request.
Photography: Contact: Christina Murphy via mail. Buys stock and assigns work. Looking for "nature, scenic, multicultural, intergenerational people shots." Model/property releases required. Uses any size b&w prints; 35mm, 2¼ × 2¼ and 4 × 5 transparencies. Photographers should query with samples first. If interested, a personal interview will be set up to see portfolio; provide résumé, promotional literature or tearsheets.
Terms: Photographers paid by the project (range: $800-5,000); per photo (range $100-400). Credit line given on most projects. Most photos purchased for one-time use. Factors used to determine payment for ms/illustration package include "nature and scope of project; complexity of illustration and continuity of work; number of illustrations." Pays illustrators $200-1,000/illustration; based on fair market value. Sends 2 complimentary copies of published work to illustrators. ABS owns all publication rights to illustrations and mss.
Tips: Illustrators and photographers: "Submit in a form that we can keep on file, if we like, such as tearsheets, postcards, photocopies, etc."

ℕ ⬚ AMIRAH PUBLISHING, P.O. Box 541146. Flushing NY 11354. Phone/fax: (718)321-9004. E-mail: amirahpbco@aol.com. Website: www.ifna.net. Estab. 1992. Specializes in fiction, educational material, multicultural material. **Manuscript Acquisitions:** Yahiya Emerick, **Art Acquisitions:** Yahiya Emerick, president. Publishes 2 young readers/year; 5 middle readers; 3 young adult titles/year. 25% of books by first-time authors. "Our goal is to produce quality books for children and young adults with a spiritually uplifting application."
Fiction: Picture books, young readers, middle readers, young adults: adventure, animal, history, multicultural, religion, Islamic. Average word length: picture books—200; young readers—1,000; middle readers—5,000; young adults—5,000. Recently published *Ahmad Deen and the Curse of the Aztec Warrior*, by Yahiya Emerick (ages 8-11); *Burhaan Khan*, by Qasim Najar (ages 6-8); *The Memory of Hands*, by Reshma Baig (ages 15 to adult).
Nonfiction: Picture books, young readers, middle readers, young adults: history, religion, Islamic. Average word length: picture books—200; young readers—1,000; middle readers—5,000; young adults—5,000. Recently published *Color and Learn Salah*, by Yahiya Emerick (ages 5-7, religious); *Learning About Islam*, by Yahiya Emerick (ages 9-11, religious); *What Islam Is All About*, by Yahiya Emerick (ages 14 +, religious).
How to Contact/Writers: Query. Nonfiction: Query. Responds to queries in 2 weeks; mss in 3 months. Publishes a book 6-12 months after acceptance. Will consider electronic submissions via disk or modem.
Illustration: Works with 2-4 illustrators/year. Reviews ms/illustration packages from artists. Query. Contact: Qasim Najar, vice president. Illustrations only: Query with samples. Contact: Yahiya Emerick, president. Responds in 1 month. Samples returned with SASE.
Photography: Works on assignment only. Contact: Yahiya Emerick, president. Uses images of the Middle East, children, nature. Model/property releases required. (31) Uses 4 × 6, matte, color prints. Submit cover letter.
Terms: Work purchased outright from authors for $1,000-3,000. Pays illustrators by the project (range: $20-40). Pays photographers by the project (range: $20-40). Sends galleys to authors; dummies to illustrators. Originals returned to artist at job's completion. Book catalog available for SASE and 2 first-class stamps. All imprints included in a single catalog. Catalog available on website.
Tips: "We specialize in materials relating to the Middle East and Muslim-oriented culture such as stories, learning materials and such. These are the only types of items we currently are publishing."

ATHENEUM BOOKS FOR YOUNG READERS, 1230 Avenue of the Americas, New York NY 10020. (212)698-2715. Website: www.simonsayskids.com. Imprint of Simon & Schuster Children's Publishing Division. Book publisher. Vice President/Associate Publisher and Editorial Director: Jonathan Lanman. Estab. 1960. **Manuscript Acquisitions:** Send queries with SASE to: Jonathan Lanman, vice president, editorial director, associate publisher; Anne Schwartz, editorial director of Anne Schwartz Books; Richard Jackson, editorial director of Richard Jackson Books; Marcia Marshall, executive editor; Caitlyn Dlouhy, senior editor. "All editors consider all types of projects." **Art Acquisitions:** Ann Bobco. Publishes 15-20 picture books/year; 4-5 young readers/year; 20-25 middle readers/year; and 10-15 young adults/year. 10% of books by first-time authors; 50% from agented writers. "Atheneum publishes original hardcover trade books for children from pre-school age through young adult. Our list includes picture books, chapter books, mysteries, biography, science fiction, fantasy, middle grade and young adult fiction and nonfiction. The style and subject matter of the books we publish is almost unlimited. We do not, however, publish textbooks, coloring or activity books, greeting cards, magazines or pamphlets or religious publications. Anne Schwartz Books is a highly selective line of books within the Atheneum imprint. The lists of Charles Scribner's Sons Books for Young Readers have been folded into the Atheneum program."

● Atheneum does not accept unsolicited manuscripts. Send query letter only. Atheneum title *The Folk Keeper*, by Franny Billingsly, won the 2000 Boston Globe-Horn Book Award for Fiction; their title *A Band of Angels*, by Deborah Hopkinson, won the Golden Kite Award for Picture Book Text. See Hopkinson's article Historical Fiction: Bringing the Past to Life for Young Readers on page 51. See Listen In: An Agent Chats with Richard Jackson, on page 83, to hear from editorial director of Atheneum imprint Richard Jackson Books.

How to Contact/Writers: Query only for all mss, regardless of length. Send letters with SASE to one of our editors at the above address. Responds to queries in 1 month; requested mss in 3 months. Publishes a book 18-24 months after acceptance. Will consider simultaneous queries from previously unpublished authors and those submitted to other publishers, "though we request that the author let us know it is a simultaneous query."

Illustration: Works with 40-50 illustrators/year. Send art samples résumé, tearsheets to Ann Bobco, Design Dept. 4th Floor, 1230 Avenue of the Americas, New York NY 10020. Samples filed. Responds to art samples only if interested.

Terms: Pays authors in royalties of 8-10% based on retail price. Pays illustrators royalty of 5-6% or by the project. Pays photographers by the project. Sends galleys and proofs to authors; proofs to illustrators. Original artwork returned at job's completion. Ms guidelines for #10 SAE and 1 first-class stamp.

A/V CONCEPTS CORP., 30 Montauk Blvd., Oakdale NY 11769. (631)567-7227. Fax: (631)567-8745. E-mail: info@edcompublishing.com. Educational book publisher. **Manuscript Acquisitions:** Laura Solimene, editorial director. **Art Acquisitions:** President: Phil Solimene, president. Publishes 6 young readers/year; 6 middle readers/year; 6 young adult titles/year. 20% of books by first-time authors. Primary theme of books and multimedia is classic literature, math, science, language arts, self esteem.

Fiction: Middle readers: hi-lo. Young adults: hi-lo, multicultural, special needs. "We hire writers to adapt classic literature."

Nonfiction: All levels: activity books. Young adults: hi-lo, multicultural, science, self help, textbooks. Average word length: middle readers—300-400; young adults—500-950.

How to Contact/Writers: Fiction: Submit outline/synopsis and 1 sample chapter. Responds to queries in 1 month.

Illustration: Works with 4-6 illustrators/year. Reviews ms/illustration packages from artists. Submit ms with 3-4 pieces of final art. Illustrations only: Query with samples. "No originals; send non-returnable material and samples only." Responds in 1 month. Samples returned with SASE; samples filed.

Photography: Submit samples.

Terms: Work purchased outright from authors (range $50-1,000). Pays illustrators by the project (range: $50-1,000). Pays photographers per photo (range: $25-250). Ms and art guidelines available for 9 × 12 SASE.

AVISSON PRESS, INC., 3007 Taliaferro Rd., Greensboro NC 27408. (336)288-6989. Fax: (336)288-6989. Estab. 1995. Specializes in multicultural material, nonfiction, YA biography. **Manuscript Acquisitions:** Martin Hester, publisher; Stephanie Todd. , Publishes 8-10 young adult titles/year. 70% of books by first-time authors.

FOR EXPLANATIONS OF THESE SYMBOLS,
SEE THE INSIDE FRONT AND BACK COVERS OF THIS BOOK

Nonfiction: Young adults: biography, multicultural. Average word length: young adults—25,000. Recently published *Mum Bet: The Life and Times of Elizabeth Freeman*, by Mary Wilds; *Young Superstars of Tennis: The Venus and Serena Williams Story; Here Comes Eleanor: A New Biography of Eleanor Roosevelt for Young People*, by Virginia Veeder Westervelt.

How to Contact/Writers: Nonfiction: Submit outline/synopsis and 2 sample chapters. Responds to queries in 2 weeks; mss in 2 months. Publishes a book 9-12 months after acceptance. Will consider simultaneous submissions.

Terms: Pays author royalty of 8-10% based on wholesale price. Offers advances (Average amount: $500). Sends galleys to authors. Book catalog available for #10 SAE and 1 first-class stamp; ms guidelines available for SASE.

Tips: "We don't use illustrated books."

☑ AVON BOOKS/BOOKS FOR YOUNG READERS, 1350 Avenue of the Americas, New York NY 10019. (212)261-6800. Fax: (212)261-6668. Website: www.harperchildrens.com. A division of The Hearst Corporation. Book publisher. Mass market paperback publisher. Imprint of HarperCollins Publishing. **Acquisitions:** Julie Richardson, senior editor and Abigail McAden, associate editor. Art Director: Barbara Sitzsimmons. Publishes 12 hardcovers, 25-30 middle readers/year, 20-25 young adults/year. 10% of books by first-time authors; 80% of books from agented writers.

Fiction: Middle readers: comedy, contemporary, problem novels, sports, spy/mystery/adventure. Young adults: contemporary, problem novels, romance. Average length: middle readers—100-150 pages; young adults—150-250 pages. Avon does not publish preschool picture books.

Nonfiction: Middle readers: hobbies, music/dance, sports. Young adults: "growing up." Average length: middle readers—100-150 pages; young adults—150-250 pages. Recent publications: *Nightmare Room*, by R.L. Stine (middle reader.

How to Contact/Writers: "Please send for guidelines before submitting." Fiction/nonfiction: Submit outline/synopsis and 3 sample chapters. Responds to mss in 3 months. Publishes a book 18-24 months after acceptance. Will consider simultaneous submissions.

Illustration: Will not review ms/illustration packages.

Terms: Pays authors in royalties of 6% based on retail price. Average advance payment is "very open." Book catalog available for 9×12 SAE and 4 first-class stamps; ms guidelines for #10 SASE.

Tips: "We have four young readers imprints: Avon Camelot, books for the middle grades; Avon Flare and Avon Tempest, young adults; and Avon hardcover. Our list includes both individual titles and series, with the emphasis on high quality recreational reading—a fresh and original writing style; identifiable, three-dimensional characters; a strong, well-paced story that pulls readers in and keeps them interested." Writers: "Make sure you really know what a company's list looks like before you submit work. Is your work in line with what they usually do? Is your work appropriate for the age group that this company publishes for? Be aware of what's in your bookstore (but not what's in there for too long!)" Illustrators: "Submit work to art directors and people who are in charge of illustration at publishers. This is usually not handled entirely by the editorial department. Do *not* expect a response if no SASE is included with your material."

☑ Ⓐ BANTAM DOUBLEDAY DELL, Books for Young Readers, imprints of Random House, Inc., 1540 Broadway, New York NY 10036. (212)354-6500. Website: www.randomhouse.com. Book publisher. Imprints: Delacorte Books for Young Readers, Doubleday Books for Young Readers, Laurel Leaf, Skylark, Starfire and Yearling Books. Vice President/Publisher: Craig Virden. Vice President/Publisher: Beverly Horowitz. **Manuscript Acquisitions:** Michelle Poploff, editorial director, paperbacks; Françoise Bui, executive editor, series; Wendy Lamb, executive editor; Karen Wojtyla, senior editor. **Art Acquisitions:** Art Director. Publishes 16 picture books; 35 middle reader hardcover books; 35 young adult hardcover titles/year. 10% of books by first-time authors; 70% of books from agented writers. "Bantam Doubleday Dell Books for Young Readers publishes award-winning books by distinguished authors and the most promising new writers."

● Bantam title *Bud, Not Buddy*, by Christopher Paul Curtis, won the 2000 Newbery Medal, the 2000 Coretta Scott King Author Award and the Golden Kite Honor Award for Fiction; their title *45th Street: Short Stories*, by Walter Dean Myers, won a Boston Globe-Horn Book Honor Award for Fiction.

Fiction: Picture books: adventure, animal, contemporary, fantasy, humor. Young readers: animal, contemporary, humor, fantasy, sports, suspense/mystery. Middle readers: adventure, animal, contemporary, humor, easy-to-read, fantasy, sports, suspense/mystery. Young adults: adventure, contemporary issues, humor, coming-of-age, suspense/mystery. Recently published *Bud, Not Buddy*, by Christopher Paul Curtis; *White Fox Chronicles*, by Gary Paulsen; and *Beetle Boy*, by Lawrence David.

Nonfiction: "Bantam Doubleday Dell Books for Young Readers publishes a very limited number of nonfiction titles."

How to Contact/Writers: Submit through agent; accepts queries from published authors. "All unsolicited manuscripts returned unopened with the following exceptions: Unsolicited manuscripts are accepted for the Delacorte Press Prize for a First Young Adult Novel contest (see Contests & Awards section) and the Marguerite de Angeli Prize for a First Middle Grade Novel contest (see Contests & Awards section)." Responds to queries in 4 months; mss in 3 months. "Simultaneous submissions must be stated as such."

Illustration: Number of illustrations used per fiction title varies considerably. Reviews ms/illustration packages from artists. Query first. Do not send originals. "If you submit a dummy, please submit the text separately." Responds to ms/art samples only if interested. Cannot return samples; samples filed. Illustrations only: Submit tearsheets, résumé, samples that do not need to be returned. Original artwork returned at job's completion.

Terms: Pays authors advance and royalty. Pays illustrators advance and royalty or flat fee.

Tips: "Writers can submit to Delacorte Contest for a First Young Adult Novel or Marguerite de Angeli Contest for contemporary or historical fiction set in North America for readers age 7-10. Send SASE for contest guidelines."

N: BAREFOOT BOOKS, 37 W. 17th St., 4th Floor E., New York NY 10011. (212)604-0505. Fax: (212)604-0074. Website: www.barefoot-books.com. Estab. 1993 in the UK; 1998 in the US. Specializes in fiction, trade books, multicultural material, nonfiction. **Manuscript Acquisitions:** Alison Keehn, associate editor. **Art Acquisitions:** Alison Keehn, associate editor. Publishes 35 picture books/year; 10 anthologies/year. 40% of books by first-time authors. "The Barefoot child represents the person who is in harmony with the natural world and moves freely across boundaries of many kinds. Barefoot Books explores this image with a range of high-quality picture books for children of all ages. We work with artists, writers and storytellers from many cultures, focusing on themes that encourage independence of spirit, promote understanding and acceptance of different traditions, and foster a life-long love of learning."

Fiction: Picture books, young readers: animal, anthology, concept, fantasy, folktales, multicultural, nature/environment, poetry, spirituality. Middle readers: anthology, folktales. Average word length: picture books—500-1,000; young readers—2,000-3,000; anthologies—10,000-20,000. Recently published *The Gigantic Turnip*, by Aleksei Tolstoy, illustrated by Niamh Sharkey (ages 1-7, picture book); *One, Two, Skip a Few*, by Roberta Arenson (ages 2-7, picture book); *Grandmothers' Stories: Wise Woman Tales from Many Cultures*, by Burleigh Mutén, illustrated by Sian Bailey (ages 6 to adult, anthology).

Nonfiction: Picture books, young readers, middle readers, young adults: multicultural, spirituality/inspirational. Average word length: young readers—3,000-20,000. Recently published *The Genius of Leonardo*, by Guido Visconti, illustrated by Bimba Landmann; *Daughters of Eve: Strong Women of the Bible*, by Lillian Hammer Ross, illustrated by Kyra Teis.

How to Contact/Writers: Fiction: Submit complete ms for picture books; outline/synopsis and 1 sample story for collections. Nonfiction: Query. Responds to queries in 1 month; mss in 2 months. Will consider simultaneous submissions and previously published work.

Illustration: Works with 45 illustrators/year. Uses color artwork only. Reviews ms/illustration packages from artists. Query for anthology/collections or send ms with dummy for picture books. Contact: Alison Keehn, associate editor. Illustrations only: Query with samples or send promo sheet and tearsheets. Contact: Alison Keehn, associate editor. Responds only if interested. Samples returned with SASE.

Terms: Pays author royalty of 5% based on retail price. Offers advances. Sends galleys to authors. Originals returned to artist at job's completion. Book catalog available for 9 × 12 SAE and 5 first-class stamps; ms guidelines available for SASE. Catalog available on website.

Tips: "We are looking for books that inspire, books that are filled with a sense of magic and wonder. We also look for strong stories from all different cultures, reflecting the ways of the individual culture while also touching deeper human truths that suggest we are all one. We welcome playful submissions for the very youngest children and also anthologies of stories or poems for older readers, all focused around a universal theme. We encourage writers and artists to visit our website and read some of our books to get a sense of our editorial philosophy and what we publish before they submit to us. Always, we encourage them to stay true to their inner voice and artistic vision that reaches out for timeless stories, beyond the momentary trends that may exist in the market today."

✓ BARRONS EDUCATIONAL SERIES, 250 Wireless Blvd., Hauppauge NY 11788. (631)434-3311 or (800)645-3476. Fax: (631)434-3723. Website: www.barronseduc.com. Book publisher. Estab. 1945. "Barrons tends to publish series of books, both for adults and children." **Acquisitions:** Wayne R. Barr, acquisitions manager. Publishes 20 picture books/year; 20 young readers/year; 20 middle reader titles/year; 10 young adult titles/year. 25% of books by first-time authors; 25% of books from agented writers.

Fiction: Picture books: animal, concept, multicultural, nature/environment. Young readers: Adventure, multicultural, nature/environment, suspense/mystery. Middle readers: adventure, horror, multicultural, nature/environment, problem novels, suspense/mystery. Young adults: horror, problem novels. Recently published *Sports Success: Winning Women in Soccer*, by Marlene Targ Brill; *Word Wizardry* by Margaret and William Kenda.

Nonfiction: Picture books: concept, reference. Young readers: how-to, reference, self help, social issues. Middle readers: hi-lo, how-to, reference, self help, social issues. Young adults: how-to, self help, social issues.

How to Contact/Writers: Fiction: Query. Nonfiction: Submit outline/synopsis and sample chapters. "Submissions must be accompanied by SASE for response." E-mailed or faxed proposals are not accepted. Responds to queries in 1 month; mss in 6-8 months. Publishes a book 1 year after acceptance. Will consider simultaneous submissions.

Illustration: Works with 10 illustrators/year. Reviews ms/illustration packages from artists. Query first; 3 chapters of ms with 1 piece of final art, remainder roughs. Illustrations only: Submit tearsheets or slides plus résumé. Responds in 3-8 weeks.

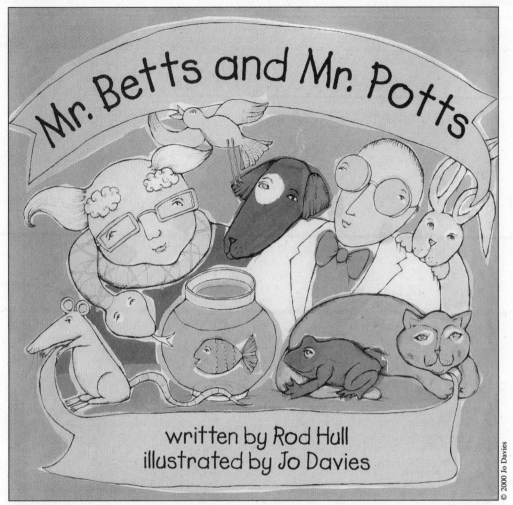

Jo Davies used gouache for the illustrations in *Mr. Betts and Mr. Potts*, published by Barefoot Books. Says associate editor, Alison Keehn, "We love the playfulness of the style, the quirkiness of the characters and the artist's lively use of color." The publisher regularly finds illustrators through sample submissions. They also use artists who work in a more classical vein.

Terms: Pays authors in royalties of 10-14% based on wholesale price or buys ms outright for $2,000 minimum. Pays illustrators by the project based on retail price. Sends galleys to authors; dummies to illustrators. Book catalog, ms/artist's guidelines for 9×12 SAE.

Tips: Writers: "We are predominately on the lookout for preschool storybooks and concept books. No YA fiction/romance or novels." Illustrators: "We are happy to receive a sample illustration to keep on file for future consideration. Periodic notes reminding us of your work are acceptable." Children's book themes "are becoming much more contemporary and relevant to a child's day-to-day activities."

BEACH HOLME PUBLISHERS, 2040 W. 12th Ave., Suite 226, Vancouver, British Columbia V6J 2G2 Canada. (604)733-4868. Fax: (604)733-4860. E-mail: bhp@beachholme.bc.ca. Website: www.beachholme.b c.ca. Book publisher. **Manuscript Acquisitions:** Michael Carroll, managing editor. **Art Acquisitions:** Michael Carroll. Publishes 5-6 young adult titles/year and 7-8 adult literary titles/year. 40% of books by first-time authors. "We publish primarily regional historical fiction. We publish young adult novels for children aged 8-12. We are particularly interested in works that have a historical basis and are set in the Pacific Northwest, or northern Canada. Include ideas for teacher's guides or resources and appropriate topics for a classroom situation if applicable."

• Beach Holme *only* accepts work from Canadian writers.

Fiction: Young adults: contemporary, folktales, history, multicultural, nature/environment, poetry. Multicultural needs include themes reflecting cultural heritage of the Pacific Northwest, i.e., first nations, Asian, East Indian, etc. Does not want to see generic adventure or mystery with no sense of place. Average word length: middle readers—15-20,000; young adults/teens—30,000-40,000. Recently published *Tiger by the Tail*, by Eric Walters (ages 9-13, young adult fiction); *The Doctor's Apprentice*, by Ann Walsh (ages 9-13, young adult fiction); and *An Island of My Own*, by Andrea Spalding (ages 9-13, young adult fiction).

How to Contact/Writers: Fiction: Submit outline/synopsis and 3 sample chapters. Responds to queries/mss in 2 months. Publishes a book 6 months-1 year after acceptance.

Illustration: Works with 4-5 illustrators/year. Responds to submissions in 2 months if interested. Samples returned with SASE; samples filed. Originals returned at job's completion.

Terms: Pays authors 10% royalty based on retail price. Offers advances (average amount: $500). Pays illustrators by the project (range: $500-1,000). Pays photographers by the project (range: $100-300). Sends galleys to authors. Book catalog available for 9×12 SAE and 3 first-class Canadian stamps; ms guidelines available with SASE.

Tips: "Research what we have previously published to familiarize yourself with what we are looking for. Please, be informed."

N BEHRMAN HOUSE INC., 11 Edison Place, Springfield NJ 07081. (973)379-7200. Fax: (973)379-7280. Book publisher. Estab. 1921. Managing Editor: Bob Tinkham. **Acquisitions:** Editorial Department. Publishes 3 young reader titles/year; 3 middle reader titles/year; and 3 young adult titles/year. 12% of books by first-time authors; 2% of books from agented writers. Publishes books on all aspects of Judaism: history, cultural, textbooks, holidays. "Behrman House publishes quality books of Jewish content—history, Bible, philosophy, holidays, ethics—for children and adults."

Fiction: All levels: Judaism.

Nonfiction: All levels: Judaism, Jewish educational textbooks. Average word length: young reader—1,200; middle reader—2,000; young adult—4,000. Published *My Jewish Year*, by Adam Fisher (ages 8-9); *Partners with God*, by Gila Gevirtz (ages 8-9); and *It's a Mitzvah!*, by Bradley Artson (adult).

How to Contact/Writers: Fiction/Nonfiction: Submit outline/synopsis and sample chapters. Responds to queries in 1 month; mss in 2 months. Publishes a book 2½ years after acceptance. Will consider simultaneous submissions.

Illustration: Works with 6 children's illustrators/year. Reviews ms/illustration packages from artists. "Query first." Illustrations only: Query with samples; send unsolicited art samples by mail. Responds to queries in 1 month; mss in 2 months.

Photography: Purchases photos from freelancers. Buys stock and assigns work. Uses photos of families involved in Jewish activities. Uses color and b&w prints. Photographers should query with samples. Send unsolicited photos by mail. Submit portfolio for review.

Terms: Pays authors in royalties of 3-10% based on retail price or buys ms outright for $1,000-5,000. Offers advance. Pays illustrators by the project (range: $500-5,000). Sends galleys to authors; dummies to illustrators. Book catalog free on request.

Tips: Looking for "religious school texts" with Judaic themes or general trade Judaica.

BENCHMARK BOOKS, Imprint of Marshall Cavendish, 99 White Plains Rd., Tarrytown NY 10591. (914)332-8888. Fax: (914)332-1888. **Manuscript Acquisitions:** Joyce Stanton, Angela Catalono, Doug Sanders and Kate Nunn. Publishes 90 young reader, middle reader and young adult books/year. "We look for interesting treatments of primarily nonfiction subjects related to elementary, middle school and high school curriculum."

Nonfiction: Most nonfiction topics should be curriculum related. Average word length for books: 2,000-20,000. All books published as part of a series.

How to Contact/Writers: Nonfiction: submit complete ms or submit outline/synopsis and 1 or more sample chapters. Responds to queries and mss in 3 months. Publishes a book 2 years after acceptance. Will consider simultaneous submissions.

Photography: Buys stock and assigns work.

Terms: Pays authors royalty based on retail price or buys work outright. Offers advances. Sends galleys to authors. Book catalog available. All imprints included in a single catalog.

✓ THE BENEFACTORY, 925 N. Milwaukee Ave., Suite 1010, Wheeling IL 60090. (847)919-1777. Fax: (847)919-2777. Website: www.readplay.com. Book publisher. Estab. 1990. **Manuscript/Art Acquisitions:** Cindy Germain, production manager. Publishes 6-12 picture books/year with the Humane Society of the United States; 6-12 picture books/year with The National Wildlife Federation. 50% of books by first-time authors. The Benefactory publishes "classic" true stories about real animals, through licenses with the Humane Society of the United States and National Wildlife Federation. Each title is accompanied by a read-along audiocassette and a plush animal. A percentage of revenues benefits the HSUS or NWF. Target age for NWF titles: 4-7; for HSUS titles: 5-10.

Nonfiction: Picture books: nature/environment; young readers: animal, nature/environment. Average word length: HSUS titles: 1,200-1,500; NWF titles: 700-800. Recently published *Chessie, the Travelin' Man*, written by Randy Houk, illustrated by Paula Bartlett (ages 5-10, picture book); *Condor Magic*, written by Lyn Littlefield Hoopes, illustrated by Peter C. Stone (ages 5-10, picture book); and *Caesar: On Deaf Ears*, written by Loren Spiotta-DiMare, illustrated by Kara Lee (ages 5-10, picture book).

How to Contact/Writers: Query only—does not accept unsolicited mss. Responds to queries in 6 weeks. Publishes a book 1 year after acceptance. Will consider simultaneous submissions. Send SASE for writer's guidelines.

Illustration: Works with 6-8 illustrators/year. Uses color artwork only. Reviews ms/illustration packages from artists. Query or send ms with dummy. Illustrations only: Send résumé, promo sheet and tearsheets to be kept on file. Responds in 6 months. Samples returned with SASE; samples filed. Send SASE for artist guidelines.

Terms: Pays authors royalty of 3-5% based on wholesale price. Offers advances (Average amount: $5,000). Pays illustrators royalty of 3-5% based on wholesale price. Sends galleys to authors; dummies to illustrators. Originals returned to artist at job's completion. Book catalog available for 8 1/2 × 11 SASE; ms and art guidelines available for SASE.

☑ BETHANY HOUSE PUBLISHERS, 11400 Hampshire Ave. S., Minneapolis MN 55438-2852. (952)829-2500. Fax: (952)829-2768. Website: www.bethanyhouse.com. Book publisher. **Manuscript Acquisitions:** Rochelle Glöege, Natasha Sperling. **Art Acquisitions:** Paul Higdon. Publishes 2 young readers/year; 18 middle-grade readers/year; and 16 young adults/year. Bethany House Publishers is a non-profit publisher seeking to publish imaginative, excellent books that reflect an evangelical worldview without being preachy. Publishes picture books under Bethany Backyard imprint.

Fiction: Series for early readers, middle readers, young adults: historical and contemporary adventure, history, humor, multicultural, suspense/mystery, religion, sports and current issues. Does not want to see poetry or science fiction. Average word length: early readers—6,000; young readers—20,000; young adults—40,000. Published *Secret of the Mezuzah*, by Mary Reeves Bell (young adult/teens, mystery series); *The Ghost of KRZY*, by Bill Myers (middle-graders, suspense/adventure/humor series); and *The Mystery of the Dancing Angels*, by Elspeth Campbell Murphy (young readers, mystery series).

Nonfiction: Young readers, middle readers, young adults: religion/devotional, self-help, social issues. Published *Can I Be a Christian Without Being Weird?*, by Kevin Johnson (early teens, devotional book); and *Hot Topics, Tough Questions*, by Bill Myers (young adult/teen, Biblically based advice).

How to Contact/Writers: Fiction/Nonfiction: Send synopsis with first three chapters. Responds in 4 months. Picture Books: does not accept unsolicited mss, query only. Publishes a book 12-18 months after acceptance. Will consider simultaneous submissions.

Illustration: Works with 12 illustrators/year. Reviews illustration samples from artists. Illustrations only: Query with samples. Responds in 2 months. Samples returned with SASE.

Terms: Pays authors royalty based on net sales. Pays illustrators by the project. Pays photographers by the project. Sends galleys to authors. Book catalog available for 11 × 14 SAE and 5 first-class stamps.

Tips: "Research the market, know what is already out there. Study our catalog before submitting material. We look for an evangelical message woven delicately into a strong plot and topics that seek to broaden the reader's experience and perspective."

☑ BEYOND WORDS PUBLISHING, INC., 20827 N.W. Cornell Rd., Hillsboro OR 97124-1808. (503)531-8700. Fax: (503)531-8773. E-mail: beyondword.com. Website: www.beyondword.com. Book publisher. Director, Children's Division: Michelle Roehm. **Acquisitions:** Barbara Mann. Publishes 6-10 picture books/year and 2 nonfiction teen books/year. 50% of books by first-time authors. "Our company mission statement is 'Inspire to Integrity,' so it's crucial that your story inspires children in some way. Our books are high quality, gorgeously illustrated, meant to be enjoyed as a child and throughout life."

Fiction: Picture books: adventure, animal, contemporary, fantasy, feminist, folktales, history, multicultural, nature/environment, spiritual. "We are looking for authors/illustrators; stories that will appeal and inspire." Average length: picture books—32 pages. Recently published *Turtle Songs*, by Margaret Wolfson, illustrated by Karla Sachi (ages 5-10, South Pacific myth).

Nonfiction: Picture books, young readers: biography, history, multicultural, nature/environment. *The Book of Goddesses*, by Kris Waldherr (all ages, multicultural historic reference); and *Girls Know Best* (compilation of 38 teen girls' writing—ages 7-15).

How to Contact/Writers: Fiction: Submit complete ms. Nonfiction: Submit outline/synopsis. Responds to queries/mss in 6 months. Will consider simultaneous submissions and previously published work.

Illustration: Works with 4-6 illustrators/year. Reviews ms/illustration packages from artists. Submit ms with 2-3 pieces of final art. "No originals please!" Illustrations only: Send résumé, promo sheet, "samples—no originals!" Responds in 6 months only if interested. Samples returned with SASE; samples filed.

Photography: Works on assignment only.

Terms: Sends galleys to authors; dummies to illustrators. Book catalog for SAE; ms and artist's guidelines for SASE.

Tips: "Please research the books we have previously published. This will give you a good idea if your proposal fits with our company."

N **BLACKBIRCH PRESS, INC.,** P.O. Box 3573, Woodbridge CT 06525. E-mail: staff@blackbirch.com. Website: www.blackbirch.com. Book publisher. Editorial Director: Beverly Larson. **Manuscript Acquisitions:** Jenifer Morse. **Art Acquisitions:** Calico Harington. Publishes 20 middle readers and 70 young adult titles/year. 15% of books by first-time authors.

Nonfiction: Picture books: animal, concept, geography, history, nature/environment, science. Young readers: animal, biography, geography, multicultural, nature/environment, special needs. Middle readers and young adults: geography, nature/environment, reference, special needs. Does not want to see dogs, spiritual, medical themes. Average word length: young adult readers—8,000-10,000; middle readers—5,000-7,000. Recently published *Bodyworks* (ages 8-10); and *Giants of Science* (biography series).

How to Contact/Writers: Nonfiction: Query. Materials will not be returned. Publishes a book 1 year after acceptance. Will consider simultaneous submissions.

Illustration: Works with 10 illustrators/year. Uses color artwork only. Reviews ms/illustration packages from artists. Submit query. Illustrations only: Query with samples; send résumé, promo sheet. Samples not returned; samples filed.

Photography: Buys photos from freelancers. Buys stock and assigns work. Uses animal, human culture, geography. Captions required. Uses 35mm, 2¼×2¼, 4×5 transparencies. Submit cover letter, published samples and promo piece.

Terms: Pays authors royalty or work purchased outright from author. Offers advances. Pays illustrators by the project or royalty. Pays photographers by the project, per photo or royalty. Original artwork returned at job's completion. Book catalog available for 8×10 SAE and 3 first-class stamps. Ms guidelines available for SASE.

BLUE SKY PRESS, 555 Broadway, New York NY 10012. (212)343-6100. Website: www.scholastic.com. Book publisher. Imprint of Scholastic Inc. **Acquisitions:** Bonnie Verberg. Publishes 15-20 titles/year. 1% of books by first-time authors. Publishes hardcover children's fiction and nonfiction including high-quality novels and picture books by new and established authors.

• Blue Sky is currently not accepting unsolicited submissions due to a large backlog of books.

Fiction: Picture books: adventure, animal, concept, contemporary, fantasy, folktales, history, humor, multicultural, nature/environment, poetry. Young readers: adventure, contemporary, fantasy, folktales, history, humor, multicultural, nature/environment, poetry. Young adults: adventure, anthology, contemporary, fantasy, history, humor, multicultural, poetry. Multicultural needs include "strong fictional or themes featuring non-white characters and cultures." Does not want to see mainstream religious, bibliotherapeutic, adult. Average length: picture books—varies; young adults—150 pages. Recently published *To Every Thing There Is a Season*, illustrated by Leo and Diane Dillon (all ages, picture book); *Bluish*, by Virginia Hamilton; *No, David!*, by David Shannon; *The Adventures of Captain Underpants*, by Dav Pilkey; and *How Do Dinosaurs Say Goodnight?*, by Jane Yolen, illustrated by Mark Teague.

How to Contact/Writers: "Due to large numbers of submissions, we are discouraging unsolicited submissions—send query with SASE only if you feel certain we publish the type of book you have written." Fiction: Query (novels, picture books). Responds to queries in 6 months. Publishes a book 1-3 years after acceptance; depending on chosen illustrator's schedule. Will not consider simultaneous submissions.

Illustration: Works with 10 illustrators/year. Uses both b&w and color artwork. Reviews illustration packages "only if illustrator is the author." Submit ms with dummy. Illustrations only: Query with samples, tearsheets. Responds only if interested. Samples returned with SASE. Original artwork returned at job's completion.

Terms: Pays 10% royalty based on wholesale price split between author and illustrators. Advance varies.

Tips: "Read currently published children's books. Revise—never send a first draft. Find your own voice, style, and subject. With material from new people we look for a theme or style strong enough to overcome the fact that the author/illustrator is unknown in the market."

✓ **BOYDS MILLS PRESS,** 815 Church St., Honesdale PA 18431. (800)490-5111. Fax: (570)253-0179. Website: www.boydsmillspress.com. Imprint: Wordsong (poetry). Book publisher. **Manuscript Acquisitions:** Beth Troop. **Art Acquisitions:** Tim Gillner. 5% of books from agented writers. Estab. 1990. "We publish a wide range of quality children's books of literary merit, from preschool to young adult."

Fiction: All levels: adventure, contemporary, history, humor, multicultural, poetry. Picture books: animal. Young readers, middle readers, young adult: problem novels, sports. Middle readers, young adults: problem novels, sports. Multicultural themes include any story showing a child as an integral part of a culture and which provides children with insight into a culture they otherwise might be unfamiliar with. "Please query us on the appropriateness of suggested topics for middle grade and young adult. For all other submissions send entire manuscript." Does not want to see talking animals, coming-of-age novels, romance and fantasy/science fiction. Recently published *Mr. Beans*, by Dayton O. Hyde (novel, ages 10 and up); and *An Alligator Ate My Brother*, by Mary Olson (picture book, ages 5-8).

Nonfiction: All levels: nature/environment, science. Picture books, young readers, middle readers: animal, multicultural. Does not want to see reference/curricular text. Recently published *Uncommon Champions*, by Marty Kaminsky (ages 12 and up) and *St. Nicholas*, by Ann Tompert (ages 6 and up).

How to Contact/Writers: Fiction/Nonfiction: Submit complete ms or submit through agent. Query on middle reader, young adult and nonfiction. Responds to queries/mss in 1 month.

Illustration: Works with 25 illustrators/year. Reviews ms/illustration packages from artists. Submit complete ms with 1 or 2 pieces of art. Illustrations only: Query with samples; send résumé and slides. Responds only if interested. Samples returned with SASE. Samples filed. Originals returned at job's completion.

Photography: Assigns work.

Terms: Authors paid royalty or work purchased outright. Offers advances. Illustrators paid by the project or royalties; varies. Photographers paid by the project, per photo, or royalties; varies. Mss/artist's guidelines available for #10 SASE.

Tips: "Picture books—with fresh approaches, not worn themes—are our strongest need at this time. Check to see what's already on the market before submitting your story."

BRIGHT LAMB PUBLISHERS, P.O. Box 844, Evans GA 30809. (706)863-2237. Fax: (706)863-9971. E-mail: brightlamb@aol.com. Website: www.brightlamb.com. Book publisher. Estab. 1995. **Contact:** Acquisitions Editor. "We publish books with product concepts or gift items to coincide with the storyline." Publishes 3 picture books/year; 3 young readers/year. 50% of books by first-time authors.
- Bright Lamb does not accept unsolicited mss or queries.

Illustration: Works with 3 illustrators/year. Reviews ms/illustration packages from artists. Send ms with dummy. Illustrations only: Query with samples; send résumé, client list and tear sheets to be kept on file. Responds only if interested.

Terms: Pays authors royalty based on wholesale price. Pays illustrators royalty based on wholesale price. Book catalog available for 4×7 SASE and 2 first-class stamps; ms guidelines available for SASE.

 BROADMAN & HOLMAN PUBLISHERS, LifeWay Christian Resources, 127 Ninth Ave. N., Nashville TN 37234. Fax: (615)251-5026. Book publisher. Senior Acquisitions & Development Editor: Gail Rothwell. Publishes 25-30 titles/year with majority being for younger readers. Only publish a few titles/yr. for ages 0-3 or 9-11. 10% of books by first-time authors. "All books have Christian values/themes."

Fiction: Middle readers, young readers: adventure, concept, contemporary, religion.

Nonfiction: Picture books: religion. Young or middle readers: self-help, social issues, religion, contemporary. Recently published: *The Word & Song Bible*, with audio by Stephen Elkins, illustrated by Tim O'Connor (Bible storybook for 10 and under); *Tails* series (3 books-3 activity books) by Karyn Henley (Bible-based picture & activity books for 4-10); *How Do I Become a Christian?* by Muriel F. Blackwell, illustrated by Betty Harper (guide to becoming a Christian for 8 and up).

How to Contact/Writers: Responds to queries in 1 week; mss in 2 months. Publishes a book 1 year after acceptance. Will consider simultaneous submissions.

Illustration: Works with 5-6 illustrators/year. Samples returned with SASE; samples filed.

Terms: Pays authors royalty 10-18% based on wholesale price. Offers variable advance. Original artwork returned at job's completion. Book catalog available for 9×12 SAE and 2 first-class stamps. Ms guidelines available for SASE.

Tips: "We're looking for picture books with good family values; Bible story re-tellings; modern-day stories for younger readers based on Bible themes and principles. Write us to ask for guidelines before submitting. We prefer a proposal to a full manuscript for middle readers."

CANDLEWICK PRESS, 2067 Massachusetts Ave., Cambridge MA 02140. (617)661-3330. Fax: (617)661-0565. E-mail: bigbear@candlewick.com. Children's book publisher. Estab. 1991. **Manuscript Acquisitions:** Liz Bicknell, editorial director; Mary Lee Donovan, executive editor; Gale Pryor, editor. **Art Acquisitions:** Ann Stott, associate art director; Anne Moore, senior book designer; Chris Paul, art director; and Julie Bushway, senior book designer. Publishes 175 picture books/year; 5 middle readers/year; and 5 young adult titles/year. 10% of books by first-time authors. "Our books are truly for children, and we strive for the very highest standards in the writing, illustrating, designing and production of all of our books. And we are not averse to risk."

Fiction: Picture books, young readers: animal, concept, contemporary, fantasy, history, humor, multicultural, nature/environment, poetry. Middle readers, young adults: animal, anthology, contemporary, fantasy, history, humor, multicultural, poetry, science fiction, sports, suspense/mystery. Recently published: *Because of Winn Dixie* (middle grade fiction); *Here Comes Mother Goose* (traditional rhyme picture book anthology).

Nonfiction: Picture books: concept, biography, geography, nature/environment. Young readers: biography, geography, nature/environment. Recently published *Castle Diary* (nonfiction).

How to Contact/Writers: Candlewick Press is accepting queries and unsolicited mss. Submit complete ms with SASE. Responds in 3 months.

Illustration: Works with 20 illustrators/year. "We prefer to see a variety of the artist's style." Reviews ms/illustration packages from artists. "General samples only please." Illustrations only: Submit résumé and portfolio to the attention of Design Dept. Responds to samples in 6 weeks. Samples returned with SASE; samples filed.

● **SPECIAL COMMENTS** by the editor of *Children's Writer's & Illustrator's Market* are set off by a bullet.

PAT BRISSON
WANDA'S
ROSES
ILLUSTRATED BY
MARYANN
COCCA-LEFFLER

Maryann Cocca-Leffler illustrated Wanda's Roses, *by Pat Brisson (Boyds Mills Press), in gouache and colored pencils on Fabriano watercolor paper. An experienced artist and author, she has never had an agent, saying, "I enjoy the chase!" Early in her career she did mailings, and she continues to visit New York City yearly to establish connections. "It's important to be a good business person." she says. "Keep your deadlines and be professional. Promote yourself and pursue the publishers that show interest."*

Terms: Pays authors royalty of 2.5-10% based on retail price. Offers advances. Pays illustrators 2.5-10% royalty based on retail price. Sends galleys to authors; dummies to illustrators. Photographers paid 2.5-10% royalty. Original artwork returned at job's completion.

CAROLRHODA BOOKS, INC., Division of the Lerner Publishing Group, 241 First Ave. N., Minneapolis MN 55401. (612)332-3344 or (800)328-4929. Fax: (612)332-7615. Website: www.lernerbooks.com. Imprint of Lerner. Lerner's other imprints are Runestone Press, Lerner Sports, LernerClassroom and First Avenue Editions. The acquisition editor for Lerner is Jennifer Zimian, who handles fiction and nonfiction for grades 5-12. Book publisher. Estab. 1969. **Acquisitions:** Rebecca Poole, submissions editor. Carolrhoda Books is a children's publisher focused on producing high-quality, socially conscious nonfiction and fiction books for young readers K through grade 4, that help them learn about and explore the world around them. List includes picture books, biographies, nature and science titles, multicultural and introductory geography books and fiction for beginning readers. Recently published *Sybil Ludington's Midnight Ride*, by Marsha Amstel, illustrated by Ellen Beier (On My Own History series, grades 1-3, nonfiction); *Totally Uncool*, by Janice Levy, illustrated by Chris Monroe (picture book); *Polar Bears*, by Dorothy Hinshaw Patent, photographs by William Muñoz (Nature Watch series, grades 3-6, nonfiction).
How to Contact/Writers: Submissions are accepted in the months of March and October only. Submissions received in any month other than March or October will be returned unopened to the sender. The Lerner Publishing group does not publish alphabet books, puzzle books, songbooks, textbooks, workbooks, religious subject matter or plays. A SASE is required for all submissions. Please allow 2-6 months for a response.

CARTWHEEL BOOKS, Imprint of Scholastic Inc., 555 Broadway, New York NY 10012. (212)343-6100. Fax: (212)343-4437. Website: www.scholastic.com. Book publisher. Vice President/Editorial Director: Bernette G. Ford. Executive Director: Grace Maccarone. **Manuscript Acquisitions:** Liza Baker, picture books; Jane Gerver, easy readers. **Art Acquisitions:** Edie Weinberg, art director. Publishes 25-30 picture books/year; 30-35 easy readers/year; 15-20 novelty/concept books/year. "With each Cartwheel list, we strive for a pleasing balance among board books and novelty books, hardcover picture books and gift books, nonfiction, paperback storybooks and easy readers. Cartwheel seeks to acquire 'novelties' that are books first; play objects second. Even without its gimmick, a Cartwheel novelty book should stand along as a valid piece of children's literature. We want all our books to be inviting and appealing, and to have inherent educational and social value. We believe that small children who develop personal 'relationships' with books and grow up with a love for reading, become book consumers, and ultimately better human beings."
Fiction: Picture books: adventure, animal, anthology, concept, contemporary, fantasy, folktales, history, humor, multicultural, nature/environment, poetry, science fiction, sports, suspense/mystery. Easy readers: adventure, animal, concept, contemporary, fantasy, history, holiday, humor, multicultural, nature/environment, poetry, science fiction. Average work length: picture books—1-3,000; easy readers—100-3,000.
Nonfiction: Picture books, young readers: animal, biography, concept, history, multicultural, nature/environment, sports. "Most of our nonfiction is either written on assignment or is within a series. We do not want to see any arts/crafts or cooking." Average word length: picture books—100-3,000; young readers—100-3,000.
How to Contact/Writers: Cartwheel Books is no longer accepting unsolicited mss; query. All unsolicited materials will be returned unread. Fiction/nonfiction: For previously published or agented authors, submit complete ms. Responds to queries in 1-2 months; mss in 3-6 months. Publishes a book 18-24 months after acceptance. Will consider simultaneous submissions; electronic submissions via disk or modem; previously published work.
Illustration: Works with 100 illustrators/year. Reviews ms/illustration packages from artists. Send ms with dummy. Illustrations only: Query with samples; arrange personal portfolio review; send promo sheet, tearsheets to be kept on file. Responds in 2 months. Samples returned with SASE; samples filed.
Photography: Buys stock and assigns work. Uses photos of kids, families, vehicles, toys, animals. Submit published samples, color promo piece.
Terms: Pays authors royalty of 2-8% based on retail price or work purchased outright for $600-5,000. Offers advances (Average amount: $3,000). Pays illustrators by the project (range: $2,000-10,000); flat fee; or advance against royalties (royalty of 1-3% based on retail price). Photographers paid by the project (range: $250-10,000); per photo (range: $250-500); or royalty of 1-3% of wholesale price. Sends galley to authors; dummy to illustrators. Originals returned to artist at job's completion. Book catalog available for 9×12 SAE and 2 first-class stamps; ms guidelines for SASE.
Tips: "Know what types of books we do. Check out bookstores or catalogs to see where your work would 'fit' best."

CHARLESBRIDGE, 85 Main St., Watertown MA 02472. (617)926-0329. Fax: (617)926-5720. E-mail: tradeeditorial@charlesbridge.com. Website: www.charlesbridge.com. Book publisher. Estab. 1980. Imprints: Talewinds and Whispering Coyote. Publishes 60% nonfiction, 40% fiction titles and picture books. Publishes nature, science, multicultural social studies and fiction picture books and board books. Charlesbridge also has an educational division. **Contact:** Trade Editorial Department, submissions editor or School Editorial Department.
Fiction: Picture books: "Strong, realistic stories with enduring themes." Considers the following categories: adventure, concept, contemporary, health, history, humor, multicultural, nature/environment, special needs, sports, suspense/mystery. Recently published: *Otto's Rainy Day*, by Natasha Yim; *Firefly Night*, by Carole Gerber.

insider report

An inside look at book marketing

Donna Spurlock's first job after graduating from Miami University in Ohio was working in a bookstore in Boston. She fell in love with bookselling and decided to become part of publishing the books that her customers wanted to read. In 1996 she joined Charlesbridge's customer service department. She soon became the customer service manager and credit manager, then the assistant to the Publicity/Promotions Coordinator. She is now the Publicity/Promotions Associate at Charlesbridge.

At what point in a book's history do you create the marketing plan?
About a year in advance we develop a marketing plan, which can include a promotional item or a novelty—an added bonus to the book that increases its inherent value. For example, we made the back endsheet of *The Big Buck Adventure* into a make-shift bank with slots for kids to save their quarters and dimes. But marketing generally concentrates on the season at hand—the months leading up to publication and the two to three months after publication.

What do you do then?
That's when we start researching specific outlets beyond bookstores. A book about trains, for example, will fit into hobbyist stores or railway gift shops. Also, we plan promotions to make the books stand out, such as book parties or events built around a specific book or author. We find out which associations or organizations would want to make the book available to their members of customers, and we contact newspapers, magazines, and newsletters that we think would be interested in promoting and reviewing the book. When the season is in full swing, the marketing team just keeps up this pace, but at the same time, we don't stop marketing or cross-promoting the backlist.

What is your most effective marketing tool?
The elements in marketing—sales, publicity, and promotion—are symbiotic. I don't think you could remove one of these and still garner the same results. Authors need to write good books, and good books need to have good editors and marketers. Direct sales, advertising, reviews and articles, author visits—all these contribute to marketing a book. But, putting books into the hands of readers—in our case, children—is what is most important, and our most effective tool is people who love bookselling. At Charlesbridge, almost every employee has a background in bookselling, whether in bookstores, libraries, or in other publishing houses.

When you are creating the marketing plan for a book, how much input do you want from an author?
I turn to authors first because they are the experts on their books. Through their research

while writing, or through associations and organizations they belong to, they can be a wellspring of leads to publicity, promotions, and sales. They're a source I want to tap into. Often, though, marketing is intuitive. For example, our book *Extraordinary Girls* is a book about girls for girls. I know I'm going to call girls' clubs, the Girl Scouts, and girl's magazines, just because that makes sense.

How involved should an author be in the marketing of her book?

Communication between authors and marketing is imperative so we can all put our best efforts behind the book. If authors don't let marketing know where they're visiting and what they're doing in the way of programs, we can't promote to local papers, local schools, and on our website. And if orders start coming in without our knowing that an author visit is pending, we won't be able to treat the orders with rush service or include posters, bookmarks, whatever would make the visit a success.

Does the marketing department influence the editorial department in deciding which manuscripts to acquire?

I wouldn't say the marketing department influences the editorial department's decisions, but we do have a voice. We have ongoing discussions about what type of books we as a company should be looking for—what type of books would enhance our list and help us grow. Our mandate at Charlesbridge is for well-written stories with interesting characters and books that educate and entertain. The marketing department has the advantage of being in contact with book buyers—retailers, wholesalers, catalog companies, and anyone else who sells books—on a daily basis. We pay close attention to trends and listen to what buyers want, whether it's books about the rain forest or books for girls. Acquisition, however, is a decision of the publishing committee, and that consists of the publisher, associate publisher, and the editorial director.

Do marketing and editorial work together after the book is in production?

Editorial does show books in production to marketing, and if we have questions about the text, illustrations, or design, we make comments. We try to think about specific placement in bookstores and how to ensure the book will look its best on the shelf. We also try to consider what customers may be looking for. We have our own personal opinions and wish-lists, which might mean adding a make-shift bank or a map of the ancient world to the text. Editorial does consider our suggestions and comments, but they are not obligated to change anything. And marketing doesn't act as an entity. We gather as individuals with our own questions, comments, and suggestions. We act as the book's test subjects.

Does marketing ever suggest book ideas to editorial?

Yes, we suggest subjects we feel would be interesting and educational. If it's a subject that everyone agrees should be addressed, editorial will then either seek out manuscripts or an author and illustrator for the project.

Where does Charlesbridge find authors for its licensed books?

In the case of the original *The M&M's® Brand Counting Book*, the author Barbara McGrath conceived of that idea and came to Charlesbridge. Sometimes authors submit original works, and sometimes the editorial department commissions authors.

Are licensed books harder or easier to market than "regular" books?
We don't approach marketing a licensed book differently than any other book. We understand that books with a product or character license have sparked controversy, but we think that if a book with M&M's®, for example, helps a child learn basic concepts or encourages that child to read, then it's a good book. All our books have educational value, which is what we try to focus on in our marketing plans. We ask ourselves what makes this book different or unique. Does it offer complete information, wonderful illustrations, or further study that would make it a book children will want to read over and over and add to their collection?

From marketing's point of view, what's the profile of a "favorite" author?
Our favorite authors go to bookstores and sign books, visit schools and libraries. They talk about their book and are in the public eye, whether they seek out these opportunities or make appearances that I have arranged. They know that author visits, interviews, features, and speaking engagements get the word out.
—Anna Olswanger

Nonfiction: Picture books: animal, biography, careers, concept, geography, health, history, multicultural, music/dance, nature/environment, religion, science, social issues, special needs, hobbies, sports. Average word length: picture books—1,500. Recently published: *Hail to the Chief*, by Don Robb and *Steam, Smoke and Steel*, by Patrick O'Brien.
How to Contact/Writers: Send ms and SASE. Accepts exclusive submissions only. Responds to mss in 3 months. Full ms only; no queries.
Illustration: Works with 5-10 illustrators/year. Uses color artwork only. Illustrations only: Query with samples; provide résumé, tearsheets to be kept on file. "Send no original artwork, please." Responds only if interested. Samples returned with SASE; samples filed. Originals returned at job's completion.
Terms: Pays authors and illustrators in royalties or work purchased outright. Ms/art guidelines available for SASE. Exclusive submissions only.
Tips: Wants "books that have humor and are factually correct. See our website for more tips."

◻ CHICAGO REVIEW PRESS, 814 N. Franklin St., Chicago IL 60610. (312)337-0747. Fax: (312)337-5985. E-mail: publish@ipgbook.com. Website: www.ipgbook.com. Book publisher. Estab. 1973. **Manuscript Acquisitions:** Cynthia Sherry, executive editor. **Art Acquisitions:** Joan Sommers, art director. Publishes 3-4 middle readers/year and "about 4" young adult titles/year. 33% of books by first-time authors; 30% of books from agented authors. "Chicago Review Press publishes high-quality, nonfiction, educational activity books that extend the learning process through hands-on projects and accurate and interesting text. We look for activity books that are as much fun as they are constructive and informative."
Nonfiction: Picture books, young readers, middle readers and young adults: activity books, arts/crafts, multicultural, history, nature/environment, science. "We're interested in hands-on, educational books; anything else probably will be rejected." Average length: young readers and young adults—175 pages. Recently published *Shakespeare for Kids*, by Margie Blumberg and Colleen Aagesen (ages 9 and up); *Civil War for Kids*, by Janis Herbert (ages 9 and up); and *Bite-Sized Science*, by John H. Falk and Kristi Rosenberg, illustrated by Bonnie Matthews (ages 3-8).
How to Contact/Writers: Enclose cover letter and no more than table of contents and 1-2 sample chapters. Send for guidelines. Responds to queries/mss in 2 months. Publishes a book 1-2 years after acceptance. Will consider simultaneous submissions and previously published work.
Illustration: Works with 6 illustrators/year. Uses primarily b&w artwork. Reviews ms/illustration packages from artists. Submit 1-2 chapters of ms with corresponding pieces of final art. Illustrations only: Query with samples, résumé. Responds only if interested. Samples returned with SASE.
Photography: Buys photos from freelancers ("but not often"). Buys stock and assigns work. Wants "instructive photos. We consult our files when we know what we're looking for on a book-by-book basis." Uses b&w prints.
Terms: Pays authors royalty of 7½-12½% based on retail price. Offers advances of $1,000-4,000. Pays illustrators by the project (range varies considerably). Pays photographers by the project (range varies considerably). Original artwork "usually" returned at job's completion. Book catalog/ms guidelines available for $3.
Tips: "We're looking for original activity books for small children and the adults caring for them—new themes and enticing projects to occupy kids' imaginations and promote their sense of personal creativity. We like activity books that are as much fun as they are constructive. Please write for guidelines so you'll know what we're looking for."

☑ **CHILDREN'S BOOK PRESS**, 2211 Mission St., San Francisco CA 94110. (415)821-3080. Fax: (415)821-3081. E-mail: cbookpress@cbookpress.org. Website: www.cbookpress.org. **Acquisitions:** Submissions Editor. Publishes 6-8 picture books/year. 50% of books by first-time authors. "Children's Book Press is a nonprofit publisher of multicultural and bilingual children's literature. We publish folktales and contemporary stories reflecting the traditions and culture of the emerging majority in the United States and from countries around the world. Our goal is to help broaden the base of children's literature in this country to include more stories from the African-American, Asian-American, Hispanic and Native American communities as well as the diverse Spanish-speaking communities throughout the Americas."
Fiction: Picture books, young readers: contemporary, folktales, history, multicultural, poetry. Average word length: picture books—800-1,600.
Nonfiction: Picture books, young readers: multicultural.
How to Contact/Writers: Submit complete ms to Submissions Editor. Responds to queries in 2-3 weeks; mss in 4 months. Publishes a book 1 year after acceptance. Will consider simultaneous submissions.
Illustration: Works with 4-5 illustrators/year. Uses color artwork only. Reviews ms/illustration packages from artists. Send ms with 3 or 4 color photocopies. Illustrations only: Send slides. Responds only of interested. Samples returned with SASE.
Terms: Pays authors and illustrators royalty of 3-8% based on wholesale price. Original artwork returned at job's completion. Book catalog available; ms guidelines available via website or with SASE.
Tips: "Vocabulary level should be approximately third grade (eight years old) or below. Keep in mind, however, that many of the young people who read our books may be nine, ten, or eleven years old or older. Their life experiences are often more advanced than their reading level, so try to write a story that will appeal to a fairly wide age range. We are especially interested in humorous stories and original stories about contemporary life from the multicultural communities mentioned above by writers *from* those communities."

CHINA BOOKS & PERIODICALS, 2929 24th St., San Francisco CA 94110. (415)282-2994. Fax: (415)282-0994. E-mail: info@chinabooks.com. Website: www.chinabooks.com. Book publisher, distributor, wholesaler. Estab. 1960. **Acquisitions:** Greg Jones, editor. Publishes 1 picture book/year; 1 middle readers/year; and 1 young adult title/year. 50% of books by first-time authors. Publishes only books about China and Chinese culture. Recently published *Sing Chinese! Popular Children's Songs & Lullabies*, by Ma Baolin and Cindy Ma (children—adults/song book); and *The Moon Maiden and Other Asian Folktales*, by Hua Long (children to age 12/folktales). "China Books is the main importer and distributor of books and magazines from China, providing an ever-changing variety of useful tools for travelers, scholars and others interested in China and Chinese culture."
Fiction: All levels: animal, anthology, folktales, history, multicultural, nature/environment.
Nonfiction: All levels: activity books, animal, arts/crafts, cooking, how-to, multicultural, music/dance, reference, textbooks. Recently published *West to East: A Young Girl's Journey to China*, by Qian Gao (young adult nonfiction travel journal).
How to Contact/Writers: Fiction/Nonfiction: Query. Responds to queries and mss in 2 months. Publishes a book 1 year after acceptance. Will consider simultaneous submissions, electronic submissions via disk or modem, previously published work.
Illustration: Works with 4-5 illustrators/year. Reviews ms/illustration packages from artists. Query. Illustrations only: Query with samples. Send résumé, promo sheet, tearsheets. Responds in 1 month only if interested. Samples returned with SASE; samples filed.
Terms: Pays authors 4-10% royalty based on wholesale price or work purchased outright. Pays illustrators and photographers by the project (range $400-1,500) or royalty based on wholesale price. Sends galleys to authors; dummies to illustrators. Originals returned to artist at job's completion. See website for guidelines.

◘ **CHRISTIAN ED. PUBLISHERS**, P.O. Box 26639, San Diego CA 92196. (619)578-4700. Senior Editor: Dr. Lon Ackelson. Managing Editor: Carol Rogers. Book publisher. Publishes 80 Bible curriculum titles/year. "We publish curriculum for children and youth, including program and student books (for youth) and take-home papers (for children)—all handled by our assigned freelance writers only."
Fiction: Young readers: contemporary. Middle readers: adventure, contemporary, suspense/mystery. "We publish fiction for Bible club take-home papers. All fiction is on assignment only."
Nonfiction: Publishes Bible curriculum and take-home papers for all ages. Recently published *All-Stars for Jesus*, by Treena Herrington and Letitia Zook, illustrated by Beverly Warren (Bible club curriculum for grades 4-6); and *Honeybees Classroom Activity Sheets*, by Janet Miller and Wanda Pelfrey, illustrated by Aiko Gilson and Terry Walderhaug (Bible club curriculum for ages 2-3).
How to Contact/Writers: Fiction/Nonfiction: Query. Responds to queries in 5 weeks. Publishes a book 1 year after acceptance. Send SASE for guidelines.
Illustration: Works with 6-7 illustrators/year. Uses primarily b&w artwork. Query; include a SASE; we'll send an application form. Contact: Carol Rogers, managing editor. Responds in 1 month. Samples returned with SASE.
Terms: Work purchased outright from authors for 3¢/word. Pays illustrators by the project (range: $300-400/book). Book catalog available for 9 × 12 SAE and 4 first-class stamps; ms and art guidelines available for SASE.
Tips: "Read our guidelines carefully before sending us a manuscript or illustrations. All writing and illustrating is done on assignment only and must be age-appropriate (preschool-6th grade)."

CHRISTIAN PUBLICATIONS, INC., 3825 Hartzdale Dr., Camp Hill PA 17011. (717)761-7044. Fax: (717)761-7273. E-mail: editors@cpi-horizon.com. Website: www.//cpi-horizon.com. Managing Editor: David Fessenden. **Manuscript Acquisitions:** George McPeek. **Art Acquisitions:** Marilynne Foster. Imprints: Christian Publications, Horizon Books. Publishes 1-2 young adult titles/year. 50% of books by first-time authors. The missions of this press are promoting participation in spreading the gospel worldwide and promoting Christian growth.

Fiction: "Not accepting unsolicited fiction."

Nonfiction: Young adults: religion. Does not want to see evangelistic/new Christian material. "Children and teens are too often assumed to have a shallow faith. We want to encourage a deeper walk with God." Average word length: young adults—25,000-40,000 words. Recently published *Grace and Guts to Live for God*, by Les Morgan (Bible study on Hebrews, 1 and 2 Peter); and *Holy Moses! And other Adventures in Vertical Living*, by Bob Hostetler. (Both are teen books which encourage a deeper commitment to God. Both illustrated by Ron Wheeler.) "Not accepting unsolicited material for age levels lower than teenage."

How to Contact/Writers: Nonfiction: Submit outline/synopsis and 2 sample chapters (including chapter one). Responds to queries in 6 weeks; mss in 2 months. Publishes a book 8-16 months after acceptance. Will consider simultaneous submissions, electronic submissions via disk or modem ("a one page, please").

Illustration: Works with 1-3 illustrators/year. Query with samples. Contact: Marilynne Foster, promotions coordinator. Responds only if interested. Samples returned with SASE; samples filed.

Terms: Pays authors royalty of 5-10% based on retail price. Offers advances. Pays illustrators by the project. Sends galleys to authors; dummies to illustrators (sometimes). Originals returned to artist at job's completion (if requested). Ms guidelines available for SASE.

Tips: "Writers: Only opportunity is in teen market, especially if you have experience working with and speaking to teens. Illustrators: Show us a few samples."

☑ **CHRONICLE BOOKS**, 85 Second St., 6th Floor, San Francisco CA 94105. (415)537-3730. Fax: (415)537-4420. Book publisher. **Acquisitions:** Victoria Rock, associate publisher, children's books; Amy Novesky, managing editor. Publishes 35-60 (both fiction and nonfiction) books/year; 5-10 middle readers, young adult nonfiction titles/year. 10-25% of books by first-time authors; 20-40% of books from agented writers.

Fiction: Picture books: animal, folktales, history, multicultural, nature/environment. Young readers: animal, folktales, history, multicultural, nature/environment, poetry. Middle readers: animal, history, multicultural, nature/environment, poetry, problem novels. Young adults: multicultural needs include "projects that feature diverse children in everyday situations." Recently published *Old Velvet*, by Mary Whitcomb; *Frank was a Monster Who Wanted to Dance*, by Keith Graves; *Penguin Dreams*, by J. Otto Seibold and Vivian Walsh.

Nonfiction: Picture books: animal, history, multicultural, nature/environment, science. Young readers: animal, arts/crafts, cooking, geography, history, multicultural and science. Middle readers: animal, arts/crafts, biography, cooking, geography, history, multicultural and nature/environment. Young adults: biography and multicultural. Recently published *Story Painter: The Life of Jacob Lawrence*, by John Duggleby; *Seven Weeks on an Iceberg*, by Keith Potter (Doodlezoo series).

How to Contact/Writers: Fiction/Nonfiction: Submit complete ms (picture books); submit outline/synopsis and 3 sample chapters (for older readers). Responds to queries/mss in 18 weeks. Publishes a book 1-3 years after acceptance. Will consider simultaneous submissions, as long as they are marked "multiple submission." Will not consider submissions by fax or e-mail. Must include SASE.

Illustration: Works with 15-20 illustrators/year. Wants "unusual art, graphically strong, something that will stand out on the shelves. Either bright and modern or very traditional. Fine art, not mass market." Reviews ms/illustration packages from artists. "Indicate if project *must* be considered jointly, or if editor may consider text and art separately." Illustrations only: Submit samples of artist's work (not necessarily from book, but in the envisioned style). Slides, tearsheets and color photocopies OK. (No original art.) Dummies helpful. Résumé helpful. "If samples sent for files, generally no response—unless samples are not suited to list, in which case samples are returned. Queries and project proposals responded to in same time frame as author query/proposals."

Photography: Purchases photos from freelancers. Works on assignment only. Wants nature/natural history photos.

Terms: Generally pays authors in royalties based on retail price "though we do occasionally work on a flat fee basis." Advance varies. Illustrators paid royalty based on retail price or flat fee. Sends proofs to authors and illustrators. Book catalog for 9×12 SAE and 8 first-class stamps; ms guidelines for #10 SASE.

Tips: "Chronicle Books publishes an eclectic mixture of traditional and innovative children's books. We are interested in taking on projects that have a unique bent to them—be it in subject matter, writing style, or illustrative technique. As a small list, we are looking for books that will lend our list a distinctive flavor. Primarily we are interested in fiction and nonfiction picture books for children ages infant-8 years, and nonfiction books for children ages 8-12 years. We are also interested in developing a middle grade/YA fiction program, and are looking for literary fiction that deals with relevant issues. Our sales reps are witnessing a resistance to alphabet books. And the market has become increasingly competitive. The '80s boom in children's publishing has passed, and the market is demanding high-quality books that work on many different levels."

☑ ♀ **CLARION BOOKS**, 215 Park Ave. S., New York NY 10003. (212)420-5889. Fax: (212)420-5855, Website: www.houghtonmifflinbooks.com/trade/. Imprint of Houghton Mifflin Company. Book publisher. Estab.

insider report

An upbeat, odd character helps illustrator's dream come true

Tara Calahan King remembers she was still in art school the first time she sketched the character who would change her life. "I had been experimenting with character development, matching different hair and expressions with different shaped heads and noses," recalls King, "when I noticed this one little girl who kept showing up in my sketchbook. I had no idea who she was, what to name her, or even what to do with her."

Tara Calahan King

King can't pinpoint the day she first sketched the puffed sleeves, gold collar and matching cummerbund onto the character's purple Little-House-on-the-Prairie frock or why she gave the child those red and white candycane-striped stockings. All she knows is that the smiling little girl with red pigtails and impossibly big glasses became more defined each time King sketched her.

It wasn't until after graduation when her friend, Kelly, recommended *Children's Writer's & Illustrator's Market*, that King excitedly shipped samples featuring the character to publishers. King put a lot of thought into her submissions. "A few of my teachers stressed how important it is to make a good impression with the samples you send. That stuck in my mind. Publishers receive so many submissions. You want to make sure yours get noticed. I took a long time deciding just what to send. I wanted to present my work well, in a fashion that showed some craftsmanship instead of just sending it loose. I wanted to show I gave it a bit of thought." King would lie awake at night obsessing over what to send.

One day, while at her job at a fast food restaurant, "the idea just came to me," says King, "It seemed so obvious. I thought 'I want to illustrate children's books, so why not send a portfolio that looks like a book?' " For the next few weeks, King spent hours every night creating hand-crafted books lined in fabric. She glued her best illustration on the cover and placed ten color copies of illustrations inside, along with a short cover letter introducing herself.

After sending her best out into the world, it was hurtful when the response wasn't what she'd hoped for. Month after month the mail brought rejections or no response at all. It looked like no one wanted King's artwork. King channelled her disappointment into refining her illustration style, gaining inspiration from illustrators she admired, such as Henrik Drescher, Lane Smith and C.F. Payne.

All the while she stayed busy serving customers at the fast food restaurant where she met Rick, the guy she would marry. To make extra money, she painted murals on children's walls and teamed up with Rick for catering gigs. Even though she much preferred the messy "hands on" process of painting and drawing, she enrolled in a computer class, to acquire "marketable skills" and was struggling through her third class, not realizing her world was about to change.

Somewhere in San Francisco, an editorial meeting was winding down. Editors at Chronicle

Books had acquired a wonderful manuscript, but still hadn't found just the right illustrator. Author Mary E. Whitcomb had sent along her own watercolors with the *Odd Velvet* manuscript, but the illustrations only showed her heroine from the back. Who could give a face to Velvet, the little girl who marched to the beat of her own drummer?

Serendipitously, King's parcel addressed to Victoria Rock arrived at Chronicle Books that morning and was sitting on the editor's desk when she returned from her meeting about the *Odd Velvet* manuscript. It must have been a magical moment when Rock opened the package and came face to face with a quirky, self-assured little girl with red pigtails who met her gaze with a disarming smile. Could this be Velvet? Later that day Rock and fellow editor Erica Jacobs contacted King for more samples and soon after sent the manuscript to King.

Tara Calahan King's illustrations landed on Chronicle Editor Victoria Rock's desk at the right time on the right day. Rock was searching for an illustrator for Mary E. Whitcomb's manuscript *Odd Velvet*, a story about an off-beat little girl who does her own thing and doesn't mind being different. A bespectacled girl with pigtails King had created had the perfect look for the character of Velvet, and Rock offered King her first picture book assignment. "It's been a dream come true that I'm able to make a living as an artist," says King.

After a quick call to her computer instructor to say "I'm not coming back!" King started reading *Odd Velvet*. Her mind raced with ideas for illustrating the other characters in the book. King identified with the story right away. It brought back a time when classmates rushed outside to play sports and games while she preferred to stay inside. She'd rather be drawing than anything else.

Now, because of a little red-headed girl she created years before, King would be able to do just that. "It's been a dream come true that I'm able to make a living as an artist," say King. Whitcomb's story and King's illustrations fit like a glove. To King's great relief, Mary Whitcomb liked the illustrations, too."That anticipation of the author's reaction is always the scary part for the illustrator. I know it was for me," says King.

Odd Velvet led to a second assignment with Chronicle, *Enemy Pie*, by Derek Munson. Then Random House tracked her down to illustrate *Superhero Max*, by Lawrence David. There's a certain momentum once you're published. But it's hard to hang in there. King's come up with a few rules for hanging on through the waiting period:

Don't take rejection as failure. Use it as fuel for your motivation."After spending so much time and thought creating my samples, it was painful to get rejected. I was in a kind of limbo at that time," says King. "I started to worry. But you know, after a while it kind of makes you mad!" Those angry feeling aren't always bad, says King. They're filled with energy. When rejection hits, turn the negative energy outward, pour all the hurt feelings and emotion into your work. "Use rejection as fuel to motivate you to keep going."

You don't have to have an agent starting out. "When I started out, I thought, 'I'll just try it on my own and see where it leads.' It's not that I don't think agents are great; it's just that you may not need one to get started," says King. She's proof that an illustrator can land assignments on her own.

Send your strongest pieces to the right contact person. Think "quality, not quantity" when choosing what to include in your portfolio. Take extra time choosing illustrations and use your creativity to come up with a unique and appropriate way to present them. It's also very important to show you can do character development, says King. "I did twelve illustrations of the little girl who became Velvet—riding her bike, doing homework, in the school cafeteria." King also stresses the importance of getting the right contact name at each publisher.

Be persistent in following up with publishers. Keep in touch with the publishers you submit your work to. Don't stop with one submission. Postcards are good for that, says King. Phone calls to editors are fine, too "but not to the point of stalking. Let publishers know you're still interested. Show them you're being productive and you've got fresh work."

Learn to budget your time. It's challenging to work from home, says King. Once you start getting assignments, you'll have to make your deadlines. "If you let things slip, it's not going to work." Now that King has a baby boy, one-year-old Ricky (whose delivery date coincided with an important book deadline), she plans her work hours very strategically, pacing herself to take advantage of Ricky's nap time. "Calendars and Post-it notes help a lot," she says. "I keep a big calendar in my office where I mark my deadlines. I figure out how much work I need to get done in a week's time. I use one of those big red china markers to mark off the deadlines as I meet them."

King was surprised at how kind editors and art directors were once she started getting assignments. "They really welcome you in." There's a lot to learn once you get your first assignment, like how to make room for text on the page and not to put characters in the book's gutters, she says. "Publishers take a lot of risks with a first-time illustrator." You have to be prepared to make revisions.

"If there's one piece of advice I'd like to leave illustrators with, it's not to give up," says King, reinforcing her cardinal rule. If you're really lucky you'll have a couple of supportive people in your life (like King's husband Rick, her friend Kelly, and her mom who attends her book signings) along the way.

—Mary Cox

Odd Velvet led to a second assignment with Chronicle for illustrator Tara Calahan King—*Enemy Pie*, by Derek Munson. Just as in her first book, for Munson's tale, King created quirky characters often drawn from unusual perspectives. In this half of a two-page spread, the main character plays checkers in a tree house with his "enemy," part of his dad's sneaky plan to show the boy that maybe his enemy isn't so bad.

1965. **Manuscript Acquisitions:** Dinah Stevenson, editorial director; Michele Coppola, editor; Virginia Buckley, contributing editor; Jennifer Green, associate editor; Julie Strauss-Gabel, associate editor. **Art Acquisitions:** Joann Hill, art director.

- Clarion title *Sector 7*, illustrated by David Wiesner, won a 2000 Caldecott Honor Medal; their title *My Rows and Piles of Coins*, illustrated by E.B. Lewis, won a 2000 Coretta Scott King Illustrator Honor Award; their title *Sir Walter Raleigh and the Quest for El Dorado*, by Marc Aronson, won the Boston Globe-Horn Book Award for Nonfiction; and their title *Ice Story: Shackleton's Lost Expedition*, by Elizabeth Cody Kimmel, won the Golden Kite Honor Award for Nonfiction.

How to Contact/Writers: Fiction and picture books: Send complete mss. Nonfiction: query. Must include SASE. Will accept simultaneous submission if informed.

Illustration: Send samples (no originals).

Terms: Pays illustrators royalty; flat fee for jacket illustration.

CLEAR LIGHT PUBLISHERS, 823 Don Diego, Santa Fe NM 87501. (505)989-9590. Fax: (505)989-9519. Book publisher. **Acquisitions:** Harmon Houghton, publisher. Publishes 4 middle readers/year; and 4 young adult titles/year.

Nonfiction: Middle readers and young adults: multicultural, American Indian only.

How to Contact/Writers: Fiction/Nonfiction: Submit complete ms with SASE. "No e-mail submissions. Authors supply art. Manuscripts not considered without art or artist's renderings." Will consider simultaneous submissions. Responds in 3 months.

Illustration: Reviews ms/illustration packages from artists. "No originals please." Submit ms with dummy and SASE.

Terms: Pays authors royalty of 10% based on wholesale price. Offers advances (average amount: up to 50% of expected net sales within the first year). Sends galleys to authors.

Tips: "We're looking for authentic American Indian art and folklore."

☑ **CONCORDIA PUBLISHING HOUSE**, 3558 S. Jefferson Ave., St. Louis MO 63118. (314)268-1187. Fax: (314)268-1329. Website: cphmall.com. Book publisher. **Manuscript Acquisitions:** Jane Wilke. **Art Acquisitions:** Ed Luhmann, art director. "Concordia Publishing House produces quality resources which communicate and nurture the Christian faith and ministry of people of all ages, lay and professional. These resources include curriculum, worship aids, books, multimedia products and religious supplies. We publish approximately 60 quality children's books each year. Most are fiction, with some nonfiction, based on a religious subject. We boldly provide Gospel resources that are Christ-centered, Bible-based and faithful to our Lutheran heritage."

Fiction: Picture books: concept, poetry, contemporary, religion. Young readers, middle readers, young adults: concept, contemporary, humor, religion, suspense/mystery. Young adults: romance. "All books must contain explicit Christian content." Recently published *The Very First Easter*, by Paul L Maier (picture book for ages 6-10); *Easter ABCs*, by Isabel Anders (novelty for ages 4-7); and *Horse Feathers*, by Dandi Daley Mackall (youth fiction, ages 12+).

Nonfiction: Picture books, young readers, middle readers: activity books, arts/crafts, religion. Young adults: religion.

How to Contact/Writers: Fiction: Submit complete ms (picture books); submit outline/synopsis and sample chapters (novel-length). May also query. Responds to queries in 1 month; mss in 3 months. Publishes a book 18 months after acceptance. Will consider simultaneous submissions. "No phone queries."

Illustration: Works with 50 illustrators/year. Illustrations only: Query with samples. Contact: Ed Luhmann, art director. Responds only if interested. Samples returned with SASE; samples filed. Originals not returned at job's completion.

Terms: Pays authors in royalties based on retail price or work purchased outright ($500-2,500). Sends galleys to author. Ms guidelines for 1 first-class stamp and a #10 envelope. Pays illustrators by the project ($1,000).

Tips: "Do not send finished artwork with the manuscript. If sketches will help in the presentation of the manuscript, they may be sent. If stories are taken from the Bible, they should follow the Biblical account closely. Liberties should not be taken in fantasizing Biblical stories."

Ⓝ **COOK COMMUNICATIONS**, 4050 Lee Vance View, Colorado Springs CO 80918. Book publisher. **Acquisitions:** Kathy Davis or Jeannie Harmon, senior editors. Publishes 15-20 picture books/year; 6-8 young readers/year; and 6-12 middle readers/year. Less than 5% of books by first-time authors; 15% of books from agented authors. "All books have overt Christian values, but there is no primary theme."

- Cook does not read unsolicited mss. Writers must query, except board books and picture books.

Illustration: Works with 15 illustrators/year. "Send color material I can keep." Query with samples; send résumé, promo sheet, portfolio, tearsheets. Responds only if interested. Samples returned with SASE; samples filed.

Terms: Pays illustrators by the project, royalty or work purchased outright. Sends dummies to illustrators. Original artwork returned at job's completion. Ms guidelines available for SASE.

☑ 🍁 **COTEAU BOOKS LTD.**, 401-2206 Dewdney Ave., Regina, Sasketchewan S4R 1H3 Canada. (306)777-0170. E-mail: coteau@coteau.coteaubooks.com. Website: www.coteaubooks.com. Thunder Creek Publishing Co-op Ltd. Book publisher. Estab. 1975. **Acquisitions:** Geoffrey Ursell, publisher. Publishes 3-4 juvenile and/or young adult books/year, 12-14 books/year. 10% of books by first-time authors. "Coteau Books publishes the finest Canadian fiction, poetry, drama and children's literature, with an emphasis on western writers."

• Coteau Books publishes Canadian writers and illustrators only; mss from the U.S. are returned unopened.

Fiction: Young readers, middle readers, young adults: adventure, contemporary, fantasy, history, humor, multicultural, nature/environment, science fiction, suspense/mystery. "No didactic, message pieces, nothing religious. No picture books. Material should reflect the diversity of culture, race, religion, creed of humankind—we're looking for fairness and balance." Recently published *Angels in the Snow*, by Wenda Young (ages 11-14); *Bay Girl*, by Betty Dorion (ages 8-11); and *The Innocent Polly McDoodle*, by Mary Woodbury (ages 8-12).

Nonfiction: Young readers, middle readers, young adult: biography, history, multicultural, nature/environment, social issues.

How to Contact/Writers: Fiction: Submit complete ms to acquisitions editor Barbara Sapergia. Include SASE or send up to 20-page sample by e-mail, as an attached file, in the Mime protocol. Responds to queries in 3-4 months; mss in 3-4 months. Publishes a book 1-2 years after acceptance. Send for guidelines.

Illustration: Works with 1-4 illustrators/year. Illustrations only: Submit nonreturnable samples. Responds only if interested. Samples returned with SASE; samples filed.

Photography: "Very occasionally buys photos from freelancers." Buys stock and assigns work.

Terms: Pays authors in royalties based on retail price. Pays illustrators and photographers by the project. Sends galleys to authors; dummies to illustrators. Original artwork returned at job's completion. Book catalog free on request with 9×12 SASE.

Tips: "Truthfully, the work speaks for itself! Be bold. Be creative. Be persistent! There is room, at least in the Canadian market, for quality novels for children, and at Coteau, this is a direction we will continue to take."

CROCODILE BOOKS, 46 Crosby St., Northampton MA 01060. (413)582-7054. Fax: (413)582-7057. E-mail: interpg@aol.com. Imprint of Interlink Publishing Group, Inc. Book publisher. **Acquisitions:** Pam Thompson, associate publisher. Publishes 4 picture books/year. 25% of books by first-time authors.

• Crocodile does not accept unsolicited mss.

Fiction: Picture books: animal, contemporary, history, spy/mystery/adventure.

Nonfiction: Picture book: history, nature/environment.

Terms: Pays authors in royalties. Sends galleys to author; dummies to illustrator.

CROSSWAY BOOKS, Good News Publishers, 1300 Crescent, Wheaton IL 60187-5800. (630)682-4300. Fax: (630)682-4785. Book Publisher. Estab. 1938. Editorial Director: Marvin Padgett. **Acquisitions:** Jill Carter. Publishes 3-4 picture books/year; and 1-2 young adult titles/year. "Crossway Books is committed to publishing books that bring Biblical reality to readers and that examine crucial issues through a Christian world view."

Fiction: Picture books: religion. Middle readers: adventure, contemporary, history, humor, religion, Christian realism. Young adults: contemporary, history, humor, religion, Christian realism. Does not want to see horror novels, romance or prophecy novels. Not looking for picture book submissions at present time. Recently published *All You Ever Need*, by Max Lucado, illustrated by Douglas Klauba (picture book); *The Unforgettable Summer*, by Joni Eareckson Tada and Steve Jensen (youth fiction); and *It's Not Funny, I've Lost My Money*, by Melody Carlson, illustrated by Steve Bjorkman (picture book).

How to Contact/Writers: Fiction: Query with outline/synopsis and up to 2 sample chapters. Responds to queries/mss in 2 months. Publishes a book 12-18 months after acceptance. Will consider simultaneous submissions.

Illustration: Works with 3-4 illustrators/year. Reviews ms/illustration packages from artists. Query. Illustrations only: Query with samples; provide résumé, promo sheet and client list. Responds to artists' queries/submissions in 2 months. Samples returned with SASE; samples filed. Originals returned at job's completion.

Terms: Pays authors royalty based on wholesale price. Pays illustrators by the project. Sends galleys to authors; dummies to illustrators. Book catalog available; ms guidelines available for SASE.

☑ **CROWN PUBLISHERS (CROWN BOOKS FOR CHILDREN)**, 1540 Broadway, New York NY 10036. (212)782-9000. Website: www.randomhouse.com/kids. Imprint of Random House, Inc. See Random House listing. Book publisher. Publisher: Simon Boughton. **Manuscript Acquisitions:** Crown BFYR Editorial Dept. **Art Acquisitions:** Isabel Warren-Lynch, art director. Publishes 20 picture books/year; 10 nonfiction titles/year. 5% of books by first-time authors; 70% of books from agented writers.

Fiction: Picture books: animal, humor, nature/environment. Young readers: history, nature/environment. Does not want to see fantasy, science fiction, poetry. Average word length: picture books—750. Recently published: *My Little Sister Ate One Hare*, by Bill Grossman; and *Me on the Map*, by Joan Sweeney.

Nonfiction: Picture books, young readers and middle readers: activity books, animal, biography, careers, health, history, hobbies, music/dance, nature/environment, religion, science, sports. Average word length: picture books—750-1,000; young readers—20,000; middle readers—50,000. Does not want to see ABCs. Recently published: *Rosie the Riviter*, by Penny Coleman (ages 9-14); and *Children of the Dust Bowl*, by Jerry Stanley (9-14 years, middle reader).

How to Contact/Writers: Fiction/nonfiction: Submit query letter. Responds to queries/mss in 3-4 months if SASE is included. Publishes book approximately 2 years after acceptance. Will consider simultaneous submissions.

Illustration: Works with 20 illustrators/year. Reviews ms/illustration packages from artists. "Submit double-spaced, continuous manuscripts; do not supply page-by-page breaks. One or two photocopies of art are fine. *Do not send original art.* Dummies are acceptable." Responds in 2 months. Illustrations only: Submit photocopies, portfolio or slides with SASE; provide business card and tearsheets. Contact: Isabel Warren-Lynch, Art Director. Original artwork returned at job's completion.

Terms: Pays authors royalty based on retail price. Advance "varies greatly." Pays illustrators by the project or royalty. Sends galleys to authors; proofs to illustrators. Book catalog for 9 × 12 SAE and 4 first-class stamps. Ms guidelines for 4½ × 9½ SASE; art guidelines available by calling (212)940-7600.

CSS PUBLISHING, 517 S. Main St., P.O. Box 4503, Lima OH 45802-4503. (419)227-1818. Fax: (419)222-4647. E-mail: acquisitions@csspub.com. Website: www.csspub.com. Book publisher. Imprints include Fairway Press and Express Press. **Manuscript Acquisitions:** Thomas Lentz. Publishes books with religious themes. "We are seeking material for use by clergy, Christian education directors and Sunday school teachers for mainline Protestant churches. Our market is mainline Protestant clergy."

Fiction: Picture books, young readers, middle readers, young adults: religion, religious poetry and humor. Needs children's sermons (object lesson) for Sunday morning worship services; dramas for Advent, Christmas or Epiphany involving children for church services; activity and craft ideas for Sunday school or mid-week services for children (particularly pre-school and first and second grade). Does not want to see secular picture books. Published *That Seeing, They May Believe*, by Kenneth Mortonson (lessons for adults to present during worship services to pre-schoolers-third graders); *What Shall We Do With This Baby?*, by Jan Spence (Christmas Eve worship service involving youngsters from newborn babies-high school youth); and *Miracle in the Bethlehem Inn*, by Mary Lou Warstler (Advent or Christmas drama involving pre-schoolers-high school youth and adult.)

Nonfiction: Picture books, young readers, middle readers, young adults: religion. Young adults only: social issues and self help. Needs children's sermons (object lesson) for Sunday morning worship services; dramas for Advent, Christmas or Epiphany involving children for church services; activity and craft ideas for Sunday school or mid-week services for children (particularly pre-school and first and second grade). Does not want to see secular picture books. Published *Mustard Seeds*, by Ellen Humbert (activity/bulletins for pre-schoolers-first graders to use during church); and *This Is The King*, by Cynthia Cowen.

How to Contact/Writers: Responds to queries in 2 weeks; mss in 3 months. Publishes a book 9 months after acceptance. Will consider simultaneous submissions.

Terms: Work purchased outright from authors. Ms guidelines and book catalog available for SASE.

☑ ▢ **MAY DAVENPORT, PUBLISHERS**, 26313 Purissima Rd., Los Altos Hills CA 94022-4539. (415)948-6499. Fax: (650)947-1373. E-mail: maydaven@aol.com. Website: www.maydavenportpublishers.com. Independent book producer/packager. Estab. 1976. **Acquisitions:** May Davenport, editor/publisher. Publishes 1-2 picture books/year; and 2-3 young adult titles/year. 99% of books by first-time authors. Seeks books with literary merit. "We like to think that we are selecting talented writers who have something humorous to write about today's unglued generation in 30,000-50,000 words for teens and young adults in junior/senior high school before they become tomorrow's 'functional illiterates.' We are interested in publishing literature that teachers in middle and high schools can use in their Language Arts, English and Creative Writing courses. There's more to literary fare than the chit-chat Internet dialog and fantasy trips on television with cartoons or humanoids." This publisher is overstocked with picture book/elementary reading material.

Fiction: Young adults (15-18): contemporary, humorous fictional literature for use in English courses in junior-senior high schools in US. Average word length: 40,000-60,000. Recently published *To Touch the Sun*, by Andrea Ross (for ages 15-18); *A Taste of the Elephant*, by Robert Norman Farley (ages 12 and up).

Nonfiction: Teens: humorous. Published *Just a Little off the Top*, by Linda Ropes (essays for teens).

How to Contact/Writers: Fiction: Query. Responds to queries/mss in 3 weeks. "We do not answer queries or manuscripts which do not have SASE attached." Publishes a book 6-12 months after acceptance.

Illustration: Works with 1-2 illustrators/year. "Have enough on file for future reference." Responds only if interested. Samples returned with SASE; samples filed. Originals returned at job's completion.

Terms: Pays authors royalties of 15% based on retail price; negotiable. Pays "by mutual agreement, no advances." Pays illustrators by the project (range: $75-350). Book catalog, ms guidelines free on request with SASE.

"PICTURE BOOKS" are for preschoolers to 8-year-olds; "Young readers" are for 5- to 8-year-olds; "Middle readers" are for 9- to 11-year-olds; and "Young adults" are for ages 12 and up. Age ranges may vary slightly from publisher to publisher.

Tips: "Create stories to enrich the non-reading 12-and-up readers. They might not appreciate your similies and metaphors and may find fault with your alliterations with the letters of the alphabet, but show them how you do it with memorable characters in today's society. Just project your humorous talent and entertain with more than two sentences in a paragraph."

N DAWN PUBLICATIONS, P.O. Box 2010, Nevada City CA 95959. (530)478-0111. Fax: (530)478-0112. E-mail: nature@dawnpub.com. Website: www.dawnpub.com. Book publisher. Publisher: Muffy Weaver. **Acquisitions:** Glenn J. Hovemann, editor. Publishes works with holistic themes dealing with nature.
Nonfiction: Picture books: animal, nature/environment. Biographies of naturalists recently published *John Muir: My Life With Nature*, by Joseph Cornell (80-page biography); and *Do Animals Have Feelings Too?*, by David L. Rice (32-page picture book).
How to Contact/Writers: Nonfiction: Query or submit complete ms. Responds to queries/mss in 3 months maximum. Publishes a book 1 year after acceptance. Will consider simultaneous submissions.
Illustration: Works with 5 illustrators/year. Will review ms/illustration packages from artists. Query; send ms with dummy. Illustrations only: Query with samples, résumé.
Terms: Pays authors royalty based on wholesale price. Offers advance. Pays illustrators by the project or royalties based on wholesale price. Book catalog available for 8½×11 SASE; ms guidelines available for SASE.
Tips: Looking for "picture books expressing nature awareness with inspirational quality leading to enhanced self-awareness. Usually no animal dialogue."

☑ DIAL BOOKS FOR YOUNG READERS, Penguin Putnam Inc., 345 Hudson St., New York NY 10014. Website: www.penguinputnam.com. Publisher: Nancy Paulsen. Editorial Director: Lauri Hornik. **Acquisitions:** Toby Sherry, Editor; Cecile Goyette, Editor. Art Director: Atha Tehon. Publishes 30 picture books/year; 3 young reader titles/year; 8 middle reader titles/year; and 6 young adult titles/year.
  ● Dial prefers submissions from agents and previously published authors.
Fiction: Picture books: adventure, animal, contemporary, folktales, history, poetry, sports, suspense/mystery. Young readers: contemporary, easy-to-read, fantasy, folktales, history, poetry, sports, mystery/adventure. Middle readers, young adults: animal, contemporary, folktales, history, poetry, sports, mystery/adventure. Published *A Year Down Yonder*, by Richard Peck (ages 10 and up); *The Magic Nesting Doll*, by Jacqueline K. Ogburn and illustrated by Laurel Long (all ages, picture book); *The Missing Mitten Mystery*, by Steven Kellogg (ages 2-6, picture book).
Nonfiction: Will consider query letters for submissions of outstanding literary merit. Picture books: animals, biography, history, sports. Young readers: animals, biography, history, sports. Middle readers: biography, history. Young adults: biography, history, contemporary. Recently published *Thanks to My Mother*, by Schoschana Rabinovici (ages 12 and up, YA) and *Dirt on Their Skirts*, by Doreen Rappaport and Lyndall Callan (ages 4-8, picture book).
How to Contact/Writers: Prefers agented material (but will respond to queries that briefly describe the ms and the author's writing credits with a SASE). Responds to queries/mss. in 2 months. "We do not supply specific guidelines, but we will send you a recent catalog if you send us a 9×12 SASE with four 33¢ stamps attached. Questions and queries should only be made in writing. We will not reply to anything without a SASE."
Illustration: Works with 25 illustrators/year. To arrange a personal interview to show portfolio, send samples and a letter requesting an interview. Art samples should be sent to Ms. Toby Sherry and will not be returned without a SASE. "No phone calls please. Only artists with portfolios that suit the house's needs will be interviewed."
Terms: Pays authors and illustrators in royalties based on retail price. Average advance payment "varies."

DK INK, Imprint of Dorling Kindersley Publishing, Inc., 95 Madision Ave., New York NY 10016. (212)213-4800. Fax: (212)213-5240. Imprint of DK Publishing, Inc. Website: www.dk.com. Book publisher. Estab. 1997. Publishes 50-60 titles/year. **Manuscript Acquisitions:** Neal Porter, publisher. **Art Acquisitions:** Dirk Kaufman, art director. "DK Ink is a distinctive imprint consisting primarily of picture books and fiction for children and adults, created by authors and illustrators you know and respect as well as exciting new talents. The main goal of these books is to edify, entertain and encourage kids to think about the human condition."
  ● DK Ink is not currently accepting queries or unsolicited manuscripts.
Fiction: Considers picture books, middle readers and young adult material. Recently published *Like, Likes, Like*, by Chris Raschka (picture book); *The Islander*, by Cynthia Rylant; *Voices in the Park*, by Anthony Browne (picture book).
Nonfiction: Considers narrative nonfiction and biography. Nonfiction is a small part of the DK Ink list.
How to Contact/Writers: Fiction: Submit complete ms. Nonfiction: Submit outline/sysnopsis' and sample chapters. Responds in 8-10 weeks.
Illustration: Submit samples to Art Director. Samples kept on file.
Terms: Pays authors royalty; offers advance. Pays illustrators royalty or flat fee, depending on assignment.

☑ DOG-EARED PUBLICATIONS, P.O. Box 620863, Middletown WI 53562-0863. (608)831-1410. (608)831-1410. Fax: (608)831-1410. E-mail: field@dog-eared.com. Website: www.dog-eared.com. Book pub-

lisher. Estab. 1977. Art Acquisitions: Nancy Field, publisher. Publishes 2-3 middle readers/year. 1% of books by first-time authors. "Dog-Eared Publications creates action-packed nature books for children. We aim to turn young readers into environmentally aware citizens and to foster a love for science and nature in the new generation.
Nonfiction: Middle readers: activity books, animal, nature/environment, science. Average word length varies. Recently published *Leapfrogging Through Wetlands*, by Margaret Anderson, Nancy Field and Karen Stephenson, illustrated by Michael Maydak (middle readers, activity book); *Ancient Forests*, by Margaret Anderson, Nancy Field and Karen Stephenson, illustrated by Sharon Torvik (middle readers, activity book); *Discovering Wolves*, by Nancy Field, Corliss Karassov, illustrated by Cary Hunkel (activity book).
How to Contact/Writers: Nonfiction: Query or submit outline/synopsis. Responds to queries/mss in 1 month. Will consider electronic submissions via disk or modem.
Illustration: Works with 2-3 illustrators/year. Reviews mss/illustration packages from artists. Submit query and a few art samples. Contact: Nancy Field, publisher. Illustrations only: Query with samples. Contact: Nancy Field, publisher. Responds only if interested. Samples not returned; samples filed.
Photography: Works on assignment only.
Terms: Pays authors royalty based on wholesale price. Offers advances(amount varies). Pays illustrators royalty based on wholesale price. Sends galleys to authors. Originals returned to artist at job's completion. Brochure available for SASE and 1 first-class stamp. Brochure available on website.

A DORLING KINDERSLEY PUBLISHING, INC., 95 Madison Ave., New York NY 10016. (212)213-4800. Fax: (212)689-1799. Website: www.dk.com. **Acquisitions:** submissions editor. Publishes 30 picture books/year; 30 young readers/year; 10 middle readers/year; and 5 young adult titles/year.
• DK works with previously published authors or agented authors only.
Nonfiction: Picture books: animal, concept, nature/environment. Middle readers: activity books, geography, history, nature/environment, reference, science, sports. Young adults: biography, careers, history, reference, science, social issues, sports. Average page count: picture books; middle readers: 32 pages; young readers: 128 pages. Recently published *Children Just Like Me: Our Favorite Stories*, by Jamila Gavin (for all ages); and *Stephen Biesty's Cross-Sections Castle* (for ages 8 and up).
How to Contact/Writers: Only interested in agented material. "Due to high volume, we are unable to accept unsolicited mss at this time. We will review policy in the future."
Illustration: Only interested in agented material. Uses color artwork only. Reviews ms/illustration packages from artists. Query with printed samples. Illustrations only: Query with samples. Send résumé and promo sheet. Responds only if interested. Samples filed.
Photography: Buys stock and assigns work. Uses color prints. Submit cover letter, résumé, published samples, color promo piece.
Terms: Pays authors royalty. Offers advances. Book catalog available for 10×13 SASE and $3 first-class postage.
Tips: "Most of our projects are generated in London where authors and illustrators are solicited."

DOWN EAST BOOKS, P.O. Box 679, Camden, ME 04843-0679. (207)594-9544. Fax: (207)594-7215. E-mail: msteere@downeast.com. Book publisher. Senior Editor: Karin Womer. **Acquisitions:** Alice Devine, associate editor, Michael Steere. Publishes 3-4 young readers and middle readers/year. 70% of books by first-time authors. "As a small regional publisher Down East Books specializes in non-fiction books with a Maine or New England theme. Down East Books' mission is to publish superbly crafted books which capture and illuminate the astonishing beauty and unique character of New England's people, culture and wild places; the very aspects that distinguish New England from the rest of the United States."
Fiction: Picture books, middle readers, young readers, young adults: animal, adventure, history, nature/environment. Young adults: suspense/mystery. Recently published *Moose, of Course!*, by Lynn Plourde, illustrated by Jim Sollers.
Nonfiction: Picture books, middle readers, young readers, young adults: animal, history, nature/environment. Recently published *Do Sharks Ever . . .?*, by Nathalie Ward, illustrated by Tessa Morgan.
How to Contact/Writers: Fiction/Nonfiction: Query. Responds to queries/mss in 1-2 months. Publishes a book 6-18 months after acceptance. Will consider simultaneous and previously published submissions.
Illustration: Works with 2-3 illustrators/year. Reviews ms/illustration packages from artists. Query. Illustrations only: Query with samples. Responds in 1-2 months. Samples returned with SASE; samples filed sometimes. Originals returned at job's completion.
Terms: Pays authors royalty (7-12% based on net receipts). Pays illustrators by the project or by royalty (7-10% based on net receipts). Sends galleys to authors; dummies to illustrators. Original artwork returned at job's completion. Book catalog available. Ms guidelines available for SASE.

☑ ♟ DUTTON CHILDREN'S BOOKS, Penguin Putnam Inc., 345 Hudson St., New York NY 10014. (212)366-3700. Website: www.penguinputnam.com. Book publisher. President and Publisher: Stephanie Owens Lurie. **Acquisitions:** Lucia Monfried, editor-in-chief. **Art Acquisitions:** Sara Reynolds, art director. Publishes approximately 60 picture books/year; 4 young reader titles/year; 10 middle reader titles/year; and 8 young adult titles/year. 10% of books by first-time authors.

insider report

Seeking stand-out stories with sparkle

When she was fifteen, Stephanie Owens Lurie reviewed a young adult novel for a local bookstore. She didn't think the author had a good "bead" on what teenagers were like, so she thought, "If only the author had . . . " That led her to think about jobs that would help writers improve their books, and in her senior year at Oberlin College, she interned in the children's book department at Dodd, Mead and Company in New York City. There, Lurie discovered she had the ability to evaluate manuscripts, and she subsequently worked as a children's book editor for Little, Brown and Simon & Schuster. When Simon & Schuster merged with Macmillan, she was named vice president/editorial director of S&S Books for Young Readers. In 1999 she moved to Dutton Children's Books where she is now president and publisher.

Stephanie Owens Lurie

How are the books you edit at Dutton different from the books you edited at Little, Brown back in 1983?
When I first started, the library market was the largest book-buying market, and it was a market that highly valued good storytelling. It was also a quieter time when buyers could take time to evaluate books, both in libraries and in independent bookstores. The smart buyers could give special attention to a subtle or midlist book. But when the chains came onto the scene, they centralized their buying in one place for the whole country. Now, store managers don't know the books until they arrive, and they don't know how to handsell. That means that books have to be louder to stand out—they have to say everything on the jacket, and they have to make an impact from across the room, with an arresting design or a punchy title. And the book has to be high-concept. By that, I mean easily summarized in a few seconds.

Does the direction in which the children's book industry is going worry you?
Yes. Because it's so difficult to launch people today, I worry about publishers' commitment to new talent. If we all keep going after the same authors and illustrators, children's books will become stale.

How are you shaping the Dutton list to distinguish it from the other Penguin-Putnam imprints?
I would like to build on the diverse Dutton backlist. For example, I'd like to publish more realistic books about nature in the tradition of *Rascal*, *Gentle Ben* and *My Side of the Mountain*. I'd like to continue publishing satisfying and realistic literature that leaves an impression, but I also want to be in touch with today's trends and offer kids books of immediate appeal.

What do you look for in a manuscript?

I look for a story that speaks to me right away, a character I feel like becoming for the duration of the book, or I look for humor, imagination, something that touches my basic emotions. I enjoy good word play-words that are fun to read aloud. The major problem with the submissions we get at Dutton is that they don't stand out in any way. They lack a sparkle that's hard to define.

Do you go out looking for new writers?

I go to a lot of writers' conferences. I call up agents to tell them what I'm looking for, and I participate in a writers' chatroom online at AOL and talk to people there.

Do you think it's helpful when editors-in-residence at writers' conferences read one manuscript page aloud to the audience and decide on the spot whether they would read further?

I think it can be helpful to the audience to know how quickly writers have to make an impression on an editor and how quickly they have to establish a voice, pace, setting, and mood. The reality is that editors often don't get beyond the cover letter itself. So I think it would be even more helpful if editors-in-residence at conferences would talk about how to write effective cover letters and query letters.

What impresses you in a query letter?

Some query letters are too bald. The writers don't take it as an opportunity to introduce themselves, or they don't have a sense of what we're publishing at Dutton. We don't get a sense of why they've chosen us. I think an effective query letter captures a writer's unique personality. It shows us that she's thought about where she's sending her manuscript and that

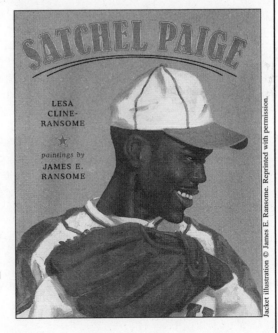

Husband and wife Lesa Cline-Ransome and James E. Ransome collaborated for the first time on *Satchel Paige* under the watch of Stephanie Owens Lurie during her tenure as president/editorial director of Simon & Schuster. "It's a stunningly illustrated picture book narrated in a folksy style," says Lurie.

Jacket illustration © James E. Ransome. Reprinted with permission.

she knows where her book would fit in the current marketplace. The effective query letter goes on to provide the hook or selling handle that we would use to present the book at our in-house launch meeting and to our sales reps. The reps use the selling handle when they pitch the book to their bookstore and library accounts. Usually reps have about thirty seconds per title to get a buyer interested.

Do you think good writing always gets published?
Not necessarily. A writer could send us a beautifully written manuscript that we just think is too quiet to stand out, or we might see a manuscript that we love but we just did the same subject and the book won a major award the previous year—so we don't feel that we can touch it. If I were a writer in this situation, I would turn to something else, or put the manuscript aside to submit later.

What are the advantages and disadvantages of being published by a large company like Penguin Putnam?
Let's start with the advantages of being published by a small publisher. Your books will probably get more attention from everyone within the house—not just from the editor, but from

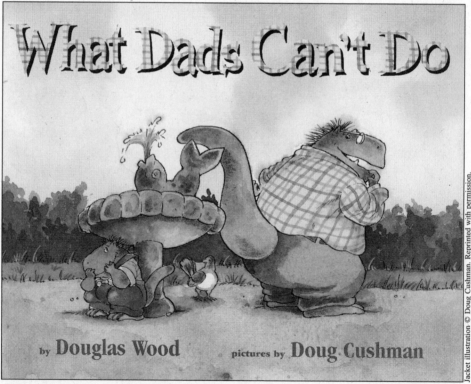

"This deceptively simple book has a clever premise that speaks directly to young children and their parents," says Stephanie Owens Lurie of *What Dads Can't Do* (Simon & Schuster). Written by Douglas Wood, illustrated by Doug Cushman, the book concedes that "there are lots of things that regular people can do but dads can't . . . Dads can't cross the street without holding hands. They can push, but they can't swing. Dads really need to be kissed good night at bedtime. It's a wonder they make it through life at all!"

marketing and sales because they have a smaller list to promote. Another benefit is targeted marketing. If you have a book for one specific segment of the population, you would probably have better success reaching your market with a small publisher that can direct its efforts there. It's unlikely that a large publisher would be able to focus its efforts that specifically.

However, the small publisher might not have the resources and the reach that a large publisher has. It would have more limited distribution. So in a setup where you have a small imprint within a large company, like we have at Dutton, you have the best of both worlds. You get individual attention from editorial and production, but you have at your disposal big sales and marketing departments organized by channels of distribution. All the outlets get covered—national chains, independent bookstores, libraries, jobbers, warehouse chains, and specialty retail.

What's the most important thing an author can do in the way of promotion?
An author has to use a grass roots effort to get the word out. She has to announce her book to friends, go to local bookstores and libraries to introduce herself, and make as many school appearances as possible. That's how the big names established themselves, by getting on the road and being tireless about promotion. In today's world, a website is a good idea too.

What should an author look for in an editor?
You need an editor who responds to your work by making suggestions that don't change your original vision, but help you to communicate that vision; an editor with helpful, specific suggestions, rather than general comments; an editor who inspires you to think harder and reach for higher levels; an editor who is willing to be the in-house advocate for your book all the way along. You should be able to reach your editor by telephone, e-mail, or letter whenever you need to. Remember, authors pay editors' salaries. Your editor needs you very much.
　—Anna Olswanger

● Dutton is temporarily not accepting new manuscripts. Dutton title *Sitting Bull and His World*, by Albert Marrin, won a 2000 Boston Globe-Horn Book Honor Award for nonfiction; their title *The Little Red Hen (Makes a Pizza)*, illustrated by Amy Walrod, won the Golden Kite Award for Picture Book Illustration in 2000.

Fiction: Picture books: adventure, animal, folktales, history, multicultural, nature/environment, poetry. Young readers: adventure, animal, contemporary, easy-to-read, fantasy, pop-up, suspense/mystery. Middle readers: adventure, animal, contemporary, fantasy, history, multicultural, nature/environment, suspense/mystery. Young adults: adventure, animal, anthology, contemporary, fantasy, history, multicultural, nature/environment, poetry, science fiction, suspense/mystery. Recently published *The Little Red Hen (Makes A Pizza)*, by Philemon Sturges, illustrated by Amy Walrod (picture book).

Nonfiction: Picture books: animal, history, multicultural, nature/environment. Young readers: animal, history, multicultural, nature/environment. Middle readers: animal, biography, history, multicultural, nature/environment. Young adults: animal, biography, history, multicultural, nature/environment, social issues. Recently published *Sitting Bull*, by Albert Marrin; *Crocodiles, Camels and Dug Out Canoes*, by Bob Zounder, illustrated by Roxie Munro.

How to Contact/Writers: Query only. Does not accept unsolicited mss. Responds to queries in 3 months. Publishes a book 12-18 months after acceptance. Will consider simultaneous submissions.

Illustration: Works with 40-60 illustrators/year. Reviews ms/illustration packages from artists. Query first. Illustrations only: Query with samples; send résumé, portfolio, slides—no original art please. Responds to art samples in 2 months. Original artwork returned at job's completion.

Photography: Will look at photography samples and photo-essay proposals.

Terms: Pays authors royalties of 4-10% based on retail price. Book catalog, ms guidelines for SASE with 8 first-class stamps. Pays illustrators royalties of 2-10% based on retail price unless jacket illustration—then pays by flat fee.

Tips: "Avoid topics that appear frequently. In nonfiction, we are looking for history, general biography, science and photo essays for all age groups." Illustrators: "We would like to see samples and portfolios from potential illustrators of picture books (full color), young novels (b&w) and jacket artists (full color)." Foresee "even more multicultural publishing, plus more books published in both Spanish and English."

☑ **E.M. PRESS, INC.**, P.O. Box 336,, Warrenton VA 20188. (540)349-9958. E-mail: empress2@erols.com. Website: www.empressinc.com. Book publisher. **Acquisitions:** Beth Miller, publisher/editor. "E.M. Press has narrowed its focus to manuscripts of local interest (Virginia, Maryland, D.C.); manuscripts by local authors; nonfiction manuscripts; and children's books. We're now publishing illustrated children's books." 50% of books by first-time authors.
Fiction: Children, young adults: folk tales, nature/environment, special needs. Recently published *New Shoes*, by Ming Wah Chen.
Nonfiction: Children, young adults: animal, arts/craft, health, history, multicultural, music/dance, nature/environment, religion, self-help, social issues. Recently published *Can You Come Here Where I Am: The Poetry and Prose of Breast Cancer Survivors*, by Rita Busch, et al.
How to Contact/Writers: Query with outline/synopsis and SASE for novel-length work and complete ms for shorter work. Responds to ms/queries in 3 months. Publishes a book 18 months after acceptance. Will consider simultaneous submissions.
Illustration: Works with 4 children's illustrators/year. Illustration packages should be submitted to Beth Miller, publisher. Responds in 3 months. Samples returned with SASE; samples kept on file. Original artwork returned at job's completion.
Terms: "We've used all means of payment from outright purchase to royalty." Offers varied advances. Sends galleys to authors. Book catalog for SASE.
Tips: "Present the most professional package possible. The market is glutted, so you must find a new approach."

EERDMAN'S BOOKS FOR YOUNG READERS, an imprint of Wm. B. Eerdmans Publishing Company, 255 Jefferson Ave. SE, Grand Rapids MI 49503. (616)459-4591. Book publisher. **Manuscript Acquisitions:** Judy Zylstra, children's book editor. **Art Acquisitions:** Gayle Brown. Publishes 10-12 picture books/year; and 3-4 middle readers/year.
Fiction: Picture books, middle readers: parables, religion, retold Bible stories, child or family issues, historical fiction, art/artists.
Nonfiction: All levels: biography, religion.
How to Contact/Writers: Fiction/Nonfiction: Query with sample chapters (novels) or submit complete ms (picture books). Responds to queries in 6 weeks; mss in 2 months.
Illustration: Works with 10-12 illustrators/year. Reviews ms/illustration packages from artists. Responds to ms/art samples in 1 month. Illustrations only: Submit résumé, slides or color photocopies. Samples returned with SASE; samples filed.
Terms: Pays authors and illustrators royalties of 5-7% based on retail price. Sends galleys to authors; dummies to illustrators. Original artwork returned at job's completion. Book catalog free on request with SASE (4 first class stamps, 9×12 envelope); ms and/or artist's guidelines free on request, with SASE.
Tips: "We are looking for material that will help children build their faith in God and explore God's world. We accept all genres."

ENSLOW PUBLISHERS INC., Box 398, 40 Industrial Rd., Berkeley Heights NJ 07922-0398. Website: www.enslow.com. Estab. 1978. **Acquisitions:** Brian D. Enslow, vice president. Publishes 100 middle reader titles/year; and 100 young adult titles/year. 30% of books by first-time authors.
Nonfiction: Young readers, middle readers, young adults: animal, biography, careers, health, history, hobbies, nature/environment, social issues, sports. "Enslow is moving into the elementary (Grades 3-4) level and is looking for authors who can write biography and suggest other nonfiction themes at this level." Average word length: middle readers—5,000; young adult—18,000. Published *Louis Armstrong*, by Patricia and Fredrick McKissack (grades 2-3, biography); and *Lotteries: Who Wins, Who Loses?*, by Ann E. Weiss (grades 6-12, issues book).
How to Contact/Writers: Nonfiction: Send for guidelines. Query. Responds to queries/mss in 2 weeks. Publishes a book 18 months after acceptance. Will not consider simultaneous submissions.
Illustration: Submit résumé, business card or tearsheets to be kept on file.
Terms: Pays authors royalties or work purchased outright. Sends galleys to authors. Book catalog/ms guidelines available for $2, along with an 8½×11 SAE and $1.67 postage.

◖ **EVAN-MOOR EDUCATIONAL PUBLISHERS**, 18 Lower Ragsdale Dr., Monterey CA 93940-5746. (408)649-5901. Fax: (408)649-6256. E-mail: editorial@evan-moor.com. Website: www.evan-moor.com. Book publisher. **Manuscript Acquisitions:** Marilyn Evans, editor. **Art Acquisitions:** Joy Evans, production director. Publishes 30-50 books/year. Less than 10% of books by first-time authors. " 'Helping Children Learn' is our motto. Evan-Moor is known for high-quality educational materials written by teachers for use in the classroom and at home. We publish teacher resource and reproducible materials in most all curriculum areas and activity books (language arts, math, science, social studies). No fiction or nonfiction literature books."

Nonfiction: Published late 1999, early 2000: *Daily Math Practice*, series, (multiple authors, book for each grade 1-6); additions to *Read & Understand*, series (*Fairytales*, grades 1-2; *Folktales & Fables*, grades 2-3; *Tall Tales*, grades 3-4; *Myths & Legends*, grades 4-6); *Daily Summer Activities*, full-color activity books for home use to aid in transition from one grade to the next; pre-kindergarten; kindergarten-grade 1; grades 1-2; grades 2-3; grades 3-4, grades 4-5.

How to Contact/Writers: Query or submit complete ms. Responds to queries in 2 months; mss in 2 months. Publishes a book 12-18 months after acceptance. Will consider simultaneous submissions if so noted. Send SASE for submission guidelines.

Illustration: Works with 8 illustrators/year. Uses b&w artwork primarily. Illustrations only: Query with samples; send résumé, tearsheets. Contact: Joy Evans, production director. Responds only if interested. Samples returned with SASE; samples filed.

Terms: Work purchased outright from authors, "dependent solely on size of project and 'track record' of author." Pays illustrators by the project (range: varies). Sends galleys to authors. Artwork is not returned. Book catalog available for 9×12 SAE; ms guidelines available for SASE.

Tips: "Writers—know the supplemental education or parent market. (These materials are *not* children's literature.) Tell us how your project is unique and what consumer needs it meets. Illustrators—you need to be able to produce quickly and be able to render realistic and charming children and animals." A number of subject areas are of ongoing interest. They include: science and math materials that emphasize "real-world," hands-on learning and critical thinking/problem solving skills; materials related to cultural diversity, global awareness; geography materials; assessment materials; and materials for parents to use with their children at home.

EXCELSIOR CEE PUBLISHING, P.O. Box 5861, Norman OK 73070-5861. (405)329-3909. Fax: (405)329-6886. Book publisher. Estab. 1989. **Manuscript Acquisitions:** J.C. Marshall.

How to Contact/Writers: Nonfiction: Query or submit outline/synopsis. Responds to queries in 1 month. Publishes a book 1 year after acceptance. Will consider simultaneous submission.

FACTS ON FILE, 11 Penn Plaza, New York NY 10001-2006. (212)967-8800. Website: www.factsonfile.com. Book publisher. Editorial Director: Laurie Likoff. **Acquisitions:** Frank Darnstadt, science and technology/nature; Nicole Bowen, American history and studies; Anne Savarese, language and literature; world studies; Jim Chambers, arts and entertainment. Estab. 1941. "We produce high-quality reference materials for the school library market and the general nonfiction trade." Publishes 25-30 young adult titles/year. 5% of books by first-time authors; 25% of books from agented writers; additional titles through book packagers, co-publishers and unagented writers.

Nonfiction: Middle readers, young adults: animal, biography, careers, geography, health, history, multicultural, nature/environment, reference, religion, science, social issues and sports.

How to Contact/Writers: Nonfiction: Submit outline/synopsis and sample chapters. Responds to queries in 8-10 weeks. Publishes a book 10-12 months after acceptance. Will consider simultaneous submissions. Sends galleys to authors. Book catalog free on request. Send SASE for submission guidelines.

Terms: Submission guidelines available via website or with SASE.

Tips: "Most projects have high reference value and fit into a series format."

☑ ☒ **FARRAR, STRAUS & GIROUX INC.**, 19 Union Square W., New York NY 10003. (212)741-6900. Fax: (212)633-2427. Book publisher. Imprint: Frances Foster Books. Children's Books Editorial Director: Margaret Ferguson. **Acquisitions:** Frances Foster, publisher, Frances Foster Books; Wesley Adams, senior editor; Janine O'Malley, assistant editor. Estab. 1946. Publishes 30 picture books/year; 15 middle reader titles/year; and 15 young adult titles/year. 10% of books by first-time authors; 20% of books from agented writers.

● Farrar title *Francie*, by Karen English, won a 2000 Coretta Scott King Author Honor Award; their title *Buttons*, written and illustrated by Brock Cole, won a 2000 Boston Globe-Horn Book Honor Award for Picture Books; their title *Speak*, by Laurie Halse Anderson, won the Golden Kite Award for Fiction in 2000.

Fiction: All levels: all categories. "Original and well-written material for all ages." Recently published *Belle Prater's Boy*, by Ruth White (ages 10 up).

Nonfiction: All levels: all categories. "We publish only literary nonfiction."

How to Contact/Writers: Fiction/Nonfiction: Query with outline/synopsis and sample chapters. Do not fax submissions or queries. Responds to queries/mss in 3 months. Publishes a book 18 months after acceptance. Will consider simultaneous submissions.

Illustration: Works with 30-60 illustrators/year. Reviews ms/illustration packages from artists. Submit ms with 1 example of final art, remainder roughs. Do not send originals. Illustrations only: Query with tearsheets. Responds if interested in 2 months. Samples returned with SASE; samples sometimes filed.

Terms: "We offer an advance against royalties for both authors and illustrators." Sends galleys to authors; dummies to illustrators. Original artwork returned at job's completion. Book catalog available for 9×12 SAE and $1.87 postage; ms guidelines for 1 first-class stamp.

Tips: "Study our catalog before submitting. We will see illustrator's portfolios by appointment. Don't ask for criticism and/or advice—it's just not possible. Never send originals. Always enclose SASE."

THE FEMINIST PRESS, 365 Fifth Ave., New York NY 10016. Website: www.feministpress.org. Estab. 1970. Acquisitions Editor: Amanda Hamlin. Publishes 3 middle readers/year. "We are a nonprofit, tax-exempt, education publishing organization interested in changing the curriculum, the classroom and consciousness."

Fiction: Middle readers, young adult: multicultural. Average word length: 20,000-30,000. Recently published *Families*, by Meredith Tax, illustrated by Maryln Hafner (ages 4-8); *Carly*, by Annegert Fuchshuber (ages 5 and up); *The Lilith Summer*, by Hadley Irwin (ages 10 and up); and *Josephina Hates Her Name*, by Diana Engel.

Nonfiction: Middle readers and young adults: biography, multicultural and social issues. Average word length: middle readers—20,000; young adult—30,000. Recently published *Aung San Su Kyi: Standing Up for Democracy in Burma*, by Bettina Ling (ages 10 and up); *Mamphela Ramphele: Challenging Apartheid in South Africa*, by Judith Harlan (ages 10 and up); and *Ela Bhatt: Uniting Women in India*, by Jyotsna Screenivasan (ages 10 and up).

How to Contact/Writers: Fiction: query. Responds to queries in 4 months; mss in 3 months. Publishes a book 18 months after acceptance. Will consider simultaneous submissions and previously published work.

Photography: Buys stock and assigns work. Contact: Dayna Navaro, production/design manager. Model/property releases required. Uses color and b&w prints. Submit published samples.

Terms: Pays authors royalty of 10% based on wholesale price. Offers advances (average amount $250). Pays illustrators and photographers by the project. Originals returned to artist at job's completion. Book catalog available for 8½×11 SAE and 4 first-class stamps. All imprints included in single catalog. Catalog available on website. Writer's guidelines available for SASE.

FENN PUBLISHING CO., 34 Nixon Rd., Bolton, Ontario L7E-1W2 Canada. Phone/fax: (905)951-6600. Fax: (905)951-6601. E-mail: fennpubs@hbfenn.com. Website: www.hbfenn.com. Estab. 1982. **Manuscript/Art Acquisitions:** C. Jordan Fenn, publisher. Publishes 35 books/year.

Fiction: Picture books: adventure, animal, folktales, multicultural, religion, sports. Young readers: adventure, animal, folktales, multicultural, religion. Middle readers: adventure, animal, health, history, multicultural, religion, special needs, sports. Young adults: adventure, animal, contemporary, folktales, health, history, multicultural, nature/environment, religion, science fiction, sports.

Nonfiction: Picture books, young readers, middle readers, activity books, animal, arts/crafts, geography, health, history, hobbies, how-to, multicultural, nature/environment, religion.

How to Contact/Writers: Fiction/Nonfiction: Query or submit complete ms. Responds to queries/mss in 2 months.

Illustration: Reviews ms/illustration packages from artists. Contact: C. Jordan Fenn, publisher. Responds only if interested. Samples not returned or filed.

FIESTA CITY PUBLISHERS, Box 5861, Santa Barbara CA 93150-5861. (805)733-1984. E-mail: fcooke3 924@aol.com. Book publisher. **Acquisitions:** Frank Cooke, president. Publishes 1 middle reader/year; 1 young adult/year. 25% of books by first-time authors. Publishes books about cooking and music or a combination of the two. "We are best known for children's and young teens' cookbooks and musical plays."

Fiction: Young adults: history, humor, musical plays.

Nonfiction: Young adult: cooking, how-to, music/dance, self-help. Average word length: 30,000. Does not want to see "cookbooks about healthy diets or books on rap music." Published *Kids Can Write Songs, Too!* (revised second printing), by Eddie Franck; *Bent-Twig*, by Frank E. Cooke, with some musical arrangements by Johnny Harris (a 3-act musical for young adolescents).

How to Contact/Writers: Query. Responds to queries in 4 days; on mss in 1 month. Publishes a book 1 year after acceptance. Will consider simultaneous submissions.

Illustration: Works with 1 illustrator/year. Will review ms/illustrations packages (query first). Illustrations only: Send résumé. Samples returned with SASE; samples filed.

Terms: Pays authors 5-10% royalty based on retail price.

Tips: "Write clearly and simply. Do not write 'down' to young adults (or children). Looking for self-help books on current subjects, original and unusual cookbooks, and books about music, or a combination of cooking and music." Always include SASE.

FIREFLY BOOKS LTD., 3680 Victoria Park Ave., Willowdale, Ontario M2H 3K1 Canada. (416)499-8412. Fax: (416)499-8313. Website: www.fireflybooks.com. Book publisher and distributor.
 • Firefly Books Ltd. does not accept unsolicited mss.

TO RECEIVE REGULAR TIPS AND UPDATES about writing and Writer's Digest publications via e-mail, send an e-mail with "SUBSCRIBE NEWSLETTER" in the body of the message to newsletter-request@writersdigest.com

FIRST STORY PRESS, Imprint of Rose Book Group, 1800 Business Park Dr., Suite 205, Clarksville TN 37040. (931)572-0806. Fax: (931)552-3200. Publisher/Editor in Chief: Judith Pierson. Contact: Acquisitions Editor. Publishes 4 books/year. 50% of books by first-time authors. Publishes books on quilt themes.
Fiction: Picture books. Average word length: picture books—700-1,500. Recently published *The Much Too Loved Quilt*, by Rachel Waterstone.
How to Contact/Writers: Fiction: Submit complete ms. Send hard copy. Responds to queries/mss in 3 months.
Illustration: Works with 3 illustrators/year. Reviews ms/illustration packages from artists. Send ms with dummy. Contact: Editor. Illustrations only: Send résumé, promo sheet and tearsheets to be kept on file. Contact: Editor. Responds only if interested. Samples returned with SASE; samples filed.
Terms: Pays authors royalty of 4-5% based on retail price or work purchased outright. Offers advances. Pays illustrators royalty of 4-5% based on retail price. Originals returned to artist. Ms guidelines available for SASE.
Tips: "SASE is always required. Do not send original artwork. Guidelines available—send SASE. Take a look at our books. We do not send out catalogs."

N ☐ ☐ FIVE STAR PUBLICATIONS, INC., P.O. Box 6698, Chandler AZ 85246-6698. (480)940-8182. Fax: (480)940-8787. E-mail: info@fivestarsupport.com. Website: www.fivestarsupport.com. Estab. 1985. Specializes in educational material, nonfiction. We are an independent book packager/producer. Publishes 7 middle readers/year.
Nonfiction: Recently published *Shakespeare for Children: The Story of Romeo & Juliet*, by Cass Foster; *The Sixty-Minute Shakespeare: Hamlet*, by Cass Foster; *The Sixty-Minute Shakespeare: Twelfth Night*, by Cass Foster.
How to Contact/Writers: Nonfiction: Query.
Illustration: Works with 3 illustrators/year. Reviews ms/illustration packages from artists. Query. Contact: Sue DeFabis, project manager. Illustrations only: Query with samples. Responds only if interested. Samples filed.
Photography: Buys stock and assigns work. Works on assignment only. Contact: Sue De Fabis, project manager. Submit letter.
Terms: Pays illustrators by the project. Pays photographers by the project. Sends galleys to authors; dummies to illustrators.

FOREST HOUSE PUBLISHING COMPANY, INC., P.O. Box 738, Lake Forest IL 60045. (847)295-8287. Fax: (847)295-8201. E-mail: info@forest-house.com. Website: www.forest-house.com. Estab. 1989. **Acquisitions:** Dianne L. Spahr, president. Imprints: HTS Books. Published 42 titles in 1999; estimates 17 titles for spring 2001. "We are not accepting any unsolicited manuscripts, until 2001."

FORWARD MOVEMENT PUBLICATIONS, 412 Sycamore St., Cincinnati OH 45202. (513)721-6659. Fax: (513)721-0729. E-mail: forwardmovement@msn.com. Website: www.forwardmovement.org. **Acquisitions:** Edward S. Gleason, editor.
Fiction: Middle readers and young adults: religion and religious problem novels, fantasy and science fiction.
Nonfiction: Religion.
How to Contact/Writers: Fiction/Nonfiction: Query. Responds in 1 month.
Illustration: Query with samples. Samples returned with SASE.
Terms: Pays authors honorarium. Pays illustrators by the project.
Tips: "Forward Movement is now exploring publishing books for children and does not know its niche. We are an agency of the Episcopal Church and most of our market is to mainstream Protestants."

☑ FREE SPIRIT PUBLISHING, 217 Fifth Ave. N., Suite 200, Minneapolis MN 55401-1299. (612)338-2068. Fax: (612)337-5050. E-mail: help4kids@freespirit.com. Website: www.freespirit.com. Book publisher. **Acquisitions:** Katrina Wentzel. Publishes 15-20 titles/year for children and teens, teachers and parents. "We believe passionately in empowering kids to learn to think for themselves and make their own good choices."
• Free Spirit no longer accepts fiction or story book submissions.
Nonfiction: "Free Spirit Publishing specializes in SELF-HELP FOR KIDS® and SELF-HELP FOR TEENS®, with an emphasis on self-esteem and self-awareness, stress management, school success, creativity, friends and family, social action, and special needs (i.e., gifted and talented, children with learning differences). We prefer books written in a natural, friendly style, with little education/psychology jargon. We need books in our areas of emphasis and prefer titles written by specialists such as teachers, counselors, and other professionals who work with youth." Recently published *Hands Are Not for Hitting*, by Martine Agassi; *Stress Can Really Get on Your Nerves!*, by Trevor Romain and Elizabeth Verdick; *Teen Angst? Naaah . . .*, by Ned Vizzini.
How to Contact/Writers: Send query letter or proposal. Responds to queries/mss in 4 months. "If you'd like materials returned, enclose a SASE with sufficient postage." Write or call for catalog and submission guidelines before sending submission. Accepts queries only by e-mail. Submission guidelines available online.
Illustration: Works with 5 illustrators/year. Submit samples to acquisitions editor for consideration. If appropriate, samples will be kept on file and artist will be contacted if a suitable project comes up. Enclose SASE if you'd like materials returned.
Photography: Submit samples to acquisitions editor for consideration. If appropriate, samples will be kept on file and photographer will be contacted if a suitable project comes up. Enclose SASE if you'd like materials returned.

Terms: Pays authors in royalties based on wholesale price. Offers advance. Pays illustrators by the project. Pays photographers by the project or per photo.

Tips: "Prefer books that help kids help themselves or that help adults help kids help themselves; that complement our list without duplicating current titles; and that are written in a direct, straightforward manner."

☑ **FREESTONE/PEACHTREE, JR.**, Peachtree Publishers, 1700 Chattahoochee Ave., Atlanta GA 30318-2112. (404)876-8761. Fax: (404)875-2578. Website: www.peachtree-online.com. Estab. 1997. **Manuscript Acquisitions:** Helen Harriss (children's, young adult). Art Acquisitions: Loraine Balesik (all). Publishes 3-4 young adult titles/year. Peachtree Jr. publishes 5 juvenile titles/year (ages 8-12) and Peachtree Publishers, Ltd. publishes 10 books a year. "We look for very good stories that are well-written, and written from the author's experience and heart with a clear application to today's young adults. We feel teens need to read about issues that are relevant to them, rather than reading adult books."

● Freestone/Peachtree, Jr. is an imprint of Peachtree Publishers. See the listing for Peachtree for submission information.

☑ **FRONT STREET BOOKS**, 20 Battery Park Ave., #403, Ashville NC 28801. (828)236-3097. Fax: (828)236-3098. Fax: (828)236-3098. E-mail: contactus@frontstreetbooks.com or roxburgh@frontstreetbooks.com. Website: www.frontstreetbooks.com. Book publisher. Estab. 1995. **Acquisitions:** Stephen Roxburgh, publisher; Nancy Zimmerman, associate publisher. Publishes 10-15 titles/year." We are a small independent publisher of books for children and young adults. We do not publish pablum: we try to publish books that will attract, if not addict, children to literature and art books that are a pleasure to look at and a pleasure to hold, books that will be revelations to young minds."

● See Front Street's website for submission guidelines and their complete catalog. Front Street focuses on fiction, but will publish poetry, anthologies, nonfiction and high-end picture books. They are not currently accepting unsolicited picture book manuscripts. Front Street title *a day, a dog*, by Gabrielle Vincent, won a 2000 Boston Globe-Horn Book Honor Award for Picture Books.

Fiction: Recently published: *Paper Trail*, by Barbara Snow Gilbert; *Myrtle of Willendorf*, by Rebecca O'Connell; *a day, a dog*, by Gabrielle Vincent (picture book).

How to Contact/Writers: Fiction: Submit cover letter and complete ms if under 30 pages; submit cover letter, one or two sample chapters and plot summary if over 30 pages. Nonfiction: Submit detailed proposal and sample chapters. Poetry: Submit no more than 25 poems. Include SASE with submissions if you want them returned. "It is our policy to consider submissions in the order in which they are received. This is a time-consuming practice, and we ask you to be patient in awaiting our response."

Illustration "If you are the artist or are working with an artist, we will be happy to consider your project." Submit ms, dummy and a sample piece of art "rendered in the manner and style representative of the final artwork."

Terms: Pays royalties.

☑ **FRONT STREET/CRICKET BOOKS**, Imprint of Carus Publishing Company, 332 S. Michigan, Suite 1100, Chicago IL 60604. Website: www.cricketsbooks.net. Imprint estab. 1999; Company estab. 1973. **Manuscript Acquisitions:** Laura Tillotson. **Art Acquisitions:** Tony Jacobson. Publishes 5 young readers, 5 middle readers and 2 young adult/year. 50% of books by first time authors. "For 25 years we've published the best children's literary magazines in America, and we're looking for the same high-quality material for our book imprint."

● Turn to First Books on page 70 to read about Front Street/Cricket author Kezi Matthews and her book *John Riley's Daughter*.

Fiction: Young readers, middle readers, young adult/teen: adventure, animal, contemporary, fantasy, history, multicultural, humor, sports, suspense/mystery, science fiction, problem novels. Recently published *Casebook of a Private (Cat's) Eye*, by Mary Stolz, illustrated by Pam Levy (middle grade); *Oh No, It's Robert*, by Barbara Seuling, illustrated by Paul Brewer (ages 7-10); *Two Suns in the Sky*, by Miriam Bat-Ami (ages 12 and up).

How to Contact/Writers: Fiction: submit complete ms. Responds to queries in 8 weeks; mss in 10-12 weeks. Publishes a book 18 months after acceptance. Will consider simultaneous submissions.

Illustration: Works with 4 illustrators/year. Use color and b&w. Illustration only: submit samples, tearsheets. Contact: Tony Jacobson. Responds only if interested. Samples returned with SASE; sample filed.

Terms: Authors paid royalty of 7-10% based on retail price. Offers advances. Illustrators paid royalty of 3% based on retail price. Sends galleys to authors; dummies to illustrators. Originals returned to artist at job's completion. Writer's guidelines available for SASE. Catalog available at website.

Tips: "At this time we are only considering chapter book and middle-grade submissions. No nonfiction or picture books. Study *Cricket* and *Spider* magazines to get an idea of our approach and to learn more of what we're looking for."

☑ **FULCRUM KIDS**, Imprint of Fulcrum Publishing, 16100 Table Mountain Parkway, #300, Golden CO 80403. (303)277-1623. Fax: (303)279-7111. E-mail: fulcrum@fulcrum-resources.com. Website: www.fulcrum-resources.com. Estab. 1984. Specializes in nonfiction and educational material. **Manuscript Acquisitions:** Naomi Horii, acquisitions editor. Publishes 4 middle readers/year. 25% of books by first-time authors. "Our mission is to make teachers' and librarians' jobs easier using quality resources."

Fiction: Looking for fiction with an educational focus.

Nonfiction: Middle and early readers: activity books, multicultural, nature/environment. Recently published *America's Mountains*, by Marianne Wallace (nature, ages 8-12); *Why the Leopard Has Spots: Dan Stories from Liberia*, written by Won-Ldy Paye and Met Lippert, illustrated by Ashley Bryan (multicultural, ages 8-12 yrs.); and *Cucumber Soup*, by Vickie Leigh Krudwig, illustrated by Craig MacFarland Brown (nature/counting), ages 3-6).

How to Contact/Writers: Submit complete ms or submit outline/synopsis and 2 sample chapters. Responds to queries in 3 weeks; mss in 2 months. Publishes a book 12-18 months after acceptance. Will consider simultaneous submissions.

Illustration: Works with 10 illustrators/year. Reviews ms/illustration packages from artists. Send ms with dummy or submit ms with 3 pieces of final art. Send résumé, promotional literature and tearsheets. Contact: Naomi Horii, acquisitions editor. Responds only if interested. Samples not returned; samples filed.

Photography: Works on assignment only.

Terms: Pays authors royalty based on wholesale price. Offers advances (Average amount: $1,500). Pays illustrators by the project (range: $300-2,000) or royalty based on wholesale price. Sends galleys to authors; dummies to illustrators. Originals returned to artist at job's completion. Book catalog available for 9×12 SAE and 77¢ postage; ms guidelines available for SASE. Catalog available on website.

Tips: "Research our line first. We are emphasizing science and nature nonfiction. We look for books that appeal to the school market and trade. Be sure to include SASE."

☑ LAURA GERINGER BOOKS, 1350 Avenue of the Americas, New York NY 10019. (212)261-6500. Website: www.harperchildrens.com. Imprint of HarperCollins Publishers. **Manuscript Acquisitions:** Laura Geringer, publisher and senior vice president. **Art Acquisitions:** Harriett Barton, art director. Publishes 10-12 picture books/year; 2 middle readers/year; 2-4 young adult titles/year.

Fiction: All levels: all subjects. Average word length: picture books—250-1,200. Recently published *If You Take a Mouse to the Movies*, by Laura Numeroff (ages 3-7, picture book); *Snowie Rolie*, by William Joyce (ages 4-8, picture book); *Three Magic Balls*, by Richard Egielski (ages 3-7, picture book).

How to Contact/Writers: Query only. Responds to queries in 2-3 months. Publishes a book 1-3 years after acceptance. Will consider simultaneous submissions.

Illustration: Works with 15-20 illustrators/year. Reviews ms/illustration packages from artists. Submit complete package. Illustrations only: Query with samples; submit portfolio for review; provide résumé, business card, promotional literature or tearsheets to be kept on file. Responds in 2-3 months. SASE for return of samples; samples kept on file.

Terms: Pays advance and royalties to be negotiated. Sends galleys to authors; proofs to illustrators. Original artwork returned at job's completion. Book catalog available for 9×11 SASE; ms/artist's guidelines available for SASE.

Tips: "Write about what you *know* and care about. Don't try to guess our needs. Don't write down to children. We are looking for fresh and original material with a strong sense of style and expression, whether it be comic or tragic, it should be deeply felt."

☑ GIBBS SMITH, PUBLISHER, P.O. Box 667, Layton UT 84090. (801)544-9800. Fax: (801)544-5582. E-mail: staylor@gibbs-smith.com. Website: gibbs-smith.com. Imprint: Gibbs Smith Junior. Book publisher. Editorial Director: Madge Baird. **Acquisitions:** Suzanne Taylor, acquisitions editor. Publishes 2-3 books/year. 50% of books by first-time authors. 50% of books from agented authors.

Fiction: Picture books: adventure, contemporary, humor, multicultural, nature/environment, suspense/mystery, western. Average word length: picture books—1,000. Recently published *Bullfrog Pops!*, by Rick Walton, illustrated by Chris McAllister (ages 4-8); and *The Magic Boots*, by Scott Emerson, illustrated by Howard Post (ages 4-8).

Nonfiction: Middle readers: activity, arts/crafts, cooking, how-to, nature/environment, science. Average word length: up to 10,000. Recently published *Hiding in a Fort*, by G. Lawson Drinkard, illustrated by Fran Lee Kirby (ages 7-12); and *Sleeping in a Sack: Camping Activities for Kids*, by Linda White, illustrated by Fran Lee (ages 7-12).

How to Contact/Writers: Fiction/Nonfiction: Submit several chapters or complete ms. Responds to queries and mss in 2 months. Publishes a book 1-2 years after acceptance. Will consider simultaneous submissions. Ms returned with SASE.

Illustration: Works with 2 illustrators/year. Reviews ms/illustration packages from artists. Query. Submit ms with 3-5 pieces of final art. Illustrations only: Query with samples; provide résumé, promo sheet, slides (duplicate slides, not originals). Responds only if interested. Samples returned with SASE; samples filed.

Terms: Pays authors royalty of 2% based on retail price or work purchased outright ($500 minimum). Offers advances (average amount: $2,000). Pays illustrators by the project or royalty of 2% based on retail price. Sends galleys to authors; color proofs to illustrators. Original artwork returned at job's completion. Book catalog available for 9×12 SAE and postage. Ms guidelines available.

Tips: "We target ages 5-11."

DAVID R. GODINE, PUBLISHER, 9 Hamilton Place, Boston MA 02108. (617)451-9600. Fax: (617)350-0250. Book publisher. Estab. 1970. Publishes 1 picture book/year; 1 young reader title/year; 1 middle reader title/year. 10% of books by first-time authors; 75% of books from agented writers. "We publish books that matter for people who care."
- This publisher is no longer considering unsolicited mss of any type.

Fiction: Picture books: adventure, animal, contemporary, folktales, nature/environment. Young readers: adventure, animal, contemporary, folk or fairy tales, history, nature/environment, poetry. Middle readers: adventure, animal, contemporary, folk or fairy tales, history, mystery, nature/environment, poetry. Young adults/teens: adventure, animal, contemporary, history, mystery, nature/environment, poetry. Recently published *The Empty Creel*, by Geraldine Pope (Paterson Prize winning book with vinyl-cut illustrations).

Nonfiction: Picture books: alphabet, animal, nature/environment. Young readers: activity books, animal, history, music/dance, nature/environment. Middle readers: activity books, animal, biography, history, music/dance, nature/environment. Young adults: biography, history, music/dance, nature/environment.

How to Contact/Writers: Query. Responds to queries in 2 weeks. Responds to solicited ms in 2 weeks (if not agented) or 2 months (if agented). Publishes a book 2 years after acceptance.

Illustration: Only interested in agented material. Works with 4-6 illustrators/year. Reviews ms/illustration packages from artists. "Submit roughs and one piece of finished art plus either sample chapters for very long works or whole ms for short works." Illustrations only: "After query, submit slides, with one full-size blow-up of art." Please do not send original artwork unless solicited. Responds to art samples in 2 weeks. Original artwork returned at job's completion. "Almost all of the children's books we accept for publication come to us with the author and illustrator already paired up. Therefore, we rarely use freelance illustrators." Samples returned with SASE; samples filed (if interested).

Terms: Pays authors in royalties based on retail price. Number of illustrations used determines final payment for illustrators. Pay for separate authors and illustrators "differs with each collaboration." Illustrators paid by the project. Sends galleys to authors; dummies to illustrators. Originals returned at job's completion. Book catalog available for SASE.

Tips: "Always enclose a SASE. Keep in mind that we do not accept unsolicited manuscripts and that we rarely use freelance illustrators."

✓ GOLDEN BOOKS, 888 Seventh Ave., New York NY 10106-4100. (212)547-6700. Imprint of Golden Books Family Entertainment Inc. **Editorial Directors:** Diane Arico, trade publishing; Lori Haskins, Road to Reading; Ellen Stamper, mass market. **Art Acquisitions:** Paula Darmofal, executive art director.
- Golden Books is not currently accepting unsolicited submissions (manuscripts or queries).

Fiction: They publish board books, novelty books, picture books, workbooks, series (mass market and trade).

✓ GREENE BARK PRESS, P.O. Box 1108, Bridgeport CT 06601-1108. (203)372-4861. Fax: (203)371-5856. E-mail: greenebark@aol.com. Website: www.greenebarkpress.com. Book publisher. **Acquisitions:** Michele Hofbauer; associate publisher. Thomas J. Greene, publisher. Publishes 4-6 picture books/year. 40% of books by first-time authors. "We publish quality hardcover picture books for children. Our books and stories are selected for originality, imagery and colorfulness. Our intention is to capture a child's attention; to fire-up his or her imagination and desire to read and explore the world through books."

Fiction: Picture books, young readers: adventure, fantasy, humor. Average word length: picture books—650; young readers—1,400. Recently published *Excuse Me, Are you a Dragon?*, written and illustrated by Rhett Ransom Pennell (for ages 3 to 8); *The Monster Encyclopedia*, by Dave Branson, illustrated by Tom Bartimole (for ages 3-8); and *A Pumpkin Story*, written and illustrated by Markio Shinju (for ages 3 to 8).

How to Contact/Writers: Responds to queries in 1 month; ms in 4 months. Publishes a book 18 months after acceptance. Will consider simultaneous submissions. Prefer to review complete mss with illustrations.

Illustrations: Works with 1-2 illustrators/year. Uses color artwork only. Reviews ms/illustration packages from artists. Submit ms with 3 pieces of final art (copies only). Illustrations only: Query with samples. Responds in 2 months only if interested. Samples returned with SASE; samples filed. Originals returned at job's completion.

Terms: Pays authors royalty of 10-12% based on wholesale price. Pays illustrators by the project (range: $1,500-3,000) or 5-7½% royalty based on wholesale price. No advances. Send galleys to authors; dummies to illustrators. Book catalog available for $2.00 fee which includes mailing. All imprints included in a single catalog. Ms and art guidelines available for SASE.

Tips: "As a guide for future publications do not look to our older backlist. Please no telephone, e-mail or fax queries."

✓ GREENHAVEN PRESS, P.O. Box 289011, San Diego CA 92128-9011. (858)485-7424. Website: www.greenhaven.com. Book publisher. Estab. 1970. **Acquisitions:** Stuart B. Miller, managing editor. Publishes 100 young adult titles/year. 35% of books by first-time authors. "Greenhaven continues to print quality nonfiction for libraries and classrooms. Our well known opposing viewpoints series is still highly respected by students and librarians in need of material on controversial social issues. In recent years, Greenhaven has also branched out with a new series covering historical and literary topics."

• Greenhaven accepts no unsolicited mss. All writing is done on a work-for-hire basis.
Nonfiction: Middle readers: biography, controversial topics, history, issues. Young adults: biography, history, nature/environment. Other titles "to fit our specific series." Average word length: young adults—15,000-25,000.
How to Contact/Writers: Query only.
Terms: Buys ms outright for $1,500-3,000. Offers advances. Sends galleys to authors. Writer's guidelines available with SASE. Book catalog available for 9 × 12 SAE and 65¢ postage.
Tips: "Get our guidelines first before submitting anything."

GREENWILLOW BOOKS, 1350 Avenue of the Americas, New York NY 10019. (212)261-6500. Website: www.harperchildrens.com. Imprint of HarperCollins. Book publisher. Senior Vice President/Publisher: Susan Hirschman. **Manuscript Acquisitions:** Submit to Editorial Department. **Art Acquisitions:** Ava Weiss, art director. Publishes 50 picture books/year; 5 middle readers books/year; and 5 young adult books/year. "Greenwillow Books publishes picture books, fiction for young readers of all ages, and nonfiction primarily for children under seven years of age. We hope you will read many children's books (especially those on our list), decide what you like or don't like about them, then write the story *you* want to tell (not what you think we want to read), and send it to us!"
Fiction: Will consider all levels of fiction; various categories.
Nonfiction: Will consider nonfiction for children under seven.
How to Contact/Writers: Submit complete ms. "If your work is illustrated, we ask to see a typed text, rough dummy, and a *copy* of a finished picture. Please do not send original artwork with your submission." Do not call. Responds to mss in 3 months. Publishes a book 18-24 months after acceptance. Will consider simultaneous submissions.
Illustration: Reviews ms/illustration packages from artists. Illustrations only: Query with samples, résumé.
Terms: Pays authors royalty. Offers advances. Pays illustrators royalty or by the project. Sends galleys to authors. Book catalog available for 9 × 12 SASE with $2.20 postage (no cash); ms guidelines available for SASE.
Tips: "You need not have a literary agent to submit to us. We accept—and encourage—simultaneous submissions to other publishers and ask only that you so inform us. Because we receive thousands of submissions, we do not keep a record of the manuscripts we receive and cannot check the status of your manuscript. We do try to respond within ten weeks' time."

GRYPHON HOUSE, P.O. Box 207, Beltsville MD 20704-0207. (301)595-9500. Fax: (301)595-0051. E-mail: kathyc@ghbooks.com. Website: www.gryphonhouse.com. Book publisher. **Acquisitions:** Kathy Charner, editor-in-chief.
Nonfiction: Parent and teacher resource books—activity books, textbooks. Recently published *The Big Messy Art Book*, by Mary Ann Kohl; *101 Easy Wacky Crazy Activities for Children*, by Kathy Lee and Carole Bibble; *The Comprehensive Infant Curriculum*, by Kay Albrecht and Linda G. Miller.
How to Contact/Writers: Query. Submit outline/synopsis and 2 sample chapters. Responds to queries/mss in 3 months. Publishes a book 18 months after acceptance. Will consider simultaneous submissions, electronic submissions via disk or modem.
Illustration: Works with 3-4 illustrators/year. Uses b&w artwork only. Reviews ms/illustration packages from artists. Submit query letter with table of contents, introduction and sample chapters. Illustrations only: Query with samples, promo sheet. Responds in 2 months. Samples returned with SASE; samples filed.
Photography: Buys photos from freelancers. Buys stock and assigns work. Submit cover letter, published samples, stock photo list.
Terms: Pays authors royalty based on wholesale price. Offers advances. Pays illustrators by the project. Pay photographers by the project or per photo. Sends edited ms copy to authors. Original artwork returned at job's completion. Book catalog and ms guidelines available via website or with SASE.
Tips: "Send a SASE for our catalog and manuscript guidelines. Look at our books, then submit proposals that complement the books we already publish or supplement our existing books. We are looking for books of creative, participatory learning experiences that have a common conceptual theme to tie them together. The books should be on subjects that parents or teachers want to do on a daily basis."

GULLIVER BOOKS, 15 E. 26th St., New York NY 10010. (212)592-1000. Imprint of Harcourt, Inc. **Acquisitions:** Elizabeth Van Doren, editorial director, Garen Thomas, senior editor. Publishes 25 titles/year.
• Gulliver only accepts mss submitted by agents, previously published authors, or SCBWI members.
Fiction: Emphasis on picture books. Also publishes middle grade and young adult.
Nonfiction: Publishes nonfiction.
How to Contact/Writers: Fiction/Nonfiction: Query or send ms for picture book.

HACHAI PUBLISHING, 156 Chester Ave., Brooklyn NY 11218-3020. (718)633-0100. Fax: (718)633-0103. E-mail: info@hachai.com. Website: www.hachai.com. Book publisher. **Manuscript Acquisitions:** Devorah

Leah Rosenfeld, submissions editor. Publishes 3 picture books/year; 3 young readers/year; 1 middle reader/year. 75% of books published by first-time authors. "All books have spiritual/religious themes, specifically traditional Jewish content. We're seeking books about morals and values; the Jewish experience in current and Biblical times; and Jewish observance, Sabbath and holidays."

• Hachai Publishing's *Nine Spoons* won the AJL Sydney Taylor Award.

Fiction: Picture books and young readers: contemporary, history, religion. Middle readers: adventure, contemporary, problem novels, religion. Does not want to see animal stories, romance, problem novels depicting drug use or violence. Recently published *As Big As An Egg*, by Rachel Sandman, illustrated by Chana Zakashanskaya (ages 3-6, picture book); and *Red, Blue, and Yellow Yarn*, by Miriam Kosman, illustrated by Valeri Gorbachev (ages 3-6, picture book).

Nonfiction: Published *My Jewish ABC's*, by Draizy Zelcer, illustrated by Patti Nemeroff (ages 3-6, picture book); *Nine Spoons* by Marci Stillerman, illustrated by Pesach Gerber (ages 5-8).

How to Contact/Wrtiers: Fiction/Nonfiction: Submit complete ms. Responds to queries/mss in 6 weeks.

Illustration: Works with 4 illustrators/year. Uses primary color artwork, some b&w illustration. Reviews ms/illustration packages from authors. Submit ms with 1 piece of final art. Contact: Devorah Leah Rosenfeld, submissions editor. Illustrations only: Query with samples; arrange personal portfolio review. Responds in 6 weeks. Samples returned with SASE; samples filed.

Terms: Work purchased outright from authors for $800-1,000. Pays illustrators by the project (range: $2,000-3,500). Book catalog, ms/artist's guidelines available for SASE.

Tips: "Write a story that incorporates a moral . . . not a preachy morality tale. Originality is the key. We feel Hachai is going to appeal to a wider readership as parents become more interested in positive values for their children."

HAMPTON ROADS PUBLISHING COMPANY, INC., 1125 Stoney Ridge Road, Charlottesville VA 22902. (804)296-2772. Fax: (804)296-5096. E-mail: hrpc@hrpub.com. Website: www.hrpub.com. Estab. 1989. **Manuscript Acquisitions:** Pat Adler, Grace Pedalino. **Art Acquisitions:** Jane Hagaman. Publishes 3 picture books/year. 60% of books by first-time authors. Mission Statement: "to work as a team to seek, create, refine and produce the best books we are capable of producing, which will impact, uplift and contribute to positive change in the world; to promote the physical, mental, emotional and financial well-being of all its staff and associates; to build the company into a powerful, respected and prosperous force in publishing in the region, the nation and the world in which we live."

Fiction: Picture books, young readers, middle readers, young adult titles: metaphysical and spiritual. Average word length: picture books—100-200; young readers—1,000-5,000; middle readers—500-4,000. Recently published *Star Babies*, by Mary Summer Rain (preschool-age 8); *The Little Soul and the Sun*, by Neale Donald Walsch (ages 7-12); *OBO*, by Robert Anderson (preschool-age 8); *Coyote Bead*, by Gerald Hausman (ages 9-14).

Nonfiction: Picture books, young readers, middle readers, young adult titles: metaphysical and spiritual. Average word length: picture books—100-200; young readers—1,000-5,000; middle readers—500-4,000. Recently published *Mountains, Meadows and Moonbeams*, by Mary Summer Rain (ages 5-8).

How to Contact/Writers: Fiction/nonfiction: submit complete ms. Responds to queries in 1 month; mss in 6 months. Publishes a book 6-12 months after acceptance. Will consider simultaneous submissions.

Illustration: Works with 2-3 illustrators/year. Reviews ms/illustration packages from artists. Submit ms with 2-3 pieces of final art (copies). Contact: Pat Adler, associate editor. Illustration only: query with samples. Contact: Jane Hagaman, art director. Responds in 1 month. Samples returned with SASE; samples not filed.

Terms: Pays authors royalty of 10-20% based on retail price. Offers advances (average amount: $1,000). Pays illustrators by the project (range: $250-1,000). Occasionally pays by royalty based on retail price. Sends galleys to authors. Original returned to artist at job's completion. Book catalog available for SASE. Writer's guidelines available for SASE.

Tips: "Please familiarize yourself with our mission statement and/or the books we publish. Preferably send manuscripts that can be recycled rather than returned. If there is no SASE, they will be recycled."

HARCOURT, INC., 525 B St., Suite 1900, San Diego CA 92101-4495. (619)231-6616. Fax: (619)699-6777. Children's Books Division includes: Harcourt Brace Children's Books (Allyn Johnston, editorial director), Gulliver Books (Elizabeth Van Doren, editorial director), Silver Whistle Books (Paula Wiseman, editorial director), Voyager Paperbacks, Odyssey Paperbacks, and Red Wagon Books. Book publisher. **Art Acquisitions:** Art Director. Publishes 50-75 picture books/year; 5-10 middle reader titles/year; 10 young adult titles/year. 20% of

Chana Zakashansky-Zverev chose watercolor and pen for the cover illustration of *Perfect Porridge* by Rochel Sandman because she knew the bright, bold colors would appeal to children. A graduate of Kiev State Art University in the Ukraine, she now works as an art director in the advertising industry. The editors at Hachai Publishing discovered Zakashansky-Zverev's work at a local art gallery. She has illustrated another of Sandman's books, *As Big As An Egg* for Hachai, as well.

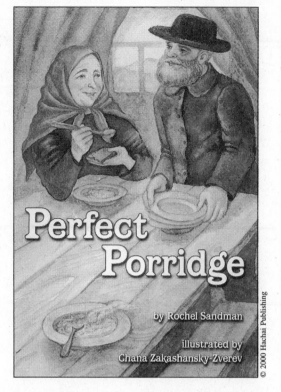

books by first-time authors; 50% of books from agented writers. "Harcourt, Inc. owns some of the world's most prestigious publishing imprints—which distinguish quality products for the juvenile, educational and trade markets worldwide."

- The staff of Harcourt's children's book department is no longer accepting unsolicited manuscripts. Only query letters from previously published authors and manuscripts submitted by agents will be considered. Harcourt title *The Babe & I*, by David Adler, won the Boston Globe-Horn Book Honor Award for Picture Book Text in 2000.

Fiction: All levels: Considers all categories. Average word length: picture books—"varies greatly"; middle readers—20,000-50,000; young adults—35,000-65,000. Recently published *Home Run*, by Robert Burleigh, illustrated by Mike Wimmer (ages 6-10, picture book/biography); *Cast Two Shadows*, by Ann Rinaldi (ages 12 and up; young adult historical fiction); *Tell Me Something Happy Before I Go to Sleep*, by Joyce Dunbar, illustrated by Debi Gliori (ages 4-8, picture book).

Nonfiction: All levels: animal, biography, concept, history, multicultural, music/dance, nature/environment, science, sports. Average word length: picture books—"varies greatly"; middle readers—20,000-50,000; young adults—35,000-65,000. Recently published *Lives of the Presidents*, by Kathleen Krull; illustrated by Kathryn Hewitt (ages 8-12, illustrated nonfiction).

How to Contact/Writers: Only interested in agented material. Fiction: Query or submit outline/synopsis. Nonfiction: Submit outline/synopsis. Responds to queries/mss in 2 months.

Illustration: Works with 150 illustrators/year. Reviews ms/illustration packages from artists. "For picture book ms—complete ms acceptable. Longer books—outline and 2-4 sample chapters." Send one sample of art; no original art with dummy. Illustrations only: Submit résumé, tearsheets, color photocopies, color stats all accepted. "Please DO NOT send original artwork or transparencies." Samples are not returned; samples filed. Responds to art samples only if interested.

Photography: Works on assignment only.

Terms: Pays authors and illustrators in royalty based on retail price. Pays photographers by the project. Sends galleys to authors; dummies to illustrators. Original artwork returned at job's completion. Book catalog available for 8×10 SAE and 4 first-class stamps; ms/artist's guidelines for business-size SASE. All imprints included in a single catalog.

Tips: "Become acquainted with Harcourt Brace's books in particular if you are interested in submitting proposals to us."

HARPERCOLLINS CHILDREN'S BOOKS, 1350 Sixth Ave., New York NY 10019. (212)261-6500. Website: www.harpercollins.com. Book publisher. Editor-in-Chief: Kate Morgan Jackson. **Art Acquisitions:** Harriett Barton, Barbara Fitzsimmon, art directors. Imprints: Laura Geringer Books, Joanna Cotler Books, Greenwillow Books. Paperback Imprints: Harper Trophy, Harper Tempest, Avon. Merchandise Imprint: Harper Festival.

● HarperCollins is not accepting unsolicited mss not addressed to a specific editor. Harper title *Monster*, by Walter Dean Myers, won the first-ever Michael L. Printz Award for excellence in literature for young adults; the title also won a 2000 Coretta Scott King Author Honor Award. Their title *Our Only May Amelia*, by Jennifer L. Holm, won a 2000 Newberry Honor Medal.

Fiction: Picture books: adventure, animal, anthology, concept, contemporary, fantasy, folktales, hi-lo, history, multicultural, nature/environment, poetry, religion. Middle readers: adventure, hi-lo, history, poetry, suspense/mystery. Young adults/teens: fantasy, science fiction, suspense/mystery. All levels: multicultural. "Artists with diverse backgrounds and settings shown in their work."

Nonfiction: Picture books: animal, arts/crafts, biography, geography, multicultural, nature/environment. Middle readers: how-to.

Illustration: Works with 100 illustrators/year. Responds only if interested. Samples returned with SASE; samples filed only if interested.

How to Contact/Writers: Nonfiction: Query.

Terms: Ms and art guidelines available for SASE.

HARVEST HOUSE PUBLISHERS, 1075 Arrowsmith, Eugene OR 97402-9197. (541)343-0123. Fax: (541)342-6410. Book publisher. Publishes 1-2 picture books/year and 2 young reader titles/year. 2-5% of books by first-time authors. Books follow a Christian theme.

● Harvest House no longer accepts unsolicited children's manuscripts.

HAYES SCHOOL PUBLISHING CO. INC., 321 Pennwood Ave., Wilkinsburg PA 15221-3398. (412)371-2373. Fax: (800)543-8771. E-mail: chayes@hayespub.com. Website: www.hayespub.com. **Acquisitions:** Mr. Clair N. Hayes. Estab. 1940. Produces folders, workbooks, stickers, certificates. Wants to see supplementary teaching aids for grades K-12. Interested in all subject areas. Will consider simultaneous and electronic submissions.

How to Contact/Writers: Query with description or complete ms. Responds in 6 weeks. SASE for return of submissions.

Illustration: Works with 3-4 illustrators/year. Responds in 6 weeks. Samples returned with SASE; samples filed. Originals not returned at job's completion.

Terms: Work purchased outright. Purchases all rights.

HEALTH PRESS, P.O. Box 1388, Santa Fe NM 87504. (505)474-0303 or (800)643-2665. Fax: (505)424-0444. E-mail: goodbooks@healthpress.com. Website: www.healthpress.com. Book publisher. **Acquisitions:** Contact Editor. Publishes 4 young readers/year; 4 middle readers/year. 100% of books by first-time authors.

Fiction: Young readers, middle readers: health, special needs. Average word length: young readers—1,000-1,500; middle readers—1,000-1,500. Recently published *Pennies, Nickels and Dimes*, by Elizabeth Murphy.

Nonfiction: Young readers, middle readers: health, special needs.

How to Contact/Writers: Submit complete ms. Responds in 1 month. Publishes a book 9 months after acceptance. Will consider simultaneous submissions.

Terms: Pays authors royalty. Sends galleys to authors. Book catalog available.

HENDRICK-LONG PUBLISHING COMPANY, P.O. Box 25123, Dallas TX 75225. Fax: (214)352-4768. E-mail: hendrick-long@worldnet.att.net. Book publisher. Estab. 1969. **Acquisitions:** Joann Long, vice president. Publishes 4 young reader titles/year; 4 middle reader titles/year. 20% of books by first-time authors. Publishes fiction/nonfiction about Texas of interest to young readers through young adults/teens.

Fiction: Middle readers: history books on Texas and the Southwest. No fantasy or poetry. Recently published *Molasses Cookies*, by Janet Kaderli, illustrated by Patricia Arnold (K-5); and *Terror from the Gulf*, by Martha Tannery Jones (grades 3-5).

Nonfiction: Middle, young adults: history books on Texas and the Southwest, biography, multicultural. Recently published *Texas Brain Twisters*, by Jodie Weddle.

How to Contact/Writers: Fiction/Nonfiction: Query with outline/synopsis and sample chapter. Responds to queries in 1 month; mss in 2 months. Publishes a book 18 months after acceptance. No simultaneous submissions. Include SASE.

Illustration: Works with 2-3 illustrators/year. Uses primarily b&w interior artwork; color covers only. Illustrations only: Query first. Submit résumé or promotional literature or photocopies or tearsheets—no original work sent unsolicited. Responds only if interested.

Terms: Pays authors in royalty based on selling price. Advances vary. Pays illustrators by the project or royalty. Sends galleys to authors; dummies to illustrators. Ms guidelines for 1 first-class stamp and #10 SAE.

Tips "Material **must** pertain to Texas or the Southwest. Check all facts about historical figures and events in both fiction and nonfiction. Be accurate."

HIGHSMITH PRESS, P.O. Box 800, Ft. Atkinson WI 53538-0800. (920)563-9571. Fax: (920)563-4801. E-mail: hpress@highsmith.com. Website: www.hpress.highsmith.com. Imprints: Highsmith Press, Alleyside Press, Upstart Books. Book publisher. **Acquisitions:** Matt Mulder, publications division director. Highsmith Press publishes library, professional books. Alleyside Press and Upstart Books publishes reading activity materials, storytelling aids, and library/study skills instructional resources for youth PreK-12 grade.

Nonfiction: All levels: reading activity books, library skills, reference, study skills. Multicultural needs include storytelling resources. Young adults: careers. Average length: 64-120 pages. Published *Researching Events*, by Maity Schrecengost (ages 8-11, study skills); *Toddle on Over*, by Robin Davis (ages 2-4, activity book); and *The Teen's Guide to the World Wide Web*, by Mimi Mandel (ages 13-18, reference).

How to Contact/Writers: Query or submit complete ms or submit outline/synopsis. Responds to queries/mss in 6 weeks. Publishes a book 6 months after acceptance. Will consider simultaneous submissions.

Illustration: Works with 6-12 illustrators/year. Responds in 1 month. Samples returned with SASE; samples filed. Originals returned at job's completion.

Terms: Pays authors royalty of 10-12% based on wholesale price. Pays illustrators by the project; varies considerably. Offers advances. Sends galleys to authors. Book catalog available for 9×12 SAE and 2 first-class stamps; ms guidelines available for SASE.

Tips: "Review our catalog and ms guidelines to see what we publish. Our complete catalog and current guidelines can be found at our website on the Internet (address above), as well as a list of projects for which we are seeking authors. We are seeking ms which help librarians and teachers to stimulate reading and how to use the Internet for instructional purposes."

HOLIDAY HOUSE INC., 425 Madison Ave., New York NY 10017. (212)688-0085. Fax: (212)421-6134. Book publisher. Estab. 1935. Vice President/Editor-in-Chief: Regina Griffin. **Acquisitions:** Assistant Editor. Publishes 35 picture books/year; 3 young reader titles/year; 10 middle reader titles/year; and 3 young adult titles/year. 20% of books by first-time authors; 10% from agented writers.

- Holiday House title *A Child's Calendar*, illustrated by Trina Schart Hyman, won a 2000 Caldecott Honor Medal.

Fiction: All levels: adventure, contemporary, ghost, historical, humor, school. Picture books, middle readers, young adults. Recently published *A Child's Calendar*, by John Updike, illustrated by Trina Schart Hyman; *I Was a Third Grade Science Project*, by M.J. Auch; and *Darkness Over Denmark*, by Ellen Levine.

Nonfiction: All levels: animal, biography, concept, contemporary, geography, historical, math, nature/environment, science, social studies.

How to Contact/Writers: Send queries only to Assistant Editor. Responds to queries in 2 months. If we find your book idea suited to our present needs, we will notify you by mail. Once a ms has been requested, the writers should send in the exclusive submission, with a S.A.S.E., otherwise the ms will not be returned.

Illustration: Works with 35 illustrators/year. Reviews ms illustration packages from artists. Send ms with dummy. Do not submit original artwork or slides. Color photocopies or printed samples are preferred. Responds only if interested. Samples returned with SASE or filed.

Terms: Pays authors and illustrators an advance against royalties. Originals returned at job's completion. Book catalog, ms/artist's guidelines available for a SASE.

Tips: "Fewer books are being published. It will get even harder for first timers to break in."

HENRY HOLT & CO., INC., 115 W. 18th St., New York NY 10011. (212)886-9200. Fax: (212)645-5832. Website: www.henryholt.com. Book publisher. **Manuscript Acquisitions:** Laura Godwin, editor-in-chief/associate publisher of Books for Young Readers dept.; Nina Ignatowicz, executive editor; Christy Ottaviano, executive editor; Reka Simonsen, editor. **Art Acquisitions:** Martha Rago, art director. Imprints: Redfeather (Reka Simonsen, editor). Publishes 20-40 picture books/year; 4-6 chapter books/year; 10-15 middle grade titles/year; 8-10 young adult titles/year. 15% of books by first-time authors; 40% of books from agented writers. "Henry Holt and Company Books for Young Readers is known for publishing quality books that feature imaginative authors and illustrators. We tend to publish many new authors and illustrators each year in our effort to develop and foster new talent."

Fiction: Picture books: animal, anthology, concept, folktales, history, humor, multicultural, nature/environment, poetry, special needs, sports. Middle readers: adventure, contemporary, history, humor, multicultural, special needs, sports, suspense/mystery. Young adults: contemporary, multicultural, problem novel, sports.

Nonfiction: Picture books: animal, arts/crafts, biography, concept, geography, history, hobbies, multicultural, music dance, nature/environment, sports. Middle readers, young readers, young adult: biography, history, multicultural, sports.

How to Contact/Writers: Fiction/Nonfiction: Submit complete ms with SASE. Responds in 3 months. Will not consider simultaneous or multiple submissions.

Illustration: Works with 50-60 illustrators/year. Reviews ms/illustration packages from artists. Random samples OK. Illustrations only: Submit tearsheets, slides. Do *not* send originals. Responds to art samples in 1 month. Samples returned with SASE; samples filed. If accepted, original artwork returned at job's completion.

Terms: Pays authors/illustrators royalty based on retail price. Sends galleys to authors; proofs to illustrators.

insider report

Whittle, revise, 'really concentrate on writing'

Kimberly Willis Holt realizes the importance of rewriting a manuscript. "I have to re-write a lot. I couldn't tell you how many drafts I write, but I know I've done at least twenty rewrites on each book," she says. Holt calls the process "whittling" because she doesn't believe in attempting too much on one rewrite. "I always know kind of where it's supposed to be—it's just getting there. And that comes through allowing myself to do a little bit on each rewrite, concentrating on one aspect of the manuscript, maybe the sensory details or the dialogue."

Kimberly Willis Holt

Holt, the author of award-winning fiction for young adults, wrote *My Louisiana Sky* (winner of the Boston Globe-Horn Book Award), *When Zachary Beaver Came to Town* (the National Book Award winner) and *Mister and Me*. She recently finished *Dancing in Cadillac Light*, about a young girl who spends time with her grandfather when he comes to live with her family. The grandfather, slightly eccentric, spends the last of his money on a Cadillac. As the girl takes rides in the new car with her grandfather, she learns about life. All of Holt's novels are set in the recent past in small Southern towns. "I think of small towns as God's country," Holt says. "I guess I romanticize them and find them idyllic, although I know there are always flaws in living in small towns too."

Perhaps because Holt moved so often as the daughter of a man in the military, she has always wanted to feel as if she belonged somewhere. Readers may find this feeling in her novels, but she resists allowing her writing to be pigeonholed. "I feel very uncomfortable when somebody wants to put me in a box. In fact, I'm afraid of the word 'theme.' I don't have a problem with a reviewer or a fifth-grade child saying, 'I think your books are about this . . .' because I think that's what we do as readers—we bring our own experiences to the page. I have a problem as a writer, telling you what my books are about."

Her current project, a contemporary short story collection, is set in Guam, a former childhood home. One of the fictional characters is a girl who, like Holt, has a military father. "Short stories are my favorite form of writing, but they are very challenging for me to write," she says. "I think I needed to break away from the novels for a while. I really wanted to try something new." Her inspiration to write about her former childhood home came during a recent visit. "It really was *organic*—some of the voices of the short stories just came to me. I'm really excited about going back and getting the opportunity to research and get to know more about these characters. Even though they're fictional, I have ideas for their background, and I need to know more about that."

Just as her experience in Guam suggests, Holt waits for the voice of her character to come to her before she begins writing. "I think the characters choose me. Sometimes the story idea comes first, but I try not to write it until the voice comes. Nine times out of ten it's a coming-of-age story. Maybe I'm still trying to make sense out of being twelve."

Holt's creative process usually begins with an idea she writes down in a notebook. Then she'll wait until she hears the character's voice, which is usually in the form of a first sentence. "I follow that voice. For a while it's nice, and then all of a sudden after chapter one or chapter two, it just sort of leaves me cold and I don't know where it's going." She forces herself to write the rough first draft and then looks for the "little gems" throughout the manuscript. She puts the first draft aside for some time and then returns and starts her whittling rewrite process.

She advises first-time authors to "really concentrate on writing. If you haven't taken a writing class, take a writing class. I took every class that was available in my area. I went to conferences inside and outside my area to network with people. That's how I got my agent. I found my agent through another agent who was at a conference. She didn't represent children's authors, but she gave me my agent's name."

In addition to classes and conferences, "get into a critique group—a good critique group. Often 'good' means not just the writing abilities of those people but their personalities—the personalities of the participants should go well together." Holt advises making writing your job. Whether it's a full-time or part-time job, report to the job as if writing were your boss.

The process of writing is the most important aspect of the business of writing for Holt. "Write every day. Make writing a part of your life, but also don't be afraid of learning from others because I think you can. I still try to think of myself as a beginner because that way I can keep on learning."

—*Karen Roberts*

Kimberly Willis Holt's novel *When Zachary Beaver Came to Town* tells of thirteen-year-old Toby Wilson who befriends Zachary Beaver, "the fattest boy in the world." Says *Booklist*, Holt "humanizes the outsider without sentimentality . . . and [reveals] the freak in all of us, and the power of redemption." Holt, who as a thirteen-year-old paid $2 to see the Fattest Boy in the World, won the National Book Award for Young People's Literature for *Zachary Beaver*.

⬜ ✅ ⬛ **HOUGHTON MIFFLIN CO.**, Children's Trade Books, 222 Berkeley St., Boston MA 02116-3764. (617)351-5000. Fax: (617)351-1111. Website: www.hmco.com. Book publisher. Vice President and Publisher: Anita Silvey. **Manuscript Aquisitions:** Hannah Rodgers, submissions coordinator. Kim Keller, assistant managing editor; Ann Rider, Margaret Raymo, senior editors; Amy Flynn, editor; Eden Edwards, Sandpiper Paperback editor; Matilda Welter, contributing editor; Walter Lorraine, Walter Lorraine Books, editor. **Art Acquisitions:** Bob Kosturko, art director. Averages 60 titles/year. Publishes hardcover originals and trade paperback reprints and originals. Imprints include Clarion Books. "Houghton Mifflin gives shape to ideas that educate, inform, and above all, delight."

• Houghton title *Henry Hikes to Fitchburg*, by D.B. Johnson, won the 2000 Boston Globe-Horn Book Award for Picture Books.

Fiction: All levels: all categories except religion. "We do not rule out any theme, though we do not publish specifically religious material." *Polkabats and Octopus Slacks*, by Calef Brown (ages 4-8, picture book); *Gathering Blue*, by Lois Lowry (ages 10-14, novel); and *The Circuit*, by Francisco Jimenez (ages 10 and up).

Nonfiction: All levels: all categories except religion. Recently published *Top of the World*, by Steve Jenkins (ages 6-10; picture book); *Once a Wolf*, by Stephen Swinburne (ages 4-8, photo); *Girls Think of Everything*, by Catherine Thimmesh, illustrated by Melissa Sweet (ages 8-12).

How to Contact/Writers: Fiction: Submit complete ms. Nonfiction: Submit outline/synopsis and sample chapters. Always include SASE. Response within 3 months.

Illustration: Works with 60 illustrators/year. Reviews ms/illustration packages from artists. Ms/illustration packages or illustrations only: Query with samples (colored photocopies are fine); provide tearsheets. Responds in 2 months. Samples returned with SASE; samples filed if interested.

Terms: Pays standard royalty based on retail price; offers advance. Illustrators paid by the project and royalty. Ms and artist's guidelines available for SASE.

✅ **HUNTER HOUSE PUBLISHERS**, P.O.Box 2914, Alameda CA 94501-0914. Fax: (510)865-4295. E-mail: acquisitions@hunterhouse.com. Website: www.hunterhouse.com. Book publisher. **Manuscript Acquisitions:** Jeanne Brondino. **Art Acquisitions:** Jinni Fontana. art director. Publishes 0-1 titles for teenage women/year. 50% of books by first-time authors; 5% of books from agented writers.

Nonfiction: Young adults: health, multicultural, self-help (self esteem), social issues. "We emphasize that all our books try to take multicultural experiences and concerns into account. We would be interested in a social issues or self-help book on multicultural issues." Books are therapy/personal growth-oriented. Does *not* want to see books for young children; fiction; illustrated picture books; autobiography. Published *Turning Yourself Around: Self-Help Strategies for Troubled Teens*, by Kendall Johnson, Ph.D.; *Safe Dieting for Teens*, by Linda Ojeda, Ph.D.

How to Contact/Writers: Query; submit overview and chapter-by-chapter synopsis, sample chapters and statistics on your subject area, support organizations or networks and marketing ideas. "Testimonials from professionals or well-known authors are crucial." Responds to queries in 1 month; mss in 3 months. Publishes a book 18 months after acceptance. Will consider simultaneous submissions.

Illustration: Works with 1 illustrator/year. Responds only if interested. Samples returned with SASE; samples filed.

Photography: Purchases photos from freelancers. Buys stock images.

Terms: Payment varies. Sends galleys to authors. Book catalog available for 9×12 SAE and $1.25 postage; ms guidelines for standard SAE and 1 first-class stamp.

Tips: Wants therapy/personal growth workbooks; teen books with solid, informative material. "We do few children's books. The ones we do are for a select, therapeutic audience. No fiction! Please, no fiction."

⬛ **HYPERION BOOKS FOR CHILDREN**, 114 Fifth Ave., New York NY 10011. (212)633-4400. Fax: (212)633-4833. An operating unit of Walt Disney Publishing Group, Inc. Book publisher. **Manuscript Acquisitions:** Katherine Tegen, editor-in-chief. **Art Acquisitions:** Ken Geist, associate publisher and creative director. 10% of books by first-time authors. Publishes various categories.

• Hyperion/Jump at the Sun title *In the Time of the Drums*, illustrated by Brian Pinkney, won the 2000 Coretta Scott King Illustrator Award; their title *Osceola: Memories of a Sharecropper's Daughter*, collected/edited by Alan Govenar, illustrated by Shane W. Evans, won a 2000 Boston Globe-Horn Book Honor Award for Nonfiction.

Fiction: Picture books, young readers, middle readers, young adults: adventure, animal, anthology (short stories), contemporary, fantasy, folktales, history, humor, multicultural, poetry, science fiction, sports, suspense/mystery. Middle readers, young adults: commercial fiction. Recently published *Sons of Liberty*, by Adele Griffin (ages 10 and up); *McDuff* series by Rosemary Wells (ages 2-5); and *Zoom Broom*, by Margie Palatini (ages 5-9).

Nonfiction: All trade subjects for all levels.

How to Contact/Writers: Only interested in agented material.

Illustration: Works with 100 illustrators/year. "Picture books are fully illustrated throughout. All others depend on individual project." Reviews ms/illustration packages from artists. Submit complete package. Illustrations only: Submit résumé, business card, promotional literature or tearsheets to be kept on file. Responds only if interested. Original artwork returned at job's completion.

Photography: Works on assignment only. Publishes photo essays and photo concept books. Provide résumé, business card, promotional literature or tearsheets to be kept on file.

Terms: Pays authors royalty based on retail price. Offers advances. Pays illustrators and photographers royalty based on retail price or a flat fee. Sends galleys to authors; dummies to illustrators. Book catalog available for 9 × 12 SAE and 3 first-class stamps; ms guidelines available for SASE.

ℕ ☙ HYPERION PRESS LIMITED, 300 Wales Ave., Winnipeg, Manitoba R2M 2S9 Canada. (204)256-9204. Fax: (204)255-7845. Book Publisher. **Acquisitions:** Dr. M. Tutiah, editor. Publishes authentic-based, retold folktales/legends for ages 4-9. "We are interested in a good story or well researched how-to material."

Fiction: Young readers, middle readers: folktales/legends. Recently published *The Wise Washerman*, by Deborah Froese, illustrated by Wang Kui; *The Cricket's Cage*, written and illustrated by Stefan Czernecki; and *The Peacock's Pride*, by Melissa Kajpust, illustrated by Jo'Anne Kelly.

How to Contact/Writers: Fiction: Query. Responds in 3 months.

Illustration: Reviews ms/illustration packages from artists. Ms/illustration packages and illustration only: Query. Samples returned with SASE.

Terms: Pays authors royalty. Pays illustrators by the project. Sends galleys to authors; dummies to illustrators. Book catalog available for 8 1/2 × 11 SAE and $2.00 postage (Canadian).

IDEALS CHILDREN'S BOOKS, an imprint of Hambleton-Hill Publishing, Inc., 1501 County Hospital Rd., Nashville TN 37218-2501. (615)254-2480. Website: www.hambleton-hill.com/icb.html. Book publisher. **Acquisitions:** Bethany Snyder. Publishes 20-30 picture books/year.

● Ideals Children's Books only accepts manuscripts from members of the Society of Children's Book Writers and Illustrators (SCBWI), agented authors, and/or previously published book authors (submit with a list of writing credits). All others will be returned unread provided a SASE has been enclosed.

Fiction: Picture books: adventure, concept, contemporary, folktales, history, humor, multicultural, nature/environment, religion, sports, suspense/mystery. Average word length: picture books—200-1,200. Recently published *Lazy Daisy*, by David Olson, illustrated by Jenny Campbell (ages 3-10); *The Littlest Red Horse*, by Charles Tazewell, illustrated by Frank Sofo (all ages); and *The Potter Giselle*, written and illustrated by Thomas Aarrestad (ages 3-7).

How to Contact/Writers: Prefers to see complete ms rather than queries. Responds in 3-6 months. Publishes a book 18-24 months after acceptance. Must include SASE for response.

Illustration: Works with 15-20 illustrators/year. Uses color artwork only. Editorial reviews ms/illustration packages from artists. Submit ms with 1 color photocopy of final art and remainder roughs. Illustrations only: Submit résumé and tearsheets showing variety of styles. Responds to art samples only if interested. "No original artwork, please." Samples returned with SASE, but prefers to keep them on file.

Terms: "All terms vary according to individual projects and authors/artists." Ms guidelines/artist guidelines via website or with SASE.

Tips: "Searching for strong storylines with realistic characters as well as 'fun for all kids' kinds of stories. We are not interested in young adult romances. We do not publish chapter books. We are not interested in alphabet books or anthropomorphism." Illustrators: "Be flexible in contract terms—and be able to show as much final artwork as possible."

ILLUMINATION ARTS, P.O. Box 1865, Bellevue WA 98009. (425)644-7185. Fax: (425)644-9274. E-mail: liteinfo@illumin.com. Website: www.illumin.com. Book publisher. Estab. 1987. "All of our books are inspirational/spiritual. We specialize in children's picture books, but our books are designed to appeal to all readers, including adults." **Acquisitions:** Ruth Thompson, editorial director. "We publish high quality children's picture books with enduring inspirational and spiritual values. We are so selective and painstaking in every detail that our company has established a reputation for producing fine quality books. Additionally we are known for our outstanding artwork."

Fiction: Average word length: picture books—1,500-3,000. Recently published *The Bonsai Bear*, by Bernard Libster, illustrated by Aries Cheung; *Dragon* written and illustrated by Jody Bergsma; and *To Sleep With the Angels*, written by H. Elizabeth Collins, illustrated by Judy Kuuisto.

How to Contact/Writers: Fiction: Submit complete ms. Responds to queries in 1 month. Publishes a book 2 years after acceptance. Will consider simultaneous submissions.

Illustration: Works with 2 illustrators/year. Uses color artwork only. Reviews ms/illustration packages from artists. Query or send ms with dummy. Illustrations only: Query with samples; send résumé and promotional literature to be kept on file. Contact: Ruth Thompson, editorial director. Responds in 1 week. Samples returned with SASE or filed.

Terms: Pays authors royalty based on wholesale price. Sends galleys to authors; dummies to illustrators. Originals returned to artist at job's completion. Book fliers available for SASE.

Tips: "Follow our guidelines. Expect considerable editing. Be patient. The market is tough. We receive 10-15 submissions a week and publish two-three books a year."

□ ✓ INCENTIVE PUBLICATIONS, INC., 3835 Cleghorn Ave., Nashville TN 37215-2532. (615)385-2934. Fax: (615)385-2967. E-mail: info@incentivepublications.com. Website: www.incentivepublications.com.

Estab. 1969. "Incentive publishes developmentally appropriate instructional aids for tots to teens." **Acquisitions:** Angela Rainer. Approximately 20% of books by first-time authors. "We publish only educational resource materials (for teachers and parents of children from pre-school age through high school). We publish *no fiction*. Incentive endeavors to produce developmentally appropriate research-based educational materials to meet the changing needs of students, teachers and parents. Books are written by teachers for teachers for the most part."

Nonfiction: Black & white line illustrated books, young reader, middle reader: activity books, arts/craft, multicultural, science, health, how-to, reference, animal, history, nature/environment, special needs, social issues, supplemental educational materials. "Any manuscripts related to child development or with content-based activities and innovative strategies will be reviewed for possible publication." Recently published *If You Don't Feed the Teachers They Eat the Students!*, by Neila Connors.

How to Contact/Writers: Nonfiction: Submit outline/synopsis, sample chapters and SASE. Usually responds to queries/mss in 1 month. Responds to queries in 6 weeks; mss in 2 months. Typically publishes a book 18 months after acceptance. Will consider simultaneous submissions.

Illustration: Works with 2-6 illustrators/year. Responds in 1 month if reply requested (send SASE). Samples returned with SASE; samples filed. Need 4-color cover art; b&w line illustration for content.

Terms: Pays authors in royalties (5-10% based on wholesale price) or work purchased outright (range: $500-1,000). Pays illustrators by the project (range: $200-1,500). Pays photographers by the project. Original artwork not returned. Book catalog and ms and artist guidelines for SAE and $1.78 postage.

Tips: Writers: "We buy only educational teacher resource material that can be used by teachers and parents (home schoolers). Please do not submit fiction! Incentive Publications looks for a whimsical, warm style of illustration that respects the integrity and age of the child. We work primarily with local artists, but not exclusively."

☑ Ⓐ ◐ JALMAR PRESS, P.O. Box 1185, Torrance CA 90745-6329. (310)816-3085. Fax: (310)816-3092. E-mail: blwjalmar@att.net. Website: www.jalmarpress.com. Subsidiary of the B.L. Winch Group, Incorporated. Book publisher. Estab. 1971. **Acquisitions:** Bradley Winch, publisher; Cathy Winch, manager. Imprint: Personhood Press. Does not publish children's picture books or books for young readers. 10% of books by first-time authors. Publishes self-esteem (curriculum content related), character education, drug and alcohol abuse prevention, peaceful conflict resolution, stress management, virtues, whole-brain learning, accelerated learning and emotional intelligence materials for counselors, teachers, and other care givers. "Our goal is to empower children to become personally and socially responsible through activities presented by teachers, counselors and other caregivers that allow them to experience being both successful and responsible. Our titles are activity-driven and develop social, emotional and ethical skills that lead to academic achievements."

• Jalmar's catalog is found on their website. Jalmar is now the exclusive distributor for Innerchoice Publishing's entire line of school counselor-oriented material (K-12).

Fiction: All levels: self-concept, self-esteem. Does not want to see "children's fiction books that have to do with cognitive learning (as opposed to affective learning) and autobiographical work." Published *Hilde Knows: Someone Cries for the Children*, by Lisa Kent, illustrated by Mikki Macklen (child abuse); and *Scooter's Tail of Terror: A Fable of Addiction and Hope*, by Larry Shles (ages 5-105). "All submissions must teach (by metaphor) in the areas listed above."

Nonfiction: All levels: activity books to develop social, emotional and ethical skills. Does not want to see autobiographical work. Published *Esteem Builders Program*, by Michele Borba, illustrated by Bob Burchett (for school use—6 books, tapes, posters).

How to Contact/Writers: Interested in all materials. Fiction/Nonfiction: Submit complete ms. Responds to queries in 2 months; mss in 2 months. Publishes a book 12-18 months after acceptance. Will consider simultaneous submissions.

Illustration: Works with 2 illustrators/year. Responds in 1 week. Samples returned with SASE; samples filed.

Terms: Pays authors 7½-15% royalty based on net receipts. Average advance varies. Pays illustrators by the project on a bid basis. Pays photographers per photo on a bid basis. Book catalog/ms guidelines free on request.

Tips: Wants "thoroughly researched, tested, practical, activity-oriented, curriculum content and grade/level correlated books on self-esteem, peaceful conflict resolution, stress management, emotional intelligence, and whole brain learning and books bridging self-esteem to various 'trouble' areas, such as 'at risk,' 'dropout prevention,' etc. Illustrators—make artwork that can be reproduced. Emotional intelligence is becoming a 'hot' category, as is character education and morality-based education."

Ⓝ ◐ ▥ JAYJO BOOKS, L.L.C., P.O. Box 213, Valley Park MO 63088-0213. (636)861-1331. Fax: (636)861-2411. E-mail: jayjobooks@aol.com. Website: http://jayjo.com. Estab. 1993. Specializes in educational material. We are an independent book packager/producer. **Manuscript Acquisitions:** Laura Ditto. Publishes 3-5 picture books/year; 3-5 young readers/year. 30% of books by first-time authors. "Our goal is to provide quality children's health education through entertainment and teaching, while raising important funds for medical research and education."

Fiction: Picture books, young readers, middle readers, young adults: health, special needs, chronic conditions. Average word length: picture books—1,500; young readers—1,500; middle readers—1,500. Recently published *Trick-or-Treat for Diabetes*, by Kim Gosselin (ages 5-10); *Taking Cystic Fibrosis to School*, by Cynthia Henry (ages 5-10); *Taking Cerebral Palsy to School*, by Mary Elizabeth Anderson (ages 5-10).

Nonfiction: Picture books, young readers, middle readers: health, special needs, chronic conditions. Average word length: picture books—1,500; young readers—1,500; middle readers—1,500.

How to Contact/Writers: Fiction/Nonfiction: Submit complete ms. Responds in 1 month. Publishes a book 2 years after acceptance. Will consider simultaneous submissions.

Illustration: Works with 2 illustrators/year. Uses color artwork only. Illustrations only: Query with samples. Contact: Laura Ditto. Responds in 1 month. Samples returned with SASE; samples filed.

Terms: Work purchased outright from authors. Pays illustrators by the project. Book catalog available for #10 SAE and 1 first-class stamp. Manuscript guidelines for SASE.

Tips: "Review our books before submitting material to see if manuscript is applicable."

[N] JEWISH LIGHTS PUBLISHING, P.O. Box 237, Rt. 4, Sunset Farm Offices, Woodstock VT 05091. (802)457-4000. Fax: (802)457-4004. E-mail: everyone@longhillpartners.com. Website: www.jewishlights.com. A division of LongHill Partners, Inc. Book publisher. Imprint: Sky Light Paths Publishing. President: Stuart M. Matlins. **Manuscript Acquisitions:** Submissions Editor. **Art Acquisitions:** Bridget Taylor. Publishes 1 picture book/year; 1 young reader/year. 50% of books by first-time authors; 50% of books from agented authors. All books have spiritual/religious themes. "Jewish Lights publishes books for people of all faiths and all backgrounds who yearn for books that attract, engage, educate and spiritually inspire. Our authors are at the forefront of spiritual thought and deal with the quest for the self and for meaning in life by drawing on the Jewish wisdom tradition. Our books cover topics including history, spirituality, life cycle, children's, self-help, recovery, theology and philosophy. We do *not* publish autobiography, biography, fiction, *haggadot*, poetry or cookbooks. At this point we plan to do only two books for children annually, and that one will be for younger children (ages 4-10)."

Fiction: Picture books, young readers, middle readers: spirituality. "We are not interested in anything other than spirituality." Recently published *God Said Amen*, by Sandy Eisenberg Sasso, illustrated by Avi Katz (ages 4-9, picture book); and *For Heaven's Sake*, by Sandy Eisenberg Sasso, illustrated by Kathryn Kunz Finney (ages 8 and up).

Nonfiction: Picture book, young readers, middle readers: activity books, spirituality. Recently published *When a Grandparent Dies: A Kid's Own Remembering Workbook for Dealing with Shiva and the Year Beyond*, by Nechama Liss-Levinson, Ph.D. (ages 7-11); and *Sharing Blessings: Children's Stories for Exploring the Spirit of the Jewish Holidays*, written by Rabbi Michael Klayman and Rahel Musleah, illustrated by Mary O'Keefe Young (ages 6-10, picture book).

How to Contact/Writers: Fiction/Nonfiction: Query with outline/synopsis and 2 sample chapters; submit complete ms for picture books. Include SASE. Responds to queries/mss in 3-4 months. Publishes a book 6 months after acceptance. Will consider simultaneous submissions and previously published work.

Illustration: Works with 2 illustrators/year. Reviews ms/illustration packages from artists. Query. Illustrations only: Query with samples; provide résumé. Samples returned with SASE; samples filed.

Terms: Pays authors royalty of 10% of revenue received. Offers advances. Pays illustrators by the project or royalty. Pays photographers by the project. Sends galleys to authors; dummies to illustrators. Book catalog available for 6½×9½ SAE and 59¢ postage; ms guidelines available for SASE.

Tips: "Explain in your cover letter why you're submitting your project to *us* in particular. (Make sure you know what we publish.)"

[N] BOB JONES UNIVERSITY PRESS, 1500 Wade Hampton Blvd., Greenville SC 29614. (803)242-5100, ext. 4316. Website: www.bju.edu/press/freelnce.html. Book publisher. Estab. 1974. **Acquisitions:** Mrs. Nancy Lohr, editor. Publishes 4 young reader titles/year; 4 middle reader titles/year; and 4 young adult titles/year. 50% of books by first-time authors. "Our books reflect the highest Christian standards of thought, feeling, and action, are uplifting or instructive and enhance moral purity. Themes advocating secular attitudes of rebellion or material-ism are not acceptable. We are looking for books that present a fully developed main character, capable of dynamic changes, who experiences the central conflict of the plot, which should have plenty of action and not be didactic in tone."

Fiction: Young readers, middle readers, young adults: adventure, animal, concept, contemporary, easy-to-read, fantasy, history, multicultural, nature/environment, sports, spy/mystery. Average word length: young readers—10,000; middle readers—30,000; young adult/teens—50,000. Published *The Treasure of Pelican Cove*, by Milly Howard (grades 2-4, adventure story); and *Right Hand Man*, by Connie Williams (grades 5-8, contemporary).

Nonfiction: Young readers, middle readers: concept, history, multicultural. Young readers, middle readers, young adults: animal, biography, geography, nature/environment. Young adults/teens: biography, history, nature/environment. Average word length: young readers—10,000; middle readers—30,000; young adult/teens—50,000. Recently published *With Daring Faith*, by Becky Davis (grades 5-8, biography); and *Someday You'll Write*, by Elizabeth Yates (how-to).

How to Contact/Writers: Fiction: "Send the complete manuscript or the first five chapters and synopsis for these genres: Christian biography, modern realism, historical realism, regional realism and mystery/adventure. Query with a synopsis and five sample chapters for these genres: fantasy and science fiction (no extra-terrestrials). Do not send stories with magical elements. We do not publish these genres: romance, poetry and drama." Nonfiction: Query or submit complete ms or submit outline/synopsis and sample chapters. Responds to queries in 3 weeks; mss in 2 months. Publishes book "approximately one year" after acceptance. Will consider simultane-ous and electronic submissions via IBM-compatible disk or modem.

Illustration: Works with 4 illustrators/year. Responds only if interested. Samples returned with SASE; samples filed.

Terms: Pays authors royalty of 7-10% based on wholesale price. Or work purchased outright ($800-1,000). Pays illustrators by the project. Originals returned to artist at job's completion. Book catalog and ms guidelines free on request. Send SASE for book catalog and mss guidelines.

Tips: "Writers—give us original, well-developed characters in a suspenseful plot that has good moral tone. Artists—be good with both color and black & white illustrations. Be willing to take suggestions and follow specific directions. Today's books for children offer a wide variety of well-done nonfiction and rather shallow fiction. With the growing trend toward increased TV viewing, parents may be less interested in good books and less able to distinguish what is worthwhile. We are determined to continue to produce high-quality books for children."

JUST US BOOKS, INC., 356 Glenwood Ave., East Orange NJ 07017. (201)676-4345. Fax: (973)677-7570. Imprint of Afro-Bets Series. Book publisher; "for selected titles" book packager. Estab. 1988. Vice President/Publisher: Cheryl Willis Hudson. **Acquisitions:** Allyson Sherwood, submissions manager. Publishes 4-6 picture books/year; "projected 6" young reader/middle reader titles/year. 33% of books by first-time authors. Looking for "books that reflect a genuinely authentic African or African-American experience. We try to work with authors and illustrators who are from the culture itself."

● Just Us Books is not accepting new mss until further notice.

Fiction: Middle readers: adventure, contemporary, easy-to-read, history, multicultural (African-American themes), romance, suspense/mystery. Average word length: "varies" per picture book; young reader—500-2,000; middle reader—5,000. Wants African-American themes. Gets too many traditional African folktales. Recently published *Glo Goes Shopping* (picture book); *Dear Corinne: Tell Somebody*, by Mari Evans (middle readers).

Nonfiction: Middle readers, biography (African-American themes). Recently published *In Praise of Our Fathers and Our Mothers: A Black Family Treasury by Outstanding Authors and Artists*.

How to Contact/Writers: Fiction/Nonfiction: Query or submit outline/synopsis for proposed title. Responds to queries/ms in 3-4 months "or as soon as possible." Publishes a book 12-18 months after acceptance. Will consider simultaneous submissions (with prior notice).

Illustration: Works with 10 illustrators/year. Reviews ms/illustration packages from artists ("but prefers to review them separately"). "Query first." Illustrations only: Query with samples; send résumé, promo sheet, slides, client list, tearsheets; arrange personal portfolio review. Responds in 2-3 weeks. Samples returned with SASE; samples filed. Original artwork returned at job's completion "depending on project."

Photography: Purchases photos from freelancers. Buys stock and assigns work. Wants "African-American and multicultural themes—kids age 10-13 in school, home and social situations."

Terms: Pays authors royalty and some work for hire depending on project. Pays illustrators by the project or royalty, or flat fee based on project. Sends galleys to authors; dummies to illustrators. Book catalog for business-size SAE and 78¢ postage; ms/artist's guidelines for business-size SAE and 78¢ postage.

Tips: "Multicultural books are tops as far as trends go. There is a great need for diversity and authenticity here. They will continue to be in the forefront of children's book publishing until there is more balanced treatment on these themes industry wide." Writers: "Keep the subject matter fresh and lively. Avoid 'preachy' stories with stereotyped characters. Rely more on authentic stories with sensitive three-dimensional characters." Illustrators: "Submit 5-10 good, neat samples. Be willing to work with an art director for the type of illustration desired by a specific house and grow into larger projects."

KAEDEN BOOKS, P.O. Box 16190, Rocky River OH 44116-6190. (440)356-0030. Fax: (440)356-5081. E-mail: books@kaeden.com. Website: kaeden.com. Book publisher. **Acquisitions:** Creative Vice President. Publishes 40 young readers/year. 50% of books by first-time authors. "Kaeden Books produces high quality, pre-reader, emergent and early reader books for classroom and reading program educators."

Fiction: Young readers: adventure, animal, concept, contemporary, health, history, humor, multicultural, nature/environment, science fiction, sports, suspense/mystery. Average word length: picture books—20-150 words; young readers—20-150 words. Recently published *The Big Fish*, by Joe Yukish, illustated by Kate Salley Palmer; *Sammy Gets A Ride*, by Karen Evans and Kathleen Urmston, illustrated by Gloria Gedeon; and *Time for a Bath*, by Jan Mader, illustrated by Karen Maizel.

Nonfiction: Young readers: activity books, animal, biography, careers, geography, health, history, hobbies, how-to, multicultural, music/dance, nature/environment, religion, science, sports. Multicultural needs include group and character diversity in stories and settings. Average word length: picture books—20-150 words; young readers—20-150 words.

How to Contact/Writers: Fiction/nonfiction: Query or submit complete ms. Do not send original transcripts. Responds to mss in 1 year. Will consider simultaneous submissions, electronic submissions via disk or modem.

Illustration: Works with 30 illustrators/year. Reviews ms/illustration packages from artists. Query. Submit art samples in color. Can be photocopies or tearsheets. Illustrations only: Query with samples. Send résumé, promo sheet, tearsheets, photocopies of work, preferably in color. Responds only if interested. Samples are filed.

Terms: Work purchased outright from authors. "Royalties to our previous authors." Offers negotiable advances. Pays illustrators by the project (range: $50-150/page). Book catalog available for 8½×11 SAE and 2 first-class stamps.

Tips: "Our books are written for emergent and fluent readers to be used in the educational teaching environment. A strong correlation between text and visual is necessary along with creative and colorful juvenile designs."

KAMEHAMEHA SCHOOLS PRESS, 1887 Makuakane St., Honolulu HI 96817. (808)842-8880. Fax: (808)842-8875. E-mail: kspress@ksbe.edu. Website: www.ksbe.edu/pubs/KSPress/catalog.html. Estab. 1933. Specializes in educational and multicultural material. **Manuscript Acquisitions:** Henry Bennett. "Kamehameha Schools Press publishes in the areas of Hawaiian history, culture, language and studies."

Nonfiction: Middle readers, young adults: biography, history, multicultural, Hawaiian folklore. Recently published *Voyage from the Past*, by Julie Stewart Williams, illustrated by Robin Yoko Burningham (Polynesian explorers and canoe voyaging).

How to Contact/Writers: Query. Responds to queries in 2 months; mss in 3 months. Publishes a book 12-18 months after acceptance.

Illustration: Uses b&w artwork only. Illustrations only: Query with samples. Responds only if interested. Samples not returned.

Terms: Work purchased outright from authors. Pays illustrators by the project. Sends galleys to authors. Book catalog available for #10 SASE and 1 first-class stamp. All imprints included in a single catalog. Catalog available on website.

Tips: "Writers and illustrators *must* be knowledgeable in Hawaiian history/culture and be able to show credentials to validate their proficiency. Greatly prefer to work with writers/illustrators available in the Honolulu area."

KAR-BEN COPIES, INC., 6800 Tildenwood Lane, Rockville MD 20852-4371. (301)984-8733. Fax: (301)881-9195. E-mail: karben@aol.com. Website: www.karben.com. Book publisher. Estab. 1975. **Manuscript Acquisitions:** Madeline Wikler, vice president. Publishes 5-10 picture books/year; 20% of books by first-time authors. All of Kar-Ben Copies' books are on *Jewish themes for young children* and families.

Fiction: Picture books, young readers: adventures, concept, contemporary, fantasy, folktales, history, humor, multicultural, religion, special needs, suspense/mystery; *must be* on a Jewish theme. Average word length: picture books—2,000. Recently published *Once Upon a Shabbos*, by Jacqueline Jules; *Baby's Bris*, by Susan Wilkowski; *Too Many Cooks*, by Edie Zolkowe; and *The Magic of Kol Nidre*, by Bruce Siegel.

Nonfiction: Picture books, young readers: activity books, arts/crafts, biography, careers, concept, cooking, history, how-to, multicultural, religion, social issues, special needs; must be of Jewish interest. Average word length: picture books—2,000. Published *Jewish Holiday Games for Little Hands*, by Ruth Brinn; *Tell Me a Mitzvah*, by Danny Siegel; *All About Hanukkah*, and *Come Let Us Welcome Shabbat*, by Judith Grones and Madeline Wikler; and *My First Jewish Word Book*, by Roz Schanzer.

How to Contact/Writers: Fiction/nonfiction: Submit complete ms. Responds to queries/ms in 6 weeks. Publishes a book 1 year after acceptance. Will consider simultaneous submissions. "Story should be short, no more than 3,000 words."

Illustration: Works with 3-4 illustrators/year. Prefers "four-color art in any medium that is scannable." Reviews ms/illustration packages from artists. Submit whole ms and sample of art (no originals). Illustrations only: Submit tearsheets, photocopies, promo sheet or anything representative that does *not* need to be returned. "Submit samples which show skill in children's book illustration." Enclose SASE for response. Responds to art samples in 2 weeks.

Terms: Pays authors in royalties of 8-10% based on wholesale price or work purchased outright (range: $500-2,000). Offers advance (average amount: $1,000). Pays illustrators royalty of 8-10% based on wholesale price or by the project (range: $500-3,000). Sends galleys to authors. Original artwork returned at job's completion. Book catalog free on request. Ms guidelines for 9×12 SAE and 2 first-class stamps.

Tips: Looks for "books for young children with Jewish interest and content, modern, non-sexist, not didactic. Fiction or nonfiction with a *Jewish* theme—can be serious or humorous, life cycle, Bible story, or holiday-related."

KEY PORTER BOOKS, 70 The Esplanade, Toronto, Ontario M5E 1R2 Canada. (416)862-7777. Fax: (416)862-2304. Book publisher. **Manuscript Acquisitions:** Susan Renouf, editor-in-chief. Publishes 4 picture books/year; and 4 young readers/year. 30% of books by first-time authors.

Fiction: Young readers, middle readers, young adult: animal, anthology, concept, health, multicultural, nature/environment, science fiction, special needs, sports, suspense/mystery. Does not want to see religious material. Average word length: picture books—1,500; young readers—5,000.

Nonfiction: Picture books: animal, history, nature/environment, reference, science. Middle readers: animal, careers, history, nature/environment, reference, science and sports. Average word length: picture books—1,500;

insider report

Illustrator/teacher offers lessons on creating picture books

Paul Yalowitz

Paul Yalowitz is an expert on two things—picture book illustration and cows. Well, "cow expert" might be a little strong. Cows are more of an underlying theme in his life. "It all started when I was giving my brother a birthday present. I was short on time, and I didn't have any wrapping paper, so I drew cow spots on the big white boxes with a magic marker." Yalowitz later decorated kitchen cabinets and walls in cow spots, recovered his sofa in cow-inspired fabric, and even bought a house next to a cow pasture.

The cows outside his window served as inspiration for the many cows Yalowitz drew for his books *Nell Nugget and the Cow Caper* (by Judith Ross Enderle and Stephanie Gordon Tessler, Simon & Schuster) and *Moonstruck: The True Story of the Cow Who Jumped Over the Moon* (by Gennifer Choldenko, Hyperion). In *Nell Nugget* there are several pages featuring forty-nine cows! "I like to make problems for myself," he says. "That was my doing. No one told me I had to draw all forty-nine cows."

Yalowitz works in colored pencil. His style is soft and textural and distinctively his own. Among his other books are *Somebody Loves You, Mr. Hatch* and *Boy, Can He Dance!* (both by Eileen Spinelli, Simon & Schuster), *Mary Veronica's Egg* (by Mary Nethery, Orchard), and his latest, *The Runaway Latkes* (by Leslie Kimmelman, Albert Whitman).

In addition to illustrating picture books for more than a decade, Yalowitz, who graduated from the School of Visual Arts in New York (www.schoolofvisualarts.edu), is an instructor at the Ringling School of Art and Design (www.rsad.edu) in Sarasota, Florida, where the transplanted New Yorker teaches classes in children's book illustration, among other illustration courses. Sit in on Children's Book Illustration 101 as he shares his insights and advice.

Tell me about the classes you teach. What are they like?
In the classroom, I want the students to enjoy what they're doing, otherwise it becomes a job. I try to mix things up on them. I invent class activities, like a kind of Pictionary ® game, where we split up into groups and compete against each other. I feel that helps them think fast and draw fast and communicate. I like to throw them curveballs every once in a while. I give regular assignments, or I'll give out a story or an article for them to illustrate, pretty straightforward. And then I'll do something that's a little bit different, like I'll give them each a bottle of hot sauce, and they have to come up with a hot sauce advertisement.

When you teach children's book illustration, what kinds of projects do you assign to your students?
I split it into three major parts. The first part is a twenty-four-page book. I give them traditional stories like *The Gingerbread Man* and *Jack and the Beanstalk*, and they do a storyboard, character sketches, thumbnails, all the development, and then maybe three pages of finished illustrations.

After that we do book jackets. I give a different fictional title to each student, and they have to write a paragraph about what that book is about, then come up with a jacket illustration. I give them things vague enough, like "Hot Dog and Cool Cat," "The Unexpected Guest," "The Neighbors," and "Omar's Big Trip." There's freedom, but it's tight enough for them to come up with something within the boundaries of the particular title.

The last project we do is a thirty-two-page book, which is anything they want to do. They can write their own story. They can use a song, or they can re-illustrate an existing story. For that, we do a full dummy and maybe four pages of finished artwork.

When you illustrated *Boy, Can He Dance!*, you added your own twist to the ending of the story. How much is an illustrator a storyteller just as a writer is?

It's more than just taking the words and illustrating exactly what they say. Everyone has his own interpretation of a story. As long as it doesn't change the story or take away from the story, I see nothing wrong with, say, throwing in a pet and letting it become a continuing joke for the reader throughout the book to watch the dog or cat to see what they're doing.

For example in *Moonstruck*, the story of the cow who jumped over the moon, the poem says, "The dish ran away with the spoon." I put all the animals in that poem in the illustrations for the story, and I had the dish run away with the spoon. But I didn't want them to run away at the beginning of the book, so I had them run away on the back of a turtle. In every picture, you can see them trying to make their escape.

It's fun for me, it's fun for the reader if you can add a little more and give your own slant and humor to it. Sometimes you can fiddle with the story slightly. In *Boy, Can He Dance!*, we wanted the story to build, so we changed the order of some of the mishaps so each one was a little bit wilder than the previous ones. The story kind of just ended with the father being proud of his son for dancing. We added a line at the end where the father finally says, "Boy, can he dance." Through the whole book, the father was kind of fighting the son's dancing. At the end he finally accepted it and found out his son really had talent, and now was proud of him. That little line helped prove the father was proud of his son.

What did you draw for that last scene?

That father was a chef at a hotel. He took his son to the restaurant with him to teach him how to be a chef. Every time he'd give the boy a chore, the boy would mess up and start dancing. At that particular hotel, they have shows and parties. The owner of the hotel came in and said one of the dancers was sick, so the boy volunteered to be a dancer. I made the show all about being a chef. So the boy ended up being a chef after all, and I took the things from earlier scenes and made the boy dance with carrots, potatoes, lemons. That was a surprise to the author.

How did you come to work in colored pencil? How do you achieve the softness along with the texture?

Growing up, pencils were a big thing to draw with. I did a lot of monsters and dinosaurs and aliens and space ships. When I went to school, I had to change those aliens and monsters into people. I still draw characters with olive-shaped heads, and they're still not quite realistic. In school, I tried all different kinds of media—I did paint and pastels and pen-and-ink—but I just kept going back to the pencil. I felt more comfortable with the pencil and just kept getting better with it.

First I do the whole illustration in black and white with a regular drawing pencil, then go over it with colored pencil. It's almost like glazing with oil paint. There are layers of different colors. I don't press hard with the pencil, so it's a very soft building of layers. That's where the texture comes from, even though it's very smooth paper. Doing the black layer first gives it the consistency throughout, so everything in the picture has some of the same color or tone in it.

When you teach a children's book illustration class, do you cover marketing, putting together promo pieces, etc.?

It's an ongoing discussion. We discuss the field and how varied it is now and different ways of trying to break into it. We talk about things to put in a portfolio and about contracts. In the course I want to get them used to what editors and art directors expect from them—creating a dummy, finished artwork, sketches, thumbnails, character sketches. I even have a "Clay Day"

Paul Yalowitz's unique colored-pencil illustration style offers interesting perspectives, soft backgrounds and lots of detail as in this illustration from *Mary Veronica's Egg*, written by Mary Nethery. Yalowitz draws his scenes in black and white, then tops his initial drawing with a layer of colored pencil thus achieving depth and texture.

where we create the main character in three dimensions to use for sketching, to see the character and turn it and light it different ways.

Is taking a class something you'd recommend to an artist interested in doing children's books?

I think it would help. There are a lot of misconceptions out there about how it works. People don't know how much the editor and art director really work with the artist and writer. Also, they think they have to have finished illustrations for the whole book. I tell them to submit just a dummy, and at the most two or three copies of finished pieces, because chances are the editor and art director are going to change things anyway.

You have to know about spacing and spreads and spots. A class would really help you with that. Everyone thinks you have to have words on every page, you have to show everything that's in the story. You can't. You edit things out, and you design it in an interesting way, not just picture-words-picture-words.

What's your advice for someone who wants to make a living illustrating picture books?

First, don't limit yourself. Don't just go for children's books and make that it. You have to keep an open mind. You don't know what's going to lead to what. Just getting your work seen is the best thing you can do. Every piece you do is an advertisement for yourself. You have to think of it that way. And be persistent. Children's books is one of the hardest illustration fields to get into. Don't give up after you've gotten your first, second, third, tenth, twentieth "no." You've just got to be at the right place at the right time.

You have such a recognizable style. Is that something you recommend to other illustrators? In a portfolio, should an illustrator stick with one distinct style?

I think if you want to go into freelancing, your work should stand out. You want to do work that no one else can do, and that's why editors and art directors will call you. I don't think it would hurt to have two or three styles at the most if you're good at, say, pen and ink and watercolor, there's no reason you have to only do one over the other.

Style is funny. You get to a certain point, and you just say, "This is the way I'm gonna draw," and that's where it stops.

In doing picture books, I would think consistency is important. If Kevin Henkes suddenly started doing funky mice instead of cute mice, it might cause a ruckus. When you get to a certain point, do you get stuck?

There are a couple different pressures. There's one that you have to keep doing the same thing because that's what people expect. Then there's the pressure that you have to change, otherwise it gets stale for you. I equate it a lot with acting. There are actors who do the same kind of roles over and over and get known for that.

I've been doing this kind of style for fifteen years now. I can look back at the beginning and see how it's slowly changed. Other people like to do an abrupt change—it's either revolution or evolution. I'm more of an evolutionist. And I think teaching keeps me fresh and open to new ideas and exposed to a lot of new work.

—Alice Pope

middle readers—15,000. Recently published *How on Earth: A Question and Answer Book About How Animals & Plants Live*, by Ron Orenstein (ages 8-10, nature/environment); *Super Skaters: World Figure Skating Stars*, by Steve Milton (ages 8 and up, sports); and *The Seven Chairs*, by Helen Lanteigne (ages 4-8).

How to Contact/Writers: Only interested in agented material from Canadian writers; *no unsolicited mss.*

Photography: Buys photos from freelancers. Buys stock and assigns work. Captions required. Uses 35mm transparencies. Submit cover letter, résumé, duplicate slides, stock photo list.

A KINGFISHER, Imprint of Larousse Kingfisher Chambers, 95 Madison Ave., New York NY 10016. (212)686-1060. Fax: (212)686-1082. Website: www.lkcpub.com.

● Kingfisher is not currently accepting unsolicited mss. All solicitations must be made by a recognized literary agent.

✓ ALFRED A. KNOPF BOOKS FOR YOUNG READERS, 1540 Broadway, New York NY 10036. (212)782-9000. Website: www.randomhouse.com/kids. Imprint of Random House Children's Books. Publishing Director: Simon Boughton. Vice-President, Editor-at-Large: Janet Schulman. Associate Publishing Director: Andrea Cascardi. Executive Art Director: Isabel Warren-Lynch. Senior Editors: Tracy Gates, Nancy Siscoe. **Acquisitions:** send mss to Knopf Editorial Department. 90% of books published through agents. "Knopf is known for high quality literary fiction and is willing to take risks with writing styles. It publishes for children ages 5 and up."

Fiction: All levels: considers all categories. Recently published *Stargirl*, by Jerry Spinelli; *The Golden Compass*, *The Subtle Knife* and *The Amber Spyglass*, all by Philip Pullman; *Spirit of Endurance*, by Jennifer Armstrong; and *And to Think That We Thought We'd Never Be Friends*, by Mary Hoberman.

How to Contact/Writers: Fiction/nonfiction: Accepts unsolicited mss. Publishes a book 12-18 months after acceptance. Will consider simultaneous submissions, but must be included as such. All mss must be accompanied by a SASE. Responds to queries/mss in 6 months.

Illustration: Reviews ms/illustration packages from artists through agent only. Illustration only: Contact: Art Director. Responds only if interested. Samples returned with SASE; samples filed.

Terms: Pays authors in royalties. Pays illustrators and photographers by the project or royalties. Original artwork returned at job's completion. Book catalog and ms guidelines free on request with 9×12 SASE and 4 first-class stamps.

LEE & LOW BOOKS, INC., 95 Madison Ave., New York NY 10016-7801. (212)779-4400. Website: www.leea ndlow.com. Book publisher. Estab. 1991. **Acquisitions:** Philip Lee, publisher; Louise May, senior editor. Publishes 12-14 picture books/year. 50% of books by first-time authors. Lee & Low publishes only picture books with multicultural themes. "Our goal is to discover new talent and produce books that reflect the multicultural society in which we live."

● Lee & Low Books is dedicated to publishing culturally authentic literature. The company makes a special effort to work with writers and artists of color and encourages new voices.

Fiction: Picture books: concept. Picture books, young readers: anthology, contemporary, history, multicultural, poetry. "We are not considering folktales, animal stories and chapter books." Picture book, middle reader: contemporary, history, multicultural, nature/environment, poetry, sports. Average word length: picture books— 1,000-1,500 words. Recently published *Ten Oni Drummers*, by Matthew Gollub, illustrated by Kazuko G. Stone (ages 2-6, picture book); and *Grandma's Purple Flowers*, written and illustrated by Adjoa J. Burrowes..

Nonfiction: Picture books: concept. Picture books, middle readers: biography, history, multicultural, science and sports. Average word length: picture books—1,500. Recently published *Crazy Horse's Vision*, by Joseph Bruchac, illustrated by S.D. Nelson (age 6 and up, picture book).

How to Contact/Writers: Fiction/Nonfiction: Submit complete ms. Responds in 4 months. Publishes a book 12-24 months after acceptance. Will consider simultaneous submissions.

Illustration: Works with 10-12 illustrators/year. Uses color artwork only. Reviews ms/illustration packages from artists. Submit ms with dummy. Illustrations only: Query with samples, résumé, promo sheet and tearsheets. Responds only if interested. Samples returned with SASE; samples filed. Original artwork returned at job's completion.

Photography: Buys photos from freelancers. Works on assignment only. Model/property releases required. Submit cover letter, résumé, promo piece and book dummy.

Terms: Pays authors royalty. Offers advances. Pays illustrators royalty plus advance against royalty. Photographers paid royalty plus advance against royalty. Sends galleys to authors; proofs to illustrators. Book catalog available for 9×12 SAE and $1.43 postage; ms and art guidelines available via website or with SASE with 33¢ postage.

Tips: "We strongly urge writers to familiarize themselves with our list before submitting. Materials will only be returned with SASE."

✓ LEGACY PRESS, Imprint of Rainbow Publishers, P.O. Box 261129, San Diego CA 92196. (858)271-7600. Book publisher. Estab. 1997. **Manuscript/Art Acquisitions:** Christy Allen, editor. Publishes 3 young readers/

year; 3 middle readers/year; 3 young adult titles/year. Published nonfiction, Bible-teaching books. "We publish growth and development books for the evangelical Christian—from a non-denominational viewpoint—that may be marketed primarily through Christian bookstores."

Nonfiction: Young readers, middle readers, young adults: reference, religion. Recently published *God's Girls* (devotions and crafts for girls age 9-12) and *Gotta Have God* (3-book series of devotionals for boys ages 2-12) both illustrated by Aline Heiser.

How to Contact/Writers: Nonfiction: Submit outline/synopsis and 3-5 sample chapters. Responds to queries in 6 weeks; on ms in 3 months. Publishes a book 18 months after acceptance. Will consider simultaneous submissions and previously published work.

Illustration: Works with 5 illustrators/year. Reviews ms/illustration packages from artists. Submit ms with 5-10 pieces of final art. Illustrations only: Query with samples to be kept on file. Responds in 6 weeks. Samples returned with SASE.

Terms: Pays authors royalty or work purchased outright. Offers advances. Pays illustrators by the project. Sends galley to authors. Book catalog available for business size SASE; ms guidelines for SASE.

Tips: "Get to know the Christian bookstore market. We are looking for innovative ways to teach and encourage children about the Christian life. No fiction, please."

LERNER PUBLICATIONS CO., 241 First Ave. N., Minneapolis MN 55401. (612)332-3344. Fax: (612)332-7615. Website: www.lernerbooks.com. Book publisher. Estab. 1959. **Manuscript Acquisitions:** Jennifer Zimian, submissions editor. Primarily nonfiction for readers of all grade levels. List includes titles encompassing nature, geography, natural and physical science, current events, ancient and modern history, world art, special interest, sports, world cultures, and numerous biography series. Some YA and middle grade fiction.

How to Contact/Writers: Submissions are accepted in the months of March and October only. The Lerner Publishing Group does not publish alphabet books, puzzle books, song books, textbooks, workbooks, religious subject matter or plays. Work received in any month other than March or October will be returned unopened. An SASE is required for authors who wish to have their materials returned. Please allow 2-6 months for a response. No phone calls please.

□ ❧ ✓ LIGHTWAVE PUBLISHING, Bold Lightwave Publishing Inc., 26275 98th Ave., Maple Ridge, British Columbia V2W 1K3 Canada. (604)462-7890. Fax: (604)462-8208. E-mail: christie@lightwavepublishing. com. Website: www.lightwavepublishing.com. Estab. 1991. Independent book packager/producer specializing in Christian material. **Text Director:** Christie Bowler. **Art Director:** Terry Van Roon. Publishes over 30 titles/year. "Our mission is helping parents pass on their Christian faith to their children."

Fiction: Picture books: religion adventure, concept. Young readers: concept, religion. Middle readers: adventure, religion. Young adults: religion.

Nonfiction: Picture books, young readers: activity books, concept, religion. Middle readers, young adults: concept, religion. Average word length: young readers—2,000; middle readers—20,000; young adults—30,000. Recently published *I Want to Know About the Ten Commandments*, by R. Osborne and K. Christie Bowler (ages 8-12, religion, teaching); *Your Child and The Christian Life*, by R. Osborne with Christie Bowler (family, religion, teaching); *107 Questions Children Ask About Prayer*, by R. Osborne et al (ages 8-12, Q&A religion, teaching).

How to Contact/Writers: Fiction/Nonfiction: Does not accept unsolicited mss. Only interested in writers who will work for hire. Query. Responds to queries in 6 weeks; mss in 2 months. Publishes book 1 year after acceptance.

Illustration: Works with 5-10 illustrators/year. Reviews ms/illustration packages from artists. Submit ms "any way the artist wants to." Contact: Terry Van Roon, art director. Responds only if interested. Samples not returned; samples filed.

Photography: Buys stock and assigns work. Model/property releases required. Uses color prints and digital.

Terms: Work purchased outright from authors. Amount varies. Pays illustrators by the project. Amount varies. Pays photographers by the project. Amount varies. Book catalog available for SASE (Canadian postage or IRC). Writer's guidelines available for SASE (Canadian postage or IRC). Catalog available on website.

Tips: "We only do work-for-hire writing illustrating. We have our own projects and ideas then find writers and illustrators to help create them. No royalties. Interested writers and illustrators are welcome to contact us. Please don't put U.S. stamps on SASE."

✓ ▢ LINNET BOOKS, Imprint of The Shoe String Press Inc., 2 Linsley St., North Haven CT 06473-2517. (203)239-2702. Fax: (203)239-2568. E-mail: sspbooks@aol.com. Website: www.shoestringpress.com or www.linnetbooks.com. Estab. 1952. Specializes in nonfiction, educational material, multicultural material. **Manuscript Acquisitions:** Diantha C. Thorpe. Imprints: Linnet Books, Linnet Professional Publications, Archon Books—Diantha C. Thorpe, acquisitions for all. Publishes 8-10 middle readers/year.

Nonfiction: Young readers: activity books, animal. Middle readers: animal, biography, geography, history, multicultural, music/dance, nature/environment, reference, science. Young adults: animal, biography, geography, history, multicultural, nature/environment, reference. Recently published *The Round Book: Rounds Kids Love to Sing*, by Margaret Read MacDonald (all ages); *Angelina Grimké: Voice of Abolition*, by Ellen H. Todras (junior high, high school); *The New African Americans*, by Brent Ashabranner (middle school).

How to Contact/Writers: Nonfiction: Query or submit outline/synopsis and 3 sample chapters. Responds to queries in 6 weeks; mss in 4 months. Publishes a book 1 year after acceptance. Will consider simultaneous submissions "only if, when we indicate serious interest, the author withdraws from other publishers."
Illustration: Uses b&w artwork only. Illustrations only: Query with samples. "We keep on file—send only disposable ones."
Photography: Buys stock. "We keep work on file, but generally our authors are responsible for photo illustrations." Uses 5×7 glossy b&w prints. Send "anything that tells us what you specialize in."
Terms: Pays authors variable royalty. Offers advances. Sends galleys to authors; dummies to illustrators. Book catalog available for 9×12 SASE.

✅ Ⓐ **LITTLE, BROWN AND COMPANY CHILDREN'S BOOKS,** Three Center Plaza, Boston MA 02108-2084. (617)227-0730. Website: www.LittleBrown.com. Book publisher. Estab. 1837. Editorial Director: Maria Modugno. Editor: Megan Tingley. Editorial Coordinator: Jamie Michalak. Art Director: Sheila Smallwood.
Art Acquisitions: Adrienne Wetmore. Publishes picture books, board books, pop-up and lift-the-flap editions, chapter books and general fiction and nonfiction titles for middle and young adult readers.

- Little, Brown does not accept unsolicited mss. In fall 2000, the publisher announced the launch of a new imprint, Megan Tingley Books. The first five titles in editor Megan Tingley's line are *The Feelings Book* and *Underwear Do's and Don'ts*, both by Todd Parr; *The Book of Bad Ideas*, by Laura Huliska-Beith; *Who Took the Cookies from the Jar?*, by Bonnie Lass & Philemon Sturges, illustrated by Ashley Wolff; and *Bravo Maurice*, by Rebecca Bond.

Fiction: Picture books: adventure, animal, contemporary, fantasy, folktales, history, humor, multicultural, nature/environment. Young adults: contemporary, health, humor, multicultural, nature/environment, suspense/mystery. Multicultural needs include "any material by, for and about minorities." Average word length: picture books—1,000; young readers—6,000; middle readers—15,000-25,000; young adults—20,000-40,000. Recently published *Tinker and Tom and the Star Baby*, by David McPhail (ages 4-8, picture book); *Miss Mary Mack*, by Mary Ann Hoberman (ages 4-8, picture book); and *Romance of the Snob Squad*, by Julie Anne Peters (ages 10 and up, young adult fiction).
Nonfiction: Picture books: nature/environment, sciences. Middle readers: arts/crafts, biography, history, multicultural, nature, self help, social issues, sports. Young adults: multicultural, self-help, social issues. Average word length: picture books—2,000; young readers—4,000-6,000; middle readers—15,000-25,000; young adults—20,000-40,000. Recently published *Exploring the Deep, Dark Sea*, by Gail Gibbons (ages 4 and up, nonfiction); and *The Girl's Guide to Life*, by Catherine Dee (ages 10 and up, nonfiction).
How to Contact/Writers: Only interested in agented material. Fiction: Submit complete ms. Nonfiction: Submit cover letter, previous publications, a proposal, outline and 3 sample chapters. Do not send originals. Responds to queries in 2 weeks. Responds to mss in 2 months.
Illustration: Works with 55 illustrators/year. Illustrations only: Query art director with samples; provide résumé, promo sheet or tearsheets to be kept on file. Responds to art samples in 2 months. Original artwork returned at job's completion.
Photography: Works on assignment only. Model/property releases required; captions required. Publishes photo essays and photo concept books. Uses 35mm transparencies. Photographers should provide résumé, promo sheets or tearsheets to be kept on file.
Terms: Pays authors royalties based on retail price. Pays illustrators and photographers by the project or royalty based on retail price. Sends galleys to authors; dummies to illustrators. Artist's and writer's guidelines for SASE.
Tips: "Publishers are cutting back their lists in response to a shrinking market and relying more on big names and known commodities. In order to break into the field these days, authors and illustrators research their competition and try to come up with something outstandingly different."

LITTLE FRIEND PRESS, 28 New Driftway, Scituate MA 02066. (781)545-1025. Estab. 1994. **Manuscript Acquisitions:** Lynne Finnegan. Publishes 2-3 picture books/year. 50% of books by first-time authors. "Several years ago a grandmother knit her grandson a special sweater that had a secret pocket knit inside. In that pocket she placed a Little Friend that stimulated the imagination of her grandson and established Little Friend Press. We are committed to providing a variety of merchandise and books to enhance the enjoyment and imagination that inspired the original Little Friend concept."
Fiction: Average word length: picture books—24-32 pages. Recently published *The Wishing Star*, by Diane R. Houghton (ages 3-7, rewards of friendship, picture book); *Aliens Took My Child*, by Mr. Hendersen (ages 3-7, humorous account of a toddler's busy day, picture book); and *What's Behind The Bump?* by Mr. Hendersen (ages 3-7, a child's perception of a mother's pregnancy).

THE SUBJECT INDEX, located in the back of this book, lists book publishers and magazines according to the fiction and nonfiction subjects they seek.

Nonfiction: Average word length: picture books—24-32 pages. Recently published *My Little Friend Goes to School*, by Evelyn M. Finnegan (ages 3-7, account of first day nursery/kindergarten).

How to Contact/Writers: Not accepting unsolicited mss for 2001 due to a large volume of submissions. Publishes a book 1 year after acceptance.

Illustration: Works with 2-3 illustrators/year. Uses color artwork only. Reviews ms/illustration packages from artists. Send résumé, promotional literature and tearsheets. Contact: Lynne Finnegan. Responds only if interested. Samples kept on file.

Terms: Pays authors royalty. Pays illustrators by the project or royalty. Sends galleys to authors; dummies to illustrators. Originals returned to artist at job's completion. Book catalog available. Writer's guidelines for SASE. All imprints included in a single catalog.

LOBSTER PRESS, 1250 René-Lévesque Blvd. W., Suite 2200, Montréal, Quebec H3B 4W8 Canada. (514)989-3121. Fax: (514)989-3168. E-mail: tompkins@lobsterpress.com. Website: www.lobsterpress.com. Estab. 1997. Manuscript and Art Acquisitions: Kathy Tompkins (fiction; Bob Kirner (nonfiction). Publishes 4 picture books/year; 4 young reader/year. Encourages books by first-time authors.

Fiction: Picture books, young readers, middle readers: adventure, animal, contemporary, health, history, multicultural, special needs, sports, suspense/mystery. Average word length: picture books—200-1,000. Recently published *From Poppa*, by Anne Carter, illustrated by Kasia Charko; *How Cold Was It*, by Jane Barclay, illustrated by Janice Donato; *Smarty Pants*, by Colleen Syder, illustrated by Suzane Lanelois.

Nonfiction: Young readers, middle readers and adults/teens: animal, biography, careers, geography, health, history, hobbies, how-to, multicultural, nature/environment, references, science, self-help, social issues, sports, travel. Average word length: middle readers—40,000. Recently published *The Lobster Kids' Guide to Exploring Montréal*, by John Symon; *The Lobster Kids' Guide to Exploring Ottawa-Hull*, by John Symon.

How to Contact/Writers: Fiction: submit complete ms. Nonfiction: submit complete ms or submit outline/ synopsis and 2 sample chapters. Responds to queries in 2 months; mss in 6 months. Publishes a book 18 months after acceptance.

Illustration: Works with 5 illustrators/year. Uses line drawings and color artwork. Reviews ms/illustration packages from artists. Query with samples. Contact: Kathy Tompkins, acquisitions editor. Illustrations only: query with samples. Contact: Kathy Tompkins, acquisitions editor. Samples not returned; samples kept on file.

Terms: Pays authors 5-10% royalty based on retail price. Offers advances (average amount: $750-1,000). Pays illustrators by the project (range: $1,000-2,000) or 2-7% royalty based on retail price. Sends galleys to authors; dummies to illustrators. Originals returned to artist at job's completion. Writer's and artist's guidelines available for SASE.

Tips: "Do not send manuscripts or samples registered mail or with fancy envelopes or bows and ribbons— everything is received and treated equally. Please do not call and ask for an appointment. We do not meet with anyone unless we are going to use their work."

LORENZ BOOKS, Imprint of Anness Publishing, Inc.
• This publisher does not accept submissions from writers in the U.S.

LOWELL HOUSE JUVENILE/ROXBURY PARK JUVENILE, 2020 Avenue of the Stars, Suite 300, Los Angeles CA 90067. (310)552-7555. Fax: (310)552-7573. Book publisher, independent book producer/packager. **Manuscript Acquisitions:** Michael Artenstein, editor-in-chief, Roxbury Park Juvenile; Brenda Pope-Ostrow, editorial director, Lowell House Juvenile. **Art Acquisitions:** Brenda Pope-Ostrow and Bret Perry. Publishes 2-4 picture books/year; 30 young readers/year; 60 middle readers/year; 5 young adult titles/year. 25% of books by first-time authors. Lowell House Juvenile is best known for its trade workbooks, especially The Gifted & Talented series and its many science titles. Roxbury Park Juvenile specializes in middle grade fiction, and sports, science, and classics for midgraders and young adults.
• Lowell House does not accept mss. Instead they generate ideas in-house then find writers to work on projects.

Fiction: Middle readers, young adults: adventure, anthology, contemporary, nature/environment, problem novels, multicultural, suspense, sports. Recently published *Qwan: the Showdown*, by A.L. Kim, cover art by Richard Kirk (ages 13 and up action novel); *Rafters*, by Nilsson Honnelly (ages 7-10, an adventure novel); *Classic Ghost Stories*; illustrated by Barbara Kiwak (ages 13 and up, collection of short scary stories); and *Shadows*, by Jonathan Schmidt (ages 10-14).

Nonfiction: Picture books, young readers: activity books, educational, arts/crafts. Middle readers: activity books, arts/crafts, social issues, multicultural, concept, cooking, geography, health, history, hobbies, reference, religion, science, sports. Young adult/teen: multicultural, reference, science, social issues, sports. Recently published *The Ultimate Soccer Almanac*, by Dan Woog (ages 10 and up); *Gifted & Talented Word Workbook for Preschoolers*, by Martha Cheney, illustrated by Kara Kaminski (ages 3-5); *101 Things Every Kid Should Know About Science*, by Samantha Beres (ages 8-12).

How to Contact/Writers: Responds to queries/mss in 1 month.

Illustration: Works with 75 illustrators/year. Send samples to give a feel for style. Include sample drawings with kids in them. Illustrations only: arrange personal portfolio review; send promo sheet, portfolio, tearsheets. Responds only if interested. Samples returned with SASE; files samples.

Photography: Buys stock and assigns work. "We're not looking for more photographers at this time."
Terms: Payment decided on project-by-project basis. Authors are paid $1,000-5,000 for outright purchase. Illustrators paid by the project ($100-1,000). Photographers paid by the project ($50-1,000).
Tips: "Send art: lots of drawings of kids, samples to keep on file. Don't be afraid to send b&w art—never see enough junior-high-aged kids! Editorial: We are interested in writing samples to lead to future jobs, but we do not accept manuscripts, preferring to generate ideas ourselves."

THE LUTTERWORTH PRESS, Imprint of James Clarke & Co. Ltd., P.O. Box 60, Cambridge England CB1 2NT. (01223)350865. Fax: (01223)366951. E-mail: publishing@lutterworth. Website: www.lutterworth.com. Book publisher. **Acquisitions:** Adrian Brink, managing director.
Fiction: All levels: adventure, animal, folktales, health, history, nature/environment, religion. Recently published *Whoever You Are* and *The Thought That Counts*, by J.J. Overell, illustrations by Robin Lawrie; *What Is God Like*, by Marie Agnés Gaudrat, illustrated by Ulises Wensell; *Carol Corsa and Mickey Morgan*, by Claire Rosemary Jane, illustrated by Robert Hutchison.
Nonfiction: All levels: activity books, animal, arts/crafts, history, nature/environment, religion, science.
How to Contact/Writers: Fiction/Nonfiction: Submit outline/synopsis and 1 or 2 sample chapters. Responds to queries in 2 weeks; ms in 6 months.
Illustration: Reviews ms illustration packages from authors. Submit ms with color or b&w copies of illustration. Illustration only: Query with samples. Responds in 3 weeks. Samples returned with SASE; samples filed.
Photography: "Occasionally" buys photos from freelancers. Send résumé and samples. Works on assignment only.
Terms: Royalty negotiable. Book catalog available for SAE.

MAGINATION PRESS, 750 First Street NE, Washington DC 20002-2984. Website: www.maginationpress.com. Book publisher. **Acquisitions:** Darcie Conner Johnston, managing editor. Publishes up to 15 picture books and young reader titles/year. "We publish books dealing with the psycho/therapeutic treatment or resolution of children's serious problems and psychological issues, many written by mental health professionals."
  • Magination Press is an imprint of the American Psychological Association. Turn to First Books on page 70 to read about two Magination Press authors: Jeanie Ransom and her book *I Don't Want to Talk About It*, and Gloria Lowell and her book *Elana's Ears*.
Fiction: Picture books, young readers, middle readers, young adult/teens: concept, health, mental health, multicultural, special needs. Recently published *My Grandma's the Mayor*, by Marjorie Pellegrino (ages 6-12); *The Very Lonely Bathtub*, by Ann Rasmussen (ages 3-7); *I Don't Know Why . . . I Guess I'm Shy*, by Barbara Cain (ages 4-8); *I Don't Have an Uncle Phil Anymore*, by Marjorie Pellegrino (ages 4-11); *Tibby Tried It*, by Sharon and Ernie Useman (ages 3-7); *Sam and Gram and Their First Day of School*, by Dianne Blomberg (ages 4-6).
Nonfiction: Picture books, young readers: concept, health, mental health, multicultural, psychotherapy, self-help, social issues, special needs.
How to Contact/Writers: Fiction/nonfiction: Submit complete ms or query. Responds to queries/mss in 6 months. Materials returned only with a SASE. Publishes a book 12-18 months after acceptance.
Illustration: Works with 10-15 illustrators/year. Reviews ms/illustration packages. Will review artwork for future assignments. We keep all samples on file.
How to Contact/Illustrators: Illustrations only: Query with samples. Original artwork returned at job's completion.
Terms: Pays authors 5-15% in royalties based on receipts minus returns. Pays illustrators by the project. Book catalog and ms guidelines on request with SASE.

MARGARET K. McELDERRY BOOKS, 1230 Sixth Ave., New York NY 10020. (212)698-2761. Fax: (212)698-2796. Website: www.simonsays.com/kidzone. Imprint of Simon & Schuster Children's Publishing Division. Editor at Large: Margaret K. McElderry. **Manuscript Acquisitions:** Emma D. Dryden, executive editor. **Art Acquisitions:** Ann Bobco, executive art director. Publishes 10-12 picture books/year; 2-4 young reader titles/year; 8-10 middle reader titles/year; and 5-7 young adult titles/year. 10% of books by first-time authors; 33% of books from agented writers. "Margaret K. McElderry Books publishes original hardcover trade books for children from pre-school age through young adult. This list includes picture books, easy-to-read books, and fiction for eight to twelve-year-olds, poetry, fantasy and young adult fiction. The style and subject matter of the books we publish is almost unlimited. We do not publish textbooks, coloring and activity books, greeting cards, magazines and pamphlets or religious publications."
  • Margaret K. McElderry Books is not currently accepting unsolicited mss. Send queries only for picture books. Send queries and 3 sample chapters for middle grade and young adult projects; also looking for strong poetry. McElderry title *King of Shadows*, by Susan Cooper, won a 2000 Boston Globe-Horn Book Honor Award for fiction.
Fiction: Young readers: adventure, contemporary, fantasy, history. Middle readers: adventure, contemporary, fantasy, humor, mystery. Young adults: contemporary, fantasy, mystery, poetry. "Always interested in publishing humorous picture books and original beginning reader stories." Average word length: picture books—500; young

readers—2,000; middle readers—10,000-20,000; young adults—45,000-50,000. Recently published *River Boy*, by Tim Bowler; *Fly Eagle, Fly*, by Christopher Gregorowski, illustrated by Niki Daly; *Ebb & Flo and The Greedy Gulls*, by Jane Simmons; *Star in the Storm*, by Joan Hiatt Harlow.

Nonfiction: Young readers, young adult teens, biography, history. Average word length: picture books—500-1,000; young readers—1,500-3,000; middle readers—10,000-20,000; young adults—30,000-45,000. *Is There Life on Mars*, by Dennis B. Fradino.

How to Contact/Writers: Fiction/nonfiction: Submit query and sample chapters with SASE; may also include brief résumé of previous publishing credits. Responds to queries in 3 weeks; mss in 4 months. Publishes a book 18 months after contract signing. Will consider simultaneous submissions (only if indicated as such).

Illustration: Works with 20-30 illustrators/year. Query with samples; provide promo sheet or tearsheets; arrange personal portfolio review. Contact: Ann Bobco, executive art director. Responds to art samples in 3 months. Samples returned with SASE or samples filed.

Terms: Pays authors royalty based on retail price. Pay illustrators royalty based on retail price. Pays photographers by the project. Sends galleys to authors; dummies to illustrators. Original artwork returned at job's completion. Ms guidelines free on request with SASE.

Tips: "We're looking for strong, original fiction. We are always interested in picture books for the youngest age reader."

☑ Ⓐ **MEADOWBROOK PRESS**, 5451 Smetana Dr., Minnetonka MN 55343. (952)930-1100. Fax: (952)930-1940. Website: www.meadowbrookpress.com. Book publisher. **Manuscript Acquisitions:** Angela Wiechmann, submissions editor. **Art Acquisitions:** Paul Woods, art director. Publishes 1-2 middle readers/year; and 2-4 young readers/year. 20% of books by first-time authors; 10% of books from agented writers. Publishes children's activity books, gift books, humorous poetry anthologies and story anthologies.

• Meadowbrook does not accept unsolicited children's picture books or novels. They are primarily a nonfiction press. The publisher offers specific guidelines for various types of submissions (such as Newfangled Fairy Tales and poetry anthologies). Be sure to specify the type of project you have in mind when requesting guidelines.

Fiction: Young readers and middle readers: anthology, folktales, humor, multicultural, poetry. "Poems and short stories representing people of color encouraged." Published *The New Adventures of Mother Goose*; *Girls to the Rescue* (short stories featuring strong girls, for ages 8-12); and *A Bad Case of the Giggles* (children's poetry anthology).

Nonfiction: Young readers, middle readers: activity books, arts/crafts, cooking, hobbies, how-to, multicultural, self help. Multicultural needs include activity books representing traditions/cultures from all over the world, and especially fairy tale/folk tale stories with strong, multicultural protagonists and diverse settings. "Books which include multicultural activities are encouraged." Average word length: varies. Recently published *Happy Anniversary!* (party book); *Free Stuff for Kids* (activity book); and *Preschooler's Play and Learn*.

How to Contact/Writers: Fiction/Nonfiction: Query or submit outline/synopsis or submit complete ms with SASE. Responds to queries/mss in 3 months. Publishes a book 1-2 years after acceptance. Send a business-sized SASE and 2 first-class stamps for free writer's guidelines and book catalog before submitting ideas. Will consider simultaneous submissions.

Illustration: Works with 10-12 illustrators/year. Reviews ms/illustration packages from artists. Submit ms with 2-3 pieces of final art. Illustrations only: Submit résumé, promo sheet and tearsheets. Responds only if interested. Samples not returned; samples filed.

Photography: Buys photos from freelancers. Buys stock and assigns work. Model/property releases required. Submit cover letter.

Terms: Pays authors in royalties of 5-7½% based on retail price. Offers average advance payment of $2,000-4,000. Pays illustrators per project. Pays photographers per photo. Originals returned at job's completion. Book catalog available for 5×11 SASE and 2 first-class stamps; ms guidelines and artists guidelines available for SASE.

Tips: "Illustrators and writers should send away for our free catalog and guidelines before submitting their work to us. Also, illustrators should take a look at the books we publish to determine whether their style is consistent with what we are looking for. Writers should also note the style and content patterns of our books. For instance, our children's poetry anthologies contain primarily humorous, rhyming poems with a strong rhythm; therefore, we would not likely publish a free-verse and/or serious poem. I also recommend that writers, especially poets, have their work read by a critical, objective person before they submit anywhere. Also, please correspond with us by mail before telephoning with questions about your submission. We work with the printed word and will respond more effectively to your questions if we have something in front of us."

▥ ▧ **MEGA-BOOKS, INC.**, 240 E. 60th St., New York NY 10022. (212)355-6200. Fax: (212)355-6303. E-mail: rfischer@propubltd.com. **President:** John Craddock. **Acquisitions:** Rusty Fischer. Book packager/producer. Produces trade paperback and mass market paperback originals and fiction and nonfiction for the educational market. Works with first-time authors, established authors and unagented writers.

• Mega-Books does not accept unsolicited mss.

Fiction: Young adult: mystery. Recently published Nancy Drew and Hardy Boys series; Pocahontas and The Lion King books (Disney).

How to Contact/Writers: Submit résumé, publishing history and clips.

Terms: Work purchased outright for $3,000 and up. Offers average 50% advance.

Tips: "Please be sure to obtain a current copy of our writers' guidelines before writing."

☑ **MERIWETHER PUBLISHING LTD.,** 885 Elkton Dr., Colorado Springs CO 80907-3557. Fax: (719)594-9916. E-mail: merpeds@aol.com. Website: www.meriwetherpublishing.com. Book publisher. Estab. 1969. Executive Editor: Arthur L. Zapel. **Manuscript Acquisitions:** Ted Zapel, educational drama; Rhonda Wray, religious drama. "We do most of our artwork in-house; we do not publish for the children's elementary market." 75% of books by first-time authors; 5% of books from agented writers. "Our niche is drama. Our books cover a wide variety of theatre subjects from play anthologies to theatrecraft. We publish books of monologs, duologs, short one-act plays, scenes for students, acting textbooks, how-to speech and theatre textbooks, improvisation and theatre games. Our Christian books cover worship on such topics as clown ministry, storytelling, banner-making, drama ministry, children's worship and more. We also publish anthologies of Christian sketches. We do not publish works of fiction or devotionals."

Fiction: Middle readers, young adults: anthology, contemporary, humor, religion. "We publish plays, not prose-fiction."

Nonfiction: Middle readers: activity books, how-to, religion, textbooks. Young adults: activity books, drama/theater arts, how-to church activities, religion. Average length: 250 pages. Recently published *Grammar Wars* by Tom Ready (language arts) and *Multicultural Plays for Young Audiences* by Roger Ellis.

How to Contact/Writers: Nonfiction: Query or submit outline/synopsis and sample chapters. Responds to queries in 3 weeks; mss in 2 months. Publishes a book 6-12 months after acceptance. Will consider simultaneous submissions.

Illustration: Works with 2 illustrators/year. Reviews ms/illustration packages from artists. Query first. Illustrations only: Query with samples; send résumé, promo sheet or tearsheets. Replies to art samples in 2 months. Samples returned with SASE. Samples kept on file. Originals returned at job's completion.

Terms: Pays authors in royalties of 10% based on retail or wholesale price. Outright purchase $200-1,000. Royalties based on retail or wholesale price. Book catalog for SAE and $2 postage; ms guidelines for SAE and 1 first-class stamp.

Tips: "We are currently interested in finding unique treatments for theater arts subjects: scene books, how-to books, musical comedy scripts, monologs and short plays for teens."

☑ **MILKWEED EDITIONS,** 1011 Washington Ave. S., Suite 300, Minneapolis MN 55415-1246. (612)332-3192. Fax: (612)215-2550. E-mail: editor@milkweed.org. Website: www.milkweed.org. Book Publisher. Estab. 1980. **Manuscript Acquisitions:** Emilie Buchwald, publisher; Elizabeth Fitz, manuscript coordinator. **Art Acquisitions:** Dale Cooney. Publishes 3-4 middle readers/year. 25% of books by first-time authors. "Milkweed Editions publishes with the intention of making a humane impact on society, in the belief that literature is a transformative art uniquely able to convey the essential experiences of the human heart and spirit. To that end, Milkweed Editions publishes distinctive voices of literary merit in handsomely designed, visually dynamic books, exploring the ethical, cultural, and esthetic issues that free societies need continually to address."

Fiction: Middle readers: adventure, animal, contemporary, fantasy, humor, multicultural, nature/environment, suspense/mystery. Does not want to see anthologies, folktales, health, hi-lo, picture books, poetry, religion, romance, sports. Average length: middle readers—90-200 pages. Recently published *The $66 Summer,* by John Armistead (multicultural, mystery); *The Ocean Within,* by V.M. Caldwell (contemporary, nature); *No Place,* by Kay Haugaard (multicultural).

How to Contact/Writers: Fiction: Submit complete ms. Responds to mss in 6 months. Publishes a book 1 year after acceptance. Will consider simultaneous submissions.

Illustration: Works with 2-4 illustrators/year. Reviews ms/illustration packages from artists. Query; submit ms with dummy. Illustrations only: Query with samples; provide résumé, promo sheet, slides, tearsheets and client list. Samples filed or returned with SASE; samples filed. Originals returned at job's completion.

Terms: Pays authors royalty of 7½% based on retail price. Offers advance against royalties. Illustrators' contracts are decided on an individual basis. Sends galleys to authors. Book catalog available for $1.50 to cover postage; ms guidelines available for SASE. Must include SASE with ms submission for its return.

☑ ⬛ **THE MILLBROOK PRESS,** P.O. Box 335, 2 Old New Milford Rd., Brookfield CT 06804. (203)740-2220. Fax: (203)775-5643. Website: www.millbrookpress.com. Book publisher. Estab. 1989. **Manuscript Acquisitions:** Editorial Assistant. **Art Acquisitions:** Associate Art Director. Publishes 20 picture books/year; 40 young readers/year; 50 middle readers/year; and 10 young adult titles/year. 10% of books by first-time authors; 20% of books from agented authors. Publishes nonfiction, concept-oriented/educational books. Publishes under Twenty-First Century Books imprint also.

Fiction: Picture books: concept. Young adults: history.

Nonfiction: All levels: animal, arts/craft, biography, cooking, geography, how-to, multicultural, music/dance, nature/environment, reference, science. Picture books: activity books, concept, hi-lo. Middle readers: hi-lo, social issues, sports. Young adults: careers, social issues. No poetry. Average word length: picture books—minimal; young readers—5,000; middle readers—10,000; young adult/teens—20,000. Published *Wildshots: The World of the Wildlife Photographer,* by Nathan Aaseng (grades 5-8, nature and photography); *Meet My Grandmother:*

She's A Children's Book Author, by Lisa Tucker McElroy, photographs by Joel Benjamin (grades 2-4, current events/history); *Little Numbers*, by Edward Packard, illustrated by Sal Murdocca (grades K-3, math/concepts); *Crafts From Your Favorite Children's Songs*, by Kathy Ross, illustrated by Vicky Enright (grades K-3, arts and crafts); *Adoption: Today's Concerns*, by Ann E. Weiss (grade 7-up, social studies).

How to Contact/Writers: Send for guidelines w/SASE *before* submitting. We do not accept certain manuscripts; guidelines give specific instructions.

Illustration: Work with approximately 30 illustrators/year. Illustrations only: Query with samples; provide résumé, business card, promotional literature or tearsheets to be kept on file. No samples returned. Samples filed. Responds only if interested.

Photography: Buys photos from freelancers. Buys stock and assigns work.

Terms: Pays author royalty of 5-7½% based on wholesale price or work purchased outright. Offers advances. Pays illustrators by the project, royalty of 3-7% based on wholesale price. Sends galleys to authors. Manuscript and artist's guidelines for SASE. Address to: Manuscript Guidelines, The Millbrook Press . . . Book catalog to 9×11 SASE. Address to: Catalogues, The Millbrook Press . . .

MIRACLE SOUND PRODUCTIONS, INC., 1560 W. Bay Area Blvd., Suite 110, Friendswood TX 77546-2668. (281)286-4575. Fax: (281)286-0009. E-mail: imsworldwd@aol.com. Website: www.storyangel.com. Book publisher. **Acquisitions:** Trey Boring, director of special projects. Estab. 1997. Publishes 2 young readers/year. 100% of books by first-time authors. Miracle Sound Productions is best known for "positive family values in multimedia products."

Fiction: Young readers. Average word length: young readers—500. Recently published *CoCo's Luck*, by Warren Chaney and Don Boyer (ages 3-8, Read-A-Long book and tape).

Illustration: Only interested in agented material. Works with 1 illustrator/year. Uses color artwork only. Reviews ms/illustration packages from artists. Submit ms with dummy. Contact: Trey W. Boring, director, special projects. Illustrations only: Send résumé and portfolio to be kept on file.

Photography: Works on assignment only. Contact: Trey W. Boring, director, special projects.

Terms: Payment negotiable for authors, illustrators and photographers.

☑ **MITCHELL LANE PUBLISHERS, INC.**, P.O. Box 619, Bear DE 19701. (302)834-9646. Fax: (302)834-4164. E-mail: mitchelllane@dpnet.net. Website: www.angelfire.com/biz/mitchelllane/index.html. Book publisher. **Acquisitons:** Barbara Mitchell, president. Publishes 20 young adult titles/year. "We publish authorized multicultural biographies of role models for children and young adults."

Nonfiction: Young readers, middle readers, young adults: biography, multicultural. Average word length: 4,000-50,000 words. Recently published *Shania Twain*, by Jim Gallagher; *Brandy*; and *Salma Hayek* (all real-life reader biographies for grades 3-8); and *Legends of Health & Fitness* (ages 10 and up).

How to Contact/Writers: Nonfiction: Query or submit outline/synopsis and 3 sample chapters. Responds to queries only if interested. Publishes a book 18 months after acceptance.

Illustration: Works with 2-3 illustrators/year. Reviews ms/illustration packages from artists. Query; arrange portfolio review, including color copies of work. Illustration only: query with samples; arrange personal portfolio review; send résumé, portfolio, slides, tearsheets. Responds only if interested. Samples not returned; samples filed.

Photography: Buys stock images. Needs photos of famous and prominent minority figures. Captions required. Uses b&w prints. Submit cover letter, résumé, published samples, stock photo list.

Terms: Pays authors 5-10% royalty based on wholesale price or work purchased outright for $250-2,000. Pays illustrators by the project (range: $40-250). Sends galleys to authors.

Tips: "Most of our assignments are work-for-hire. Submit résumé and samples of work to be considered for future assignments."

☑ **MONDO PUBLISHING**, 980 Avenue of the Americas, New York NY 10018. (212)268-3560. Fax: (212)268-3561. Website: www.mondopub.com. Book publisher. **Acquisitions:** editorial staff. Publishes 60 picture and chapter books/year. 10% of books by first-time authors. Publishes various categories. "Our motto is 'creative minds creating ways to create lifelong readers.' We publish for both educational and trade markets, aiming for the highest quality books for both."

● Mondo Publishing only accepts agented material and work from previously published authors.

Fiction: Picture books, young readers, middle readers: adventure, animal, contemporary, fantasy, folktales, history, humor, multicultural, nature/environment, poetry, sports. Multicultural needs include: stories about children in different cultures or about children of different backgrounds in a U.S. setting. Recently published *My Lucky Hat*, by Kevin O'Malley (ages 5-9); *Hairy Tuesday*, by Uri Orlev (ages 6-10); and *Twiddle Twins* series by Howard Goldsmith (ages 6-10, adventure chapter books).

Nonfiction: Picture books, young readers, middle readers: animal, biography, geography, how-to, multicultural, nature/environment, science, sports. Recently published *Touch the Earth*, by Jane Baskwill (ages 6-10); and *Thinking About Ants*, by Barbara Brenner (ages 5-10, animals).

How to Contact/Writers: Accepting mss from agented or previously published writers only. Fiction/Nonfiction: Query or submit complete ms. Responds to queries in 1 month; mss in 6 months. Will consider simultaneous submissions. Mss returned with SASE. Queries must also have SASE.

Illustration: Works with 40 illustrators/year. Reviews ms/illustration packages from illustrators. Illustration only: Query with samples, résumé, portfolio. Responds only if interested. Samples returned with SASE; samples filed. Send attention: Art Department.

Photography: Occasionally uses freelance photographers. Buys stock images. Uses mostly nature photos. Uses color prints, transparencies.

Terms: Pays authors royalty of 2-5% based on wholesale/retail price. Offers advance based on project. Pays illustrators by the project (range: 3,000-9,000), royalty of 2-4% based on retail price. Pays photographers by the project or per photo. Sends galleys to authors depending on project. Originals returned to artists at job's completion. Book catalogs available for 9×12 SASE with $3.20 postage.

Tips: "Prefer illustrators with book experience or a good deal of experience in illustration projects requiring consistency of characters and/or setting over several illustrations. Prefer manuscripts targeted to trade market plus crossover to educational market."

☑ **MOREHOUSE PUBLISHING CO.**, 4775 Linglestown Rd., Harrisburg PA 17112. (717)541-8130. Fax: (717)541-8136. Website: www.morehousegroup.com. Book publisher. Estab. 1884. Publisher: Mark J.H. Fretz. **Manuscript Acquisitions:** Mark J.H. Fretz, editorial director. **Art Acquisitions:** Debbie Dortch, managing editor. Publishes 4-6 picture books/year. 25% of books by first-time authors. "Morehouse is a publisher and provider of books, church curricula, church resources materials and communications services for the Episcopal Church and other mainline church groups and organizations."

Fiction: Picture Books: spirituality, religion. Wants to see new and creative approaches to theology for children. Recently published *Bless This Day*, by Anne E. Kitch, illustrated by Joni Oeltjenbruns.

Nonfiction: Picture Books: religion and prayers.

How to Contact/Writers: Fiction/nonfiction: Submit ms (1,500 word limit). Responds to mss in 1 month. Publishes a book 2 years after acceptance.

Illustration: Works with 2-3 illustrators/year. Reviews ms/illustration packages from artists. Submit 3 chapters of ms with 1 piece of final art. Illustrations only: Submit résumé, tearsheets. Responds to art samples in 2 weeks. Samples returned with SASE; samples filed.

Terms: Pays authors royalty based on net price. Offers modest advance payment. Pays illustrators royalty based on net price. Sends galleys to authors. Book catalog free on request if SASE ($2 postage) is supplied.

Tips: "Morehouse Publishing seeks books that wrestle with important theological questions in words and images that children can relate to and understand."

☑ **MORGAN REYNOLDS PUBLISHING**, 620 S. Elm St., Suite 384, Greensboro NC 27406. (336)275-1311. Fax: (336)275-1152. E-mail: info@morganreynolds.com. Website: www.morganreynolds.com. **Acquisitions:** Laura Shoemaker, editor. Book publisher. Publishes 18 young adult titles/year. 50% of books by first-time authors. Morgan Reynolds publishes nonfiction books for juvenile and young adult readers. We prefer lively, well-written biographies of interesting figures for our biography series. Subjects may be contemporary or historical. Books for our Great Events series shold be insightful and exciting looks at critical periods.

● Morgan Reynolds has added two new series: Makers of the Media and Women in Sciences, directed toward the YA reader.

Nonfiction: Middle readers, young adults/teens: biography, history. Average word length: 17,000-20,000. Recently published *Edgar Rice Burroughs: Creator of Tarzan*, by William J. Boerst; *Women's Rights and Nothing Less: The Story of Elizabeth Cady Stanton*, by Lisa Fredericksen Bohannon; and *Carl Sagan: In Touch With the Cosmos*, by Jeremy Byman.

How to Contact/Writers: Prefers to see entire ms. Query; submit outline/synopsis with 3 sample chapters. Responds to queries in 6 weeks; mss in 6 weeks. Publishes a book 1 year after acceptance. Will consider simultaneous submissions.

Terms: Pays authors negotiated price. Offers advances. Sends galleys to authors. Ms guidelines available for SASE. Visit website for complete catalog.

Tips: "We are open to suggestions—if you have an idea that excites you, send it along. Recent trends suggest that the field is open for younger, smaller companies. Writers, especially ones starting out, should search us out."

MORROW JUNIOR BOOKS

● Morrow Junior was incorporated into HarperCollins Children's Books.

MOUNT OLIVE COLLEGE PRESS, 634 Henderson St., Mount Olive NC 28365. (919)658-2502. Book publisher. Estab. 1990. **Acquisitions:** Pepper Worthington, editor. Publishes 1 middle reader/year. 85% of books by first-time authors.

THE AGE-LEVEL INDEX, located in the back of this book, lists book publishers and magazines according to the age-groups for which they need material.

Fiction: Middle readers: animal, humor, poetry. Average word length: middle readers—3,000 words.

Nonfiction: Middle readers: nature/environment, religion, self help. Average word length: middle readers—3,000 words.

How to Contact/Writers: Submit complete ms or outline/synopsis and 3 sample chapters. Responds to queries in 6-12 months. Publishes a book 1 year after acceptance.

Illustration: Uses b&w artwork only. Submit ms with 50% of final art. Contact: Pepper Worthington, editor. Responds in 6-12 months if interested. Samples not returned.

Terms: Payment negotiated individually. Book catalog available for SAE and 1 first-class stamp.

N̄: NATIONAL GEOGRAPHIC SOCIETY, 1145 17th St. NW, Washington DC 20036. (202)828-5492. Fax: (202)429-5727. E-mail: jtunstal@ngs.org. Website: www.nationalgeographic.com. Estab. 1888. Specializes in nonfiction and multicultural trade books. **Acquisitions:** Jo Tunstall. Publishes 8 picture books, 15 middle readers and 2 reference books/year. 10% of books by first-time authors.

Fiction: Picture books, young readers: adventure, folktales, history, multicultural, nature/environment.

Nonfiction: Picture books, young readers, middle readers: animal, biography, concept, geography, history, multicultural, nature/environment, reference, science.

How to Contact/Writers: Fiction: Submit outline/synopsis and 2 sample chapters. Nonfiction: Submit complete manuscript or submit outline/synopsis and 2 sample chapters. Responds to mss/queries in 6 months. Publishes a book 2 years after acceptance. Will consider simultaneous submissions and electronic submissions via e-mail.

Illustration: Works with 4-8 illustrators/years. Review ms/illustration packages from artists. Ms/illustration packages: Submit ms with three pieces of finished art. Contact: Jo Tunstall, assistant editor. Illustrations only: Query with samples. Contact: Jo Tunstall. Reports back only if interested.

Photography: Buys stock and assigns work. Contact: Jo Tunstall. Uses color and b&w prints and 35mm or 4×5 transparencies. Send cover letter and published samples.

Terms: Sends galleys to authors, dummies to illustrators. Original artwork returned at job's completion. Book catalog available for 9×12 SASE.

TOMMY NELSON, Imprint of Thomas Nelson, Inc., P.O. 24100, Nashville TN 37214. (615)889-9000. Fax: (615)902-3330. Website: www.tommy.nelson.com. Book publisher. **Acquisitions:** Laura Minchew, Senior Vice President/Publisher. Publishes 15 picture books/year; 20 young readers/year; and 25 middle readers/year. Evangelical Christian publisher.

Fiction: Picture books: concept, humor, religion. Young readers: adventure, concept, humor, religion. Middle readers: adventure, humor, religion, sports, suspense/mystery. Young adults: adventure, problem novels, religion, sports, suspense/mystery. Recently published Todays Girls.com series (12 books), created by Terry Brown; and The Jay Jay board books, by Porch Light Entertainment.

Nonfiction: Picture books, young readers: activity books, religion, self help. Middle readers, young adults: reference, religion, self help. Recently published *The Ultimate Guide to Home Schooling*, by Debra Bell; and *The Adventure in Odyssey Devotional*, by Focus on the Family.

How to Contact/Writers: Does not accept unsolicited mss, queries or proposals.

Illustration: Query with samples. Responds only if interested. Samples filed. Contact: Karen Phillips, art director.

Terms: Pays authors royalty of 5% based on wholesale price or work purchased outright. Offers advances of $1,000 and up. Pays illustrators by the project or royalty.

Tips: "Know the CBA market—and avoid preachiness."

NEW HOPE, Imprint of Woman's Missionary Union, P.O. Box 12065, Birmingham AL 35202-2065. (205)991-8100. Website: www.newhopepubl.com. Book publisher. **Acquisitions:** Amy Cain. **Art Acquisitions:** Rachael Crutchfield (New Hope Publishers). Publishes 1-2 picture books/year; 1-2 young readers/year; and 1-2 middle readers/year. 75% of books by first-time authors. "Our goal is to equip and motivate children and adults to share the hope of Christ."

Fiction: All levels: multicultural, religion. Multicultural fiction must be related to Christian concepts.

Nonfiction: All levels: multicultural, religion. Multicultural nonfiction must be related to Christian concepts, particularly women reaching beyond themselves to share the hope of Christ.

How to Contact/Writers: Submit complete ms. Responds to queries in 6 weeks; mss in 3 months. Publishes a book 2 years after acceptance. Will consider simultaneous submissions.

Illustration: Works with 3-4 illustrators/year. Reviews ms/illustration packages from artists. Send ms with dummy. Illustrations only: query with samples (color copies). Responds only if interested. Samples not returned; samples filed.

Photography: Buy stock already on file. Model/property releases required.

Terms: Pays authors royalty of 5-10% based on retail price or work purchased outright (depends on length). Pays illustrators by the project, or by royalty. Sends galleys to author. Originals returned to artist at job's completion, if requested. Book catalog available for 10×12 SAE and 3 first-class stamps; ms guidelines for SASE.

Tips: "Obtain the catalog first to see the kinds of material we publish."

NORTH WORD PRESS, Creative Publishing International, 5900 Green Oak Dr., Minnetonka MN 55343. (612)936-4700. Fax: (612)932-0380. Estab. 1985. Publishes 2-3 picture books/year; 4-6 middle readers/year. 60% of books by first-time authors.

Nonfiction: Picture books, middle readers: animal, nature/environment. Average word length: picture books— 900; middle readers—3,000. Recently published *Foxes for Kids*, by Shuler (ages 8-12); *Children of the Earth . . . Remember*, by Schimmel (all ages); and *Wildflowers, Blooms & Blossoms*, by Burns (ages 8-12).

How to Contact/Writers: Nonfiction: query or submit complete ms. Responds to queries and ms in 3 months. Publishes a book 1 year after acceptance. Will consider simultaneous submissions and previously published work.

Illustration: Works with 2-3 illustrators/year. Uses color artwork only. Reviews ms/illustration packages from artists. Query or submit ms with 4-5 pieces of final art. Contact: acquisitions editor. Illustrations only: query with samples. Responds in 3 months. Samples returned with SASE; samples kept on file.

Photography: Buys stock. Contact: photo researcher. Uses nature and wildlife images. Model/property releases required; captions required. Uses 35mm, 2¼×2¼ and 4×5 color transparencies. Submit cover letter, résumé, dupe sample, slides and stock photo list.

Terms: Purchases transcripts or pays authors royalty based on wholesale price. Offers advances. Pays illustrators by the project. Pays photographer by the project or by the photo. Sends galleys to authors; dummies to illustrators. Originals returned to artist at job's completion. Book catalog available for 9×12 SAE and 7 first-class stamps; ms and art guidelines available for SASE. All imprints included in a single catalog.

☑ ◖ THE OLIVER PRESS, INC., Charlotte Square, 5707 W. 36th St., Minneapolis MN 55416-2510. (952)926-8981. Fax: (952)926-8965. E-mail: queries@oliverpress.com. Website: www.oliverpress.com. Book publisher. **Acquisitions:** Denise Sterling, Jenna Anderson. Publishes 8 young adult titles/year. 10% of books by first-time authors. "We publish collective biographies of people who made an impact in one area of history, including science, government, archaeology, business and crime. Titles from The Oliver Press can connect young adult readers with their history to give them the confidence that only knowledge can provide. Such confidence will prepare them for the lifelong responsibilities of citizenship. Our books will introduce students to people who made important discoveries and great decisions."

Nonfiction: Middle reader, young adults: biography, history, multicultural, social issues, history of science and technology. "Authors should only suggest ideas that fit into one of our existing series. We would like to add to our Innovators series on the history of technology." Average word length: young adult—20,000 words. Recently published *You Are the Explorer*, by Nathan Aaseng (ages 10 and up, history); *Women Who Led Nations*, by Joan Axelrod-Contrada (ages 10 and up, collective biography); *Communications: Sending the Message*, by Thomas Streissgath (ages 10 and up, collective biography); and *Puritans, Pilgrims, and Merchants: Founders of the Northeastern Colonies*, by Kieran Doherty (ages 10 and up, collective biography).

How to Contact/Writers: Nonfiction: Query with outline/synopsis. Responds in 6 months. Publishes a book approximately 1 year after acceptance.

Photography: Buys photos from freelancers. Buys stock images. Looks primarily for photos of people in the news. Captions required. Uses 8×10 b&w prints. Submit cover letter, résumé and stock photo list.

Terms: Pays authors negotiable royalty. Work purchased outright from authors (fee negotiable). Pays photographers per photo (negotiable). Sends galleys to authors upon request. Book catalog and ms guidelines available for SASE.

Tips: "Authors should read some of the books we have already published before sending a query to The Oliver Press. Authors should propose collective biographies for one of our existing series."

☑ ◖ ORCA BOOK PUBLISHERS, P.O. Box 5626 Station B, Victoria, British Columbia V8R 6S4 Canada. (604)380-1229. Fax: (604)380-1892. Book publisher. Estab. 1984. Publisher: R. Tyrrell. **Acquisitions:** Maggie deVries, children's book editor. Publishes 10 picture books/year; 4 middle readers/year; and 4 young adult titles/ year. 25% of books by first-time authors. "We only consider authors who are Canadian or who live in Canada."

• Orca no longer considers nonfiction.

Fiction: Picture books: animals, contemporary, history, nature/environment. Middle readers: contemporary, history, nature/environment, problem novels. Young adults: adventure, contemporary, history, multicultural, nature/environment, problem novels, suspense/mystery. Average word length: picture books—500-2,000; middle readers—20,000-35,000; young adult—25,000-45,000. Published *Tall in the Saddle*, by Anne Carter, illustrated by David McPhail (ages 4-8, picture book); *Me and Mr. Mah*, by Andrea Spalding, illustrated by Janet Wilson (ages 5 and up, picture book); and *Alone at Ninety Foot*, by Katherine Holubitsky (young adult).

How to Contact/Writers: Fiction: Submit complete ms if picture book; submit outline/synopsis and 3 sample chapters. Nonfiction: Query with SASE. "All queries or unsolicited submissions should be accompanied by a SASE." Responds to queries in 2 months; mss in 3 months. Publishes a book 18-24 months after acceptance.

Illustration: Works with 8-10 illustrators/year. Reviews ms/illustration packages from artists. Submit ms with 3-4 pieces of final art. "Reproductions only, no original art please." Illustrations only: Query with samples; provide résumé, slides. Responds in 2 months. Samples returned with SASE; samples filed.

Terms: Pays authors royalty of 5% for picture books, 10% for novels, based on retail price. Offers advances (average amount: $2,000). Pays illustrators royalty of 5% minimum based on retail price and advance on royalty.

Sends galleys to authors. Original artwork returned at job's completion if picture books. Book catalog available for legal or 8½×11 manila SAE and $2 first-class postage. Ms guidelines available for SASE. Art guidelines not available.

Tips: "American authors and illustrators should remember that the U.S. stamps on their reply envelopes cannot be posted in any country outside of the U.S."

☑ ORCHARD BOOKS, 95 Madison Ave., New York NY 10016. (212)951-2600. Fax: (212)213-6435. Website: www.scholastic.com. Imprint of Scholastic, Inc. Book publisher. President and Publisher: Judy V. Wilson. **Manuscript Acquisitions:** Ana Cerro, editor. **Art Acquisitions:** Mina Greenstein, art director. "We publish between 60 and 70 books yearly including fiction, poetry, picture books, and some illustrated nonfiction." 10-25% of books by first-time authors.

● Orchard is not accepting unsolicited mss; query letters only.

Fiction: All levels: animal, anthology, contemporary, fantasy, folktales, history, humor, multicultural, nature/environment, poetry, science fiction, sports, suspense/mystery. Recently published *Some Babies*, by Amy Schwartz; *Mouse in Love*, by Kraus and Aruego Dewey; *Pete and Polo's Big School Adventure*, by Reynolds.

Nonfiction: Picture books, young readers: animal, history, multicultural, nature/environment, science, social issues. "We rarely publish nonfiction." Recently published *While You're Waiting for the Food to Come*, by Eric Muller.

How to Contact/Writers: Query only with SASE. Responds in 3 months.

Illustration: Works with 40 illustrators/year. Art director reviews ms/illustration portfolios. Submit "tearsheets or photocopies or photostats of the work." Responds to art samples in 1 month. Samples returned with SASE. No disks or slides, please.

Terms: Most commonly an advance against list royalties. Sends galleys to authors; dummies to illustrators. Original artwork returned at job's completion. Book catalog free on request with 8½×11 SAE with 4 oz. postage.

Tips: "Read some of our books to determine first whether your manuscript is suited to our list."

▯ OTTENHEIMER PUBLISHERS, 5 Park Center Court, Suite 300, Owings Mills MD 21117-5001. (410)902-9100. Fax: (410)902-7210. E-mail: bholland@ottenheimerpub.com. Imprints: Dream House, Halo Press. Independent book producer/packager. Estab. 1896. **Acquisitions:** Betsy Crowley. Publishes 2 picture books/year; 30 early readers/year. 20% of books by first-time authors. "We publish series; rarely single-tile ideas. Early learning, religious, Beatrix Potter, activity books. We do lots of novelty formats and always want more ideas for inexpensive and creative packaging concepts. We are sticker book and pop-up book experts."

Nonfiction: Picture books: activity books, animal, concept, early learning novelty formats, geography, nature/environment, reference, religion. Recently published *My Bible Alphabet Block Pop-Up Book* (ages 3-6); *Wonders of Nature* (ages 3-6); and *Classic Christmas Sticker Books* (ages 3-6).

How to Contact/Writers: Query only. Currently not accepting unsolicited mss. Responds to queries/mss in 2 months. Publishes a book 6 months to 1 year after acceptance. Will consider simultaneous submissions; previously published work.

Illustration: Works with 8 illustrators/year. Reviews ms/illustration packages from artists. Query. Illustrations only: Send promo sheet and tearsheets to be kept on file. Responds only if interested. Samples returned with SASE; samples kept on file.

Photography: Buys stock images.

Terms: Pays authors royalty of 5-10% based on wholesale price or work purchased outright for $200-1,000. Offers advances. Pays illustrators by the project (range: $200-16,000). Sends galleys to authors. Originals returned to artist at job's completion. Ms guidelines for SASE.

Tips: "Don't submit single stories; we want series concepts for early learners, ages three to seven."

OUR CHILD PRESS, P.O. Box 74, Wayne PA 19087-0074. (610)964-0606. Fax: (610)964-0938. E-mail: ocp98@aol.com. Website: www.ourchildpress.com. Book publisher. **Acquisitions:** Carol Hallenbeck, president. 90% of books by first-time authors.

Fiction/Nonfiction: All levels: adoption, multicultural, special needs. Published *Don't Call Me Marda*, written and illustrated by Sheila Kelly Welch; *Is That Your Sister?* by Catherine and Sherry Burin; and *Oliver: A Story About Adoption*, by Lois Wichstrom.

How to Contact/Writers: Fiction/Nonfiction: Query or submit complete ms. Responds to queries/mss in 6 months. Publishes a book 6-12 months after acceptance.

Illustration: Works with 1 illustrator/year. Reviews ms/illustration packages from artists. Ms/illustration packages and illustration only: Query first. Submit résumé, tearsheets and photocopies. Responds to art samples in 2 months. Samples returned with SASE; samples kept on file.

Terms: Pays authors in royalties of 5-10% based on wholesale price. Pays illustrators royalties of 5-10% based on wholesale price. Original artwork returned at job's completion. Book catalog for business-size SAE and 52¢ postage.

Tips: "Won't consider anything not related to adoption."

☑ ▱ **OUR SUNDAY VISITOR, INC.**, 200 Noll Plaza, Huntington IN 46750. (219)356-8400. Fax: (219)359-9117. E-mail: booksed@osv.com; jlindsey@osv.com; mdubriel@osv.com. Website: www.osv.com. Book publisher. **Acquisitions:** Jacquelyn M. Lindsey, Michael Dubruiel. Art Director: Eric Schoenig. Publishes primarily religious, educational, parenting, reference and biographies. OSV is dedicated to providing books, periodicals and other products that serve the Catholic Church.

● Our Sunday Visitor, Inc., is publishing only those children's books that tie in to sacramental preparation. Contact the acquisitions editor for manuscript guidelines and a book catalog.

Nonfiction: Picture books, middle readers, young readers, young adults. Recently published *I Am Special*, by Joan and Paul Plum, illustrated by Andee Most (3-year-old activity book).

How to Contact/Writers: Query, submit complete ms, or submit outline/synopsis, and 2-3 sample chapters. Responds to queries in 2 months; mss in 2 months. Publishes a book 18-24 months after acceptance. Will consider simultaneous submissions, electronic submissions via disk or modem, previously published work.

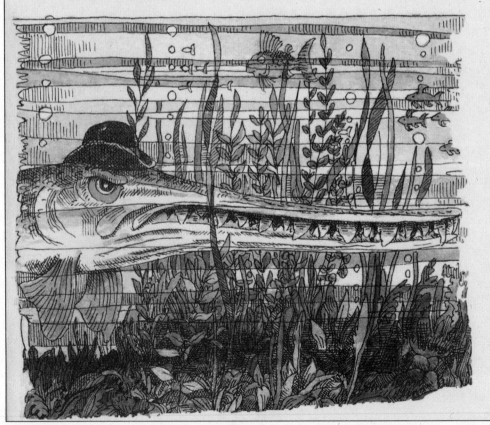

Log Garfish

A Paul Bunyan Tall Tale

retold by R. Hugh Rice   illustrated by Bruce MacDonald

© Bruce MacDonald

Sending out samples helped Bruce MacDonald land the assignment of illustrating *Log Garfish*, by R. Hugh Rice, published by Richard C. Owen Publishers, Inc. It also helped that he was very professional and easy to work with, according to art director, Janice Boland, who advises illustrators to keep a publisher's audience in mind when sending samples. "Many artists send sophisticated art to us," says Boland. "We publish books for 5- to 8-year-old children."

Illustration: Reviews ms/illustration packages from artists. Contact: Jacquelyn Lindsey or Michael Dubruiel, acquisitions editors. Illustration only: Query with samples. Contact: Aquisitions Editor. Responds only if interested. Samples returned with SASE; samples filed. Original artwork returned at job's completion.
Photography: Buys photos from freelancers. Contact: Acquisitions Editor.
Terms: Pays authors royalty of 10-12% net. Pays illustrators by the project (range: $200-1,500). Sends galleys to authors; dummies to illustrators. Book catalog available for SASE; ms guidelines available for SASE.
Tips: "Stay in accordance with our guidelines."

THE OVERMOUNTAIN PRESS, P.O. Box 1261, Johnson City TN 37605. (423)926-2691. Fax: (423)929-2464. E-mail: bethw@overmtn.com. Website: www.overmtn.com. Also www.silverdaggermysteries.com. Estab. 1970. Specializes in regional history trade books. **Manuscript Acquisitions:** Elizabeth L. Wright, senior editor. Publishes 3 picture books/year; 2 young readers/year; 2 middle readers/year. 50% of books by first-time authors. "We are primarily a publisher of southeastern regional history, and we have recently published several titles for children. Children's books about southern Appalachia are of special interest."
Fiction: Picture books: folktales, history. Young readers, middle readers: folktales, history, suspense/mystery. Average word length: picture books—800-1,000; young readers—5,000-10,000; middle readers—20-30,000. Recently published *Bloody Mary: The Mystery of Amanda's Magic Mirror*, by Patrick Bone (young, middle reader); *Zebordee's Miracle*, by Ann G. Cooper, illustrated by Adam Hickam (pre-elementary, picture book); and *Appalachian ABCs*, by Francie Hall, illustrated by Kent Oehm (pre-elementary, picture book).
Nonfiction: Picture books, young readers, middle readers: biography (regional), history (regional). Average word length: picture books—800-1,000; young readers—5,000-10,000; middle readers—20-30,000. Recently published *Ten Friends: A Child's Story About the Ten Commandments*, written and illustrated by Gayla Dowdy Seale (preschool-elementary, picture book).
How to Contact/Writers: Fiction/Nonfiction: Submit outline/synopsis and 2 sample chapters. Responds to queries in 2 months; mss in 6 months. Publishes book 1 year after acceptance. Will consider simultaneous submissions and previously published work.
Illustration: Works with 4 illustrators/year. Uses color artwork only. Reviews ms/illustration packages from artists. Send ms with dummy with at least 3 color copies of sample illustrations. Illustrations only: Send résumé. Responds only if interested. Samples not returned; samples filed.
Terms: Pays authors royalty of 5-15% based on wholesale price. Pays illustrators royalty of 5-10% based on wholesale price or by author/illustrator negotiations (author pays). Sends galleys to authors; dummies to illustrators. Originals sometimes returned to artist at job's completion. Book catalog available for 8½×11 SAE and 4 first-class stamps; ms guidelines available for SASE. All imprints included in a single catalog. Catalog available on website.
Tips: "Because we are fairly new in the children's market, we will not accept a manuscript without complete illustrations. We are compiling a database of freelance illustrators which is available to interested authors. Please call if you have questions regarding the submission process or to see if your product is of interest. The children's market is HUGE! If the author can find a good local publisher, he or she is more likely to get published. We are currently looking for authors to represent our list in the new millennium. At this point, we are accepting regional (Southern Appalachian) manuscripts only. *Please* call if you have a question regarding this policy."

RICHARD C. OWEN PUBLISHERS, INC., P.O. Box 585, Katonah NY 10536. (914)232-3903. Fax: (914)232-3977. Website: www.rcowen.com. Book publisher. **Acquisitions:** Janice Boland, children's books editor/art director. Publishes 20 picture story books/year. 90% of books by first-time authors. We publish "child-focused books, with inherent instructional value, about characters and situations with which five-, six-, and seven-year-old children can identify—books that can be read for meaning, entertainment, enjoyment and information. We include multicultural stories that present minorities in a positive and natural way. Our stories show the diversity in America."
Fiction: Picture books, young readers: adventure, animal, contemporary, folktales, hi-lo, humor, multicultural, nature/environment, poetry, science fiction, sports, suspense/mystery. Does not want to see holiday, religious themes, moral teaching stories. "No talking animals with personified human characteristics, jingles and rhymes, alphabet books, stories without plots, stories with nostalgic views of childhood, soft or sugar-coated tales. No stereotyping." Average word length: 40-200 words. Recently published *Digging to China*, by Katherine Goldsby, illustrated by Viki Woodworth; *The Red-Tailed Hawk*, by Lola Schaefer, illustrated by Stephen Taylor; and *Dogs at School*, by Suzanne Hardin, illustrated by Jo-Ann Friar.
Nonfiction: Picture books, young readers: animals, careers, hi-lo, history, how-to, music/dance, geography, multicultural, nature/environment, science, sports. Multicultural needs include: "Good stories respectful of all heritages, races, cultural—African-American, Hispanic, American Indian." Wants lively stories. No "encyclopedic" type of information stories. Average word length: 40-250 words. Recently published *New York City Buildings*, by Ann Mace, photos by Tim Holmstron.
How to Contact/Writers: Fiction/nonfiction: Submit complete ms. "*Must* request guidelines first with #10 SASE." Responds to mss in 18 months. Publishes a book 2-3 years after acceptance. Will consider simultaneous submissions.

Illustration: Works with 20 illustrators/year. Uses color artwork only. Illustration only: Send color copies/reproductions or photos of art or provide tearsheets; do not send slides. Must request guidelines first. Responds only if interested; samples filed.

Photography: Buys photos from freelancers. Contact: Janice Boland, art director. Wants photos that are child-oriented; candid shots; not interested in portraits. "Natural, bright, crisp and colorful—of children and of interesting subjects and compositions attractive to children. If photos are assigned, we buy outright—retain ownership and all rights to photos taken in the project." Sometimes interested in stock photos for special projects. Uses 35mm, 2¼×2¼, color transparencies.

Terms: Pays authors royalties of 5% based on wholesale price or outright purchase (range: $25-500). Offers no advances. Pays illustrators by the project (range: $100-2,500). Pays photographers by the project (range: $100-2,000) or per photo ($100-150). Original artwork returned 12-18 months after job's completion. Book brochure, ms/artists guidelines available for SASE.

Tips: Seeking "stories (both fiction and nonfiction) that have charm, magic, impact and appeal; that children living in today's society will want to read and reread; books with strong storylines, child-appealing language, action and interesting, vivid characters. Write for the ears and eyes and hearts of your readers—use an economy of words. Visit the children's room at the public library and immerse yourself in the best children's literature."

N: PACIFIC PRESS, P.O. Box 5353. Nampa ID 83653-5353. (208)465-2574. Fax: (208)465-2531. E-mail: booksubmissions@pacificpress.com. Website: www.pacificpress.com. Estab. 1874. Specializes in Christian material. **Manuscript Acquisitions:** Tim Lale. **Art Acquisitions:** Randy Maxwell, creative director. Publishes 1 picture book/year; 1 young readers/year; 2 middle readers/year. 5% of books by first-time authors. Pacific Press brings the Bible and Christian lifestyle to children.

Fiction: Picture books, young readers, middle readers, young adults: Religion. Average word length: picture books—100; young readers—1,000; middle readers—15,000; young adults—40,000. Recently published *The Cat in the Cage and Other Great Stories*, by Jerry Thomas; *Detective Zack and the Secret of Blackloch Castle*, by Jerry Thomas.

Nonfiction: Picture books, young readers, middle readers, young adults: religion. Average word length: picture books—100; young readers—1,000; middle readers—15,000; young adults—40,000. Recently published *Before I Was a Kid*, by Rita Spears-Stewart; *God Spoke to a Girl*, by Dorothy Nelson; *My Talents for Jesus*, by Charles Mills.

How to Contact/Writers: Fiction/Nonfiction: Query or submit outline/synopsis and 3 sample chapters. Responds to queries in 2 months; mss in 3 months. Publishes a book 6-9 months after acceptance. Will consider electronic submissions via disk or modem.

Illustration: Works with 2 illustrators/year. Uses color artwork only. Query. Responds only if interested. Samples returned with SASE.

Photography: Buys stock and assigns work. Model/property releases required.

Terms: Pays author royalty of 6-15% based on wholesale price. Offers advances (Average amount: $1,500). Pays illustrators royalty of 6-15% based on wholesale price. Pays photographers royalty of 6-15% based on wholesale price. Sends galleys to authors. Originals returned to artist at job's completion. Book catalog available for 10×12 SAE and 5 first-class stamps; ms guidelines for SASE. All imprints included in a single catalog. Catalog available on website www.adventistbookcenter.com.

Tips: Pacific Press is owned by the Seventh-day Adventist Church. The Press rejects all material that is not Bible-based.

PACIFIC VIEW PRESS, P.O. Box 2657, Berkeley CA 94702. (510)849-4213. Fax: (510)843-5835. E-mail: PVP@sirius.com. Book publisher. **Acquisitions:** Pam Zumwalt, president. Publishes 1-2 picture books/year. 50% of books by first-time authors. "We publish unique, high-quality introductions to Asian cultures and history for children 8-12, for schools, libraries and families. Our children's books focus on hardcover illustrated nonfiction. We look for titles on aspects of the history and culture of the countries and peoples of the Pacific Rim, especially China, presented in an engaging, informative and respectful manner. We are interested in books that all children will enjoy reading and using, and that parents and teachers will want to buy."

Nonfiction: Young readers, middle readers: Asia-related multicultural only. Recently published *Kneeling Carabao and Dancing Giants: Celebrating Filipino Festivals*, by Rena Krasno, illustrated by Ileana C. Lee (ages 8-12, nonfiction on festivals and history of Philippines); and *Made in China: Ideas and Inventions from Ancient China*, by Suzanne Williams, illustrated by Andrea Fong (ages 10-12, nonfiction on history of China and Chinese inventions).

How to Contact/Writers: Query with outline and sample chapter. Responds in 3 months.

Illustration: Works with 2 illustrators/year. Responds only if interested. Samples returned with SASE.

Terms: Pays authors royalty of 8-12% based on wholesale price. Pays illustrators by the project (range: $2,000-5,000).

Tips: "We welcome proposals from persons with expertise, either academic or personal, in their area of interest. While we do accept proposals from previously unpublished authors, we would expect submitters to have considerable experience presenting their interests to children in classroom or other public settings and to have skill in writing for children."

PARENTING PRESS, INC., P.O. Box 75267, Seattle WA 98125. (206)364-2900. Fax: (206)364-0702. E-mail: office@parentingpress.com. Website: www.parentingpress.com. Book publisher. Estab. 1979. Publisher: Carolyn Threadgill. **Acquisitions:** Elizabeth Crary, (parenting) and Carolyn Threadgill (children and parenting). Publishes 4-5 books/year for parents or/and children and those who work with them. 40% of books by first-time authors. "Parenting Press publishes educational books for children in story format—no straight fiction. Our company publishes books that help build competence in parents and children. We are known for practical books that teach parents and can be used successfully by parent educators, teachers, and educators who work with parents. We are interested in books that help people feel good about themselves because they gain skills needed in dealing with others. We are particularly interested in material that provides 'options' rather than 'shoulds.' "

● Parenting Press's guidelines are available on their website.

Fiction: Picture books: concept. Publishes social skills books, problem-solving books, safety books, dealing-with-feelings books that use a "fictional" vehicle for the information. "We rarely publish straight fiction." Recently published *I Can't Wait, I Want It, My Name Is Not Dummy*, by Elizabeth Crary, illustrations by Marina Megale (ages 3-8, social skill building); *Telling Isn't Tattling*, by Kathryn Hammerseng, illustrations by Dave Garbot (ages 4-12, personal safety); and 4 toddler board books on expressing feelings.

Nonfiction: Picture books: health, social skills building. Young readers: health, social skills building books. Middle readers: health, social skills building. No books on "new baby; coping with a new sibling; cookbooks; manners; books about disabilities (which we don't publish at present); animal characters in anything; books that tell children what they should do, instead of giving options." Average word length: picture books—500-800; young readers—1,000-2,000; middle readers—up to 10,000. Published *Kids to the Rescue*, by Maribeth and Darwin Boelts (ages 4-12).

How to Contact/Writers: Query. Responds to queries/mss in 3 months, "after requested." Publishes a book 18 months after acceptance. Will consider simultaneous submissions.

Illustrations: Works with 3-5 illustrators/year. Reviews ms/illustration packages from artists. "We do reserve the right to find our own illustrator, however." Query. Illustrations only: Submit "résumé, samples of art/drawings (no original art); photocopies or color photocopies okay." Responds only if interested. Samples returned with SASE; samples filed, if suitable.

Terms: Pays authors royalties of 3-8% based on wholesale price. Pays illustrators (for text) by the project; 3-5% royalty based on wholesale price. Pays illustrators by the project ($250-3,000). Sends galleys to authors; dummies to illustrators. Book catalog/ms/artist's guidelines for #10 SAE and 1 first-class stamp.

Tips: "Make sure you are familiar with the unique nature of our books. All are aimed at building certain 'people' skills in adults or children. Our publishing for children follows no trend that we find appropriate. Children need nonfiction social skill-building books that help them think through problems and make their own informed decisions."

PAULIST PRESS, 997 Macarthur Blvd., Mahwah NJ 07430. (201)825-7300. Fax: (201)825-8345. Website: www.paulistpress.com. Book publisher. Estab. 1865. **Acquisitions:** Therese Johnson Borchard, editor. Publishes 9-11 picture books/year; 8-10 young reader titles/year; and 3-4 middle reader titles/year. 80% of books by first-time authors; 30% of books from agented writers. "Our goal is to produce books that 'heal with kid-appeal,' 'share the goodness,' and delight in diversity."

Fiction: Picture books, young readers, middle readers and young adults: interested mainly in books providing an accessible introduction to basic religious and family values, but not preachy. Recently published *I Hate Goodbyes*, by Kathleen Szaj, illustrated by Mark A. Hicks; Walking With God series: *Spirit!, Yes, I Can!, Imagine!* and *Where Is God?*, by Heidi Bratton; *Elizabeth, Who is NOT a Saint*, by Kathleen Szaj, illustrated by Mark A. Hicks; and *Little Blessings*, by Sally Ann Conan, illustrated by Kathy Rogers.

Nonfiction: All levels: biography, concept, multicultural, religion, self help, social issues.

How to Contact/Writers: Fiction/nonfiction: Submit complete ms. Responds to queries/mss in 6-8 months. Publishes a book 12-16 months after acceptance.

Illustration: Works with 10-12 illustrators/year. Editorial reviews all varieties of ms/illustration packages from artists. Submit complete ms with 1 piece of final art (photocopy only) remainder roughs. Illustrations only: Submit résumé, tearsheets. Reports on art samples in 6-8 months.

Photography: Buys photos from freelancers. Works on assignment only. Uses inspirational photos.

Terms: Pays authors royalty of 6-8% based on retail price. Offers average advance payment of $500. Pays illustrators by the project (range: $50-100) or royalty of 2-6% based on retail price. Pays photographers by the project (range: $25-150; negotiable). Factors used to determine final payment: color art, b&w, number of illustrations, complexity of work. Pay for separate authors and illustrators: Author paid by royalty rate; illustrator paid by flat fee, sometimes by royalty. Sends galleys to authors; dummies to illustrators. Original artwork returned at job's completion, "if requested by illustrator."

Tips: "We cannot be responsible for unsolicited manuscripts. Please send copies, not originals. We try to respond to all manuscripts we receive—please understand if you have not received a response within six months the manuscript does not fit our current publishing plan. We look for authors who diligently promote their work."

☑ **PEACHTREE PUBLISHERS, LTD.**, 1700 Chattahoochee Ave., Atlanta GA 30318-2112. (404)876-8761. Fax: (404)875-2578. E-mail: peachtree@mindspring.com. Website: www.peachtree-online.com. Book publisher. Imprints: Peachtree Jr. and Freestone. Estab. 1977. **Acquisitions:** Helen Harriss, Sarah Helyar Smith. **Art Director:** Loraine Balcsik. Publishes 20 titles/year.

Fiction: Picture books: adventure, animal, concept, history, nature/environment. Young readers: adventure, animal, concept, history, nature/environment, poetry. Middle readers: adventure, animal, history, nature/environment, sports. Young adults: fiction, mystery, adventure. Does not want to see science fiction, romance.

Nonfiction: Picture books: animal, history, nature/environment. Young readers, middle readers, young adults: animal, biography, nature/environment. Does not want to see religion.

How to Contact/Writers: Fiction/Nonfiction: Submit complete ms. Responds to queries in 3 months; mss in 4 months. Publishes a book 1-1½ years after acceptance. Will consider simultaneous and previously published submissions.

Illustration: Works with 8-10 illustrators/year. Illustrations only: Query with samples, résumé, slides, color copies to keep on file. Responds only if interested. Samples returned with SASE; samples filed.

Terms: Ms guidelines for SASE, or call for a recorded message.

N: PEEL PRODUCTIONS, P.O. Box 546, Columbus NC 28722. (828)894-8838. Fax: (828)894-8839. E-mail: editor@peelbooks.com. Book publisher. **Acquisitions:** Susan Dubosque, editor. Publishes 1 picture book/year; and 5 how-to-draw books/year.

Nonfiction: Young readers, middle readers: activity books (how to draw).

How to Contact/Writers: Fiction/Nonfiction: Submit outline/synopsis and 2 sample chapters. Responds to queries in 1 month; mss in 6 weeks. Publishes a book 1 year after acceptance. Will consider simultaneous submissions.

Terms: Pays authors royalty. Offers advances. Sends galleys to authors. Book catalog available for SAE and 2 first-class stamps. Ms guidelines available for SASE.

☑ ⬙ **PELICAN PUBLISHING CO. INC.**, P.O. Box 3110, Gretna LA 70054-3110. (504)368-1175. E-mail: editorial@pelicanpub.com. Website: www.pelicanpub.com. Book publisher. Estab. 1926. **Manuscript Acquisitions:** Nina Kooij, editor-in-chief. **Art Acquisitions:** Tracey Clements, production manager. Publishes 12 young readers/year and 2 middle reader titles/year. 20% of books from agented writers. "Pelican publishes hardcover and trade paperback originals and reprints. Our children's books (illustrated and otherwise) include history, holiday, and regional."

Fiction: Young readers: history, holiday and regional. Middle readers: Louisiana history. Multicultural needs include stories about African-Americans, Irish-Americans, Jews, Asian-Americans, Cajuns and Hispanics. Does not want animal stories, general Christmas stories, "day at school" or "accept yourself" stories. Maximum word length: 1,100 young readers; middle readers—40,000. Recently published *The Warlord's Puzzle*, by Virginia Walton Pilegarde (ages 5-8, folktale).

Nonfiction: Young readers: history. Middle readers: Louisiana history. Recently published *The Governors of Louisiana*, by Miriam G. Reeves (ages 8-12, biography).

How to Contact/Writers: Fiction/Nonfiction: Query. Responds to queries in 1 month; mss in 3 months. Publishes a book 9-18 months after acceptance.

Illustration: Works with 9 illustrators/year. Reviews ms/illustration packages from artists. Query first. Illustrations only: Query with samples (no originals). Responds only if interested. Samples returned with SASE; samples kept on file.

Terms: Pays authors in royalties; buys ms outright "rarely." Sends galleys to authors. Illustrators paid by "various arrangements." Book catalog and ms guidelines available for SASE.

Tips: "No anthropomorphic stories, pet stories (fiction or nonfiction), fantasy, poetry, science fiction or romance. Writers: Be as original as possible. Develop characters that lend themselves to series and always be thinking of new and interesting situations for those series. Give your story a strong hook—something that will appeal to a well-defined audience. There is a lot of competition out there for general themes. We look for stories with specific 'hooks' and audiences, and writers who actively promote their work."

PENGUIN PUTNAM INC., 345 Hudson St., New York NY 10014. See listings for Dial Books for Young Readers, Dutton Children's Books, Philomel Books, Puffin Books, G.P. Putnam's Sons and Viking Children's Books.

⬙ ☑ ⬚ **PERFECTION LEARNING CORPORATION**, Cover to Cover, 10520 New York, Des Moines IA 50322. (515)278-0133. Fax: (515)278-2980. E-mail: acquisitions@plconline.com. Website: www.perfectionlearning.com. Book publisher, independent book producer/packager. **Manuscript Acquisitions:** S. Thies (K-12 books), Rebecca Christian (curriculum). **Art Acquisitions:** Randy Messer, art director. Publishes 20 early chapter books/year; 40-50 middle readers/year; 25 young adult titles/year.

● Perfection Learning Corp. publishes *all* hi-lo children's books on a variety of subjects.

Publishing simple, straightforward stories to delight and challenge young readers

Kathy Landwehr

Kathy Landwehr laughingly remembers a much-loved book from her childhood, *Run With the Horseman*, and how it prompted her mother to suggest she go to work for Peachtree Publishers when she grew up. "I thought she was crazy, and of course, I had no intention of doing anything my mother told me to do." Fast forward to the present, where Landwehr is associate publisher at Peachtree, managing the editorial and production departments and seeing projects through the acquisition stage all the way through to the creation of the physical book. "What can I say," she concedes. "My mother was right."

Based in Atlanta, Georgia, Peachtree Publishers is a general trade publisher which focuses on books for children and young adults, self-help titles and guides to the American South. At book shows, their products routinely attract clients with their clever titles and bright, whimsical illustrations. Although Peachtree is a smaller company, Landwehr sees advantages for authors and illustrators. "Because we are smaller, we are very focused on each and every book we publish. We pay a lot of attention to a book's development, sales and marketing. There's a level of attention that I don't think a large corporation is able to give."

That attention has paid off in lots of award-winning books for Peachtree. A quick look at their website, www.peachtree-online.com, offers an impressive list of books and the honors they've accumulated. It also offers proof that Peachtree knows and loves its audience—children and the adults who read to them.

"There is an assumption that children have a shorter attention span," says Landwehr, "that you have to capture children's eyes with funky MTV kind of design and things that are very pop-culture oriented. I don't think that's necessarily the case, but I think the marketplace is responding as if it were."

Still, it must be difficult for book publishers to compete against the fast-paced action of video games, animated movies and computers. "My personal opinion," says Landwehr, "is that it's not a very pleasant way to see the world. It's exhausting, it's overstimulating and it results in very little satisfaction. There are a lot of children who ultimately find comfort in something that's simple, straightforward, well done and not distracting with a lot of bells and whistles. I have hopes that we'll defeat the 'Nintendoization' of our society."

To that end, Landwehr looks for writing that deals with timeless subject matter. Since it takes eighteen to twenty-four months to develop and publish a book, trendy topics are a poor investment risk. But no subject is taboo, if the author handles it well. Most of Peachtree's children's titles are fiction with a lot of humorous aspects. "What we look for is a unique voice that communicates information or tells a story in a new and appealing way. We also look for somebody who we think will be a career writer, who we'll have the opportunity to work with on many projects."

Landwehr points to author Carmen Agra Deedy's *The Library Dragon* as an example of one of Peachtree's most popular books. "We have done enormously well with *The Library Dragon*. It's very funny. Carmen is a wonderful professional storyteller. She and Michael White, who illustrated the book, worked very intensely together, so it's very organic in the way that it developed. Everything flows wonderfully. It also has a very gentle, subtle message about the importance of reading and children's access to books. Librarians love it. Most everybody loves it."

The Library Dragon comes pretty close to Landwehr's description of the perfect children's book: a seamless integration of illustration and design; a writer and illustrator working closely to make the book as strong as it can be; and an educational benefit tucked into a story that's completely enjoyable on a purely literary level.

For those wanting to break into the children's book market, Landwehr advises talking to other writers, joining writer's groups, taking classes and attending conferences. "Southern publishing, and probably all publishing, is very friendly, very chatty. The best thing to do is to keep pitching and, whenever possible, to make a personal contact. A lot of the writers we work with have had really positive associations with the SCBWI conferences."

It also helps to interact with kids a lot. Says Landwehr, "We've loved working with the writers who have been teachers or librarians or have been connected with children in some way before they decided to become children's writers. I think they have an understanding of

Illustration © Suzy Schultz. Reprinted with permission of Peachtree Publishers.

In her debut book for children, author Adrian Fogelin offers "a moving, coming-of-age story of a young white girl who overcomes family prejudice and cultural differences when she befriends a black girl in a small working-class town." This sort of timeless subject matter is perfect for Peachtree Publishers's Peachtree Junior imprint, producing quality titles for readers 8-12.

what children are interested in and how you reach them."

Landwehr cautions aspiring writers to avoid taking the low road when crafting a story. "There's a very basic level of bathroom humor that goes over easily but doesn't make a good book. It doesn't last. The best children's books have something in them that appeals to the poor, beleaguered adult who may have to reread it a million times."

Another peeve is writers who submit stories that are really "saccharine and precious." Landwehr's years in the industry tell her that these are the people who haven't actually talked to children. "It's a good idea for writers to read their manuscripts and develop them with kids and get their feedback. Not only do kids really love the experience, they're also brutally honest."

It becomes very clear in talking to Landwehr that she loves children and has a great respect for them. As a result, she and her staff are dedicated to working with talented authors and artists and putting together imaginative books that delight and challenge young readers every step of the way. For that, we can all be glad Kathy Landwehr listened to her mother.

—*Cindy Duesing*

Peachtree editor Kathy Landwehr calls *The Library Dragon*, by Carmen Agra Deedy, practically a perfect children's book. Deedy's collaboration with illustrator Michael P. White offers a seamless integration of illustration and design, and an educational benefit tucked into a story that's completely enjoyable on a literary level.

Illustration © Michael P. White. Reprinted with permission of Peachtree Publishers.

Fiction: All levels: adventure, animal, contemporary, fantasy, folktales, history, humor, multicultural, nature/environment, poetry, science fiction—special needs, sports, suspense/mystery. Average word length: early chapter books—4,000; middle readers—10,000-14,000; young adults: 10,000-30,000. Recently published *Holding the Yellow Rabbit*; and *Prairie Meeting*.

Nonfiction: All levels: activity, animal, biography, careers, geography, health, history, hobbies, multicultural, nature/environment, science, self-help, social issues, special needs, sports. Multicultural needs include stories, legends and other oral tradition narratives by authors who are of the culture. Does not want to see ABC books. Average word length: early chapter books—4,000; middle readers—10,000-14,000; young adults—10,000-14,000.

How to Contact/Writers: Fiction/Nonfiction: Submit a few sample chapters and synopsis. Responds to queries in 6 months; mss in 6 months. Publishes a book 18 months after acceptance.

Illustration: Works with 15-20 illustrators/year. Illustration only: Query with samples; send résumé, promo sheet, client list, tearsheets. Contact: Randy Messer, art director. Responds only if interested. Samples returned with SASE; samples filed.

Photography: Buys photos from freelancers. Contact: Randy Messer, art director. Buys stock and assigns work. Uses children. Uses color or up to 8×10 b&w glossy prints; 2¼×2¼, 4×5 transparencies. Submit cover letter, client list, stock photo list, promo piece (color or b&w).

Terms: Pays authors "depending on going rate for industry." Offers advances. Pays illustrators by the project. Pays photographers by the project. Original artwork returned on a "case by case basis."

Tips: "Our materials are sold through schools for use in the classroom. Talk to a teacher about his/her needs."

PHILOMEL BOOKS, Penguin Putnam Inc., 345 Hudson St., New York NY 10014. (212)414-3610. Website: www.penguinputnam.com. Putnam Books. Book publisher. Estab. 1980. **Manuscript Acquisitions:** Patricia Gauch, editorial director; Emily Earle, assistant editor; Michael Green, senior editor. **Art Acquisitions:** Gina DiMassi, design assistant. Publishes 18 picture books/year; 2 middle-grade/year; 2 young readers/year; 4 young adult/year. 5% of books by first-time authors; 80% of books from agented writers. "We look for beautifully written, engaging manuscripts for children and young adults."

• Philomel Books is not accepting unsolicited manuscripts.

Fiction: All levels: adventure, animal, anthology, contemporary, fantasy, folktales, hi-lo, history, humor, poetry, sports, multicultural. Middle readers, young adults: problem novels, science fiction, suspense/mystery. No concept picture books, mass-market "character" books, or series. Average word length: 1,000 for picture books; 1,500 young readers; 14,000 middle readers; 20,000 young adult.

Nonfiction: Picture books, young readers, middle readers: hi-lo. "Creative nonfiction on any subject." Average word length: 2,000 for picture books; 3,000 young readers; 10,000 middle readers.

How to Contact/Writers: Not accepting unsolicited mss. Fiction: Submit outline/synopsis and first two chapters. Nonfiction: Query. Responds to queries in 3 months; mss in 4 months.

Illustration: Works with 20-25 illustrators/year. Reviews ms/illustration packages from artists. Query with art sample first. Illustrations only: Query with samples. Send résumé and tearsheets. Responds to art samples in 1 month. Original artwork returned at job's completion. Samples returned with SASE or kept on file.

Terms: Pays authors in royalties. Average advance payment "varies." Illustrators paid by advance and in royalties. Sends galleys to authors; dummies to illustrators. Book catalog, ms guidelines free on request with SASE (9×12 envelope for catalog).

Tips: Wants "unique fiction or nonfiction with a strong voice and lasting quality. Discover your own voice and own story—and persevere." Looks for "something unusual, original, well-written. Fine art. The genre (fantasy, contemporary, or historical fiction) is not so important as the story itself and the spirited life the story allows its main character. We are also interested in receiving adolescent novels, particularly novels that contain regional spirit, such as a story about a young boy or girl written from a Southern, Southwestern or Northwestern perspective."

PHOENIX LEARNING RESOURCES, 12 W. 31st St., New York NY 10001-4415. (212)629-3887. (212)629-5648. E-mail: john@phoenixlr.com. Website: www.phoenixlr.com. Book publisher. Executive Vice President: John A. Rothermich. Publishes 20 textbooks/year. Publisher's goal is to provide proven skill building materials in reading, language, math and study skills for today's student, grades K-adult.

Nonfiction: Middle readers, young readers, young adults: hi-lo, textbooks. Recently published *Reading for Concepts*, Third Edition.

How to Contact/Writers: Nonfiction: Submit outline/synopsis. Responds to queries in 2 weeks; mss in 1 month. Will consider simultaneous submissions and previously published work.

Photography: Buys stock. Contact: John A. Rothermich, executive vice president. Uses color prints and 35mm, 2¼×2¼, 4×5 transparencies. Submit cover letter.

Terms: Pays authors royalty based on wholesale price or work purchased outright. Pays illustrators and photographers by the project. Sends galleys to authors. Book catalog available for SASE.

Tips: "We look for classroom-tested and proven materials."

▣ ▢ PIANO PRESS, P.O. Box 85, Del Mar CA 92014-0085. (858)481-5651. Fax: (858)755-1104. E-mail: PianoPress@aol.com. Website: www.pianopress.com. Estab. 1999. Specializes in fiction, educational material, multicultural material, nonfiction. **Manuscript Acquisitions:** Elizabeth C. Axford, M.A., editor. "We publish music-related books, either fiction or nonfiction, songbooks and poetry."

Fiction: Picture books, young readers, middle readers, young adults: folktales, multicultural, poetry, music. Average word length: picture books—1,500-2,000. Recently published *Shadows from the Clouds—A Collection of Poems*, by Elizabeth C. Axford.

Nonfiction: Picture books, young readers, middle readers, young adults: multicultural, music/dance. Average word length: picture books—1,500-2,000. Recently published *Merry Christmas Happy Hanukkah—A Multilingual Songbook & CD*, by Elizabeth C. Axford.

How to Contact/Writers: Fiction/Nonfiction: Query. Responds to queries in 2 months; mss in 4 months. Publishes a book 1 year after acceptance. Will consider simultaneous submissions, electronic submissions via disk or modem.

Illustration: Works with 1 or 2 illustrators/year. Reviews ms/illustration packages from artists. Query. Contact: Elizabeth C. Axford, editor. Illustrations only: Query with samples. Contact: Elizabeth C. Axford, editor. Responds in 2 months. Samples returned with SASE; samples filed.

Photography: Buys stock and assigns work. Contact: Elizabeth C. Axford, editor. Looking for seasonal, music-related, multicultural. Model/property releases required. Uses glossy or flat, color or b&w prints. Submit cover letter, résumé, client list, published samples, stock photo list.

Terms: Pays author royalty of 8-12% based on retail price. Pays illustrators royalty of 8-12% based on retail price. Pays photographers royalty of 8-12% based on retail price. Sends galleys to authors; dummies to illustrators. Originals returned to artist at job's completion. Book catalog available for #10 SAE and 2 first-class stamps. All imprints included in a single catalog. Catalog available on website.

Tips: "We are looking for music-related material only for any juvenile market. Query first before submitting anything."

✓ THE PLACE IN THE WOODS, "Different" Books, 3900 Glenwood Ave., Golden Valley MN 55422-5302. (763)374-2120. Book publisher. **Acquisitions:** Roger Hammer, publisher/editor; Kathryn Smitley, special editor. Publishes 2 elementary-age titles/year and 1 middle readers/year; 1 young adult titles/year. 100% of books by first-time authors. Books feature primarily diversity/multicultural storyline and illustration.

Fiction: All levels: adventure, animal, contemporary, fantasy, folktales, hi-lo, history, humor, poetry, multicultural, special needs.

Nonfiction: All levels: hi-lo, history, multicultural, special needs. Multicultural themes must avoid negative stereotypes. "Generally, we don't publish nonfiction, but we would look at these."

How to Contact/Writers: Fiction/Nonfiction: Submit complete ms. Responds to queries/mss in 1 month with SASE. "No multiple or simultaneous submissions. Please indicate a time frame for response."

Illustration: Works with 4 illustrators/year. Uses primarily b&w artwork only. Reviews ms/illustration packages from authors. Query; submit ms. Contact: Roger Hammer, editor. Illustration only: Query with samples. Responds in 1 month. Include SASE. "We buy all rights."

Photography: Buys photos from freelancers. Works on assignment only. Uses photos that appeal to children. Model/property releases required; captions required. Uses any b&w prints. Submit cover letter and samples with SASE.

Terms: Work purchased outright from authors ($50-250). Pays illustrators by the project (range: $10-500). Pays photographers per photo. For all contracts, "initial payment repeated with each printing." Original artwork not returned at job's completion. Guidelines available for SASE.

PLAYERS PRESS, INC., P.O. Box 1132, Studio City CA 91614-0132. (818)789-4980. Book publisher. Imprints: Showcase Publishing; Gaslight Productions; Health Watch Books. Estab. 1965. Vice President/Editorial: Robert W. Gordon. **Manuscript Acquisitions:** Attention: Editor. **Art Acquisitions:** Attention: Art Director. Publishes 7-25 young readers dramatic plays and musicals/year; 2-10 middle readers dramatic plays and musicals/year; and 4-20 young adults dramatic plays and musicals/year. 35% of books by first-time authors; 1% of books from agented writers.

Fiction: Picture books, middle readers, young readers, young adults: history. Young adults: health, suspense/mystery. Recently published *Tower of London*, a play by William Hezlep; *Punch and Judy*, a play by William-Alan Landes; and *Silly Soup!*, by Carol Kerty (a collection of short plays with music and dance).

Nonfiction: Picture books, middle readers, young readers, young adults. "Any children's nonfiction pertaining to the entertainment industry, performing arts and how-to for the theatrical arts only." Needs include, activity, arts/crafts, careers, history, how-to, music/dance, reference and textbook. Published *Stagecrafter's Handbook*, by I.E. Clark; and *New Monologues for Readers Theatre*, by Steven Porter. Recently published *Assignments in Musical Theatre Acting & Directing*, by Jacque Wheeler and Halle Laughlin (how-to on teaching or learning to a musical theater actor or director); and *Theatre for Children in the United States: A History*, by Nellie McCaslin (complete history of children's theater from the turn of the century through 1996).

How to Contact/Writers: Fiction/nonfiction: Submit plays or outline/synopsis and sample chapters of entertainment books. Responds to queries in 1 month; mss in 1 year. Publishes a book 10 months after acceptance. No simultaneous submissions.

Illustration: Works with 2-6 illustrators/year. Use primarily b&w artwork. Illustrations only: Submit résumé, tearsheets. Responds to art samples in 1 week only if interested. Samples returned with SASE; samples filed.

Terms: Pays authors royalties based on wholesale price. Pay illustrators by the project (range: $5-5,000). Pays photographers by the project (up to 1,000); royalty varies. Sends galleys to authors; dummies to illustrators. Book catalog and ms guidelines available for SASE.

Tips: Looks for "plays/musicals and books pertaining to the performing arts only. Illustrators: send samples that can be kept for our files."

N □ PLAYHOUSE PUBLISHING, 655 W. Market St., Akron OH 44303. (330)762-6800. Fax: (330)762-2230. E-mail: info@playhousepublishing.com. Website: www.playhousepublishing.com. Specializes in mass market Christian and educational material. **Acquisitions:** Deborah D'Andrea, creative director. Imprints: Picture Me Books, Nibble Me Books. Publishes 10-15 picture books/year, 2-5 young readers/year. 50% of books by first-time authors. "Playhouse Publishing is dedicated to finding imaginative new ways to inspire young minds to read, learn and grow—one book at a time."

Fiction: Picture books: adventure, animal, concept, fantasy, folktales, humor, nature/environment, sports. Young readers: adventure, animal. Average word length: picture books—75; young readers—500. Recently published: *Picture Me as Mom's Little Helper*, illustrated by Wendy Rasmussen (age 2-7, board book); *Picture Me in the Circus*, by Heather Rhoades (age 1-5, board book); and *Cool School Story*, by Katina Jones, illustrated by Hoffman, Ottinger, Zaidan (age 4-8, picture book/early reader).

How to Contact/Writers: Fiction: Query or submit outline/synopsis. Reports on queries/mss in 2-4 months. Publishes a book 18 months after acceptance. Will consider simultaneous submissions and electronic submissions via disk or modem.

Illustration: Works with 7 illustrators/year. Uses color artwork only. Reviews ms/illustration packages. Query or submit ms with 1-2 pieces of final art. Illustrations only: Query with samples. Send résumé, promosheet and tearsheets. Contact: Deborah D'Andrea, creative director. Reports back in 1 month. Samples returned with SASE.

Photography: Works on assignment only. Model/property release required. Uses color prints.

Terms: Work purchased outright from authors. Illustrators and photographers paid by the project. Book catalog available for 9×12 SASE. All imprints included in single catalog. Catalog available online.

☑ PLEASANT COMPANY PUBLICATIONS, 8400 Fairway Place, Middleton WI 53562-0998. (608)836-4848. Fax: (608)836-1999. Website: www.americangirl.com. Book publisher. Editorial Director: Judy Woodburn. **Manuscript Acquisitions:** Erin Falligant, submissions editor. Jodi Evert, editorial director fiction/picture books; Michelle Watkins, editorial director, American Girl Library. Andrea Weiss, contemporary fiction; Peg Ross, History Mysteries; Yvette LaPierre, senior editor. **Art Acquisitions:** Jane Varda, senior art director. Imprints: The American Girls Collection, American Girl Library, History Mysteries, AG Fiction. Publishes 60 middle readers/year. 40% of books by first-time authors. Publishes fiction and nonfiction for girls 7 and up. "Pleasant Company's mission is to educate and entertain girls with high-quality products and experiences that build self-esteem and reinforce positive social and moral values."

● Pleasant Company publishes *American Girl* magazine. See the listing for *American Girl* in the Magazines section.

Fiction: Middle readers: adventure, animal, contemporary, fantasy, history, suspense/mystery. Recently published *Changes for Josefina*, by Valerie Tripp, illustrated by Jean-Paul Tibbles (ages 7-12, historical fiction); *Ceiling of Stars*, by Ann Howard Creel (ages 10 an up, contemporary fiction); *Smuggler's Treasure*, by Sarah Masters Buckey (ages 10 an up, historical fiction/mystery).

Nonfiction: Middle readers: activity books, arts/crafts, cooking, history, hobbies, how-to, self help, sports. Recently published *The Care and Keeping of You*, by Valerie Lee Schaefer, illustrated by Norm Bendell (ages 8 and up, self help); *Ooops! The Manners Guide for Girls*, by Nancy Holyoke, illustrated by Debbie Tilley (ages 8 and up, self help); and *Josefina's Cookbook, Pleasant Company* (ages 7-12, cooking).

How to Contact/Writers: Fiction/nonfiction: Query or submit entire ms. Responds to queries/mss in 2 months. Will consider simultaneous submissions.

Illustration: Works with 10 illustrators/year. Reviews ms/illustration packages from artists. Illustrations only: Query with samples. Contact: Jane Varda, senior art director. Responds only if interested. Samples returned with SASE; copies of samples filed.

Photography: Buys stock and assigns work. Submit cover letter, published samples, promo piece.

Terms: Pays authors royalty or work purchased outright. Pays illustrators by the project. Pays photographers by the project. Sends galleys to authors; dummies to illustrators. Originals returned to artist at job's completion. Book catalog available for 8½×11 SAE and 4 first-class stamps. All imprints included in a single catalog.

N POLYCHROME PUBLISHING CORPORATION, 4509 N. Francisco, Chicago IL 60625. (312)478-4455. Fax: (312)478-0786. E-mail: polypub@earthlink.net. Website: http://home.earthlink.net/~polypub/. Book publisher. Contact: Editorial Board. Publishes 2-4 picture books/year; 1-2 middle readers/year; and 1-2 young adult titles/year. 50% of books are by first-time authors. Stories focus on children of Asian ancestry in the United States.

Fiction: All levels: adventure, contemporary, history, multicultural, problem novels, suspense/mystery. Middle readers, young adults: anthology. Multicultural needs include Asian American children's experiences. Not interested in animal stories, fables, fairy tales, folk tales. Published *Nene and the Horrible Math Monster*, by Marie Villanueva; *Stella: On the Edge of Popularity*, by Lauren Lee.

Nonfiction: All levels: multicultural. Multicultural needs include Asian-American themes.

How to Contact/Writers: Fiction/Nonfiction: Submit complete ms along with an author's bio regarding story background. Responds to queries in 4 months; mss in 6 months. Publishes a book 1-2 years after acceptance. Will consider simultaneous submissions.

Illustration: Works with 4-6 illustrators/year. Reviews ms/illustration packages from artists. Submit ms with bio of author, story background and photocopies of sample illustrations. Contact: Editorial Board. Illustrations only: Query with résumé and samples (can be photocopies) of drawings of multicultural children. Responds only if interested. Samples returned with SASE; samples filed "only if under consideration for future work."

Terms: Pays authors royalty of 2-10% based on wholesale price. Work purchased outright ($25 minimum). Pays illustrators 2-10% royalty based on wholesale price. Sends galleys to authors; dummies to illustrators. Book catalog available for #10 SAE and 52¢. Ms guidelines available for SASE.

Tips: Wants "stories about experiences that will ring true with Asian Americans."

✔ PROMETHEUS BOOKS, 59 John Glenn Dr., Amherst NY 14228-2197. Fax: (716)564-2711. E-mail: slmpbooks@aol.com or slmitchell@prometheusbooks.com. Website: www.PrometheusBooks.com. Book publisher. Estab. 1969. **Acquisitions:** Steven L. Mitchell, editor-in-chief. **Art Acquisitions:** Jacqueline Cooke. Publishes 1-2 titles/year. 40% of books by first-time authors; 50% of books from agented writers. "We hope more books will be published that focus on real issues children face and real questions they raise. Our primary focus is to publish children's books with alternative viewpoints: humanism, free thought, skepticism toward the paranormal, moral values, critical reasoning, human sexuality, and independent thinking based upon science and reasoning. Our niche is the parent who seeks informative books based on these principles. We are dedicated to offering customers the highest-quality books. We are also committed to the development of new markets both in North America and throughout the world."

Nonfiction: All levels: sex education, moral education, critical thinking, nature/environment, science, self help, skepticism, social issues. Average word length: picture books—2,000; young readers—10,000; middle readers—20,000; young adult/teens—60,000. Recently published *Sasquaches From Outer Space: Exploring the Weirdest Mysteries Ever*, by Tim Yule (ages 8 and up); and *Saving Emily*, by Nicholas Read (ages 10 and up).

How to Contact/Writers: Submit complete ms with sample illustrations (b&w). Responds to queries in 1-3 weeks; mss in 1-2 months. Publishes a book 12-18 months after acceptance. SASE required for return of ms/proposal.

Illustration: Works with 1-2 illustrators/year. "We will keep samples in a freelance file, but freelancers are rarely used." Reviews ms/illustration packages from artists. "Prefer to have full work (manuscript and illustrations); will consider any proposal." Include résumé, photocopies.

Terms: Pays authors royalty of 5-15% based on wholesale price. "Author hires illustrator; we do not contract with illustrators." Pays photographers per photo (range: $50-100). Sends galleys to author. Book catalog is free on request.

Tips: We do not accept projects with anthropomorphic characters. We stress realistic children in realistic situations. "Books should reflect secular humanist values, stressing nonreligious moral education, critical thinking, logic, and skepticism. Authors should examine our book catalog to learn what sort of manuscripts we're looking for."

PUFFIN BOOKS, Penguin Putnam Inc., 345 Hudson St., New York NY 10014-3657. (212)366-2000. Website: www.penguinputnam.com/yreaders. Imprint of Penguin Putnam Inc. **Acquisitions:** Sharyn November, senior editor; Joy Peskin, editor. Publishes trade paperback originals (very few) and reprints. Publishes 175-200 titles/year. Receives 300 queries and mss/year. 1% of books by first-time authors; 5% from unagented writers. "Puffin Books publishes high-end trade paperbacks and paperback originals and reprints for preschool children, beginning and middle readers, and young adults."

Fiction: Picture books, young adult novels, middle grade and easy-to-read grades 1-3. "We publish mostly paperback reprints. We publish few original titles." Recently published *Go and Come Back*, by Joan Abelelove.

Nonfiction: Biography, children's/juvenile, illustrated book, young children's concept books (counting, shapes, colors). Subjects include education (for teaching concepts and colors, not academic), women in history. " 'Women in history' books interest us." Reviews artwork/photos. Send color photocopies. Recently published *Rachel Carson: Pioneer of Ecology*, by "Fadlinski" (history); *Grandma Moses*, by O'Neill Ruff (history). Publishes the Alloy Books series.

How to Contact/Writers: Fiction: Submit complete picture book ms or 3 sample chapters with SASE. Nonfiction: Submit 5 pages of ms with SASE. "It could take up to 5 months to get response." Publishes book 1 year after acceptance. Will consider simultaneous submissions, if so noted.

Terms: Pays royalty. Offers advance (varies). Book catalog for 9×12 SASE with 7 first-class stamps; send request to Marketing Department.

G.P. PUTNAM'S SONS, Penguin Putnam Inc., 345 Hudson St., New York NY 10014. (212)366-2000. Website: www.penguinputnam.com. Book publisher. **Manuscript Acquisitions:** Kathy Dawson, senior editor; Susan Kochan, editor. **Art Acquisitions:** Cecilia Yung, art director, Putnam and Philomel. Publishes 22 picture books/year; 13 middle readers/year; and 2 young adult titles/year. 5% of books by first-time authors; 50% of books from agented authors.

> ● Putnam titles *Getting Near to Baby*, by Audrey Couloumbis, and *26 Fairmount Ave.*, by Tomie dePaola, won 2000 Newbery Honor Medals. Turn to First Books on page 70 to read more about Putnam author Catherine Atkins and her book *When Jeff Comes Home*.

Fiction: Picture books: animal, concept, contemporary, humor, multicultural, special needs. Young readers: adventure, contemporary, history, humor, multicultural, special needs, suspense/mystery. Middle readers: adventure, contemporary, history, humor, multicultural, problem novels, special needs, sports, suspense/mystery. Young adults: contemporary, history, problem novels, special needs. "Multicultural books should reflect different cultures accurately but unobtrusively." Regarding special needs, "stories about physically or mentally challenged children should portray them accurately and without condescension." Does not want to see series, romances. Very little fantasy. Average word length: picture books—200-1,500; middle readers—10,000-30,000; young adults—40,000-50,000. Recently published *Raising Sweetness*, by Diane Stanley, illustrated by Brian Karas (ages 4-8); and *Amber Brown Sees Red*, by Paula Danziger (ages 7-10).

Nonfiction: Picture books: animal, concept, nature/environment. Subject must have broad appeal but inventive approach. Average word length: picture books—200-1,500. Recently published *Sacred Places*, by Philemon Sturges, illustrated by Giles Laroche (all ages, 32 pages).

How to Contact/Writers: Fiction/nonfiction: Query with outline/synopsis and 3 sample chapters. Unsolicited picture book mss only. Responds to queries in 2-3 weeks; mss in 4-10 weeks. Publishes a book 2 years after acceptance. Will consider simultaneous submissions on queries only.

Illustration: Works with 40 illustrators/year. Reviews ms/illustration packages from artists. Ms/illustration packages and illustration only: Query. Responds only if interested. Samples returned with SASE; samples filed.

Terms: Pays authors royalty based on retail price. Pays illustrators by the project or royalty based on retail price. Sends galleys to authors. Original artwork returned at job's completion. Books catalog and ms and artist's guidelines available for SASE.

Tips: "Study our catalogs and get a sense of the kind of books we publish, so that you know whether your project is likely to be right for us.

RAGWEED PRESS, P.O. Box 2023, Charlottetown, Prince Edward Island C1A 7N7 Canada. (902)566-5750. Fax: (902)566-4473. E-mail: editor@ragweed.com. Website: www.ragweed.com or www.gynergy.com (feminist imprint). Book publisher. **Contact:** Managing Editor. Publishes 1 picture book/year; 2 young adult titles/year. 20% of books by first-time authors.

> ● Ragweed accepts work from Canadian authors only.

Fiction: Young readers: adventure, multicultural, suspense/mystery. Middle readers, young adults: adventure, anthology, contemporary, history, multicultural. Average word length: picture books—1,000-24 pages (full color illustration); middle readers: 96 pages; young adults: 256 pages. Recently published *Light the Way Home*, by Nancy L.M. Russell (young adult adventure).

How to Contact/Writers: Fiction: Submit complete ms. Responds to queries/mss in 5-6 months. Publishes a book 6 months from final ms, "up to 2 years before editorial process is completed." Will consider simultaneous submissions.

Illustration: Works with 1-2 illustrators/year. Uses color artwork only. Reviews illustration packages from artists. Query with samples. Contact: Managing Editor. Samples returned with SASE if requested; samples filed.

Terms: Pays authors/illustrators royalty of 5-10% based on retail price. Sends galleys to authors. Original artwork returned at job's completion. Book catalog available for 9×12 SAE and 2 first-class stamps Canadian or IRC; ms and art guidelines available via website or with SASE.

Tips: "Submit in writing—phone calls won't get results. We do look at everything we receive and make our decision based on our needs. Be patient."

RAINBOW BOOKS, P.O. Box 261129, San Diego CA 92196. (858)271-7600. Book publisher. Estab. 1979. **Acquisitions:** Christy Allen, editor. Publishes 5 young readers/year; 5 middle readers/year; and 5 young adult titles/year. 50% of books by first-time authors. "Our mission is to publish Bible-based, Christ-centered materials that contribute to and inspire spiritual growth and development."

Nonfiction: Young readers, middle readers, young adult/teens: activity books, arts/crafts, how-to, reference, religion. Does not want to see traditional puzzles. Recently published *Worship Bulletins for Kids*, by Mary Rose Pearson and Jeanne Grieser (series of 2 books for ages 3-12).

How to Contact/Writers: Nonfiction: Submit outline/synopsis and 3-5 sample chapters. Responds to queries in 6 weeks; mss in 3 months. Publishes a book 18 months after acceptance. Will consider simultaneous submissions, submissions via disk and previously published work.

Illustration: Works with 2-5 illustrators/year. Reviews ms/illustration packages from artists. Submit ms with 2-5 pieces of final art. Illustrations only: Query with samples. Responds in 6 weeks. Samples returned with SASE; samples filed.

Terms: For authors, work purchased outright (range: $500 and up). Pays illustrators by the project (range: $300 and up). Sends galleys to authors. Book catalog available for 10×13 SAE and 2 first-class stamps; ms guidelines available for SASE.

Tips: "Our Rainbow imprint carries reproducible books for teachers of children in Christian ministries, including crafts, activities, games and puzzles. Our Legacy imprint (new in '97) handles nonfiction titles for children and adults in the Christian realm, such as Bible story books, devotional books, and so on. Please write for guidelines and study the market before submitting material."

☑ **RAINTREE STECK-VAUGHN**, A Harcourt Company, 15 E. 26th St., New York NY 10010. Fax: (646)936-3713. Book publisher. Publishing Directors: Frank Sloan and Walter Kossmann. Art Director: Max Brinkmann. Publishes 30 young readers/year; 30 middle readers/year; 20 young adults/year.
   ● Raintree Steck-Vaughn publishes strictly nonfiction titles.
Nonfiction: Picture books, young readers, middle readers: animal, biography, geography, health, history, multi-cultural, nature/environment, science, sports. Young adults: biography, careers, geography, health, history, sports. Average page length: young readers—32; middle readers—48; young adults: 64-128. Recently published: *Indian Nation* series (Indian tribes); *Discovering Science* series (science); and *Making of America* series (American history).
How to Contact/Writers: Nonfiction: query. Responds to queries/mss in 3-4 months.
Illustration: Contact Max Brinkman.
Photography: Contact Max Brinkman.
Terms: Pays authors royalty or flat fee. Offers advance. Sends galleys to authors. Book catalog available for 9×12 SAE and $3 first-class postage. Ms guidelines available for SASE.
Tips: "Request a catalog so you're not proposing books similar to those we've already done. Always include SASE."

Ⓐ ☐ **RANDOM HOUSE BOOKS FOR YOUNG READERS**, 201 E. 50th St., New York NY 10022. (212)572-2600. Random House, Inc. Book publisher. Estab. 1935. "Random House Books aims to create books that nurture the hearts and minds of children, providing and promoting quality books and a rich variety of media that entertain and educate readers from 6 months to 12 years." Vice President/Publishing Director: Kate Klimo. Vice President/Associate Publishing Director/Art Director: Cathy Goldsmith. **Acquisitions:** Easy-to-Read Books (step-into-reading and picture books): Heidi Kilgras, executive editor. Nonfiction: Alice Jonaitis, senior editor. First Stepping Stones and middle grade fiction: Mallory Loehr, editor-in-chief. Fantasy & Science Fiction: Alice Alfonsi, senior editor. Baby & Toddler Books: Apple Jane Jordan. 100% of books published through agents; 2% of books by first-time authors.
   ● Random House accepts only agented material.
Fiction: Picture books: animal, easy-to-read, history, humor, sports. Young readers: adventure, animal, easy-to-read, history, sports, suspense/mystery. Middle readers: adventure, history, sports, suspense/mystery. Published works of Dr. Seuss, P.D. Eastman and the Berenstein Bears; *The Story of Babar*; the Step into Reading beginning reader series; the Junie B. Jones series; the Magic Tree House series; *The Protector of the Small Quartet*, by Tamora Pierce; and *The Phantom Tollbooth*, by Norman Juster.
Nonfiction: Picture books: animal. Young readers: animal, biography, hobbies. Middle readers: biography, history, science, hobbies, sports.
How to Contact/Writers: Fiction/Nonfiction: Submit through agent only. Publishes a book 12-18 months after acceptance. Will consider simultaneous submissions.
Illustration: Reviews ms/illustration packages from artists through agent only.
Terms: Pays authors in royalties; sometimes buys mss outright. Sends galleys to authors. Book catalog free on request.

☑ **RED DEER PRESS**, Rm 813, Mackimmie Library Tower, 2500 University Dr. NW, Calgary, Alberta T2N 1N4 Canada. (403)220-4334. Fax: (403)210-8191. E-mail: khanson@ucalgary.ca. Imprints: Northern Lights Books for Children, Northern Lights Young Novels. Book publisher. Estab. 1975. **Manuscript/Art Acquisitions:** Peter Carver, children's editor. Publishes 2 picture books/year; 2 young adult titles/year. 50% of books by first-time authors. Red Deer Press is known for their "high-quality international children's program that tackles risky and/or serious issues for kids."
Fiction: Picture books, young readers: adventure, contemporary, fantasy, folktales, history, humor, multicultural, nature/environment, poetry; middle readers, young adult/teens: adventure, contemporary, fantasy, folktales, hi-lo, history, humor, multicultural, nature/environment, problem novels, suspense/mystery. Recently published *The Polar Bear's Gift*, written by Jeanne Bushey, illustrated by Vladyana Langer Krykorka (ages 4-8); *Graveyard Girl: Stories*, by Wendy Lewis (14+); *Monkey Mountain Books*, by Ted Staunton (3 books—early reader series 7-10).
How to Contact/Writers: Fiction/Nonfiction: Query or submit outline/synopsis. Responds to queries in 6 months; ms in 8 months. Publishes a book 18 months after acceptance. Will consider simultaneous submissions.
Illustration: Works with 4-6 illustrators/year. Illustrations only: Query with samples. Responds only if interested. Samples not returned; samples filed for six months.

Photography: Buys stock and assigns work. Model/property releases required. Submit cover letter, résumé and color promo piece.

Terms: Pays authors royalty (negotiated). Occasionally offers advances (negotiated). Pays illustrators and photographers by the project or royalty (depends on the project). Sends galleys to authors. Originals returned to artist at job's completion. Guidelines not available.

Tips: "Red Deer Press is currently not accepting children's manuscripts unless the writer is an established Canadian children's writer with an original project that fits its publishing program. Writers, illustrators and photographers should familiarize themselves with RD Press's children's publishing program."

■ RED WHEELBARROW PRESS, INC., P.O. Box 33143, Austin TX 78764. (512)441-4191. E-mail: publisher@rwpress.com. Website: www.rwpress.com. Estab. 1997. Trade book publisher specializing in fiction (with slant) and educational material. **Manuscript Acquisitions:** L.C. Sajbel, publisher.
  • Red Wheelbarrow is currently not accepting submissions.

RISING MOON, (imprint of Northland Publishing), P.O. Box 1389, Flagstaff AZ 86002-1389. (520)774-5251. Fax: (520)774-0592. E-mail: editorial@northlandpub.com. Website: www.northlandpub.com. Book publisher. **Manuscript Acquisitions:** Aimee Jackson, editor. **Art Acquisitions:** Lois Rainwater, art director. Publishes 10-12 picture books/year; 10% of books by first-time authors. "Rising Moon is committed to publishing educational and entertaining books with contemporary, universal themes that all children, in all regions of the U.S., will enjoy. We are best known for our attention to illustrative style and design, as well as for our heart-warming multicultural tales."

Fiction: Picture books: humor, contemporary, multicultural, nature/environment, poetry. All levels: multicultural. "Multicultural needs include stories with characters/plots that have to do with multicultural Hispanic aspects. No religion, science fiction, anthology. Average word length: picture books—300-1,500. Recently published *Dirty Birdy Feet*, by Rick Winter, illustrated by Mike Lester (ages 4-7); *Jane vs. the Tooth Fairy*, by Betsy Jay; illustrated by Lori Oslecki (ages 5-8); and *Chewy Louie*, written and illustrated by Howie Schneider (ages 5-8).

Nonfiction: Picture books: activity books, animal, nature/environment, sports. Young readers: activity books, arts/crafts, nature/environment, sports.

How to Contact/Writers: We no longer accept unsolicited submissions.

Illustration: Works with 10-12 illustrators/year. Uses color artwork only. Reviews ms/illustration packages from artists. Submit ms with 3 pieces of final art (color copy). Illustrations only: Contact: art director with résumé, samples, promo sheet, slides, tearsheets. Samples returned with SASE; samples filed.

Terms: Pays authors royalty based on retail or wholesale price. Pays illustrators by the project or royalty based on retail or wholesale price. Sends galleys to authors; dummies to illustrators. Originals returned at job's completion. Catalog and writer's and artist's guidelines available for SASE.

Tips: "No phone, fax or e-mail queries or submissions. Follow standard submission guidelines carefully and research us by visiting our website. (check SCBWI if unsure how to submit manuscripts). Does not accept unsolicited picture books. Especially looking for contemporary stories with humor and message."

■ RONSDALE PRESS, 3350 W. 21st Ave., Vancouver, British Columbia V6S 1G7 Canada. (604)738-4688. Fax: (604)731-4548. E-mail: ronhatch@pinc.com. Website: ronsdalepress.com. Book publisher. Estab. 1988. **Manuscript/Art Acquisitions:** Veronica Hatch, children's editor. Publishes 2 children's books/year. 80% of titles by first-time authors. "Ronsdale Press is a Canadian literary publishing house that publishes 8 to 10 books each year, two of which are children's titles. Of particular interest are books involving children exploring and discovering new aspects of Canadian history."

Fiction: Middle readers, young adults: animal, contemporary, history, multicultural, nature/environment, poetry, problem novels. Average word length: for middle readers and young adults—40,000. Recently published *Tangled in Time*, by Lynne Fairbridge (ages 8-15); *The Keeper of the Trees*, by Beverley Brenna (ages 8-12); and *The Ghouls' Night Out*, by Janice MacDonald, illustrated by Pamela Breeze Currie (ages 6-10), *Eyewitness*, by Margaret Thompson (ages 9-15).

Nonfiction: Middle readers, young adults: animal, biography, history, multicultural, social issues. Average word length: young readers—90; middle readers—90.

How to Contact/Writers: Fiction/Nonfiction: Submit complete ms. Responds to queries in 2 weeks; ms in 2 months. Publishes a book 1 year after acceptance. Will consider simultaneous submissions.

Illustrations: Works with 2 illustrators/year. Reviews ms/illustration packages from artists. Submit ms with dummy. Responds in 2 weeks. Samples returned with SASE. Originals returned to artist at job's completion.

Terms: Pays authors royalty of 10-12% based on retail price. Pays illustrators by the project $800-1,200. Sends galleys to authors; dummies to illustrators. Book catalog available for 8½×11 SAE and $1 postage; ms and art guidelines available for SASE.

Tips: "Ronsdale Press publishes well-written books that have a new slant on things or books that can take an age-old story and give it a new spin. We are particularly interested in novels for middle readers and young adults with a historical component that offers new insights into a part of Canada's history. We publish only Canadian authors."

Howie Schneider created this delightful cover for his book, *Chewy Louie*, with colored pencil and pen and ink. "Howie's illustrative style is a perfect match for his humorous writing," says Rising Moon editor Aimee Jackson. "His illustrations made us laugh out loud when we first saw them." Schneider is a well-known cartoonist whose work has appeared in *The New Yorker*, *Redbook*, *Esquire* and many others. He first came to the attention of the staff at Rising Moon through his agent who had previously worked with the publisher. Schneider advises aspiring illustrators to be persistent in their goals and never give up.

THE ROSEN PUBLISHING GROUP INC., 29 E. 21st St., New York NY 10010. (212)777-3017. Fax: (212)777-0277. E-mail: rosened@erols.com. **Art Acquisitions:** Gregory Payan, photo manager. Imprints: Rosen (Young Adult) (Erin M. Hovanec, acquisitions editor); Rosen Central (Amy Gelman Haugesag, acquisitions editor); PowerKids Press (Kristin Ward, acquisitions editor). Publishes 120 young adult books/year.

Nonfiction: Picture books: health, hi-lo, nature/environment, science, self-help, social issues, special needs, sports. Young readers: animal, biography, careers, cooking, geography, health, hi-lo, history, multicultural, nature/environment, religion, science, self-help, social issues, special needs. Middle readers: biography, careers, geography, health, history, hobbies, multicultural, nature/environment, religion, science, self-help, social issues, special needs, sports. Young adult: biography, careers, health, hi-lo, history, multicultural, nature/environment, reference, religion, science, self-help, social issues, special needs, sports. Average word length: young readers—800-950; middle readers—5,000-7,500; young adults—between 8,000 and 30,000. Recently published *Body Talk: A Girl's Guide to What's Happening to Your Body.*

How to Contact/Writers: Nonfiction: Query or submit outline/synopsis. Responds in 6 weeks. Publishes a book 1 year after acceptance.

Photography: Buys stock and assigns work. Contact: Gregory Payan, photo manager.

Terms: Book catalog available—no SASE or postage necessary. Offers ms and photographer's guidelines.

Tips: "Our list is specialized, and we publish only in series. Authors should familiarize themselves with our publishing program and policies before submitting."

ST. ANTHONY MESSENGER PRESS, 1615 Republic St., Cincinnati OH 45210-1298. (513)241-5615. Fax: (513)241-0399. E-mail: stanthony@americancatholic.org. Website: www.AmericanCatholic.org. Book publisher. Managing Editor: Lisa Biedenbach. **Manuscript Acquisitions:** Katie Carroll. 25% of books by first-time authors. Imprints include Franciscan Communications (print and video) and Ikonographics (video). "Through print and electronic media marketed in North America and worldwide, we endeavor to evangelize, inspire and inform those who search for God and seek a richer Catholic, Christian, human life. We also look for books for parents and religious educators."

Fiction: Picture books, middle readers, young readers: religion.

Nonfiction: Picture books, young readers, middle readers, young adults: religion. "We like all our resources to include anecdotes, examples, etc., that appeal to a wide audience. All of our products try to reflect cultural and racial diversity." Recently published *Friend Jesus: Prayers for Children*, by Gaynell Bordes Cronin; *Growing Up a Friend of Jesus: A Guide to Discipleship for Children*, by Francoise Darcy-Berube and John Paul Berube (middle readers); *Can You Find Jesus? Introducing Your Child to the Gospel*, by Philip Gallery and Janet Harlow (ages 5-10); *God Is Calling* (family based catechetical program for ages 11-14 and under 10); and *Can You Find Bible Heroes? Introducing Your Child to the Old Testament*, by Philip Gallery and Janet Harlow (ages 5-10).

How to Contact/Writers: Query or submit outline/synopsis and sample chapters. Responds to queries in 1 month; mss in 2 months. Publishes a book 12-18 months after acceptance.

Illustration: Works with 2 illustrators/year. "We design all covers and do most illustrations in-house, unless illustrations are submitted with text." Reviews ms/illustration packages from artists. Query with samples, résumé. Contact: Mary Alfieri, art director. Responds to queries in 1 month. Samples returned with SASE; samples filed. Originals returned at job's completion.

Photography: Purchases photos from freelancers. Contact: Mary Alfieri, art director. Buys stock and assigns work.

Terms: Pays authors royalties of 10-12% based on net receipts. Offers average advance payment of $1,000. Pays illustrators by the project. Pays photographers by the project. Sends galleys to authors. Book catalog and ms guidelines free on request.

Tips: "Know our audience—Catholic. We seek popularly written manuscripts that include the best of current Catholic scholarship. Parents, especially baby boomers, want resources for teaching children about the Catholic faith for passing on values. We try to publish items that reflect strong Catholic Christian values."

☑ ST. MARY'S PRESS, Christian Brothers Publications, 702 Terrace Heights, Winona MN 55987-1320. (507)457-7900 or (800)533-8095. Fax: (507)457-7990. Website: www.smp.org. Book publisher. "Our mission is to significantly advance the ministry of sharing the Good News among youth . . . employing all appropriate settings, means, and media." **Contact:** Steve Nagel.

Fiction: Young adults: history, mystery, science fiction, all topics that "both give insight into the struggle of teens to become healthy, hopeful adults and also shed light on Catholic experience, history or cultures."

How to Contact/Writers: Query with cover letter and sample chapter. Cover letter should include personal bio including background and experience; a tentative title; table of contents; date of availability for final ms; estimated word count; author's address, phone numbers and Social Security number. SASE. Simultaneous submissions are okay with notification.

Terms: Payment varies.

Tips: "Here are key questions to ask yourself before submitting: does my work further SMP's publishing program and mission? Am I clearly in touch with the needs of my audience? Has my book been critiqued by those who are qualified to do so? If you wish to learn more about us, call our toll free number and ask for a free catalog."

N ◻ **FRANK SCHAFFER PUBLICATIONS FAMILY OF COMPANIES**, 23740 Hawthorne Blvd., Torrance CA 90505. (310)378-1133. Fax: (310)791-5468. E-mail: FSPEditor@aol.com. Website: www.frankscha ffer.com. Estab. 1978. Specializes in educational material, Christian material. **Manuscript Acquisitions:** Douglas Rife, vice president of product development. **Art Acquisitions:** Michelle St. Marie, creative director. Imprints: Grace Publications and Shining Star (Janie Schmidt, editorial director); TotLine Publications (Mina McMullin, editorial director); Fearon Teacher Aids and Good Apple (Kristin Eclov, editorial director); Judy/Instructo (Stephanie Oberc, editorial director); Frank Schaffer Publications (Jeanine Manfro, editorial director). "We produce supplementary educational materials from pre-school to grade 8 and a limited amount for grades 9-12."
Nonfiction: Picture books: activity books, animal, arts/crafts, multicultural, music/dance, nature/environment, science. Young readers, middle readers, young adults: activity books, animal, arts/crafts, biography, careers, concept, geography, health, history, multicultural, music/dance, nature/environment, religion, science, self-help. Nonfiction: Query, submit complete ms, outline/synopsis or sample chapters. Responds to queries in 3 months; mss in 6 months. Publishes a book 1 year after acceptance. Will consider simultaneous submissions.
Illustration: Reviews ms/illustration packages from artists. Query, send ms with dummy, or submit ms. Contact: Michelle St. Marie, creative director. Illustrations only: Query with samples. Contact: Michelle St. Marie, creative director. Responds only if interested. Samples returned with SASE; samples filed.
Photography: Sometimes buys stock or works on assignment only. Contact: Michelle St. Marie, creative director. Query.
Terms: Pays author royalty and work purchased outright. Payment for illustration and photography varies project to project. Sometimes sends galleys to authors; dummies to illustrators, if requested. Book catalog available for 8½×11 SASE. Offers writer's and artist's guidelines.
Tips: "For teacher materials, visit educational stores to see what is being offered."

N ♥ **SCHOLASTIC CANADA LTD.**, 175 Hillmount Rd., Markham, Ontario L6C 1Z7 Canada. (905)887-READ. Fax: (905)887-1131. Website: www.scholastic.com; for ms/artist guidelines: www.scholastic.ca/guideline .html. Imprints: North Winds Press (contact Joanne Richter); Les Éditions Scholastic (contact Sylvie Andrews, French editor). **Acquisitions:** Sandra Bogart Johnston, editor, children's books. Publishes hardcover and trade paperback originals. Publishes 30 titles/year; imprint publishes 4 titles/year. 3% of books from first-time authors; 50% from unagented writers. Canadian authors, theme or setting required.
Fiction: Children's/juvenile, young adult. Recently published *After the War*, by Carol Matas (novel).
Nonfiction: Animals, history, hobbies, nature, recreation, science, sports. Reviews artwork/photos as part of ms package. Send photocopies. Recently published *Whose Bright Idea Was It?*, by Larry Verstraete (about amazing inventions).
How to Contact/Writers: Query with synopsis, 3 sample chapters and SASE. Nonfiction: Query with outline, 1-2 sample chapters and SASE. Responds in 3 months. Publishes book 1 year after acceptance.
Terms: Pays 5-10% royalty on retail price. Offers advance: $1,000-5,000 (Canadian). Book catalog for 8½×11 SAE with 2 first-class stamps (IRC or Canadian stamps only).

✓ ♥ **SCHOLASTIC INC.**, 555 Broadway, New York NY 10012. (212)343-6100. Website: www.scholastic. com. Estab. 1920. Senior Vice President and publisher: Jean Feiwel. **Manuscript Acquisitions:** Scholastic Press: Elizabeth Szabla, editorial director; Blue Sky Press: Bonnie Verburg, editorial director; Trade Paperback: Craig Walker, vice president and editorial director; Cartwheel Books: Bernette Ford, vice president and editorial director; Arthur A. Levine Books: Arthur Levine, editorial director; Scholastic Reference: Wendy Barrish, editorial director. **Art Acquisitions:** David Saylor, creative director. "We are proud of the many fine, innovative materials we have created—such as classroom magazines, book clubs, book fairs, and our new literacy and technology programs. But we are most proud of our reputation as 'The Most Trusted Name in Learning.' "
● Scholastic is not interested in receiving ideas for more fiction paperback series. They do not accept unsolicited mss. Scholastic title *Black Hands, White Sails: The Story of African-American Whalers*, by Patricia C. and Frederick L. McKissack, won a 2000 Coretta Scott King Author Honor Award; their title *Black Cat*, written and illustrated by Christopher Myers, won a 2000 Coretta Scott King Illustrator Honor Award; and their title *Space Station Science: Life in Free Fall*, by Marianne J. Dyson won the Golden Kite Award for Nonfiction in 2000.
Illustration: Works with 50 illustrators/year. Does not review ms/illustration packages. Illustrations only: send promo sheet and tearsheets.Responds only if interested. Samples not returned. Original artwork returned at job's completion.
Terms: All contracts negotiated individually; pays royalty. Sends galleys to author; dummies to illustrators.

♥ **SCHOLASTIC PRESS**, 555 Broadway, New York NY 10012. (212)343-6100. Website: www.scholastic.c om. Book publisher. Imprint of Scholastic Inc. **Manuscript Acquisitions:** Dianne Hess, executive editor (picture book fiction/nonfiction); Lauren Thompson, senior editor (picture book fiction/nonfiction); Tracy Mack, senior editor (picture book, middle grade, YA). **Art Acquisitions:** David Saylor, Scholastic Press, Reference, Paperback; Edie Weinberg, Cartwheel Books. Publishes 60 titles/year. 1% of books by first-time authors.
● Scholastic Press title *Red-Eyed Tree Frog*, by Joy Cowley, illustrated with photos by Nic Bishop, won a 1999 Boston Globe-Horn Book Award for picture books.

Class clown makes it big with a cavalcade of kooky characters

Growing up funny in Ohio fits the Dav Pilkey profile. The fact that the thirty-five-year-old author and illustrator of more than thirty books was a feisty class clown will come as no surprise. But discovering that some teachers met his lively spirit with unbridled harshness may be a shocker. And knowing his dreams endured in spite of it all is bound to leave you inspired.

Dav Pilkey

Modern medicine calls the condition Attention Deficit Disorder. But elementary school officials called Pilkey's creative energy trouble. "I remember one teacher who used to rip up my books and tell me I'd better start taking life more seriously because I couldn't spend the rest of my days making silly books," Pilkey says. "Fortunately, I wasn't a very good listener."

Pilkey's high school principal was even more direct. "He said, 'I know you think you're special because you can draw, but let me tell you something. Artists are a-dime-a-dozen. You will never make a living as an artist.' Those words haunted me for many years," Pilkey remembers. "How delightful it was to prove him wrong."

Proof started stacking up after Pilkey enrolled as an art student at Kent State University in Ohio. He entered his book, "World War Won" in the National Written & Illustrated by . . . Awards Contest for Students, a fifteen-year-old tradition sponsored by Landmark Editions, Inc., a publisher in Kansas City, Missouri. Branded a winner, Landmark published the book a year later. And he's been following his bliss ever since.

Reaching out to *all* kids—kids some grown-ups see as good *and* bad—is Pilkey's top priority. "I think it's a good thing for kids to hear that some successful grown-ups weren't so successful in school," he says. " I wish I'd heard that when I was a kid. It would have been a real comfort to me."

That same, reassuring essence shines from every Pilkey illustration and book. In *Dog Breath*, Pilkey's 1994 classic, the Tosis children search for a bad breath cure, until their afflicted dog, Hally beats the burglars with his smelly, slobbery kiss. In 1998's *Silly Gooses*, a scornful flockmate warns the main character, "You had better stop being so silly, or you will never find a wife," just as a slap-happy spouse drops as if from heaven.

From *Dumb Bunnies* to *Captain Underpants*, Pilkey's message is clearly getting through. "I get letters all the time from classrooms of children with special needs," he says. "They all seem to be inspired by the fact that I was just like them, but I still turned out okay. One classroom told me I was an even better role model than all the wrestlers!"

As if top dogging a wrestler wasn't enough, Pilkey added an electronic extension to his reach, www.pilkey.com. "I think the website has been up about three years now," he says. "From my perspective, the Web gives me a chance to reach out to my fans without having to leave the comfort and privacy of my own home. I don't travel well."

Captain Underpants and the Perilous Plot of Professor Poopypants (Scholastic) is the fourth in Dav Pilkey's series of epic novels featuring the silly super hero. Captain Underpants emerged in *The Adventures of Captain Underpants*. Friends George and Harold hypnotize their crusty principal Mr. Krupp with a 3-D Hypno-Ring, and he takes on the identity of the comic book character they'd created.

Designed to be super kid-friendly (like Pilkey himself), the site is also a must for adults. "My hope is that teachers and librarians will use it to download cool stuff to share with kids," Pilkey admits. "I'm hoping it will be a fun, easy and free resource to help adults bring the books to life in their classrooms and libraries."

With the click of a mouse, educators have the chance to participate in a www.pilkey.com treasure hunt. They can download Dav Pilkey coloring sheets. They can adopt Pilkey as their "teacher of the month." They can even use Pilkey's personal ADD story as an inspiration for students who might be learning impaired.

Technical glitches have made it hard to update his cyber stop. "But I'm now in the process of learning how to do that kind of thing myself," Pilkey says. "Again, my goal is for the site to be as big and funny as possible, with an endless supply of fun, free resources for people to download."

Keeping his books fresh hasn't been as challenging. "I just try to make the books as funny and smart as possible," he says. But he admits his confidence stems first from his illustrations. "I probably see myself as an illustrator first. Drawing is something I have complete, total, 100% confidence in. I can't say the same thing about writing."

Does Pilkey's 'Net head inclination mean he's going all electronic anytime soon? "No," he says . . . I don't think so. (I hope not)." Pilkey sees no future for e-books in the realm of children's literature, "and I rarely illustrate electronically. The only time I use the computer is if an illustration contains lettering that needs to be warped into perspective."

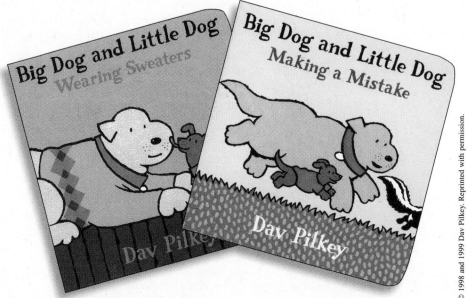

The versatile Dav Pilkey has written and illustrated picture books, epic novels, and even a series of board books starring Big Dog and Little Dog. These books, written for baby-preschool level, include *Wearing Sweaters*, *Making a Mistake*, *Getting in Trouble* and *Going for a Walk*, along with the series' first title, simply, *Big Dog and Little Dog* (all Harcourt Red Wagon Books).

For now, Pilkey is content to write traditional children's books in a totally twisted way. "The most important thing about what I do is that it makes children laugh," he says. "I could probably get my old job at the gas station back, if this writing thing didn't pan out. But this is my dream . . . to keep doing what I'm doing for as long as I possibly can.

"It's the coolest job in the world," he says. "I get to draw cartoons and write stories about underwear . . . what's not to like?"

—Kelly Milner Halls

Editor's note: For more information on the The National Written and Illustrated By . . . Awards Contest, write to Landmark Editions, Inc., P.O. Box 270169, Kansas City, MO 64127.i

Fiction: All levels: adventure, animal, anthology, concept, contemporary, fantasy, health, history, humor, multicultural, nature/environment, poetry, religion, science fiction, sports, suspense/mystery. Picture books: concept, folktales. Middle readers: folktales, problem novels, romance. Young adults: problem novels, romance. Multicultural needs include: strong fictional or nonfictional themes featuring non-white characters and cultures. Does not want to see mainstream religious, bibliotherapeutic, adult. Average word length: picture books—varies; young adults—150 pages. Recently published *Black Cat*, by Christopher Meyers.

Nonfiction: All levels: animal, biography, history, multicultural, music/dance, nature/environment, science, social issues, sports. Picture books: concept. Multicultural needs "usually best handled on biography format." Average word length: picture book—varies; young adults—150 pages. Recently published *Black Hands, White Sails*, by Patricia C. and Frederick L. McKissack.

How to Contact/Writers: Fiction: "Send query with 1 sample chapter and synopsis. (don't call!) only if you feel certain we publish the type of book you have written." Nonfiction: young adult titles: query. Picture books: submit complete ms. Responds in 1-3 months.

Illustrations: Works with 30 illustrators/year. Uses both b&w and color artwork. Contact: Editorial Submissions. Illustration only: Query with samples; send tearsheets. Responds only if interested. Samples returned with SASE. Original artwork returned at job's completion.

Photography: Buys photos from freelancers. Contact: Photo Research Dept. Buys stock and assigns work. Uses photos to accompany nonfiction. Model/property releases required; captions required. Submit cover letter, résumé, client list, stock photo list.

Terms: Pays authors by varying royalty (usually standard trade roles) or outright purchase (rarely). Offers variable advance. Pays illustrators by the project (range: varies) or standard royalty based on retail price. Pays photographers by the project or royalty. Sends galleys to authors.

Tips: "Read *currently* published children's books. Revise, rewrite, rework and find your own voice, style and subject. We are looking for authors with a strong and unique voice who can tell a great story and have the ability to evoke genuine emotion. Children's publishers are becoming more selective, looking for irresistable talent and fairly broad appeal, yet still very willing to take risks, just to keep the game interesting."

N̄ Ā SEASTAR BOOKS, Division North-South Books Inc., 1123 Broadway, Suite 800, New York NY 10010. (212)463-9736. E-mail: seastar@northsouth.com. Website: www.northsouth.com. Specializes in fiction, trade books. **Manuscript Acquisitions:** Andrea Schneeman, editor-in-chief. **Art Acquisitions:** Ellen Friedman, art director. Publishes 15 picture books/year; 5 young readers/year; 5 middle readers/year; 5 young adult titles/year. 5% of books by first-time authors. "SeaStar is a publisher of literary hardcover (and some paperback) books for children ages 4-14. We seek to present a 'constellation of stars' rather than a dizzying universe of titles, with an emphasis on picture books, fiction and fine illustration. We will consider work in almost any 'category' but are not interested in formula/genre-oriented/mass market or textbook-oriented material."

• SeaStar Books only considers agented manuscripts but will consider unagented material from SCBWI members.

Fiction: Recently published *Aesop's Fables*, by Jerry Pinkney (ages 5-9, illustrated fable collection); *Gus & Gertie and the Missing Pearl*, by Joan Lowery Nixon; illustrated by Diane de Groat (ages 7-10, illustrated easy-to-read); *The Dark Portal*, by Robin Jarvis (ages 10 and up, middle grade/young adult). "Again, we will consider nonfiction with a wide range of categories, but our nonfiction list is limited to approximately 5 titles/year. Will only consider trade-oriented nonfiction."

Nonfiction: Recently published *Out of Sight*, by Seymour Simon (ages 5-9, photo essay); *Picture This: How Pictures Work*, by Molly Bang (ages 10 and up, illustrated nonfiction).

How to Contact/Writers: Only interested in agented material. Will consider unagented material by members of SCBWI. Fiction: Submit complete ms for picture books; or submit outline/synopsis and 3 sample chapters for chapter books. Nonfiction: Submit outline/synopsis and 3 sample chapters. Responds to mss in 3 months. Publishes a book 2 years after acceptance. Will consider previously published work.

Illustration: Works with 15 illustrators/year. Submit ms with dummy and copies of about 3-5 pieces of final art. Contact: Andrea Schneeman, editor-in-chief. Illustrations only: Send promo sheet, tearsheets, "Nothing that needs to be returned." Responds in 3 months only if ms is submitted. Samples returned with SASE but prefers not to have to return samples.

Photography: Buys stock.

Terms: Pays author royalty of 1-6¼% if picture book author; 10-12½% if no art in book. Pays illustrators 1-6¼% if a separate author and illustrator are involved; 10-12½% if author and illustrator are the same. Sends galleys to authors; dummies to illustrators. Originals returned to artist at job's completion. All imprints included in a single catalog. Catalog available on website.

N: SEEDLING PUBLICATIONS, INC., 4522 Indianola Ave., Columbus OH 43214-2246. (614)267-7333. Fax (614)267-4205. E-mail: Sales@SeedlingPub.com. Website: www.SeedlingPub.com. **Acquisitions:** Josie Stewart, vice president. 20% of books by first-time authors. Publishes books for the beginning reader in English and Spanish. "Natural language and predictable text are requisite to our publications. Patterned text acceptable, but must have a unique storyline. Poetry, books in rhyme, full-length picture books or chapter books are not being accepted at this time. Illustrations are not necessary."

Fiction: Beginning reader books: adventure, animal, fantasy, hi-lo, humor, multicultural, nature/environment, special needs. Multicultural needs include stories which include children from many cultures and Hispanic-centered storylines. All mss to be published in Spanish must be submitted in both English and Spanish. Does not want to see texts longer than 16 pages or over 150-200 words or stories in rhyme. Average word length: young readers—100. Recently published *Treasure in the Attic*, by Linda Kulp and *Before the Fridge*, by Heather Flanders (ages 3-7, paperback early reader).

Nonfiction: Beginning reader books: animal, concept, hi-lo, multicultural, music/dance, nature/environment, science, special needs, sports. Does not want to see texts longer than 16 pages or over 150-200 words. Average word length: young readers—100. Recently published *Magnets*, by Josie Stewart and Lynn Salem (ages 3-7, early reader).

How to Contact/Writers: Fiction/Nonfiction: Submit complete ms. Responds in 6 months. Publishes a book 1-2 years after acceptance. Will consider simultaneous submissions.

Illustration: Works with 4-5 illustrators/year. Uses color artwork only. Reviews ms/illustration packages from artists. Submit ms with dummy. Illustrations only: Send color copies. Responds only if interested. Samples returned with SASE only; samples filed if interested.

Photography: Buys photos from freelancers. Works on assignment only. Model/property releases required. Uses color prints and 35mm transparencies. Submit cover letter and color promo piece.

Terms: Pays authors royalty of 5% based on retail price or work purchased outright. Pays illustrators and photographers by the project. Original artwork is not returned at job's completion. Book catalog available for 2 first-class stamps.

Tips: "Follow our guidelines carefully and test your story with children and educators."

☐ 17TH STREET PRODUCTIONS, (formerly Daniel Weiss Associates, Inc.), 11th Floor, 33 W. 17th St., New York NY 10011. (212)645-3865. Fax: (212)633-1236. Independent book producer/packager. Estab. 1987. **Manuscript Acquisitions:** Judy Goldschmidt, editorial assistant. **Art Acquisitions:** Paul Matarazzo, art director (illustrations); Mike Rivilis, associate art director (ms/illustration packages). Publishes 30 young readers/year; 40 middle readers/year; and 70 young adults/year. 25% of books by first-time authors. "We do mostly series! We mainly publish middle grade and YA series and hire writers for books in these series. As a book packager, we work with the larger publishing houses."

Fiction: Middle readers: sports. Young adults: fantasy, romance. Recently published *5vtt Senior Year* #8; *Major Who*, Thoroughbred #34; *On The Track.*

Nonfiction: Young adults. Recently published *Ultimate Cheerleading Handbook Scene* series.

How to Contact/Writers: Send SASE for guidelines to write for series currently in production. No unsolicited mss.

Illustration: Works with 20 illustrators/year. Reviews ms/illustration packages from artists. Submit query. Illustrations only: Provide promo sheet. Responds in 2 months. Samples returned with SASE. Original artwork returned at job's completion.

Terms: Pays authors royalty on work purchased outright from authors. Offers advances. Pays illustrators by the project.

☐ SILVER MOON PRESS, 160 Fifth Ave., New York NY 10010. (212)242-6499. E-mail: mail@silvermoonpress. com. Website: www.silvermoonpress.com. Publisher: David Katz, marketing assistant. Managing Editor: Carmen McCain. **Acquisitions:** Karin Lillebo, marketing assistant. Book publisher. Publishes 2 books for grades 4-6. 25% of books by first-time authors; 10% books from agented authors. "We publish books of entertainment and educational value and develop books which fit neatly into curriculum for grades 4-6. Silver Moon Press publishes mainly American historical fiction with a strong focus on the Revolutionary War and Colonial times. History comes alive when children can read about other children who lived when history was being made!''

Fiction: Middle readers: historical, multicultural and mystery. Average word length: 14,000. Recently published *A Message for General Washington*, by Vivian Schurfranz; and *A Secret Party in Boston Harbor*, by Kris Hemphill (both historical fiction, ages 8-12); *Treason Stops at Oyster Bay*, by Anna Leah Sweetzer.

How to Contact/Writers: Fiction: Query. Send synopsis and/or a few chapters, along with a SASE. Responds to queries in 2-4 weeks; mss in 1-2 months. Publishes a book 1-2 years after acceptance. Will consider simultaneous submissions or previously published work.

Illustration: Works with 2-3 illustrators/year. Reviews ms/illustration packages from artists. Query. Illustrations only: Query with samples, résumé, client list. Responds only if interested. Samples returned with SASE; samples filed. Original artwork returned at job's completion.

Photography: Buys photos from freelancers. Buys stock and assigns work. Uses archival, historical, sports photos. Captions required. Uses color, b&w prints; 35mm, 2¼×2¼, 4×5, 8×10 transparencies. Submit cover letter, résumé, published samples, client list, promo piece.

Terms: Pays authors royalty or work purchased outright. Pays illustrators by the project, royalty. Pays photographers by the project, per photo, royalty. Sends galleys to authors; dummies to illustrators. Book catalog available for 8½×11 SAE and 77¢ postage.

SIMON & SCHUSTER BOOKS FOR YOUNG READERS, 1230 Avenue of the Americas, New York NY 10020. (212)698-7000. Fax: (212)698-2796. Website: www.simonsayskids.com. Imprint of Simon & Schuster Children's Publishing Division. Vice President/Associate Publisher: Steve Geck. **Manuscript Acquisitions:** David Gale, editorial director; Jessica Schulte, editor; Kevin Lewis, senior editor; Amy Hampton-Knight, associate editor; John Rudolph, assistant editor; Emily Thomas, editorial assistant. **Art Acquisitions:** Paul Zakris, art director. Publishes 75 books/year. "We publish high-quality fiction and nonfiction for a variety of age groups and a variety of markets. Above all we strive to publish books that will offer kids a fresh perspective on their world."

- Simon & Schuster Books for Young Readers does not accept unsolicited manuscripts. Simon & Schuster title *Hard Love*, by Ellen Wittlinger, won a 2000 Michael L. Printz Honor Award and the Lambda Literary Award; their title *With All My Heart, With All My Mind*, edited by Sandy Asher won the 2000 National Jewish Book Award.

Fiction: Picture books: animal, concept. Middle readers, young adult: adventure, suspense/mystery. All levels: anthology, contemporary, history, humor, poetry, nature/environment. Recently published *Click, Clack, Moo: Cows That Type*, by Doreen Cronin, illustrated by Betty Lewin; *The Janitor's Boy*, by Andrew Clements; and *When Kambia Elaine Flew in From Neptune*, by Lori Aurelia Williams.

Nonfiction: All levels: biography, history, nature/environment. Picture books: concept. "We're looking for picture book or middle grade nonfiction that has a retail potential. No photo essays." Recently published *Author Talk*, edited by Leonard S. Marcus; and *Wall Street Wizard*, by Jay Liebowitz.

How to Contact/Writers: Accepting query letters only. Responds to queries/mss in 1-2 months. Publishes a book 2-4 years after acceptance. Will consider simultaneous submissions.

Illustration: Works with 70 illustrators/year. Do not submit original artwork. Editorial reviews ms/illustration packages from artists. Submit query letter to Submissions Editor. Illustrations only: Query with samples; samples filed. Provide promo sheet, tearsheets. Responds only if interested. Originals returned at job's completion.

Terms: Pays authors royalty (varies) based on retail price. Pays illustrators or photographers by the project or royalty (varies) based on retail price. Original artwork returned at job's completion. Ms/artist's guidelines available via website or free on request (call (212)698-2707.).

Tips: "We're looking for picture books centered on a strong, fully-developed protagonist who grows or changes during the course of the story; YA novels that are challenging and psychologically complex; also imaginative and humorous middle-grade fiction. And we want nonfiction that is as engaging as fiction. Our imprint's slogan is 'Reading You'll Remember.' We aim to publish books that are fresh, accessible and family-oriented; we want them to have an impact on the reader."

SOMERVILLE HOUSE BOOKS LIMITED, 24 Dinnick Crescent, Toronto, Ontario M4N 1L5 Canada. (416)489-7769. Fax: (416)486-4458. E-mail: sombooks@goodmedia.com. Website: www.sombooks.com. Somerville publishes books and develops products. **Acquisitions:** Jane Somerville, publisher/president. Produces 20-30 titles/year in nonfiction and novelty formats.

- Somerville is currently accepting unsolicited mss in the areas of natural science, activities, sports and novelty formats.

Nonfiction: Young readers and middle readers: activity books, animal, arts/crafts, cooking, geography, history, hobbies, music/dance, nature/environment, science, sports. Recently published *The Hummingbird Book and Feeders*, by Neil Dawe; and *The Titanic Book and Submersible Model*, by Steve Santini.

How to Contact/Writers: Only interested in agented material. Responds to queries/mss in 2-3 months.

Illustration: Works with 20-30 illustrators/year. Responds only if interested. Samples not returned; samples filed.

insider report

Creating children's books takes the effort, talent of many

For many people, writing seems like a solitary profession. The thought of spending day after day alone, staring at a computer screen, can be enough to scare someone away from pursuing a career as an author. But for Robie H. Harris, whose books *It's Perfectly Normal: Changing Bodies, Growing Up, Sex, and Sexual Health* and *It's So Amazing!: A Book About Eggs, Sperm, Birth, Babies, and Families* focus on sexual health for kids, the writing process has been far from lonely. In fact, her first book dealing with sex, *It's Perfectly Normal*, came about after many discussions with family, teachers, and child specialists. And collaboration played an important role with her subsequent titles, *It's So Amazing!*, *Happy Birth Day!*, and *Hi New Baby!* (all published by Candlewick Press) and *Good-bye Mousie* (Margaret K. McElderry Books).

Robie H. Harris

Harris never intended to write books on sexuality for kids. But when an editor for another publisher asked her to do a book for children about HIV/AIDS, she started to consider the subject seriously. "The topic had never crossed my mind," says Harris. "But I said to that editor, 'If I were talking with my own kids about HIV when they were in elementary school, I would want to talk about it in the context of healthy sexuality. There are a whole lot of things that kids need to know before in order to stay healthy. They need to know how their bodies work, what happens during puberty, what's the same and what's different about females and males, how babies are made and, of course, about HIV/AIDS, and lots more.' "

In fact, Harris outlined a potential book in that editor's office that day and went home and told her kids, who were then in their late teens, about her conversation with the editor. "I asked my kids, 'What was helpful when your dad and I talked to you about sex? What did you still need to know? And what should I put in this book that I didn't think about?' " And that's when the great collaboration began. "We talked, and that night I made about ten phone calls to science teachers, other parents, and our pediatrician. My kids talked to their friends, and I talked with them, too. And they were very open." The editor decided, however, that he still wanted a book focusing on HIV/AIDS. But by then Harris knew she was going to do her own book about sexual health, one which would be comprehensive and would include HIV/AIDS.

From the start, Harris realized she'd have to learn not only how to present sensitive sexual topics to kids but also the specific science of the facts of life. "We wanted to be absolutely sure the information in the books is as accurate as possible and would really work for kids, particularly for *It's Perfectly Normal* and *It's So Amazing!* because these books deal with topics that can be difficult and tough—as well as fascinating—for kids. We also realized these books are also about human biology and are really about how each one of us grows up. That's why I always feel in writing for children—no matter what the topic—that our responsibility is to the kids who are our audience," says Harris.

Photo: Stewart Clements

And this responsibility comes through in the way the books are written. Topics like the fertilization of an egg by a sperm, the stages of pregnancy, puberty, heterosexuality and homosexuality, masturbation, and others are clearly explained in a way that makes them *perfectly normal*. Harris's use of a cartoon bird and bee as narrators in *It's So Amazing!* and *It's Perfectly Normal* allows kids to be more comfortable with the subject matter. "The bird and the bee are the voices of kids," explains Harris. The bird is curious and wants to know everything about sex while the bee is resistant and would rather read books about earth science than hear about where babies come from. Young readers are able to identify with the personality most like their own.

In order to get her books right, however, Harris had to do her research. And looking at the pages of thank-yous in the back of *It's So Amazing!* and *It's Perfectly Normal*, it's clear that her research was extensive. "I talked to everybody from pediatricians to teachers, librarians, social workers, psychologists, reproductive biologists, child development experts, HIV/AIDS experts and clergy members," says Harris.

For writers doing research, Harris advises that when asking people to help, the first thing you say is that your book is for children. She followed this plan and was never once turned down. In fact, she established many beneficial relationships that lasted through the entire process of creating the books. "I felt strongly about getting the science as accurate and as up-to-date as possible." At one point she read an article in *The New York Times* Science section about reproductive biologist, Jeffrey Pudney, Ph.D. who had been doing research on sperm. "I picked up the phone, got his number from information, and said, 'Hi, my name is Robie Harris, and I'm writing a book on sexual health for kids.'" From this call she developed an important contact with Dr. Pudney, who spent many hours going over the materials with Harris and her illustrator, Michael Emberley. "Jeffrey is so passionate about biology that he was an extraordinary teacher

Several years after writing *It's Perfectly Normal* for readers ages 10-14, Robie H. Harris once again teamed up with illustrator Michael Emberley for *It's So Amazing*, written for younger readers. A starred review in *The Horn Book* called their effort "a friendly and sensitive guide for younger children." Harris and Emberley once again employed a cartoon bird and bee to help guide readers through the text.

for us. He felt excited because he wanted the kids to be excited about science and health when they read our books and looked at the cartoon illustrations."

Harris also went to parents for input on her manuscript; however, when some of the parents asked if they could read a draft of the book to their children, Harris asked them to wait. Unlike many writers who jump eagerly at any chance to share their work with their intended audience, Harris says, "It made me nervous, not because I didn't want the parents to read it to their kids, but because the book was not finished yet. I felt it would be irresponsible to pass on any information inadvertently that might not have been quite right or inaccurate at that point in the writing process."

All the research Harris did was part of the collaborative process. "I work best through collaboration. I love to work closely with the illustrator and all the people I showed the text to beyond the editor—all the parents, kids, teachers, librarians, health professionals, scientists, and child development experts." Nevertheless, through this research she realized she had to write about topics that were so difficult to even think about—like sexual abuse—because it would have been a disservice to kids not to include them.

"The most difficult part about writing the section on abuse," says Harris, "happened when I talked to Eli Newberger, M.D. He said what can be confusing for kids is that sometimes the abuse feels good. I said to him, 'How am I going to write that?' But he said he knew I could do it because it is very important for children to know." Although this section was an incredible challenge for Harris and Emberley, its inclusion in the book actually helped a girl who was being abused. "I read an article about a ten-year-old girl who read the chapter in *It's Perfectly Normal* on sexual abuse and who then went to her mother and said her father was abusing her. The father was convicted, and the book was even used in the trial. And even though this chapter was so difficult to write, it was absolutely worth doing—just for this one child."

In order to present these difficult topics clearly, Harris worked closely with illustrator Michael Emberley. Although most publishers find illustrators after the book has been written, and as a rule authors and illustrators don't collaborate, Harris's process was different. She started working with Emberley early on—even before the book was sold to a publisher. "We were concerned with how to make this book accessible to kids," says Harris. A crucial part of this accessibility was ensuring that the illustrations showed children of different shapes, sizes, and ethnicities.

Harris met with Emberley constantly to find the best ways of presenting the information in the books. "We had to be very confident about every double-page spread in the book," says Harris. "We asked if the information would be appropriate, would it be fun? We set out to create a book that would work for many kids, so that one child would be able to read the boxes of text or look at the pictures, while another could read the discussion between the bird and the bee, and another to look at a diagram or even start at the beginning and go all the way to the end. I believe brilliant books can be done even when the author and illustrator never meet. I feel extremely lucky to have a working relationship with someone I respect highly and who really wants to do what is in the best interest of the child." For his research, Emberley even attended an actual birth to learn how to draw a newborn.

The entire process—from the day she started thinking about writing *It's Perfectly Normal* to when the book was finished—took about five years. "When you collaborate it does take longer," says Harris. She eventually took her manuscript and Emberley's drawings to Candlewick Press because she was impressed with editor Amy Ehrlich, who felt the book was an important project and shared Harris's vision for the book and how it should be produced. And although Candlewick was a new press at the time, its sister company, the established Walker Books in the United Kingdom, gave the press more than thirty years of experience. Working with Candlewick meant even more collaboration. "There were a ton of meetings with editors that were critical. But Michael and I met even more, and that was the most important collaboration."

For Harris the collaborative process has paid off. "As a writer you can spend a lot of time alone. I feel very lucky that I was able to so closely work with Michael and everyone else. I learn so much from them. It's more effort and time, but ultimately, if you are lucky, I believe you end up with a better book."

—*Donya Dickerson*

Robie H. Harris's most recent collaboration with illustrator Michael Emberley, *Hi New Baby!*, rejoins the family featured in their book *Happy Birth Day*, this time dealing with new sibling issues, as a little girl adjusts to life with her new baby brother.

☑ **SOUNDPRINTS**, 353 Main Ave., Norwalk CT 06851-1552. (203)846-2274. Fax: (203)846-1776. E-mail: sndprnts@ix.netcom.com. Website: www.soundprints.com. Estab. 1987. Specializes in trade books, educational material, multicultural material, nonfiction. **Manuscript Acquisitions:** Chelsea Shriver, editorial assistant. **Art Acquisitions:** Scott Findlay. Publishes 4 picture books/year; 8 young readers/year. Soundprints publishes children's books accompanied by plush toys and read-along cassettes that deal with wildlife, history and nature. All content must be accurate and realistic and is curated by experts for veracity.

Fiction: Picture books: animal. Young readers: animal, multicultural, nature/environment. Middle readers: history, multicultural.

Nonfiction: Picture books: animals. Young readers: animal, multicultural, natuare/environment. Middle readers: history, multicultural. *Koala Country: Story of an Australian Eucalyptus Forest*, by Deborah Dennard, illustrated by James McKinnon (grades 1-4); *Box Turtle at Silver Pond*, by Susan Korman, illustrated by Stephen Mucclesi (grades ps-2); *Bear on His Own*, by Laura Gales Gatvin (ages 18 months to 3 years).

How to Contact/Writers: Fiction/Nonfiction: Query. Responds in 3 months. Publishes book 2 years after acceptance.

Illustration: Works with 12 illustrators/year. Uses color artwork only. Query. Contact: Chelsea Shriver, editorial assistant. Query with samples. Samples not returned.

Photography: Works on assignment only.

Terms: Work purchased outright from authors for $1,000-2,500. Pays illustrators by the project. Book catalog available for SASE; ms and art guidelines available for SASE. Catalog available on website.

☑ **SOURCEBOOKS, INC.**, 1935 Brookdale Rd., Suite 139, Naperville IL 60563-9245. (630)961-3900. Fax: (630)961-2168. Website: www.sourcebooks.com. Book publisher. **Manuscript Acquisitions:** Todd Stocke, editorial director; Hillel Black, agented manuscripts; Deborah Werksman, gift, humor, relationships. **Art Acquisitions:** Norma Underwood, director of production.
How to Contact/Writers: Fiction/Nonfiction: Query or submit outline/synopsis. Responds to queries/mss in 3 months. Publishes a book 1 year after acceptance. Will consider simultaneous submissions, electronic submissions via disk or modem and previously published work.
Illustration: Works with 10 illustrators/year. Reviews ms/illustration packages from artists. Query. Illustrations only: Query with samples. Samples returned with SASE; samples filed.
Photography: Buys stock.
Terms: Send galleys to authors. Originals returned to artist at job's completion. Book catalog for 9 × 12 SASE. All imprints included in a single catalog. Ms guidelines available for SASE.

◘ **THE SPEECH BIN, INC.**, 1965 25th Ave., Vero Beach FL 32960. (561)770-0007. Fax: (561)770-0006. Book publisher. Estab. 1984. **Acquisitions:** Jan J. Binney, senior editor. Publishes 10-12 books/year. 50% of books by first-time authors; less than 15% of books from agented writers. "Nearly all our books deal with treatment of children (as well as adults) who have communication disorders of speech or hearing or children who deal with family members who have such disorders (e.g., a grandparent with Alzheimer's disease or stroke)."
● The Speech Bin is currently overstocked with fiction.
Fiction: Picture books: animal, easy-to-read, fantasy, health, special needs. Young readers, middle readers, young adult: health, special needs.
Nonfiction: Picture books, young readers, middle readers, young adults: activity books, health, textbooks, special needs.
How to Contact/Writers: Fiction/Nonfiction: Query. Responds to queries in 6 weeks; mss in 3 months. Publishes a book 10-12 months after acceptance. "Will consider simultaneous submissions *only* if notified; too many authors fail to let us know if manuscript is simultaneously submitted to other publishers! We *strongly* prefer sole submissions. No electronic or faxed submissions."
Illustration: Works with 4-5 illustrators/year ("usually in-house"). Reviews ms/illustration packages from artists. Ms/illustration packages and illustration only: "Query first!" Submit tearsheets (no original art). SASE required for reply or return of material. No electronic or faxed submissions without prior authorization.
Photography: Buys stock and assigns work. Looking for scenic shots. Model/property releases required. Uses glossy b&w prints, 35mm or 2¼ × 2¼ transparencies. Submit résumé, business card, promotional literature or tearsheets to be kept on file.
Terms: Pays authors in royalties based on selling price. Pay illustrators by the project. Photographers paid by the project or per photo. Sends galleys to authors. Original artwork returned at job's completion. Book catalog for $1.43 postage and 9 × 12 SAE; ms guidelines for #10 SASE.
Tips: "No calls, please. All submissions and inquiries must be in writing."

☑ **STANDARD PUBLISHING**, 8121 Hamilton Ave., Cincinnati OH 45231. (513)931-4050. Fax: (513)931-0950. E-mail: customerservice@standardpub.com. Website: www.standardpub.com. Book publisher. Estab. 1866. Director, Children's Publishing: Diane Stortz. **Manuscript Acquisitions:** Lise Caldwell, children's editor, Ruth Frederick, Church Resources. **Art Acquisitions:** Coleen Davis, art director. Imprints: Bean Sprouts™ Children's Books, Church Resources. Number and type of books varies yearly. Many projects are written in-house. No juvenile or young adult novels. 25-40% of books by first-time authors; 1% of books from agented writers. "We publish well-written, upbeat books with a Christian perspective. Books are fun with relevancy in Christian education."
● Standard publishes *Encounter*, *Kidz Chat* and *Live Wire*, all listed in Magazines. Also see listing for Standard Publishing in the Greeting Cards, Puzzles & Games section.
Fiction: Adventure, animal, contemporary, Bible stories. Average word length: board/picture books—400-1,000. Recent publications: *Noah! Noah!*, by Jennifer Stewart.
Nonfiction: Bible background, nature/environment, devotions. Average word length: 400-1,000. Recently published *Pattycake Devotions*, by Christine Tangiold, illustrated by Norma Garris (board books).
How to Contact/Writers: Responds in 6 weeks on queries, mss in 3 months.
Illustration: Works with 20 new illustrators/year. Illustrations only: Submit cover letter and photocopies. Responds to art samples only if interested. Samples returned with SASE; samples filed.
Terms: Pays authors royalties based on net price or work purchased outright (range varies by project). Pays illustrators (mostly) by project. Pays photographers by the photo. Sends galleys to authors on most projects. Book catalog available for $2 and 8½ × 11 SAE; ms guidelines for letter-size SASE.
Tips: "We look for manuscripts that help draw children into a relationship with Jesus Christ; help children develop insights about what the Bible teaches; make reading an appealing and pleasurable activity."

STEMMER HOUSE PUBLISHERS, INC., 2627 Caves Rd., Owings Mills MD 21117-9919. (410)363-3690. Fax: (410)363-8459. E-mail: stemmerhouse@home.com. Website: www.stemmer.com. Book publisher. Estab.

1975. **Acquisitions:** Barbara Holdridge, president. Publishes 1-3 picture books/year. "Sporadic" numbers of young reader, middle reader titles/year. 60% of books by first-time authors. "Stemmer House is best known for its commitment to fine illustrated books, excellently produced."
Fiction: Picture books: animal, folktales, multicultural, nature/environment. Middle readers: folktales, nature/environment. Does not want to see anthropomorphic characters. Published *How Pleasant to Know Mr. Lear: Poems by Edward Lear*, illustrated by Bohdan Butenko; and *The Marvelous Maze*, by Maxine Rose Schur, illustrated by Robin DeWitt and Patricia DeWitt-Grush.
Nonfiction: Picture books: animal, multicultural, nature. All level: animals, nature/environment. Multicultural needs include Native American, African. Recently published *A Duck in a Tree*, by Jennifer A. Loomis, photographs by the author; *The Bird Alphabet Encyclopedia Coloring Book*, by Julia Pinkham; *Ask Me If I'm a Frog*, by Ann Milton, illustrated by Jill Chambers.
How to Contact/Writers: Fiction/Nonfiction: Query or submit outline/synopsis and sample chapters. Responds to queries/mss in 1 week. Publishes a book 18 months after acceptance. Will consider simultaneous submissions. No submissions via e-mail.
Illustration: Works with 2-3 illustrators/year. Uses color artwork only. Reviews ms/illustration packages from artists. Query first with several photocopied illustrations. Illustrations only: Submit tearsheets and/or slides (with SASE for return). Responds in 2 weeks. Samples returned with SASE; samples filed "if noteworthy."
Terms: Pays authors royalties of 4-10% based on wholesale price. Offers average advance payment of $300. Pays illustrators royalty of 4-10% based on wholesale price. Pays photographers 4-10% royalty based on wholesale price. Sends galleys to authors. Original artwork returned at job's completion. Book catalog and ms guidelines for 9 × 12 SASE.
Tips: Writers: "Simplicity, literary quality and originality are the keys." Illustrators: "We want to see ms/illustration packages—don't forget the SASE!"

N: THE STORY PLACE, 1735 Brantley Rd., #1611, Ft. Myers FL 33902-3920. Fax: (775)206-7437. E-mail: tsp@thestoryplace.com. Website: www.thestoryplace.com. Estab. 1998. Specializes in mass market books, fiction, nonfiction. **Manuscript Acquisitions:** Brian Smith. **Art Acquisitions:** Katie Hughey. Publishes 2 picture books/year; 1 young readers/year. 100% of books by first-time authors. "The Story Place focuses on new and different ideas that fill the void in children's publishing today."
Fiction: Picture books, young readers: all categories. Middle readers, young adults: adventure, animal, fantasy, folktales, humor, nature/environment, religion, sports. Average word length: picture books—50-500; young readers—100-2,000. Recently published *Leo Hamilton's Odd Collection of Animal and Insect Stories Volume I, Leo Hamilton's Odd Collection of Animal and Insect Stories Volume II, Leo Hamilton Presents: Children's Dream Adventures*, all by Leo Hamilton, illustrated by Jessica Larkin (ages 4-11, animal, humor).
Nonfiction: Picture books, young readers: all categories. Middle readers, young adults: animal, nature/environment. Average word length: picture books—50-500; young readers—100-2,000.
How to Contact/Writers: Fiction/Nonfiction: Submit complete ms. Responds in 1 month. Publishes a book 10-18 months after acceptance. Will consider simultaneous submissions, electronic submissions via disk or modem.
Illustration: Uses both color and b&w artwork. Reviews ms/illustration packages from artists. Submit ms with dummy. Contact: Brian Smith, publishing director. Samples returned.
Terms: Pays author royalty of 10-40% or work purchased outright. Sends galleys to authors. Originals returned to artist at job's completion. Book catalog available for 9 × 12 SAE and 3 first-class stamps. Manuscript guidelines available for SASE.
Tips: "Research our guidelines, read our books to get an idea of what we publish. As for the market in general, research, research, research."

SUNBELT MEDIA, INC./EAKIN PRESS, P.O. Box 90159, Austin TX 78709. (512)288-1771. Fax: (512)288-1813. E-mail: eakinpub@sig.net. Website: www.eakinpress.com. Book publisher. Estab. 1978. President: Ed Eakin. Publishes 25 books for young readers/year. 50% of books by first-time authors; 5% of books from agented writers.
Fiction: Picture books: animal. Middle readers, young adults: history, sports. Average word length: picture books—3,000; young readers—10,000; middle readers—15,000-30,000; young adults—30,000-50,000. "90% of our books relate to Texas and the Southwest."
Nonfiction: Picture books: animal. Middle readers and young adults: history, sports. Recently published *Abuelito Eats with his Fingers*, by Janice Levy, illustrated by Layne Johnson.
How to Contact/Writers: Fiction/Nonfiction: Query. Responds to queries in 2 weeks; mss in 6 weeks. Publishes a book 18 months after acceptance. Will consider simultaneous submissions.
Illustration: Reviews ms/illustration packages from artists. Query. Illustrations only: Submit tearsheets. Responds to art samples in 2 weeks.
Terms: Pays authors royalties of 10-15% based on net to publisher. Pays for separate authors and illustrators: "Usually share royalty." Pays illustrators royalty of 10-15% based on net to publisher. Sends galleys to authors. Book catalog $1 available via website or with SASE; writer guidelines available with SASE.
Tips: Writers: "Be sure all elements of manuscript are included—include bio of author or illustrator." Submit books relating to TX only.

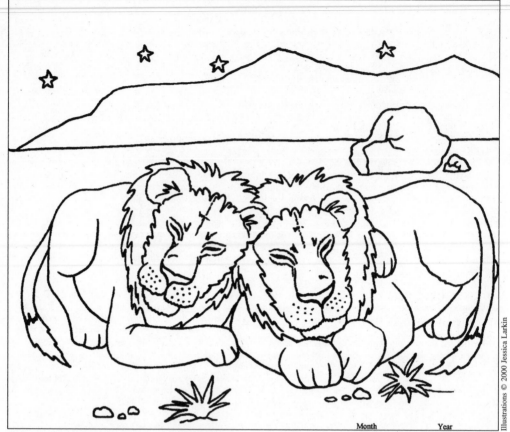

Month   Year

Illustrations © 2000 Jessica Larkin

This black-ink line drawing by Jessica Larkin appeared in *Leo Hamilton's Odd Collection of Animal and Insect Stories*, a coloring/storybook published by The Story Place. The publishers were so pleased with her work, they asked her to do the illustrations for a second volume of *Leo* stories, as well as a third book, *Leo Hamilton Presents Children's Dream Adventures*. Larkin relies on word-of-mouth to get assignments. She emphasizes the importance of being willing to try new styles and techniques as a way to improve skill levels. "Know your personal motivation before starting a project," she says, "and be assertive."

SUPER MANAGEMENT, Smarty Pants A/V, 15104 Detroit, Suite 2, Lakewood OH 44107-3916. (216)221-5300. Fax: (216)221-5348. Estab. 1988. Specializes in mass market books, fiction, educational material, Christian material, audio with each book. **Acquisitions:** S. Tirk, CEO/President. Publishes 12 young readers/ year. 5% of books by first-time authors. "We do mostly the classics or well known names such as Paddington Bear."

Fiction: Picture books: adventure, animal, folktales, multicultural, nature/environment, poetry. Average word length: young readers—24 pages. Recently published *The Best of Mother Goose*, from the "Real M.G."; *Beatrix Potter, Paddington Bear.*

Nonfiction: Picture books, young readers: activity books, animal, music/dance, nature/environment. Average word length: picture books—24 pages; middle readers—24 pages.

How to Contact/Writers: Fiction: Submit complete ms. Responds in 3 weeks. Publishes a book 6-12 months after acceptance. Will consider simultaneous submissions and previously published work.

Illustration: Only interested in agented material. Works with several illustrators/year. Uses color artwork only. Reviews ms/illustration packages from artists. Submit ms with dummy with return prepaid envelope. Contact: S. Tirk, CEO/President. Illustrations only: send promo sheet. Contact: S. Tirk, CEO/President. Responds in 3 weeks to queries. Samples returned with SASE.

Photography: Works on assignment only. Model/property releases required. Uses color prints. Submit color promo piece.

Terms: Pays author negotiable royalty. Buys artwork and photos outright. Manuscript and art guidelines available for SASE.

Tips: "We deal with mostly children's classics and well-known characters."

N ☐ ⊞ TEACHER IDEAS PRESS, Libraries Unlimited, P.O. Box 6633, Englewood CO 80511-6633. (303)770-1220. Fax: (303)220-8843. E-mail: lu-books@lu.com. Website: www.lu.com/tip. Estab. 1965. Specializes in educational material, multicultural material. Independent book packager/producer.
Nonfiction: Young readers, middle readers, young adult: activity books, multicultural, reference, teacher resource books. Recently published *Science Through Children's Literature, 2000*, by Butzow (grades K-6, lit-based activity book); *More Novels & Plays: 30 Creative Teaching Guides for Grades 6-12*, by Worthington; and *Native Americans Today: Resources & Activities for Educators*, by Hirschfelder (grades 4-8).
How to Contact/Writers: Nonfiction: Query or submit outline/synopsis. Responds to queries in 6 weeks. Publishes a book 6-9 months after acceptance. Will consider simultaneous submissions or electronic submissions via disk of modem.
Terms: Pays authors royalty of 10-15%. Send galleys to authors. Book catalog available for 9 × 12 SASE and 5 first-class stamps. Writer's guidelines available for SASE. Catalog available online at www.lu.com.
Tips: "We encourage queries from writers with classroom experience as teachers, although we will consider others. Activity books, annotated bios, story collections with supplemental materials, and books with many reproducibles are welcome for consideration."

THROUGH THE BIBLE PUBLISHERS, Treasure Publishing and Treasure Systems, 1133 Riverside, Suite B, Fort Collins CO 80524-3216. (970)484-8483. Fax: (970)495-6700. E-mail: ataylor@throughthebible.com. Website: www.throughthebible.com. Book publisher. **Acquisitions:** Andrea Taylor, editor. "Through the Bible Publishers exists to assist the Church of Jesus Christ in fulfilling the Great Commission. We create, market and distribute Christian education resources which feature excellence in biblical content, educational methodology and product presentation. Our primary responsibility is to serve the local and international Church.
Nonfiction: Bible study resources for elementary children ages 6-12, preschool (ages 2-5) and junior/senior high school (ages 13-18). Recently published *DiscipleLand* curriculum.
How to Contact/Writers: Query with writing sample and SASE. Freelance writers send résumé with samples of children's writing to acquisition editor.
Illustration: Freelance designers send résumé and samples to art director.
Terms: Freelance writers/illustrators work for hire contracts only.
Tips: "Our present interests is children's Bible curriculum. No fiction, please."

☑ TILBURY HOUSE, PUBLISHERS, 2 Mechanic St., #3, Gardiner ME 04345. (207)582-1899. Fax: (207)582-8227. E-mail: tilbury@tilburyhouse.com. Website: www.tilburyhouse.com. Book publisher. Publisher: Jennifer Elliott. Publishes 1-3 young readers/year.
Fiction: Young readers, middle readers: multicultural, nature/environment. Special needs include books that teach children about tolerance and honoring diversity.
Nonfiction: Young readers, middle readers: multicultural, nature/environment. Published *Talking Walls* and *Who Belongs Here?* both by Margy Burns Knight, illustrated by Anne Sibley O'Brien (grades 3-8); *Stone Wall Secrets*, by Kristine and Robert Thorson, illustrated by Gustav Moore; *Everybody's Somebody's Lunch*, by Cherie Mason, illustrated by Gustav Moore.
How to Contact/Writers: Fiction/Nonfiction: Submit outline/synopsis. Responds to queries/mss in 1 month. Publishes a book 1-2 years after acceptance. Will consider simultaneous submissions "with notification."
Illustration: Works with 2 illustrators/year. Illustrations only: Query with samples. Contact: J. Elliott, associate publisher. Responds in 1 month. Samples returned with SASE. Original artwork returned at job's completion.
Photography: Buys photos from freelancers. Contact: J. Elliott, publisher. Works on assignment only.
Terms: Pays authors royalty based on wholesale price. Pays illustrators/photographers by the project; royalty based on wholesale price. Sends galleys to authors. Book catalog available for 6 × 9 SAE and 55¢ postage.
Tips: "We are primarily interested in children's books that teach children about tolerance in a multicultural society and honoring diversity. We are also interested in books that teach children about environmental issues."

TOR BOOKS, Forge, Orb, 175 Fifth Ave., New York NY 10010. E-mail: benjamin.yots@stmartins.com. Website: www.tor.com. Publisher, Middle Grade and Young Adult Division: Kathleen Doherty. Children's, Young Adult Editor: Jonathan Schmidt. Educational Sales Coordinator: Benjamin Yots. Publishes 5-10 middle readers/year; 5-10 young adults/year.
Fiction: Middle readers, young adult titles: adventure, animal, anthology, concept, contemporary, fantasy, folktales, health, history, humor, multicultural, nature/environment, problem novel, science fiction, special needs, sports, suspense/mystery. "We are interested and open to books which tell stories from a wide range of perspectives. We are interested in materials that deal with a wide range of issues." Average word length: middle readers—10,000; young adults—30,000-60,000. Published *Mind Quakes: Stories to Shatter Your Brain* and *Scorpions Shards*, by Neal Shusterman (ages 8 and up); and *From One Experience to Another*, edited by Helen and Jerry Weiss (ages 10 and up).

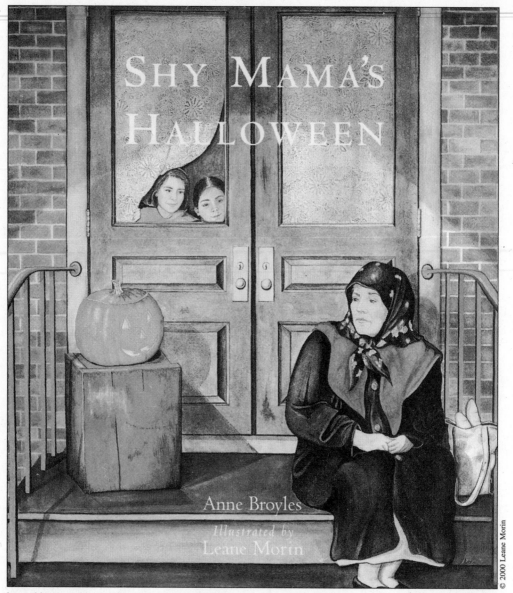

SHY MAMA'S
HALLOWEEN

Anne Broyles

Illustrated by
Leane Morin

Leane Morin combines realism with a wonderful ability to capture expressive faces in her illustrations for *Shy Mama's Halloween*, published by Tilbury House. Besides the actual time spent painting, Morin also went to great pains researching the time period to make sure her depictions of an immigrant family in the 1930s were accurate. Publisher Jennifer Elliott reports that Morin's work was a big success at Book Expo, and *Publishers Weekly* chose one of her pieces for their Children's Fall Roundup listings.

Nonfiction: Middle readers and young adult: activity books, geography, history, how-to, multicultural, nature/environment, science, social issues. Does not want to see religion, cooking. Average word length: middle readers—10,000-15,000; young adults—40,000. Published *Strange Unsolved Mysteries*, by Phyllis Rabin Emert; *Stargazer's Guide* (to the Galaxy), by Q.L. Pearce (ages 8-12, guide to constellations, illustrated).

How to Contact/Writers: Fiction/Nonfiction: Submit outline/synopsis and 3 sample chapters or complete ms. Responds to queries in 3 weeks; mss in 6 months.

Illustration: Works with 40 illustrators/year. Reviews ms/illustration packages from artists. Query with samples. Contact: Jonathan Schmidt. Responds only if interested. Samples returned with SASE; samples kept on file.

Terms: Pays authors royalty. Offers advances. Pays illustrators by the project. Book catalog available for 9 × 12 SAE and 3 first-class stamps. Submission guidelines available with SASE.

Tips: "Know the house you are submitting to, familiarize yourself with the types of books they are publishing. Get an agent. Allow him/her to direct you to publishers who are most appropriate. It saves time and effort."

TRADEWIND BOOKS, 2216 Stephens St., Vancouver, British Columbia V6K 3W6 Canada.(604)730-0153. Fax: (604)730-0154. E-mail: tradewindbooks@yahoo.com. Website: tradewindbooks.com. Estab. 1994. Trade book publisher. **Manuscript Acquisitions:** Michael Katz, publisher. **Art Acquisitions:** Carol Frank, art director. Publishes 3 picture books/year. 25% of books by first-time authors.

Fiction: Picture books: adventure, animal, multicultural, folktales. Average word length: 900 words. Recently published *Mr. Belinsky's Bagels*; *Mama God, Papa God*; *Wherever Bears Be*, and *The Girl Who Lost Her Smile*.

Nonfiction: Picture books: animal and nature/environment.

How to Contact/Writers: Fiction: Submit complete ms. Will consider simultaneous submissions. Do not send query letter. Responds to mss in 6 weeks.

Illustration: Works with 3-4 illustrators/year. Uses color artwork only. Reviews ms/illustration packages from artists. Send ms with dummy. Illustrations only: Query with samples. Responds only if interested. Samples returned with SASE; samples filed.

Photography: Works on assignment only. Uses color prints.

Terms: Royalties negotiable. Offers advances against royalties. Originals returned to artist at job's completion. Book catalog available for 3 × 5 SAE and 3 first-class stamps. Catalog available on website. Unsolicited submissions accepted only if authors have read at least 3 books published by Tradewind Books. Submissions must include a reference to these books.

TRANSWORLD PUBLISHERS LIMITED, 61-63 Uxbridge Rd., London W5 5SA England. Phone: (0208)579-2652. Fax: (0208)231-6737. E-mail: childrens.editorial@transworld-publishers.co.uk. Imprints are Doubleday, Picture Corgi (ages 3-6), Corgi Pups (ages 5-8), Young Corgi (ages 6-9), Corgi Yearling (ages 8-11), Corgi (ages 10 +), Corgi Freeway (ages 11 +) and Bantam Books (ages 10 +). Book publisher. Publisher, Children's and Young Adult Publishing: Philippa Dickinson. Publishes 10 picture books/year; 12 young readers/year; 12 middle readers/year; and a few young adult titles/year.

Fiction: Picture books: adventure, animal, anthology, contemporary, fantasy, folktales, humor, multicultural, nature/environment, poetry, suspense/mystery. Young readers: adventure, animal, anthology, contemporary, fantasy, folktales, humor, multicultural, nature/environment, poetry, sports, suspense/mystery. Middle readers: adventure, animal, anthology, contemporary, fantasy, folktales, humor, multicultural, nature/environment, problem novels, romance, sports, suspense/mystery. Young adults: adventure, contemporary, fantasy, humor, multicultural, nature/environment, problem novels, romance, science fiction, suspense/mystery. Average word length: picture books—800; young readers—1,500-6,000; middle readers—10,000-15,000; young adults—20,000-45,000. Recently published *Dangerous Reality*, by Malorie Blackman (ages 8 and up, computer-assisted adventure); *The Dare Game*, by Jacqueline Wilson (ages 10 and up, contemporary); and *Billy the Bird*, by Dick King-Smith (ages 6-8, animal novel).

How to Contact/Writers: Submit outline/synopsis and 3 sample chapters to Children's Editorial. Responds to queries in 1 month; mss in 2 months. Will consider simultaneous and previously published submissions.

Illustration: Works with 50 illustrators/year. Reviews ms/illustration packages from artists. Submit ms with dummy. Contact: Penny Walker. Illustrations only: Query with samples. Responds in 1 month. Samples are returned with SASE (IRC).

Photography: Buys photos from freelancers. Contact: Tracey Hurst, art department. Buys stock images. Photo captions required. Uses color or b&w prints. Submit cover letter, published samples.

Terms: Pays authors royalty. Offers advances. Pays illustrators by the project or royalty. Pays photographers by the project or per photo. Sends galleys to authors; dummies to illustrators.

TRICYCLE PRESS, Imprint of Ten Speed Press, P.O. Box 7123, Berkeley CA 94710. (510)559-1600. Fax: (510)559-1637. E-mail: kate@tenspeed.com. Website: www.tenspeed.com. Estab. 1971. **Acquisitions:** Nicole Geiger, editor. Imprints: Ten Speed Press and Celestial Arts. Publishes 8 picture books/year; 5 activity books/year; 3 young readers/year; 5 young adult/year. 30% of books by first-time authors. "Tricycle Press looks for something outside the mainstream; books that encourage children to look at the world from a different angle."

Fiction: Picture books, young readers, middle reader: adventure, animal, contemporary, folktales, history, multicultural, nature/environment. Picture books, young readers: concept. Middle readers: anthology. Average word length: picture books—1,200. Recently published *Hurry Granny Annie*, by Arlene Alda (ages 4-7, picture book); *Why I Will Never Ever Ever Ever Finish This Book*, by Remy Charlip (ages 6-12, picture book); *Never Let Your Cat Make Lunch for You*, by Lee Harris, illustrated by Debbie Tilley (ages 4-7, picture book).

Nonfiction: Picture books, middle readers, young readers: activity books, animal, arts/crafts, concept, cooking, hobbies, how-to, nature/environment, science, self help, social issues. Young readers: activity books, arts/crafts, health, how-to, nature/environment, science, self help, social issues. Picture books, middle readers: concept, hobbies. Young adult: hobbies. Recently published *G is for Googol: A Math Alphabet Book*, by David M. Schwartz (ages 9 and up, picture book); *Honest Pretzels and 64 Other Amazing Recipes for Cooks Ages 8 & Up*, by Mollie Katzen (activity book); and *Pumpkin Circle: The Story of a Garden*, by George Levenson, photography by Shmuel Thaler (ages 5-8, nonfiction picture book).

How to Contact/Writers: Fiction: Submit complete ms for picture books. Submit outline/synopsis and 2-3 sample chapters for chapter book. "No queries!" Nonfiction: Submit complete ms. Responds to mss in 5 months. Publishes a book 1-2 years after acceptance. Welcomes simultaneous submissions and previously published work. Do not send original artwork; copies only, please.

Illustration: Works with 9 illustrators/year. Uses color and b&w. Reviews ms/illustration package from artists. Submit ms with dummy and/or 2-3 pieces of final art. Illustrations only: Query with samples, promo sheet, tearsheets. Contact: Nicole Geiger. Responds only if interested. Samples returned with SASE; samples filed. Original artwork returned at job's completion unless work for hire.

Photography: Works on assignment only. Contact: Nicole Geiger. Uses 35mm transparencies. Submit samples.

Terms: Pays authors royalty. Offers advances. Pays illustrators by the project or royalty. Pays photographers royalty and by the project. Sends galleys to authors. Book catalog for 9×12 SASE ($1.01). Ms guidelines for SASE.

Tips: "We are looking for something a bit outside the mainstream and with lasting appeal (no one-shot-wonders). Lately we've noticed a sacrifice of quality writing for the sake of illustration."

A TROLL COMMUNICATIONS, 100 Corporate Dr., Mahwah NJ 07430. (201)529-4000. Website: www.troll.com. Book publisher. **Acquisitions:** Marian Frances, editor.

● Troll Communications only accepts agented mss and are not currently accepting unsolicited manuscripts; they are open to receiving samples from illustrators.

Fiction: Picture books: animal, contemporary, folktales, history, nature/environment, poetry, sports, suspense/mystery. Young readers: adventure, animal, contemporary, folktales, history, nature/environment, poetry, science fiction, sports, suspense/mystery. Middle readers: adventure, anthology, animal, contemporary, fantasy, folktales, health-related, history, nature/environment, poetry, problem novels, romance, science fiction, sports, suspense/mystery. Young adults: problem novels, romance and suspense/mystery.

Nonfiction: Picture books: activity books, animal, biography, careers, history, hobbies, nature/environment, sports. Young readers: activity books, animal, biography, careers, health, history, hobbies, music/dance, nature/environment, sports. Middle readers: activity books, animal, biography, careers, health, history, hobbies, music/dance, nature/environment, sports. Young adults: health, music/dance.

How to Contact/Writers: Currently not accepting unsolicited mss. Fiction: Query or submit outline/synopsis and 3 sample chapters. Nonfiction: Query. Responds in 4 weeks.

Illustration: Reviews ms/illustration packages from artists. Contact: Marian Frances, editor. Illustrations only: Query with samples; provide résumé, promotional literature or tearsheets to be kept on file. Responds in 4 weeks.

Photography: Interested in stock photos. Model/property releases required.

Terms: Pays authors royalty or work purchased outright. Pays illustrators by the project or royalty. Photographers paid by the project.

✓ TROPHY BOOKS, 1350 Avenue of the Americas, New York NY 10019. (212)261-6500. Fax: (212)261-6668. Website: www.harpercollins.com. Subsidiary of HarperCollins Children's Books Group. Book publisher. Vice President/Editorial Director: Ginee Seo. Editor: Susan Rich. Associate Editor: Susan Chang. Publishes 6-9 chapter books/year, 25-30 middle grade titles/year, 20 reprint picture books/year, 10-15 young adult titles/year.

● Trophy is primarily a paperback reprint imprint. They publish a limited number of chapter book, middle grade and young adult manuscripts each year.

TURTLE BOOKS, 866 United Nations Plaza, Suite 525, New York NY 10017. (212)644-2020. Website: www.turtlebooks.com. Book Publisher. Estab. 1997. **Acquisitions:** John Whitman. "Turtle Books publishes only picture books for very young readers. Our goal is to publish a small, select list of quality children's books each spring and fall season. As often as possible, we will publish our books in both English and Spanish editions."

Fiction: Picture books: adventure, animal, concept, contemporary, fantasy, folktales, hi-lo, history, humor, multicultural, nature/environment, religion, sports, suspense/mystery. Recently published: *The Legend of Mexicatl*, by Jo Harper, illustrated by Robert Casilla (the story of Mexicatl and the origin of the Mexican people); *Vroom, Chugga, Vroom-Vroom*, by Anne Miranda, illustrated by David Murphy (a number identification book in the form of a race car story); *The Crab Man*, by Patricia VanWest, illustrated by Cedric Lucas (the story of a young Jamaican boy who must make the difficult decision between making an income and the ethical treatment of animals); and *Prairie Dog Pioneers*, by Jo and Josephine Harper, illustrated by Craig Spearing (the story of a young girl who doesn't want to move, set in 1870s Texas).

How to Contact/Writers: Send complete ms. "Queries are a waste of time." Response time varies.
Illustrators: Works with 6 illustrators/year. Responds to artist's queries/submissions only if interested. Samples returned with SASE only.
Terms: Pays royalty. Offers advances.

TURTLE PRESS, P.O. Box 290206, Wethersfield CT 06129-0206. (860)529-7770. Fax: (860)529-7775. E-mail: editorial@turtlepress.com. Website: www.turtlepress.com. Estab. 1990. Publishes trade books. Specializes in nonfiction, multicultural material. **Manuscript Acquisitions:** Cynthia Kim. Publishes 1 young reader/year; 1 middle reader/year. 40% of books by first-time authors.
Fiction: Middle readers, young adults: multicultural, sports. Recently published *A Part of the Ribbon: A Time Travel Through Adventure the History of Korea*.
Nonfiction: Young readers, middle readers, young adults: multicultural, sports. Recently published *Martial Arts Training Diary for Kids* and *Everyday Warriors*.
How to Contact/Writers: Fiction/Nonfiction: Query. Nonfiction: Query. Responds to queries in 1 month; 2 months on mss. Publishes a book 12-18 months after acceptance. Will consider simultaneous submissions.
Photography: Buys stock.
Terms: Pays authors royalty of 8-12%. Offers advances against royalties of $1,000. Pays illustrators by the project. Sends galleys to authors. Book catalog available for 6×9 SAE and 3 first-class stamps; ms guidelines for SASE. All imprints included in a single catalog. Catalog available on website.
Tips: "We focus on martial arts and related cultures."

N TWO LIVES PUBLISHING, 508 N. Swarthmore Ave., #1, Ridley Park PA 19078-3222. (610)532-2024. Fax: (610)532-2790. E-mail: info@twolives.com. Website: www.twolives.com. Estab. 1999. Specializes in trade books. **Manuscript Acquisitions:** Bobbie Combs. Publishes 6 picture books/year. 100% of books by first-time authors. "Two Lives Publishing is committed to creating and distributing quality children's books for children in gay and lesbian families."
Fiction: Picture books: anthology, concept, contemporary, multicultural, poetry, special needs. Young readers, middle readers: adventure, anthology, contemporary, humor, multicultural, poetry, special needs. Young adults: adventure, anthology, contemporary, multicultural, poetry, special needs.
Nonfiction: Picture books, young readers, middle readers, young adults: activity books, arts/crafts, biography, concept, history, hobbies, how-to, reference, social issues, special needs.
How to Contact/Writers: Fiction/Nonfiction: Submit complete ms. Responds to queries/mss 1 month. Publishes a book 1 year after acceptance. Will consider simultaneous submissions, electronic submissions via disk or modem, previously published work.
Illustration: Works with 4 illustrators/year. Reviews ms/illustration packages from artists. Submit ms with dummy. Contact: Bobbie Combs. Illustrations only: send résumé, portfolio. Contact: Bobbie Combs. Responds in 1 month. Samples returned with SASE.
Terms: Pays author royalty of 5-7½% based on retail price; or work purchased outright from authors for $500-1,000. Offers advances (Average amount: $1,000). Pays illustrators royalty of 5-7½% based on retail price. Sends galleys to authors; dummies to illustrators. Originals returned to artist at job's completion. Book catalog available for 8½×11 SAE and 6 first-class stamps; ms and art guidelines available for SASE. All imprints included in a single catalog.

N A TYNDALE HOUSE PUBLISHERS, INC., 351 Executive Dr., P.O. Box 80, Wheaton IL 60189. (630)668-8300. Book publisher. Estab. 1962. **Manuscript Acquisitions:** Karen Watson. **Art Acquisitions:** Beth Sparkman.Publishes approximately 20 Christian children's titles/year.
  • Tyndale House no longer reviews unsolicited mss. Only accepts agented material.
Fiction: Middle readers: adventure, religion, suspense/mystery.
Nonfiction: Picture books: religion. Young readers: Christian living, Bible, devotionals.
How to Contact/Writers: Only interested in agented material. "Request children's writer guidelines from (630)668-8310 ext. 836 for more information."
Illustration: Uses full-color for book covers, b&w or color spot illustrations for some nonfiction. Illustrations only: Query with photocopies (color or b&w) of samples, résumé. Contact: Talinda Laubach.
Photography: Buys photos from freelancers. Works on assignment only.
Terms: Pay rates for authors and illustrators vary.
Tips: "All accepted manuscripts will appeal to Evangelical Christian children and parents."

UAHC PRESS, 633 Third Ave., New York NY 10017. (212)650-4120. Fax: (212)650-4119. E-mail: press@uahc .org. Website: www.uahc.press.org. Book publisher. Estab. 1876. **Manuscript/Art Acquisitions:** Rabbi Hara Person, managing editor. Publishes 4 picture books/year; 2 young readers/year; 2 middle readers/year; 2 young adult titles and 4 textbooks/year. "The Union of American Hebrew Congregations Press publishes textbooks for the religious classroom, children's tradebooks and scholarly work of Jewish education import—no adult fiction and no YA fiction."
Fiction: Picture books, young readers, middle readers: religion. Average word length: picture books—150; young readers—500; middle readers—3,000. Recently published *A Tree Trunk Seder*, written and illustrated by Camille

Kress (toddler's board book); *Hello, Hello, Are You There, God?* written by Molly Cone and illustrated by Rosalind Charney Kaye (ages 3-7, short stories); and *Come Let Us Be Joyful! The Story of Hava Nagila*, written by Fran Manuskin and illustrated by Rosalind Charney Kaye (ages 3-7, Jewish fiction).

Nonfiction: Picture books, young readers, middle readers, young adult/teens: religion. Average word length: picture books—150; young readers—500; middle readers—3,000; young adult/teens—20,000. Recently published *My Jewish Holiday Fun Book*, written and illustrated by Ann Koffsky (ages 5-9, activity book); *Until the Messiah Comes*, by Kenneth Roseman (ages 10-13, do-it-yourself Jewish adventure); and *Chocolate Chip Challah: And Other Twists on the Jewish Holiday Table*, written and illustrated by Lisa Rauchwerger (an interactive family cookbook).

How to Contact/Writers: Fiction: Submit outline/synopsis and 2 sample chapters. Nonfiction: Submit complete ms. Responds to queries/ms in 4 months. Publishes a book 18 months-2 years after acceptance. Will consider simultaneous submissions.

Illustration: Works with 5 illustrators/year. Reviews ms/illustration packages from artists. Send ms with dummy. Illustrations only: Send portfolio to be kept on file. Responds in 2 months. Samples returned with SASE. Looking specifically for Jewish themes.

Photography: Buys stock and assigns work. Uses photos with Jewish content. Prefer modern settings. Submit cover letter and promo piece.

Terms: Offers advances. Pays photographers by the project (range: $200-3,000) or per photo (range:$20-100). Book catalog free; ms guidelines for SASE.

Tips: "Look at some of our books. Have an understanding of the Reform Jewish community. We sell mostly to Jewish congregations and day schools.' "

UNITY HOUSE, 1901 NW Blue Pkwy., Unity Village MO 64065-0001. (816)524-3550, ext. 3190. Fax: (816)251-3552. Website: www.unityworldhq.org. Book publisher. Estab. 1896. Publishes "spiritual, metaphysical, new thought publications." **Manuscript Acquisitions:** Raymond Teague. Other imprints: Wee Wisdom. Publishes 1 picture book every two years.

Fiction: All levels: religion. Recently published *I Turn to the Light*, by Connie Bowen (picture book); *Adventures of the Little Green Dragon*, by Mari Prirette Ulmer, illustrated by Mary Maass (picture book anthology); and *The Sunbeam and the Wave*, by Harriet Hamilton, illustrated by Connie Bowen (picture book).

Nonfiction: All levels: religion.

How to Contact/Writers: Fiction/Nonfiction: Submit outline/synopsis and 1-3 sample chapters. Responds to queries/mss in up to 2 months. Publishes a book approximately 1 year after acceptance. Will consider simultaneous submission or previously self-published work. Writer's guidelines and catalog available upon request.

Illustration: Reviews ms/illustration packages from artists. Query. Contact: Raymond Teague, associate editor.

Terms: Pays authors royalty of 10-15% based on retail price or work purchased outright. Offers advances (Average amount: $1,500). Book catalog available.

Tips: "Read our Writer's Guidelines and study our catalog before submitting. All of our publications reflect Unity's spiritual teachings, but the presentations and applications of those teachings are wide open."

VIKING CHILDREN'S BOOKS, Penguin Putnam Inc., 345 Hudson St., New York NY 10014-3657. (212)366-2000. Website: www.penguinputnam.com. **Acquisitions:** Judy Carey, associate editor, all types of fiction; Cathy Hennessy, associate editor, all types of fiction; Jill Davis, senior editor, nonfiction; Melanie Cecka, senior editor, easy-to-read and fiction. **Art Acquisitions:** Denise Cronin, Viking Children's Books. Publishes hardcover originals. Publishes 80 books/year. Receives 7500 queries/year. 25% of books from first-time authors; 33% from unagented writers. "Viking Children's Books is known for humorous, quirky picture books, in addition to more traditional fiction and publishes the highest quality trade books for children including fiction, nonfiction, and novelty books for pre-schoolers through young adults." Publishes book 1-2 years after acceptance of artwork. Hesitantly accepts simultaneous submissions.

● Viking title *Joseph Had a Little Overcoat*, written and illustrated by Simms Taback, won the 2000 Caldecott Medal.

Fiction: All levels: adventure, animal, anthology, contemporary, hi-lo, humor, multicultural, suspense/mystery, easy-to-read, history, poetry, religion, sports. Middle readers, young adults/teens: problem novels, fantasy, romance, science fiction. Recently published *Busy, Busy City Street*, by Cari Meister (picture book); *Calling the Swan*, by Jean Thesman (young adult novel); and *Cody Unplugged*, by Betsy Duffry (middle grade).

Nonfiction: Picture books: activity books, biography, concept. Young readers, middle readers, young adult: biography, history, reference, religion, science, sports. Middle readers: animal, biography, geography, hi-lo, history, hobbies, multicultural, music/dance, nature/environment, religion, science, social issues, sports. Young adult/teens: animal, biography, cooking, geography, hi-lo, history, multicultural, music/dance, nature/environment, reference, religion, science, social issues, sports.

Illustration: Works with 40 illustrators/year. Responds to artist's queries/submissions only if interested. Samples returned with SASE or samples filed. Originals returned at job's completion.

How to Contact/Writers: Picture books: submit entire ms and SASE. Novels: submit outline with 3 sample chapters and SASE. Nonfiction: query with outline, one sample chapter and SASE. Responds to queries/mss in 8 months.

insider report

Balancing the business and creativity of book publishing

Deborah Brodie grew up in a suburb of Kansas City, Missouri, but decided at the age of twelve that she wanted to live in New York City. She moved to Manhattan when she was eighteen and earned degrees from the Jewish Theological Seminary and Columbia University. After her first job as managing editor of a magazine, she founded Bonim Books, a children's book imprint at Hebrew Publishing Company. Four years later, she joined Viking Children's Books. As planned, she never left New York City and recently celebrated her twenty-first anniversary at Viking.

Photo: Nathan Englander

Deborah Brodie

How did the merger of Penguin and Putnam affect your job as Executive Editor?
The resources for marketing, distribution, promotion, and publicity are better than ever. But the market is so competitive these days that it's more of a challenge to nurture authors or illustrators who need a long time to develop or books that are considered midlist.

Does your department work more closely with marketing now?
Yes, but even though we sometimes second-guess what books marketing will like, I want to stress that the marketing department is also under siege from the market in general. When a children's book does extremely well, the expectation is that the house will duplicate that success each year. Everyone, from management to the authors themselves, has that expectation.

What goes on at Viking editorial meetings?
We have informal, collegial meetings for our department every four to eight weeks. We bring manuscripts that we're undecided about or solicit opinions about how to encourage an author, even if we can't accept her manuscript. Sometimes we ask for text ideas for illustrators we want to work with.

How is the Viking imprint different from the other Penguin-Putnam imprints?
We all do a range. Grosset does only mass market, but Putnam, Dial, Dutton, and Viking do everything from board books to literary YA. You will find some of every genre and age group on every list. The differences are in personalities of editors—what they're good at, what they want to emphasize. For example, Viking is known for doing picture books with very hip, sophisticated downtown art.

What else are you looking for at Viking?

I'm looking for fiction with a fresh voice, good plot, strong characterization, and an author who is willing to revise. The department is overwhelmed by hundreds of submissions each week, and even though we still work with authors who don't have agents and we still accept unsolicited manuscripts, it's increasingly hard for all of us to find enough time to read submissions.

What impresses you in a query letter?

I don't like query letters because I can't get enough of an idea about the manuscript from them. Maybe query letters work for nonfiction where the main point is to hook the reader, but for fiction, I don't care beforehand what the book is about. I care only how it is written, so I need to see the complete manuscript. If I get a query and I'm interested, by the time I get around to reading the sample, making notes, contacting the author, and getting the whole manuscript, I will have forgotten what was in the original query. I would rather have fresh energy for the whole thing the first time through.

What do you want in a cover letter?

No gimmicks, no résumés—we're not hiring you to be on staff. Be sure to include the most obvious information, like your address and phone number. The manuscript should also have your name and the page number on every page. You can learn the basics from talking to other writers and from joining SCBWI (Society of Children's Book Writers and Illustrators). Children's book publishing is so competitive that you need to submit as professionally as possible in order to increase your chances of being published.

"The strongly individual characters in *Dreamland* stay with us," says Viking editor Deborah Brodie. "Right from the first chapter, even with a shadow already hovering over Caitlin's life, we experience Sarah Dessen's trademark ability to make us laugh, no matter what."

What do you wish writers, both new and established, knew about publishing?

How things work. Publishing has always been a business, even in the old days when it was a "gentlemen's' business," and that mix of business and creativity makes it exciting. So to get published and published well today, you have to be businesslike. Don't type one line to each page in a picture book manuscript, for example, and don't include your own illustrations (or your mother-in-law's) unless you're a professional illustrator. Know about the publishing house you're submitting to. At Viking we publish almost no science fiction, so if you have a science fiction manuscript, you're better off going to a house where they love that genre and have a number of science fiction titles on their list.

It's important to be well read, to join SCBWI, to take as many classes as possible, and for some people, to be in a critique group because that can help you move ahead. Read a lot of children's books and know the possibilities—why a picture book has 32 pages, for example, what makes a picture book vibrant and appealing, why you would want to read it again.

Why do you teach writing?

I teach in the M.F.A. in Creative Writing program at The New School because on an obvious, practical level, it's a source of new writers for me as an editor. The students are willing to

Jacket illustration © 2000 S.D. Schindler. Reprinted with permission of Viking, a division of Penguin Putnam.

Hog Music

by M. C. Helldorfer
illustrated by S. D. Schindler

"Mary Claire Helldorfer transforms her research into 19th-century American history so that Lucy's adventure along the National Public Road is a joyous adventure for us, too," says Viking editor Deborah Brodie of Helldorfer's picture book *Hog Music*. "Then illustrator Steven Schindler transforms our genteel, sanitized image of those days."

spend the time, money, and effort to take courses, so they're showing a commitment to becoming more professional. In my office, I have to make a decision: do I publish it—yes or no? At The New School, the question is "What can I do to help this student improve her writing and meet her potential?" For me, teaching touches on the core reason that I went into publishing, and children's publishing especially—it's the chance to work with someone and focus on the writing without the distraction of a practical agenda.

Teaching also touches on the reason I'm an editor and not an editor-in-chief or editorial director. I've never wanted to be in administration. I've turned down jobs over the years because I've wanted to be the teacher, not the principal, so to speak. I want to deal directly with authors and illustrators.

What do you achieve as a teacher that you don't achieve as an editor?
I spend more time with more people at a less developed stage of their writing. I've heard some of my published students say, "She spends more time with me than my editor does."

In what direction do you think children's book publishing is going?
With only a few large publishers and fewer doors to open, I imagine the future will hold more small publishers. But the one thing that will never change is the collaborative nature of publishing—the supportive, mutually nourishing relationship of editor, author and illustrator. I am confident that won't change.
—*Anna Olswanger*

Terms: Pays 2-10% royalty on retail price or flat fee. Advance negotiable.
Tips: Mistake often made is that "authors disguise nonfiction in a fictional format."

✅ **WALKER AND COMPANY**, Books for Young Readers, 435 Hudson St., New York NY 10014. (212)727-8300. Fax: (212)727-0984. Website: www.walkerbooks.com. Division of Walker Publishing Co. Inc. Book publisher. Estab. 1959. **Manuscript Acquisitions:** Emily Easton, publisher; Timothy Travaglini, editor. Publishes 16 picture books/year; 4-6 middle readers/year; 2-4 young adult titles/year. 5% of books by first-time authors; 65% of books from agented writers.
Fiction: Picture books: animal, history, multicultural. Young readers: contemporary, history, humor, multicultural. Middle readers: animal, contemporary, history, multicultural, humor. Young adults: contemporary and historical fiction. Recently published *The Baboon King*, by Anton Quintana, *My Life, Take Two*, by Paul Many; *Bad Dog*, by Nina Laden
Nonfiction: Young readers: biography, animals. Middle readers: animal, biography, health, history, multicultural, reference, social issues. Young adults: biography, health, history, multicultural, reference, social issues, sports. Published *The Sound That Jazz Makes*, by Carole Boston Weatherford, illustrated by Eric Velasquez; *Slinky Scaly, Slithery Snakes*, by Dorothy H. Patent, illustrated by Kendahl Jubb; *Girl Thoughts*, by Judith Harlan. Multicultural needs include "contemporary, literary fiction and historical fiction written in an authentic voice. Also high interest nonfiction with trade appeal."
How to Contact/Writers: Fiction/nonfiction: Submit outline/synopsis and sample chapters; query for novels. Responds to queries/mss in 3 months. Send SASE for writer's guidelines.
Illustration: Works with 10-12 illustrators/year. Uses color artwork only. Editorial department reviews ms/illustration packages from artists. Query or submit ms with 4-8 samples. Illustrations only: Tearsheets. "Please do not send original artwork." Responds to art samples only if interested. Samples returned with SASE.
Terms: Pays authors royalties of 5-10%; pays illustrators royalty or flat fee. Offers advance payment against royalties. Original artwork returned at job's completion. Sends galleys to authors. Book catalog available for 9×12 SASE; ms guidelines for SASE.
Tips: Writers: "Make sure you study our catalog before submitting. We are a small house with a tightly focused list. Illustrators: "Have a well-rounded portfolio with different styles." Does not want to see folktales, ABC books, paperback series, genre fiction. "Walker and Company is committed to introducing talented new authors and illustrators to the children's book field."

WHISPERING COYOTE PRESS, INC.

- All submissions should be directed to Charlesbridge. See their listing on page 111.

WHITECAP BOOKS, 351 Lynn Ave., North Vancouver, British Columbia V7J 2C4 Canada. (604)980-9852. E-mail: whitecap@whitecap.ca. Book publisher. **Acquisitions:** Robin Rivers, editorial director. Publishes 4 young readers/year; and 2 middle readers/year.

Fiction: Picture books for children 3-7.

Nonfiction: Young readers, middle readers: animal, nature/environment. Does not want to see text that writes down to children. Recently published *Welcome to the World of Octopuses*, by Diane Swanson (ages 5-7); *Animals Eat the Weirdest Things*, by Diane Swanson (ages 8-11); and *Whose Feet Are These*, by Wayne Lynch (ages 5-7).

How to Contact/Writers: Nonfiction: Query. Responds to queries in 1 month; ms in 3 months. Publishes a book 6 months after acceptance. Will consider simultaneous submissions. Please send international postal voucher if submission is from US.

Illustration: Works with 1-2 illustrators/year. Reviews ms/illustration packages from artists. Query. Illustrations only: Query with samples—"never send original art." Contact: Robin Rivers. Samples returned with SASE with international postal voucher for Canada if requested.

Photography: Buys stock. "We are always looking for outstanding wildlife photographs." Uses 35mm transparencies. Submit cover letter, client list, stock photo list.

Terms: Pays authors a negotiated royalty or purchases work outright. Offers advances. Pays illustrators by the project or royalty (depends on project). Pays photographers per photo (depends on project). Originals returned to artist at job's completion unless discussed in advance. Ms guidelines available for SASE with international postal voucher for Canada.

Tips: "Writers and illustrators should spend time researching what's already available on the market. Whitecap specializes in nonfiction for children and adults. Whitecap Fiction focuses on humorous events or extraordinary animals. Please review previous publications before submitting."

ALBERT WHITMAN & COMPANY, 6340 Oakton St., Morton Grove IL 60053-2723. (847)581-0033. Fax: (847)581-0039. Website: www.awhitmanco.com. Book publisher. Estab. 1919. **Manuscript Acquisitions:** Kathleen Tucker, editor-in-chief. **Art Acquisitions:** Scott Piehl, designer. Publishes 30 books/year. 15% of books by first-time authors; 15% of books from agented authors.

- Albert Whitman title *Red Berry Wool*, illustrated by Tim Coffey, won the Golden Kite Honor Award for Picture Book Illustration. Coffey and the book's editor, Wendy McClure, were featured in the *2000 Children's Writer's & Illustrator's Market* First Books article.

Fiction: Picture books, young readers, middle readers: adventure, animal, concept, contemporary, health, history, humor, multicultural, nature/environment, special needs. Middle readers: problem novels, suspense/mystery. "We are interested in contemporary multicultural stories—stories with holiday themes (except Christmas) and exciting distinctive novels. We publish a wide variety of topics and are interested in stories that help children deal with their problems and concerns. Does not want to see "religion-oriented, ABCs, pop-up, romance, counting." Published *Jungle Halloween*, by Maryann Cocca-Leffler; *Mommy Far, Mommy Near: An Adoption Story*, by Carol A. Peacock, illustrated by Shawn Costello Brownell; and *Dirt Boy*, by Erik Jon Slangerup, illustrated by John Manders.

Nonfiction: Picture books, young readers, middle readers: animal, biography, concept, geography, health, history, hobbies, multicultural, music/dance, nature/environment, special needs. Middle readers: careers. Middle readers, young adults: biography, social issues. Does not want to see "religion, any books that have to be written in or fictionalized biographies." Recently published *Shelter Dogs*, by Peg Kehret; *I Have a Weird Brother Who Digested a Fly*, by Joan Hulub, illustrated by Patrick Girouard; and *The Riches of Oseola McCarty*, by Evelyn Coleman, illustrated by Daniel Minter.

How to Contact/Writers: Fiction/Nonfiction: Submit complete ms. Responds to queries in 6 weeks; mss in 4 months. Publishes a book 18 months after acceptance. Will consider simultaneous submissions "but let us know if it is one."

Illustration: Works with 30 illustrators/year. Uses more color art than b&w. Reviews ms/illustration packages from artists. Illustrations only: Query with samples. Send slides or tearsheets. Samples returned with SASE; samples filed. Originals returned at job's completion. Responds in 2 months.

Photography: Publishes books illustrated with photos but not stock photos—desires photos all taken for project. "Our books are for children and cover many topics; photos must be taken to match text. Books often show a child in a particular situation (e.g., kids being home-schooled, a sister whose brother is born prematurely)." Photographers should query with samples; send unsolicited photos by mail.

Terms: Pays authors royalty. Offers advances. Pays illustrators and photographers royalty. Sends galleys to authors; dummies to illustrators. Original artwork returned at job's completion. Ms/artist's guidelines available for SASE, or on website. Book catalogs available with 9×12 SASE and $1.43 in postage.

Tips: "In both picture books and nonfiction, we are seeking stories showing life in other cultures and the variety of multicultural life in the U.S. We also want fiction and nonfiction about mentally or physically challenged children—some recent topics have been autism, asthma, diabetes. Look up some of our books first, to be sure your submission is appropriate for Albert Whitman & Co."

◻ **JOHN WILEY & SONS, INC.**, 605 Third Ave., New York NY 10158. (212)850-6206. Fax: (212)850-6095. Website: www.wiley.com. Book publisher. **Acquisitions:** Kate Bradford, senior editor. Publishes 18 middle readers/year; 2 young adult titles/year. 10% of books by first-time authors. Publishes educational, nonfiction: primarily history, science, and other activities.
Nonfiction: Middle readers: activity books, animal, arts/crafts, biography, cooking, geography, health, history, hobbies, how-to, nature/environment, reference, science, self help. Young adults: activity books, arts/crafts, health, hobbies, how-to, nature/environment, reference, science, self help. Average word length middle readers—20,000-40,000. Recently published: *Teresa Weatherspoon's Basketball for Girls* (ages 8 and up, sports); *Civil War Days*, in the American Kids in History series (ages 8-12, history/activity).
How to Contact/Writers: Query. Submit outline/synopsis, 2 sample chapters and an author bio. Responds to queries in 1 month; mss in 3 months. Publishes a book 1 year after acceptance. Will consider simultaneous and previously published submissions.
Illustration: Works with 6 illustrators/year. Uses primarily black & white artwork. Reviews ms/illustration packages from artists. Query. Illustrations only: Query with samples, résumé, client list. Responds only if interested. Samples filed. Original artwork returned at job's completion. No portfolio reviews.
Photography: Buys photos from freelancers.
Terms: Pays authors royalty of 10-12% based on wholesale price, or by outright purchase. Offers advances. Pays illustrators by the project. Photographers' pay negotiable. Sends galleys to authors. Book catalog available for SASE.
Tips: "We're looking for topics and writers that can really engage kids' interest—plus we're always interested in a new twist on time-tested subjects."

☑ ⛉ **WILLIAMSON PUBLISHING CO.**, Box 185, Charlotte VT 05445. (802)425-2102. Fax: (802)425-2199. E-mail: susan@williamsonbooks.com. Website: www.williamsonbooks.com. Book publisher. Estab. 1983.
Manuscript Acquisitions: Susan Williamson, editorial director. **Art Acquisitions:** Jack Williamson, publisher. Publishes 12-15 young readers titles/year. 50% of books by first-time authors; 10% of books from agented authors. Publishes "very successful nonfiction series (Kids Can!® Series—3,000,000 sold) on subjects such as nature, creative play, arts/crafts, geography. Successfully launched *Little Hands®* series for ages 2-6 and recently introduced the new *Kaleidoscope Kids®* series (age 7 and up) and *Quick Starts™ for Kids!* (ages 7+). Our mission is to help every child fulfill his/her potential and experience personal growth.
Nonfiction: Hands-on activity books, arts/crafts, biography, careers, geography, health, hobbies, how-to, math, multicultural, music/dance, nature/environment, science, self-help, social issues. Does not want to see textbooks, picture books, poetry, fiction. "We are looking for books in which learning and doing are inseparable." Published *Gizmos and Gadgets*, by Jill Hauser, illustrated by Michael Kline (ages 6-12, exploring science); *Alphabet Art*, by Judy Press (ages 2-6, early learning skills); and *Ancient Greece!*, by Avery Hart and Paul Mantell, illustrated by Michael Kline (age 7 and up, learning history through activities and experience).
How to Contact/Writers: Query with outline/synopsis and 1 sample chapter. Responds to queries in 4 months; mss in 4 months. Publishes book, "depending on graphics, about 1 year" after acceptance. Writers may send a SASE for guidelines. Please do not query via e-mail.
Illustration: Works with 8 illustrators and 8 designers/year. "We're interested in expanding our illustrator and design freelancers." Uses primarily b&w artwork; some 2-color and 4-color. Responds only if interested. Samples returned with SASE; samples filed. Please do not send samples via e-mail.
Photography: Buys photos from freelancers; uses archival art and photos.
Terms: Pays authors royalty based on wholesale price or purchases outright. Pays illustrators by the project. Pays photographers per photo. Sends galleys to authors. Book catalog available for 8½×11 SAE and 5 first-class stamps; ms guidelines available for SASE.
Tips: "We're interested in interactive learning books with a creative approach packed with interesting information, written for young readers ages 2-6 and 7-14. In nonfiction children's publishing, we are looking for authors with a depth of knowledge shared with children through a warm, embracing style. We are *not* interested in picture books. Our publishing philosophy is based on the idea that all children can succeed and have positive learning experiences. Children's lasting learning experiences involve participation."

⊡ **WINSLOW PRESS**, 115 E. 23rd St., 10th Floor, New York NY 10010. E-mail: winslow@winslowpress.com. Website: www.winslowpress.com. Estab. 1997. **Acquisitions:** Sarah Nielsen, assistant editor. **Art Acquisitions:** Design Department. Produces 10 picture books and young readers/year; 7 middle readers/year; 3 young adult titles/year. 25% of books by first-time authors. "We connect the magic of the book to the wonder of the Web. We have an innovative Web program that features all our books."
 ● Turn to First Books on page 70 to read about Winslow Press author Teri Daniels and her book *The Feet in the Gym.*
Fiction: Will consider all age-levels and subjects. Average length: picture books and young readers—32 pages; middle readers—100 pages; young adult—250 pages. Recently published: *Apples, Apples, Apples*, by Nancy Elizabeth Wallace (picture book); *The Runaway Tortilla*, by Eric A. Kimmel (picture books); and *Aria of the Sea*, by Dia Calhoun (young adult novel).
Nonfiction: Will consider all age-levels and subject. "We have not published any non-fiction as of yet, but we are interested in pursuing a nonfiction program."

How to Contact/Writers: Fiction/nonfiction: Query, submit complete ms, or submit outline/synopsis and 3 sample chapters. Responds to queries/mss in 1 month. Will consider simultaneous submissions and previously published work.

Illustration: Works with 20 illustrators/year. Will review ms/illustration packages from artists. Submit mss with photocopies of artwork (color and b&w). Do not send original art. Contact: Sarah Nielsen. Illustrations only: Send tearsheets or photocopies of work. Do not send original art. Contact: Design Department. Responds only if interested. Samples not returned.

Photography: Buys stock images. Contact: Design Department. Submit cover letter and stock photo list.

Terms: Payment varies. Sends galleys to authors; dummies to illustrators. Original artwork returned at job's completion. Book catalog available for 9×12 SASE with 3 first-class stamps. Submission guidelines available for SASE. Catalog available online. "All of our books can be seen on our website."

☑ **WM KIDS**, Imprint of White Mane Publishing Co., Inc., P.O. Box, 152, 63 W. Burd St., Shippensburg PA 17257. (717)532-2237. Fax: (717)532-6110. E-mail: marketing@whitemane.com. Book publisher. Estab. 1987.
Acquisitions: Harold Collier. White Mane Books (Martin Gordon, acquisitions editor), Burd Street Press, White Mane Kids, Ragged Edge Press (Harold Collier, acquisitions editor). Publishes 10 middle readers/year. 50% of books are by first-time authors.

Fiction: Middle readers, young adults: history. Average word length: middle readers—30,000. Recently published *Shenandoah Autumn*, by Mauriel Joelyn (grades 5 and up); *House of Spies*, by Margaret W. Blair (grades 5 and up); *The Powder Monkey*, by Carol Campbell (grades 5 and up). Also, *Retreat from Gettysburg*, by Kathleen Ernst (historical fiction); *Rebel Hart*, by Eddie Hemingway & Jackie Shields (historical fiction); *Young Heroes of Gettysburg*, by William Thomas Vennor (historical fiction).

Nonfiction: Middle readers, young adults: history. Average word length: middle readers—30,000.

How to Contact/Writers: Fiction: Query. Nonfiction: Submit outline/synopsis and 2-3 sample chapters. Responds to queries in 1 month; mss in 3 months. Publishes a book 1 year after acceptance. Will consider simultaneous submissions.

Illustration: Works with 3 illustrators/year. Reviews ms/illustration packages from artists. Submit ms with 3 pieces of final art. Contact: Harold Collier, acquisitions editor. Responds in 1 month. Samples returned with SASE.

Photography: Buys stock and assigns work. Submit cover letter and portfolio.

Terms: Pays authors royalty of 7-10%. Pays illustrators by the project. Pays photographers by the project. Sends galleys for review. Originals returned to artist at job's completion. Book catalog and writer's guidelines available for SASE. All imprints included in a single catalog.

🅽 🅾 **THE WRIGHT GROUP**, 19201 120th Ave. NE, Bothell WA 98011. (800)523-2371. Fax: (800)543-7323. Website: www.wrightgroup.com. Specializes in fiction and nonfiction educational and multicultural material. **Manuscripts Acquisitions:** Amanda Balkwill. **Art Acquisitions:** Debra Lee, Art Director—Product. Publishes 100+ young readers, 50+ middle readers/year. "The Wright Group is dedicated to improving literacy by providing outstanding tutorials for students and teachers."

Fiction: Picture books, young readers: adventure, animal, concept, contemporary, fantasy, folktales, hi-lo, history, humor, multicultural, nature/environment, poetry, sports, suspense/mystery. Middle readers: adventure, animal, contemporary, fantasy, folktales, hi-lo, history, humor, multicultural, nature/environment, poetry, problem novels. Average word length: young readers—50-5,000; middle readers—3,000-10,000. Recenty published: *Wild Crayons*, by Joy Cowley (young reader fantasy); *The Gold Dust Kids*, by Michell Dionetti (historical fiction chapter book for young readers); and *Watching Josh*, by Deborah Eaton (middle reader mystery).

Nonfiction: Picture books, young readers, middle readers: animal, biography, careers, concept, geography, health, hi-lo, history, how-to, multicultural, nature/environment, science, sports. Average word length: young readers 50-3,000. Recently published: *Iditarod*, by Joe Ramsey (young reader); and *The Amazing Ant*, by Sara Sams (young reader); and *Chameleons*, by Nic Bishop (young reader).

How to Contact/Writers: Fiction/Nonfiction: Submit complete manuscript or submit outline/synopsis and 3 sample chapters. Responds to queries in 2 weeks; mss in 3 months. Publishes a book 8 months after acceptance. Will consider previously published work.

Illustration Query with samples. Contact: Debra Lee, art director—product. Responds only if interested. Samples kept on file.

Photography: Buys stock and assigns work. Contact: Debra Lee. Model/property release and captions required. Uses 8½×11 color prints. Submit published samples, promo pieces.

Terms: Work purchased outright from authors ($500-2,400). Illustrators paid by the project. Photographers paid by the project ($3,500-5,000) or per photo ($300-350). Book catalog available online.

Tips: "Much of our illustration assignments are being done by offsite developers, so our level of commission in this area is minimal."

Magazines

Children's magazines are a great place for unpublished writers and illustrators to break into the market. Illustrators, photographers and writers alike may find it easier to get book assignments if they have tearsheets from magazines. Having magazine work under your belt shows you're professional and have experience working with editors and art directors and meeting deadlines.

But magazines aren't merely a breaking-in point. Writing, illustration and photo assignments for magazines let you see your work in print quickly, and the magazine market can offer steady work and regular paychecks (a number of them pay on acceptance). Book authors, illustrators and photographers may have to wait a year or two before receiving royalties from a project. The magazine market is also a good place to use research material that didn't make it into a book project you're working on. You may even work on a magazine idea that blossoms into a book project.

TARGETING YOUR SUBMISSIONS

It's important to know the topics typically covered by different children's magazines. To help you match your work with the right publications, we've included several indexes in the back of this book. The **Subject Index** lists both book and magazine publishers by the fiction and nonfiction subjects they're seeking. **If you're a photographer**, the **Photography Index** lists children's magazines that use photos from freelancers. Using these two indexes in combination, you can quickly narrow your search of markets that suit your work. For instance, if you photograph sports, compare the Magazine list in the Photography Index with the list under Sports in the Subject Index. Highlight the markets that appear on both lists, then read those listings to decide which magazines might be best for your work.

If you're a writer, use the Subject Index in conjunction with the **Age-Level Index** to narrow your list of markets. Targeting the correct age group with your submission is an important consideration. Most rejection slips are sent because a writer has not targeted a manuscript to the correct age. Few magazines are aimed at children of all ages, so you must be certain your manuscript is written for the audience level of the particular magazine you're submitting to. Magazines for children (just as magazines for adults) may also target a specific gender.

If you're a poet, refer to the **Poetry Index** to find which magazines publish poems.

Each magazine has a different editorial philosophy. Language usage also varies between periodicals, as does the length of feature articles and the use of artwork and photographs. Reading magazines *before* submitting is the best way to determine if your material is appropriate. Also, because magazines targeted to specific age groups have a natural turnover in readership every few years, old topics (with a new slant) can be recycled.

Since many kids' magazines sell subscriptions through direct mail or schools, you may not be able to find a particular publication at bookstores or newsstands. Check your local library, or send for copies of the magazines you're interested in. Most magazines in this section have sample copies available and will send them for a SASE or small fee.

Also, many magazines have submission guidelines and theme lists available for a SASE. (Visit www.writersdigest.com for a searchable database of more than 1,500 writers guidelines.) Check magazines' websites, too. Many offer excerpts of articles, submission guidelines and theme lists and will give you a feel for the editorial focus of the publication.

For an illustrator's perspective on children's magazines, see the Insider Report with **Phyllis Pollema-Cahill** on page 233.

Information on magazines listed in the previous edition but not included in this edition of *Children's Writer's & Illustrator's Market* **may be found in the General Index.**

ADVOCATE, PKA'S PUBLICATION, PKA Publication, 301A Rolling Hills Park, Prattsville NY 12468. (518)299-3103. **Publisher**: Patricia Keller. Bimonthly tabloid. Estab. 1987. Circ. 12,000. "*Advocate* advocates good writers and quality writings. We publish art, fiction, photos and poetry. *Advocate*'s submitters are talented people of all ages who do not earn their livings as writers. We wish to promote the arts and to give those we publish the opportunity to be published through a for-profit means rather than in a not-for-profit way. We do this by selling advertising and offering reading entertainment."
- Gaited Horse Association newsletter is now included in our publication. Horse-oriented stories, poetry, art and photos are currently needed.

Fiction: Middle readers and young adults/teens: adventure, animal, contemporary, fantasy, folktales, health, humorous, nature/environment, problem-solving, romance, science fiction, sports, suspense/mystery. Looks for "well written, entertaining work, whether fiction or nonfiction." Buys approximately 42 mss/year. Average word length: 1,500. Byline given. Wants to see more humorous material, nature/environment and romantic comedy.

Nonfiction: Middle readers and young adults/teens: animal, arts/crafts, biography, careers, concept, cooking, fashion, games/puzzles, geography, history, hobbies, how-to, humorous, interview/profile, nature/environment, problem-solving, science, social issues, sports, travel. Buys 10 mss/year. Average word length: 1,500. Byline given.

Poetry: Reviews poetry any length.

How to Contact/Writers: Fiction/nonfiction: send complete ms. Responds to queries in 6 weeks/mss in 2 months. Publishes ms 2-18 months after acceptance.

Illustration: Uses b&w artwork only. Uses cartoons. Reviews ms/illustration packages from artists. Submit a photo print (b&w or color), an excellent copy of work (no larger than 8×10) or original. Illustrations only: "Send previous unpublished art with SASE, please." Responds in 2 months. Samples returned with SASE; samples not filed. Credit line given.

Photography: Buys photos from freelancers. Model/property releases required. Uses color and b&w prints. Send unsolicited photos by mail with SASE. Responds in 2 months. Wants nature, artistic and humorous photos.

Terms: Pays on publication. Acquires first rights for mss, artwork and photographs. Pays in copies. Original work returned upon job's completion. Sample copies for $4. Writer's/illustrator/photo guidelines for SASE.

Tips: "Artists and photographers should keep in mind that we are a b&w paper."

AIM MAGAZINE, America's Intercultural Magazine, P.O. Box 1174, Maywood IL 60153-8174. **Contact:** Ruth Apilado (nonfiction), Mark Boone (fiction). **Photo Editor:** Betty Lewis. Quarterly magazine. Circ. 8,000. Readers are high school and college students, teachers, adults interested in helping, through the written word, to create a more equitable world. 15% of material aimed at juvenile audience.

Fiction: Young adults/teens: adventure, folktales, humorous, history, multicultural, "stories with social significance." Wants stories that teach children that people are more alike than they are different. Does not want to see religious fiction. Buys 20 mss/year. Average word length: 1,000-4,000. Byline given.

Nonfiction: Young adults/teens: biography, interview/profile, multicultural, "stuff with social significance." Does not want to see religious nonfiction. Buys 20 mss/year. Average word length: 500-2,000. Byline given.

How to Contact/Writers: Fiction: Send complete ms. Nonfiction: Query with published clips. Responds to queries in 2 weeks; mss in 6 weeks. Will consider simultaneous submissions.

Illustration: Buys 6 illustrations/issue. Preferred theme: Overcoming social injustices through nonviolent means. Reviews ms/illustration packages from artists. Query first. Illustrations only: Query with tearsheets. Responds to art samples only if interested. Samples returned with SASE or filed. Original artwork returned at job's completion "if desired." Credit line given.

Photography: Wants "photos of activists who are trying to contribute to social improvement."

Terms: Pays on acceptance. Buys first North American serial rights. Pays $15-25 for stories/articles. Pays in contributor copies if copies are requested. Pays $25 for b&w cover illustration. Photographers paid by the project. Sample copies for $5.

Tips: "We need material of social significance, stuff that will help promote racial harmony and peace and illustrate the stupidity of racism."

N AMERICAN CAREERS, Career Communications, Inc., 6701 W. 64th St., Overland Park KS 66202. (913)362-7788. Fax: (913)362-4864. **Articles Editor:** Mary Pitchford. **Art Director:** Jerry Kanabel. Quarterly magazine. Estab. 1990. Circ. 400,000. Publishes career and education information for middle and high school students.

Nonfiction: Buys 20 mss/year. Average word length: 300-800. Byline given.

How to Contact/Writers: Nonfiction: Query with published clips. Responds to queries in 2 months. Publishes ms 6 months after acceptance. Will consider simultaneous submissions, electronic submission via disk or modem. **Tips:** Send a query with résumé and clips.

AMERICAN CHEERLEADER, Lifestyle Publications LLC, 250 W. 57th St., Suite 420, New York NY 10107. (212)265-8890. Fax: (212)265-8908. E-mail: editors@americancheerleader.com. Website: www.americancheerle ader.com. **Editorial Director:** Julie Davis. **Managing Editor:** Meredith Cristiano. Bimonthly magazine. Estab. 1995. Circ. 200,000. Special interest teen magazine for kids who cheer.
Nonfiction: Young adults: biography, interview/profile (sports personalities), careers, fashion, beauty, health, how-to (cheering techniques, routines, pep songs, etc.), problem-solving, sports, cheerleading specific material. "We're looking for authors who know cheerleading." Buys 20 mss/year. Average word length: 750-2,000. Byline given.
How to Contact/Writers: Query with published clips. Responds to queries/mss in 3 months. Publishes ms 3 months after acceptance. Will consider electronic submission via disk or modem.
Illustration: Buys 6 illustrations/issue; 30-50 illustrations/year. Works on assignment only. Reviews ms/illustra tion packages from artists. Illustrations only: Query with samples; arrange portfolio review. Responds only if interested. Samples filed. Originals not returned at job's completion. Credit line given.
Photography: Buys photos from freelancers. Looking for cheerleading at different sports games, events, etc. Uses 35mm, 2¼×2¼ transparencies and 5x7 prints. Query with samples; provide résumé, business card, tear sheets to be kept on file. "After sending query, we'll set up an interview." Responds only if interested.
Terms: Pays on publication. Buy all rights for mss, artwork and photographs. Pays $100-1,000 for stories. Pays illustrators $50-200 for b&w inside, $100-300 for color inside. Pays photographers by the project $300-750; per photo (range: $25-100). Sample copies for $5.
Tips: "Authors: We invite proposals from freelance writers who are involved in or have been involved in cheerleading—i.e. coaches, sponsors or cheerleaders. Our writing style is upbeat, and 'sporty' to catch and hold the attention of our teen readers. Articles should be broken down into lots of sidebars, bulleted lists, etc. Photogra phers and illustrators must have teen magazine experience or high profile experience."

AMERICAN GIRL, Pleasant Company, 8400 Fairway Place, P.O. Box 620986, Middleton WI 53562-0984. (608)836-4848. E-mail: im_agmag_editor@pleasantco.com. Website: www.americangirl.com. **Editor:** Kristi Thom. **Managing Editor:** Barbara Stretchberry. **Contact:** Editorial Dept. Assistant. Bimonthly magazine. Estab. 1992. Circ. 750,000. "For girls ages 8-12. We run fiction and nonfiction, historical and contemporary."
Fiction: Middle readers: contemporary, historical, multicultural, suspense/mystery, good fiction about anything. No preachy, moralistic tales or stories with animals as protagonists. Only a girl or girls as characters—no boys. Buys approximately 6 mss/year. Average word length: 1,000-2,300. Byline given.
Nonfiction: Any articles aimed at girls ages 8-12. Buys 3-10 mss/year. Average word length: 600. Byline sometimes given.
How to Contact/Writers: Fiction: Send complete ms. Nonfiction: Query with published clips. Responds to queries/mss in 6-12 weeks. Will consider simultaneous submissions.
Illustration: Works on assignment only.
Terms: Pays on acceptance. Buys first North American serial rights. Pays $500 minimum for stories; $300 minimum for articles. Sample copies for $3.95 and 9×12 SAE with $1.93 in postage (send to Editorial Depart ment Assistant). Writer's guidelines free for SASE.
Tips: "Keep (stories and articles) simple but interesting. Kids are discriminating readers, too. They won't read a boring or pretentious story. We're looking for short (maximum 175 words) how-to stories and short profiles of girls for 'Girls Express' section, as well as word games, puzzles and mazes."

☑ APPLESEEDS The Magazine for Young Readers, Cobblestone Publishing, 30 Grove St., Suite C, Peterborough NH 03458. E-mail: barbara_burt@posthavard.edu. Website: cobblestonepub.com/pages/writersAP Pguides.html. **Editor:** Barbara Burt. Magazine published monthly except June, July and August. *AppleSeeds* is a theme-based social studies magazine from Cobblestone Publishing for ages 7-10. Published 9 times/year.
   ● *AppleSeeds* is aimed toward readers ages 7-10. *AppleSeeds* themes for 2001 include Clara Barton, Amazon Adventures and Exploring the Oceans. At press time, Cobblestone Publishing was purchased by Carus Publishing. No editorial changes were planned.
How to Contact/Writers: Nonfiction: Query only. See website for submission guidelines and theme list.

**FOR EXPLANATIONS OF THESE SYMBOLS,
SEE THE INSIDE FRONT AND BACK COVERS OF THIS BOOK**

Tips: "Submit queries specifically focused on the theme of an upcoming issue. We look for unusual perspectives, original ideas, and excellent scholarship. We accept no unsolicited manuscripts. Writers should check our website at cobblestonepub.com/pages/writersAPPguides/html for current guidelines, topics, and query deadlines. We use very little fiction. Illustrators should not submit unsolicited art."

ARCHAEOLOGY'S DIG, Archaeological Institute of America, 135 William St., New York NY 10038. (212)732-5154. (212)732-5707. E-mail: editor@dig.archaeology.org. Website: www.archaeology.org. Editor-in-Chief: Stephen Hanks. Art Director: Ken Feisel. Photo Editor: Jarrett Lobell. Bimonthly magazine. Estab. 1999. Circ. 60,000. An archaeology magazine for kids ages 8-13. Publishes entertaining and educational stories about discoveries, dinosaurs, etc.
Nonfiction: Middle readers, young adults: biography, games/puzzles, history, science, archaeology. Buys 15-20 mss/year. Average word length: 400-1,000. Byline given.
How to Contact/Writers: Nonfiction: Query with published clips. Responds to queries/mss in 1 month. Publishes ms 2-3 months after acceptance. Will consider simultaneous submissions and electronic submission via disk or modem.
Illustration: Buys 10-15 illustrations/issue; 60-75 illustrations/year. Uses color artwork only. Works on assignment only. Reviews ms/illustration packages from artists. Query. Contact: Ken Feisel, art director. Illustrations only: Query with samples. Arrange portfolio review. Send tearsheets. Contact: Ken Feisel, art director. Responds in 2 months only if interested. Samples not returned; samples filed. Credit line given.
Photography: Uses anything related to archaeology, history, artifacts, dinosaurs and current archaeological events that relate to kids. Uses color prints and 35mm transparencies. Provide résumé, business card, promotional literature or tearsheets to be kept on file. Responds only if interested.
Terms: Pays on publication. Buys all rights for mss. Buys first North American rights for artwork and photos. Original artwork returned at job's completion. Pays 50¢/word. Additional payment for ms/illustration packages and for photos accompanying articles. Pays illustrators $1,000 and up for color cover; $150-2,000 for color inside. Pays photographers by the project (range: $500-1,000). Pays per photo (range: $100-500).
Tips: "We are looking for writers who can communicate archaeological and paleontological concepts in a conversational style for kids. Writers should have some idea where photography can be located to support their work."

BABYBUG, Carus Publishing Company, P.O. Box 300, Peru IL 61354. (815)224-6656. **Editor**: Paula Morrow. **Art Director:** Suzanne Beck. Published 10 times/year (every 6 weeks). Estab. 1994. "A listening and looking magazine for infants and toddlers ages 6 to 24 months, *Babybug* is 6 ¼ × 7, 24 pages long, printed in large type (26-point) on high-quality cardboard stock with rounded corners and no staples."
Fiction: Looking for very simple and concrete stories, 4-6 short sentences maximum.
Nonfiction: Must use very basic words and concepts, 10 words maximum.
Poetry: Maximum length 8 lines. Looking for rhythmic, rhyming poems.
How to Contact/Writers: "Please do not query first." Send complete ms with SASE. "Submissions without SASE will be discarded." Responds in 3 months.
Illustration: Uses color artwork only. Works on assignment only. Reviews ms/illustration packages from artists. "The manuscripts will be evaluated for quality of concept and text before the art is considered." Contact: Suzanne Beck. Illustrations only: Send tearsheets or photo prints/photocopies with SASE. "Submissions without SASE will be discarded." Responds in 3 months. Samples filed.
Terms: Pays on publication for mss; after delivery of completed assignment for illustrators. Buys first rights with reprint option or (in some cases) all rights. Original artwork returned at job's completion. Rates vary ($25 minimum for mss; $250 minimum for art). Sample copy for $5. Guidelines free for SASE.
Tips: "*Babybug* would like to reach as many children's authors and artists as possible for original contributions, but our standards are very high, and we will accept only top-quality material. Before attempting to write for *Babybug*, be sure to familiarize yourself with this age child." (See listings for *Cricket*, *Cicada*, *Ladybug*, *Muse* and *Spider*.)

N **BLABBER MOUTH, the mouth of teens**, Deva Communications, P.O. Box 417, Mendon MA 01756. (508)529-6630. Fax: (508)529-6039. E-mail: submit@blabbermouthonline.com. Website: www.blabbermouthonline.com. **Articles Editor:** Amy Saunders. Bimonthly magazine currently changing from newsletter to magazine format. Estab. 1999. *Blabber Mouth* focuses on teenagers' interests and issues. We profile teens with hobbies and businesses; cover issues like preparing for college; and publish teen writing and artwork. Fiction, nonfiction, and art of various kinds is accepted. Most of our contributors are teenagers, but we don't exclude those older or younger. 100% of publication aimed at juvenile market.
Fiction: Middle readers, young adults: adventure, animal, contemporary, fantasy, health, history, humorous, multicultural, nature/environment, problem-solving, science fiction, sports, suspense/mystery. Average word length: maximum 1,000 but will consider longer pieces.
Nonfiction: Middle readers, young adults: animals, arts/crafts, biography, careers, cooking, games/puzzles, geography, health, history, hobbies, how-to, humorous, interview/profile, math, multicultural, nature/environment, problem-solving, science, social issues, sports, travel. Average word length: maximum 1,000 but will consider longer pieces. Byline given.
Poetry: Reviews poetry. All styles accepted. Maximum length: 50 lines. Unlimited poems per submission.

How to Contact/Writers: Fiction/nonfiction: Submit complete ms. Responds to queries in 1 month; mss in 3 months. Publishes ms 3 months after acceptance. Will consider simultaneous submissions, electronic submission via disk or modem, previously published work.

Illustration: Buys 1 illustration/issue; 6 illustrations/year. Reviews ms/illustration packages from artists. Query. Contact: Amy Saunders, editor. Illustrations only: Query with samples; send portfolio. Contact: Amy Saunders, editor. Responds only if interested. Samples returned with SASE; samples filed. Credit line given.

Photography: Looking for artistic, photojournalism type photos, though other types will be considered. Uses color and b&w prints. Query with samples. Responds only if interested.

Terms: Currently non-paying. Buys one-time rights for mss. Original artwork returned at job's completion. Pays with contributor's copies if the contributor requests a copy of the issue his/her work is published in. Sample copies for $2.25 US; $3 non-US. Writer's/illustrator's/photo guidelines for SASE.

Tips: Our audience and contributors are multicultural, coming from around the world. We particularly like personal experiences ranging from battling with a disease to how I learned to memorize facts in school. If you submit a pencil drawing, please darken the lines; otherwise it may not scan properly. Always have your name and complete address (including Zip code and country) on everything you submit.

☑ **BOYS' LIFE,** Boy Scouts of America, 1325 W. Walnut Hill Lane, P.O. Box 152079, Irving TX 75015-2079. (214)580-2366. Website: www.bsa.scouting.org. **Editor-in-Chief:** J.D. Owen. **Managing Editor:** W.E. Butterworth, IV. **Articles Editor:** Michael Goldman. **Fiction Editor:** Rich Haddaway. **Director of Design:** Joseph P. Connolly. **Art Director:** Eric Ottinger. Monthly magazine. Estab. 1911. Circ. 1,300,000. *Boys' Life* is "a 4-color general interest magazine for boys 8 to 18 who are members of the Cub Scouts, Boy Scouts or Venturers; a 4-color general interest magazine for all boys."

Fiction: Middle readers: adventure, animal, contemporary, fantasy, history, humor, problem-solving, science fiction, sports, spy/mystery. Does not want to see "talking animals and adult reminiscence." Buys 12 mss/year. Average word length: 1,000-1,500. Byline given.

Nonfiction: "Subject matter is broad. We cover everything from professional sports to American history to how to pack a canoe. A look at a current list of the BSA's more than 100 merit badge pamphlets gives an idea of the wide range of subjects possible. Even better, look at a year's worth of recent issues. Column headings are science, nature, earth, health, sports, space and aviation, cars, computers, entertainment, pets, history, music and others." Average word length: 500-1,500. Columns 300-750 words. Byline given.

How to Contact/Writers: Fiction: Send complete ms with SASE. Nonfiction: query with SASE for response. Responds to queries/mss in 2 months.

Illustration: Buys 10-12 illustrations/issue; 100-125 illustrations/year. Works on assignment only. Reviews ms/illustration packages from artists. "Query first." Illustrations only: Send tearsheets. Responds to art samples only if interested. Samples returned with SASE. Original artwork returned at job's completion.

Terms: Pays on acceptance. Buys first rights. Pays $750-1,500 for fiction; $400-1,500 for major articles; $150-400 for columns; $250-300 for how-to features. Pays illustrators $1,500-3,000 for color cover; $100-1,500 color inside. Sample copies for $3 plus 9×12 SASE. Writer's/illustrator's/photo guidelines available for SASE.

Tips: "We strongly urge you to study at least a year's issues to better understand the type of material published. Articles for *Boys' Life* must interest and entertain boys ages 8 to 18. Write for a boy you know who is 12. Our readers demand crisp, punchy writing in relatively short, straightforward sentences. The editors demand well-reported articles that demonstrate high standards of journalism. We follow *The New York Times* manual of style and usage. All submissions must be accompanied by SASE with adequate postage."

☑ **BOYS' QUEST,** The Bluffton News Publishing and Printing Co., 103 N. Main St., Bluffton OH 45817. (419)358-4610. Fax: (419)358-5027. **Articles Editor:** Marilyn Edwards. **Art Submissions:** Diane Winebar. Bimonthly magazine. Estab. 1995. "*Boys' Quest* is a magazine created for boys from 6 to 13 years, with youngsters 8, 9 and 10 the specific target age. Our point of view is that every young boy deserves the right to be a young boy for a number of years before he becomes a young adult. As a result, *Boys' Quest* looks for articles, fiction, nonfiction, and poetry that deal with timeless topics, such as pets, nature, hobbies, science, games, sports, careers, simple cooking, and anything else likely to interest a young boy."

Fiction: Young readers, middle readers: adventure, animal, history, humorous, nature/environment, problem-solving, sports, jokes, building, cooking, cartoons, riddles. Does not want to see violence, teenage themes. Buys 30 mss/year. Average word length: 200-500. Byline given.

Nonfiction: Young readers, middle readers: animal, arts/crafts, biography, cooking, games/puzzles, history, how-to, humorous, math, problem-solving, science. Prefer photo support with nonfiction. Buys 30 mss/year. Average word length: 200-500. Byline given.

Poetry: Reviews poetry. Maximum length: 21 lines. Limit submissions to 6 poems.

How to Contact/Writers: All writers should consult the theme list before sending in articles. To receive current theme list, send a SASE. Fiction/Nonfiction: Query or send complete ms (preferred). Send SASE with correct postage. No faxed material. Responds to queries in 2 weeks; mss in 3 weeks (if rejected); 4 months (if scheduled). Publishes ms 3 months-3 years after acceptance. Will consider simultaneous submissions and previously published work.

Illustration: Buys 6 illustrations/issue; 36-45 illustrations/year. Uses b&w artwork only. Works on assignment only. Reviews ms/illustration packages from artists. Send ms with dummy. Illustrations only: Query with samples, arrange portfolio review. Send portfolio, tearsheets. Responds in 2 weeks. Samples returned with SASE; samples filed. Credit line given.

Photography: Photos used for support of nonfiction. "Excellent photographs included with a nonfiction story is considered very seriously." Model/property releases required. Uses b&w, 5×7 or 3×5 prints. Query with samples; send unsolicited photos by mail. Responds in 3 weeks.

Terms: Pays on publication. Buys first North American serial rights for mss. Buys first rights for artwork. Pays 5¢/word for stories and articles. Additional payment for ms/illustration packages and for photos accompanying articles. Pays $150-200 for color cover. Pays photographers per photo (range: $5-10). "*Boys' Quest*, as a new publication, is aware that its rates of payment are modest at this time. But we pledge to increase those rewards in direct proportion to our success. Meanwhile, we will strive to treat our contributors and their work with respect and fairness. That treatment, incidentally, will include quick decision on all submissions." Originals returned to artist at job's completion. Sample copies for $4. Writer's/illustrator's/photo guidelines free for SASE.

Tips: "We are looking for lively writing, most of it from a young boy's point of view—with the boy or boys directly involved in an activity that is both wholesome and unusual. We need nonfiction with photos and fiction stories—around 500 words—puzzles, poems, cooking, carpentry projects, jokes and riddles. Nonfiction pieces that are accompanied by black and white photos are far more likely to be accepted than those that need illustrations. We will entertain simultaneous submissions as long as that fact is noted on the manuscript." (See listing for *Hopscotch*.)

BREAD FOR GOD'S CHILDREN, Bread Ministries, Inc., P.O. Box 1017, Arcadia FL 34265-1017. (863)494-6214. Fax: (863)993-0154. E-mail: bread@desoto.net. **Editor:** Judith M. Gibbs. Bimonthly magazine. Estab. 1972. Circ. 10,000 (US and Canada). "*Bread* is designed as a teaching tool for Christian families." 85% of publication aimed at juvenile market.

Fiction: Young readers, middle readers, young adult/teen: adventure, religious, problem-solving, sports. Looks for "teaching stories that portray Christian lifestyles without preaching." Buys approximately 20 mss/year. Average word length: 900-1,500 (for teens); 600-900 (for young children). Byline given.

Nonfiction: Young readers, middle readers: animal. All levels: how-to. "We do not want anything detrimental to solid family values. Most topics will fit if they are slanted to our basic needs." Buys 3-4 mss/year. Average word length: 500-800. Byline given.

Illustration: "The only illustrations we purchase are those occasional good ones coming with a story we accept."

How to Contact/Writers: Fiction/nonfiction: Send complete ms. Responds to mss in 3 weeks-6 months "if considered for use." Will consider simultaneous submissions and previously published work.

Terms: Pays on publication. Pays $10-50 for stories; $25 for articles. Sample copies free for 9×12 SAE and 5 first-class stamps (for 2 copies).

Tips: "We want stories or articles that illustrate overcoming by faith and living solid, Christian lives. Know our publication and what we have used in the past . . . know the readership . . . know the publisher's guidelines. Stories should teach the value of morality and honesty without preaching. Edit carefully for content and grammar."

 CALLIOPE, Exploring World History, Cobblestone Publishing Company, 30 Grove St., Suite C, Peterborough NH 03458. (603)924-7209. Website: www.cobblestonepub.com. **Managing Editor:** Lou Waryncia. **Art Director:** Ann Dillon. Magazine published 9 times/year. "*Calliope* covers world history (East/West), and lively, original approaches to the subject are the primary concerns of the editors in choosing material."

• At press time, Cobblestone Publishing was purchased by Carus Publishing. No editorial changes were planned. *Calliope* themes for 2001 include Fall of Rome, Norman Conquest, The Medici and The Black Death.

Fiction: Middle readers and young adults: adventure, folktales, plays, history, biographical fiction. Material must relate to forthcoming themes. Word length: up to 800.

Nonfiction: Middle readers and young adults: arts/crafts, biography, cooking, games/puzzles, history. Material must relate to forthcoming themes. Word length: 300-800.

Poetry: Maximum line length: 100. Wants "clear, objective imagery. Serious and light verse considered."

How to Contact/Writers: "A query must consist of the following to be considered (please use nonerasable paper): a brief cover letter stating subject and word length of the proposed article; a detailed one-page outline explaining the information to be presented in the article; an extensive bibliography of materials the author intends to use in preparing the article; a self-addressed stamped envelope. Writers new to *Calliope* should send a writing sample with query. If you would like to know if your query has been received, please also include a stamped postcard that requests acknowledgment of receipt. In all correspondence, please include your complete address

---

● **SPECIAL COMMENTS** by the editor of *Children's Writer's & Illustrator's Market* are set off by a bullet.

as well as a telephone number where you can be reached. A writer may send as many queries for one issue as he or she wishes, but each query must have a separate cover letter, outline, bibliography and SASE. Telephone queries are not accepted. Handwritten queries will not be considered. Queries may be submitted at any time, but queries sent well in advance of deadline *may not be answered for several months*. Go-aheads requesting material proposed in queries are usually sent five months prior to publication date. Unused queries will be returned approximately three to four months prior to publication date."

Illustration: Illustrations only: Send tearsheets, photocopies. Original work returned upon job's completion (upon written request).

Photography: Buys photos from freelancers. Wants photos pertaining to any forthcoming themes. Uses b&w/color prints, 35mm transparencies. Send unsolicited photos by mail (on speculation).

Terms: Buys all rights for mss and artwork. Pays 20-25¢/word for stories/articles. Pays on an individual basis for poetry, activities, games/puzzles. "Covers are assigned and paid on an individual basis." Pays photographers per photo ($15-100 for b&w; $25-100 for color). Sample copy for $4.95 and SAE with $1.05 postage. Writer's/illustrator's/photo guidelines for SASE. (See listings for *AppleSeeds*, *Cobblestone*, *Faces*, *Footsteps* and *Odyssey*.)

CAMPUS LIFE, Christianity Today, International, 465 Gundersen Dr., Carol Stream IL 60188. (630)260-6200. Fax: (630)260-0114. E-mail: clmag@campuslife.net. Website: www.campuslife.net. **Articles and Fiction Editor:** Chris Lutes. **Design Director:** Doug Johnson. Bimonthly magazine. Estab. 1944. Circ. 100,000. "Our purpose is to help Christian high school students navigate adolescence with their faith intact."

Fiction: Young adults: humorous, problem-solving. Buys 5-6 mss/year. Byline given.

Poetry: Reviews poetry.

How to Contact/Writers: Fiction/nonfiction: Query.

Illustration: Works on assignment only. Reviews illustration packages from artists. Contact: Doug Johnson, design director. Illustrations only: Query; send promo sheet. Contact: Doug Johnson, design director. Responds only if interested. Credit line given.

Photography: Looking for photos depicting lifestyle/authentic teen experience. Model/property release required. Uses 8×10 glossy prints and 35mm, 2¼×2¼, 4×5 transparencies. Query with samples. Responds only if interested.

Terms: Pays on acceptance. Original artwork returned at job's completion. Writer's/illustrator's/photo guidelines for SASE.

CAREER WORLD, General Learning Communications, 900 Skokie Blvd., Suite 200, Northbrook IL 60062-4028. (847)205-3000. Fax: (847)564-8197. **Articles Editor:** Carole Rubenstein. Monthly (school year) magazine. Estab. 1972. A guide to careers, for students grades 6-12.

Nonfiction: Young adults/teens: education, how-to, interview/profile, career awareness and development. Byline given.

How to Contact/Writers: Nonfiction: Query with published clips and résumé. "We do not want any unsolicited manuscripts." Responds to queries in 2 weeks.

Illustration: Buys 5-10 illustrations/year. Works on assignment only. Reviews ms/illustration packages from artists. Ms/illustration packages and illustration only: Query; send promo sheet and tearsheets. Credit line given.

Photography: Purchases photos from freelancers.

Terms: Pays on publication. Buys all rights for ms. Pays $150 and up for articles. Pays illustrators by the project. Writer's guidelines free, but only on assignment.

CAREERS & COLLEGES, E.M. Guild, 989 Avenue of the Americas, New York NY 10018. (212)563-4688. (212)967-2531. Website: www.careersandcolleges.com. **Editorial Director:** Don Rauf. Magazine published 4 times during school year (September, November, January, March). Circ. 250,000. "*Careers & Colleges* provides juniors and seniors in high school with useful, thought-provoking, and hopefully entertaining reading on career choices, higher education and other topics that will help prepare them for life after high school. Each issue focuses on a specific single theme: How to Get Into College; How to Pay for College; Careers; and Life After High School."

● *Careers & Colleges* has recently been redesigned.

Nonfiction: Young adults/teens: careers, college, health, how-to, humorous, interview/profile, personal development, problem-solving, social issues, sports, travel. Wants more celebrity profiles. Buys 20-30 mss/year. Average word length: 1,000-1,500. Byline given.

How to Contact/Writers: Nonfiction: Query. Responds to queries in 6 weeks. Will consider electronic submissions via disk or modem.

Illustration: Buys 8 illustrations/issue; buys 32 illustrations/year. Works on assignment only. Reviews ms/illustration packages from artists. Query first. Illustrations only: Send tearsheets, cards. Responds to art samples in 3 weeks if interested. Original artwork returned at job's completion. Credit line given.

Terms: Pays on acceptance plus 30 days. Buys first North American serial rights. Pays $100-600 for assigned/unsolicited articles. Additional payment for ms/illustration packages "must be negotiated." Pays $300-1,000 for color illustration; $200-700 for b&w/color inside illustration. Pays photographers by the project. Sample copy $2.50 with SAE and $1.25 postage; writer's guidelines free with SASE.

Tips: "We look for articles with great quotes, good reporting, good writing. Articles must be rich with examples and anecdotes, and must tie in with our mandate to help our teenaged readers plan their futures."

CARUS PUBLISHING COMPANY, P.O. Box 300, Peru IL 61354. See listing for *Babybug*, *Cicada*, *Click*, *Cricket*, *Ladybug*, *Muse* and *Spider*.
 • At press time, Carus Publishing purchased Cobblestone Publishing, publisher of *AppleSeeds*, *Calliope*, *Cobblestone*, *Faces*, *Footsteps* and *Odyssey*.

CATHOLIC FAITH & FAMILY, Circle Media, 33 Rossotto Dr., Hamden CT 06514. (203)288-5600. Fax: (203)288-5157. E-mail: editor@twincircle.com. **Articles Editor:** Loretta G. Seyer. **Art Director:** Tom Brophy. Biweekly tabzine. Estab. 1965. Circ. 18,000. 5% of publication aimed at children.
Nonfiction: Buys hundreds of mss/year. Average word length: 450-2,000. Byline given.
How to Contact/Writers: Nonfiction: Send complete ms. Responds to queries in 2 months; mss in 6 months. Will consider electronic submission via disk or modem.
Illustration: Uses color artwork only. Reviews ms/illustration packages from artists. Query; send ms with dummy. Illustrations only: Query with samples. Contact: Loretta G. Seyer, editor. Responds in 3 months. Samples returned with SASE. Credit line given.
Photography: Needs photos depicting family-oriented activities. Uses color glossy prints and 35mm, $2\frac{1}{4} \times 2\frac{1}{4}$, 4×5 or 8×10 transparencies. Query with samples; call. Responds in 3 months.
Terms: Pays on publication. Buys first North American rights. Buys one-time rights for artwork. Original artwork returned at job's completion. Pays $75-300 for articles. Pays illustrators $75-100 for color cover; $25-50 for color inside. Pays photographers per photo. Sample copies for SASE. Writer's/illustrator's/photo guidelines for SASE.
Tips: "We need photos of families—parents, kids, grandparents and combos for our publication. They should be showing a variety of emotions and activities."

[N] CATHOLIC FORESTER, Catholic Order of Foresters, P.O. Box 3012, 355 Shuman Blvd., Naperville IL 60566-7012. (630)983-4900. Fax: (630)983-3384. **Articles Editor:** Patricia Baron. **Art Director:** Keith Halla. Bimonthly magazine. Estab. 1883. Circ. 100,000. Targets members of the Catholic Order of Foresters. In addition to the organization's news, it offers general interest pieces on health, finance, travel, family life. Also use inspirational and humorous fiction.
Fiction: Young readers, middle readers, young adults: humorous, nature/environment, religious. Buys 10-20 mss/year. Average word length: 500-1,500.
Nonfiction: Picture-oriented material, young readers, young adults: cooking, games/puzzles. Buys 10 mss/year. Average word length: 500-1,500. Byline given.
How to Contact/Writers: Fiction/nonfiction: Submit complete ms. Responds in 2-3 months. Will consider previously published work.
Illustration: Buys 8-12 illustrations/issue. Uses color artwork only. Works on assignment only.
Photography: Buys photos with accompanying ms only.
Terms: Pays on acceptance. Buys first North American serial rights, reprint rights, one-time rights. Sample copies for 9×12 SAE and 3 first-class stamps. Writer's guidelines free for SASE.

[N] [icons] CHICKADEE, The Owl Group, 179 John St., Suite 500, Toronto, Ontario M5T 3G5 Canada. (416)340-2700. Fax: (416)340-9769. E-mail: owl@owlkids.com. Website: www.owlkids.com. Contact: Angela Keenlyside, managing editor. Magazine published 9 times/year. Estab. 1979. Circ. 110,000. "*Chickadee* is a hands-on publication designed to interest 6- to 9-year-olds in science, nature and the world around them. It features games, stories, crafts, experiments. Every effort is made to provide *Chickadee* readers with fresh ideas that are offered in an innovative and surprising way. Lively writing and a strong visual component are necessary strengths in any piece written for *Chickadee*."
Fiction: Picture-oriented material, new readers: animal, humorous, nature/environment. Does not want to see religious, anthropomorphic animal, romance material, material that talks down to kids. Buys 8 mss/year. Average word length: 800-900. Byline given.
Nonfiction: Picture-oriented material, new readers: animal (facts/characteristics), arts/crafts, games/puzzles, humorous, nature/environment, science. Does not want to see religious material. Buys 2-5 mss/year. Average word length: 300-800. Byline given.
Poetry: Limit submissions to 5 poems at a time.
How to Contact/Writers: Fiction/nonfiction: Send complete ms. SAE and international postage coupon for answer and return of ms. Responds to mss in 3 months unless return postage is missing. Will consider simultaneous submissions. "We prefer to read complete manuscript on speculation."
Illustration: Buys 3-5 illustrations/issue; 40 illustrations/year. Preferred theme or style: realism/humor (but not cartoons). Works on assignment only. Illustration only: Send promo sheet. Responds to art samples only if interested. Samples returned with SASE. Credit line given.
Photography: Looking for animal (mammal, insect, reptile, fish, etc.) and nature photos. Uses 35mm and $2\frac{1}{4} \times 2\frac{1}{4}$ transparencies. Write to request photo package for $1 money order, attention Ekaterina Gitlin, researcher.

Terms: Pays on publication. Buys all rights for mss. Buys one-time rights for photos. Original artwork returned at job's completion. Pays $10-250 for stories. Pays illustrators $100-650 for color inside, pays photographers per photo (range: $100-350). Sample copies for $4. Writer's guidelines free. All requests must include SAE and international postage coupon.

Tips: "The magazine publishes fiction and nonfiction that encourages kids to read and learn more about the world around them. The majority of *Chickadee*'s content is stories, puzzles, activities and observation games for young kids to enjoy on their own. Each issue also includes a longer story or poem that can be enjoyed by older kids." (See listings for *Chirp* and *OWL*.)

CHILD LIFE, Children's Better Health Institute, P.O. Box 567, Indianapolis IN 46206. Parcels and packages: please send to 1100 Waterway Blvd., 46202. (317)636-8881. **Editor:** Lise Hoffman. **Art Director:** Phyllis Lybarger. Magazine published 8 times/year. Estab. 1921. Circ. 80,000. Targeted toward kids ages 9-11. Focuses on health, sports, fitness, nutrition, safety, academic excellence, general interests, and the nostalgia of *Child Life's* early days. "We publish jokes, riddles and poems by children." Kids should include name, address, phone number (for office use) and school photo. "No mass duplicated, multiple submissions."

   ● *Child Life* is no longer accepting manuscripts for publication. See listings for *Children's Playmate*, *Humpty Dumpty's Magazine*, *Jack And Jill*, *Turtle Magazine* and *U*S*Kids*.

Tips: "We use kids' submissions from our age range—9 to 11. Those older or younger should try one of our sister publications: *Children's Digest, Children's Playmate, Humpty Dumpty's Magazine, Jack And Jill, Turtle Magazine, U*S*Kids.*"

CHILDREN'S DIGEST, Children's Better Health Institute, 1100 Waterway Blvd., P.O. Box 567, Indianapolis IN 46206. (317)634-1100. Parcels and packages please send to 1100 Waterway Blvd., Indianapolis IN 46202. **Editor:** Lisa Hoffman. Art Director: Penny Rasdall. Magazine published 8 times/year. Estab. 1950. Circ. 110,000. For preteens; focuses on health, sports, fitness, nutrition, safety, academic excellence, general interest, and the nostalgia of *Child's Life's* early days. "We publish jokes, riddles, and poems by children." Kids should include name, address, phone numbers (for office use), and school photo. No mass duplicated, multiple submissions.

   ● *Children's Digest* is no longer accepting manuscripts for publication.

Tips: We use submissions from our age range—9-11. Those older or younger should try one of our sister publications: *Children's Playmate, Humpty Dumpty's Magazine, Jack and Jill, Turtle Magazine, U*S* Kids.*

CHILDREN'S PLAYMATE, Children's Better Health Institute, 1100 Waterway Blvd., Box 567, Indianapolis IN 46206. (317)636-8881. **Editor:** Terry Harshman. **Art Director:** Chuck Horsman. Magazine published 8 times/year. Estab. 1929. Circ. 135,000. For children ages 6-8 years; approximately 50% of content is health-related.

Fiction: Young readers: animal, contemporary, fantasy, history, humorous, sports, suspense/mystery/adventure. Buys 25 mss/year. Average word length: 300-500. Byline given.

Nonfiction: Young readers: arts/crafts, biography, cooking, games/puzzles, health, history, how-to, humorous, safety, science, sports. Buys 16-20 mss/year. Average word length: 300-500. Byline given.

Poetry: Maximum length: 20-25 lines.

How to Contact/Writers: Fiction/nonfiction: Send complete ms. Responds to mss in 3 months.

Illustration: Works on assignment only. Reviews ms/illustration packages from artists. Query first.

Photography: Buys photos with accompanying ms only. Model/property releases required; captions required. Uses 35mm transparencies. Send completed ms with transparencies.

Terms: Pays on publication for illustrators and writers. Buys all rights for mss and artwork; one-time rights for photos. Pays 17¢/word for stories. Pays minimum $25 for poems. Pays $275 for color cover illustration; $35-90 for b&w inside; $70-155 for color inside. Pays photographers per photo (range: $10-75). Sample copy $1.75. Writer's/illustrator's guidelines for SASE. (See listings for *Child Life, Children's Digest, Humpty Dumpty's Magazine, Jack and Jill, Turtle Magazine* and *U*S* Kids.*)

CHIRP, The Owl Group, 179 John St., Suite 500, Toronto, Ontario M5T 3G5 Canada. E-mail: owl@owlkids.com. ca. Website: www.owl.on.ca. **Editor-in-chief:** Marybeth Leatherdale. **Creative Director:** Tim Davin. Published monthly during school year. *Discovery* magazine for children ages 3-6. "*Chirp* aims to introduce preschool non-readers to reading for pleasure about the world around them."

Fiction: Picture-oriented material: nature/environment, adventure, animal, multicultural, problem-solving, sports. Word length: 250 maximum.

Nonfiction: Picture-oriented material: fun, easy craft ideas, animal, games/puzzles, how-to, multicultural, nature/environment, problem-solving.

Poetry: Wants rhymes and poetry. Maximum length: 8 lines.

How to Contact/Writers: Query. Responds to queries/mss in 1 month.

Illustration: Uses approximately 15 illustrations/issue; 135 illustrations/year. Samples returned with SASE. Originals returned at job's completion. Credit line given.

Terms: Pays on acceptance. Buys all rights. Pays on publication. Pays writers $250 (Canadian); illustrators $150-650 (Canadian); photographers paid per photo ($150-375 Canadian). Sample copies available for $4 (Canadian).

Tips: "*Chirp* editors prefer to read completed manuscripts of stories and articles, accompanied by photographs or suggestions of visual references where they are appropriate. All craft ideas should be based on materials that are found around the average household." (See listings for *Chickadee* and *OWL*.)

CICADA, Carus Publishing Company, P.O. Box 300, 315 Fifth St., Peru IL 61354. (815)224-6656. Fax: (815)224-6615. E-mail: CICADA@caruspub.com. Website: www.cicadamag.com. **Editor-in-Chief:** Marianne Carus. **Executive Editor:** Deborah Vetter. **Senior Editor:** John D. Allen. **Senior Art Director:** Ron McCutchan. Bimonthly magazine. Estab. 1998. *Cicada* publishes fiction and poetry with a genuine teen sensibility, aimed at the high school and college-age market. The editors are looking for stories and poems that are thought-provoking but entertaining.
Fiction: Young adults: adventure, animal, contemporary, fantasy, history, humorous, multicultural, nature/environment, romance, science fiction, sports, suspense/mystery, stories that will adapt themselves to a sophisticated cartoon, or graphic novel format. Buys up to 60 mss/year. Average word length: about 5,000 words for short stories; up to 15,000 for novellas only—we run one novella per issue.
Nonfiction: Young adults: first-person, coming-of-age experiences that are relevant to teens and young adults (example-life in the Peace Corps). Buys 6 mss/year. Average word length: about 5,000 words. Byline given.
Poetry: Reviews serious, humorous, free verse, rhyming (if done well) poetry. Maximum length: up to 25 lines. Limit submissions to 5 poems.
How to Contact/Writers: Fiction/nonfiction: send complete ms. Responds to mss in 10 weeks. Publishes ms 1-2 years after acceptance. Will consider simultaneous submissions if author lets us know.
Illustration: Buys 20 illustrations/issue; 120 illustrations/year. Uses color artwork for cover; b&w for interior. Works on assignment only. Reviews ms/illustration packages from artists. Send ms with 1-2 sketches and samples of other finished art. Contact: Ron McCutchan, senior art director. Illustrations only: Query with samples. Contact: Ron McCutchan, senior art director. Responds in 6 weeks. Samples returned with SASE; samples filed. Credit line given.
Photography: Wants documentary photos (clear shots that illustrate specific artifacts, persons, locations, phenomena, etc., cited in the text) and "art" shots of teens in photo montage/lighting effects etc. Uses b&w 4×5 glossy prints. Submit portfolio for review. Responds in 6 weeks.
Terms: Pays on publication. Buys first rights for mss. Buys one-time, first publication rights for artwork and photographs. Pays up to 25¢/word for mss; up to $3/line for poetry. Pays illustrators $750 for color cover; $50-150 for b&w inside. Pays photographers per photo (range: $50-150). Sample copies for $8.50. Writer's/illustrator's/photo guidelines for SASE.
Tips: "Please don't write for a junior high audience. We're looking for good character development, strong plots, and thought-provoking themes for young people in high school and collge. Don't forget humor!" (See listings for *Babybug, Click, Cricket, Ladybug, Muse* and *Spider*.)

CLASS ACT, Class Act, Inc., P.O. Box 802, Henderson KY 42419-0802. E-mail: classact@henderson.net. Website: www.henderson.net/~classact. **Articles Editor:** Susan Thurman. Monthly, September-May. Newsletter. Estab. 1993. Circ. 300. "We are looking for practical, ready-to-use ideas for the English/language arts classroom (grades 6-12)."
Nonfiction: Young adults/teens: games/puzzles, how-to. Does not want to see esoteric material; no master's theses; no poetry (except articles about how to write poetry). Buys 20 mss/year. Average word length: 200-2,000. Byline given.
How to Contact/Writers: Send complete ms. E-mail submissions (no attachments) and submissions on disk using Word encouraged. Responds to queries/mss in 1 month. Usually publishes ms 3-12 months after acceptance. Will consider simultaneous submissions. Must send SASE.
Terms: Pays on acceptance. Pays $10-40 per article. Buys all rights. Sample copy for $3 and SASE.
Tips: "We're only interested in language arts-related articles for teachers and students. Writers should realize teens often need humor in classroom assignments. In addition, we are looking for teacher-tested ideas that have already worked in the classroom. We currently have more puzzles than we need and are looking for prose rather than puzzles. Be clever. We've already seen a zillion articles on homonyms and haikus. If a SASE isn't sent, we'll assume you don't want a response."

COBBLESTONE: Discover American History, Cobblestone Publishing Co., 30 Grove St., Suite C, Peterborough NH 03458. (603)924-7209. Fax: (603)924-7380. Website: www.cobblestonepub.com. **Editor:** Meg Chorlian. **Art Director:** Ann Dillon. **Managing Editor:** Lou Warnycia. Magazine published 9 times/year. Circ. 33,000. "*Cobblestone* is theme-related. Writers should request editorial guidelines which explain procedure and list upcoming themes. Queries must relate to an upcoming theme. It is recommended that writers become familiar with the magazine (sample copies available)."

● At press time, Cobblestone Publishing was purchased by Carus Publishing. No editorial changes were planned. At press time, *Cobblestone* was revising their writers guidelines. See their website for updated information. *Cobblestone* themes for 2001 include Jefferson Davis, The Mill Girls, Panama Canal and German Mexicans.

Nonfiction: Middle readers (school ages 8-14): activities, biography, games/puzzles (no word finds), history (world and American), interview/profile, science, travel. All articles must relate to the issue's theme. Buys 120 mss/year. Average word length: 600-800. Byline given.

Poetry: Up to 100 lines. "Clear, objective imagery. Serious and light verse considered." Pays on an individual basis. Must relate to theme.

How to Contact/Writers: Fiction/nonfiction: Query. "A query must consist of all of the following to be considered: a brief cover letter stating the subject and word length of the proposed article, a detailed one-page outline explaining the information to be presented in the article, an extensive bibliography of materials the author intends to use in preparing the article, a self-addressed stamped envelope. Writers new to *Cobblestone* should send a writing sample with query. If you would like to know if your query has been received, please also include a stamped postcard that requests acknowledgement of receipt. In all correspondence, please include your complete address as well as a telephone number where you can be reached. A writer may send as many queries for one issue as he or she wishes, but each query must have a separate cover letter, outline, bibliography and SASE. Telephone queries are not accepted. Handwritten queries will not be considered. Queries may be submitted at any time, but queries sent well in advance of deadline *may not be answered for several months*. Go-aheads requesting material proposed in queries are usually sent five months prior to publication date. Unused queries will be returned approximately three to four months prior to publication date."

Illustration: Buys 4 color illustrations/issue; 36 illustrations/year. Preferred theme or style: Material that is simple, clear and accurate but not too juvenile. Sophisticated sources are a must. Works on assignment only. Reviews ms/illustration packages from artists. Query. Illustrations only: Send photocopies, tearsheets, or other nonreturnable samples. "Illustrators should consult issues of *Cobblestone* to familiarize themselves with our needs." Responds to art samples in 2 weeks. Samples returned with SASE; samples not filed. Original artwork returned at job's completion (upon written request). Credit line given.

Photography: Photos must relate to upcoming themes. Send transparencies and/or color prints. Submit on speculation.

Terms: Pays on publication. Buys all rights to articles and artwork. Pays 20-25¢/word for articles/stories. Pays on an individual basis for poetry, activities, games/puzzles. Pays photographers per photo ($15-100 for b&w; $25-100 for color). Sample copy $4.95 with 7½×10½ SAE and 5 first-class stamps; writer's/illustrator's/photo guidelines free with SAE and 1 first-class stamp.

Tips: Writers: "Submit detailed queries which show attention to historical accuracy and which offer interesting and entertaining information. Study past issues to know what we look for. All feature articles, recipes, activities, fiction and supplemental nonfiction are freelance contributions." Illustrators: "Submit color samples, not too juvenile. Study past issues to know what we look for. The illustration we use is generally for stories, recipes and activities." (See listings for *AppleSeeds*, *Calliope*, *Faces*, *Footsteps* and *Odyssey*.)

☑ **COBBLESTONE PUBLISHING COMPANY**, 30 Grove St., Suite C, Peterborough NH 03458. See listings for *AppleSeeds*, *Calliope*, *Cobblestone*, *Faces*, *Footsteps* and *Odyssey*.
 • At press time, Cobblestone Publishing was purchased by Carus Publishing, publisher of *Babybug*, *Cicada*, *Click*, *Cricket*, *Ladybug*, *Muse* and *Spider*.

COLLEGE BOUND MAGAZINE, Ramholtz Publishing, Inc., 2071 Clove Rd., Staten Island NY 10304. (718)273-5700. Fax: (718)273-2539. E-mail: editorial@collegebound.net. Website: www.collegebound.net. **Articles Editor:** Gina LaGuardia. **Art Director:** Giulio Rammairone. Monthly magazine and website. Estab. 1987. Circ. 75,000 (regional); 750,000 (national). *College Bound Magazine* is written by college students for high school juniors and seniors. It is designed to provide an inside view of college life, with college students from around the country serving as correspondents. The magazine's editorial content offers its teen readership personal accounts on all aspects of college, from living with a roommate, choosing a major, and joining a fraternity or sorority, to college dating, interesting courses, beating the financial aid fuss, and other college-bound concerns. *College Bound Magazine* is published six times regionally throughout the tri-state area. Special issues include the Annual National Edition (published each February) and Fall and Spring California and Chicago issues. The magazine also has an award-winning World Wide Web site, *CollegeBound.NET*, at www.collegebound.net.

Nonfiction: Young adults: careers, college prep, fashion, health, how-to, interview/profile, problem-solving, social issues, college life. Buys 70 mss/year. Average word length: 400-1,100 words. Byline given.

How to Contact/Writers: Nonfiction: Query with published clips. Responds to queries in 5 weeks; mss in 6 weeks. Publishes ms 2-3 months after acceptance. Will consider electronic submission via disk or modem, previously published work (as long as not a competitor title).

Illustration: Buys 2-3 illustrations/issue. Uses color artwork only. Works on assignment only. Reviews ms/illustration packages from artists. Query. Contact: Giulio Rammiarone, art director. Illustrations only: Query with samples. Responds in 2 months. Samples kept on file. Credit line given.

Terms: Pays on publication. Buys first North American serial rights, all rights or reprint rights for mss. Buys first rights for artwork. Originals returned if requested, with SASE. Pays $25-100 for articles 30 days upon publication. All contributors receive 2 issues with payment. Pays illustrators $25-125 for color inside. Sample copies free for #10 SASE and $3 postage. Writer's guidelines for SASE.

Tips: "Review the sample issue and get a good feel for the types of articles we accept and our tone and purpose."

N **CosmoGIRL!**, Hearst Corporation, 1790 Broadway, 11th Floor, New York NY 10019. (212)841-8473. Fax: (212)582-7067. E-mail: inbox@cosmogirl.com. Website: www.cosmogirl.com. **Articles Editor:** Lauren Smith. **Art Director:** Lisa Shapiro. **Photo Editor:** Georgia Paralemos. Monthly magazine. Estab. 1999. Circ. 850,000. "We deal with issues of interest to teen girls—fashion, beauty, fitness, boys. Most important in *CosmoGIRL!*, though, is the 'inner girl' that exists in our readers."

Nonfiction: Young adult/teen: arts/crafts, careers, concept, fashion, health, how-to, interview/profile, problem-solving, social issues. Buys 40 mss/year from freelancers. Word length: 250-1,400. Byline given.

How to Contact/Writers: Query with published clips. Responds to queries/mss in 2 months. Published mss 4 months after acceptance. Considers simultaneous submissions and electronic submissions via disk or modem.

Illustration: Buys 4 illustrations/issue, 25 illustrations/year from freelancers. Uses color artwork only. Send portfolio and tearsheets. Contact: Lisa Shapiro, art director. Responds only if interested. Credit line given.

Photography: Buys photos separately. Looking for real-life girl situations. Model/property release required. Uses 2¼×2¼ transparencies. Submit portfolio for review. Responds only if interested.

Terms: Pays on publication. Buys all rights for mss. Original artwork returned at job's completion. Pays $1/word for stories. Guidelines available for SASE.

Tips: "Please truly know *CosmoGIRL!* when submitting story ideas. We look for real-life hints for our readers, not generic teen reporting. Pitch articles for specific section."

CRICKET MAGAZINE, Carus Publishing, Company, P.O. Box 300, Peru IL 61354. (815)224-6656. **Articles/Fiction Editor-in-Chief:** Marianne Carus. **Executive Editor:** Deborah Vetter. **Senior Editor:** John D. Allen. **Associate Editor:** Julia M. Messina. **Art Director:** Ron McCutchan. Monthly magazine. Estab. 1973. Circ. 71,000. Children's literary magazine for ages 9-14.

Fiction: Middle readers, young adults/teens: adventure, animal, contemporary, fantasy, folk and fairy tales, history, humorous, multicultural, nature/environment, science fiction, sports, suspense/mystery. Buys 140 mss/year. Maximum word length: 2,000. Byline given.

Nonfiction: Middle readers, young adults/teens: animal, arts/crafts, biography, environment, experiments, games/puzzles, history, how-to, interview/profile, natural science, problem-solving, science and technology, space, sports, travel. Multicultural needs include articles on customs and cultures. Requests bibliography with submissions. Buys 40 mss/year. Average word length: 1,200. Byline given.

Poetry: Reviews poems, 1-page maximum length. Limit submissions to 5 poems or less.

How to Contact/Writers: Send complete ms. Do not query first. Responds to mss in 3 months. Does not like but will consider simultaneous submissions. SASE required for response.

Illustration: Buys 35 illustrations (14 separate commissions)/issue; 425 illustrations/year. Uses b&w and full-color work. Preferred theme or style: "strong realism; strong people, especially kids; good action illustration; no cartoons. All media, but prefer other than pencil." Reviews ms/illustration packages from artists "but reserves option to re-illustrate." Send complete ms with sample and query. Illustrations only: Provide tearsheets or good quality photocopies to be kept on file. SASE required for response/return of samples. Responds to art samples in 2 months.

Photography: Purchases photos with accompanying ms only. Model/property releases required. Uses color transparencies, b&w glossy prints.

Terms: Pays on publication. Buys first publication rights in the English language. Buys first publication rights plus promotional rights for artwork. Original artwork returned at job's completion. Pays up to 25¢/word for unsolicited articles; up to $3/line for poetry. Pays $750 for color cover; $75-150 for b&w, $150-250 for color inside. Pays $750 for color cover; $75-150 for b&w, $150-250 for color inside. Writer's/illustrator's guidelines for SASE.

Tips: Writers: "Read copies of back issues and current issues. Adhere to specified word limits. *Please* do not query." Illustrators: "Edit your samples. Send only your best work and be able to reproduce that quality in assignments. Put name and address on *all* samples. Know a publication before you submit—is your style appropriate?" (See listings for *Babybug*, *Cicada*, *Click*, *Ladybug*, *Muse* and *Spider*.)

CRUSADER, Calvinist Cadet Corps, P.O. Box 7259, Grand Rapids MI 49510. (616)241-5616. Fax: (616)241-5558. **Editor:** G. Richard Broene. **Art Director:** Robert DeJonge. Magazine published 7 times/year. Circ. 13,000. "Our magazine is for members of the Calvinist Cadet Corps—boys aged 9-14. Our purpose is to show how God is at work in their lives and in the world around them. Our magazine offers nonfiction articles and fast-moving fiction—everything to appeal to interests and concerns of boys, teaching Christian values subtly."

Fiction: Middle readers, young adults/teens: adventure, humorous, multicultural, problem-solving, religious, sports. Buys 12 mss/year. Average word length: 900-1,500.

Nonfiction: Middle readers, young adults/teens: arts/crafts, games/puzzles, hobbies, how-to, humorous, interview/profile, problem-solving, science, sports. Buys 6 mss/year. Average word length: 400-900.

How to Contact/Writers: Fiction/nonfiction: Send complete ms. Responds to queries in 1 month; on mss in 1-2 months. Will consider simultaneous submissions.

Illustration: Buys 1 illustration/issue; buys 6 illustrations/year. Works on assignment only. Reviews ms/illustration packages from artists. Responds in 5 weeks. Samples returned with SASE. Originals returned to artist at job's completion. Credit line given.

Photography: Buys photos from freelancers. Wants nature photos and photos of boys.

Terms: Pays on acceptance. Buys first North American serial rights; reprint rights. Pays 4-5¢/word for stories/articles. Pays illustrators $50-200 for b&w/color cover or b&w inside. Sample copy free with 9×12 SAE and 4 first-class stamps.

Tips: "Our publication is mostly open to fiction; send SASE for a list of themes (available yearly in January). We use mostly fast-moving fiction that appeals to a boy's sense of adventure or sense of humor. Avoid preachiness; avoid simplistic answers to complicated problems; avoid long dialogue with little action. Articles on sports, outdoor activities, bike riding, science, crafts, etc. should emphasize a Christian perspective but avoid simplistic moralisms."

THE CRYSTAL BALL, The Starwind Press, P.O. Box 98, Ripley OH 45167. (937)392-4549. E-mail: susannah @techgallery.com. Articles/Fiction Editor: Marlene Powell. **Assistant Editor:** Susannah C. West. Quarterly magazine. Estab. 1997. Circ. 1,000. Publishes science fiction and fantasy for young adults.

Fiction: Young adults: fantasy, folktale, science fiction. Buys 8-12 mss/year. Average word length: 1,500-5,000. Byline given.

Nonfiction: Young adults: biography, how-to, interview/profile, science. Buys 8-12 mss/year. Average word length: 1,000-3,000.

Poetry: Only publishes poetry by kids.

How to Contact/Writers: Fiction: send complete ms. Nonfiction: query. Responds to queries and mss in 4 months. Publishes ms 6-12 months after acceptance. Will consider previously published work if published in noncompeting market.

Illustration: Buys 6-8 illustrations/issue; 24-32 illustrations/year. Uses b&w camera ready artwork only. Works on assignment only. Reviews ms/illustration packages from artists. Send ms with dummy. Contact: Marlene Powell, editor. Illustrations only: query with samples. Contact: Marlene Powell, editor. Responds in 4 months if SASE enclosed. Samples kept on file. Credit line given.

Photography: Looking for photos to illustrate nonfiction pieces. Uses b&w, line shots or already screened. Responds in 3 months.

Terms: Pays on acceptance. Buys first North American serial rights for mss, artwork and photos. Original artwork returned at job's completion if requested. Pays $5-20 for stories and articles. Additional payment for photos accompanying article. Pays illustrators $5-20 for b&w inside and cover. Pays photographers per photo (range: $5-20). Sample copies for $3. Writer's/illustrator's guidelines for SASE.

Tips: Be familiar with the science fiction/fantasy genre.

DISCOVERIES, Children's Ministries, 6401 The Paseo, Kansas City MO 64131. (816)333-7000. Fax: (816)333-4439. E-mail: vfolsom@nazarene.org. **Editor**: Virginia Folsom. **Executive Editor**: Randy Cloud. **Assistant Editor:** Emily Freeburg. Weekly tabloid. "*Discoveries* is a leisure-reading piece for third and fourth graders. It is published weekly by WordAction Publishing. The major purpose of the magazine is to provide a leisure-reading piece which will build Christian behavior and values and provide reinforcement for Biblical concepts taught in the Sunday School curriculum. The focus of the reinforcement will be life-related, with some historical appreciation. *Discoveries'* target audience is children ages eight to ten in grades three and four. The readability goal is third to fourth grade."

Fiction: Middle readers: adventure, contemporary, humorous, religious. "Fiction—stories should vividly portray definite Christian emphasis or character-building values, without being preachy. The setting, plot and action should be realistic." 500 word maximum. Byline given.

Nonfiction: Game/puzzles, history (all Bible-related) and Bible "trivia."

How to Contact/Writers: Fiction: Send complete ms. Responds to queries/mss in 1 month.

Terms: Pays "approximately one year before the date of issue." Buys multi-use rights. Pays 5¢/word. Contributor receives 4 complimentary copies of publication. Sample copy free for #10 SASE with 1 first-class stamp. Writer's/artist's guidelines free with #10 SAE.

Tips: "*Discoveries* is committed to reinforcement of the Biblical concepts taught in the Sunday School curriculum. Because of this, the themes needed are mainly as follows: faith in God, obedience to God, putting God first, choosing to please God, accepting Jesus as Savior, finding God's will, choosing to do right, trusting God in hard times, prayer, trusting God to answer, importance of Bible memorization, appreciation of Bible as God's Word to man, Christians working together, showing kindness to others, witnessing." (See listing for *Power and Light*.)

DISCOVERY, John Milton Society for the Blind, 475 Riverside Dr., Room 455, New York NY 10115. (212)870-3335. Fax: (212)870-3229. E-mail: ipeck@jmsblind.org. Website: www.jmsblind.org. **Assistant Editor**: Ingrid Peck. **Executive Director & Editor**: Darcy Quigley. Quarterly braille magazine. Estab. 1935. Circ. 2,000. "*Discovery* is a free Christian braille magazine for blind and visually impaired youth ages 8-18. 95% of material is

AUGUST 6, 2000

DISCOVERY trails

FOR KIDS IN SEARCH OF THE TRUTH!

Taken For A Ride

© 1999 Randall Rider

Randy Rider used pen and ink augmented in Photoshop for this illustration that appeared in *Discovery Trails*, a piece of Sunday School literature produced by Gospel House Publishing. Rider does four promotional mailings per year to get his work in the hands of art directors. He praises Gospel House for being open to new ideas. "They give you room to do great work!"

stories, poems, quizzes and educational articles, reprinted from 20 Christian and other magazines for youth. Original pieces from individual authors must be ready to print with little or no editing involved. We cannot offer reprint fees. Christian focus."

Fiction: Young readers, middle readers, young adults/teens: all categories and issues pertaining to blind; adventure, animal, contemporary, fantasy, folktales, health, history, humorous, multicultural, nature/environment, problem solving, religious. Does not want stories in which blindness is described as a novelty. It should be part of a story with a larger focus. Buys less than 10 mss/year. Average word length: 1,500 words (maximum). Byline given.

Nonfiction: Young readers, middle readers, young adults/teens: animal, biography, careers, concept, cooking, games/puzzles, geography, health, history, hobbies, how-to, humorous, interview/profile, multicultural, nature/environment, problem solving, religion, science, social issues. Also want inspirational stories involving visually impaired. Buys less than 10 mss/year. Average word length: 1,500 words (maximum). Byline given.

Poetry: Reviews poetry. Maximum length: 500 words.

How to Contact/Writers: Fiction/nonfiction: Send complete ms. Responds to queries/mss in 6-8 weeks. Publishes ms 3-12 months after acceptance. Will consider simultaneous submissions, previously published work.

Terms: Acquires reprint rights. Authors do not receive payment, only sample copy. Sample copies free with SASE.

Tips: "95% of the material in *Discovery* is reprinted from Christian and other periodicals for youth. Previously unpublished material must therefore be ready to print with little or no editing involved. Please send complete manuscripts or request our 'Writers' Guidelines' which includes a list of periodicals we reprint from."

✔ **DISCOVERY TRAILS**, Gospel Publishing House, 1445 N. Boonville Ave., Springfield MO 65802-1894. (417)862-2781. E-mail: rl-discoverytrails@gph.org. Website: www.radiantlife.org. **Articles Editor:** Sinda S.

Zinn. **Art Director:** Dale Gehris. Quarterly take-home paper. Circ. 40,000. "*Discovery Trails* provides fiction stories that promote Christian living through application of biblical principles. Puzzles and activities are fun ways to learn more about God's Word and "bytes" of information are provided to inspire readers to be in awe of God's wonderful creation."

Fiction: Middle readers: adventure, animal, contemporary, humorous, nature/environment, problem-solving, religious, suspense/mystery. Buys 100 or less mss/year.

Nonfiction: Middle readers: animal, arts/crafts, how-to, humorous, nature/environment, problem-solving, religion. Buys 50-100 mss/year. Average word length: 200-500. Byline given.

Poetry: Reviews poetry. Limit submissions, at one time, to 2 poems.

How to Contact/Writers: Fiction/nonfiction: Send complete ms. Responds in 1 month. Publishes ms 15-24 months after acceptance. Will consider simultaneous submissions or previously published work. Please indicate such.

Illustration: Buys 1 illllustration issue; 50-60 illustrations/year from assigned freelancers. Uses color artwork only. Works on assignment only. Send promo sheet, portfolio. Contact: Dale Gehris, art coordinator. Responds only if interested. Samples returned with SASE; samples filed. Credit line given.

Terms: Pays on acceptance. Pays authors 7-10¢ per word. Buys first rights or reprint rights for mss. Buys reprint rights for artwork. Original artwork returned at job's completion. Sample copies for 6×9 SAE and 2 first-class stamps. Writer's guidelines for SASE.

☑ DOLPHIN LOG, The Cousteau Society, 870 Greenbriar Circle, Suite 402, Chesapeake VA 23320. (800)441-4395. Website: www.dolphinlog.org. **Editor:** Lisa Rao. Bimonthly magazine for children ages 7-13. Circ. 80,000. Entirely nonfiction subject matter encompasses all areas of science, natural history, marine biology, ecology and the environment as they relate to our global water system. The philosophy of the magazine is to delight, instruct and instill an environmental ethic and understanding of the interconnectedness of living organisms, including people. Of special interest are articles on ocean- or water-related themes which develop reading and comprehension skills.

Nonfiction: Middle readers, young adult: animal, games/puzzles, geography, interview/profile, nature/environment, science, ocean. Multicultural needs include indigenous peoples, lifestyles of ancient people, etc. Does not want to see talking animals. No dark or religious themes. Buys 10 mss/year. Average word length: 500-700. Byline given.

How to Contact/Writers: Nonfiction: Query first. Responds to queries in 3 months; mss in 6 months.

Illustration: Buys 1 illustration/issue; buys 6 illustrations/year. Preferred theme: Biological illustration. Reviews ms/illustration packages from artists. Illustrations only: Query; send résumé, promo sheet, slides. Responds to art samples in 2 months only if interested. Credit line given to illustrators.

Photography: Wants "sharp, colorful pictures of sea creatures. The more unusual the creature, the better." Submit duplicate slides only.

Terms: Pays on publication. Buys first North American serial rights; reprint rights. Pays $75-250 for articles. Pays $100-400 for illustrations. Pays $75-200/color photos. Sample copy $2.50 with 9×12 SAE and 3 first-class stamps. Writer's/illustrator's guidelines free with #10 SASE.

Tips: Writers: "Write simply and clearly and don't anthropomorphize." Illustrators: "Be scientifically accurate and don't anthropomorphize. Some background in biology is helpful, as our needs range from simple line drawings to scientific illustrations which must be researched for biological and technical accuracy."

Ⓝ DRAMATICS, Educational Theatre Association, 2343 Auburn Ave., Cincinnati OH 45219. (513)421-3900. E-mail: dcorathers@etassoc.org. Website: www.etassoc.org. **Articles Editor:** Don Corathers. **Art Director:** William Johnston. Published monthly September-May. Estab. 1929. Circ. 40,000. "Dramatics is for students (mainly high school age) and teachers of theater. Mix includes how-to (tech theater, acting, directing, etc.), informational, interview, photo feature, humorous, profile, technical. "We want our student readers to become a more discerning and appreciative audience. Material is directed to both theater students and their teachers, with strong student slant."

Fiction: Young adults: drama (one-act and full-length plays.) Does not want to see plays that show no understanding of the conventions of the theater. No plays for children, no Christmas or didactic "message" plays. "We prefer unpublished scripts that have been produced at least once." Buys 5-9 plays/year. Emerging playwrights have better chances with short plays, 10 minute or one-act.

Nonfiction: Young adults: arts/crafts, careers, how-to, interview/profile, multicultural (all theater-related). "We try to portray the theater community in all its diversity." Does not want to see academic treatises. Buys 50 mss/year. Average word length: 750-3,000. Byline given.

How to Contact/Writers: Send complete ms. Responds in 3 months (longer for plays). Published ms 3 months after acceptance. Will consider simultaneous submissions and previously published work occasionally.

Illustration: Buys 0-2 illustrations/year. Works on assignment only. Arrange portfolio review; send résumé, promo sheets and tearsheets. Responds only if interested. Samples returned with SASE; sample not filed. Credit line given.

Photography: Buys photos with accompanying ms only. Looking for "good-quality production or candid photography to accompany article. We very occasionally publish photo essays." Model/property release and captions required. Uses 5×7 or 8×10 b&w glossy prints and 35mm transparencies. Query with résumé of credits. Responds only if interested.

Terms: Pays on acceptance. Buys one-time rights, occasionally reprint rights. Buys one-time rights for artwork and photos. Original artwork returned at job's completion. Pays $100-400 for plays; $50-300 for articles; up to $100 for illustrations. Pays photographers by the project or per photo. Sometimes offers additional payment for ms/illustration packages and photos accompanying a ms. Sample copy available for $2.50 and 9×12 SAE. Writer's and photo guidelines available for SASE.

Tips: "Obtain our writer's guidelines and look at recent back issues. The best way to break in is to know our audience—drama students, teachers and others interested in theater—and write for them. Writers who have some practical experience in theater, especially in technical areas, have an advantage, but we'll work with anybody who has a good idea. Some freelancers have become regular contributors."

DYNAMATH, Scholastic Inc., 555 Broadway, New York NY 10012-3999. (212)343-6458. **Editor:** Matt Friedman. **Art Director:** Deborah Dinger. Monthly magazine. Estab. 1981. Circ. 225,000. Purpose is "to make learning math fun, challenging and uncomplicated for young minds in a very complex world."

Nonfiction: Middle readers: animal, arts/crafts, cooking, fashion, games/puzzles, health, history, hobbies, how-to, humorous, math, multicultural, nature/environment, problem-solving, science, social issues, sports—all must relate to math and science topics.

How to Contact/Writers: Nonfiction: Query with published clips, send ms. Responds to queries in 1 month; mss in 6 weeks. Publishes ms 4 months after acceptance. Will consider simultaneous submissions.

Illustration: Buys 4 illustrations/issue. Illustration only: Query first; send résumé and tearsheets. Responds on submissions only if interested. Credit line given.

Terms: Pays on acceptance. Buys all rights for mss, artwork, photographs. Originals returned to artist at job's completion. Pays $50-350 for stories. Pays artists $800-1,000 for color cover illustration; $100-800 for color inside illustration. Pays photographers $300-1,000 per project.

Tips: See listings for *Junior Scholastic, Scholastic Math Magazine, Science World* and *Superscience*.

☑ **ENCOUNTER**, (formerly *Straight*), Standard Publishing, 8121 Hamilton Ave., Cincinnati OH 45231. (513)931-4050. Fax: (513)931-0950. E-mail: kcarr@standardpub.com. Website: standardpub.com. **Articles/Fiction Editor:** Kelly Carr. Magazine published quarterly in weekly parts. Circ. 32,000.

Fiction: Young adults/teens: adventure, contemporary, health, humorous, multicultural, nature/environment, problem solving, religious, romance, sports. Does not want to see science fiction, fantasy, historical. "All should have religious perspective." Byline given. "We purchase very few fiction pieces."

Nonfiction: Young adults/teens: biography, careers, health, hobbies, how-to, humorous, interview/profile, multicultural, nature/environment, problem-solving, quizzes, religion, social issues, sports. Does not want to see devotionals. Byline given.

Poetry: Reviews poetry from teenagers only.

How to Contact/Writers: Fiction/nonfiction: Query or send complete ms. Responds to queries in 2 weeks; mss in 2 months. Will consider simultaneous submissions.

Illustration: Uses color artwork only. Preferred theme or style: Realistic, cartoon (full-color only). Works on assignment only. Query first. Illustrations only: Submit promo sheets or tearsheets. Samples returned with SASE. Responds only if interested. Credit line given.

Photography: Buys photos from freelancers. Looking for photos of contemporary, modestly dressed teenagers. Model/property release required. Uses 35mm transparencies. Photographer should request themes.

Terms: Pays on acceptance. Buys first rights and second serial (reprint rights) for mss. Buys one-time rights for artwork; one-time rights for photos. Pays 6-8¢/word for stories; 6-8¢/word for articles. Pays photographers per photo (range: $75-125). Sample copies for 9×12 SAE and 2 first-class stamps. Writer's/illustrator's guidelines for business SASE.

Tips: "Remember we are a publication for Christian teenagers. Each fiction or nonfiction piece should address modern-day issues from a religious perspective. We are trying to become more racially diverse. Writers, illustrators and photographers should keep this in mind and submit more material with African-Americans, Hispanics, Asian-Americans, etc. as the focus. The main characters of all pieces should be contemporary teens who cope with modern-day problems using Christian principles. Stories should be uplifting, positive and character-building, but not preachy. Conflicts must be resolved realistically, with thought-provoking and honest endings. Nonfiction is preferred. We use articles on current issues from a Christian point of view and humor. Nonfiction pieces should concern topics of interest to teens, including school, family life, recreation, friends, part-time jobs, dating and music." This magazine publishes writing/art/photos by teenagers. Be realistic! Get involved with teenagers. Go where they go; watch what they watch; read what they read. Don't just assume that you know what today's teens are interested in. Ask for our theme list and guidelines—we publish accordingly. (See listings for *Kidz Chat* and *Live Wire*.)

☑ **FACES, People, Places & Cultures**, Cobblestone Publishing, Inc., 30 Grove St., Peterborough NH 03458. (603)924-7209. Fax: (603)924-7380. E-mail: facesmag@yahoo.com. Website: www.cobblestonepub.com. **Edi-**

tor: Elizabeth Crooker Carpentiere. **Managing Editor**: Lou Waryncia. **Art Director**: Ann Dillon. Magazine published 9 times/year (September-May). Circ. 15,000. *Faces* is a theme-related magazine; writers should send for theme list before submitting ideas/queries. Each month a different world culture is featured through the use of feature articles, activities and photographs and illustrations.

● At press time, Cobblestone Publishing, Inc. was purchased by Carus Publishing. No editorial changes were planned. *Faces* themes for 2001 include Saudi Arabia, Vatican City, Finland and South Africa.

Fiction: Middle readers, young adults/teens: adventure, folktales, history, multicultural, plays, religious, travel. Does not want to see material that does not relate to a specific upcoming theme. Buys 9 mss/year. Maximum word length: 800. Byline given.

Nonfiction: Middle readers and young adults/teens: animal, anthropology, arts/crafts, biography, cooking, fashion, games/puzzles, geography, history, how-to, humorous, interview/profile, nature/environment, religious, social issues, sports, travel. Does not want to see material not related to a specific upcoming theme. Buys 63 mss/year. Average word length: 300-800. Byline given.

Poetry: Clear, objective imagery; up to 100 lines. Must relate to theme.

How to Contact/Writers: Fiction/nonfiction: Query with published clips and 2-3 line biographical sketch. "Ideas should be submitted six to nine months prior to the publication date. Responses to ideas are usually sent approximately four months before the publication date."

Illustration: Buys 3 illustrations/issue; buys 27 illustrations/year. Preferred theme or style: Material that is meticulously researched (most articles are written by professional anthropologists); simple, direct style preferred, but not too juvenile. Works on assignment only. Roughs required. Reviews ms/illustration packages from artists. Illustrations only: Send samples of b&w work. "Illustrators should consult issues of *Faces* to familiarize themselves with our needs." Responds to art samples only if interested. Samples returned with SASE. Original artwork returned at job's completion (upon written request). Credit line given.

Photography: Wants photos relating to forthcoming themes.

Terms: Pays on publication. Buys all rights for mss and artwork. Pays 20-25¢/word for articles/stories. Pays on an individual basis for poetry. Covers are assigned and paid on an individual basis. Pays illustrators $50-300 for color inside. Pays photographers per photo ($25-100 for color). Sample copy $4.95 with 7½ × 10½ SAE and 5 first-class stamps. Writer's/illustrator's/photo guidelines via website or free with SAE and 1 first-class stamp.

Tips: "Writers are encouraged to study past issues of the magazine to become familiar with our style and content. Writers with anthropological and/or travel experience are particularly encouraged; *Faces* is about world cultures. All feature articles, recipes and activities are freelance contributions." Illustrators: "Submit b&w samples, not too juvenile. Study past issues to know what we look for. The illustration we use is generally for retold legends, recipes and activities." (See listing for *Apple Seeds, Calliope, Cobblestone, Footsteps* and *Odyssey*.)

Focus on the Family CLUBHOUSE; Focus on the Family CLUBHOUSE JR., Focus on the Family, 8605 Explorer Dr., Colorado Springs CO 80920. (719)531-3400. Fax: (719)531-3499. Website: www.family.org. **Editor:** Jesse Florea. **Art Director:** Timothy Jones. Monthly magazine. Estab. 1987. Combined circulation is 210,000. "*Focus on the Family Clubhouse* is a 24-page Christian magazine, published monthly, for children ages 8-12. Similarly, *Focus on the Family Clubhouse Jr.* is published for children ages 4-8. We want fresh, exciting literature that promotes biblical thinking, values and behavior in every area of life."

Fiction: Young readers, middle readers: adventure, contemporary, multicultural, nature/environment, religious. Middle readers: history, sports, science fiction. Multicultural needs include: "interesting, informative, accurate information about other cultures to teach children appreciation for the world around them." Buys approximately 6-10 mss/year. Average word length: *Clubhouse*, 500-1,400; *Clubhouse Jr.*, 250-1,100. Byline given on all fiction and puzzles.

Nonfiction: Young readers, middle readers: arts/crafts, cooking, games/puzzles, how-to, multicultural, nature/environment, religion, science. Young readers: animal. Middle readers, young adult/teen: interview/profile. Middle readers: sports. Buys 3-5 mss/year. Average word length: 200-1,000. Byline given.

Poetry: Wants to see "humorous or biblical" poetry for 4-8 year olds. Maximum length: 250 words.

How to Contact/Writers: Fiction/nonfiction: send complete ms. Responds to queries/mss in 6 weeks.

Illustration: Buys 8 illustrations/issue. Uses color artwork only. Works on assignment only. Reviews ms/illustration packages from artists. Submit ms with rough sketches. Contact: Tim Jones, art director. Illustrations only: Query with samples, arrange portfolio review or send tearsheets. Contact: Tim Jones, art director. Responds in 3 months. Samples returned with SASE; samples kept on file. Credit line given.

Photography: Buys photos from freelancers. Uses 35mm transparencies. Photographers should query with samples; provide résumé and promotional literature or tearsheets. Responds in 2 months.

Terms: Pays on acceptance. Buys first North American serial rights for mss. Buys first rights or reprint rights for artwork and photographs. Original artwork returned at job's completion. Additional payment for ms/illustration packages. Pays writers $100-300 for stories; $50-150 for articles. Pays illustrators $300-700 for color cover; $200-700 for color inside. Pays photographers by the project or per photo. Sample copies for 9 × 12 SAE and 3 first-class stamps. Writer's/illustrators/photo guidelines for SASE.

Tips: "Test your writing on children. The best stories avoid moralizing or preachiness and are not written *down* to children. They are the products of writers who share in the adventure with their readers, exploring the characters they have created without knowing for certain where the story will lead. And they are not always explicitly Christian, but are built upon a Christian foundation (and, at the very least, do not contradict biblical views or values)."

FOOTSTEPS, The Magazine of African American History, Cobblestone Publishing Co., 30 Grove St., Suite C, Peterborough NH 03458. (603)924-7204 or (800)821-0115. Fax: (608)924-7380. Website: www.cobblestonepub.com. **Editor:** Charles F. Baker. Magazine on African American history for readers ages 8-14.
  ● At press time, Cobblestone Publishing Co. was purchased by Carus Publishing. No editorial changes were planned. *Footsteps* won a 2000 Parent's Choice Gold Award.
Fiction: Middle readers: adventure, history, multicultural. Word length: up to 700 words.
Nonfiction: Middle readers: history, interviews/profile. Word length: 300-750 words.
Terms: Writer's guidelines available on website.
Tips: "We are looking for articles that are lively, age-appropriate, and exhibit an original approach to the theme of the issue. Cultural sensitivity and historical accuracy are extremely important." (See listings for *AppleSeeds, Calliope, Cobblestones, Faces,* and *Odyssey.*)

FOR SENIORS ONLY, Campus Communications, Inc., 339 N. Main St., New York NY 10956. (914)638-0333. **Publisher:** Darryl Elberg. **Articles/Fiction Editor:** Judi Oliff. **Art Director:** David Miller. Semiannual magazine. Estab. 1971. Circ. 350,000. Publishes career-oriented articles for high school students, college-related articles, and feature articles on travel, etc.
Fiction: Young adults: health, humorous, sports, travel. Byline given.
Nonfiction: Young adults: careers, games/puzzles, health, how-to, humorous, interview/profile, social issues, sports, travel. Buys 4-6 mss/year. Average word length: 1,000-2,500. Byline given.
How to Contact/Writers: Fiction/nonfiction: Send complete ms. Publishes ms 2-4 months after acceptance. Will consider simultaneous submissions, electronic submissions via disk or modem and previously published work.
Illustration: Reviews ms/illustration packages from artists. Query; submit complete package with final art; submit ms with rough sketches. Illustrations only: Query; send slides. Responds only if interested. Samples not returned; samples kept on file. Original work returned upon job's completion. Credit line given.
Photography: Model/property release required. Uses $5\frac{1}{2} \times 8\frac{1}{2}$ and $4\frac{7}{8} \times 7\frac{3}{8}$ color prints; 35mm and 8×10 transparencies. Query with samples; send unsolicited photos by mail. Responds only if interested.
Terms: Pays on publication. Buys exclusive magazine rights. Payment is byline credit. Writer's/illustrator's/photo guidelines for SASE.

FOX KIDS MAGAZINE, Peter Green Design/Fox Kids Network, 4219 W. Burbank Blvd., Burbank CA 91505. (818)953-2210. Fax: (818)953-2220. E-mail: bananadog@aol.com. Website: www.foxkids.com. **Articles Editor:** Scott Russell. **Art Director:** Tim Sims. Quarterly magazine. Estab. 1990. Circ. 4 million. Features "fun and hip articles, games and activities for Fox Kids Club members ages 6-13, promoting Fox Kids shows."
Nonfiction: Young readers, middle readers, young adults/teens: animals, arts/crafts, concept, games/puzzles, how-to, humorous, science, nature/environment, sports. Middle readers, young adult: interview/profile, hobbies. Any material tied in to a Fox Kids Network show or one of our other features (no religious material). Buys 16 mss/year. Average word length: 100-300.
How to Contact/Writers: Nonfiction only: Query with published clips. Responds to queries/mss in 2-3 months. Publishes mss 2-6 months after acceptance. Will consider simultaneous submissions and electronic submissions via disk or modem.
Illustration: Buys 5 illustrations/issue. Uses color artwork only. Works on assignment only. Prefers "cartoon character work, must be *on model.*" Reviews ms/illustration packages from artists. Query. Illustrations only: Send résumé, promo sheet, tearsheets. Responds only if interested. Samples returned with SASE; samples filed. Original work returned at job's completion. Credit line given.
Photography: Buys photos from freelancers. Uses a variety of subjects, depending on articles. Model/property release required. Uses color prints and 4×5 or 35mm transparencies. Query with résumé, business card, tearsheets. Responds only if interested.
Terms: Pays 30 days from acceptance. Buys all rights. Pays $100-400 for stories/articles. Additional payment for ms/illustration packages and for photos accompanying articles. Sample writer's guidelines for SASE.
Tips: "Practice. Read. Come up with some new and creative ideas. Our articles are almost always humorous. We try to give kids cutting-edge information. All of our articles are tied into Fox Kids shows."

A SELF-ADDRESSED, STAMPED ENVELOPE (SASE) should always be included with submissions within your own country. When sending material to other countries, include a self-addressed envelope (SAE) and International Reply Coupons (IRCs).

☑ **THE FRIEND MAGAZINE**, The Church of Jesus Christ of Latter-day Saints, 50 E. North Temple, Salt Lake City UT 84150-3226. (801)240-2210. **Editor:** Vivian Paulsen. **Art Director:** Mark Robison. Monthly magazine for 3-11 year olds. Estab. 1971. Circ. 350,000.

Fiction: Picture material, young readers, middle readers: adventure, animal, contemporary, folktales, history, humorous, problem-solving, religious, ethnic, sports, suspense/mystery. Does not want to see controversial issues, political, horror, fantasy. Average word length: 400-1,000. Byline given.

Nonfiction: Picture material, young readers, middle readers: animal, arts/crafts, biography, cooking, games/puzzles, history, how-to, humorous, problem-solving, religious, sports. Does not want to see controversial issues, political, horror, fantasy. Average word length: 400-1,000. Byline given.

Poetry: Reviews poetry. Maximum length: 20 lines.

How to Contact/Writers: Fiction/nonfiction: Send complete ms. Responds to mss in 2 months.

Illustration: Illustrations only: Query with samples; arrange personal interview to show portfolio; provide résumé and tearsheets for files.

Terms: Pays on acceptance. Buys all rights for mss. Pays 9-11¢/word for unsolicited fiction articles; $25 and up for poems; $10 for recipes, activities and games. Contributors are encouraged to send for sample copy for $1.50, 9×11 envelope and four 33¢ stamps. Free writer's guidelines.

Tips: "*The Friend* is published by The Church of Jesus Christ of Latter-day Saints for boys and girls up to twelve years of age. All submissions are carefully read by the *Friend* staff, and those not accepted are returned within two months when a self-addressed, stamped envelope is enclosed. Submit seasonal material at least eight months in advance. Query letters and simultaneous submissions are not encouraged. Authors may request rights to have their work reprinted after their manuscript is published."

GIRLS' LIFE, Monarch, 4517 Harford Rd., Baltimore MD 21214. (410)254-9200. Fax: (410)254-0991. Website: www.girlslife.com. **Executive Editor**: Kelly White. **Creative Director**: Chun Kim. Bimonthly magazine. Estab. 1994. General interest magazine for girls, ages 9-15.

Nonfiction: Interview/profile, multicultural, nature/environment, new products, party ideas, skin care, social issues, sports, travel, health, hobbies, humorous. Buys appoximately 25 mss/year. Word length varies. Byline given. "No fiction!"

How to Contact/Writers: Nonfiction: Query with published clips or send complete ms on spec only. Responds in 2 weeks. Publishes ms 3 months after acceptance. Will consider simultaneous submissions. No phone calls. No e-mail.

Illustration: Buys 4 illustrations/issue. Uses color artwork only. Works on assignment only. Reviews ms/illustration packages from artists. Send ms with dummy. Illustration only: Query with samples; send tearsheets. Contact: Chun Kim, creative director. Responds only if interested. Samples returned with SASE; samples filed. Credit line given.

Photography: Buys photos from freelancers. Uses 35mm transparencies. Provide samples. Responds only if interested.

Terms: Pays on publication. Original artwork returned at job's completion. Pays $500-800 for features; $150-350 for departments. Sample copies available for $5. Writer's guidelines for SASE.

Tips: "Don't call with queries. Make query short and punchy."

Ⓝ **GUIDE MAGAZINE**, Review and Herald Publishing Association, 55 W. Oak Ridge Dr., Hagerstown MD 21740. (301)393-4038. Fax: (301)393-4055. E-mail: guide@rhpa.org. Website: www.guidemagazine.org. **Articles Editor**: Randy Fishell. **Designer**: Brandon Reese. Weekly magazine. Estab. 1953. Circ. 32,000. "Ours is a weekly Christian journal written for middle readers and young adults (ages 10-14), presenting true stories relevant to the needs of today's young person, emphasizing positive aspects of Christian living."

Nonfiction: Middle readers, young adults/teens: adventure, animal, character-building, contemporary, games/puzzles, humorous, multicultural, problem-solving, religious. "We need true, or based on true, happenings, not merely true-to-life. Our stories and puzzles must have a spiritual emphasis." No violence. No articles. "We always need humorous adventure stories." Buys 150 mss/year. Average word length: 500-600 minimum, 1,000-1,200 maximum. Byline given.

How to Contact/Writers: Nonfiction: Send complete ms. Responds in 1 month. Will consider simultaneous submissions. "We can only pay half of the regular amount for simultaneous submissions." Responds to queries/mss in 6 weeks. Credit line given.

Terms: Pays on acceptance. Buys first North American serial rights; first rights; one-time rights; second serial (reprint rights); simultaneous rights. Pays 6-12¢/word for stories and articles. "Writer receives several complimentary copies of issue in which work appears." Sample copy free with 6×9 SAE and 2 first-class stamps. Writer's guidelines for SASE.

Tips: "Children's magazines want mystery, action, discovery, suspense and humor—no matter what the topic. For us, truth is stronger than fiction."

☑ **GUIDEPOSTS FOR KIDS**, P.O. Box 638, Chesterton IN 46304. Fax: (219)926-3839. E-mail: gp4k@guideposts.org. Website: www.gp4k.com. **Editor-in-Chief**: Mary Lou Carney. **Managing Editor:** Rosanne Tolin. **Assistant Editor**: Allison Payne. **Art Director**: Mike Lyons. **Photo Editor**: Julie Brown. Bimonthly magazine.

Estab. 1990. Circ. 200,000. "*Guideposts for Kids* is published bimonthly by Guideposts for kids 7-12 years old (emphasis on upper end of that age bracket). It is a value-centered, direct mail magazine that is *fun* to read. It is *not* a Sunday school take-home paper or a miniature *Guideposts*."

Fiction: Middle readers: adventure, animal, contemporary, fantasy, folktales, historical, humorous, multicultural, nature/environment, problem-solving, science fiction, sports, suspense/mystery. Multicultural needs include: Kids in other cultures—school, sports, families. Does not want to see preachy fiction. "We want real stories about real kids doing real things—conflicts our readers will respect; resolutions our readers will accept. Problematic. Tight. Filled with realistic dialogue and sharp imagery. No stories about 'good' children always making the right decision. If present at all, adults are minor characters and *do not* solve kids' problems for them." Buys approximately 10 mss/year. Average word length: 500-1,400. Byline given.

Nonfiction: Middle readers: animal, current events, games/puzzles, history, how-to, humorous, interview/profile, multicultural, nature/environment, problem-solving, profiles of kids, science, seasonal, social issues, sports. "Make nonfiction issue-oriented, controversial, thought-provoking. Something kids not only *need* to know but *want* to know as well." Buys 20 mss/year. Average word length: 200-1,300. Byline usually given.

How to Contact/Writers: Fiction: Send complete ms. Nonfiction: Query or send ms. Responds to queries/ mss in 6 weeks.

Illustration: Buys 10 illustrations/issue; 60 illustrations/year. Uses color artwork only. Works on assignment only. Reviews ms/illustration packages from artists. Contact: Mike Lyons, art director. Illustration only: Query; send résumé, tearsheets. Responds only if interested. Credit line given.

Photography: Looks for "spontaneous, *real* kids in action shots."

Terms: Pays on acceptance. Buys all rights for mss. Buys first rights for artwork. "Features range in payment from $300-450; fiction from $250-500. We pay higher rates for stories exceptionally well-written or well-researched. Regular contributors get bigger bucks, too." Additional payment for ms/illustration packages "but we prefer to acquire our own illustrations." Pays illustrators $400-800/page. Pays photographers by the project (range: $300-1,000) or per photo (range: $100-500). Sample copies for $3.25. Writer's guidelines free for SASE.

Tips: "Make your manuscript good, relevant and playful. No preachy stories about Bible-toting children. *Guideposts for Kids* is not a beginner's market. Study our magazine. (Sure, you've heard that before—but it's *necessary!*) Neatness *does* count. So do creativity and professionalism. SASE essential." (See listings for *Guideposts for Teens*.)

GUIDEPOSTS FOR TEENS, P.O. Box 638, Chesterton IN 46304. (219)929-4429. Fax: (219)926-3839. E-mail: gp4t@guideposts.org. **Editor-in-Chief:** Mary Lou Carney. **Art Director:** Michael Lyons. **Photo Editor:** Julie Brown. Bimonthly magazine. Estab. 1998. "We are a value-centered magazine that offers teens advice, humor and true stories—lots of true stories. These first-person (ghostwritten) stories feature teen protagonists and are filled with action, adventure, overcoming adversity and growth—set against the backdrop of God at work in everyday life."

Nonfiction: Young adults: how-to, humorous, interview/profile, social issues, sports, true stories, most embarrassing moments. Average word length: 300-1,500. Byline sometimes given.

How to Contact/Writers: Nonfiction: Query. Responds to queries/mss in 6 weeks. Will consider simultaneous submissions or electronic submission via disk or modem. Send SASE for writer's guidelines.

Illustration: Uses color artwork only. Works on assignment only. Reviews ms/illustration packages from artists. Query. Contact: Michael Lyons, art director. Illustrations only: Query with samples. Responds only if interested. Samples kept on file. Credit line given.

Photography: Buys photos separately. Wants location photography and stock; digital OK. Uses color prints and 35mm, 2¼×2¼, 4×5 or 8×10 transparencies. Query with samples; provide web address. Responds only if interested.

Terms: Pays on acceptance. Buys all rights for mss. Buys one-time rights for artwork. Original artwork returned at job's completion. Pays $300-500 for true stories; $100-300 for articles. Additional payment for photos accompanying articles. Pays illustrators $125-1,500 for color inside (depends on size). Pays photographers by the project (range: $100-1,000). Sample copies for $4.50 from: Guideposts, 39 Seminary Hill Rd., Carmel NY 10512. Attn: Special Handling.

Tips: "Language and subject matter should be current and teen-friendly. No preaching, please! For illustrators: We get illustrators from two basic sources: submissions by mail and submissions by Internet. We also consult major illustrator reference books. We prefer color illustrations, "on-the-edge" style. We accept art in almost any digital or reflective format." (See listing for *Guideposts for Kids*.)

HIGHLIGHTS FOR CHILDREN, 803 Church St., Honesdale PA 18431. (570)253-1080. **Manuscript Coordinator:** Beth Troop. **Art Director:** Janet Moir McCaffrey. Monthly magazine. Estab. 1946. Circ. 2.8 million. "Our motto is 'Fun With a Purpose.' We are looking for quality fiction and nonfiction that appeals to children, encourages them to read, and reinforces positive values. All art is done on assignment."

Fiction: Picture-oriented material, young readers, middle readers: adventure, animal, contemporary, fantasy, folktales, history, humorous, multicultural, problem-solving, sports. Multicultural needs include first person accounts of children from other cultures and first-person accounts of children from other countries. Does not want to see war, crime, violence. "We see too many stories with overt morals." Would like to see more suspense/ stories/articles with world culture settings, sports pieces, action/adventure and stories with children in contemporary settings. Buys 150 mss/year. Average word length: 400-800. Byline given.

Nonfiction: Picture-oriented material, young readers, middle readers: animal, arts/crafts, biography, careers, games/puzzles, geography, health, history, hobbies, how-to, interview/profile, multicultural, nature/environment, problem solving, science, sports. Multicultural needs include articles set in a country *about* the people of the country. "We have plenty of articles with Asian and Spanish settings." Does not want to see trendy topics, fads, personalities who would not be good role models for children, guns, war, crime, violence. "We'd like to see more nonfiction for younger readers—maximum of 600 words. We still need older-reader material, too—600-900 words." Buys 200 mss/year. Maximum word length: 900. Byline given.

How to Contact/Writers: Send complete ms. Responds to queries in 1 month; mss in 6 weeks.

Illustration: Buys 25-30 illustrations/issue. Preferred theme or style: Realistic, some stylization, cartoon style acceptable. Works on assignment only. Reviews ms/illustration packages from artists. Illustrations only: photocopies, promo sheet, tearsheets, or slides. Résumé optional. Portfolio only if requested. Contact: Janet Moir McCaffrey, art director. Responds to art samples in 6 weeks. Samples returned with SASE; samples filed. Credit line given.

Terms: Pays on acceptance. Buys all rights for mss. Pays $100 and up for unsolicited articles. Pays illustrators $1,000 for color cover; $25-200 for b&w inside, $100-500 for color inside. Sample copies $3.95 and 9×11 SASE with 4 first-class stamps. Writer's/illustrator's guidelines free with SASE.

Tips: "Know the magazine's style before submitting. Send for guidelines and sample issue if necessary." Writers: "At *Highlights* we're paying closer attention to acquiring more nonfiction for young readers than we have in the past." Illustrators: "Fresh, imaginative work encouraged. Flexibility in working relationships a plus. Illustrators presenting their work need not confine themselves to just children's illustrations as long as work can translate to our needs. We also use animal illustrations, real and imaginary. We need party plans, crafts and puzzles—any activity that will stimulate children mentally and creatively. We are always looking for imaginative cover subjects. Know our publication's standards and content by reading sample issues, not just the guidelines. Avoid tired themes, or put a fresh twist on an old theme so that its style is fun and lively. We'd like to see stories with subtle messages, but the fun of the story should come first. Write what inspires you, not what you think the market needs."

N HOLIDAYS & SEASONAL CELEBRATIONS, Teaching & Learning Company, 1204 Buchanan, P.O. Box 10, Carthage IL 62321. (217)357-2591. Fax: (217)357-6789. **Contact:** Articles Editor or Art Director. Quarterly magazine. Estab. 1995. "Every submission must be seasonal or holiday-related. Materials need to be educational and consistent with grades pre-K through 3 development and curriculum."

Fiction: Young readers: health, multicultural, nature/environment; must be holiday or seasonal-related. Buys 8 mss/year. Byline given.

Nonfiction: Young readers: arts/crafts, cooking, games/puzzles, geography, how-to, math, multicultural, nature/environment, science. "We need holiday and seasonally related ideas from all cultures that can be used in the classroom." Buys 150 mss/year. Byline given.

Poetry: Reviews holiday or seasonal poetry.

How to Contact/Writers: Fiction: Query. Nonfiction: Send complete ms. Responds to queries in 2 months; mss in 3 months. Publishes ms 4-12 months after acceptance. Will consider electronic submissions via disk or modem.

Illustration: Buys 70 illustrations/issue; 300 illustrations/year. Uses b&w and color artwork. Works on assignment only. "Prefers school settings with lots of children; b&w sketches at this time." Reviews ms/illustration packages from artists. Submit ms with rough sketches. Illustrations only: submit résumé, promo sheet, tearsheets, sketches of children. Responds in 1 month. Samples returned with SASE; samples filed. Credit line sometimes given.

Terms: Pays on publication. Buys all rights. Pays $20-75 for stories; $10-125 for articles. Additional payment for ms/illustration packages. Pays illustrators $150-300 for color cover; $10-15 for b&w inside. Pays photographers per photo. Sample copy available for $4.95. Writer's/illustrator's guidelines for SASE.

Tips: "95% of our magazine is written by freelancers. Writers must know that this magazine goes to teachers for use in the classroom, grades pre-K through 3. Also 90% of our magazine is illustrated by freelancers. We need illustrators who can provide us with 'cute' kids grades pre-K through 3. Representation of ethnic children is a must. Because our magazine is seasonal, it is essential that we receive manuscripts approximately 8-12 months prior to the publication of that magazine. Too often we receive a holiday-related article way past the deadline."

✓ HOPSCOTCH, The Magazine for Girls, The Bluffton News Publishing and Printing Company, 103 N. Main St., Bluffton OH 45817. (419)358-4610. **Editor:** Marilyn Edwards. **Contact:** Diane Winebar, editorial assistant. Bimonthly magazine. Estab. 1989. Circ. 14,000. For girls from ages 6-12, featuring traditional subjects—pets, games, hobbies, nature, science, sports, etc.—with an emphasis on articles that show girls actively involved in unusual and/or worthwhile activities."

Fiction: Picture-oriented material, young readers, middle readers: adventure, animal, history, humorous, nature/environment, science fiction, sports, suspense/mystery. Does not want to see stories dealing with dating, sex, fashion, hard rock music. Buys 30 mss/year. Average word length: 300-700. Byline given.

Nonfiction: Picture-oriented material, young readers, middle readers: animal, arts/crafts, biography, cooking, games/puzzles, geography, hobbies, how-to, humorous, math, nature/environment, science. Does not want to see pieces dealing with dating, sex, fashion, hard rock music. "Need more nonfiction with quality photos about a *Hopscotch*-age girl involved in a worthwhile activity." Buys 46 mss/year. Average word length: 400-700. Byline given.

Poetry: Reviews traditional, wholesome, humorous poems. Maximum word length: 300; maximum line length: 20. Will accept 6 submissions/author.

How to Contact/Writers: All writers should consult the theme list before sending in articles. To receive a current theme list, send a SASE. Fiction: Send complete ms. Nonfiction: Query, send complete ms. Responds to queries in 2 weeks; on mss in 2 months. Will consider simultaneous submissions.

Illustration: Buys illustrations for 6-8 articles/issue; buys 50-60 articles/year. "Generally, the illustrations are assigned after we have purchased a piece (usually fiction). Occasionally, we will use a painting—in any given medium—for the cover, and these are usually seasonal." Uses b&w artwork only for inside; color for cover. Review ms/illustration packages from artists. Query first or send complete ms with final art. Illustrations only: Send résumé, portfolio, client list and tearsheets. Responds to art samples with SASE in 2 weeks. Credit line given.

Photography: Purchases photos separately (cover only) and with accompanying ms only. Looking for photos to accompany article. Model/property releases required. Uses 5×7, b&w prints; 35mm transparencies. Black and white photos should go with ms. Should show girl or girls ages 6-12.

Terms: For mss: pays a few months ahead of publication. For mss, artwork and photos, buys first North American serial rights; second serial (reprint rights). Original artwork returned at job's completion. Pays 5¢/word and $5-10/photo. "We always send a copy of the issue to the writer or illustrator." Text and art are treated separately. Pays $150-200 for color cover. Photographers paid per photo (range: $5-15). Sample copy for $4. Writer's/illustrator's/photo guidelines free for #10 SASE.

Tips: "Remember we publish only six issues a year, which means our editorial needs are extremely limited. Please look at our guidelines and our magazine . . . and remember, we use far more nonfiction than fiction. If decent photos accompany the piece, it stands an even better chance of being accepted. We believe it is the responsibility of the contributor to come up with photos. Please remember, our readers are 6-12 years—most are 7-10—and your text should reflect that. Many magazines try to entertain first and educate second. We try to do the reverse of that. Our magazine is more simplistic, like a book to be read from cover to cover. We are looking for wholesome, non-dated material." (See listing for *Boys' Quest*.)

☑ **HUMPTY DUMPTY'S MAGAZINE**, Children's Better Health Institute, 1100 Waterway Blvd., P.O. Box 567, Indianapolis IN 46206. (317)636-8881. Fax: (317)684-8094. Website: www.humptydumptymag.org. **Editor:** Sheila Rogers. **Art Director:** Rebecca Ray. Magazine published 8 times/year—Jan/Feb; Mar; April/May; June; July/Aug; Sept; Oct/Nov; Dec. *HDM* is edited for children ages 4-6. It includes fiction (easy-to-reads; read alouds; rhyming stories; rebus stories), nonfiction articles (some with photo illustrations), poems, crafts, recipes, and puzzles. Content encourages development of better health habits.
- *Humpty Dumpty's* publishes material promoting health and fitness with emphasis on simple activities, poems and fiction.

Fiction: Picture-oriented stories: adventure, animal, contemporary, fantasy, folktales, health, humorous, multicultural, nature/environment, problem-solving, science fiction, sports. Does not want to see "bunny-rabbits-with-carrot-pies stories! Also, talking inanimate objects are very difficult to do well. Beginners (and maybe everyone) should avoid these." Buys 8-10 mss/year. Maximum word length: 300-400. Byline given.

Nonfiction: Picture-oriented articles: animal, arts/crafts, concept, games/puzzles, health, how-to, humorous, nature/environment, no-cook recipes, science, social issues, sports. Buys 6-10 mss/year. Prefers very short nonfiction pieces—200 words maximum. Byline given.

How to Contact/Writers: Send complete ms. Nonfiction: Send complete ms with bibliography if applicable. "No queries, please!" Responds to mss in 3 months. Send seasonal material at least 8 months in advance.

Illustration: Buys 13-16 illustrations/issue; 90-120 illustrations/year. Preferred theme or style: Realistic or cartoon. Works on assignment only. Illustrations only. Query with slides, printed pieces or photocopies. Contact: Rebecca Ray, art director. Samples are not returned; samples filed. Responds to art samples only if interested. Credit line given.

Terms: Writers: Pays on publication. Artists: Pays within 1-2 months. Buys all rights. "One-time book rights may be returned if author can provide name of interested book publisher and tentative date of publication." Pays up to 22¢/word for stories/articles; payment varies for poems and activities. 10 complimentary issues are provided to author with check. Pays $250 for color cover illustration; $35-90 per page b&w inside; $70-155 for color inside. Sample copies for $1.75. Writer's/illustrator's guidelines free with SASE.

Tips: Writers: "Study current issues and guidelines. Observe word lengths and adhere to requirements. Submit what you do best. Don't send your first, second, or even third drafts. Polish your piece until it's as perfect as you can make it." Illustrators: "Please study the magazine before contacting us. Your art must have appeal to three-to seven-year-olds." (See listings for *Child Life, Children's Digest, Children's Playmate, Jack and Jill, Turtle Magazine* and *U*S* Kids*.)

N I.D., David C. Cook Publishing Co., 4050 Lee Vance View, Colorado Springs CO 80918. Fax: (719)536-3296. E-mail: northamg@cookministries.org. Website: www.cookministries.org. **Editor**: Glynese Northam. **Senior Designer**: Jeffrey P. Barnes. **Designer**: Joe Matisek. Weekly magazine. Estab. 1991. Circ. 100,000. "*I.D.* is a class-and-home paper for senior high Sunday school students. Stories relate to Bible study."
Nonfiction: Young adults/teens: animal, arts/crafts, biography, careers, concept, geography, health, history, how-to, humorous, interview/profile, multicultural, nature/environment, problem solving, religion, science, social issues, sports. "Sometimes material sent to us is too 'preachy.' " Buys 20 mss/year. Average word length: 600-1,000. Byline sometimes given if written in the first person.
How to Contact/Writers: Send complete ms. Responds in 6 months. Publishes ms 15 months after acceptance. Will consider simultaneous submissions.
Illustrations: Buys 5 illustrations/issue; 30 illustrations/year. Uses b&w and color artwork. Reviews ms/illustration packages from artists. Submit ms with rough sketches. Illustrations only: Query. Works on assignment only. Responds only if interested.
Terms: Pays on acceptance. Pays $50-300 for stories and articles.

✔ INSIGHT, Teens Meeting Christ, (formerly *Insight Magazine*), 55 W. Oak Ridge Dr., Hagerstown MD 21740. (301)393-4037. Fax: (301)393-4055. E-mail: insight@rhpa.org. Website: http://insightmagazine.org. **Articles Editor**: Lori Peckham. **Art Director**: Doug Bendall. **Photo Editor**: Doug Bendall. Weekly magazine. Estab. 1970. Circ. 20,000. "Our readers crave true stories written by teens or written about teens that convey or portray a spiritual truth." 100% of publication aimed at teen market.
Nonfiction: Young adults: animal, biography, fashion, health, humorous, interview/profile, multicultural, nature/environment, problem-solving, social issues, sports, travel: first-person accounts preferred. Buys 200 mss/year. Average word length: 500-1,500. Byline given.
Poetry: Reviews poetry. Publishes poems written by teens. Maximum length: 250-500 words.
How to Contact/Writers: Nonfiction: Send complete ms. Responds to queries in 1-2 months. Publishes ms 6-12 months after acceptance. Will consider simultaneous submissions, electronic submission via disk or modem, previously published work.
Illustration: Works on assignment only. Reviews ms/illustration packages from artists. Query. Contact: Doug Bendall, design. Illustrations only: Query with samples. Contact: Doug Bendall, designer. Samples kept on file. Credit line given.
Photography: Looking for photos that will catch a teen's eye with unique elements such as juxtaposition. Model/property release required; captions not required but helpful. Uses color prints and 35mm, 2¼×2¼, 4×5, 8×10 transparencies. Query with samples; provide business card, promotional literature or tearsheets to be kept on file. Responds only if interested.
Terms: Pays on acceptance. Buys first North American serial rights for mss. Buys one-time rights for artwork and photos. Original artwork returned at job's completion. Pays $10-100 for stories; $10-100 for articles. Pays illustrators $100-300 for b&w (cover); $100-300 for color cover; $100-300 for b&w (inside), $100-300 for color inside. Pays photographers by the project. Sample copies for 9×14 SAE and 4 first-class stamps.
Tips: "Do your best to make your work look 'hip,' 'cool' appealing to teens."

INTEEN, Urban Ministries, Inc., 1551 Regency Ct., Calumet City IL 60409. (708)868-7100, ext. 239. Fax: (708)868-7105. E-mail: umil551@aol.com. **Editor**: Katara A. Washington. **Art Acquisitions**: Larry Taylor. Quarterly magazine. Estab. 1970. "We publish Sunday school lessons for urban teens and features for the same group."
● Contact *Inteen* for guidelines. They work on assignment only—do not submit work.
Nonfiction: Young adults/teens: careers, games/puzzles, how-to, interview/profile, religion. "We make 40 assignments/year."
Terms: Pays $75-150 for stories.

JACK AND JILL, Children's Better Health Institute, 1100 Waterway Blvd., P.O. Box 567, Indianapolis IN 46206. (317)636-8881. **Editor**: Daniel Lee. **Art Director**: Emilie Frazier. Magazine published 8 times/year. Estab. 1938. Circ. 360,000. "Write entertaining and imaginative stories *for* kids, not just *about* them. Writers should understand what is funny to kids, what's important to them, what excites them. Don't write from an adult 'kids are so cute' perspective. We're also looking for health and healthful lifestyle stories and articles, but don't be preachy."
Fiction: Young readers and middle readers: adventure, contemporary, folktales, health, history, humorous, nature, sports. Buys 30-35 mss/year. Average word length: 700. Byline given.
Nonfiction: Young readers, middle readers: animal, arts/crafts, cooking, games/puzzles, history, hobbies, how-to, humorous, interview/profile, nature, science, sports. Buys 8-10 mss/year. Average word length: 500. Byline given.
Poetry: Reviews poetry.

insider report

Illustrators: Find your window of opportunity in children's magazines

Most children's illustrators are so focused on picture books, they often overlook golden opportunities in other markets. One of the best-kept secrets of successful illustrators is the simple, yet effective strategy of alternating assignments between children's books and magazines. It makes for a rewarding, balanced career. Just ask Phyllis Pollema-Cahill.

Phyllis Pollema-Cahill

Pollema-Cahill lives in Colorado at the foot of Pikes Peak, with her husband Jeff and two cats, Mickey and Patches. Pollema-Cahill earned her living for years as a graphic designer until fate presented a window of opportunity for her to try her dream career. These days, Pollema-Cahill balances her time between illustration, gardening, cooking, reading YA novels, speaking French, and hosting her own website for illustrators, www.phyl-liscahill.com. In between book projects, Pollema-Cahill works on a variety of challenging assignments for magazines, such as *Jack and Jill*, *Discovery Trails* and *Highlights for Children*. She wouldn't have it any other way.

You illustrate both for children's books and magazines. Which market do you prefer?
I wouldn't want to choose one over the other. They both have their advantages. There are several things I like about magazine work. The assignments are easier to fit into my schedule, since they can be as simple as one spot illustration or a five-page story as opposed to a thirty-two-page picture book. Also since magazine assignments are smaller, there are fewer pages in which you have to keep your characters consistent.

Magazine assignments also add variety to my schedule. For example, if I'm working on a book, I can take a few days and work on a magazine assignment that's on a totally different subject with different characters and come back to the book refreshed. With magazines you also get to see your work in print sooner and get smaller, more frequent paychecks. There can also be regular, repeat assignments from magazine publishers, which in this crazy freelance world can add some very welcome stability.

Would you advise other children's illustrators to try the magazine market?
I definitely would. With magazines your work is seen by so many more kids every month. *Highlights* has a circulation of three million. It's in all the doctors' and dentists' offices. Almost everyone knows of it or remembers it from their childhood. How many book print runs even approach the one-million mark? Books may last longer, but people collect magazines too. There are also many magazines buying art every month. It's a healthy market.

Also, it keeps us busy drawing for kids and improving our skills. To me it's much more fun than having to do other types of work to make ends meet. If you're new to the business it will give you great experience in working with art directors, preparing art for printing and meeting deadlines. Plus it gives you publishing credits. There are many small regional and religious magazines who might not have very big budgets, but they're a good place for illustrators to get a start.

Do you think magazine illustration can actually end up being a springboard to a career into books?

I know there are illustrators who think of magazines as a stepping stone to doing books. There are also illustrators who don't do magazine illustration at all and concentrate only on books. They may do other types of illustration, do the speaking circuit, or have other jobs such as teaching or graphic design to support themselves. I think magazines are a great end in and of themselves. Illustrators are missing out on a great opportunity by not pursuing them. About one-third of my income comes from magazine illustration. I want to concentrate all my efforts on illustrating for kids, and magazine illustration helps me do that.

How does working for magazines differ from working for book publishers?

It's pretty much the same, but there are a few minor differences. With a magazine you're one of many illustrators and photographers who contribute, whereas picture books have to stand on their own by your sole efforts. While pacing and page turns are part of magazines, they're crucial in picture books. Books can be larger, more involved projects. For those reasons I'd say magazine illustration is probably easier. There's less pressure on the individual artist— unless you're the cover artist, of course.

Where do you find magazine markets, and what's the best way to approach them?

Landing assignments from magazines differs from landing book assignments in that magazine offices are all over the country, not concentrated in New York, so you can't take your portfolio and see many of them in one trip. Direct mail is really the best way to reach magazine publishers.

This watercolor illustration was created by Phyllis Pollema-Cahill for a folktale titled "The Moonfish." The story (written by Caroline Stutson) and art appeared in the October 1999 issue of *Highlights for Children*. "This story took place at dusk. I used a nice blue-violet palette," says Pollema-Cahill. "I also did research on the coast of Baja, California and its plant life."

Reprinted with permission.

I got started doing magazine illustration by using *Children's Writer's & Illustrator's Market*, sending for and studying copies of the magazines and mailing out my samples only to those who used work similar to mine. Most publishers will send sample copies for a SASE and a small check. It's worth the time and trouble. I have three filing cabinet drawers full of magazines and book publishers' catalogs. Another good source is the public library's children's section.

I worked as a creative director in the marketing department of a large publishing house, so I know how important it is to study and target your market. Also, before I mailed anything I read various books and newsletter articles on how to prepare my samples and put together a professional-looking mailing. There's a lot of material out there to help us, and it's so important to do your homework first.

How do you develop a style that is recognizable/individual? Was there a moment when you hit on the perfect style for you, or was it more of a gradual development?
I think it comes from your soul and from putting in the work. You work at it until it feels right to you, and then, because you can't draw any other way and be true to yourself, the work becomes unique.

Your website offers links to some portfolio critique services. Have you ever used such a service and if so, was it worth it?
Yes, I've paid to have my portfolio critiqued several times and have always found it worthwhile. You get so close to your own work and your struggle with it that you don't see it objectively. Also if you're new to this market, you don't have the experience and knowledge that someone else might have. I've also gotten assignments through portfolio critiques.

Tell me about one of your more memorable or challenging magazine assignments.
My most challenging one was a spread for *Guideposts for Kids*. The story was set in 1885 and included a crowd of Russian peasants pushing and pulling a 12,000 pound bell toward the Russian Church of St. Mary Magdalene on the Mount of Olives. I do a lot of religious illustrations, but this had such specific details, even down to the Russian inscription on the bell. I figured out what buildings existed on the Mount of Olives at that time, what archeological digs were started or not, how Russian bells vary from other bells. I knew how much the bell weighed, but I didn't know how that translated into actual size. In comparing it to other bells, I learned how much the Liberty Bell weighed, but couldn't find its height. I ended up calling

Phyllis Pollema-Cahill's illustration accompanied a story called "Getting A-Head (for Business)," by Gary L. Blackwood, in the June 1999 issue of *Jack and Jill* magazine. "The story is about a young girl whose father builds her a lemonade stand. After a difficult afternoon selling lemonade, where almost everything that could go wrong did, she rents her stand to a friend," says Pollema-Cahill. "I loved showing the different facial expressions."

Reprinted with permission.

Independence Hall in Philadelphia and asking a staff member how tall the Liberty Bell was, and then I did some simple algebra. I also called my friend who lived in Israel to learn what the winter weather was like, and I researched the clothing of the peasants.

You've researched everything from Korean horsehair hats to the nesting habits of puffins. Is such research common with magazine assignments?

Most of the time it's assumed that I'll do the research. Illustrators usually consider it part of their job. Sometimes art directors supply photocopies of reference material, which is helpful. I usually do my own additional research. I like to feel confident I know the subject and am not making any mistakes. I think it's very important to go the extra mile to give kids accurate images. It adds authenticity and integrity to the illustrations. Plus, learning new things is a fun part of my job. I know I've gotten assignments because I do thorough research.

Sometimes I spend hours on research, and other times it's really fast because I'm already familiar with the subject or it's easy to find what I need. When I research I usually check my reference books, clip file and the Internet first. (I'm always on the lookout for good reference material.) Then I'll usually go to the public library. I head to the children's section first, because the books there have the best photos and they explain things simply and clearly.

Sometimes finding just the right image or information takes some creativity. I've gone to museums and antique shops, rented videos, sketched from life, talked to experts. A couple months ago I was crawling around under a horse-drawn wagon to study the undercarriage.

Not to sound New Age or mystical, but have you experienced any serendipitous happenings that seemed to come along when you needed them and help you take a positive direction in your career?

New Age and mystical is good! There's no question in my mind that our beliefs and thoughts influence events and that serendipity occurs when you're on the right track, following your heart's desire. Two books that have been very helpful to me are *The Artist's Way*, by Julia Cameron and *Creative Visualization*, by Shakti Gawain.

I wanted to illustrate for children since art school, but for various reasons (mainly fear) I continued to work in graphic design. I was listening to the tape "Reflections" on *The Artist's Way* every day in my car, while driving back and forth to a job I was getting pretty fed up with. (I had the tape almost memorized, I'd listened to it so many times.) An artist I'd recently started working with told me about his friend who illustrated children's books for a publisher in Denver. I took a chance and sent off some samples to this publisher and soon had my first book contract. A month or so later the division I was working for (at my day job) was sold. I was laid off, received a fairly large severance check and knew it was time to pursue my dream of becoming a full-time children's illustrator.

There have been other instances of serendipity in my career since then. Getting involved in SCBWI, making friends in the business, networking and keeping a positive attitude have been so important to me.

What are your ultimate goals as an artist?

To be able to have my art look as good as the images I have in my imagination. To develop my abilities so they don't limit me in any way from expressing what I want to in my illustrations.

—*Mary Cox*

How to Contact/Writers: Fiction/nonfiction: Send complete ms. Responds to mss in 3 months.

Illustration: Buys 15 illustrations/issue; 120 illustrations/year. Responds only if interested. Samples not returned; samples filed. Credit line given.

Terms: Pays on publication; minimum 17¢/word. Pays illustrators $275 for color cover; $35-90 for b&w, $70-155 for color inside. Pays photographers negotiated rate. Sample copies $1.25. Buys all rights.

Tips: See listings for *Child Life*, *Children's Digest*, *Children's Playmate*, *Humpty Dumpty's Magazine*, *Turtle Magazine* and *U*S* Kids*. Publishes writing/art/photos by children.

JUMP, For Girls Who Dare to be Real, Weider, 21100 Erwin St., Woodland Hills CA 91367. Fax: (818)594-0972. E-mail: letters@jumponline.com. Website: www.jumponline.com. **Contact:** Elizabeth Sosa, editorial assistant. **Editor:** Lori Berger. **Managing Editor:** Maureen Meyers. Monthly magazine for a female teen audience. Estab. 1997. Circ. 350,000.

Nonfiction: Young adults/teens: general interest, how-to, interview/profile, new product, personal experience. *Jump* columns include Busted! (quirky, bizarre and outrageous trends, news, quotes—6 items, 50 words each); The Dish (food and nutrition for teens—1,500 words); Jump On . . . In, Music, Sports, Body & Soul (small news and trend items on sports, health, music, etc.—6 items, 75 words each).

How to Contact/Writers: Nonfiction: Query with published clips. Responds to queries in 1 month. Publishes ms 4 months after acceptance. Will consider simultaneous submissions.

Terms: Pays on publications. Buys all rights. Pays 50¢-$1/word.

Tips: "Writers must read our magazine before submitting queries. We'll turn away queries that clearly show the writer isn't familiar with the content of the magazine."

KIDS' WALL STREET NEWS, Kids' Wall Street News, Inc., P.O. Box 1207, Rancho Santa Fe CA 92067. (760)591-7681. Fax: (760)591-3731. E-mail: info@kwsnews.com. Website: www.kwsnews.com. **Contact:** Kate Allen, editor-in-chief. Bimonthly magazine. Estab. 1996. *"Kids' Wall Street News* hopes to empower and educate America's youth so they will be better prepared for today and their future. This bimonthly magazine covers world and business news, financial information, computer updates, the environment, adventure and much more."

Nonfiction: Young adults/teens: animal, biography, careers, finance, geography, health, history, interview/profile, nature/environment, science, social issues, sports, travel. Buys 130 mss/year. Average word length: 250-550. Byline given.

How to Contact/Writers: Nonfiction: Query with published clips. Responds to queries in 2-3 months. Will consider simultaneous submissions and electronic submission via disk or modem.

Terms: Pays on publication. Buys exclusive magazine rights for mss. Samples copies for 9×12 SAE and $1.70 postage (6 first-class stamps).

Tips: *"Kids' Wall Street News* generally assigns specific subject matter for articles. There is a heavy financial slant to the magazine."

KIDZ CHAT, Standard Publishing, 8121 Hamilton Ave., Cincinnati OH 45231. (513)931-4050. **Editor:** Gary Thacker. Weekly magazine. Circ. 55,000.

• *Kidz Chat* has decided to reuse much of the material that was a part of the first publication cycle. They will not be sending out theme lists because of this policy.

Tips: See listings for *Encounter* and *Live Wire*.

LADYBUG, The Magazine for Young Children, Carus Publishing Company, P.O. Box 300, Peru IL 61354. (815)224-6656. **Editor-in-Chief:** Marianne Carus. **Editor:** Paula Morrow. **Art Director:** Suzanne Beck. Monthly magazine. Estab. 1990. Circ. 130,000. Literary magazine for children 2-6, with stories, poems, activities, songs and picture stories.

Fiction: Picture-oriented material: adventure, animal, fantasy, folktales, humorous, multicultural, nature/environment, problem-solving, science fiction, sports, suspense/mystery. "Open to any easy fiction stories." Buys 50 mss/year. Average word length 300-850 words. Byline given.

Nonfiction: Picture-oriented material: activities, animal, arts/crafts, concept, cooking, humorous, math, nature/environment, problem-solving, science. Buys 35 mss/year.

Poetry: Reviews poems, 20-line maximum length; limit submissions to 5 poems. Uses lyrical, humorous, simple language.

How to Contact/Writers: Fiction/nonfiction: Send complete ms. Queries not accepted. Responds to mss in 3 months. Publishes ms up to 2 years after acceptance. Will consider simultaneous submissions if informed. Submissions without SASE will be discarded.

Illustration: Buys 12 illustrations/issue; 145 illustrations/year. Prefers "bright colors; all media, but use watercolor and acrylics most often; same size as magazine is preferred but not required." To be considered for future assignments: Submit promo sheet, slides, tearsheets, color and b&w photocopies. Responds to art samples in 3 months. Submissions without SASE will be discarded.

Terms: Pays on publication for mss; after delivery of completed assignment for illustrators. For mss, buys first publication rights; second serial (reprint rights). Buys first publication rights plus promotional rights for artwork.

Original artwork returned at job's completion. Pays 25¢/word for prose; $3/line for poetry. Pays $750 for color (cover) illustration, $50-100 for b&w (inside) illustration, $250/page for color (inside). Sample copy for $4. Writer's/illustrator's guidelines free for SASE.

Tips: Writers: "Get to know several young children on an individual basis. Respect your audience. We want less cute, condescending or 'preachy-teachy' material. Less gratuitous anthropomorphism. More rich, evocative language, sense of joy or wonder. Keep in mind that people come in all colors, sizes, physical conditions. Be inclusive in creating characters. Set your manuscript aside for at least a month, then reread critically." Illustrators: "Include examples, where possible, of children, animals, and—most important—action and narrative (i.e., several scenes from a story, showing continuity and an ability to maintain interest). (See listings for *Babybug*, *Cicada*, *Cricket*, *Muse* and *Spider*.)

☑ LISTEN, Drug-Free Possibilities for Teens, The Health Connection, 55 West Oak Ridge Dr., Hagerstown MD 21740. (301)393-4019. Fax: (301)393-4055. E-mail: listen@healthconnection.org. **Editor:** Larry Becker. Monthly magazine, 9 issues. Estab. 1948. Circ. 50,000. "*Listen* offers positive alternatives to drug use for its teenage readers. Helps them have a happy and productive life by making the right choices."

Fiction: Young adults: health, humorous, problem-solving peer pressure. Buys 50 mss/year. Average word length: 1,000-1,200. Byline given.

Nonfiction: Young adults: biography, games/puzzles, hobbies, how-to, health, humorous, problem solving, social issues, drug-free living. Wants to see more factual articles on drug abuse. Buys 50 mss/year. Average word length: 1,000-1,200. Byline given.

How to Contact/Writers: Fiction/nonfiction: Query. Responds to queries in 6 weeks; mss in 2 months. Will consider simultaneous submissions, electronic submission via disk or e-mail and previously published work.

Illustration: Buys 8-10 illustrations/issue; 72 illustrators/year. Reviews ms/illustration packages from artists. Ms/illustration packages and illustration only: Query. Contact: Ed Guthero, designer. Responds only if interested. Originals returned at job's completion. Samples returned with SASE. Credit line given.

Photography: Purchases photos from freelancers. Photos purchased with accompanying ms only. Uses color and b&w photos; 35mm, 2¼×2¼. Query with samples. Looks for "youth oriented—action (sports, outdoors), personality photos."

Terms: Pays on acceptance. Buys exclusive magazine rights for ms. Buys one-time rights for artwork and photographs. Pays $50-200 for stories/articles. Pay illustrators $500 for color cover; $75-225 for b&w inside; $135-450 for color inside. Pays photographers by the project (range: $125-500); pays per photo (range: $125-500). Additional payment for ms/illustration packages and photos accompanying articles. Sample copy for $1 and 9×12 SASE and 2 first class stamps. Writer's guidelines free with SASE.

Tips: "*Listen* is a magazine for teenagers. It encourages development of good habits and high ideals of physical, social and mental health. It bases its editorial philosophy of primary drug prevention on total abstinence from tobacco, alcohol, and other drugs. Because it is used extensively in public high school classes, it does not accept articles and stories with overt religious emphasis. Four specific purposes guide the editors in selecting materials for *Listen*: (1) To portray a positive lifestyle and to foster skills and values that will help teenagers deal with contemporary problems, including smoking, drinking, and using drugs. This is *Listen*'s primary purpose. (2) To offer positive alternatives to a lifestyle of drug use of any kind. (3) To present scientifically accurate information about the nature and effects of tobacco, alcohol, and other drugs. (4) To report medical research, community programs, and educational efforts which are solving problems connected with smoking, alcohol, and other drugs. Articles should offer their readers activities that increase one's sense of self-worth through achievement and/or involvement in helping others. They are often categorized by three kinds of focus: (1) Hobbies. (2) Recreation. (3) Community Service.

LIVE WIRE, Standard Publishing Co., 8121 Hamilton Ave., Cincinnati OH 45231. (513)931-4050. Fax: (513)931-0950. E-mail: standardpub@attmail.com. Website: www.standardpub.com. **Articles Editor:** Margie Redford. **Art Director:** Sandy Wimmer. **Photo Editor:** Sandy Wimmer. Newspaper published quarterly in weekly parts. Estab. 1997. Circ. 40,000. "*Live Wire* is a weekly publication geared to preteens (10-12 year olds). 'who want to connect to Christ.' Articles are in a news brief format that feature current events and profiles. We publish true stories about kids, puzzles, activities, interview."

Nonfiction: Middle readers: animal, arts/crafts, biography, cooking, games/puzzles, religion, geography, health, history, how-to, humorous, interview/profile, multicultural, nature/environment, science, sports. Buys 50-70 mss/year. Average word length: 250-350. Byline given.

Poetry: Reviews poetry from preteens only. Limit submissions to 5 poems.

How to Contact/Writers: Nonfiction: Send complete ms. Responds to queries in 1-2 weeks; mss in 2-3 months. Ms published 1 year after acceptance. Accepts simultaneous submissions and previously published work.

Illustration: Buys 4 illustrations/issue; 200 illustrations/year. Uses color artwork only. Works on assignment only. Reviews ms/illustration packages from artists. Ms/illustration packages: query first.

Terms: Pays on acceptance. Buys first rights or reprint rights for mss. Buys full rights for artwork; one-time use for photos. Pays 3-7¢ per word for articles. Additional payment for photos accompanying articles. Pays illustrators $100-200 for color cover, $25-125 for color inside. Pays photographers per photo (range: $100-150). Writer's guidelines for SASE.

Tips: "Articles should be appealing and fun. Multicultural material should deal specifically with missionary families or kids." (See listings for *Encounter* and *Kidz Chat*.)

MUSE, Carus Publishing, 332 S. Michagan Ave, Suite 1100, Chicago IL 60604. (312)939-1500. Fax: (312)939-8150. E-mail: muse@caruspub.com. Website: www.musemag.com **Editor:** Diana Lutz. **Art Director:** John Grandits. **Photo Editor:** Carol Parden. Estab. 1996. Circ. 100,000. "The goal of *Muse* is to give as many children as possible access to the most important ideas and concepts underlying the principal areas of human knowledge. It will take children seriously as developing intellects by assuming that, if explained clearly, the ideas and concepts of an article will be of interest to them. Articles should meet the highest possible standards of clarity and transparency aided, wherever possible, by a tone of skepticism, humor, and irreverence."
 ● *Muse* is published in cooperation of the Cricket Magazine Group and *Smithsonian* magazine.
Nonfiction: Middle readers, young adult: animal, biography, history, interview/profile, math, multicultural, nature/environment, problem-solving, science, social issues. Buys 60-75 mss/year. Length: 1,000-2,500 words. Work on commision only. "Each article must be about a topic that children can understand. The topic must be a 'large' one that somehow connects with a fundamental tennet of some discipline or area of practical knowledge. The topic and presentation must lead to further questioning and exploration; it must be open-ended rather than closed. The treatment of the topic must be of the competence one would expect of an expert in the field in which the topic resides. It must be interesting and hold the reader's attention, not because of the way it is written, but because of the compelling presentation of the ideas it describes."
How to Contact/Writers: Nonfiction: Query with résumé, writing samples, published clips, detailed story ideas and SASE. Will consider simultaneous submissions, electronic submissions via disk or modem or previously published work.
Illustration: Buys 6 illustrations/issue; 40 illustrations/year. Uses color artwork only. Works on assignment only. Reviews ms/illustration packages. Send ms with dummy. Illustrations only: Query with samples. Send résumé, promo sheet and tearsheets. Responds only if interested. Samples returned with SASE. Credit line given.
Photography: Needs vary. Query with samples. Responds only if interested.
Terms: Pays within 60 days of acceptance. Buys first publications rights; all rights for feature articles. Pays 50¢/word for assigned articles; 25¢/word for unsolicited manuscripts. Writer's guidelines and sample copy available for $5.
Tips: "*Muse* may on occasion publish unsolicited manuscripts, but the easiest way to be printed in *Muse* is to send a query. However, manuscripts may be submitted to the Cricket Magazine Group for review, and any that are considered suitable for *Muse* will be forwarded. Such manuscripts will also be considered for publication in *Cricket*, *Spider* or *Ladybug*." (See listing for *Babybug*, *Cricket*, *Ladybug* and *Spider*.)

NATIONAL GEOGRAPHIC WORLD, National Geographic Society, 1145 17th St. NW, Washington DC 20036-4688. (202)857-7000. Fax: (202)775-6112. **Editor:** Melina Bellows. **Art Director:** Ursula Vosseler. **Photo Editor:** Chuck Herron. Monthly magazine. Estab. 1975. Circ. 870,000.
Nonfiction: Young readers, middle readers, young adult/teens: animal, arts/crafts, biography, cooking, games/puzzles, geography, history, hobbies, how-to, interview/profile, multicultural, nature/environment, science, sports, travel. Middle readers, young adult/teens: social issues. "We do not review or buy unsolicited manuscripts, but do use freelance writers."
Illustration: Buys 100% of illustrations from freelancers. Works on assignment only. Query. Illustrations only: Query with samples. Responds in 2 months. Samples returned with SASE; samples filed. Credit line given.
Photography: Buys photos separately. Looking for active shots, funny, strange animal close-ups. Uses 35mm transparencies. Query with samples. Responds in 2 months.
Terms: Pays on acceptance. Buys all rights for mss and artwork. Originals returned to artist at job's completion. Writers get 3 copies of issue their work appears in. Pays photographers by the project. Sample copies for 9×12 SAE and 2 first-class stamps; photo guidelines available free for SASE.
Tips: "Most story ideas are generated in-house and assigned to freelance writers. Query with cover letter and samples of your writing for children or young adults. Keep in mind that *World* is a visual magazine. A story will work best if it has a very tight focus and if the photos show children interacting with their surroundings as well as with each other."

NATURE FRIEND MAGAZINE, 2727 Press Run Rd., Sugarcreek OH 44681. (330)852-1900. Fax: (330)852-3285. **Articles Editor:** Marvin Wengerd. Monthly magazine. Estab. 1983. Circ. 9,000.
Fiction: Picture-oriented material, conversational, no talking animal stories.
Nonfiction: Picture-oriented material, animal, how-to, nature. No talking animal stories. No evolutionary material. Buys 100 mss/year. Average word length: 500. Byline given.
How to Contact/Writers: Nonfiction: Send complete ms. Responds to mss in 4 months. Will consider but must note simultaneous submissions.
Illustration: Buys approximately 8 illustrations/issue from freelancers; 96 illustrations/year. Responds to artist's submissions in 1 month. Works on assignment only. Credit line given.
Terms: Pays on publication. Buys one-time rights. Pays $15-75. Payment for illustrations: $15-80/b&w, $50-100/color inside. Two sample copies and writer's guidelines for $5 with 7½×10½ SAE and $1.47 postage. Writer's/illustrator's guidelines for $2.50.

Tips: Looks for "main articles, puzzles and simple nature and science projects. Needs conversationally-written stories about unique animals or nature phenomena. Please examine samples and writer's guide before submitting." Current needs: science and nature experiments.

NEW MOON: The Magazine For Girls & Their Dreams, New Moon Publishing, Inc., P.O. Box 3620, Duluth MN 55803-3620. (218)728-5507. Fax: (218)728-0314. E-mail: girl@newmoon.org. Website: www.newm oon.org. **Managing Editors:** Deb Mylin and Bridget Grosser. Bimonthly magazine. Estab. 1992. Circ. 25,000. *New Moon* is for every girl who wants her voice heard and her dreams taken seriously. *New Moon* portrays strong female role models of all ages, backgrounds and cultures now and in the past. 100% of publication aimed at juvenile market.

Fiction: Middle readers, young adults: adventure, animal, contemporary, fantasy, folktales, history, humorous, multicultural, nature/environment, problem-solving, religious, science fiction, sports, suspense/mystery, travel. Buys 3 mss/year from adults and 3 mss/year from girls. Average word length: 900-1,200. Byline given.

Nonfiction: Middle readers, young adults: animal, arts/crafts, biography, careers, cooking, games/puzzles, health, history, hobbies, humorous, interview/profile, math, multicultural, nature/environment, problem-solving, science, social issues, sports, travel, stories about real girls. Does not want to see how-to stories. Wants more stories about real girls doing real things written by girls. Buys 6-12 adult-written mss/year. 30 girl-written mss/year. Average word length: 600. Byline given.

How to Contact/Writers: Fiction/Nonfiction: Does not return or acknowledge unsolicited mss. Send only copies. Responds only if interested. Will consider simultaneous submissions and electronic submission e-mail.

Illustration: Buys 6-12 illustrations/year from freelancers. *New Moon* seeks 4-color cover illustrations as well as b&w illustrations for inside. Reviews ms/illustrations packages from artists. Query. Submit ms with rough sketches. Illustration only: Query; send portfolio and tearsheets. Samples not returned; samples filed. Responds in 6 months only if interested. Credit line given.

Terms: Pays on publication. Buys all rights for mss. Buys one-time rights, reprint rights, for artwork. Original artwork returned at job's completion. Pays 6-12¢/word for stories; 6-12¢/word for articles. Pays in contributor's copies. Pays illustrators $400 for color cover; $50-300 for b&w inside. Sample copies for $6.50. Writer's/cover art guidelines for SASE or available on website.

Tips: "Please refer to a copy of *New Moon* to understand the style and philosophy of the magazine. Writers and artists who understand our goals have the best chance of publication. We're looking for stories about real girls; women's careers, and historical profiles. We publish girl's and women's writing only." Publishes writing/art/ photos by girls.

N **NICK JR. MAGAZINE,** Nickelodeon Magazines, Inc., 1515 Broadway, 40th Floor, New York NY 10036. (212)258-7500. Fax: (212)846-1752. Website: www.nickjr.com. **Articles Editor:** Wendy Smolen, deputy editor. **Art Director:** Don Morris. Bimonthly magazine. Estab. 1999. Circ. 500,000. A magazine where kids play to learn and parents learn to play. 50% of publication aimed at juvenile market.

Fiction: Picture-oriented material: adventure, animal, contemporary, humorous, multicultural, nature/environment, problem-solving, sports. Byline sometimes given.

Nonfiction: Picture-oriented material: animal, arts/crafts, concept, cooking, games/puzzles, hobbies, how-to, humorous, math, multicultural, nature/environment, problem-solving, science, social issues, sports. Byline sometimes given.

How to Contact/Writers: Only interested in agented material. Fiction/nonfiction: Query or submit complete ms. Responds to queries/mss in 3-12 weeks. Will consider simultaneous submissions.

Illustration: Only interested in agented material. Works on assignment only. Reviews ms/illustration packages from artists. Query or send ms with dummy. Contact: Wendy Smolen, deputy editor. Illustrations only: arrange portfolio review; send résumé, promo sheet and portfolio. Contact: Josh Klenert, art director. Responds only if interested. Samples not returned; samples kept on file. Credit line sometimes given.

Photography: Looking for photos of children. Model/property release required. Query with résumé of credits; provide résumé, business card, promotional literature or tearsheets. Responds only if interested.

Terms: Writer's guidelines for SASE.

V **ODYSSEY, Adventures in Science,** Cobblestone Publishing, Inc., 30 Grove St., Suite C, Peterborough NH 03458. (603)924-7209. Fax: (603)924-7380. E-mail: odyssey@cobblestonepub.com. Website: www.odyssey magazine.com. (Also see www.cobblestonepub.com.) **Editor:** Elizabeth E. Lindstrom. **Managing Editor:** Lou Waryncia. **Art Director:** Ann Dillon. Magazine published 9 times/year. Estab. 1979. Circ. 22,000. Magazine covers earth, general science and technology, astronomy and space exploration for children ages 10-16. All material must relate to the theme of a specific upcoming issue in order to be considered.

• At press time, Cobblestone Publishing was purchased by Carus Publishing. No editorial changes were planned. *Odyssey* won 2000 Parents' Choice Silver Award. *Odyssey* themes for 2001 include The Fate of the Universe, Pop Quiz: Bubbleology, The Science of Leonardo da Vinciz and Nanotechnology.

Fiction: Middle readers and young adults/teens: science fiction, science, astronomy. Does not want to see anything not theme-related. Average word length: 900-1,200 words.

Bridget Grosser, managing editor at *New Moon* magazine, found artist Tricia Tusa through her listing in *Picturebook*. Says Grosser, "Tricia's work has a storybook quality to it—we needed the illustrator to be accomplished at capturing the feel of a fairytale." Adds Tusa, "I recommend buying one page to advertise your work in annuals like *Workbook* or *Picturebook*." This illustration, done in watercolor and pen and ink, was commissioned for a story about what makes a girl really beautiful.

New Moon • www.newmoon.org • May/June 2000 • 41

Nonfiction: Middle readers and young adults/teens: interviews, activities. Don't send anything not theme-related. Average word length: 750-2,000, depending on section article is used in.

How to Contact/Writers: "A query must consist of all of the following to be considered (please use noneras-able paper): a brief cover letter stating the subject and word length of the proposed article; a detailed one-page outline explaining the information to be presented in the article; an extensive bibliography of materials the author intends to use in preparing the article; a SASE. Writers new to *Odyssey* should send a writing sample with query. If you would like to know if your query has been received, please also include a stamped postcard that requests acknowledgment of receipt. In all correspondence, please include your complete address as well as a telephone number and e-mail address where you can be reached. A writer may send as many queries for one issue as he or she wishes, but each query must have a separate cover letter, outline, bibliography, and SASE. Telephone queries are not accepted. Handwritten queries will not be considered. Queries may be submitted at any time, but queries sent well in advance of deadline *may not be answered for several months.* Go-aheads requesting material proposed in queries are usually sent four months prior to publication date. Unused queries will be returned approximately three to four months prior to publication date."

Illustration: Buys 3 illustrations/issue; 27 illustrations/year. Works on assignment only. Reviews ms/illustration packages from artists. Query. Contact: Beth Lindstrom, editor. Illustration only: Query with samples. Send tear-sheets, photocopies. Responds in 2 weeks. Samples returned with SASE; samples not filed. Original artwork returned upon job's completion (upon written request).

Photography: Wants photos pertaining to any of our forthcoming themes. Uses b&w and color prints; 35mm transparencies. Photographers should send unsolicited photos by mail on speculation.

Terms: Pays on publication. Buys all rights for mss and artwork. Pays 20-25¢/word for stories/articles. Covers are assigned and paid on an individual basis. Pays photographers per photo ($15-100 for b&w; $25-100 for color). Sample copy for $4.95 and SASE with $2 postage. Writer's/illustrator's/photo guidelines for SASE. (See listings for *Apple Seeds, Calliope, Cobblestone, Faces* and *Footsteps.*)

ON COURSE, A Magazine for Teens, General Council of the Assemblies of God, 1445 Boonville Ave., Springfield MO 65802-1894. (417)862-2781. Fax: (417)866-1146. E-mail: oncourse@ag.org. **Editor:** Melinda Booze. **Art Director:** David Danielson. Quarterly magazine. Estab. 1991. Circ. 166,000. *On Course* is a magazine to empower students to grow in a real-life relationship with Christ.

Fiction: Young adults: Christian discipleship, contemporary, humorous, multicultural, problem-solving, sports. Average word length: 1,000. Byline given.

Nonfiction: Young adults: careers, interview/profile, multicultural, religion, social issues, college life, Christian discipleship.

How to Contact/Writers: Works on assignment basis only.

Illustration: Buys 4 illustrations/issue; 16 illustrations/year. Uses color artwork only. Reviews ms/illustration packages from artists. Query. Illustration only: Query with samples or send résumé, promo sheet, slides, client list and tearsheets. Contact Melinda Booze, editor. Responds only if interested. Originals not returned at job's completion. Credit line given.

Photography: Buys photos from freelancers. "Teen life, church life, college life; unposed; often used for illustrative purposes." Model/property releases required. Uses color glossy prints and 35mm or 2¼×2¼ trans-parencies. Query with samples; send business card, promotional literature, tearsheets or catalog. Responds only if interested.

Terms: Pays on acceptance. Buys first or reprint rights for mss. Buys one-time rights for photographs. Pays 10¢/word for stories/articles. Pays illustrators and photographers "as negotiated." Sample copies free for 9×11 SAE. Writer's guidelines for SASE.

N ON THE LINE, Mennonite Publishing House, 616 Walnut Ave., Scottdale PA 15683. (724)887-8500. Fax: (724)887-3111. E-mail: otl@mph.org. **Editor:** Mary Clemens Meyer. Magazine published monthly. Estab. 1970. Circ. 5,500. "*On The Line* is a children's magazine for ages 9-14, emphasizing self-esteem and Christian values. Also emphasizes multicultural awareness, care of the earth and accepting others with differences."

Fiction: Middle readers, young adults: contemporary, history, humorous, nature/environment, problem-solving, religious, science fiction, sports. "No fantasy or fiction with animal characters." Buys 45 mss/year. Average word length: 1,000-1,800. Byline given.

Nonfiction: Middle readers, young adults: arts/crafts, biography, cooking, games/puzzles, health, history, hob-bies, how-to, humorous, sports. Does not want to see articles written from an adult perspective. Average word length: 200-600. Byline given.

Poetry: Wants to see light verse, humorous poetry.

How to Contact/Writers: Fiction/nonfiction: Send complete ms. "No queries, please." Responds to mss in 1 month. Will consider simultaneous submissions. Prefers no e-mail submissions.

Illustration: Buys 5-6 illustrations/issue; buys 60 illustrations/year. "Inside illustrations are done on assignment only to accompany our stories and articles—our need for new artists is limited." Looking for new artists for cover illustrations—full-color work. Illustrations only: "Prefer samples they do not want returned; these stay in our files." Responds to art samples only if interested.

Terms: Pays on acceptance. For mss buys one-time rights; second serial (reprint rights). Buys one-time rights for artwork and photos. Pays 3-5¢/word for assigned/unsolicited articles. Pays $50 for full-color inside illustration; $150 for full-color cover illustration. Photographers are paid per photo, $25-50. Original artwork returned at job's completion. Sample copy free with 7×10 SAE. Free writer's guidelines.
Tips: "We focus on the age 12-13 group of our age 9-14 audience."

OWL, The Discovery Magazine for Children, Bayard Press, 179 John St., Suite 500, Toronto, Ontario M5T 3G5 Canada. (416)340-2700. Fax: (416)340-9769. E-mail: owl@owlkids.com. Website: www.owlkids.com. **Editor:** Elizabeth Siegel. **Creative Director:** Tim Davin. **Photo Editor:** Katherine Murray. Monthly magazine. Circ. 75,000. "*OWL* helps children over eight discover and enjoy the world of science, nature and technology. We look for articles that are fun to read, that inform from a child's perspective, and that motivate hands-on interaction. *OWL* explores the reader's many interests in the natural world in a scientific, but always entertaining, way."
Nonfiction: Middle readers: animal, biology, games/puzzles, high-tech, humor, nature/environment, science, social issues, sports, travel. Especially interested in puzzles and game ideas: logic, math, visual puzzles. Does not want to see religious topics, anthropomorphizing. Buys 6 mss/year. Average word length: 500-1,500. Byline given.
How to Contact/Writers: Nonfiction: Query with published clips. Responds to queries/mss in 3-4 months.
Illustration: Buys 3-5 illustrations/issue; 40-50 illustrations/year. Uses color artwork only. Preferred theme or style: lively, involving, fun, with emotional impact and appeal. "We use a range of styles." Works on assignment only. Illustrations only: Send tearsheets and slides. Responds to art samples only if interested. Original artwork returned at job's completion.
Photography: Looking for shots of animals and nature. "Label the photos." Uses 2¼×2¼ and 35mm transparencies. Photographers should query with samples.
Terms: Pays on publication. Buys first North American and world rights for mss, artwork and photos. Pays $200-500 (Canadian) for assigned/unsolicited articles. Pays up to $650 (Canadian) for illustrations. Photographers are paid per photo. Sample copies for $4.28. Writer's guidelines for SAE (large envelope if requesting sample copy) and money order for $1 postage (no stamps please).
Tips: Writers: "*OWL* is dedicated to entertaining kids with contemporary and accurate information about the world around them. *OWL* is intellectually challenging but is never preachy. Ideas should be original and convey a spirit of humor and liveliness." (See listings for *Chickadee* and *Chirp*.)

POCKETS, Devotional Magazine for Children, The Upper Room, 1908 Grand, P.O. Box 340004, Nashville TN 37203-0004. (615)340-7333. Fax: (615)340-7267. E-mail: pockets@upperroom.org. Website: www.upperroom.org/pockets. **Articles/Fiction Editor:** Lynn W. Gilliam. **Art Director:** Chris Schechner, Suite 207, 3100 Carlisle Plaza, Dallas TX 75204. Magazine published 11 times/year. Estab. 1981. Circ. 96,000. "*Pockets* is a Christian devotional magazine for children ages 6-12. Stories should help children experience a Christian lifestyle that is not always a neatly wrapped moral package but is open to the continuing revelation of God's will."
Fiction: Picture-oriented, young readers, middle readers: adventure, contemporary, folktales, multicultural, nature/environment, problem-solving, religious. Does not want to see violence or talking animal stories. Buys 40-45 mss/year. Average word length: 800-1,400. Byline given.
Nonfiction: Picture-oriented, young readers, middle readers: cooking, games/puzzles, interview/profile, religion. Does not want to see how-to articles. "Our nonfiction reads like a story." Multicultural needs include: stories that feature children of various racial/ethnic groups and do so in a way that is true to those depicted. Buys 10 mss/year. Average word length: 800-1,600. Byline given.
How to Contact/Writers: Fiction/nonfiction: Send complete ms. "Prefer not to deal with queries." Responds to mss in 6 weeks. Will consider simultaneous submissions.
Illustration: Buys 40-50 illustrations/issue. Preferred theme or style: varied; both 4-color and 2-color. Works on assignment only. Illustrations only: Send promo sheet, tearsheets.

POWER AND LIGHT, Children's Ministries, 6401 The Paseo, Kansas City MO 64131-1284. (816)333-7000. Fax: (816)333-4439. E-mail: mprice@nazarene.org. Website: www.nazarene.org. **Editor:** Matt Price. Weekly story paper. "*Power and Light* is a leisure-reading piece for fifth and sixth graders. It is published weekly by the Department of Children's Ministries of the Church of the Nazarene. The major purposes of *Power and Light* are

"PICTURE-ORIENTED MATERIAL" is for preschoolers to 8-year-olds; "Young readers" are for 5- to 8-year-olds; "Middle readers" are for 9- to 11-year-olds; and "Young adults/teens" are for ages 12 and up. Age ranges may vary slightly from magazine to magazine.

to provide a leisure-reading piece which will build Christian behavior and values; provide reinforcement for Biblical concepts taught in the Sunday School curriculum. The focus of the reinforcement will be life-related, with some historical appreciation. *Power and Light*'s target audience is children ages 11-12 in grades 5 and 6."

Fiction: Middle readers, young adults: adventure, contemporary, humorous, multicultural, preteen issues, problem solving, religious. "Avoid fantasy, science fiction, abnormally mature or precocious children, personification of animals. Also avoid extensive cultural or holiday references, especially those with a distinctly American frame of reference. Our paper has an international audience. We need stories involving multicultural preteens in realistic settings dealing with realistic problems with God's help." Average word length: 500-700. Byline given.

Nonfiction: Middle readers, young adults: archaeological, biography, history, games/puzzles, how-to, interview/profile, problem-solving, religion, social issues, travel. Multicultural needs include: ethnics and cultures—other world areas especially English-speaking.

How to Contact/Writers: Send complete ms. Responds to queries/mss in 2 months. Publishes ms 2 years after acceptance.

Photography: Buys "b&w archaeological/Biblical for inside use.

Terms: Pays on publication. "Payment is made approximately one year before the date of issue." Buys multiple use rights for mss. Purchases all rights for artwork and first/one-time rights for photographs. Pays 5¢/word for stories/articles. Writer's guidelines for SASE.

Tips: Writers: "Themes and outcomes should conform to the theology and practices of the Church of the Nazarene, Evangelical Friends, Free Methodist, Wesleyan and other Bible-believing Evangelical churches." We look for bright, colorful illustrations; concise, short articles and stories. Keep it realistic and contemporary. Request guidelines first!" (See listing for *Discoveries*.)

RANGER RICK, National Wildlife Federation, 8925 Leesburg Pike, Vienna VA 22184. (703)790-4000. Website: www.nwf.org. **Editor:** Gerald Bishop. **Design Director:** Donna Miller. Monthly magazine. Circ. 600,000. "Our audience ranges from ages 7 to 12, though we aim the reading level of most material at 9-year-olds or fourth graders."

Fiction: Middle readers: animal (wildlife), fables, fantasy, humorous, multicultural, plays, science fiction. Average word length: 900. Byline given.

Nonfiction: Middle readers: animal (wildlife), conservation, humorous, nature/environment, outdoor adventure, travel. Buys 15-20 mss/year. Average word length: 900. Byline given.

How to Contact/Writers: No longer accepting unsolicited queries/mss.

Illustration: Buys 5-7 illustrations/issue. Preferred theme: nature, wildlife. Works on assignment only. Illustrations only: Send résumé, tearsheets. Responds to art samples in 2 months.

Terms: Pays on acceptance. Buys exclusive first-time worldwide rights and non-exclusive worldwide rights thereafter to reprint, transmit, and distribute the work in any form or medium. Original artwork returned at job's completion. Pays up to $700 for full-length of best quality. For illustrations, buys one-time rights. Pays $150-250 for b&w; $250-1,200 for color (inside, per page) illustration. Sample copies for $2.15 plus a 9×12 SASE.

Tips: "Fiction and nonfiction articles may be written on any aspect of wildlife, nature, outdoor adventure and discovery, domestic animals with a 'wild' connection (such as domestic pigs and wild boars), science, conservation or related subjects. To find out what subjects have been covered recently, consult our cumulative index on our website and the *Children's Magazine Guide*, which is available in many libraries. The National Wildlife Federation (NWF) discourages the keeping of wildlife as pets, so the keeping of such pets should not be featured in your copy. Avoid stereotyping of any group. For instance, girls can enjoy nature and the outdoors as much as boys can, and mothers can be just as knowledgeable as fathers. The only way you can write successfully for *Ranger Rick* is to know the kinds of subjects and approaches we like. And the only way you can do that is to read the magazine. Recent issues can be found in most libraries or are available from our office for $2.15 plus 9×12 SASE."

☑ **READ**, Weekly Reader Corporation, 200 First Stamford Place, P.O. Box 120023, Stamford CT 06912-0023. Fax: (203)705-1661. E-mail: sbarchers@weeklyreader.com. Website: www.weeklyreader.com. **Editor:** Suzanne Barchers. Magazine published 18 times during the school year. Language arts periodical for use in classrooms for students ages 12-16; motivates students to read and teaches skills in listening, comprehension, speaking, writing and critical thinking.

Fiction: Wants short stories, narratives and plays to be used for classroom reading and discussions. Middle readers, young adult/teens: adventure, animal, contemporary, fantasy, folktales, history, humorous, multicultural, nature/environment, problem solving, sports. Average word length: 1,000-2,500.

Nonfiction: Middle readers, young adult/teen: animal, games/puzzles, history, humorous, problem solving, social issues.

How to Contact: Responds to queries/mss in 6 weeks.

Illustration: Buys 2-3 illustrations/issue; 20-25 illustration jobs/year. Responds only if interested. Samples returned with SASE. Credit line given.

Terms: Pays on publication. Rights purchased varies. Pays writers $100-800 for stories/articles. Pays illustrators $650-850 for color cover; $125-750 for b&w and color inside. Pays photographers by the project (range: $450-650); per photo (range: $125-650). Samples copies free for digest-sized SAE and 3 first-class stamps.

Suzanne Hankins regularly uses *Children's Writer's & Illustrator's Market* and the Internet to find new publishers to whom she can market her work. This illustration, done in watercolor applied with brush and pen, appeared in an issue of *READ* magazine as an accompaniment to "The Sea Dragon of Fife," written by Jane Yolen. The staff at *READ* was looking for an elegant, fun, fantastical style, and Hankins' work fit the story's mood and theme beautifully. The audience for *READ* is children, ages 11-17.

Tips: "We especially like plot twists and surprise endings. Stories should be relevant to teens and contain realistic conflicts and dialogue. Plays should have at least 12 speaking parts for classroom reading. Avoid formula plots, trite themes, underage material, stilted or profane language, and sexual suggestion. Get to know the style of our magazine as well as our teen audience. They are very demanding and require an engaging and engrossing read. Grab their attention, keep the pace and action lively, build to a great climax, and make the ending satisfying and/ or surprising. Make sure characters and dialogue are realistic. Do not use cliché, but make the writing fresh— simple, yet original. Obtain guidelines and planned editorial calendar first. Be sure submissions are relevant."

N: SCHOOL MATES, USCF's Magazine for Beginning Chess Players, United States Chess Federation, 3054 Rt. 9W, New Windsor NY 12553. (914)562-8350. Fax: (914)561-CHES. **Editor:** Peter Kurzdorfen. **Graphic Designer:** Jami Anson. Bimonthly magazine. Estab. 1987. Circ. 30,000. Magazine for beginning chess players. Offers instructional articles, features on famous players, scholastic chess coverage, games, puzzles, occasional fiction, listing of chess tournaments.
Fiction: Young readers, middle readers, young adults: chess. Middle readers: humorous (chess-related). Average word length: 500-2,500 words.
Nonfiction: Young readers, middle readers, young adults: games/puzzles, chess. Middle readers, young adults: interview/profile (chess-related). "No *Mad Magazine* type humor. No sex, no drugs, no alcohol, no tobacco. No stereotypes. We want to see chess presented as a wholesome, non-nerdy activity that's fun for all. Good sportsmanship, fair play, and 'thinking ahead' are extremely desirable in chess articles. Also, celebrities who play chess."
Poetry: Infrequently published. Must be chess related.
How to Contact/Writers: Send complete ms. Responds to queries/mss in 5 weeks.
Illustration: Buys 10-25 illustrations/year. Prefers b&w and ink; cartoons OK. Illustration only: Query first. Responds only if interested. Credit line sometimes given. "Typically, a cover is credited while an illustration inside gets only the artist's signature in the work itself."
Photography: Purchases photos from freelancers. Wants "action shots of chess games (at tournament competitions), well-done portraits of popular chess players."
Terms: Pays on publication. Buys one-time rights for mss, artwork and photos. For stories/articles, pays $20-100. Pays illustrators $50-75 for b&w cover; $20-50 for b&w inside. Pays photographers per photo (range: $25-75). Sample copies free for 9×12 SAE and 2 first-class stamps. Writer's guidelines free on request.
Tips: Writers: "Lively prose that grabs and sustains kids' attention is desirable. Don't talk down to kids or over their heads. Don't be overly 'cute.' " Illustration/photography: "Whimsical shots are often desirable."

SCIENCE WEEKLY, Science Weekly Inc., P.O. Box 70638, Chevy Chase MD 20813. (301)680-8804. Fax: (301)680-9240. E-mail: sciencew@erols.com. **Editor:** Deborah Lazar. Magazine published 16 times/year. Estab. 1984. Circ. 200,000.
   ● *Science Weekly* uses freelance writers to develop and write an entire issue on a single science topic. Send résumé only, not submissions. Authors must be within the greater DC, Virginia, Maryland area. *Science Weekly* works on assignment only.
Nonfiction: Young readers, middle readers, (K-8th grade): science/math education, education, problem-solving.
Terms: Pays on publication. Prefers people with education, science and children's writing background. *Send résumé.* Samples copies free with SAE and 2 first-class stamps. Follow what is asked for by a publication when submitting materials—if it says résumé only, just send a résumé. If it says a specific locale only, don't send if you are outside of this area. It is a waste of your valuable time and the time of the publication to go through materials it cannot use.

☑ SEVENTEEN MAGAZINE, Primedia, 850 Third Ave., New York NY 10022. (212)407-9700. Fax: (212)407-9899. Website: http://seventeen.com. **Editor-in-Chief:** Patrice G. Adcroft. **Executive Editor:** Roberta Caploe, fiction. **Deputy Editor:** Tamara Glenny. **Art Director:** Carol Pagliuco. Monthly magazine. Estab. 1944. Circ. 2.5 million. "*Seventeen* is a young woman's first fashion and beauty magazine."
Fiction: "We consider all good literary short fiction." Buys 6-12 mss/year. Average word length: 800-4,000. Byline given.
Nonfiction: Young adults: animal, beauty, entertainment, fashion, careers, health, hobbies, how-to, humorous, interview/profile, multicultural, relationships, religion, social issues, sports. Buys 150 mss/year. Word length: Varies from 800-1,000 words for short features and monthly columns to 800-2,500 words for major articles. Byline given.
How to Contact/Writers: Fiction: Send complete ms. Nonfiction: Query with published clips or send complete ms. "Do not call." Responds to queries/mss in 3 months. Will consider simultaneous submissions.
Terms: Pays on acceptance. Strongly recommends requesting writers guidelines with SASE and reading recent issues of the magazine.

☑ SHARING THE VICTORY, Fellowship of Christian Athletes, 8701 Leeds, Kansas City MO 64129. (816)921-0909. Fax: (816)921-8755. Website: www.fca.org. **Articles/Photo Editors:** David Smale, Allen Palmeri. **Art Director:** Frank Grey. Magazine published 9 times a year. Estab. 1982. Circ. 80,000. "Purpose is to present to coaches and athletes, and all whom they influence, the challenge and adventure of receiving Jesus Christ as Savior and Lord."

Nonfiction: Young adults/teens: interview/profile, sports. Buys 30 mss/year. Average word length: 700-1,200. Byline given.

Poetry: Reviews poetry. Maximum length: 50-75 words.

How to Contact/Writers: Nonfiction: Query with published clips. Responds in 3 weeks. Publishes ms 3 months after acceptance. Will consider simultaneous submissions, electronic submissions via disk or modem and previously published work. Writer's guidelines available on website.

Photography: Purchases photos separately. Looking for photos of sports action. Uses color, b&w prints and 35mm transparencies.

Terms: Pays on publication. Buys first rights and second serial (reprint) rights. Pays $50-200 for assigned and unsolicited articles. Photographers paid per photo (range: $50-100). Sample copies for 9×12 SASE and $1. Writer's/photo guidelines for SASE.

Tips: "Be specific—write short. Take quality, sharp photos that are useable." Wants interviews and features, articles on athletes with a solid Christian base; be sure to include their faith and testimony. Interested in colorful sports photos.

☑ **SKIPPING STONES, A Multicultural Children's Magazine**, P.O. Box 3939, Eugene OR 97403. (541)342-4956. E-mail: skipping@efn.org. Website: www.efn.org/~skipping. **Articles/Photo/Fiction Editor:** Arun N. Toké. Bimonthly magazine. Estab. 1988. Circ. 2,500. "*Skipping Stones* is a multicultural, nonprofit children's magazine designed to encourage cooperation, creativity and celebration of cultural and ecological richness. We encourage submissions by minorities and under-represented populations."

- Send SASE for *Skipping Stones* guidelines and theme list for detailed descriptions of the topics they're looking for.

Fiction: Middle readers, young adult/teens: contemporary, meaningful, humorous. All levels: folktales, multicultural, nature/environment. Multicultural needs include: bilingual or multilingual pieces; use of words from other languages; settings in other countries, cultures or multi-ethnic communities.

Nonfiction: All levels: animal, biography, cooking, games/puzzles, history, humorous, interview/profile, multicultural, nature/environment, creative problem-solving, religion and cultural celebrations, sports, travel, social and international awareness. Does not want to see preaching or abusive language; no poems by authors over 18 years old; no suspense or romance stories for the sake of the same. Average word length: 500-750. Byline given.

How to Contact/Writers: Fiction: Query. Nonfiction: Send complete ms. Responds to queries in 1 month; mss in 4 months. Will consider simultaneous submissions; reviews artwork for future assignments. Please include your name on each page.

Illustration: Prefers color and/or b&w drawings, especially by teenagers and young adults. Will consider all illustration packages. Ms/illustration packages: Query; submit complete ms with final art; submit tearsheets. Responds in 4 months. Credit line given.

Photography: Black & white photos preferred, but color photos with good contrast are welcome. Needs: youth 7-17, international, nature, celebration.

Terms: Acquires first or reprint rights for mss and artwork; reprint rights for photographs. Pays in copies for authors, photographers and illustrators. Sample copies for $5 with SAE and 4 first-class stamps. Writer's/illustrator's guidelines for 4×9 SASE.

Tips: "We want material meant for children and young adults/teenagers with multicultural or ecological awareness themes. Think, live and write as if you were a child—naturally, uninhibited." Wants "material that gives insight on cultural celebrations, lifestyle, custom and tradition, glimpse of daily life in other countries and cultures. Photos, songs, artwork are most welcome if they illustrate/highlight the points. Translations are invited if your submission is in a language other than English. Upcoming themes will include cultural celebrations, living abroad, challenging disability, hospitality customs of various cultures, cross-cultural communications, African, Asian and Latin American cultures, indigenous architecture, humor, international, creative problem solving and turning points in life."

☑ **SOCCER JR., The Soccer Magazine for Kids**, Scholastic Inc., 27 Unquowa Rd., Fairfield CT 06430-5015. (203)259-5766. Fax: (203)256-1119. E-mail: jschoff@soccerjr.com. Website: www.soccerjr.com. **Articles/Fiction Editor:** Jill Schoff. Bimonthly magazine. Estab. 1992. Circ. 100,000. *Soccer Jr.* is for soccer players 8-14 years old. "The editorial focus of *Soccer Jr.* is on the fun and challenge of the sport. Every issue contains star interviews, how-to tips, lively graphics, action photos, comics, games, puzzles and contests. Fair play and teamwork are emphasized in a format that provides an off-the-field way for kids to enjoy the sport."

Fiction: Middle readers, young adults/teens: sports (soccer). Does not want to see "cute," preachy or "moralizing" stories. Buys 3-4 mss/year. Average word length: 1,000-2,000. Byline given.

Nonfiction: Young readers, middle readers, young adults/teens: sports (soccer). Buys 10-12 mss/year.

How to Contact/Writers: Fiction: Send complete ms. Nonfiction: Send query letter. Responds to mss in 6 weeks. Publishes ms 3-12 months after acceptance. Will consider simultaneous submissions.

Illustration: Buys 2 illustrations/issue; 20 illustrations/year. Works on assignment only. Illustrations only: Send samples to be filed. Samples not returned; samples kept on file. "We have a small pool of artists we work from but look for new freelancers occasionally, and accept samples for consideration." Credit line given.

Terms: Pays on acceptance. Buys first rights for mss. Pays $50-600 for stories. Pays illustrators $300-750 for color cover; $50-200 for b&w inside; $75-300 for color inside. Pays photographers per photo (range: $75-300). Sample copies for 9×12 SAE and 5 first-class stamps.

Tips: "We ask all potential writers to understand *Soccer Jr.*'s voice. We write to kids, not to adults. We request a query for any feature ideas, but any fiction pieces can be sent complete. All submissions, unless specifically requested, are on a speculative basis. Please indicate if a manuscript has been submitted elsewhere or previously published. Please give us a brief personal bio, including your involvement in soccer, if any, and a listing of any work you've had published. We prefer manuscripts in Microsoft Word, along with an attached hard copy." The magazine also accepts stories written by children.

SPELLBOUND MAGAZINE, Eggplant Productions, P.O. Box 2248, Schiller Park IL 60176. (847)928-9925. Fax: (801)720-0706. E-mail: spellbound@eggplant-productions.com. Website: www.eggplantproductions. com/spellbound. **Articles Editor:** Raechel Henderson Moon. Quarterly magazine. Estab. 1999. Circ. less than 200. "*Spellbound Magazine*'s goal is to introduce new readers to the fantasy genre in all its wonderful forms. We publish intelligent fiction, nonfiction and poetry to excite kids. We like artwork that is fun."

• *Spellbound* only accepts e-mail submissions. All postal submissions are returned unread.

Fiction: Middle readers, young adults: fantasy, folktale, multicultural. Buys 20 mss/year. Average word length: 500-2,500. Byline given.

Nonfiction: Middle readers, young adults: myths/legends. Buys 1-2 mss/year. Average word length: 500-1,000. Byline given.

Poetry: Reviews free verse, traditional, rhyming poetry. Maximum length: 36 lines. Limit submissions to 5 poems.

How to Contact/Writers: Fiction: Send complete ms. Nonfiction: Query. Responds to queries in 2 weeks; mss in 1 month. Publishes ms 6 months after acceptance. Will consider simultaneous submissions; only considers electronic submission via modem.

Illustration: Buys 3-4 illustrations/issue; 12-16 illustrations/year. Uses b&w artwork only. Reviews ms/illustration packages from artists. Submit through e-mail to spellbound@eggplant-productions.com. Contact: Raechel Henderson Moon, editor. Illustrations only: Query with samples. Contact: Raechel Henderson Moon, editor. Responds in 2 weeks. Samples kept on file. Credit line given.

Terms: Pays on publication.Buys first world English-language rights for mss. Buys one-time rights for art. Pays $5 stories; $5 for articles. Artists are paid 2 contributor copies per interior art and 3 contributor copies for cover art. Sample copies for $5.

Tips: "Keep in mind that this is a market for children, but don't let that limit your work. We see too much that preaches or talks down to readers or that relies on old plot lines. Write the kind of story or poem that you would like to have read when you were 11. Then send it our way."

SPIDER, The Magazine for Children, Carus Publishing Company, P.O. Box 300, Peru IL 61354. (815)224-6656. Website: www.cricketmag.com. **Editor-in-Chief:** Marianne Carus. **Assistant Editor:** Tracy Schoenle. **Art Director:** Tony Jacobson. Monthly magazine. Estab. 1994. Circ. 85,000. *Spider* publishes high-quality literature for beginning readers, primarily ages 6-9.

Fiction: Young readers: adventure, animal, contemporary, fantasy, folktales, history, humorous, multicultural, nature/environment, problem-solving, science fiction, sports, suspense/mystery. "Authentic, well-researched stories from all cultures are welcome. No didactic, religious, or violent stories, or anything that talks down to children." Average word length: 300-900. Byline given.

Nonfiction: Young readers: animal, arts/crafts, cooking, games/puzzles, geography, history, math, multicultural, nature/environment, problem-solving, science. "Well-researched articles on all cultures are welcome. Would like to see more games, puzzles and activities, especially ones adaptable to *Spider*'s takeout pages. No encyclopedic or overtly educational articles." Average word length: 300-800. Byline given.

Poetry: Serious, humorous, nonsense rhymes. Maximum length: 20 lines.

How to Contact/Writers: Fiction/nonfiction: Send complete ms. Responds to mss in 3 months. Publishes ms 3-4 years after acceptance. Will consider simultaneous submissions and previously published work.

Illustration: Buys 20 illustrations/issue; 240 illustrations/year. Uses color artwork only. "Any medium—preferably one that can wrap on a laser scanner—no larger than 20×24. We use more realism than cartoon-style art." Works on assignment only. Reviews ms/illustration packages from artists. Submit ms with rough sketches. Illustrations only: Send promo sheet and tearsheets. Responds in 6 weeks. Samples returned with SASE; samples filed. Credit line given.

Photography: Buys photos from freelancers. Buys photos with accompanying ms only. Model/property releases required; captions required. Uses 35mm or 2¼×2¼ transparencies. Send unsolicited photos by mail; provide résumé and tearsheets. Responds in 6 weeks.

Terms: Pays on publication for text; within 45 days from acceptance for art. Buys first, one-time or reprint rights for mss. Buys first and promotional rights for artwork; one-time rights for photographs. Original artwork returned at job's completion. Pays 25¢/word for stories/articles. Authors also receive 2 complimentary copies of the issue in which work appears. Additional payment for ms/illustration packages and for photos accompanying articles. Pays illustrators $750 for color cover; $200-300 for color inside. Pays photographers per photo (range: $25-75). Sample copies for $4. Writer's/illustrator's guidelines for SASE.

Tips: Writers: "Read back issues before submitting." (See listings for *Babybug, Cicada, Cricket, Click, Muse* and *Ladybug*.)

N: SPORTS ILLUSTRATED FOR KIDS, 135 W. 50th St., New York NY 10020-1393. (212)522-1212. Fax: (212)522-0120. Website: www.sikids.com. **Art Director:** Beth Bugler. **Photo Editor:** Andrew McCloskey. Monthly magazine. Estab. 1989. Circ. 950,000. Each month *SI Kids* brings the excitement, joy, and challenge of sports to life for boys and girls ages 8-14 via: action photos, dynamic designs, interactive stories; a spectrum of sports: professional, extreme, amateur, women's and kids; profiles, puzzles, playing tips, sports cards; posters, plus drawings and writing by kids. 100% of publication aimed at juvenile market.

Nonfiction: Middle readers, young adults: biography, games/puzzles, interview/profile, sports. Buys less than 20 mss/year. Average word length: 500-700. Byline given.

How to Contact/Writers: Nonfiction: Query. Responds in 4-6 weeks. Will consider simultaneous submissions.

Illustration: Only interested in agented material. Buys 50 illustrations/year. Works on assignment only. Reviews ms/illustration packages from artists. Submit ms/illustration package with SASE. Contact: Beth Bugler, art director. Illustrations only: Send promo sheet and samples. Contact: Beth Bugler, art director. Responds in 1 month. Samples kept on file. Credit line given.

Photography: Looking for action sports photography. Uses color prints and 35mm transparencies. Submit portfolio for review. Responds in 1 month.

Terms: Pays 25% on acceptance 75% on publication. Buys all rights for mss. Buys all rights for artwork. Buys all rights for photos. Original artwork returned at job's completion. Pays $500 for 500-600 word articles. by the project—$400; $500/day; per photo (range: $75-1,000). Sample copies free for 9 × 12 SASE. Writer's guidelines for SASE.

Tips: (48) as edited.

STANDARD PUBLISHING, 8121 Hamilton Ave., Cincinnati OH 45231. See listings for *Encounter, Kidz Chat* and *Live Wire*.

N: STORY FRIENDS, Mennonite Publishing House, 616 Walnut Ave., Scottdale PA 15683. (724)887-8500. Fax: (724)887-3111. E-mail: RSTUTZ@mph.org. **Editor:** Rose Mary Stutzman. **Art Director:** Jim Butti. Estab. 1905. Circ. 7,000. Monthly story paper that reinforces Christian values for children ages 4-9.

Fiction: Picture-oriented material: contemporary, humorous, multicultural, nature/environment, problem-solving, religious, relationships. Multicultural needs include fiction or nonfiction pieces which help children be aware of cultural diversity and celebrate differences while recognizing similarities. Buys 45 mss/year. Average word length: 300-800. Byline given.

Nonfiction: Picture-oriented: animal, humorous, interview/profile, multicultural, nature/environment. Buys 10 mss/year. Average word length: 300-800. Byline given.

Poetry: Average length: 4-12 lines.

How to Contact/Writers: Fiction/nonfiction: Send complete ms. Responds to mss in 10 weeks. Will consider simultaneous submissions.

Illustration: Works on assignment only. Send tearsheets with SASE. Responds in 2 months. Samples returned with SASE; samples filed. Credit line given.

Photography: Occasionally buys photos from freelancers. Wants photos of children ages 4-8.

Terms: Pays on acceptance. Buys one-time rights or reprint rights for mss and artwork. Original artwork returned at job's completion. Pays 3-5¢/word for stories and articles. Pays photographers $15-30 per photo. Writer's guidelines free with SAE and 2 first-class stamps.

Tips: "Become immersed in high quality children's literature."

TODAY'S CHRISTIAN TEEN, Marketing Partners Inc., P.O. Box 100, Morgantown PA 19543. (610)372-1111. Fax: (610)372-8227. E-mail: tcpubs@mkpt.com. **Articles Editor:** Elaine Williams. Publishes issues of interest to teenagers from a conservative biblical view.

Nonfiction: Young adults: health, religion, social issues. Buys 10 mss/year. Average word length: 800-1,100. Byline given.

How to Contact/Writers: Nonfiction: send complete ms. Responds to queries in 2 weeks; mss in 3 months. Publishes ms 1 year after acceptance. Will consider simultaneous submissions, electronic submissions via disk or modem and previously published work.

Terms: Pays on publication. Pays $75-150 for articles. Sample copies free for 9 × 12 SAE with 4 first-class stamps. Writer's guidelines for SASE.

Tips: "Make articles applicable to conservative teens with a biblical perspective—something they can use, not just entertainment."

TOGETHER TIME, WordAction Publishing Co., 6401 The Paseo, Kansas City MO 64131. (816)333-7000. Fax: (816)333-4439. E-mail: mhammer@nazarene.org. Website: www.nazarene.org or www.nphdirect.com. **Contact:** Melissa Hammer. Weekly magazine. Estab. 1981. Circ. 27,000. "*Together Time* is a story paper that correlates with the WordAction Sunday School Curriculum. Each paper contains a Bible story and 2 activities. It is designed to connect Sunday School learning with the daily living experiences and growth of children three and four years old. All submissions must agree with the theology and practices of the Nazarene and other holiness denominations."

Nonfiction: Picture-oriented material: arts/crafts, songs, recipes.

Poetry: Reviews poetry. Maximum length: 8 lines. Limit submissions to 10 poems.

How to Contact/Writers: Fiction: Send complete ms. Responds to queries/mss in 1 month. Publishes ms 1 year after acceptance.

Terms: Pays on publication. Buys multi-use rights. "Writers receive payment and contributor copies." Sample copies for #10 SAE and 1 first-class stamp. Writer's guidelines for SASE.

Tips: "Make sure the material you submit is geared to three- and four-year-old children. Request a theme list with the guidelines and try to submit stories that correlate with specific issues."

TOUCH, GEMS Girls' Clubs, Box 7259, Grand Rapids MI 49510. (616)241-5616. Fax: (616)241-5558. E-mail: sara@gemsgc.org. Website: www.gospelcom.net/gems. **Editor:** Jan Boone. **Managing Editor:** Sara Lynne Hilton. Monthly (with combined May/June issue and July/August newsletter) magazine. Circ. 16,000. "*Touch* is designed to help girls ages 9-14 see how God is at work in their lives and in the world around them."

Fiction: Middle readers: adventure, animal, contemporary, health, history, humorous, multicultural, nature/environment, problem-solving, religious, sports. Does not want to see unrealistic stories and those with trite, easy endings. Buys 30 mss/year. Average word length: 400-1,000. Byline given.

Nonfiction: Middle readers: animal, arts/crafts, careers, cooking, fashion, games/puzzles, health, hobbies, how-to, humorous, nature/environment, multicultural, problem-solving, religious, social issues, sports, travel. Buys 9 mss/year. Average word length: 200-800. Byline given.

How to Contact/Writers: Send for annual update for publication themes. Fiction/nonfiction: Send complete ms. Responds to mss in 1 month. Will consider simultaneous submissions.

Illustration: Buys 3 illustrations/year. Prefers ms/illustration packages. Works on assignment only. Responds to submissions in 1 month. Samples returned with SASE. Credit line given.

Terms: Pays on publication. Buys first North American serial rights, first rights, second serial (reprint rights) or simultaneous rights. Original artwork not returned at job's completion. Pays $5-30 for stories; $5-30 for assigned articles; $5-30 for unsolicited articles. "We send complimentary copies in addition to pay." Pays $25-75 for color cover illustration; $25-50 for color inside illustration. Pays photographers by the project ($25-75 per photo). Writer's guidelines for SASE.

Tips: Writers: "The stories should be current, deal with adolescent problems and joys, and help girls see God at work in their lives through humor as well as problem-solving."

TURTLE MAGAZINE, For Preschool Kids, Children's Better Health Institute, 1100 Waterway Blvd., P.O. Box 567, Indianapolis IN 46206. (317)636-8881. **Editor:** Terry Harshman. **Art Director:** Bart Rivers. Monthly/bimonthly magazine published 8 times/year. Circ. 300,000. *Turtle* uses read-aloud stories, especially suitable for bedtime or naptime reading, for children ages 2-5. Also uses poems, simple science experiments, easy recipes and health-related articles.

Fiction: Picture-oriented material: adventure, contemporary, fantasy, health-related, history, holiday themes, humorous, multicultural, nature/environment, problem-solving, sports, suspense/mystery. "We need very simple experiments illustrating basic science concepts. Also needs action rhymes to foster creative movement. Avoid stories in which the characters indulge in unhealthy activities. Buys 30 mss/year. Average word length: 100-300. Byline given.

Nonfiction: Picture-oriented material: animal, arts/crafts, cooking, games/puzzles, geography, health, multicultural, nature/environment, science, sports. Buys 24 mss/year. Average word length: 100-300. Byline given.

Poetry: "We're especially looking for short poems (4-8 lines) and slightly longer action rhymes to foster creative movement in preschoolers. We also use short verse on our back cover."

How to Contact/Writers: Fiction/nonfiction: "Prefer complete manuscript to queries." Responds to mss in 3 months.

Photography: Buys photos from freelancers with accompanying ms only.

Terms: Pays on publication. Buys all rights for mss/artwork; one-time rights for photographs. Pays up to 22¢/word for stories and articles (depending upon length and quality) and 10 complimentary copies. Pays $25 minimum for poems. Pays $30-70 for b&w inside. Sample copy $1.75. Writer's guidelines free with SASE.

Tips: "Our need for health-related material, especially features that encourage fitness, is ongoing. Health subjects must be age-appropriate. When writing about them, think creatively and lighten up! Always keep in mind that in order for a story or article to educate preschoolers, it first must be entertaining—warm and engaging, exciting, or genuinely funny. Here the trend is toward leaner, lighter writing. There will be a growing need for interactive activities. Writers might want to consider developing an activity to accompany their concise manuscripts." (See listings for *Child Life*, *Children's Digest*, *Children's Playmate*, *Humpty Dumpty's Magazine*, *Jack and Jill* and *U*S* Kids*.)

U*S* KIDS, Children's Better Health Institute, 1100 Waterway Blvd., P.O. Box 567, Indianapolis IN 46206. (317)636-8881. **Editor:** Nancy S. Axelrod. **Art Director:** Rebecca Ray. Magazine published 8 times a year. Estab. 1987. Circ. 230,000.

Fiction: Young readers: adventure, animal, contemporary, health, history, humorous, multicultural, nature/environment, problem-solving, sports, suspense/mystery. Buys limited number of stories/year. Average word length: 500-800. Byline given.

Nonfiction: Young readers: animal, arts/crafts, cooking, games/puzzles, health, history, hobbies, how-to, humorous, interview/profile, multicultural, nature/environment, science, social issues, sports, travel. Wants to see interviews with kids ages 5-10, who have done something unusual or different. Buys 16-24 mss/year. Average word length: 400. Byline given.

Poetry: Maximum length: 8-24 lines.

How to Contact/Writers: Fiction: Send complete ms. Responds to queries and mss in 2-3 months. Nonfiction: Publishes ms 6 months after acceptance.

Illustration: Buys 8 illustrations/issue; 70 illustrations/year. Color artwork only. Works on assignment only. Reviews ms/illustration packages from artists. Query. Illustrations only: Send résumé and tearsheets. Responds only if interested. Samples returned with SASE; samples kept on file. Does not return originals. Credit line given.

Photography: Purchases photography from freelancers. Looking for photos that pertain to children ages 5-10. Model/property release required. Uses color and b&w prints; 35mm, 2¼×2¼, 4×5 and 8×10 transparencies. Photographers should provide résumé, business card, promotional literature or tearsheets to be kept on file. Responds only if interested.

Terms: Pays on publication. Buys all rights for mss. Purchases all rights for artwork. Purchases one-time rights for photographs. Pays 25¢/word minimum. Additional payment for ms/illustration packages. Pays illustrators $155/page for color inside. Photographers paid by the project or per photo (negotiable). Sample copies for $2.95. Writer's/illustrator/photo guidelines for #10 SASE.

Tips: "Write clearly and concisely without preaching or being obvious." (See listings for *Child Life, Children's Digest, Children's Playmate, Humpty Dumpty's Magazine, Jack and Jill* and *Turtle Magazine*.)

☑ **W.O.W. (Wild Outdoor World),** Suites 16-20, P.O. Box 1349, Helena MT 59624. (406)449-1335. Fax: (406)442-9197. **Editorial Director:** Carolyn Zieg Cunningham. **Executive Editor:** Kay Morton Ellerhoff. **Design Editor:** Bryan Knaff. Publishes 5 issues/year. Estab. 1993. Circ. 200,000. "A magazine for young conservationists (age 8-12)." W.O.W. is distributed in fourth grade classrooms throughout the US.

Nonfiction: Middle readers: adventure (outdoor), animal, nature/environment, sports (outdoor recreation), travel (to parks, wildlife refuges, etc.). Average word length: 800 maximum. Byline given.

How to Contact/Writers: Nonfiction: Query. Responds in 6 months.

Illustration: Buys 2 illustrations/issue; 12-15 illustrations/year. Prefers work on assignment. Reviews ms/illustration packages from artists. Illustrations only: Query; send slides, tearsheets. Responds in 2 months. Samples returned with SASE; samples sometimes filed. Credit line given.

Photography: *Must* be submitted in 20-slide sheets and individual protectors, such as KYMAC. Looks for "children outdoors—camping, fishing, doing 'nature' projects." Model/property releases required. Photo captions required. Uses 35mm transparencies. Does not accept unsolicited photography. Contact: Theresa Morrow Rush, photo editor. Responds in 2 months.

Terms: Pays 30-60 days after publication. Buys one-time rights for mss. Purchases one-time rights for photographs. Original work returned at job's completion. Pays $100-300 for articles; $50 for fillers. Pays illustrators variable rate for b&w inside; $250 color cover; $35-100 color inside. Pays photographers $150 for full inside; per photo (range: $125-300); $375 for cover photo. Sample copies for $3.95 and 8½×11 SAE. Writer's/illustrator's/photo guidelines for SASE.

Tips: "We are seriously overloaded with manuscripts and do not plan to buy very much new material in the next year."

N WEEKLY READER, Weekly Reader Corporation, 200 First Stamford Place, Stamford CT 06912-0023. (203)705-3500. Website: www.weeklyreader.com. **Managing Editor:** Bill Walter (grades 2-4). **Executive Art Director:** Sandy Forrest. Weekly magazine. Estab. 1902. Circ. 9 million. Classroom periodicals bring news to kids from pre-K to high school in 17 grade-specific periodicals. Publication aimed at juvenile market.

Illustration: Uses color artwork only. Works on assignment only. Illustrations only: Query with samples or send tearsheets. Contact: Sandy Forrest, executive art director. Responds only if interested. Samples returned with SASE; samples filed. Credit line given.

Photography: Uses color prints. Query with samples, Provide tearsheets. Responds only if interested.

Terms: Pays 30 days after submission of invoice. Buys all rights for mss. Buys one-time usage for artwork. Buys one-time usage for photos. Original artwork returned at job's completion. Pays illustrators $400-800 for color cover.

Tips: Please do not call to see if samples were received, as many arrive daily.

☑ WHAT! A MAGAZINE, What! Publishers Inc. 108-93 Lombard Ave., Winnipeg, Manitoba R3B 3B1 Canada. (204)957-5638. Fax: (204)943-8991. E-mail: l.malkin@m2ci.mb.ca. **Articles Editor:** Leslie Malkin. **Art Director:** Brian Kauste. Magazine published 6 times/year. Estab. 1987. Circ. 250,000. "Informative and entertaining teen magazine for both genders. Articles deal with issues and ideas of relevance to Canadian teens. The magazine is distributed through schools so we aim to be cool and responsible at the same time."

Nonfiction: Young adults (14 and up): biography, careers, concept, health, how-to, humorous, interview/profile, nature/environment, science, social issues, sports. "No cliché teen stuff. Also, we're getting too many heavy pitches lately on teen pregnancy, AIDS, etc." Buys 8 mss/year. Average word length: 675-2,100. Byline given.
How to Contact/Writers: Nonfiction: Query with published clips. Responds to queries/mss in 2 months. Publishes ms 2 months after acceptance.
Terms: Pays on publication plus 30 days. Buys first rights for mss. Pays $100-500 (Canadian) for articles. Sample copies when available for 9×12 and $1.45 (Canadian). Writer's guidelines free for SASE.
Tips: "Teens are smarter today than ever before. Respect that intelligence in queries and articles. Aim for the older end of our age-range (14-19) and avoid cliché. Humor works for us almost all the time."

N: WINNER, The Health Connection, 55 W. Oakridge Dr., Hagerstown MD 21740. (301)393-4010. Fax: (301)393-4055. E-mail: Listen@healthconnection.org. **Articles Editor:** Anita Jacobs. **Art Director:** Kimberly Haupt. Monthly magazine (September-May). (4) Estab. 1958. Publishes articles that will promote choosing a positive lifestyle for children in grades 4-6.
Fiction: Young readers, middle readers: contemporary, health, nature/environment, problem-solving, anti-tobacco, alcohol and drugs. Byline sometimes given.
Nonfiction: Young readers, middle readers: biography, games/puzzles, health, hobbies, how-to, problem-solving, social issues. Buys 20 mss/year. Average word length: 600-800. Byline sometimes given.
How to Contact/Writers: Fiction/nonfiction: Query. Responds in 6 weeks. Publishes ms 6-12 months after acceptance. Will consider simultaneous submissions, electronic submission via disk or modem.
Illustration: Buys 3 illustrations/issue; 30 illustrations/year. Uses color artwork only. Works on assignment only. Reviews ms/illustration packages from artists. Send ms with dummy. Contact: Kimberly Haupt, art director. Responds only if interested. Samples returned with SASE.
Terms: Pays on acceptance. Buys first rights for mss. Original artwork returned at job's completion. Additional payment for ms/illustration packages. Sometimes additional payment when photos accompany articles. Pays $200-400 for color inside. Writer's and illustrator's guidelines free for SASE. Sample magazine $1.00; include 9x12 envelope with 2 first-class stamps.
Tips: Keep material upbeat and positive for elementary age children.

WITH, The Magazine for Radical Christian Youth, Faith & Life Press, 722 Main, P.O. Box 347, Newton KS 67114. (316)283-5100. Fax: (316)283-0454. E-mail: deliag@gcmc.org. **Editor:** Carol Duerksen. Published 6 times a year. Circ. 5,800. Magazine published for Christian teenagers, ages 15-18. "We deal with issues affecting teens and try to help them make choices reflecting a radical Christian faith."
Fiction: Young adults/teens: contemporary, fantasy, humorous, multicultural, problem-solving, religious, romance. Multicultural needs include race relations, first-person stories featuring teens of ethnic minorities. Buys 15 mss/year. Average word length: 1,000-2,000. Byline given.
Nonfiction: Young adults/teens: first-person teen personal experience (as-told-to), how-to, humorous, multicultural, problem-solving, religion, social issues. Buys 15-20 mss/year. Average word length: 1,000-2,000. Byline given.
Poetry: Wants to see religious, humorous, nature. "Buys 1-2 poems/year." Maximum length: 50 lines.
How to Contact/Writers: Send complete ms. Query on first-person teen personal experience stories and how-to articles. (Detailed guidelines for first-person stories, how-tos, and fiction available for SASE.) Responds to queries in 3 weeks; mss in 6 weeks. Will consider simultaneous submissions.
Illustration: Buys 6-8 assigned illustrations/issue; buys 64 assigned illustrations/year. Uses b&w and 2-color artwork only. Preferred theme or style: candids/interracial. Reviews ms/illustration packages from artists. Query first. Illustrations only: Query with portfolio (photocopies only) or tearsheets. Responds only if interested. Credit line given.
Photography: Buys photos from freelancers. Looking for candid photos of teens (ages 15-18), especially ethnic minorities. Uses 8×10 b&w glossy prints. Photographers should send unsolicited photos by mail.
Terms: Pays on acceptance. For mss buys first rights, one-time rights; second serial (reprint rights). Buys one-time rights for artwork and photos. Original artwork returned at job's completion upon request. Pays 6¢/word for unpublished manuscripts; 4¢/word for reprints. Will pay more for assigned as-told-to stories. Pays $10-25 for poetry. Pays $50-60 for b&w cover illustration and b&w inside illustration. Pays photographers per project (range: $120-180). Sample copy for 9×12 SAE and 4 first-class stamps. Writer's/illustrator's guidelines for SASE.
Tips: "We want stories, fiction or nonfiction, in which high-school-age youth of various cultures/ethnic groups are the protaganists. Stories may or may not focus on cross-cultural relationships. We're hungry for stuff that makes teens laugh—fiction, nonfiction and cartoons. It doesn't have to be religious, but must be wholesome. Most of our stories would not be accepted by other Christian youth magazines. They would be considered too gritty, too controversial, or too painful. Our regular writers are on the *With* wavelength. Most writers for Christian youth magazines aren't." For writers: "Fiction and humor are the best places to break in. Send SASE and request guidelines." For photographers: "If you're willing to line up models and shoot to illustrate specific story scenes, send us a letter of introduction and some samples of your work."

☑ **WRITER'S INTL. FORUM, "For Those Who Write to Sell,"** Bristol Services Intl., P.O. Box 2109, Sequim WA 98382. E-mail: services@bristolservicesintl.com. Website: www.bristolservicesintl.com. **Editor:** Sandra E. Haven. Estab. 1990. "Periodic writing competitions held exclusively at our website." Up to 25% aimed at writers of juvenile literature. "We have published past winning short stories and essays along with a professional critique. Website includes writing lessons and information."
Fiction: Middle readers, young readers, young adults/teens: adventure, contemporary, fantasy, humorous, nature/environment, problem-solving, religious, romance, science fiction, suspense/mystery. "No experimental formats; no picture books; no poetry. No stories for children under age eight. Byline and bio information printed.
How to Contact/Writers: Send SASE or see website to determine if a contest is currently open. Only send a manuscript if a contest is open.
Terms: See details at website.

☒ **YES MAG, Canada's Science Magazine for Kids,** Peter Piper Publishing Inc., 4175 Francisco Place, Victoria, British Columbia V8N 6H1 Canada. Phone/fax: (250)477-5543. E-mail: shannon@yesmag.bc.ca. Website: www.yesmag.bc.ca. **Articles Editor:** Shannon Hunt. **Art/Photo Director:** David Garrison. Quarterly magazine. Estab. 1996. Circ. 15,000. "*YES Mag* is designed to make science accessible, interesting, exciting, and FUN. Written for children ages 8 to 14, *YES Mag* covers a range of topics including science and technology news, environmental updates, do-at-home projects and articles about Canadian students and scientists."
Nonfiction: Middle readers: animal, health, math, nature/environment, science. Buys 70 mss/year. Average word length: 250-1,250. Byline given.
How to Contact/Writers: Nonfiction: Query with published clips or send complete ms (on spec only). Responds to queries/mss in 3 weeks. Publishes ms 3 months after acceptance. Will consider simultaneous submissions, electronic submission via disk or modem, previously published work.
Illustration: Buys 2 illustrations/issue; 10 illustrations/year. Uses color artwork only. Works on assignment only. Reviews ms/illustration packages from artists. Query. Contact: David Garrison, art director. Illustration only: Query with samples. Contact: David Garrison, art director. Responds in 3 weeks. Samples filed. Credit line given.
Photography: "Looking for science, technology, nature/environment photos based on current editorial needs." Photo captions required. Uses color prints. Provide résumé, business card, promotional literature, tearsheets if possible. Responds in 3 weeks.
Terms: Pays on publication. Buys one-time rights for mss. Buys one-time rights for artwork/photos. Original artwork returned at job's completion. Pays $25-125 for stories and articles. Sample copies for $3.50. Writer's guidelines for SASE.
Tips: "We do not publish fiction or science fiction. Visit our website for more information, sample articles and writers guidelines. We accept queries via e-mail. Articles relating to the physical sciences and mathematics are encouraged."

☑ **YM,** 685 Third Ave., New York NY 10017. (212)499-2000. Fax: (212)499-1698. E-mail: annemarie@ym.com. **Editor:** Annemarie Iverson. **Executive Editor:** Ellen Seidman. "*YM* is a national magazine for girls ages 12-24 to help guide them through the joys and challenges of young adulthood."
Nonfiction: "*YM* covers dating, psychology, entertainment, friendship, self-esteem, human interest and news trends. All articles should be lively and empowering and include quotes from experts and real teens. We do not publish fiction or poetry." Word length: 800-2,000 words.
How to Contact/Writers: Nonfiction: Query with SASE. (Write "query" on envelope.) Responds to queries in 4-6 weeks; mss in 1-2 months.
Terms: Pays on acceptance. Rates vary. Sample copies available for $2.50.

🅽 **YOUNG & ALIVE,** Christian Record Services, P.O, Box 6097, Lincoln NE 68506. (402)488-0981. Fax: (402)488-7582. E-mail: crsnet@compuserve.com. Website: www.christianrecord.org. **Articles Editor:** Ms. Gaylena Gibson. Quarterly magazine. Estab. 1976. Circ. 25,000. "We seek to provide wholesome, entertaining material for teens and others through age 25."
Nonfiction: Young adult/teen: animal, biography, careers, games/puzzles, health, history, humorous, interview/profile, multicultural, nature/environment, problem-solving, religion ("practical Christianity"), sports, travel. Buys 40-50 mss/year from freelancers. Word length: 700-1,400. Byline given.
How to Contact/Writers: Send complete manuscript. Responds to queries in 2 months, mss in 5 months. Published a manuscript "at least 2 years" after acceptance. Considers simultaneous submissions and previously published work. "Please don't send the work as a previously published piece; send a clean copy."
Illustration: Works on assignment only. Reviews ms/illustration packages from artists. Send manuscript with dummy. Contact: Gaylena Gibson, editor.
Photography: Buys photos with accompanying ms only. Model/property release required; captions required. Uses color or b&w 3×5 or 8×10 prints.
Terms: Pays on acceptance. Buys one-time rights for ms and photos. Original artwork returned at job's completion. Pays 4-5¢/word for stories/article. Pays $25-40 for b&w inside illustration. Pays photographers by the projects ($25-75). Sample copies available for 8×10 SASE and 5 first-class stamps. Writers guidelines available for SASE.

Tips: "Hold the reader's attention with an interesting beginning, a complete middle, and a satisfactory ending that ties everything together. Use proper grammar, punctuation and spelling. Use clean white paper (no pages ripped from another magazine)."

YOUNG SALVATIONIST, The Salvation Army, 615 Slaters Lane, P.O. Box 269, Alexandria VA 22314-1112. (703)684-5500. Fax: (703)684-5534. E-mail: ys@usn.salvationarmy.org. Website: publications.salvationarmyusa .org. Published 10 times/year. Estab. 1984. Circ. 50,000. **Managing Editor:** Tim Clark. "We accept material with clear Christian content written for high school age teenagers. *Young Salvationist* is published for teenage members of The Salvation Army, an evangelical part of the Christian Church that focuses on living the Christian life."
Fiction: Young adults/teens: contemporary, humorous, problem-solving, religious. Buys 10-11 mss/year. Average word length: 750-1,200. Byline given.
Nonfiction: Young adults/teens: religious—careers, concept, interview/profile, how-to, humorous, multicultural, problem-solving, social issues, sports. Buys 40-50 mss/year. Average word length: 750-1,200. Byline given.
How to Contact/Writers: Fiction/nonfiction: Query with published clips or send complete ms. Responds to queries/mss in 1 month. Will consider simultaneous submissions.
Illustrations: Buys 3-5 illustrations/issue; 20-30 illustrations/year. Reviews ms/illustration packages from artists. Send ms with art. Illustrations only: Query; send résumé, promo sheet, portfolio, tearsheets. Responds only if interested. Samples returned with SASE; samples filed. Credit line given.
Photography: Purchases photography from freelancers. Looking for teens in action.
Terms: Pays on acceptance. Buys first North American serial rights, first rights, one-time rights or second serial (reprint) rights for mss. Purchases one-time rights for artwork and photographs. Original artwork returned at job's completion "if requested." For mss, pays 10-15¢/word; 10¢/word for reprints. Pays $60-150 color (cover) illustration; $60-150 b&w (inside) illustration; $60-150 color (inside) illustration. Pays photographers per photo (range: $60-150). Sample copy for 9×12 SAE and 4 first-class stamps. Writer's guidelines for #10 SASE.
Tips: "Ask for theme list/sample copy! Write 'up,' not down to teens. Aim at young *adults*, not children." Wants "less fiction, more 'journalistic' nonfiction."

YOUTH UPDATE, St. Anthony Messenger Press, 1615 Republic St., Cincinnati OH 45210. (513)241-5615. E-mail: carolann@americancatholic.org. Website: www.AmericanCatholic.org. **Articles Editor:** Carol Ann Morrow. **Art Director:** June Pfaff Daley. Monthly newsletter. Estab. 1982. Circ. 28,000. "Each issue focuses on one topic only. *Youth Update* addresses the faith and Christian life questions of young people and is designed to attract, instruct, guide and challenge its audience by applying the gospel to modern problems and situations. The students who read *Youth Update* vary in their religious education and reading ability. Write for average high school students. These students are 15-year-olds with a C+ average. Assume that they have paid attention to religious instruction and remember a little of what 'sister' said. Aim more toward 'table talk' than 'teacher talk.'"
Nonfiction: Young adults/teens: religion. Buys 12 mss/year. Average word length: 2,200-2,300. Byline given.
How to Contact/Writers: Nonfiction: Query. Responds to queries/mss in 3 months. Will consider computer printout and electronic submissions via disk.
Photography: Buys photos from freelancers. Uses photos of teens (high-school age) with attention to racial diversity and with emotion.
Terms: Pays on acceptance. Buys first North American serial rights for mss. Buys one-time rights for photographs. Pays $75-500 for articles. Pays photographers per photo ($50-75 minimum). Sample copy free with #10 SASE. Writer's guidelines free on request.
Tips: "Read the newsletter yourself—3 issues at least. In the past, our publication has dealt with a variety of topics including: dating, Lent, teenage pregnancy, baptism, loneliness, violence, confirmation and the Bible. When writing, use the *New American Bible* as translation. Interested in church-related topics."

ZILLIONS For Kids From Consumer Reports, Consumers Union, 101 Truman Ave., Yonkers NY 10703-1057. (914)378-2551. Fax: (914)378-2985. Website: www.zillions.org. **Articles Editor:** Karen McNulty. **Art Director:** Rob Jenter. Bimonthly magazine. Estab. 1980. Circ. 300,000. "*Zillions* is the Consumer Reports for kids (with heavy emphasis on fun!) We offer kids information on product tests, ads and fads, money smarts, and more."
● *ZILLIONS* works on assignment only. They do not accept unsolicited manuscripts; query first.
Nonfiction: Children/young adults: arts/crafts, careers, games/puzzles, health, hobbies, how-to, humorous, nature/environment, problem-solving, social issues, sports. "Will consider story ideas on kid money matters, marketing to kids and anything that educates kids to be smart consumers." Buys 10 mss/year. Average word length: 800-1,000.
How to Contact/Writers: Nonfiction: Query with résumé and published clips. "We'll contact if interested (within a few months probably)." Publishes ms 2 months after acceptance.
Terms: Pays on publication. Buys all rights for ms. Pays $1,000 for articles. Writer's guidelines for SASE.
Tips: "Read the magazine!"

Greeting Cards, Puzzles & Games

In this section you'll find companies that produce puzzles, games, greeting cards and other items (like coloring books, stickers and giftwrap) especially for kids. These are items you'll find in children's sections of bookstores, toy stores, department stores and card shops.

Because these markets create an array of products, their needs vary greatly. Some may need the service of freelance writers for greeting card copy or slogans for buttons and stickers. Others are in need of illustrators for coloring books or photographers for puzzles. Artists should send copies of their work that art directors can keep on file—never originals. Carefully read through the listings to find companies' needs, and send for guidelines and catalogs if they're available, just as you would for book or magazine publishers.

If you'd like to find out more about the greeting card industry beyond the market for children, there are a number of resources to help you. The Greeting Card Association is a national trade organization for the industry. For membership information, contact the GCA at 1030 15th NW, Suite 870, Washington DC 20005. (202)393-1778. *Greetings Etc.* (Edgel Communications), is a quarterly trade magazine covering the greeting card industry. For information call (978)262-9611. Illustrators should check out *Greeting Card Designs*, by Joanne Fink (PBC Intl. Inc.). For a complete list of companies, consult the latest edition of *Artist's & Graphic Designer's Market* (Writer's Digest Books). Writers should see *You Can Write Greeting Cards*, by Karen Ann Moore and *How to Write & Sell Greeting Cards, Bumper Stickers, T-shirts and Other Fun Stuff*, by Molly Wigand (both Writer's Digest Books).

Information on greeting card, puzzle and game companies listed in the previous edition but not included in this edition of *Children's Writer's & Illustrator's Market* may be found in the General Index.

N **AMCAL**, 2500 Bisso Lane, #500, Concord CA 94520. (925)689-9930. Fax: (925)689-0108. Website: www.amcalart.com. Vice President/Creative Development: Judy Robertson. Estab. 1975. Cards, calendars, desk diaries, boxed Christmas cards, journals, mugs, and other high quality gift and stationery products.
Illustration: Receives over 150 submissions/year. "AMCAL publishes high quality full color, narrative and decorative art for a wide market from traditional to contemporary. "Currently we are very interested in country folk art and decorative styles. Know the trends and the market. Juvenile illustration should have some adult appeal. We don't publish cartoon, humorous or gag art, or bold graphics. We sell to mostly small, exclusive gift retailers. Submissions are always accepted for future lines." To contact, send samples, photocopies, slides and SASE for return of submission. Responds in approximately 1 month. Pays on publication. Pay negotiable/usually advance on royalty. Rights purchased negotiable. Guideline sheets for #10 SASE and 1 first-class stamp.
Tips: To learn more about AMCAL and our products, please visit our website at: www.amcalart.com.

N **ARISTOPLAY, LTD.**, 8122 Main St., Dexter MI 48130. (734)424-0123. Fax: (734)424-0124. Website: www.aristoplay.com. Art Director: Doreen Consiglio. Estab. 1979. Produces educational board games and card decks, activity kits—all educational subjects. 100% of products are made for kids or have kids' themes.
Illustration: Needs freelance illustration and graphic designers (including art directors) for games, card decks and activity kits. Makes 2-4 illustration assignments/year. To contact, send cover letter, résumé, published samples or color photocopies. Responds back in 1 month if interested. For artwork, pays by the project, $500-5,000. Pays on acceptance (½-sketch, ½-final). Buys all rights. Credit line given.
Photography: Buys photography from freelancers. Wants realistic, factual photos.
Tips: "Creating board games requires a lot of back and forth in terms of design, illustration, editorial and child testing; the more flexible you are, the better. Also, factual accuracy is important." Target age group 4-14. "We are an educational game company. Writers and illustrators working for us must be willing to research the subject and period of focus."

N AVANTI PRESS, INC., 155 W. Congress, Suite 200, Detroit MI 48226. (313)961-0022. Submit images to this address: Avanti, 6 W. 18th St., 12th Floor, New York NY 10011. (212)414-1025. Fax: (212)414-1055. Website: www.avantipress.com. Contact: Editing Dept.. Estab. 1979. Greeting card company. Publishes photographic greeting cards—nonseasonal and seasonal.

Photography: Purchases photography from freelancers. Buys stock and assigns work. Buys approximately 150 stock images/year. Makes approximately 150 assignments/year. Wants "narrative, storytelling images, graphically strong and colorful!" Accepts only photographs. Uses b&w/color prints; 35mm, 2¼×2¼ and 4×5 transparencies. To contact, "Call for submission guidelines or visit our Website. Pays either a flat fee or a royalty which is discussed at time of purchase." Pays on acceptance. Buys exclusive product rights (world-wide card rights). Credit line given. Photographer's guidelines for SASE.

Tips: At least 75% of products have kids' and pets themes. Submit seasonal material 9 months-1 year in advance. "All images submitted should express some kind of sentiment which either fits an occasion or can be versed and sent to the recipient to convey some feeling."

AVONLEA TRADITIONS, INC., 17075 Leslie St., Units 12-15, Newmarket, Ontario L3Y-8E1 Canada. (905)853-1777. Fax: (905)853-1763. Website: www.avonlea-traditions.com. President: Kathryn Morton. Estab. 1988. Giftware importer and distributor. Designs, imports and distributes products related to Canada's most famous storybook, *Anne of Green Gables*, and other Canadian themes. Publishes greeting cards (blank), novelties, quarterly newsletter, website.

Writing: Makes 2 writing assignments/month.

Illustration: Needs freelance illustration for stationery and packaging for giftware. Makes 2-3 illustration assignments/month; 24/year. Prefers romantic, Victorian, storybook artwork. To contact, send color photocopies and promo pieces. Responds only if interested. Materials not returned; materials filed. For other artwork, pays by the hour (range: $10-25). Pays on publication. Buys all rights. Credit line sometimes given.

Photography: Works on assignment only. Wants product photos. Uses transparencies. To contact, send portfolio and promo piece. Responds only if interested. Materials not returned; material filed. Pays on usage. Buys all rights. Credit line sometimes given.

Tips: "We strongly prefer artists/writers who are Canadian. Also give preference to those located in the Toronto area. Submit seasonal material 6 months in advance."

THE BEISTLE COMPANY, P.O. Box 10, Shippensburg PA 17257. (717)532-2131. Fax: (717)532-7789. E-mail: beistle@mail.cvn.net. Website: www.beistle.com. Product Manager: C. Michelle Luhrs-Wiest. Estab. 1900. Paper products company. Produces decorations and party goods, posters—baby, baptism, birthday, holidays, educational, wedding/anniversary, graduation, ethnic themes, and New Year parties. 50% of products are made for kids or have kids' themes.

Illustration: Needs freelance illustration for decorations, party goods, school supplies, point-of-purchase display materials and gift wrap. Makes 100 illustration assignments/year. Prefers fanciful style, cute 4- to 5-color illustration in gouache and/or computer illustration. To contact, send cover letter, résumé, client list, promo piece. To query with specific ideas, phone, write or fax. Responds only if interested. Materials returned with SASE; materials filed. Pays by the project or by contractual agreement; price varies according to type of project. Pays on acceptance. Buys all rights. Artist's guidelines available for SASE.

Photography: Buys photography from freelancers. Buys stock and assigns work. Makes 30-50 assignments/year. Wants scenic landscapes and product still life displays. Uses 35mm, 2¼×2¼, 4×5 transparencies. To contact, send cover letter, résumé, slides, client list, promo piece. Responds only if interested. Materials returned if accompanied with SASE; materials filed. Pays on acceptance. Buys first rights. Credit line sometimes given—depends on project. Guidelines available for SASE.

Tips: Submit seasonal material 6 months in advance.

N CARDMAKERS, P.O. Box 236, 66 High Bridge Rd., Lyme NH 03768-0236. (603)795-4422. Fax: (603)795-4222. E-mail: info@cardmakers.com. Website: cardmakers.com. Owner: Peter Diebold. Estab. 1978. "We publish whimsical greeting cards with an emphasis on Christmas and business-to-business."

Writing: To contact, send cover letter and writing samples with SASE. Responds in 3 months. Returns materials if accompanied by SASE. Pays on acceptance. Buys all rights. Credit line given. Writer's guidelines available for SASE.

Illustration: Needs freelance illustration for greeting cards. Makes 30-50 illustration assignments/year. Looking for happy holidays, "activity" themes—nothing with an "edge." To contact, send cover letter, published samples, color photocopies, promo pieces and SASE. Query with specific ideas, keep it simple. Responds in 3 months. Materials returned with SASE. For greeting cards, pays flat fee of $100-400. Pays on acceptance. Credit line given. Artist's guidelines available for SASE.

Photography: Buys stock images. Wants humor. To contact, send cover letter, published samples, SASE. Responds in 3 months. Returns material with SASE. Pays per photo (range: $100-400 for b&w, $100-400 for color). Pays on acceptance. Buys exclusive product rights. Credit line given. Guidelines available for SASE.

Tips: Submit seasonal material 9 months in advance. "Be brief. Be polite. We look at all our mail. No calls, no fax, no e-mails. Worst times to submit—September-December. The best submissions we see are simple, right to the point, color samples with a 'check-off' stamped, return post card eliciting comments/expression of interest."

© MCMXCIX Cardmakers/Peter Diebold

Coming up with a Christmas card for a company that sells aquariums and fish supplies isn't the easiest thing in the world, but artist Susan Drawbaugh proved she was up to the task. She used watercolor and a fine-tipped Rapidograph pen to draw the Santa figure, then scanned it into Photoshop where she created the water and fish using the airbrush tool. "The best part for me is getting bits of humorous details in anywhere I can so the viewer has fun finding them," she says. Drawbaugh put together a four-page full-color brochure showcasing various pieces she's done, then mailed them off to publishers.

COURAGE CARDS, 3915 Golden Valley Rd., Golden Valley MN 55422. (763)520-0211. Fax: (763)520-0299. E-mail: artsearch@courage.org. Website: www.courage.cords.org. Art and Production: Laura Brooks. Estab. 1959. Nonprofit greeting card company. Courage Cards helps support Courage Center, a nonprofit provider of rehabilitation services for children and adults with disabilities. Published holiday/seasonal greeting cards. 10% of products are made for kids or have kid's themes.
Illustration: Needs freelance illustration for children's greeting cards. Makes 40 illustration assignments/year. Prefers colorful holiday, peace, ethnic, diversity art. Uses color artwork only. To contact, request guidelines and application—send art with submission. Responds in 3 months performs annual art search. Returns materials if accompanied by SASE. For greeting cards, pays flat fee of $350. Pays on publication. Buys reprint rights. Credit line given.
Tips: "Please contact us for specific guidelines for the annual art search."

CREATE-A-CRAFT, P.O. Box 941293, Plano TX 75094-1293. Contact: Editor. Estab. 1967. Greeting card company. Produces greeting cards (create-a-card), giftwrap, games (create-a-puzzle), coloring books, calendars (create-a-calendar), posters, stationery and paper tableware products for all ages.
Writing: Needs freelance writing for children's greeting cards and other children's products. Makes 5 writing assignments/year. For greeting cards, accepts both rhymed and unrhymed verse ideas. Other needs for freelance writing include rhymed and unrhymed verse ideas on all products. **To contact, send via recognized agent only.** Responds only if interested. Material not returned. For greeting cards pay depends on complexity of project. Pays on publication. Buys all rights. Writer's guidelines available for SASE and $2.50—includes sample cards.
Illustration: Works with 3 freelance artists/year. Buys 3-5 designs/illustrations/year. Primary age concentration is 4-8 year old market. Prefers artists with experience in cartooning. Works on assignment only. Buys freelance designs/illustrations mainly for greetings cards and T-shirts. Also uses freelance artists for calligraphy, P-O-P displays, paste-up and mechanicals. Considers pen & ink, watercolor, acrylics and colored pencil. Prefers humorous and "cartoons that will appeal to families. Must be cute, appealing, etc. No religious, sexual implications or off-beat humor." Produces material for all holidays and seasons. Contact only through artist's agent. Some

samples are filed; samples not filed are not returned. Responds only if interested. Write for appointment to show portfolio of original/final art, final reproduction/product, slides, tearsheets, color and b&w. Original artwork is not returned. "Payment depends upon the assignment, amount of work involved, production costs, etc. involved in the project." Pays after all sales are tallied. Buys all rights. For guidelines and sample cards, send $2.50 and #10 SASE.

Tips: Submit 6 months in advance. "Demonstrate an ability to follow directions exactly. Too many submit artwork that has no relationship to what we produce. No phone calls accepted. Follow directions given. Do not ignore them. We do not work with anyone who does not follow them."

CREATIF LICENSING CORP., 31 Old Town Crossing, Mt. Kisco NY 10549. (914)241-6211. E-mail: creatif @usa.net. Website: http://members.aol.com/creatiflic. President: Paul Cohen. Estab. 1975. Gift industry licensing agency. Publishes greeting cards, puzzles, posters, calendars, fabrics, home furnishings, all gifts. 50% of products are made for kids or have kids' themes.

Illustration: Needs freelance illustration for children's greeting cards, all gift and home furnishings. Makes many illustration assignments/month. To contact, send cover letter, résumé, client list, published samples, photocopies, portfolio, promo piece and SASE. Responds in 1 month. Materials returned with SASE; materials filed. For greeting cards, pays royalty and advance. For other artwork, pays royalty and advance. Pays on acceptance or publication. Artist's and submission guidelines are available on website. Does not accept images via e-mail.

Tips: Submit seasonal material 8-12 months in advance.

N: CURRENT, INC., 1005 E. Woodmen Rd., Colorado Springs CO 80920. (719)531-2087. Fax: (719)531-2564. E-mail: dmgrignano@currentinc.com. Website: www.currentcatalog.com. Editorial: Mar Porter. Art Manager: Dana Grignano. Estab. 1950. Greeting card company, paper products company. Publishes cards (classroom valentines), notecards, calendars, business-to-business papers, scrapbooking supplies, giftwraps etc. Products geared for all ages, children to adult. Greeting cards (thank you's, stationery), novelties (classroom valentines), calendars (kids activity calendars, teacher calendars). 50% of products are made for kids or have kid's themes.

Writing: Needs freelance writing for children's greeting cards and activity calendars. Makes 20 writing assignments/year. For greeting cards, accepts both rhymed and unrhymed verse ideas. To contact, send cover letter and writing samples. To query for specific ideas, submit idea on 3×5 cards. Responds in 2 weeks. Returns material accompanied by SASE. For greeting cards, pays flat fee of $25-150. Pays on publication. Credit line sometimes given. Writer's guidelines available for SASE.

Illustration: Needs freelance illustration for children's greeting cards. Makes 20 illustration assignments/month. Uses everything from charming and sweet to bright, bold, graphic, fun characters or sweet fuzzy characters. To contact, send published samples, photocopies and promo pieces. To query with specific ideas, submit idea with SASE. Materials returned with SASE; material filed. For greeting cards, pays flat fee of $50-500. Pays on publication or on acceptance. Buys all rights. Credit line sometimes given. Artist's guidelines available for SASE.

Photography: Buys stock and assigns work. Buys up to 60 stock images/year.

DESIGN DESIGN INC., P.O. Box 2266, Grand Rapids MI 49501. (616)774-2448. Fax: (616)774-4020. President: Don Kallil. Creative Director: Tom Vituj. Estab. 1986. Greeting card company. 5% of products are made for kids or have kids themes.

Writing: Needs freelance writing for children's greeting cards. Prefers both rhymed and unrhymed verse ideas. To contact, send cover letter and writing samples. Materials returned with SASE; materials not filed. For greeting cards, pays flat fee. Buys all rights or exclusive product rights; negotiable. No credit line given. Writer's guidelines for SASE.

Illustration: Needs freelance illustration for children's greeting cards and related products. To contact, send cover letter, published samples, color or b&w photocopies, color or b&w promo pieces or portfolio. Returns materials with SASE. Pays by royalty. Buys all rights or exclusive product rights; negotiable. Artist's guidelines available for SASE. Do not send original art.

Photography: Buys stock and assigns work. Looking for the following subject matter: babies, animals, dog, cats, humorous situations. Uses 4×5 transparencies or high quality 35mm slides. To contact, send cover letter with slides, stock photo list, color copies, published samples and promo piece. Materials returned with SASE; materials not filed. Pays royalties. Buys all rights or exclusive product rights; negotiable. Photographer's guidelines for SASE. Do not send original photography.

Tips: Seasonal material must be submitted 1 year in advance.

FAX-PAX USA, INC., 37 Jerome Ave., Bloomfield CT 06002. (860)242-3333. Fax: (860)242-7102. Editor: Stacey L. Savin. Contact: Mike Flynn. Estab. 1990. Buys 1 freelance project/year. Publishes art and history flash cards. Needs include US history, natural history.

Writing/Illustration: Buys all rights. Pays on publication. Cannot return material.

Tips: "We need concise, interesting, well-written 'mini-lessons' on various subjects including U.S. and natural history."

GALLERY GRAPHICS, INC., 2400 S. Hwy. 59, P.O. Box 502, Noel MO 64854-0502. (417)475-6191. Fax: (417)475-6494. E-mail: badgerow@gallerygraphics.com. Website: www.gallerygraphics.com. Marketing Director: Terri Galvin. Estab. 1979. Greeting card, paper products company. Specializes in products including prints, cards, calendars, stationery, magnets, framed items, books, flue covers and sachets. We market towards all age groups. Publishes reproductions of children's books from the 1800's. 10% of products are made for kids or have kid's themes.

Illustration: Needs freelance illustration for children's greeting cards, other children's products. Makes 8 illustration assignments/year. Prefers children, angels, animals in any medium. Uses color artwork only. To contact, send cover letter, published samples, photocopies (prefer color), promo pieces. Responds in 3 weeks. "We'll return materials at our cost. If artist can send something we can file, that would be ideal. I'll usually make copies." For greeting cards, pays flat fee of $100-700, or royalty of 5-7% for life of card. Pays on sales. Buys exclusive product rights. Credit line sometimes given.

Tips: "We've significantly increased our licensing over the last year. Most of these are set up on a 5% royalty basis. Submit various art subjects."

☑ **HOW RICH UNLIMITED**, LLC, 245 Eighth Ave., Suite 2304, New York NY 10016. (212)686-6281. Fax: (212)213-0055. E-mail: HowRichUnlimited@aol.com. Website: howrichunlimited.com. Owner: H.J. Fleischer. Contact: Mike Flynn. Toy designer, licensing agent and manufacturer. Designs, licenses, manufactures toys, gifts and related products. Manufactures novelties (educational, impulse, creative), puzzles, games; publishes booklets. 100% of products are made for kids or have kids' themes.

Illustration: Needs freelance illustration for toy concepts. Makes 12 illustration assignments/year. Uses both color and b&w artwork. To contact, send cover letter, résumé, published samples, portfolio, photocopies, promo pieces. To query with specific ideas, write to request disclosure form first. Responds in 3 weeks. Materials returned with SASE; materials filed. For other artwork, pays by the hour($10); negotiable royalty. Pays on acceptance. Credit line sometimes given.

Photography: Works on assignment only. Uses transparencies. To contact, send cover letter, published samples, portfolio, promo piece. Responds only if interested. Materials returned; materials filed. Pays on acceptance. Credit line sometimes given.

Tips: Submit seasonal material 6 months in advance. Concept submissions require prototype or detailed professionally presented illustrations. "Interested in unique toy/game/product concepts."

INTERCONTINENTAL GREETINGS LTD., 176 Madison Ave., New York NY 10016. (212)683-5830. Fax: (212)779-8564. Art Director: Haeran Park. Estab. 1964. 100% of material freelance written and illustrated. Intended for greeting cards, scholastic products (notebook covers, pencil cases), novelties (gift bags, mugs), tin gift boxes, shower and bedding curtains. 30-40% of products are made for kids or have kids' themes.

Writing: "We use very little writing except for humor." Makes 4 writing assignments/year. To contact, send cover letter, résumé, client list and writing samples with SASE. Responds in 6 weeks. Pays advance of $20-100 and royalty of 20% for life. Pays on publication. Contracts exclusive product rights. Credit line sometimes given.

Illustration: Needs children's greeting cards, notebook cover, photo albums, gift products. Makes 3 illustration assignments/month. Prefers primarily greeting card subjects, suitable for gift industry. To contact, send cover letter, résumé, client list, published samples, photocopies, slides and promo piece with SASE. Responds in 6 weeks. For greeting cards pays 20% royalty for life. For other artwork pays 20% royalty for life. Pays on publication. Buys exclusive product rights for contract period of 2 years. Credit line sometimes given.

Photography: Needs stylized and interesting still lifes, studio florals, all themed toward the paper and gift industry. Guidelines available for SASE.

Tips: Target group for juvenile cards: ages 1-10. Illustrators: "Use clean colors, not muddy or dark. Send a neat, concise sampling of your work. Include some color examples, a SASE to issue return of your samples if wanted."

☑ **INTERNATIONAL PLAYTHINGS, INC.**, 75D Lackawanna Ave., Parsippany NJ 07054-1712. (973)316-2500. Fax: (973)316-5883. E-mail: lindag@intplay.com. Website: www.intplay.com. Product Manager: Linda Golowko. Estab. 1968. Toy/game company. Distributes and markets children's toys, games and puzzles in specialty toy markets. 100% of products are made for kids or have kids' themes.

Illustration: Needs freelance illustration for children's puzzles and games. Makes 10-20 illustration assignments/year. Prefers fine-quality, original illustration for children's puzzles. Uses color artwork only. To contact, send published samples, slides, portfolio, or color photocopies or promo pieces. Responds in 1 month only if interested. Materials filed. For artwork, pays by the project (range: $500-2,000). Pays on publication. Buys one-time rights, negotiable.

**FOR EXPLANATIONS OF THESE SYMBOLS,
SEE THE INSIDE FRONT AND BACK COVERS OF THIS BOOK**

Tips: "Mail correspondence only, please. No phone calls. Send child-themed art, not cartoon-y. Use up-to-date themes and colors."

JILLSON & ROBERTS GIFT WRAPPINGS, 5 Watson Ave., Irvine CA 92618. (949)859-8781. Art Director: Josh Neufeld. Estab. 1973. Paper products company. Makes gift wrap/gift bags. 20% of products are made for kids or have kids' themes.

Illustration: Needs freelance illustration for children's gift wrap. Makes 6-12 illustration assignments/year. Wants children/baby/juvenile themes. To contact, send cover letter. Responds in 1 month. Returns material with SASE; materials filed. For wrap and bag designs, pays flat fee of $250. Pays on publication. Rights negotiable. Artist's guidelines for SASE.

Tips: Seasonal material should be submitted up to 3½ months in advance. "We produce two lines of gift wrap per year: one everyday line and one Christmas line. The closing date for everyday is June 30th and Christmas is September 15."

J.T. MURPHY COMPANY, 200 W. Fisher Ave., Philadelphia PA 19120. Greeting card company. Publishes greeting cards. 30% of products are made for kids or have kids' themes.

Writing: To contact, send writing samples. Materials returned with SASE. Pays on acceptance.

Illustration: Needs freelance illustration for children's greeting cards.

NOVO CARD PUBLISHERS, INC., 3630 W. Pratt Ave., Lincolnwood IL 60712. (847)763-0077. Fax: (847)763-0020. E-mail: novo@novocards.com. Contact: art production. Estab. 1926. Greeting card company. Company publishes greeting cards, note/invitation packs and gift envelopes for middle market. Publishes greeting cards (Novo Card/Cloud-9). 20% of products are made for kids or have kids' themes.

Writing: Needs freelance writing for children's greeting cards. Makes 400 writing assignments/year. Other needs for freelance writing include invitation notes. To contact send writing samples. To query with specific ideas, write to request disclosure form first. Responds in approximately 1 month only if interested. Materials returned only with SASE. For greeting cards, pays flat fee of $2/line. Pays on acceptance. Buys all rights. Credit line sometimes given. Writer's guidelines available for SASE.

Illustration: Needs freelance illustration for children's greeting cards. Makes 1,000 illustration assignments/year. Prefers just about all types: traditional, humor, contemporary, etc. To contact, send published samples, slides and color photocopies. To query with specific ideas write to request disclosure form first. Responds in approximately 1 month if interested. Materials returned with SASE. For greeting cards, pay negotiable. Pays on acceptance. Buys all greeting card and stationary rights. Credit line sometimes given. Artist's guidelines available for SASE.

Photography: Buys stock and assigns work. Buys more than 100 stock images/year. Wants all types. Uses color and b&w prints; 35mm transparencies. To contact, send slides, stock photo list, published samples, paper copies acceptable. Responds in approximately 1 month. Materials returned with SASE. Pays negotiable rate. Pays on acceptance. Buys all greeting card and stationary rights. Credit line sometimes given. Guidelines for SASE.

Tips: Submit seasonal material 10-12 months in advance. "Novo has extensive lines of greeting cards: everyday, seasonal (all) and alternative lives (over 24 separate lines of note card packs and gift enclosures). Our lines encompass all types of styles and images."

N: NRN DESIGNS, 5142 Argosy Ave., Long Beach CA 92649. (714)898-6363. Fax: (714)898-0015. Website: nrndesigns.com. Art Director: Linda Braun. Estab. 1984. Paper products company. Publishes imprintables. 25% of products are made for kids or have kid's themes.

Writing: Needs freelance writing for children's greeting cards. Responds in 1 month.

Illustration: Needs freelance illustration for children's imprintables. Uses color artwork only. To contact, send published samples. Responds in 2 months. Materials returned with SASE; materials filed.

Tips: Submit seasonal material anytime.

☑ P.S. GREETINGS/FANTUS PAPER PRODUCTS, 5730 North Tripp Ave., Chicago IL 60646. (773)267-6069 or (800)334-2141. Fax: (773)267-6055. Website: www.psg-fpp.com. Art Director: Jennifer Dodson. Estab. 1950. Greeting card company. Publishes boxed and individual counter greeting cards. Seasons include: Christmas, every major holiday and everyday. 30% of products are made for kids or have kid's themes.

Writing: Needs freelance writing for children's greeting cards. Makes 10-20 writing assignments/year. To contact, send writing samples. Responds in 1 month. Material returned only if accompanied with SASE. For greeting cards, pays flat fee/line. Pays on acceptance. Buys greeting card rights. Credit line given. Writer's guidelines free with SASE.

Illustration: Needs freelance illustration for children's greeting cards. Makes about 10-20 illustration assignments/year. Open to all mediums, all themes. To contact, send published samples, color promo pieces and color photocopies only. Responds in 1 month. Returns materials with SASE. For greeting cards, pays flat fee of $250-400. Pays on acceptance. Buys greeting card rights. Credit line given. Artist's guidelines free with SASE.

Photography: Buys photography from freelancers. Buys and assigns work. Buys 5-10 stock images/year. Makes 5-10 assignments/year. Wants florals, animals, seasonal (Christmas, Easter, valentines, etc.). Uses 35mm transparencies. To contact, send slides. Responds in 6 weeks. Materials returned with SASE; materials filed. Pays on acceptance. Buys greeting card rights. Credit line given. Photographer's guidelines free with SASE.
Tips: Seasonal material should be submitted 8 months in advance.

✓ **PLUM GRAPHICS INC.**, P.O. Box 136, Prince St. Station, New York NY 10012. (212)337-0999. Fax: (212)633-9910. E-mail: plumgraphi@aol.com. Owner: Yvette Cohen. Estab. 1983. Greeting card company. Produces die-cut greeting cards for ages 5-105. Publishes greeting cards, message boards and journals.
Writing: Needs freelance writing for greeting cards. Makes 4 writing assignments/year. Looks for "greeting card writing which is fun." To contact, send SASE for guidelines. Contact: Michelle Reynoso. Responds in 2 months. Materials returned with SASE; materials filed. For greeting cards, pays flat fee of $40. Pays on publication. Buys all rights. Writer's guidelines available for SASE.
Illustration: Needs freelance illustration for greeting cards. Makes 10-15 freelance illustration assignments/year. Prefers very tight artwork that is fun and realistic. Uses color artwork only. To contact, send b&w photocopies. Contact: Yvette Cohen. Responds only if interested. Materials returned with SASE; materials filed. For greeting cards, pays flat fee of $350-450 "plus $50 each time we reprint." Pays on publication. Buys exclusive product rights. Credit line given.
Tips: "Go to a store and look at our cards and style before submitting work."

RED FARM STUDIO, 1135 Roosevelt Ave., P.O. Box 347, Pawtucket RI 02862. (401)728-9300. Contact: Production Coordinator. Estab. 1949. Greeting card company. Publishes coloring books and paintables. 20% of products are made for kids or have kids' themes.
Illustration: Needs freelance illustration for tweens' and teens' greeting cards, coloring books and paintables. Makes 1 illustration assignment/month; 6-12/year. Any medium accepted. For first contact, request art guidelines with SASE. Responds in 1 month. Returns materials with SASE. Appropriate materials are kept on file. "We work on assignment using ink line work (coloring books) or pencil renderings (paintables)." Buys all rights. Credit line given, and artist may sign artwork. Artist's guidelines for SASE.
Tips: Majority of freelance assignments made during January-May/yearly. "Research companies before sending submissions to determine whether your styles are compatible."

RESOURCE GAMES, 2704 185th Ave. NE, Redmond WA 98052. (425)883-3143. Fax: (425)883-3136. Website: www.resourcegames.com. Owner: John Jaquet. Estab. 1987. Educational game manufacturer. Resource Games manufactures a line of high-quality geography theme board and card games for ages 6 and up. Publishes games. 100% of products made for kids or have kids' themes.
Tips: "We are always on the lookout for innovative educational games for the classroom and the home. If accepted, we enter into royalty agreements ranging from 5-10%."

Ⓝ ROYAL CONSUMER PRODUCTS, INC., 108 Main St., Norwalk CT 06851. (203)847-85800. Fax: (203)849-9177. E-mail: kwebdale@mafcote.com. Website: www.mafcote.com. Marketing, Consumer Products Division: Krista Webdale (writing). General Manager, Sonburn Papers: Steve Shopoff. Marketing (art/photography). Estab. 1890s. Paper products company. Produces social/designer stationery for imprinting and scrapbooking; ink jet papers for school, home and office use; posterboard to mass retail and schools; paper lace doilies and disposable kitchen accessories to hotels/airlines and at retail. Manufactured novelties (Royal Lace, Royal Brites ink jet papers) and stationery (Sonburn Designer Stationery and Social Papers). 40% of products are made for kids or have kid's themes.
Writing: Needs freelance writing for press releases and ads, direct mail pieces. Makes 6 writing assignments/year. To contact, send cover letter, résumé, client list, writing samples and fee schedule. To query for specific ideas, use IBM compatible programs only. Responds only if interested. Materials returned with SASE; material filed. For children's papers, pays flat fee of $50-450. For other writing, pays by the project (range: $50-250). Pays on acceptance. Buys all rights; negotiable. Credit line sometimes given.
Illustration: Needs freelance illustration for children's designer stationery and scrapbook papers. Makes 80-100 illustration assignments/year. Only accepts original hand drawn or hand painted designs—no computer-generated work accepted. Contact Steve Shopoff at Sonburn (800)527-7505. To contact, send cover letter, résumé, photocopies and promo pieces. Write to request disclosure form first. Responds only if interested. Materials returned with SASE; material filed. For greeting cards, pays flat fee of $150-250. For other artwork, pays by the project (range: $150). Buys exclusive product rights. Credit line sometimes given.
Photography: Buys stock and assigns work. Buys 4-5 stock images/year. Makes 7-10 assignments/year. Need photo of children using products for press releases, consumer interest for packaging, miscellaneous for contests, sweepstakes or direct mail. Uses color prints; and 35mm, 2¼ × 2¼ transparencies. To contact, send cover letter, stock photo list, published samples, client list and promo piece. Responds only if interested. Material returned with SASE; materials filed. Pays per photo (range: $20-200 for b&w, $20-200 for color); by the hour ($50-100); by the day ($400-800); by the project ($150-1,500). Pays on acceptance. Rights negotiable. Credit line sometimes given.

Tips: Submit seasonal material 6-8 months in advance. "Be persistent. Don't be turned off if we cannot use your work for months after initial contact. Be upbeat and friendly—makes it more appealing to develop work relationship."

SHULSINGER SALES, INC., 50 Washington St., Brooklyn NY 11201. (718)852-0042. Fax: (718)935-9691. President: Miriam Gutfeld. Estab. 1979. Greeting card, novelties and paper products company. "We are a Judaica company, distributing products such as greeting cards, books, paperware, puzzles, games, novelty items—all with a Jewish theme." Publishes greeting cards, novelties, coloring books, children's books, giftwrap, tableware and puzzles. 60% of products are made for kids or have kids' themes to party stories, temples, bookstores, supermarkets and chain stores.

Writing: Looks for greeting card writing which can be sent by children to adults and sent by adults to children (of all ages). Makes 10-20 freelance writing assignments/year. To contact, send cover letter. To query with specific ideas, write to request disclosure form first. Responds in 2 weeks. Materials returned with SASE; materials filed. For greeting cards, pays flat fee (this includes artwork). Pays on acceptance. Buys exclusive product rights.

Illustration: Needs freelance illustration for children's greeting cards, books, novelties, games. Makes 10-20 illustration assignments/year. "The only requirement is a Jewish theme." To contact, send cover letter and photocopies, color if possible. To query with specific ideas, write to request disclosure form first. Responds in 2 weeks. Returns materials with SASE; materials filed. For children's greeting cards, pays flat fee (this includes writing). For other artwork, pays by the project. Pays on acceptance. Buys exclusive product rights. Credit line sometimes given. Artist's guidelines not available.

Tips: Seasonal material should be submitted 6 months in advance. "An artist may submit an idea for any item that is related to our product line. Generally, there is an initial submission of a portfolio of the artist's work, which will be returned at the artist's expense. If the art is appropriate to our specialized subject matter, then further discussion will ensue regarding particular subject matter. We request a sampling of at least 10 pieces of work, in the form of tearsheets, or printed samples, or high quality color copies that can be reviewed and then kept on file if accepted. If art is accepted and published, then original art will be returned to artist. Shulsinger Sales, Inc. maintains the right to re-publish a product for a mutually agreed upon time period. We pay an agreed upon fee per project."

☑ STANDARD PUBLISHING, 8121 Hamilton Ave., Cincinnati OH 45231. (513)931-4050. Fax: (513)931-0950. Directors: Diane Stortz (children's series) and Ruth Frederick (church resources). Art Director: Colleen Davis. Estab. 1866. Publishes children's books and teacher helps for the religious market. 75% of products are made for kids or have kids' themes.

• Standard also has a listing in Book Publishers.

Writing: Considers Christian puzzle books, activity books and games. Responds in 3 months. Payment method varies. Credit line given.

Illustration: Needs freelance illustration for puzzle, activity books, teacher helps. Makes 6-10 illustration assignments/year. To contact, send cover letter and photocopies. Responds in 3 months if interested. Payment method varies. Credit line given.

Photography: Buys a limited amount of photos from freelancers. Wants mature, scenic and Christian themes.

Tips "Many of our projects are developed in-house and assigned. Study our catalog and products; visit Christian bookstores. We are currently looking for Bible-based word puzzles and activities."

TALICOR, INC., 4741 Murriet St., Chino CA 91710-5156. (909)517-1962. Fax: (909)517-1962. E-mail: webmaster@talicor.com. Website: www.talicor.com. President: Lew Herndon. Estab. 1971. Game and puzzle manufacturer. Publishes games and puzzles (adults' and children's). 70% of products are made for kids or have kids' themes.

Writing: Makes 1 writing assignment/month; 12/year.

Illustration: Needs freelance illustration for games and puzzles. Makes 12 illustration assignments/year. To contact, send promo piece. Responds in 6 months. Materials returned with SASE; materials filed. For artwork, pays by the hour, by the project or negotiable royalty. Pays on acceptance. Buys negotiable rights.

Photography: Buys stock and assigns work. Buys 6 stock images/year. Wants photos with wholesome family subjects. Makes 6 assignments/year. Uses 4×5 transparencies. To contact, send color promo piece. Responds only if interested. Materials returned with SASE; materials filed. Pays per photo, by the hour, by the day or by the project (negotiable rates). Pays on acceptance. Buys negotiable rights.

Tips: Submit seasonal material 6 months in advance.

Play Publishers & Producers

Writing plays for children and family audiences is a special challenge. Whether creating an original work or adapting a classic, plays for children must hold the attention of audiences that often include children and adults. Using rhythm, repetition and dramatic action are effective ways of holding the attention of kids. Pick subjects children can relate to, and never talk down to them.

Theater companies often have limited budgets so plays with elaborate staging and costumes often can't be produced. Touring companies want simple sets that can be moved easily. Keep in mind that they may have as few as three actors, so roles may have to be doubled up.

Many of the companies listed here produce plays with roles for adults and children, so check the percentage of plays written for adult and children's roles. Most importantly, study the types of plays a theater wants and doesn't want. Many name plays they've recently published or produced, and some have additional guidelines or information available. For more listings of theaters open to submissions of children's and adult material and information on contests and organizations for playwrights, consult *Dramatists Sourcebook* (Theatre Communications Group, Inc.).

Information on play publishers listed in the previous edition but not included in this edition of *Children's Writer's & Illustrator's Market* may be found in the General Index.

A.D. PLAYERS, 2710 W. Alabama, Houston TX 77098. (713)526-2721. Fax: (713)522-5475. E-mail: adplayer@hearn.org. Website: www.adplayers.org. Estab. 1967. Produces 4-5 children's plays/year in new Children's Theatre Series; 5 musicals/year. Produces children's plays for professional productions.
- A.D. Players has received the Dove family approval stamp; an award from the Columbia International Film & Video Festival; and a Silver Angel Award.

Needs: 99-100% of plays/musicals written for adult roles; 0-1% for juvenile roles. "Cast must utilize no more than five actors. Need minimal, portable sets for proscenium or arena stage with no fly space and no wing space." Does not want to see large cast or set costumes or New Age themes. Recently produced plays: *Samson: The Hair Off His Head*, by William Shryoch (courage and obedience for preK-grade 6); *The Wizard of Oz*, by Danny Siebert (new adaptation for preK-grade 6).

How to Contact: Send script with SASE. No tapes or pictures. Will consider simultaneous submissions and previously performed work. Responds in 9 months.

Terms: Buys some residual rights. Pay negotiated. Submissions returned with SASE.

Tips: "Children's musicals tend to be large in casting requirements. For those theaters with smaller production capabilities, this can be a liability for a script. Try to keep it small and simple, especially if writing for theaters where adults are performing for children. We are interested in material that reflects family values, emphasizes the importance of responsibility in making choices, encourages faith in God and projects the joy and fun of telling a story."

ALABAMA SHAKESPEARE FESTIVAL, #1 Festival Dr., Montgomery AL 36117. (334)271-5300. Fax: (334)271-5348. E-mail: pr4bard@wsnet.com. Website: www.asf.net. Artistic Director: Kent Thompson. Estab. 1972. Produces 1 children's play/year.

Needs: Produces children's plays for professional LORT (League of Regional Theaters) theatre. 90% of plays/musicals written for adult roles; 10% for juvenile roles. Must have moderate sized casts (2-10 characters); have two stages (750 seat house/250 seat house). Interested in works for the Southern Writers' Project (contact ASF for information). Does not want to see plays exclusively for child actors. Recently produced plays: *Wiley and the Hairy Man*, by Susan Zeder (southern folk tale for elementary ages); *Androcles and the Lion*, by Aurand Harris (folktale for elementary ages).

How to Contact: Plays: Query first with synopsis, character breakdown and set description; scripts which meet/address the focus of the Southern Writers' Project. Musicals: Query with synopsis, character breakdown and set description; scripts which meet/address the focus of the Southern Writers' Project. Will consider simultaneous submissions and previously performed work. Responds in 1 year.

Terms: Submissions returned with SASE.

Tips: "Created in 1991 by Artistic Director Kent Thompson, the Alabama Shakespeare Festival's Southern Writers' Project is an exploration and celebration of its rich Southern cultural heritage. In an attempt to reach this goal the project seeks: to provide for the growth of a 'new' voice for Southern writers and artists; to encourage new works dealing with Southern issues and topics including those that emphasize African American experiences; to create theatre that speaks in a special way to ASF's unique and racially diverse audiences. In this way the Southern Writers' Project strives to become a window to the complexities and beauty found in this celebrated region of our country, the South."

☑ AMERICAN STAGE, P.O. Box 1560, St. Petersburg FL 33731. (727)823-1600. Website: www.americansta ge.org. Artistic Director: Ken Mitchell. Managing Director: Lee Manwaring Lowry. Estab. 1977. Produces 3 children's plays/year. Produces children's plays for professional children's theater program, mainstage, school tour, performing arts halls.

Needs: Limited by budget and performance venue. Subject matter: classics and original work for children (ages K-12) and families. Recently produced plays: *Schoolhouse Rock Live!*, by Lynn Ahrens and Bob Borough (5-adult); *The Gifts of the Magi*, by Mark St. Germain and Randy Courts (6-adults). Does not want to see plays that look down on children. Approach must be that of the child or fictional beings or animals.

How to Contact: Query with synopsis, character breakdown and set description. Will consider simultaneous submissions and previously performed work.

Terms: Purchases "professional rights." Pays writers in royalties (6-8%); $25-35/performance. SASE for return of submission.

Tips: Sees a move in plays toward basic human values, relationships and multicultural communities.

Ⓝ APPLE TREE THEATRE, 595 Elm Place, Suite 210, Highland Park IL 60035. (847)432-8223. Fax: (847)432-5214. Produces 3 children's plays/year.

Needs: Produces professional, daytime and educational outreach programs for grades 4-9. 98% of plays written for adult roles; 2% for juvenile roles. Uses a unit set and limited to 9 actors. No musicals. Straight plays only. Does not want to see: "children's theater," i.e. . . . Peter Rabbit, Snow White. Material *must* be based in social issues. Recently produced plays: *Devil's Arithmetic*, adapted from the novel by Jane Yolen (about the Holocaust, ages 10-up); *Roll of Thunder, Hear My Cry*, adapted from the novel by Mildred Taylor (about Civil rights, racial discrimination in Mississippi in 1930s, ages 10-up).

How to Contact: Query first. Query with synopsis, character breakdown and set description. Will consider simultaneous submissions and previously performed work. Responds in 2 months.

Terms: Pay negotiated per contract. Submissions returned with SASE.

Tips: "Never send an unsolicited manuscript. Include reply postcard for queries."

BAKER'S PLAYS, P.O. Box 699222, Quincy MA 02269-9222. (617)745-0805. Fax: (617)745-9891. E-mail: info@bakersplays.com. Website: www.bakersplays.com. Associate Editor: Raymond Pape. Estab. 1845. Publishes 20 plays/year; 2 musicals/year.

Needs: Adaptations of both popular and lesser known folktales. Subject matter: full lengths for family audience and full lengths and one act plays for teens." Recently published plays: *Broadway Cafe*, by Cohen and Spencer (musical for young adults for ages 12-25); *Willabella Witch's Last Spell*, by Thomas Hischar (a witch wants to quit her job for ages 8-18).

How to Contact: Submit complete ms, score and tape of songs. Responds in 6-8 months.

Terms: Obtains worldwide rights. Pays writers in production royalties (amount varies) and book royalties.

Tips: "Know the audience you're writing for before you submit your play anywhere. 90% of the plays we reject are not written for our market. When writing for children, never be afraid to experiment with language, characters or story. They are fertile soil for fresh, new ideas."

Ⓝ BARTER THEATRE EDUCATION WING, P.O. Box 867, Abingdon VA 24212. (540)628-2281, ext. 318. Fax: (540)628-4551. E-mail: btplayers@naxs.net. Website: www.bartertheatre.com. Artistic Director: Richard Rose. Education Director: Jeremy Baker. Estab. 1933. Produces 2-4 children's plays and 1 children's musical/ year.

Needs: "We produce 'By Kids for Kids' productions as well as professional and semi-professional children's productions. 5-10% of plays/musicals written for adult roles; 90% written for juvenile roles. Recently produced plays: *Sleeping Beauty* (fairytale for all ages); and *Winnie the Pooh* (classic for all ages).

How to Contact: Query with synopsis, character breakdown and set description. Will consider simultaneous submissions and previously performed work. Responds only if interested.

Terms: Pays for performance ($20-60). Submissions returned with SASE.

Tips: "Find creative, interesting material for children K-12. Don't talk below the audience."

BILINGUAL FOUNDATION OF THE ARTS, 421 N. Avenue 19th, Los Angeles CA 90031. (323)225-4044. Fax: (323)225-1250. E-mail: bfateatro@aol.com. Artistic Director: Margarita Galban. Contact: Agustín Coppola, dramaturg. Estab. 1973. Produces 6 children's plays/year; 4 children's musicals/year.

Needs: Produces children's plays for professional productions. 60% of plays/musicals written for adult roles; 40% for juvenile roles. No larger than 8 member cast. Recently produced plays: *Second Chance*, by A. Cardona and A. Weinstein (play about hopes and fears in every teenager for teenagers); *Choices*, by Gannon Daniels (violence prevention, teens).

How to Contact: Plays: Query with synopsis, character breakdown and set description and submit complete ms. Musicals: Query with synopsis, character breakdown and set description and submit complete ms with score. Will consider simultaneous submissions and previously performed work. Responds in 6 months.

Terms: Pays royalty; per performance; buys material outright; "different with each play."

Tips: "The plays should reflect the Hispanic experience in the U.S."

☑ **BIRMINGHAM CHILDREN'S THEATRE**, P.O. Box 1362, Birmingham AL 35201-1362. (205)458-8181. Fax: (205)458-8895. E-mail: bertb@bct123.org. Website: www.bct123.org. Managing Director: Bert Brosowsky. Estab. 1947. Produces 8-10 children's plays/year; some children's musicals/year.

Needs: "BCT is an adult professional theater performing for youth and family audiences September-May." 99% of plays/musicals written for adult roles; 1% for juvenile roles. "Our 'Wee Folks' Series is limited to four cast members and should be written with preschool-grade 1 in mind. We prefer interactive plays for this age group. We commission plays for our 'Wee Folks' Series (preschool-grade 1), our Children's Series (K-6) and our Young Adult Series (6-12)." Recently produced plays: *Queen of Hearts*, by Jean Pierce (pre-1st grade); *Thomas Edison: Wizard at Work*, by Joe Zelner (4th-8th grade). No adult language. Will consider musicals, interactive theater for Wee Folks Series. Prefer children's series and young adult series limited to 4-7 cast members.

How to Contact: Query first, query with synopsis, character breakdown and set description. Responds in 4 months.

Terms: Buys negotiable rights. Submissions returned with SASE.

Tips: "We would like our commissioned scripts to teach as well as entertain. Keep in mind the age groups (defined by each series) that our audience is composed of. Send submissions to the attention of Bert Brosowsky, managing director."

CALIFORNIA THEATRE CENTER, P.O. Box 2007, Sunnyvale CA 94087. (408)245-2979. Fax: (408)245-0235. E-mail: ctc@ctcinc.org. Website: www.ctcinc.org. Resident Director: Will Huddleston. Estab. 1975. Produces 15 children's plays and 1 musical for professional productions.

Needs: 75% of plays/musicals written for adult roles; 20% for juvenile roles. Prefers material suitable for professional tours and repertory performance; one-hour time limit, limited technical facilities. Recently produced *Most Valuable Player*, by Mary Hall Surface (U.S. history for grades 3 and up); *Sleeping Beauty*, by Gayle Cornelison (fairy tale for ages K-5).

How to Contact: Query with synopsis, character breakdown and set description. Send to: Will Huddleston. Will consider previously performed work. Responds in 6 months.

Terms: Rights negotiable. Pays writers royalties; pays $35-50/performance. Submissions returned with SASE.

Tips: "We sell to schools, so the title and material must appeal to teachers who look for things familiar to them. We look for good themes, universality. Avoid the cute."

☑ **CHILDREN'S STORY SCRIPTS, Baymax Productions**, PMB 130, 2219 W. Olive Ave., Burbank CA 91506-2648. (818)787-5584. E-mail: baymax@earthlink.net. Editor: Deedra Bebout. Estab. 1990. Produces 1-10 children's scripts/year.

Needs: "Except for small movements and occasionally standing up, children remain seated in Readers Theatre fashion." Publishes scripts sold primarily to schools or wherever there's a program to teach or entertain children. "All roles read by children except K-2 scripts, where kids have easy lines, leader helps read the narration. Prefer multiple cast members, no props or sets." Subject matter: scripts on all subjects that dovetail with classroom subjects. Targeted age range—K-8th grade, 5-13 years old. Recently published plays: *A Clever Fox*, by Mary Ellen Holmes (about using one's wits, grades 2-4); *Memories of the Pony Express*, by Sharon Gill Askelson (grades 5-8). No stories that preach a point, no stories about catastrophic disease or other terribly heavy topics, no theatrical scripts without narrative prose to move the story along, no monologues or 1-character stories.

How to Contact: Submit complete ms. Will consider simultaneous submissions and previously performed work (if rights are available). Responds in 2 weeks.

Terms: Purchases all rights; authors retain copyrights. "We add support material and copyright the whole package." Pays writers in royalties (10-15% on sliding scale, based on number of copies sold). SASE for reply and return of submission.

Tips: "We're only looking for stories related to classroom studies—educational topics with a freshness to them. Our scripts mix prose narration with character dialogue—we do not publish traditional, all-dialogue plays." Writer's guidelines packet available for business-sized SASE with 2 first-class stamps. Guidelines explain what Children's Story Scripts are, give 4-page examples from 2 different scripts, give list of suggested topics for scripts.

CIRCA '21 DINNER THEATRE, P.O. Box 3784, Rock Island IL 61204-3784. (309)786-2667. Fax: (309)786-4119. Website: circa21.com. Producer: Dennis Hitchcock. Estab. 1977. Produces 3 children's musicals/year.

Needs: Produces children's plays for professional productions. 95% of musicals written for adult roles; 5% written for juvenile roles. "Prefer a cast of four to eight—no larger than ten. Plays are produced on mainstage sets." Recently produced plays: *Aladdin and Little Mermaid*, by Ted Morris and Bill Johnson (ages 5-12).
How to Contact: Send complete script with audiotape of music. Responds in 3 months.
Terms: Payment negotiable.

☑ **I.E. CLARK PUBLICATIONS**, P.O. Box 246, Schulenburg TX 78956-0246. (979)743-3232. Fax: (979)743-4765. E-mail: ieclark@cvtv.net. General Manager: Donna Cozzaglio. Estab. 1956. Publishes 3 or more children's plays/year; 1 or 2 children's musicals/year.
Needs: Publishes plays for all ages. Published plays: *Little Women*, by Thomas Hischak (dramatization of the Alcott novel for family audiences); *Heidi*, by Ann Pugh, music by Betty Utter (revision of our popular musical dramatization of the Johanna Spyri novel). Does not want to see plays that have not been produced.
How to Contact: Submit complete ms and audio or video tape. Will consider simultaneous submissions and previously performed work. Responds in 4 months.
Terms: Pays writers in negotiable royalties. SASE for return of submission.
Tips: "We publish only high-quality literary works. Request a copy of our writer's guidelines before submitting. Please send only one manuscript at a time and be sure to include videos and audiotapes."

COLUMBIA ENTERTAINMENT COMPANY, % Betsy Phillips, 309 Parkade, Columbia MO 65202-1447. (573)874-5628. Artistic Director: Betsy Phillips. Estab. 1988. Produces 2-4 children's plays/year; 0-1 children's musicals/year.
Needs: "We produce children's theatre plays. Our theatre school students act all the roles. We cast adult and children roles with children from theatre school. Each season we have 5 plays done by adults (kid parts possible)—3 theatre school productions. We need large cast plays-20+, as plays are produced by theater school classes (ages 12-14). Any set changes are completed by students in the play." Musical needs: Musicals must have songs written in ranges children can sing. Recently produced: *Comedia Del Delight*, by Claudia Haas and Richard Cash (a spoof of 16th century Italian commedia, all ages).
How to Contact: Plays: Submit complete ms; use SASE to get form. Musicals: Submit complete ms and score; tape of music must be included, use SASE to get entry form. Will consider simultaneous submissions and previously performed work. Responds in 2-6 months.
Terms: Buys production (sans royalties) rights on mss. "We have production rights sans royalties for one production. Production rights remain with author." Pays $250 1st prize. Submissions returned with SASE.
Tips: "Please write a play/musical that appeals to all ages. We always need lots of parts, especially for girls."

Ⓝ **CONNECTICUT STRATFORD SHAKESPEARE FESTIVAL THEATRE**, 1850 Elm St., Stratford CT 06615. (203)378-1200 ext. 103. Fax: (203)378-9777. E-mail: joeywish@hotmail.com or /dpict@aol.com. Website: www.stratfordfeset.com. Artistic Director: Louis S. Burke. Re-estab. 2000. Planning to produce 2-3 children's plays/year; at least 1 children's musical/year.
Needs: Produces children's plays for professional productions. 80% of plays/musicals written for adult roles; 20% for juvenile roles. Musical needs: Prefers musicals with name recognition—classic stories, or well-known modern children's tales. Recently produced plays: *Babe, the Sheep-Pig*, by David Wood (based on the book from which the film was based for all ages); *The Princess and the Pea*, by Joey Wishnia (for future production, based on the Hans C. Andersen story for all ages).
How to Contact: Plays: Query with synopsis, character breakdown and set description; and a few pages to assess the writing (dialog sample). Musicals: Query with synopsis, character breakdosn and set description; some dialog pages and a sample of at least 2 songs on cassette or CD. Will consider simultaneous submissions, electronic submissions via disk/modem, previously performed work. Responds in 6-8 weeks.
Terms: Rights negotiable Lort B contract.

CONTEMPORARY DRAMA SERVICE, Division of Meriwether Publishing Ltd., 885 Elkton Dr., Colorado Springs CO 80907-3557. (719)594-4422. Fax: (719)594-9916. E-mail: merpcds@aol.com. Website: www.meriwe therpublishing.com. Executive Editor: Arthur L. Zapel. Estab. 1979. Publishes 60 children's plays/year; 15 children's musicals/year.
Needs: Prefer shows with a large cast. 50% of plays/musicals written for adult roles; 50% for juvenile roles. Recently published plays: *The Night the Animals Sang*, by Katherine Barb (Sunday school pageant for ages 10-12); *Fairy Tales Go to Court*, by Steve and Laura Dingledine(fairy tale spoof/satire for middle school grades). "We publish church plays for elementary level for Christmas and Easter. Most of our secular plays are for teens or college level." Does not want to see "full-length, three-act plays unless they are adaptations of classic works or have unique comedy appeal."
How to Contact: Query with synopsis, character breakdown and set description; "query first if a musical." Will consider simultaneous submissions or previously performed work. Responds in 1 month.
Terms: Purchases first rights. Pays writers royalty (10%) or buys material outright for $200-1,000. SASE for return of submission.

Tips: "If the writer is submitting a musical play, an audiocassette of the music should be sent. We prefer plays with humorous action. We like comedies, spoofs, satires and parodies of known works. A writer should provide credentials of plays published and produced. Writers should not submit items for the elementary age level."

N! DALLAS CHILDREN'S THEATER, 2215 Cedar Springs, Dallas TX 75201. Website: www.dct.org. Artistic Director: Robyn Flatt. Estab. 1984. Produces 10 children's plays/year.
Needs: Produces children's plays for professional theater. 80% of plays/musicals written for adult roles; 20% for juvenile roles. Prefer cast size between 8-12. Musical needs: "We do produce musical works, but prefer nonmusical. Availability of music tracks is a plus." Does not want to see: anything not appropriate for a youth/family audience. Recently produced plays: *Bless Cricket, Toothpaste, and Tommy Tune*, by Linda Daugherty (explores a young girl's relationship with her older brother who has Down Syndrome); *Island of the Blue Dolphins*, by Burgess Clark based on book by Scott O'Dell (survival story of a young Indian girl living alone for 18 years on a deserted island. Based on popular youth novel.)
How to Contact: Plays: Query with synopsis, character breakdown and set description. Musicals: Query with synopsis, character breakdown and set description. Will consider previously performed work. Responds only if interested.
Terms: Rights are negotiable. Pay is negotiable. Submissions returned with SASE.
Tips: "We are most interested in substantive works for a student/youth/family audience. Material which enlightens aspects of the global community, diverse customs and perspectives, adaptations of classical and popular literature, myth, and folk tale. Topics which focus on the contemporary concerns of youth, families, and our diverse communities are also of great interest. Full-length works are preferred rather than one-acts or classroom pieces."

DRAMATIC PUBLISHING, INC., 311 Washington St., Woodstock IL 60098. (815)338-7170. Fax: (815)338-8981. E-mail: plays@dramaticpublishing.com. Website: www.dramaticpublishing.com. Acquisitions Editor: Linda Habjan. Estab. 1885. Publishes 10-15 children's plays/year; 4-6 children's musicals.
Needs: Recently published: *The Cay*, by Dr. Gayle Cornelison and Robert Taylor; *The Dream Thief*, by Robert Schenkkan (fantasy classic by Pulitzer-prize-winning author); and *Alexander and the Terrible, Horrible, No Good, Very Bad Day*, book lyrics by Judith Viorst and Shelly Markham (for family audiences).
How to Contact: Submit complete ms/score and cassette/video tape (if a musical); include SASE if materials are to be returned. Responds in 6 months. Pays writers in royalties.
Tips: "Scripts should be from ½ to 1½ hours long and not didactic or condescending. Original plays dealing with hopes, joys and fears of today's children are preferred to adaptations of old classics."

N! DRAMATICS MAGAZINE, 2343 Auburn Ave., Cincinnati OH 45219-2815. (513)421-3900. Fax: (513)421-7077. Website: www.etassoc.org. Assistant Editor: Laura C. Kelley. Estab. 1929. Publishes 6 children's plays/year.
Needs: Most of plays written for high school actors. 14-18 years old (grades 9-12) appropriate for high school production and study.
How to Contact: Plays: Submit complete ms. Musicals: Not accepted. Will consider simultaneous submissions, electronic submissions via disk/modem, previously performed work. Responds in 3 months.
Terms: Buys one-time publication rights. Payment varies. Submissions returned with SASE.
Tips: Consider our readers, who are savvy high school theater students and teachers.

☑ EARLY STAGES CHILDREN'S THEATRE @ STAGES REPERTORY THEATRE, 3201 Allen Parkway, Suite 101, Houston TX 77019. (713)527-0220. Fax: (713)527-8669. E-mail: chesleyk@stagestheatre.com. Artistic Director: Chesley Krohn. Early Stages Director: Chesley Krohn. Estab. 1978. Produces 5 children's plays/year; 1-2 children's musicals/year.
Needs: In-house professional children's theatre. 100% of plays/musicals written for adult roles. Cast size must be 8 or less. Performances are in 2 theaters—Arena has 230 seats; Thrust has 180 seats. Musical needs: Shows that can be recorded for performance; no live musicians. Recently produced plays: *The Firebird: A Russian Fairy Tale*, by Kate Pogue (story of courage, for ages 4 yr.-adult); *Tombigee: The Spirit of the Swamp*, by Nancy Hovasse/Bruce Halverson (ecology—an endangered swamp, for ages 4-adult).
How to Contact: Plays/musicals: Query with synopsis, character breakdown and set description. Will consider simultaneous submissions and previously performed work. Responds only if interested.
Terms: Mss optioned exclusively. Pays 3-8% royalties. Submissions returned with SASE.
Tips: "Select pieces that are intelligent, as well as entertaining, and that speak to a child's potential for understanding. We are interested in plays/musicals that are imaginative and open to full theatrical production."

N! EL CENTRO SU TEATRO, 4725 High, Denver CO 80216. (303)296-0219. Fax: (303)296-4614. Artistic Director: Anthony J. Garcia. Estab. 1971. Produces 2 children's plays/year.
Needs: "We are interested in plays by Chicanos or Latinos that speak to that experience. We do not produce standard musicals. We are a culturally specific company." Recently produced *Joaquim's Christmas*, by Anthony J. Garcia (children's Christmas play for ages 7-15); and *The Dragonslayer*, by Silviana Woods (young boy's relationship with grandfather for ages 7-15). Does not want to see "cutesy stuff."

How to Contact: Query with synopsis, character breakdown and set description. Will consider simultaneous submissions and previously performed work. Responds in 6 months. Buys regional rights.
Terms: Pays writers per performance: $35 1st night, $25 subsequent. Submissions returned with SASE.
Tips: "People should write within their realm of experience but yet push their own boundaries. Writers should approach social issues within the human experience of their character."

ELDRIDGE PUBLISHING CO. INC., P.O. Box 1595, Venice FL 34284-1595. (941)496-4679. Fax: (941)493-9680. E-mail: info@histage.com. Website: www.histage.com or www.95church.com. Editor: Nancy Vorhis. Estab. 1906. Publishes approximately 25 children's plays/year; 4-5 children's musicals/year.
Needs: Prefers simple staging; flexible cast size. "We publish for junior and high school, community theater and children's theater (adults performing for children), all genres, also religious plays." Recently published plays: *Oliver T*, by Craig Sodaro ("Oliver Twist" reset behind 1950s TV for ages 12-14); *teensomething*, book, music, lyrics by Michael Mish (a revue of teen life for ages 12-19). Prefers work which has been performed or at least had a staged reading.
How to Contact: Submit complete ms, score and tape of songs (if a musical). Will consider simultaneous submissions ("please let us know, however"). Responds in 3 months.
Terms: Purchases all dramatic rights. Pays writers royalties of 50%; 10% copy sales; buys material outright for religious market.
Tips: "Try to have your work performed, if at all possible, before submitting. We're always on the lookout for comedies which provide a lot of fun for our customers. But other more serious topics which concern teens, as well as intriguing mysteries and children's theater programs are of interest to us as well. We know there are many new talented playwrights out there, and we look forward to reading their fresh scripts."

ENCORE PERFORMANCE PUBLISHING, P.O. Box 692, Orem UT 84059. (801)225-0605. Fax: (807)765-0489. E-mail: encoreplay@aol.com. Website: www.Encoreplay.com. Contact: Mike Perry. Estab. 1978. Publishes 20-30 children's plays/year; 10-20 children's musicals/year.
Needs: Prefers close to equal male/female ratio if possible. Adaptations for K-12 and older. 60% of plays written for adult roles; 40% for juvenile roles. Recently published plays: *Boy Who Knew No Fear*, by G. Riley Mills/Mark Levenson (adaptation of fairy tale, ages 8-16); *Two Chains*, by Paul Burton (about drug abuse, ages 11-18).
How to Contact: Query first with synopsis, character breakdown, set description and production history. Will only consider previously performed work. Responds in 2 months.
Terms: Purchases all publication and production rights. Author retains copyright. Pays writers in royalties (50%). SASE for return of submission.
Tips: "Give us issue and substance, be controversial without offense. Use a laser printer! Don't send an old manuscript. Make yours look the most professional."

N: FLORIDA STUDIO THEATRE, 1241 N. Palm Ave., Sarasota FL 34236. (941)366-9017. Artistic Director: Richard Hopkins. Estab. 1980. Produces 3 children's plays/year; 1-3 children's musicals/year.
Needs: Produces children's plays for professional productions. 50% of plays/musicals written for adult roles; 50% for juvenile roles. "Prefer small cast plays that use imagination more than heavy scenery." Will consider simultaneous submissions and previously performed work.
How to Contact: Query with synopsis, character breakdown and set description. Responds in 3 months. Rights negotiable. Pay negotiable. Submissions returned with SASE.
Tips: "Children are a tremendously sophisticated audience. The material should respect this."

THE FOOTHILL THEATRE COMPANY, P.O. Box 1812, Nevada City CA 95959-1812. (530)265-9320. Fax: (530)265-9325. E-mail: ftc@foothilltheatre.org. Website: www.foothilltheatre.org. Literary Manager: Gary Wright. Estab. 1977. Produces 0-2 children's plays/year; 0-1 children's musicals/year. Professional nonprofit theater.
Needs: 95% of plays/musicals written for adult roles; 5% for juvenile roles. "Small is better, but will consider anything." Produced *Peter Pan*, by J.M. Barrie (kids vs. grownups, for all ages); *Six Impossible Things Before Breakfast*, by Lee Potts & Marilyn Hetzel (adapted from works of Lewis Carroll, for all ages). Does not want to see traditional fairy tales.
How to Contact: Query with synopsis, character breakdown and set description. Will consider simultaneous submissions and previously performed work. Responds in 6 months.
Terms: Buys negotiable rights. Payment method varies. Submissions returned with SASE.
Tips: "Trends in children's theater include cultural diversity, real life issues (drug use, AIDS, etc.), mythological themes with contemporary resonance. Don't talk down to or underestimate children. Don't be preachy or didactic—humor is an excellent teaching tool."

N: SAMUEL FRENCH, INC., 45 W. 25th St., New York NY 10010. (212)206-8990. Fax: (212)206-1429. Senior Editor: Lawrence Harbison. Estab. 1830. Publishes 2 or 3 children's plays/year; "variable number of musicals."

Needs: Subject matter: "all genres, all ages. No puppet plays. No adaptations of any of those old 'fairy tales.' No 'Once upon a time, long ago and far away.' No kings, princesses, fairies, trolls, etc."
How to Contact: Submit complete ms and demo tape (if a musical). Responds in 8 months.
Terms: Purchases "publication rights, amateur and professional production rights, option to publish next 3 plays." Pays writers "book royalty of 10%; variable royalty for professional and amateur productions. SASE for return of submissions.
Tips: "Children's theater is a very tiny market, as most groups perform plays they have created themselves or have commissioned."

HAYES SCHOOL PUBLISHING CO. INC., 321 Pennwood Ave., Wilkinsburg PA 15221. (412)371-2373. Fax: (412)371-6408. Estab. 1940.
Needs: Wants to see supplementary teaching aids for grades K-12. Interested in all subject areas, especially music, foreign language (French, Spanish, Latin), early childhood education.
How to Contact: Query first with table of contents, sample page of activities. Will consider simultaneous and electronic submissions. Responds in 6 weeks.
Terms: Purchases all rights. Work purchased outright. SASE for return of submissions.

HEUER PUBLISHING COMPANY, P.O. Box 248, Cedar Rapids IA 52406. (319)364-6311. Fax: (319)364-1771. E-mail: editor@hitplays.com. Website: www.hitplays.com. Associate Editor: Geri Albrecht. Estab. 1928. Publishes 10-15 plays/year for young audiences and community theaters; 5 musicals/year.
Needs: "We publish plays and musicals for schools and community theatres (amateur)." 100% for juvenile roles. Single sets preferred. Props should be easy to find and costumes, other than modern dress, should be simple and easy to improvise. Stage effects requiring complex lighting and/or mechanical features should be avoided. Musical needs: "We need musicals with large, predominantly female casts. We publish plays and musicals for middle, junior and senior high schools." Recently published plays: *Mushroom Blues*, by Ray Sheers (Marx Brothers style comedy in three acts for all ages); *Lost City of the Nunus*, by Martin Follose (group of young archaeologists find adventure deep in the jungle in this three act comedy for all ages).
How to Contact: Plays: Query with synopsis. Musicals: Query with synopsis. Will consider simultaneous submissions and previously performed work. Responds in 2 months.
Terms: Buys amateur rights. Pays royalty or purchases work outright. Submissions returned with SASE.
Tips: "We sell almost exclusively to junior and smaller senior high schools so the subject matter and language should be appropriate for schools and young audiences."

⚄ LAGUNA PLAYHOUSE YOUTH THEATRE, P.O. Box 1747, Laguna Beach CA 92652. (949)497-2787. Fax: (949)376-8185. E-mail: jlauderdale@lagunaplayhouse.com. Artistic Director: Joe Lauderdale. Estab. 1986. Produces 6-8 children's plays/year; 1-2 children's musicals/year.
Needs: The Laguna Playhouse is an L.R.C theatre company with an amateur youth theatre. 40% of plays/musicals written for adult roles; 60% for juvenile roles. "We especially look for small touring shows based on existing children's literature." Musical needs: Small combos of 4-7 people with some doubling of instruments possible. Recently produced plays: *Charlotte's Web*, by Joseph Robinette (friendship, family); *45 Minutes From Broadway*, by George M. Cohan adapted by June Walker Rogers (classic musical, family).
How to Contact: Submit letter of intent and synopsis. Musicals should also submit recording. Responds in 6 months.
Terms: Pays 5-8% royalties.
Tips: "Although the majority of our work is literary based and for younger audiences, we produce at least one original work that is targeted for junior high and high school. This piece for older audiences should be educational, enlightening and entertaining."

☑ NEBRASKA THEATRE CARAVAN, 6915 Cass St., Omaha Ne 68132. (402)553-4890, ext. 154. Fax: (402)553-6288. E-mail: caravan@omahaplayhouse.com. Director: Marya Lucca-Thyberg. Estab. 1976. Produces 2 children's plays/year; 1-2 children's musicals/year.
Needs: Produces children's plays for professional productions with a company of 5-6 actors touring. 100% of plays/musicals written for adult roles; setting must be adaptable for easy touring. 75 minute show for grades 7-12; 60 minutes for elementary. Musical need: 1 piano or keyboard accompaniment. Recently produced plays: *A Thousand Cranes*, by Kathryn Schultz Miller (Sadako Susaki, for ages K-8).
How to Contact: Plays: query with synopsis, character breakdown and set description. Musicals: query first. Will consider simultaneous submissions and previously performed work. Responds in 3 months.
Terms: Pays $35-40/performance; pays commission—option 1—own outright, option 2—have right to produce at any later date—playwright has right to publish and produce. Submissions returned with SASE.
Tips: "Be sure to follow guidelines."

☑ THE NEW CONSERVATORY THEATRE CENTER, 25 Van Ness Ave., San Francisco CA 94102-6033. (415)861-4914. Fax: (415)861-6988. E-mail: nctcsf@yahoo.com. Website: www.nctcsf.org. Executive Director: Ed Decker. Estab. 1981. Produces 6 children's plays/year; 1 children's musical/year.

Needs: Limited budget and small casts only. Produces children's plays as part of "a professional theater arts training program for youths ages 4-19 during the school year and 2 summer sessions. The New Conservatory also produces educational plays for its touring company. We do not want to see any preachy or didactic material." Recently produced plays: *Aesop's Funky Fables*, adapted by Dyan McBride (fables, for ages 4-9); *A Little Princess*, by Frances Hodgson Burnett, adapted by June Walker Rogers (classic story of a young girl, for ages, 5-10).

How to Contact: Query with synopsis, character breakdown and set description, or submit complete ms and score. Responds in 3 months.

Terms: Rights purchased negotiable. Pays writers in royalties. SASE for return of submission.

Tips: "Wants plays with name recognition, i.e., *The Lion, the Witch and the Wardrobe* as well as socially relevant issues. Plays should be under 50 minutes in length."

NEW PLAYS INCORPORATED, P.O. Box 5074, Charlottesville VA 22905-0074. (804)979-2777. Fax: (804)984-2230. E-mail: patwhitton@aol.com. Website: www.newplaysforchildren.com. Publisher: Patricia Whitton Forrest. Estab. 1964. Publishes 3-4 plays/year; 1 or 2 children's musicals/year.

Needs: Publishes "generally material for kindergarten through junior high." Recently published: *Same But Different*, by Coleen Jennings (middle school exploration of multicultural experiences); *Princess and the Pea*, by Travis Tyne (fairy tale for ages 7-12). Does not want to see "adaptations of titles I already have. No unproduced plays; no junior high improvisations. Read our catalog."

How to Contact: Submit complete ms and score. Will consider simultaneous submissions and previously performed work. Responds in 2 months (usually).

Terms: Purchases exclusive rights to sell acting scripts. Pays writers in royalties (50% of production royalties; 10% of script sales). SASE for return of submission.

Tips: "Write the play you really want to write (not what you think will be saleable) and find a director to put it on."

THE OPEN EYE THEATER, P.O. Box 959, Margaretville NY 12455. Phone/fax: (914)586-1660. E-mail: openeye@catskill.net. Website: www.theopeneye.com. Producing Artistic Director: Amie Brockway. Estab. 1972 (theater). Produces 3 plays/year for a family audience. Most productions are with music but are not musicals.

Needs: "Casts of various sizes. Technical requirements are kept to a minimum for touring purposes." Produces professional productions combining professional artists and artists-in-training (actors of all ages). Recently produced plays: *The Weaver and the Sea*, by Julia Steiny, music by Dennis Livingston (myth, family); *Hoop*, by Pamela Monk (the Cardiff Giant, family).

How to Contact: "No videos or cassettes. Letter of inquiry only." Will consider previously performed work. Responds in 6 months.

Terms: Rights agreement negotiated with author. Pays writers one-time fee or royalty negotiated with publisher. SASE for return of submission.

Tips: "Send letter of inquiry only. We are interested in plays for a multigenerational audience (8-adult)."

☑ **PHOENIX THEATRE'S COOKIE COMPANY**, 100E. McDowell, Phoenix AZ 85004. (602)258-1974. Fax: (602)253-3626. E-mail: phoenixtheatre@yahoo.com. Website: phoenixtheatre.net. Artistic Director: Alan J. Prewitt. Estab. 1980. Produces 4 children's plays/year.

Needs: Produces theater with professional adult actors performing for family audiences. 95% of plays/musicals written for adult roles; 5% for juvenile roles. Requires small casts (4-7), small stage, mostly 1 set, flexible set or ingenious sets for a small space. "We're just starting to do plays with music—no musicals per se." Does not want to see larger casts, multiple sets, 2 hour epics. Recently produced *Holidays on the Prairie*, by Alan J. Prewitt (a single mother with children faces the Santa Fe Trail, for ages 4-12); *The Sleeping Beauty*, by Alan J. Prewitt (classic tale gets "truthful parent" twist, for ages 4-12)).

How to Contact: Plays/musicals: Query with synopsis, character breakdown and set description. Will consider simultaneous submissions. Responds only if interested within 1 month.

Terms: Submissions returned with SASE.

Tips: "Only submit innovative, imaginative work that stimulates imagination and empowers the child. We specialize in producing original scripts based on classic children's literature."

PIONEER DRAMA SERVICE, P.O. Box 4267, Englewood CO 80155-4267. (303)779-4035. Fax: (303)779-4315. E-mail: editors@pioneerdrama.com. Website: www.pioneerdrama.com. Submissions Editor: Beth Somers. Publisher: Steven Fendrich. Estab. 1960. Publishes more than 10 new plays and musicals/year.

Needs: "We are looking for plays up to 90 minutes long, large casts and simple sets." Publishes plays for ages middle school-12th grade and community theatre. Recently published plays/musicals: *Bah, Humbug! Scrooge's Christmas Carol*, book by R.J. Ryland, music and lyrics by Bill Francoeur; *Scheherazade, Legend of the Arabian Nights*, by Susan Pargman. Wants to see "script, scores, tapes, pics and reviews."

How to Contact: Query with synopsis, character breakdown, running time and set description. Submit complete ms and score (if a musical) with SASE. Will consider simultaneous submissions, CAD electronic submissions via disk or modem, previously performed work. Contact: Beth Somers, submissions editor. Responds in 4 months. Send for writer's guidelines.

Terms: Purchases all rights. Pays writers in royalties (10% on sales, 50% royalties on productions). Research Pioneer through catalog and website.
Tips: "Research the company. Include a cover letter and a SASE."

PLAYERS PRESS, INC., P.O. Box 1132, Studio City CA 91614-0132. (818)789-4980. Vice President: R. W. Gordon. Estab. 1965. Publishes 10-20 children's plays/year; 3-12 children's musicals/year.
Needs: Subject matter: "We publish for all age groups." Recently published: *African Folk Tales*, by Carol Korty (for ages 10-14).
How to Contact: Query with synopsis, character breakdown and set description; include #10 SASE with query. Considers previously performed work only. Responds to query in 1 month; submissions in 1 year.
Terms: Purchases stage, screen, TV rights. Payment varies; work purchased possibly outright upon written request. Submissions returned with SASE.
Tips: "Submit as requested—query first and send only previously produced material. Entertainment quality is on the upswing and needs to be directed at the world, no longer just the U.S. Please submit with two #10 SASEs plus ms-size SASE. Please do not call."

 PLAYS, The Drama Magazine for Young People, P.O. Box 600160, Newton MA 02460. E-mail: lizpreston@mediaone.net. Website: www.playsmag.com. Managing Editor: Elizabeth Preston. Estab. 1941. Publishes 70-75 children's plays/year.
Needs: "Props and staging should not be overly elaborate or costly. There is little call among our subscribers for plays with only a few characters; ten or more (to allow all students in a class to participate, for instance) is preferred. Our plays are performed by children in school from lower elementary grades through junior-senior high." 100% of plays written for juvenile roles. Subject matter: Audience is lower grades through junior/senior high. Recently published plays: *Fitness is the Fashion*, by Anne Coulter Martens (putting the "kick" back into romance); *The Case of the Punjabi Ruby*, by Frank Willmeut (auction of valuable gem comes to a screeching halt); *Safety Circus*, by Claire Boike (look before you leap!, for middle/lower grades); *Matchmaking for Mother*, by Helen Louise Miller (middle-grade play about brother and sister trying to marry off their hardworking mom); and senior high adaptation of *The Prince and the Pauper*, by Mark Twain. "Send nothing downbeat—no plays about drugs, sex or other 'heavy' topics."
How to Contact: Query first on adaptations of folk tales and classics; otherwise submit complete ms. Responds in 3 weeks.
Terms: Purchases all rights. Pay rates vary. Guidelines available; send SASE. Sample copy $4.
Tips: "Get your play underway quickly. Keep it wholesome and entertaining. No preachiness, heavy moral or educational message. Any 'lesson' should be imparted through the actions of the characters, not through unbelievable dialogue. Use realistic situations and settings without getting into downbeat, depressing topics. No sex, drugs, violence, alcohol."

 RIVERSIDE CHILDREN'S THEATRE, 3280 Riverside Park Dr., Vero Beach FL 32963. (561)234-8052. Fax: (561)234-4407. E-mail: ret@riversidetheatre.com. Website: www.riversidetheatre.com. Education Director: Linda Downey. Estab. 1980. Produces 4 children's plays/year; 2 children's musicals/year.
Needs: Produces amateur youth productions. 100% of plays/musicals written for juvenile roles. Musical needs: For children ages 6-18. Produced plays: *The Beloved Dently*, by Dory Cooney (pet bereavement, general); *Taming of the Shrew*, by Shakespeare (general).
How to Contact: Plays/musicals: Query with synopsis, character breakdown and set description. Will consider simultaneous submissions, electronic submissions via disk/modem and previously performed work. Responds only if interested.
Terms: Pays royalty or $40-60 per performance. Submissions returned with SASE.
Tips: "Interested in youth theatre for children ages 6-18 to perform."

 SEATTLE CHILDREN'S THEATRE, P.O. Box 9640, Seattle WA 98109. Fax: (206)443-0442. Website: www.sct.org. Literary Manager and Dramaturg: Tobin A. Maheras. Estab. 1975. Produces 5 full-length children's plays/year; 1 full-length children's musical/year. Produces children's plays for professional productions (September-June).

**FOR EXPLANATIONS OF THESE SYMBOLS,
SEE THE INSIDE FRONT AND BACK COVERS OF THIS BOOK**

Needs: 95% of plays/musicals written for adult roles; 5% for juvenile roles. "We generally use adult actors even for juvenile roles." Prefers no turntable, no traps. Produced plays: *The King of Ireland's Son*, by Paula Wing (mythology and Hero Quest for ages 8 and older); *Pink and Say*, by Oyamo (adaptation from Patricia Polacco). Does not want to see anything that condescends to young people—anything overly broad in style.

How to Contact: Accepts agented scripts or those accompanied by a professional letter of recommendation (director or dramaturg). Responds in 1 year.

Terms: Rights vary. Payment method varies. Submissions returned with SASE.

Tips: "Please *do not* send unsolicited manuscripts. We prefer sophisticated material (our weekend performances have an audience that is half adults)."

STAGE ONE: THE LOUISVILLE CHILDREN'S THEATRE, 501 W. Main, Louisville KY 40202-2957. (502)589-5946. Fax: (502)588-5910. E-mail: stageone@kca.org. Website: www.stageone.org. Producing Director: Moses Goldberg. Estab. 1946. Produces 6-8 children's plays/year; 1-4 children's musicals/year.

Needs: Stage One is an Equity company producing children's plays for professional productions. 100% of plays/musicals written for adult roles. "Sometimes we do use students in selected productions." Produced plays: *Pinocchio*, by Moses Goldberg, music by Scott Kasbaum (ages 8-12); and *John Lennon & Me*, by Cherie Bennett (about cystic fibrosis; peer acceptance for ages 11-17). Does not want to see "camp or condescension."

How to Contact: Submit complete ms, score and tape of songs (if a musical); include the author's résumé if desired. Will consider simultaneous submissions, electronic submissions via disk or modem and previously performed work. Responds in 4 months.

Terms: Pays writers in royalties (5-6%) or $25-75/performance.

Tips: Looking for "stageworthy and respectful dramatizations of the classic tales of childhood, both ancient and modern; plays relevant to the lives of young people and their families; and plays directly related to the school curriculum."

☑ **THEATREWORKS/USA**, 151 W. 26th, 7th Floor, New York NY 10001. (212)647-1100. Fax: (212)924-5377. Artistic Director: Barbara Pasternack. Assistant Artistic Director: Michael Alltop. Estab. 1960. Produces 3-4 children's plays and musicals/year.

Needs: Cast of 5 or 6 actors. Play should be 1 hour long, tourable. Professional children's theatre comprised of adult equity actors. 100% of shows are written for adult roles. Produced plays: *Curious George*, book and lyrics by Thomas Toce, music by Tim Brown (adaptation, for grades K-3); *Little Women*, by Allan Knee, incidental music by Kim Oler and Alison Hubbard (adaptation, for grades 4-8). No fractured, typical "kiddy theater" fairy tales or shows written strictly to teach or illustrate.

How to Contact: Query first with synopsis, character breakdown and sample songs. Will consider previously performed work. Responds in 3 months.

Terms: Pays writers royalties of 6%. SASE for return of submission.

Tips: "Plays should be not only entertaining, but 'about something.' They should touch the heart and the mind. They should not condescend to children."

Young Writer's & Illustrator's Markets

The listings in this section are special because they publish work of young writers and artists (under age 18). Some of the magazines listed exclusively feature the work of young people. Others are adult magazines with special sections for the work of young writers. There are also a few book publishers listed that exclusively publish the work of young writers and artists. Many of the magazines and publishers listed here pay only in copies, meaning authors and illustrators receive one or more free copies of the magazine or book to which they contributed.

As with adult markets, markets for children expect writers to be familiar with their editorial needs before submitting. Many of the markets listed will send guidelines to writers stating exactly what they need and how to submit it. You can often get these by sending a request with a self-addressed, stamped envelope (SASE) to the magazine or publisher, or by checking a publication's website (a number of listings include web addresses). In addition to obtaining guidelines, read through a few copies of any magazines you'd like to submit to—this is the best way to determine if your work is right for them.

A number of kids' magazines are available on newsstands or in libraries. Others are distributed only through schools, churches or home subscriptions. If you can't find a magazine you'd like to see, most editors will send sample copies for a small fee.

Before you submit your material to editors, take a few minutes to read Before Your First Sale on page 8 for more information on proper submission procedures. You may also want to check out two other sections—Contests & Awards and Conferences & Workshops. Some listings in these sections are open to students (some exclusively)—look for the phrase **"open to students"** in bold. Additional opportunities for writers can be found in *Market Guide for Young Writers* (Writer's Digest Books) and *A Teen's Guide to Getting Published: the only writer's guide written by teens for teens*, by Danielle and Jessica Dunn (Prufrock Press). More information on these books are given in the Helpful Resources section in the back of this book.

Information on companies listed in the previous edition but not included in this edition of *Children's Writer's & Illustrator's Market* **may be found in the General Index.**

THE ACORN, 1530 Seventh St., Rock Island IL 61201. (309)788-3980. Newsletter. Estab. 1989. Editor: Betty Mowery. Audience consists of "kindergarten-12th grade students, parents, teachers and other adults. Purpose in publishing works for children: "to expose children's manuscripts to others and provide a format for those who might not have one. We want to showcase young authors who may not have their work published elsewhere and present wholesome writing material that will entertain and educate—audience grades K-12." Children must be K-12 (put grade on manuscripts). Guidelines available for SASE.

Magazines: 100% of magazine written by children. Uses 6 fiction pieces (500 words); 20 pieces of poetry (32 lines). No payment; purchase of a copy isn't necessary to be printed. Sample copy $3. Subscription $10 for 4 issues. Submit mss to Betty Mowery, editor. Send complete ms. Will accept typewritten, legibly handwritten and/or computer printout. Include SASE. Responds in 1 week. Will not respond without SASE.

Artwork: Publishes artwork by children. Looks for "all types; size 4×5. Use black ink in artwork." No payment. Submit artwork either with ms or separately to Betty Mowery. Include SASE. Responds in 1 week.

Tips: "My biggest problem is not having names on the manuscripts. If the manuscript gets separated from the cover letter, there is no way to know whom to respond to. Always put name, age or grade and address on manuscripts, and if you want your material returned, enclose a SASE. Don't send material with killing of humans or animals, or lost love poems or stories."

AMELIA MAGAZINE, 329 "E" St., Bakersfield CA 93304-2031. (805)323-4064. Magazine. Published quarterly. Strives to offer the best of all genres. Purpose in publishing works for children: wants to offer first opportunities to budding writers. Also offers the annual Amelia Student Scholarship ($500) for high school students. Submissions from young writers must be signed by parent, teacher or guardian verifying originality. Guidelines are not specifically for young writers; they cover the entire gamut of publication needs. For sample of past winner send $3 and SASE.

Magazines: 3% of magazine written by children. Uses primarily poetry, often generated by teachers in creative writing classes. Uses 1 story in any fiction genre (1,500 words); 4 pieces of poetry, usually haiku (3 lines). Would like to receive more general poetry from young writers. Pays in copies for haiku; $2-10 for general poetry. Regular $35 rate for fiction or nonfiction. Submit mss to Frederick A. Raborg, editor. Submit complete ms (teachers frequently submit student's work). Will accept typewritten ms. Include SASE. Responds in 3 weeks.

Artwork: Publishes artwork and photography by children. Looks for photos no smaller than 5×7; artwork in any medium; also cartoons. Pays $5-20 on publication. Submit well-protected artwork with SASE. Submit artwork/photos to Frederick A. Raborg, Jr., editor. Include SASE. Responds in 3 weeks. Sample issue: $10.95.

Tips: "Be neat and thorough. Photos should have captions. Cartoon gaglines ought to be funny; try them out on someone before submitting. We want to encourage young writers because the seeds of literary creativity are sown quite young with strong desires to read and admiration for the authors of those early readings."

AMERICAN GIRL, 8400 Fairway Place, Middleton WI 53562. (608)836-4848. Fax: (608)831-7089. Website: www.americangirl. Contact: Magazine Department Assistant. Bimonthly magazine. Audience consists of girls ages 8-12 who are joyful about being girls. Purpose in publishing works by young people: "self-esteem boost and entertainment for readers. *American Girl* values girls' opinions and ideas. By publishing their work in the magazine, girls can share their thoughts with other girls! Young writers should be 8-12 years old. We don't have writer's guidelines for children's submissions. Instruction for specific solicitations appears in the magazine."

Magazines: 5% of magazine written by young people. "A few pages of each issue feature articles that include children's answers to questions or requests that have appeared in a previous issue of *American Girl*." Pays in copies. Submit to address listed in magazine. Will accept legibly handwritten ms. Include SASE. Responds in 3 months.

Tips: "Please, no stories, poems, etc. about American Girls Collection Characters (Felicity, Samantha, Molly, Kirsten, Addy or Josefina). Inside *American Girl*, there are several departments that call for submissions. Read the magazine carefully and submit your ideas based on what we ask for."

☑ **BEYOND WORDS PUBLISHING, INC.**, 20827 NW Cornell Rd., Suite 500, Hillsboro OR 97124-9808. (503)531-8700. Fax: (503)531-8773. E-mail: barbara@beyondword.com. Website:www.beyondword.com. Book publisher. Managing Editor of Children's Department: Barbara Mann. Publishes 2-3 books by children/year. Looks for "books that inspire integrity in children ages 5-15 and encourage creativity and an appreciation of nature." Wants to "encourage children to write, create, dream and believe that it is possible to be published. The books must be unique, be of national interest, and the child author must be personable and promotable." Writer's guidelines available with SASE.

Books: Holds yearly writing contests for activity/advice books written by and for children/teens. Also publishes nonfiction advice books for and by children, such as joke books or guides for kids about pertinent concerns. Submit mss to Barbara Mann, managing editor. Responds in 6 months.

Artwork/Photography: Publishes artwork by children. Submit artwork to Barbara Mann, managing editor.

Tips: "Write about issues that affect your life. Trust your own instincts. You know best!"

🅽 ☑ **CHICKADEE MAGAZINE**, 179 John St., Suite 500, Toronto, Ontario M5T 3G5 Canada. (416)340-2700. Magazine published 9 times/year. "*Chickadee* is for children ages 6-9. Its purpose is to entertain and educate children about science, nature and the world around them. We publish children's drawings to give readers the chance to express themselves. Drawings must relate to the topics that are given in the 'All Your Own' section of each issue."

Artwork: Publishes artwork by children. No payment given. Mail submissions with name, age and return address for thank you note. Submit to Mitch Butler, All Your Own Editor. Responds in 4 months.

☑ **CHILDREN WRITING FOR CHILDREN NONPROFIT (CWC)**, 7142 Dustin Rd., Galena OH 43021-7959. (800)759-7171. Website: www.cwcbooks.org. Executive Director: Susan Schmidt. Purpose of organization: A non-profit corporation established to educate the public at large about children's issues through literary works created by children and to celebrate and share the talents of children as authors. Books must be written and/or illustrated by children and young adults. "We look for kids to write about personal experiences that educate and reveal solutions to problems." Open submissions are accepted. Books published to date include those dealing with cancer, child abuse, cerebral palsy, Tourette's syndrome and avoiding teen violence.

Books: Publishing focus is on nonfiction writings about children's issues such as peer pressure, illness, and special challenges or opportunities. Stories with educational value are preferred. Writer's guidelines available with SASE. Pays royalties, but no advances. Will accept typewritten, legibly handwritten and computer-printed ms. Include SASE for ms return and/or comments. Responds in 6 months.

Artwork/Photography: Publishes books with artwork and/or photography accompanying nonfiction stories written and illustrated by children. Please submit photocopies of art—no originals please.

Tips: Write about personal experiences in challenging situations, painting a word picture of the people involved, the story, how you resolved or responded to the situation and what you learned or gained from the experience.

CICADA, Carus Publishing Company, P.O. Box 300, 315 Fifth St., Peru IL 61354. (815)224-6656. Fax: (815)224-6615. E-mail: cicada@caruspub.com. Website: www.cicadamag.com. Editor-in-chief: Marianne Carus. Editor: Deborah Vetter. Senior Editor: John D. Allen. Senior Art Director: Ron McCutchan.
- *Cicada* publishes work of writers and artists of high-school age. See the *Cicada* listing in the Magazines section for more information, or check their website or copies of the magazine.

☑ ⬙ THE CLAREMONT REVIEW, 4980 Wesley Rd., Victoria, British Columbia Canada V8Y 1Y9. (604)658-5221. Fax: (250)658-5387. E-mail: aurora@home.com. Website: www.members.home.net/review. Magazine. Publishes 2 books/year by young adults. Publishes poetry and fiction with literary value by students aged 13-19 anywhere in North America. Purpose in publishing work by young people: to provide a literary venue. Sponsors annual poetry contest.

Magazines: Uses 10-12 fiction stories (200-2,500 words); 30-40 poems. Pays in copies. Submit mss to editors. Submit complete ms. Will accept typewritten mss. SASE. Responds in 6 weeks (except during the summer).

Artwork: Publishes artwork by young adults. Looks for b&w copies of imaginative art. Pays in copies. Send picture for review. Negative may be requested. Submit art and photographs to editors. SASE. Responds in 6 weeks.

Tips: "Read us first—it saves disappointment. Know who we are and what we publish. We're closed July and August. SASE a must. American students send I.R.C.'s as American stamps *do not* work in Canada. Thanks."

CREATIVE KIDS, P.O. Box 8813, Waco TX 76714-8813. (800)998-2208. Fax: (254)756-3339. E-mail: creative_kids@prufrock.com. Website: www.prufrock.com. Editor: Libby Lindsey. Magazine published 4 times/year. Estab. 1979. "All material is by children, for children." Purpose in publishing works by children: "to create a product that provides children with an authentic experience and to offer an opportunity for children to see their work in print. *Creative Kids* contains the best stories, poetry, opinion, artwork, games and photography by kids ages 8-14." Writers ages 8-14 must have statement by teacher or parent verifying originality. Writer's guidelines available on request with SASE.

Magazines: Uses "about 6" fiction and nonfiction stories (800-900 words); poetry, plays, ideas to share (200-750 words) per issue. Pays "free magazine." Submit mss to submissions editor. Will accept typewritten mss. Include SASE. Responds in 1 month.

Artwork/Photography: Publishes artwork and photos by children. Looks for "any kind of drawing, cartoon, or painting." Pays "free magazine." Send original or a photo of the work to submissions editor. Include SASE. Responds in 1 month.

Tips: "*Creative Kids* is a magazine by kids, for kids. The work represents children's ideas, questions, fears, concerns and pleasures. The material never contains racist, sexist or violent expression. The purpose is to provide children with an authentic experience. A person may submit one piece of work per envelope. Each piece must be labeled with the student's name, birth date, grade, school, home address and school address. Include a photograph, if possible. Recent school pictures are best. Material submitted to *Creative Kids* must not be under consideration by any other publication. Items should be carefully prepared, proofread and double checked (perhaps also by a parent or teacher). All activities requiring solutions must be accompanied by the correct answers. Young writers and artists should always write for guidelines and then follow them."

☑ CREATIVE WITH WORDS, Thematic anthologies, Creative with Words Publications, P.O. Box 223226, Carmel CA 93922. Fax: (831)655-8627. E-mail: cwwpub@usa.net. Website: members.tripod.com/CreativeWithWords. Editor: Brigitta Geltrich. Nature Editor: Bert Hower. Publishes 14 anthologies/year. Estab. 1975. "We publish the creative writing of children (4 anthologies written by children; 4 anthologies written by adults; 4-6 anthologies written by all ages)." Audience consists of children, schools, libraries, adults, reading programs. Purpose in publishing works by children: to offer them an opportunity to get started in publishing. "Work must be of quality, typed, original, unedited, and not published before; age must be given (up to 19 years old) and home address." SASE must be enclosed with all correspondence and mss. Writer's guidelines and theme list available on request with SASE, via e-mail or on website.

Books: Considers all categories except those dealing with sensationalism, death, violence, pornography and overly religious. Uses fairy tales, folklore items (up to 1,500 words) and poetry (not to exceed 20 lines, 46 characters across). Published *Nature Series: Seasons, Nature, School, Love* and *Relationships* (all children and adults). Pays 20% discount on each copy of publication in which fiction or poetry by children appears. Best of the month is published on website, and author receives one free copy of issue. Submit mss to Brigitta Geltrich, editor. Query; child, teacher or parent can submit; teacher and/or parents must verify originality of writing. Will accept typewritten and/or legibly handwritten mss. SASE. "Will not go through agents or overly protective 'stage mothers'." Responds in 1 month after deadline of any theme.

Artwork/Photography: Publishes b&w artwork, b&w photos and computer artwork by children (language art work). Pays 20% discount on every copy of publication in which work by children appears. Submit artwork to Brigitta Geltrich, editor, and request info on payment.

Tips: "Enjoy the English language, life and the world around you. Look at everything from a different perspective. Look at the greatness inside all of us. Be less descriptive and use words wisely. Let the reader experience a story through a viewpoint character, don't be overly dramatic. Match illustrations to the meaning of the story or poem."

✓ **FREE SPIRIT PUBLISHING INC.**, 217 Fifth Ave. N, Suite 200, Minneapolis MN 55401-1299. (612)338-2068. Fax: (612)337-5050. E-mail: help4kids@freespirit.com. Website: www.freespirit.com. Publishes 15-20 books/year. "We specialize in SELF-HELP FOR KIDS® and SELF-HELP FOR TEENS®. We aim to help kids help themselves. We were the *first* publisher of self-help materials for children, and today we are the *only* publisher of SELF-HELP FOR KIDS® materials. Our main audience is children and teens, but we also publish for parents, teachers, therapists, youth workers and other involved in caring for kids. Our main interests include the development of self-esteem, self-awareness, creative thinking and problem-solving abilities, assertiveness and making a difference in the world. We do not publish fiction or poetry. We do accept submissions from young people ages 14 and older; however, please send a letter from a parent/guardian/leader verifying originality." Request catalog, author guidelines, and "student guidelines" before submitting work. Send SASE.

Books: Publishes self-help for kids, how-to, classroom activities. Pays advance and royalties. Submit mss to acquisitions editor. Send query and sample table of contents. Will accept typewritten mss. SASE required. Responds in 3-4 months.

Artwork/Photography: Submit samples to acquisitions editor.

Tips: "Free Spirit publishes very specific material, and it helps when writers request and study our catalog before submitting work to us, and refer to our author guidelines (our catalog and guidelines are available by mail or via our website.) We do not accept general self-help books, autobiographies or children's books that feature made-up stories. Our preference is books that help kids to gain self-esteem, succeed in school, stand up for themselves, resolve conflicts and make a difference in the world. We do not publish books that have animals as the main characters."

N HIGH SCHOOL WRITER, P.O. Box 718, Grand Rapids MN 55744-0718. (218)326-8025. Fax: (218)326-8025. E-mail: writer@mx3.com. Editor: Barbara Eiesland. Magazine published monthly during the school year. "The *High School Writer* is a magazine written *by* students *for* students. All submissions must exceed contemporary standards of decency." Purpose in publishing works by young people: to provide a real audience for student writers—and text for study. Submissions by junior high and middle school students accepted for our junior edition. Senior high students' works are accepted for our senior high edition. Students attending schools that subscribe to our publication are eligible to submit their work." Writer's guidelines available on request.

Magazines: Uses fiction, nonfiction (2,000 words maximum) and poetry. Submit mss to Barbara Eiesland, editor. Submit complete ms (teacher must submit). Will accept typewritten, computer-generated (good quality) mss.

Tips: "Submissions should not be sent without first obtaining a copy of our guidelines (see page 2 of every issue). Also, submissions will not be considered unless student's school subscribes."

N HIGHLIGHTS FOR CHILDREN, 803 Church St., Honesdale PA 18431. (570)253-1080. Magazine. Published monthly. "We strive to provide wholesome, stimulating, entertaining material that will encourage children to read. Our audience is children ages 2-12." Purpose in publishing works by young people: to encourage children's creative expression.

Magazines: 15-20% of magazine written by children. Uses stories and poems. Also uses jokes, riddles, tongue twisters. Features that occur occasionally: "What Are Your Favorite Books?" (8-10/year), Recipes (8-10/year), "Science Letters" (15-20/year). Special features that invite children's submissions on a specific topic occur several times per year. Recent examples include "Pet Stories," "Favorite Songs," "Kids at Work," and "Help the Cartoonists." Pays in copies. Submit complete ms to the editor. Will accept typewritten, legibly handwritten and computer printout mss. Responds in 6 weeks.

Artwork: Publishes artwork by children. Pays in copies. No cartoon or comic book characters. No commercial products. Submit b&w or color artwork for "Our Own Pages." Features include "Creatures Nobody Has Ever Seen" (5-8/year) and "Illustration Job" (18-20/year). Responds in 6 weeks.

✓ ❧ **KWIL KIDS PUBLISHING, The Little Publishing Company That Kwil Built**, Kwilville, P.O. Box 29556, Maple Ridge, British Columbia V2X 2V0 Canada. Phone/fax: (604)465-9101. E-mail: kwil@telus.n et. Website: www.members.home.com/kwilkids/. Publishes greeting cards, newspaper column, newsletter and web page. Publishes weekly column in local paper, four quarterly newsletters. "*Kwil Kids* come in all ages, shapes and sizes—from 4-64 and a whole lot more! Kwil does not pay for the creative work of children but provides opportunity/encouragement. We promote literacy, creativity and written 'connections' through written and artistic expression and publish autobiographical, inspirational, fantastical, humorous stories of gentleness, compassion, truth and beauty. Our purpose is to foster a sense of pride and enthusiasm in young writers and artists, to celebrate the voice of youth and encourage growth through joy-filled practice and cheerleading, not criticism." Must include name, age, school, address and parent signature (if a minor). Will send guideline upon request and an application to join "The Kwil Club."

Books: Publishes autobiographical, inspirational, creative stories (alliterative, rhyming refrains, juicy words) fiction; short rhyming and non-rhyming poems (creative, fun, original, expressive, poetry). Length: 1,000 words for fiction; 8-16 lines for poetry. No payment—self-published and sold "at cost" only (1 free copy). Submit mss to Kwil publisher. Submit complete ms; send copy only—expect a reply but will not return ms. Will accept typewritten and legibly handwritten mss and e-mail. Include SASE. Publishes greeting cards with poems, short stories and original artwork. Pays 5¢ royalty on each card sold (rounded to the nearest dollar and paid once per year) as a fundraiser. Responds in 1 month.
Newsletter: 95% of newsletter written by young people. Uses 15 short stories, poems, jokes (20-100 words). No payment—free newsletters only. Submit complete ms. Will accept typewritten and legibly handwritten mss and e-mail. Kwil answers every letter in verse. Responds in April, August and December.
Artwork: Publishes artwork and photography by children with writing. Looks for black ink sketches to go with writing and photos to go with writing. Submit by postal mail only; white background for sketches. Submit artwork/photos to Kwil publisher. Include SASE. Responds in 3 months.
Tips: "We love stories that teach a lesson or encourage peace, love and a fresh, new understanding. Just be who you are and do what you do. Then all of life's treasures will come to you."

☑ **MERLYN'S PEN: Fiction, Essays, and Poems by America's Teens**, P.O. Box 910, East Greenwich RI 02818. (800)247-2027. Fax: (401)885-5222. Website: www.merlynspen.com. Magazine. Published annually. "By publishing student writing, *Merlyn's Pen* seeks to broaden and reward the young author's interest in writing, strengthen the self-confidence of beginning writers and promote among all students a positive attitude toward literature. We publish 75 manuscripts annually by students in grades 6-12. The entire magazine is dedicated to young adults' writing. Our audience is classrooms, libraries and students from grades 6-12." Writers must be in grades 6-12 and must send a completed *Merlyn's Pen* cover sheet with each submission. When a student is accepted, he/she, a parent and a teacher must sign a statement of originality. Writer's guidelines available at www.merlynspen.com.
Magazines: Uses 20 short stories (no word limit); plays; 8 nonfiction essays (no word limit); 25 pieces of poetry; letters to the editor; editorials; reviews of previously published works. Published authors receive 3 contributor's copies and payment of $20-200. Also, a discount is offered for additional copies of the issue. Submit up to 3 titles at one time. Will only accept typewritten mss. Responds in 10 weeks.
Tips: "All manuscripts and artwork must be accompanied by a completed copy of *Merlyn's Pen* official cover sheet for submissions. Call to request cover sheet, or download from our website."

☑ **NATIONAL GEOGRAPHIC WORLD**, 1145 17th St. NW, Washington DC 20036-4688. (202)857-7000. Fax: (202)775-6112. Website: www.nationalgeographic.com. Illustrations Director: Chuck Herron. Magazine published monthly. Picture magazine for ages 9-12. Purpose in publishing work by young people: to encourage in young readers a curiosity about the world around them.
   ● *National Geographic World* does not accept unsolicited manuscripts.
Tips: Publishes art, letters, poems, games, riddles, jokes and craft ideas by children in mailbag section only. No payment given. Send by mail to: Submissions Committee. "Sorry, but *World* cannot acknowledge or return your contributions."

☑ **NEW MOON: The Magazine For Girls & Their Dreams**, New Moon Publishing, Inc., P.O. Box 3620, Duluth MN 55803-3620. (218)728-5507. Fax: (218)728-0314. E-mail: girl@newmoon.org. Website: www.newmoon.org. Managing Editors: Deb Mylin and Bridget Grosser. Magazine. Published bimonthly. *New Moon*'s primary audience is girls ages 8-14. "We publish a magazine that listens to girls." More than 70% of *New Moon* is written by girls. Purpose in publishing work by children/teens: "We want girls' voices to be heard. *New Moon* wants girls to see that their opinions, dreams, thoughts and ideas count." Writer's guidelines available for SASE or online.
Magazine: 75% of magazine written by young people. Buys 3 fiction mss/year (900-1,200 words); 30 nonfiction mss/year (600 words). Submit to Deb Mylin, managing editor. Submit query, complete mss for fiction and nonfiction. Will accept typewritten, legibly handwritten mss and disk (IBM compatible). "We do not return or acknowledge unsolicited material. Do not send originals—we will not return any materials." Responds in 6 months if interested.
Artwork/Photography: Publishes artwork and photography by children. Looks for cover and inside illustrations. Pay negotiated. Submit art and photographs to Deb Mylin, managing editor. "We do not return unsolicited material."
Tips: "Read *New Moon* to completely understand our needs."

VISIT THE WRITER'S DIGEST WEBSITE at www.writersdigest.com for hot new markets, daily market updates, writers' guidelines and much more.

☑ **POTLUCK CHILDREN'S LITERARY MAGAZINE**, P.O. Box 546, Deerfield IL 60015-0546. Fax: (847)317-9492. E-mail: nappic@aol.com. Website: www.potluckmagazine.com. Quarterly magazine. "We look for works with imagery and human truths. Occasionally we will work with young authors on editing their work. We are available to the writer for questions and comments. The purpose of *Potluck* is to encourage creative expression and to supply young writers with a forum in which they can be heard. We also provide informative articles to help them become better writers and to prepare them for the adult markets. For example, recent articles dealt with work presentation, tracking submissions and rights." Writer's guidelines available on request with a SASE.

Magazines: 99% of magazine written by young people. Uses fiction (300-400 words); nonfiction (300-400 words); poetry (30 lines); book reviews (150 words). Pays with copy of issue published. Submit mss to Susan Napoli Picchietti, editor. Submit complete ms; teacher may send group submissions, which have different guidelines and payment schedules. Will accept typewritten and e-mailed mss. Include SASE. Responds 6 weeks after deadline.

Artwork/Photography: Publishes artwork by young artists. Looks for all types of artwork—no textured works. Must be 8½ × 11 only. Pays in copies. Do not fold submissions. If you want your work returned, you must include proper postage and envelope. Color photo copy accepted. Submit artwork to Susan Napoli Picchietti, editor. Include SASE. Responds in 6 weeks.

Tips: "Relax—observe and acknowledge all that is around you. Life gives us a lot to draw on. Don't get carried away with style—let your words speak for themselves. If you want to be taken seriously as a writer, you must take yourself seriously. The rest will follow. Enjoy yourself and take pride in every piece, even the bad—they keep you humble."

☑ **SKIPPING STONES**, Multicultural Children's Magazine, P.O. Box 3939, Eugene OR 97403. (541)342-4956. Website: www.efn.org/~skipping. Articles/Poems/Fiction Editor: Arun N. Toké. 5 issues a year. Estab. 1988. Circulation 2,500. "*Skipping Stones* is a multicultural, nonprofit, children's magazine to encourage cooperation, creativity and celebration of cultural and environmental richness. It offers itself as a creative forum for communication among children from different lands and backgrounds. We prefer work by children under 18 years old. International, minorities and under-represented populations receive priority, multilingual submissions are encouraged."

● *Skipping Stones'* theme for the 2001 Youth Honor Awards is multicultural and nature awareness. Send SASE for guidelines and more information on the awards.

Magazines: 50% written by children. Uses 5-10 fiction short stories and plays (500-750 words); 5-10 nonfiction articles, interviews, letters, history, descriptions of celebrations (500-750 words); 15-20 poems, jokes, riddles, proverbs (250 words or less) per issue. Pays in contributor's copies. Submit mss to Mr. Arun Toké, editor. Submit complete ms for fiction or nonfiction work; teacher and parents can also submit their contributions. Submissions should include "cover letter with name, age, address, school, cultural background, inspiration piece, dreams for future." Will accept typewritten, legibly handwritten and computer/word processor mss. Include SASE. Responds in 4 months. Accepts simultaneous submissions.

Artwork/Photography: Publishes artwork and photography for children. Will review all varieties of ms/illustration packages. Wants comics, cartoons, b&w photos, paintings, drawings (preferably ink & pen or pencil), 8 × 10, color photos OK. Subjects include children, people, celebrations, nature, ecology, multicultural. Pays in contributor's copies.

Terms: "*Skipping Stones* is a labor of love. You'll receive complimentary contributor's (up to four) copies depending on the length of your contribution and illustrations." Responds to artists in 4 months. Sample copy for $5 and 4 first-class stamps.

Tips: "Let the 'inner child' within you speak out—naturally, uninhibited." Wants "material that gives insight on cultural celebrations, lifestyle, custom and tradition, glimpse of daily life in other countries and cultures. Please, no mystery for the sake of mystery! Photos, songs, artwork are most welcome if they illustrate/highlight the points. Upcoming features: Living abroad, turning points in life, inspirations, outstanding moments in life, religions and cultures from around the world, Hawaii and more."

SKYLARK, Purdue University Calumet, 2200 169th St., Hammond IN 46323-2094. (219)989-2273. Fax: (219)989-2165. Editor: Pamela Hunter. Young Writers' Editor: Shirley Jo Moritz. Annual magazine. Circ. 1,000. 20% of material written by juvenile authors. Presently accepting material by children. "*Skylark* wishes to provide a vehicle for creative writing of all kinds (with emphasis on an attractive synthesis of text and layout), especially by writers ages 5-18, who live in the Illinois/Indiana area and who have not ordinarily been provided with such an outlet. Children need a place to see their work published alongside that of adults." Proof of originality is required from parents or teachers for all authors. Age or grade of submitter must be provided, too. "We feel that creativity should be nurtured as soon as possible in an individual. By publishing young, promising authors and illustrators in the same magazine which also features work by adults, perhaps we will provide the impetus for a young person to keep at his/her craft." Writer's guidelines available upon request with a SASE.

Magazines: 20% of magazine written by young people. In previous issues, *Skylark* has published mysteries, fantasy, humor, good narrative fiction stories (400-800 words), personal essays, brief character sketches, nonfiction stories (400-650 words), poetry (no more than 20 lines). Does not want to see material that is obviously religious or sexual. Pays in contributor's copies. Two copies per piece published (if two poems are published by

Young

*Illustration by Isaiah Stroup, Grade 6
University Elementary, Bloomington, Indiana*

Shirley Jo Moritz

Editor

Readers responded enthusiastically to Isaiah Stroup's flamingo, which appeared in *Skylark* magazine. Stroup, who was a sixth grader when he created this piece, was a student of art teacher Dr. Martyna Bellessis in the Gifted and Talented program at Monroe County Community School Corporation, Bloomington, Indiana. *Skylark* features the work of these students in every issue. Editor-in-chief, Pamela Hunter, explains, "*Skylark* has always encouraged young artists and young writers to submit their work. Our readers marveled at this young artist's sophistication."

one author, that author receives three (3) complimentary copies.) Submit ms to Shirley Jo Moritz, Young Writers' editor. Submit complete ms. Prefers typewritten ms. Must include SASE for response or return of material. Responds in 3 months. Byline given.

Artwork/Photography: Publishes artwork and photographs by children. Looks for "photos of animals, landscapes and sports, and for artwork to go along with text." Pays in contributor's copies. One copy per each piece of artwork published. Artwork and photos may be b&w or color. Use unlined paper. Do not use pencil and no copyrighted characters. Markers are advised for best reproduction. Include name and address on the back of each piece. Also, provide age or grade of artist. Package properly to avoid damage. Submit artwork/photos to Pamela Hunter, editor-in-chief. Include SASE. Responds in 5 months.

Tips: "We're looking for literary work. Follow your feelings, be as original as you can and don't be afraid to be different. You are submitting to a publication that accepts work by adults and young people alike. Be responsible. Abide by our guidelines, especially the one concerning an SASE for return of your work or notification of acceptance. Check your manuscript for correct grammar and spelling. If the editor receives two manuscripts that have equally promising content, that editor will always select the work that requires less proofreading corrections."

N SNAKE RIVER REFLECTIONS, 1863 Bitterroot Dr., Twin Falls ID 83301. (208)734-0746. E-mail: william@micron.net. E-mail submissions accepted, permission to publish on Internet needed. Website: www.geoc ities.com/sagebrush_wlkr/index.html. Newsletter. Publishes 12 times/year. Proof of originality required with submissions. Guidelines available on request with #10 SASE or at website.

Magazines: 5% of magazine's poems written by children. Uses poetry (30 lines maximum). Pays in copies only. Submit mss to William White, editor. Submit complete ms. Will accept typewritten and legibly handwritten mss. #10 SASE. Responds in 1 month.

SPRING TIDES, 824 Stillwood Dr., Savannah GA 31419. (912)925-8800. Annual magazine. Audience consists of children 5-12 years old. Purpose in publishing works by young people: to promote and encourage writing. Requirements to be met before work is published: must be 5-12 years old. Writers guidelines available on request.

Magazines: 100% of magazine written by young people. Uses 5-6 fiction stories (1,200 words maximum); autobiographical experiences (1,200 words maximum); 15-20 poems (20 lines maximum) per issue. Writers are not paid. Submit complete ms or teacher may submit. Will accept typewritten mss. SASE. Responds in 2 months.

Artwork: Publishes artwork by children. "We have so far used only local children's artwork because of the complications of keeping and returning pieces."

STONE SOUP, The Magazine by Young Writers and Artists, Children's Art Foundation, P.O. Box 83, Santa Cruz CA 95063. (831)426-5557. Fax: (831)426-1161. E-mail: editor@stonesoup.com. Website: www.stone soup.com. Articles/Fiction Editor, Art Director: Ms. Gerry Mandel. Magazine published 6 times/year. Circ. 20,000. "We publish fiction, poetry and artwork by children through age 13. Our preference is for work based on personal experiences and close observation of the world. Our audience is young people through age 13, as well as parents, teachers, librarians." Purpose in publishing works by young people: to encourage children to read and to express themselves through writing and art. Writer's guidelines available upon request with a SASE.

Magazines: Uses animal, contemporary, fantasy, history, problem-solving, science fiction, sports, spy/mystery/ adventure fiction stories. Uses 5-10 fiction stories (100-2,500 words); 5-10 nonfiction stories (100-2,500 words); 2-4 poems per issue. Does not want to see classroom assignments and formula writing. Buys 65 mss/year. Byline given. Pays on publication. Buys all rights. Pays $25 each for stories and poems, $25 for book reviews. Contributors also receive 2 copies. Sample copy $4. Free writer's guidelines. "We don't publish straight nonfiction, but we do publish stories based on real events and experiences." Send complete ms to Ms. Gerry Mandel, editor. Will accept typewritten and legibly handwritten mss. Include SASE. Responds in 1 month.

Artwork/Photography: Publishes any type, size or color artwork/photos by children. Pays $15 for b&w or color illustrations. Contributors receive 2 copies. Sample copy $4. Free illustrator's guidelines. Send originals if possible. Send submissions to Ms. Gerry Mandel, editor. Include SASE. Responds in 1 month. Original artwork returned at job's completion. All artwork must be by children through age 13.

Tips: "Be sure to enclose a SASE. Only work by young people through age 13 is considered. Whether your work is about imaginary situations or real ones, use your own experiences and observations to give your work depth and a sense of reality. Read a few issues of our magazine to get an idea of what we like."

N STUDENTSWRITE.COM., P.O. Box 90046, San Antonio TX 78209. E-mail: editor@studentswrite.com. Website: www.studentswrite.com. Website. New work posted monthly; archive also available. "Our audience is young writers 12-19, their teachers and their parents." Purpose in publishing works by young people: to give them an opportunity to publish their work online along with other talented young writers, and to show them that they can be published authors. Children must be 12-19 years old. "We do send a form for them to sign after their work is accepted that states that their work is original." Writer's guidelines available on request; e-mail guidelines@studentswrite.com for instantaneous response.

Magazines: 50% of web page written by young people. Uses 1 fiction story (800-2,000 words) or 1 opinionated essay, personal experience, etc. (800-2,000 words), 3 poems (maximum 30 lines) per issue. "Very experienced young writers may submit articles discussing the art and business of writing; relate experience in cover letter."

Submit mss to Susan Currie, editor. Include SASE. Responds in 1 month. Work must be typed. E-mail submissions are encouraged and preferred. We will ask for contributors' word processing file upon acceptance, which can be e-mailed or sent on disk. Articles by adults on various writing and publishing topics are desperately needed; send mss (preferred over queries).

Tips: "Be persistent and careful in your submissions! Keep trying until you've published. We also need articles on the art and business of writing from adults. We appreciate cover letters!"

☑ ☑ **VIRGINIA WRITING**, Longwood College, 201 High St., Farmville VA 23909-1839. (804)395-2160. Fax: (804)392-6441. E-mail: tdean@longwood.lwc.com. Website: www.lwc.edu/vawriting. Submit entries to: Billy C. Clark, editor. Magazine published twice yearly. "*Virginia Writing* publishes prose, poetry, fiction, nonfiction, art, photography, music and drama from Virginia high school students and teachers. The purpose of the journal is to give "promising writers, artists and photographers, the talented young people of Virginia, an opportunity to have their works published. Our audience is mainly Virginia high schools, Virginia public libraries, Department of Education offices, and private citizens. The magazine is also used as a supplementary text in many of Virginia's high school classrooms. The children must be attending a Virginia high school, preferably in no less than 9th grade (though some work has been accepted from 8th graders). Originality is strongly encouraged. The guidelines are in the front of our magazine or available with SASE." No profanity or racism accepted.

● *Virginia Writing* is the recipient of 15 national awards, including the 1997 Golden Shoestring Honor Award, eight Distinguished Achievement Awards for Excellence in Educational Journalism and the Golden Lamp Honor Award as one of the top four educational magazines in the U.S. and Canada.

Magazines: 85% of magazine written by children. Uses approximately 7 fiction and nonfiction short stories and essays, 56 poems per issue. Submit complete ms. Will accept only typewritten mss. All works (writings, art, and photography) must be titled. Responds in 4 months, "but must include SASE to receive a reply in the event manuscript is not accepted."

Artwork/Photography: Publishes artwork by children. Considers all types of artwork, including that done on computer. Color slides of artwork are acceptable. All original work is returned upon publication in a non-bendable, well protected package. Responds as soon as possible.

Tips: "All works should be submitted with a cover letter describing student's age, grade and high school currently attending. Submit as often as you like and in any quantity. We cannot accept a work if it features profanity or racism."

☑ **WORD DANCE**, Playful Productions, Inc., P.O. Box 10804, Wilmington DE 19850-0804. (302)894-1950. Fax: (302)894-1957. E-mail: playful@worddance.com. Website: www.worddance.com. Director: Stuart Unger. Magazine. Published quarterly. "We're a magazine of creative writing and art that is for *and* by children in kindergarten through grade eight. We give children a voice."

Magazines: Uses adventure, fantasy, humorous, etc. (fiction); travel stories, poems and stories based on real life experiences (nonfiction). Publishes 250 total pieces of writing/year; maximum length: 3 pages. Submit mss to Stuart Ungar, articles editor. Sample copy $3. Free writer's guidelines and submissions form. SASE. Responds in 9 months.

Artwork: Illustrations accepted from young people in kindergarten through grade 8. Accepts illustrations of specific stories or poems and other general artwork. Must be high contrast. Query. Submit complete package with final art to art director. SASE. Responds in 8 months.

Tips: "Submit writing that falls into one of our specific on-going departments. General creative writing submissions are much more competitive."

THE WRITERS' SLATE, (The Writing Conference, Inc.), P.O. Box 27288, Overland Park KS 66225-7288. (913)681-8894. Fax: (913)681-8894. E-mail: jbushman@writingconference.com. Website: www.writingconference.com. Magazine. Publishes 3 issues/year. *The Writers' Slate* accepts original poetry and prose from students enrolled in kindergarten-12th grade. The audience is students, teachers and librarians. Purpose in publishing works by young people: to give students the opportunity to publish and to give students the opportunity *to read* quality literature written by other students. Writer's guidelines available on request.

Magazines: 90% of magazine written by young people. Uses 10-15 fiction, 1-2 nonfiction, 10-15 other mss per issue. Submit mss to Dr. F. Todd Goodson, editor, Kansas State University, 364 Bluemont Hall, Manhattan KS 66506-5300. Submit complete ms. Will accept typewritten mss. Responds in 1 month. Include SASE with ms if reply is desired.

Artwork: Publishes artwork by young people. Bold, b&w, student artwork may accompany a piece of writing. Submit to Dr. F. Todd Goodson, editor. Responds in 1 month.

Tips: "Always accompany submission with a letter indicating name, home address, school, grade level and teacher's name. If you want a reply, submit a SASE."

Resources
Agents & Art Reps

This section features listings of literary agents and art reps who either specialize in or represent a good percentage of children's writers or illustrators. While there are a number of children's publishers who are open to nonagented material, using the services of an agent or rep can be beneficial to a writer or artist. Agents and reps can get your work seen by editors and art directors more quickly. They are familiar with the market and have insights into which editors and art directors would be most interested in your work. Also, they negotiate contracts and will likely be able to get you a better deal than you could get on your own.

Agents and reps make their income by taking a percentage of what writers and illustrators receive from publishers. The standard percentage for agents is 10-15 percent; art reps generally take 25-30 percent. We have not included any agencies in this section that charge reading fees.

WHAT TO SEND

When putting together a package for an agent or rep, follow the guidelines given in their listings. Most agents open to submissions prefer initially to receive a query letter describing your work. (For tips on queries, see Writing Effective Query Letters on page 22.) For novels and longer works, some agents ask for an outline and a number of sample chapters, but you should send these only if you're asked to do so. Never fax or e-mail a query letter or sample chapters to agents without their permission. Just as with publishers, agents receive a large volume of submissions. It may take them a long time to reply, so you may want to query several agents at one time. It's best, however, to have a complete manuscript considered by only one agent at a time. Always include a self-addressed, stamped envelope (SASE).

For initial contact with art reps, send a brief query letter and self-promo pieces. Again, follow the guidelines given in the listings. If you don't have a flier or brochure, send photocopies. (For tips on creating promotional material see For Illustrators: Super Self-Promotion Strategies on page 44.) Always include a SASE.

An Organization for Agents

In some listings of agents you'll see references to AAR (The Association of Authors' Representatives). This organization requires its members to meet an established list of professional standards and code of ethics.

The objectives of AAR include keeping agents informed about conditions in publishing and related fields; encouraging cooperation among literary organizations; and assisting agents in representing their author-clients' interests. Officially, members are prohibited from directly or indirectly charging reading fees. They offer writers a list of member agents on their website or through the mail (for $7 plus 55¢ postage). They also offer a list of recommended questions an author should ask an agent. They can be contacted at AAR, P.O. Box 237201, Ansonia Station NY 10003. Website: www.aar-online.org.

For those who both write and illustrate, some agents listed will consider the work of author/illustrators. Read through the listings for details.

As you consider approaching agents and reps with your work, keep in mind that they are very choosy about who they take on to represent. Your work must be high quality and presented professionally to make an impression on them. For insights from an art rep on what impresses him in a submission, read the Insider Report with Leighton O'Connor of Leighton & Company on page 291. For more listings of agents and more information and tips see *Guide to Literary Agents*; for additional listing of art reps see *Artist's & Graphic Designer's Market* (both Writer's Digest Books).

Information on agents and art reps listed in the previous edition but not included in this edition of *Children's Writer's & Illustrator's Market* may be found in the General Index.

AGENTS

BOOKS & SUCH, 3093 Maiden Ln., Altadena CA 91001. (626)797-1716. Fax: (626)398-0246. E-mail: jkgboo ks@aol.com. **Contact:** Janet Kobobel Grant. Estab. 1996. Associate member of CBA. Represents 25 clients. 17% of clients are new/unpublished writers. Specializes in "general and inspirational fiction, romance, specializes in the Christian booksellers market but is expanding into the ABA market as well as children's and young adult market."
- Before becoming an agent, Ms. Grant was an editor for Zondervan and managing editor for *Focus on the Family*.
Represents: 34% juvenile books. Considers: nonfiction, fiction, picture books, young adult.
How to Contact: Query with SASE. Considers simultaneous queries. Responds in 1 month on queries; 6 weeks on mss. Returns material only with SASE.
Recent Sales: The Hidden Diary series, by Sandra Byrd (Bethany House).
Needs: Actively seeking "material appropriate to the Christian market or that would crossover to the ABA market as well." Obtains new clients through recommendations and conferences.
Terms: Agent receives 15% commission on domestic and foreign sales. Offers written contract. 2 months notice must be given to terminate contract. Charges for postage, photocopying, fax and express mail.
Tips: "The heart of my motivation is to develop relationships with the authors I serve, to do what I can to shine the light of success on them, and to help be a caretaker of their gifts and time."

☑ **ANDREA BROWN LITERARY AGENCY, INC.**, P.O. Box 371027, Montara CA 94037-1027. (650)728-1783. E-mail: ablit@home.com. **President:** Andrea Brown. Estab. 1981. Member of AAR, SCBWI and Authors Guild. 10% of clients are new/previously unpublished writers. Specializes in "all kinds of children's books—illustrators and authors."
- Prior to opening her agency, Brown served as an editorial assistant at Random House and Dell Publishing and as an editor with Alfred A. Knopf.
Member Agents: Andrea Brown, Laura Rennert.
Represents: 98% juvenile books. Considers: nonfiction (animals, anthropology/archaeology, art/architecture/design, biography/autobiography, current affairs, ethnic/cultural interests, history, how-to, nature/environment, photography, popular culture, science/technology, sociology, sports); fiction (historical, science fiction); picture books, young adult.
How to Contact: Query. Responds in 1 month on queries; 3 months on mss.
Needs: Mostly obtains new clients through recommendations, editors, clients and agents.
Terms: Agent receives 15% commission on domestic sales; 20% on foreign sales. Written contract.
Tips: Query first. "Taking on very few picture books. Must be unique—no rhyme, no anthropomorphism. Do not call, or fax queries or manuscripts." Agents at Andrea Brown Literary Agency attend Austin Writers League; SCBWI, Orange County Conferences; Mills College Childrens Literature Conference (Oakland CA); Asilomar (Pacific Grove CA); Maui Writers Conference, Southwest Writers Conference; San Diego State University Writer's Conference; Big Sur Children's Writing Workshop (Director). Recent sales include *All About The 50 States*, by Bill Giftman (Random House); *Music Teacher from the Black Lagoon*, by Mike Thaler (Scholastic); *Jill Tater and Seti*, by Ellen Jackson (Houghton-Mifflin).

PEMA BROWNE LTD., HCR Box 104B, Pine Rd., Neversink NY 12765-9603. (914)985-2936. Website: www.geocities.com/~pemabrowneltd. **Contact:** Perry Browne or Pema Browne ("Pema rhymes with Emma"). Estab. 1966. Member of SCBWI. Represents 50 clients. Handles selected commercial fiction, nonfiction, romance, business, new age, reference, pop culture, juvenile and children's picture books.

● Prior to opening their agency, Perry Browne was a radio and TV performer; Pema Browne was a fine artist and art buyer.

Member Agents: Pema Browne (children's fiction and nonfiction, adult nonfiction); Perry Browne (adult fiction and nonfiction).

Represents: 35% juvenile books. Considers: nonfiction, fiction, picture books, young adult.

How to Contact: Query with SASE. No fax queries. No e-mail queries. Responds in 3 weeks on queries; within 6 weeks on mss. Prefers to be the only reader. "We do not review manuscripts that have been sent out to publishers."Returns materials only with SASE.

Needs: Actively seeking nonfiction, juvenile, middle grade, some young adult, picture books. Obtains new clients through "editors, authors, *LMP, Guide to Literary Agents* and as a result of longevity!"

Terms: Agent receives 15% commission on domestic sales; 20% on foreign sales.

Tips: "In nonfiction, one must have credentials to lend credence to a proposal. Make sure of margins, double-space and use clean, dark type." This agency sold 25 books in the last year.

DWYER & O'GRADY, INC., P.O. Box 239, Lempster NH 03605-0239. (603)863-9347. Fax: (603)863-9346. E-mail: dosouth@mindspring.com. **Contact:** Elizabeth O'Grady. Estab. 1990. Member of SCBWI. Represents 20 clients. Represents only writers and illustrators of children's books.

● Dwyer & O'Grady is currently not accepting new clients.

Member Agents: Elizabeth O'Grady (children's books); Jeff Dwyer (children's books).

Represents: 100% juvenile books. Considers: nonfiction, fiction, picture books, young adult.

Recent Sales: *Moon Over Blind Eye*, by N. Tarpley/E.B. Lewis (Knopf Byr); *Louisa May & Mr. Thoreau's Flute*, by J. Duhlar/M.Azarian (Dial Byr); *Gleam & Glow*, by E. Bunting/P. Sylvada (Harcourt).

Needs: Obtains new clients through referrals or direct approach from agent to writer whose work they've read.

Terms: Agent receives 15% commission on domestic sales; 20% on foreign sales. Offers written contract. Thirty days notice must be given to terminate contract. Charges for "photocopying of longer manuscripts or mutually agreed upon marketing expenses."

Tips: Agents from Dwyer & O'Grady attend Book Expo; American Library Association; Society of Children's Book Writers & Illustrators conferences. Clients include: Kim Ablon, Tom Bodett, Odds Bodkin, Donna Clair, Pat Lowery Collins, Leonard Jenkins, Rebecca Rule, Steve Schuch, Virginia Stroud, Natasha Tarpley, Zong-Zhou Wang, Rashida Watson, Jabari Pesim and Peter Sylvada, Pegi Deitz Shea, Mary Azarian, and E.B. Lewis.

☑ **ETHAN ELLENBERG LITERARY AGENCY**, 548 Broadway, #5-E, New York NY 10012. (212)431-4554. Fax: (212)941-4652. E-mail: eellenberg@aol.com. Website: http://EthanEllenberg.com. **Contact:** Ethan Ellenberg. Estab. 1983. Represents 70 clients. 10% of clients are new/previously unpublished writers. Children's books are an important area for us.

● Prior to opening his agency, Ellenberg was contracts manager of Berkley/Jove and associate contracts manager for Bantam.

Represents: "We do a lot of children's books." Considers: nonfiction, fiction, picture books, young adult.

How to Contact: Children's submissions—send full ms. Young adults—send outline plus 3 sample chapters. Accepts queries by e-mail; does not accept attachments to e-mail queries or fax queries. Considers simultaneous queries and submissions. Responds in 10 days on queries; 3-4 weeks on mss. Returns materials only with SASE.

Terms: Agent receives 15% on domestic sales; 10% on foreign sales. Offers written contract, "flexible." Charges for "direct expenses only: photocopying, postage."

Tips: "We do consider new material from unsolicited authors. Write a good clear letter with a succinct description of your book. We prefer the first three chapters when we consider fiction, but for children's book submissions, we prefer the full manuscript. For all submissions you must include SASE for return or the material is discarded. It's always hard to break in, but talent will find a home. We continue to see natural storytellers and nonfiction writers with important books." This agency sold over 100 titles in the last year, including *Puppy and Me* series, by Julia Noonan (Scholastic).

FLANNERY LITERARY, 1140 Wickfield Court, Naperville IL 60563-3300. (630)428-2682. Fax: (630)428-2683. **Contact:** Jennifer Flannery. Estab. 1992. Represents 33 clients. 90% of clients are new/previously unpublished writers. Specializes in children's and young adult, juvenile fiction and nonfiction.

● Prior to opening her agency, Ms. Flannery was an editorial assistant.

Represents: 95% juvenile books. Considers: nonfiction, fiction, picture books, young adult.

How to Contact: Query. Responds in 3 weeks on queries; 5 weeks on mss.

Needs: Obtains new clients through referrals and queries.

Terms: Agent receives 15% commission on domestic sales; 20% on foreign sales. Offers written contract, binding for life of book in print, with 30 day cancellation clause. 100% of business is derived from commissions on sales.

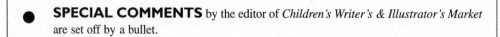

● **SPECIAL COMMENTS** by the editor of *Children's Writer's & Illustrator's Market* are set off by a bullet.

Tips: "Write an engrossing succinct query describing your work." Jennifer Flannery attends SCBWI conferences. Flannery Literary sold 20 titles in the last year.

KIRCHOFF/WOHLBERG, INC., AUTHORS' REPRESENTATION DIVISION, 866 United Nations Plaza, #525, New York NY 10017. (212)644-2020. Fax: (212)223-4387. Director of Operations: John R. Whitman. Estab. 1930s. Member of AAR. Represents 50 authors. 10% of clients are new/previously unpublished writers. Specializes in juvenile through young adult trade books and textbooks.
Member Agents: Liza Pulitzer-Voges (juvenile and young adult authors).
Represents: 80% juvenile books, 5% young adult. "We are interested in any original projects of quality that are appropriate to the juvenile and young adult trade book markets. But we take on very few new clients as our roster is full."
How to Contact: "Send a query that includes an outline and a sample; SASE required." Responds in 1 month on queries; 2 months on mss. Please send queries to the attention of Liza Pulitzer-Voges.
Needs: "Usually obtains new clients through recommendations from authors, illustrators and editors."
Terms: Agent receives standard commission "depending upon whether it is an author only, illustrator only, or an author/illustrator book." Offers written contract, binding for not less than 1 year.
Tips: Kirchoff/Wohlberg has been in business since 1930 and sold over 50 titles in the last year."

✔ **BARBARA S. KOUTS, LITERARY AGENT**, P.O. Box 560, Bellport NY 11713. (631)286-1278. **Contact:** Barbara Kouts. Estab. 1980. Member of AAR. Represent 50 clients. 10% of clients are new/previously unpublished writers. Specializes in adult fiction and nonfiction and children's books.
Represents: 60% juvenile books. Considers: nonfiction, fiction, picture books, young adult.
How to Contact: Query. Responds in 3 days on queries; 6 weeks on mss.
Needs: Obtains new clients through recommendations from others, solicitation, at conferences, etc.
Terms: Agent receives 15% commission on domestic sales; 20% on foreign sales. Charges for photocopying.
Tips: "Write, do not call. Be professional in your writing." Recent sales of this agency include *Dancing on the Edge*, by Han Nolan (Harcourt Brace); *Cendrillon*, by Robert San Souci (Simon & Schuster).

⟦N⟧ **LEIGHTON & COMPANY, INC.**, 7 Washington St., Beverly MA 01915. (978)921-0887. Fax: (978) 921-0223. E-mail: leighton@leightonreps.com. Website: www.leightonreps.com. **Contact:** Leighton O'Connor. Commercial Illustration Representatives and Literary Agents. Estab. 1986. Member of the SCBWI and GAG. Represents 35 illustrators and 10 writers. Markets include: publishing/books; advertising agencies; corporations/clients direct; design firms; editorial/magazines.
Represents: Illustration and children's book manuscripts. "Looking for fresh manuscripts for simple picture books from writers and illustrators." Does not handle novels, chapter books, nonfiction or young adult books.
How to Contact: For illustrators, send an e-mail with link to website or send non-returnable samples by mail. No attachments. Only responds if interested. For writers, please e-mail short synopsis on manuscript. Will respond to all inquires for manuscripts.
Terms: Rep receives 25%-30% commission for commercial artwork and 10-20% for manuscripts. Illustration advertising costs (if needed) are split: 75% paid by talent; 25% by representative." For promotional purpose illustrators must supply artwork for two websites and printed samples for promotion." Advertises in *Black Book*, *Showcase*, *Graphic Artists Guild Directory* and *Workbook*.
Tips: "Currently we have a full stable of illustrators, but when we do solicit new talent, it's from referrals, direct mail or their website. Only send a portfolio when requested. Send nonreturnable samples or enclose a SASE. We like to handle manuscripts that are unusual, a little off beat and very visual. Please no stories about bunnies, fairies, dragons or monsters. Do some research on our website before you e-mail a submission. It's also very important to get the correct spelling and address of the agent. Follow-up e-mails are always better then phone calls."

✔ **RAY LINCOLN LITERARY AGENCY**, Elkins Park House, Suite 107-B, 7900 Old York Rd., Elkins Park PA 19027. (215)635-0827. Fax: (215)782-8882. **Contact:** Mrs. Ray Lincoln. Estab. 1974. Represents 30 clients. 35% of clients are new/previously unpublished writers. Specializes in biography, nature, the sciences, fiction in both adult and children's categories.
Member Agents: Jerome A. Lincoln.
Represents: 20% juvenile books. Considers nonfiction, fiction, young adult, chapter and picture books.
How to Contact: Query first, then on request send outline, 2 sample chapters and SASE. "I send for balance of manuscript if it is a likely project." Responds in 2 weeks on queries; 1 month on mss.
Needs: Obtains new clients usually from recommendations.
Terms: Agent receives 15% commission on domestic sales; 20% on foreign sales. Offers written contract, binding "but with notice, may be cancelled." Charges only for overseas telephone calls. "I request authors to do manuscript photocopying themselves. Postage or shipping charge on manuscripts accepted for representation by agency."
Tips: "I always look for polished writing style, fresh points of view and professional attitudes." Recent sales of this agency include *The Blandeys Family*, by Barbara Robinson (HarperCollins); *Stargirl*, by Jerry Spinelli (Knopf); *Moe McTooth*, by Eileen Spinelli (Houghton Mifflin); and *Towanda and Me*, by Susan Katz (Orchard Books).

GINA MACCOBY LITERARY AGENCY, P.O. Box 60, Chappaqua NY 10514. (914)238-5630. **Contact:** Gina Maccoby. Estab. 1986. Represents 35 clients. Represents writers and illustrators of children's books.
Represents: 33% juvenile books. **Considers:** nonfiction, fiction, young adult.
How to Contact: Query with SASE. "Please, no unsolicited mss." Considers simultaneous queries and sub-misssions. Responds in 2 months. Returns materials only with SASE.
Needs: Usually obtains new clients through recommendations from own clients.
Terms: Agent receives 15% commission on domestic sales; 25% on foreign sales. Charges for photocopying. May recover certain costs such as airmail postage to Europe or Japan or legal fees.
Tips: This agency sold 18 titles last year including *The Art of Keeping Cool*, by Janet Taylor Lisle.

☑ THE NORMA-LEWIS AGENCY, 311 W. 43rd St., Suite 602, New York NY 10036. (212)664-0807.
Contact: Norma Liebert. Estab. 1980. 50% of clients are new/previously unpublished writers. Specializes in juvenile books (pre-school to high school).
Represents: 60% juvenile books. **Considers:** nonfiction, fiction, picture books, middle grade young adult.
How to Contact: Prefers to be only reader. Responds in 6 weeks. Returns materials only with SASE.
Terms: Agent receives 15% commission on domestic sales; 20% on foreign sales.

STERNIG & BYRNE LITERARY AGENCY, 3209 S. 55th St., Milwaukee WI 53219-4433. (414)328-8034.
Fax: (414)328-8034. E-mail: jackbyrne@aol.com. **Contact:** Jack Byrne. Estab. 1950s. Member of SFWA and MWA. Represents 30 clients. 20% of clients are new/unpublished writers. Sold 17 titles in the last year. "We have a small, friendly, personal, hands-on teamwork approach to marketing."
Member Agents: Jack Byrne.
Represents: 30% juvenile books. **Considers:** nonfiction, fiction, young adult.
How to Contact: Query. Considers simultaneous queries; no simultaneous submissions. Responds in 3 weeks on queries; 3 months on mss. Returns materials only with SASE. "No SASE equals no return."
Needs: Actively seeking science fiction/fantasy. Does not want to receive romance, poetry, textbooks, highly specialized nonfiction.
Terms: Agent receives 15% commission on domestic sales; 20% on foreign sales. Offers written contract, open/non binding. 60 days notice must be given to terminate contract.
Tips: "Don't send first drafts; have a professional presentation . . . including cover letter; know your field (read what's been done . . . good and bad)." Reads *Publishers Weekly*, etc. to find new clients. Looks for "whatever catches my eye."

S©OTT TREIMEL NEW YORK, 434 Lafayette St., New York NY 10003. (212)505-8353. Fax: (212)505-0664. E-mail: mescottyt@earthlink.net. **Contact:** Scott Treimel. Estab. 1995. Represents 26 clients. 15% of clients are new/unpublished writers. Specializes in children's books, all genres: from concept board books through young adult novels: tightly focused segments of the trade and educational markets.
   ● Prior to opening his agency, Treimel was a rights agent for Scholastic, Inc.; a book packager and rights agent for United Feature Syndicate; the founding director of Warner Bros. Worldwide Publishing, a freelance editor; and a rights consultant for HarperCollins Children's Books.
Represents: 100% juvenile books. Considers all juvenile fiction and most nonfiction areas. No religious books.
How to Contact: Query with SASE. For picture books, send entire ms. Does not accept queries by fax or e-mail. No multiple submissions. Requires "30-day exclusive on requested manuscripts." Returns materials only with SASE or discards.
Needs: Actively seeking picture book illustrators, picture book authors, first chapter books, middle-grade fiction and young adult fiction. Obtains most clients through recommendations.
Terms: Agent receives 15% commission on domestic sales; 20% on foreign sales. Offers verbal or written contract, binding on a "contract-by-contract basis." Charges for photocopying, overnight/express postage, messengers and book orders.
Tips: Attends Society of Children's Book Writers & Illustrators Conferences (Los Angeles, August). Sold 20 titles in the last year.

WECKSLER-INCOMCO, 170 West End Ave., New York NY 10023. (212)787-2239. Fax: (212)496-7035.
Contact: Sally Wecksler. Estab. 1971. Represents 25 clients. 50% of clients are new/previously unpublished writers. "However, I prefer writers who have had something in print." Specializes in nonfiction with illustrations (photos and art).
   ● Prior to becoming an agent, Wecksler was an editor at *Publishers Weekly*; publisher with the international department of R.R. Bowker; and international director at Baker & Taylor.
Member Agents: Joann Amparan (general, children's books), S. Wecksler (general, foreign rights/co-editions, fiction, illustrated books, children's books).
Represents: 25% juvenile books. **Considers:** nonfiction, fiction, picture books.
How to Contact: Query with outline plus 3 sample chapters. Include brief bio. Responds in 1 month on queries; 2 months on mss.

Needs: Actively seeking "illustrated books for adults or children with beautiful photos or artwork." Does not want to receive "science fiction or books with violence." Obtains new clients through recommendations from others and solicitations.

Terms: Agent receives 12-15% commission on domestic sales; 20% on foreign sales. Offers written contract, binding for 3 years.

Tips: "Make sure a SASE is enclosed. Send three chapters and outline, clearly typed or word processed manuscript, double-spaced, written with punctuation and grammar in approved style. *We do not like to receive presentations by fax.*"

WRITERS HOUSE, 21 W. 26th St., New York NY 10010. (212)685-2400. Fax: (212)685-1781. Estab. 1974. Member of AAR. Represents 280 clients. 50% of clients were new/unpublished writers. Specializes in all types of popular fiction and nonfiction. No scholarly, professional, poetry or screenplays.

Member Agents: Amy Berkower (major juvenile authors); Merrilee Heifetz (quality children's fiction); Susan Cohen (juvenile and young adult fiction and nonfiction); Susan Ginsberg; Fran Lebowitz (juvenile and young adult); Robin Rue (YA fiction).

Represents: 35% juvenile books. Considers: nonfiction, fiction, picture books, young adult.

How to Contact: Query. Responds in 1 month on queries.

Needs: Obtains new clients through recommendations from others.

Terms: Agent receives 15% commission on domestic sales; 20% on foreign sales. Offers written contract, binding for 1 year.

Tips: "Do not send manuscripts. Write a compelling letter. If you do, we'll ask to see your work."

☑ **WRITERS HOUSE**, (West Coast Office), 3368 Governor Dr., #224F, San Diego CA 92122. (858)678-8767. Fax: (858)678-8530. **Contact:** Steven Malk.

Represents: Nonfiction, fiction, picture books, young adult.

How to Contact: Query. Responds in 6-8 weeks to queries.

Tips: "Be professional. Enclose a SASE. Put time and thought into your query letter."

ART REPS

N· ARTCO/GAIL THURM, 232 Madison Ave., Suite 512, New York NY 10016. (212)889-8777. Fax: (212)447-1475. E-mail: artco1@mindspring.com. Website: www.artcorep.com. **Contact:** Gail Thurm. Commercial illustration representative. Estab. 1980. Member of Graphic Artists Guild. Represents 43 illustrators. Approximately 25% of artwork handled is children's book illustration. Staff includes Gail Thurm, Jeff Palmer. Currently open to illustrators seeking representation. Open to both new and established illustrators. Submission guidelines available for #10 SASE.

Handles: Illustration.

Recent Sales: *Follow the Moon*, illustrated by Suzanne Duranceau (HarperCollins/Laura Geringer); *Whitefish Will Rides Again*, by Mort Drucker (HarperCollins/Michael di Capua); *Tomatoes From Mars*, by Mort Drucker (HarperCollins di Capua); *Driftwood Cove*, by Ron Lightburn (Doubleday Canada Ltd. BC Prize Winner). Represents Sue Hughes, Sally Vitsky, Tim Barnes, Ron Lightburn, Mort Drucker, Inkwell Studios, Suzanne Duranceau.

Terms: Offers written contract. Advertising costs are split: approximately 70% paid by illustrators; 30% paid by rep. Requires portfolio and tearsheets for promotional purposes. Advertises in *Picturebook, American Showcase, Creative Black Book, Workbook, Directory of Illustration.*

How to Contact: For first contact, send any of the following: photostats, SASE (required for return of materials), slides, direct mail flier/brochure, photographs, tearsheets, photocopies. Responds only if interested. Portfolio should include tearsheets, slides and photocopies. Finds illustrators through recommendations from other, queries/solicitations, conferences.

☑ **ARTISTS INTERNATIONAL**, 17 Wheaton Rd., New Preston CT 06791. (860)868-1011. Fax: (860)868-1272. E-mail: artsintl@javanet.com. Website: www.artistsinternational.com. **Contact:** Michael Brodie. Commercial illustration representative. Estab. 1970. Represents 20 illustrators. Specializes in children's books. Markets include: design firms; editorial/magazines; licensing.

Handles: Illustration.

Terms: Rep receives 30% commission. No geographic restrictions. Advertising costs are split: 70% paid by talent; 30% paid by representative.

How to Contact: For first contact, send slides, photocopies and SASE. Reports in 1 week.

Tips: Obtains new talent through recommendations from others, solicitation, conferences, *Literary Market Place*, etc. "SAE with example of your work; no résumés please."

☑ **ASCIUTTO ART REPS., INC.**, 1712 E. Butler Circle, Chandler AZ 85225. (480)899-0600. Fax: (480)899-3636. **Contact:** Mary Anne Asciutto. Children's illustration representative. Estab. 1980. Member of SPAR, Society of Illustrators. Represents 12 illustrators. Specializes in children's illustration for books, magazines, posters, packaging, etc. Markets include: publishing/packaging/advertising.

Handles: Illustration only.

Terms: Rep receives 25% commission. No geographic restrictions. Advertising costs are split: 75% paid by talent; 25% paid by representative. For promotional purposes, talent should provide "prints (color) or originals within an 8½×11 size format."

How to Contact: Send a direct mail flier/brochure, tearsheets, photocopies and SASE. Reports in 2 weeks. After initial contact, send appropriate materials if requested. Portfolio should include original art on paper, tearsheets, photocopies or color prints of most recent work. If accepted, materials will remain for assembly.

Tips: In obtaining representation "be sure to connect with an agent who handles the kind of accounts you (the artist) *want*."

☑ **CAROL BANCROFT & FRIENDS**, 121 Dodgingtown Rd., P.O. Box 266, Bethel CT 06801. (203)748-4823 or (800)720-7020. Fax: (203)748-4581. E-mail: artists@carolbancroft.com. Website: www.carolbancroft.com. **Owner:** Carol Bancroft. Illustration representative for children's publishing. Estab. 1972. Member of SPAR, Society of Illustrators, Graphic Artists Guild. Represents 40 illustrators. Specializes in illustration for children's publishing—text and trade; any children's-related material. Clients include Scholastic, Houghton Mifflin, Harper-Collins, Dutton, Harcourt Brace.

Handles: Illustration for children of all ages. Seeking multicultural and fine artists.

Terms: Rep receives 25-30% commission. Advertising costs are split: 75% paid by talent; 25% paid by representative. For promotional purposes, talent must provide "laser copies (not slides), tearsheets, promo pieces, good color photocopies, etc.; 6 pieces or more is best; narrative scenes and children interacting." Advertises in *RSVP*, *Picture Book*.

How to Contact: Send samples and SASE."

Tips: "We're looking for artists who can draw animals and people with energy and, above all, imagination. They need to show characters in an engaging way with action in situational settings. Must be able to take a character through a story."

☑ **SAM BRODY, ARTISTS & PHOTOGRAPHERS REPRESENTATIVE & CONSULTANT**, 77 Winfield St., Apt. 4, E. Norwalk CT 06855-2138. Phone/fax: (203)854-0805 (for fax, add 999). E-mail: sambrody@bigplanet.com. **Contact:** Sam Brody. Commercial illustration and photography representative and broker. Estab. 1948. Member of SPAR. Represents 4 illustrators, 3 photographers, 2 designers. Markets include: advertising agencies; corporations/client direct; design firms; editorial/magazines; publishing/books; sales/promotion firms.

Handles: Consultant.

Terms: Agent receives 30% commission. Exclusive area representation is required. For promotional purposes, talent must provide back-up advertising material, i.e., cards (reprints—*Workbook*, etc.) and self-promos.

How to Contact: For first contact, send bio, direct mail flier/brochure, tearsheets. Reports in 3 days or within 1 day if interested. After initial contact, call for appointment or drop off or mail in appropriate materials for review. Portfolio should include tearsheets, slides, photographs. Obtains new talent through recommendations from others, solicitation.

Tips: Considers "past performance for clients that I check with and whether I like the work performed."

PEMA BROWNE LTD., HCR Box 104B, Pine Rd., Neversink NY 12762. (914)985-2936 or (914)985-2062. Fax: (914)985-7635. **Contact:** Pema Browne or Perry Browne. Commercial illustration representative. Estab. 1966. Represents 10 illustrators. Specializes in general commercial. Markets include: all publishing areas; children's picture books; collector plates and dolls; advertising agencies. Clients include HarperCollins, Thomas Nelson, Bantam Doubleday Dell, Nelson/Word, Hyperion, Putnam. Client list available upon request.

Handles: Illustration. Looking for "professional and unique" talent.

Terms: Rep receives 30% commission. Exclusive area representation is required. For promotional purposes, talent must provide color mailers to distribute. Representative pays mailing costs on promotion mailings.

How to Contact: For first contact, send query letter, direct mail flier/brochure and SASE. If interested will ask to mail appropriate materials for review. Portfolios should include tearsheets and transparencies or good color photocopies, plus SASE. Obtains new talent through recommendations and interviews (portfolio review).

Tips: "We are doing more publishing—all types—less advertising." Looks for "continuity of illustration and dedication to work."

☑ **CORNELL & MCCARTHY, LLC**, 2-D Cross Hwy., Westport CT 06880. (203)454-4210. Fax: (203)454-4258. E-mail: cmartreps@aol.com. Website: http://cornellandmccarthy.com. **Contact:** Merial Cornell. Children's book illustration representative. Estab. 1989. Member of SCBWI and Graphic Artists Guild. Represents 30 illustrators. Specializes in children's books: trade, mass market, educational.

A SELF-ADDRESSED, STAMPED ENVELOPE (SASE) should always be included with submissions within your own country. When sending material to other countries, include a self-addressed envelope (SAE) and International Reply Coupons (IRCs).

Handles: Illustration.

Terms: Agent receives 25% commission. Advertising costs are split: 75% paid by talent; 25% paid by representative. For promotional purposes, talent must provide 10-12 strong portfolio pieces relating to children's publishing.

How to Contact: For first contact, send query letter, direct mail flier/brochure, tearsheets, photocopies and SASE. Responds in 1 month. Obtains new talent through recommendations, solicitation, conferences.

Tips: "Work hard on your portfolio."

CREATIVE FREELANCERS MANAGEMENT, INC., 99 Park Ave., #210A, New York NY 10016. (800)398-9544. Fax: (203)532-2927. Website: www.freelancers.com. **Contact:** Marilyn Howard. Commercial illustration representative. Estab. 1988. Represents 30 illustrators. "Our staff members have art direction, art buying or illustration backgrounds." Specializes in children's books, advertising, architectural, conceptual. Markets include: advertising agencies; corporations/client direct; design firms; editorial/magazines; paper products/greeting cards; publishing/books; sales/promotion firms.

Handles: Illustration. Artists must have published work.

Terms: Rep receives 30% commission. Exclusive area representation is preferred. Advertising costs are split: 75% paid by talent; 25% paid by representative. For promotional purposes, talent must provide "printed pages to leave with clients. Co-op advertising with our firm could also provide this. Transparency portfolio preferred if we take you on, but we are flexible." Advertises in *American Showcase*, *Workbook*.

How to Contact: For first contact, send tearsheets or "whatever best shows work." Responds back only if interested.

Tips: Looks for experience, professionalism and consistency of style. Obtains new talent through "word of mouth and website."

☑ DWYER & O'GRADY, INC., P.O. Box 239, Lempster NH 03605. (603)863-9347. Fax: (603)863-9346. E-mail: dosouth@mindspring.com. **Contact:** Elizabeth O'Grady. Agents for children's picture book artists and writers. Estab. 1990. Member of Society of Illustrators, SCBWI, ABA. Represents 12 illustrators and 12 writers. Staff includes Elizabeth O'Grady, Jeffrey Dwyer. Specializes in children's picture books (middle grade and young adult). Markets include: publishing/books, audio/film.

• Dwyer & O'Grady is currently not accepting new clients.

Handles: Illustrators and writers of children's books.

Terms: Receives 15% commission domestic, 20% foreign. Additional fees are negotiable. Exclusive representation is required (world rights). Advertising costs are paid by representative. For promotional purposes, talent must provide both color slides and prints of at least 20 sample illustrations depicting the figure with facial expression.

Ⓝ HANNAH REPRESENTS, 14431 Ventura Blvd., #108, Sherman Oaks CA 91423. (818)378-1644. E-mail: hannah.robinson@mciworld.com. **Contact:** Hannah Robinson. Literary representative for illustrators. Estab. 1997. Represents 8 illustrators. 100% of artwork handled is children's book illustration. Looking for established illustrators only.

Handles: Manuscript/illustration packates. Looking for illustrators with book already under contract.

Terms: Receives 15% commission. Offers written contract. Advertises in *Picturebook*.

How to Contact: For first contact, send SASE and tearsheets. Responds only if interested. Call to schedule an appointment. Portfolio should include photocopies. Finds illustrators through recommendations from other, conferences, queries/solicitations, international.

Tips: Present a carefully developed range of characterization illustrations that are world-class enough to equal those in the best children's books.

HK PORTFOLIO, 666 Greenwich St., New York NY 10014. (212)675-5719. E-mail: harriet@hkportfolio.com. Website: www.hkportfolio.com. **Contact:** Harriet Kasak or Mela Bolinao. Commercial illustration representative. Estab. 1986. Member of SPAR, Society of Illustrators and Graphic Artists Guild. Represents 50 illustrators. Specializes in illustration for juvenile markets. "Sub-agent for Peters, Fraser & Dunlop (London)." Markets include: advertising agencies; editorial/magazines; publishing/books.

Handles: Illustration.

Recent Sales: *The Book of Bad Ideas*, by Laura Huliska-Beith (Little, Brown); *Dogeared*, by Amanda Harvey (Random House).

Terms: Rep receives 25% commission. No geographic restrictions. Advertising costs are split: 75% paid by talent; 25% paid by representative. Advertises in *American Showcase*, *Picturebook*, *Black Book*.

How to Contact: No geographic restrictions. For first contact, send query letter, direct mail flier/brochure, tearsheets, slides, photographs, photostats and SASE. Responds in 1 week. After initial contact, drop off or mail in appropriate materials for review. Portfolio should include tearsheets, slides, photographs, photostats, photocopies.

Tips: Leans toward highly individual personal styles.

KIRCHOFF/WOHLBERG, ARTISTS' REPRESENTATION DIVISION, 866 United Nations Plaza, #525, New York NY 10017. (212)644-2020. Fax: (212)223-4387. **Director of Operations:** John R. Whitman. Estab.

1930. Member of SPAR, Society of Illustrators, AIGA, Association of American Publishers, Bookbuilders of Boston, New York Bookbinders' Guild. Represents over 50 illustrators. Artist's Represenative: Elizabeth Ford. Specializes in juvenile and young adult trade books and textbooks. Markets include: publishing/books.
Handles: Illustration and photography (juvenile and young adult).
Terms: Rep receives 25% commission. Exclusive representation to book publishers is usually required. Advertising costs paid by representative ("for all Kirchoff/Wohlberg advertisements only"). "We will make transparencies from portfolio samples; keep some original work on file." Advertises in *American Showcase, Art Directors' Index, Society of Illustrators Annual*, children's book issues of *Publishers Weekly*.
How to Contact: Please send all correspondence to the attention of Elizabeth Ford. For first contact, send query letter, "any materials artists feel are appropriate." Responds in 6 weeks. "We will contact you for additional materials." Portfolios should include "whatever artists feel best represents their work. We like to see children's illustration in any style."

Ⓝ LEIGHTON & COMPANY, INC., 7 Washington St., Beverly MA 01915. (978)921-0887. Fax: (978) 921-0223. E-mail: leighton@leightonreps.com. Website: www.leightonreps.com. **Contact:** Leighton O'Connor. Commercial Illustration Representatives and Literary Agents. Estab. 1986. Member of the SCBWI and GAG. Represents 35 illustrators and 10 writers. Markets include: publishing/books; advertising agencies; corporations/clients direct; design firms; editorial/magazines.
Handles: Illustration and children's book manuscripts. "Looking for fresh manuscripts for simple picture books from writers and illustrators." Does not handle novels, chapter books, nonfiction or young adult books.
Terms: Rep receives 25%-30% commission for commercial artwork and 10-20% for manuscripts. Illustration advertising costs (if needed) are split: 75% paid by talent; 25% by representative." For promotional purpose illustrators must supply artwork for two websites and printed samples for promotion." Advertises in *Black Book, Showcase, Graphic Artists Guild Directory* and *Workbook*.
How to Contact: For illustrators, send an e-mail with link to website or send non returnable samples by mail. No attachments. Only responds if interested. For writers, please e-mail short synopsis on manuscript. Will respond to all inquires for manuscripts.
Tips: "Currently we have a full stable of illustrators, but when we do solicit new talent, it's from referrals, direct mail or their website. Only send a portfolio when requested. Send nonreturnable samples or enclose a SASE. We like to handle manuscripts that are unusual, a little off beat and very visual. Please no stories about bunnies, fairies, dragons or monsters. Do some research on our website before you e-mail a submission. It's also very important to get the correct spelling and address of the agent. Follow-up e-mails are always better then phone calls."

☑ LINDGREN & SMITH, 250 W. 57th St., #521, New York NY 10107. (212)397-7330. Fax: (212)397-7334. E-mail: pat@lindgrensmith.com. Website: www.lindgrensmith.com. **Assistant:** Pamela Wilson. Commercial illustration representative. Estab. 1984. Member of SPAR. Markets include children's books, advertising agencies; corporations/client direct; design firms; editorial/magazines; paper products/greeting cards; publishing/books.
Handles: Illustration.
Recent Sales: *Chicken Chuck*, by Steven Salerno, illustrator (Winslow Press); *Friend Frog*, by Lori Lohstoeter, illustrator (Harcourt); *The Christmas Treasury*, by Valerie Sokolova illustrator (Golden).
Terms: Exclusive representation is required. Advertises in *American Showcase, The Workbook, The Black Book* and *Picturebook*.
How to Contact: For first contact, send direct mail flier/brochure, tearsheets, photocopies. "We will respond by mail or phone."
Tips: "Check to see if your work seems appropriate for the group. We only represent experienced artists who have been professionals for some time. The request that you send will be one of many received—it must be excellent in all ways—a good, simple postcard will do for first contact."

Ⓝ NACHREINER BOIE ART FACTORY, 925 Elm Grove Rd., Elm Grove WI 53122. (262)785-1940. Fax: (262)785-1611. E-mail: nbart@execpc.com. Website: www.expecpc.com/artfactory. **Contact:** Tom Stockl. Commercial illustration representative. Estab. 1978. Represents 9 illustrators. 10% of artwork handled is children's book illustration. Staff includes Tom Stockl and Tom Nachreiner.Currently open to illustrators seeking representation. Open to both new and established illustrators.
Handles: Illustration.
Recent Sales: Represents Tom Buchs, Tom Nachreiner, Todd Dakins, Linda Godfrey, Larry Mikec, Bill Scott, Amanda Aquino.
Terms: Receives 25-30% commission. Offers written contract. Advertising costs are split: 75% paid by illustrators; 25% paid by rep. "We try to mail samples of all our illustrators at one time and we try to update our website; so we ask the illustrators to keep up with new samples." Advertises in *Picturebook, Workbook*.
How to Contact: For first contact, send query letter, tearsheets. Responds only if interested. Call to schedule an appointment. Portfolio should include tearsheets. Finds illustrators through queries/solicitations.
Tips: "Have a unique style."

insider report

Tips from a rep: 'You're only as good as your worst piece'

Leighton O'Connor of Leighton & Company, Inc., started out as a rep more than a dozen years ago. He began his career representing photographers, as he was a photographer himself for a time. "I started an industrial photography business and shot fun things like shoes, power supplies, widgets, and other exciting products. I enjoyed the business end of things, but my photo career was not doing the trick for me," he says.

So O'Connor stopped the photographing part, stuck with the business part and began to rep photographers, eventually taking on a few illustrators. He enjoyed representing illustrators so much, he finally decided to do that exclusively.

Leighton O'Connor

Probably the first rep to take his business online, O'Connor created a presence on the Internet in 1996. "I saw the amazing potential," he says. "Now I thank the Web gods every day." O'Connor's website, www.leighton-reps.com, is easy to navigate, and includes attractive icons leading to all the site's features, among them the portfolios of the illustrators he represents. Leighton & Company's stable of illustrators work in a number of areas, including, of course, children's books. He reps children's book illustrators Scott Nash (*Six Hogs on a Scooter, Oh, Tucker!*), Linda Bronson (*The Babies Are Landing, Teatime With Emma Buttersnap*) and others.

When shopping the work of commercial illustrators, O'Connor may send two thousand postcards to potential buyers. For his children's book illustrators, he prepares more personal packages. If one of his illustrators has a new book out, he'll send copies of that book to a number of editors, or he'll send a package of books by six or seven different illustrators to a group of editors, working to gear packages to specific editors' tastes. He prefers to work with editors at larger houses. "They have better distribution, and their sales are higher."

O'Connor's initial contact with an editor might be through an e-mail telling about his website. "That piques their curiosity, editors visit the site and ask for samples. I think the Internet has changed the business as far as submissions. It changes the way I send things to editors. One of the main ways writers are finding out about me is through my website. They can actually send their manuscripts to me through e-mail and get a response sometimes in a matter of days."

O'Connor is open to receiving manuscripts and illustration samples, but he's most interested in illustrators who can write as well. "That's something that editors really like because it streamlines the production process," he says. "I may pick up an illustrator/writer on a per project basis rather than repping them fully."

He is also open to manuscripts without illustrations. "I'm taking on more writers right now than illustrators and author/illustrators." About 95% submit through e-mail. (O'Connor offers e-mail submission guidelines for writers on his website.)

"I'm very simpleminded," O'Connor jokes, "so the stories I take on have to be simple. I have to be able to envision the illustrations. Because I represent picture books, I look for a good story that can be illustrated well."

O'Connor stresses the importance of researching agents and reps before submitting manuscripts to them. "I do picture books. I've gotten novels. I've gotten mysteries. I've gotten chapter books. I've gotten synopses not even telling me the name of the story they're pitching," he says. "Leighton & Company is listed in directories. You can find out anything about me on my website."

Researching agencies is also a key consideration for illustrators before submitting samples. "They need to check the agencies out. They should find out which illustrators the agencies represent and the types of work their artists do. Then they need to put together a decent package, from the envelope to the samples.

"You're only as good as your worst piece," O'Connor says. "Send your best stuff—not all your stuff. Be choosy. You can't show five different styles. I like one consistent body of work."

O'Connor also advises illustrators to produce samples that show they can illustrate a story, not simply spot illustrations. "They've got to have backgrounds; they've got to show situations, characters interacting. Facial expressions are very important." He often recommends illustrators find a story, or write one themselves, and create illustrations for that story. "Then the editors will know the illustrator is very comfortable illustrating a story."

Leighton & Company Inc.
ARTISTS' REPRESENTATIVES
http://www.leightonreps.com

portfolios　artist search　get samples　stock illustration　e-mail　children's books　online estimator　contact us

Art rep Leighton O'Connor offers a great website for anyone interested in the artists he represents. When logging on to www.leightonreps.com, visitors find eye-catching icons leading them to portfolios, children's books, stock art and more. You can search for artists by name, technique, or field of expertise, and even get an online estimate for an illustration project.

The Web is a very effective promotional tool for illustrators, too. O'Connor finds that children's book editors actively look for illustrators on the Web. "A website is a great lead-generator for illustrators. It's a good way to introduce yourself to children's book editors. But you have to promote the site—mention it on your voicemail, on all your promo pieces, on the back of your car," whatever it takes to get the word out about it. "And once you get editors there, then you have to have pieces to send them."

Editors, O'Connor says, have a tougher time finding illustrators than finding manuscripts. "Editors get so many manuscripts via the mail. But, they tell me it's very difficult to find good illustrators. They look for a lot of different criteria for children's book illustrators—do they like the person, do they like the style, can the illustrator convey the concept throughout the book? Editors also want illustrators they can have a relationship with, not just do one book."

—*Alice Pope*

N THE NEIS GROUP, P.O. Box 174, 11440 Oak Dr., Shelbyville MI 49344. (616)672-5756. Fax: (616)672-5757. E-mail: neisgroup@wmis.net. Website: www.neisgroup.com. **Contact:** Judy Neis. Commercial Illustration representative. Estab. 1982. Represents 45 illustrators. 60% of artwork handled is children's book illustration. Currently open to illustrators seeking representation. Looking for established illustrators only.
Handles: Illustration, photography and illustration/manuscript packages.
Recent Sales: Represents Lyn Bayer, Pam Thomson, Don Sharp, Terry Workman, Liz Conrad, Garry Colby, Clint Hansen, Don McLean, Donna Christensen, Peg Magover.
Terms: Receives 25% commission. Advertising costs are split: 75% paid by illustrator; 25% paid by rep. "I prefer porfolios on CD, color printouts and e-mail capabilities whenever possible." Advertises in *Picturebook, American Showcase, Creative Black Book.*
How to Contact: For first contact, send bio, tearsheets, direct mail flier/brochure. Reports back only if interested. After initial contact, drop off portfolio of non-returnables. Portfolio should include tearsheets, photocopies. Obtains new talent through recommendations from others and queries/solicitations.

N WANDA NOWAK/CREATIVE ILLUSTRATION AGENCY, 231 E. 76th St. ??, New York NY 10021. (212)535-0438. Fax: (212)535-1629. E-mail: wandanowak@aol.com. Website: www.wandanow.com. **Contact:** Wanda Nowak. Commercial illustration representative. Estab. 1996. Member of Graphic Artists Guild. Represents 16 illustrators. 25% of artwork handled is children's book illustration. Staff includes Wanda Nowak. Open to both new and established illustrators.
Handles: Illustration. Looking for "unique, individual style."
Recent Sales: *Emilie Chollart (HarperCollins), Buhet (Intervisual Books), Herve Blandon (Winslow Press), Frederique Bertrand (Random House).* Represents Martin Matje, Emilie Chollat, Herve Blandon, Thea Kliros, Pierre Pratt, Frederique Bertrand, Ilya Bereimckas, Boris Kulikov, Yayo, Charlene Potts, Donald Saof, Beatriz Vidal, Christiana Sun.
Terms: Receives 30% commission. Exclusive representation required. Offers written contract. Advertising costs are split: 70% paid by illustrators; 30% paid by rep. Advertises in *Picturebook, Workbook, The Alternative Pick.*
How to Contact: For first contact, send SASE. Responds only if interested. Drop off portfolio. Portfolio should include tearsheets. Finds illustrators through recommendations from other, sourcebooks like *CA Picture Bok, Black Book*, exhibitions.
Tips: Develop your own style, send a little illustrated story, which will prove you can carry a character in different situations with facial expressions etc.

N THE PENNY & STERMER GROUP, 2031 Holly Dr., Prescott AZ 86305. (520)708-9446 (West Coast); (212)505-9342 (East Coast). Fax: (520)708-9447. E-mail: carollee@primenet.com. Website: www.pennystermergroup.com. **Contact:** Carol Lee Stermer. Commercial illustration representative. Estab. 1978. Represents 8 illustrators. 50% of artwork handled is children's book illustration. Currently open to illustrators seeking representation. Open to both new and established illustrators.
Handles: Illustration. "We handle all types—humor, picture book, nonfiction, licensing, educational and trade, workbooks—everything for the children's market."
Recent Sales: Represents Rick Stromoski, Thomas Payne, Julia Noonan, Joanna Borerro and John Mantha.
Terms: Receives 30% commission. Advertises in *Picturebook, American Showcase, Creative Black Book, Directory of Illustration.*
How to Contact: For first contact, send promos to be kept on file; anything returnable must be sent with SASE. Finds illustrators through recommendations from others, queries/solicitations, conferences.

Tips: "Our agency is unique. We take each artist's specialties and market them directly to clients looking for their special talents. We're always interested in contacting new publishers for projects, and also in receiving promos from new illustrators and professional children's book illustrators seeking non-exclusive representation."

☑ **S.I. INTERNATIONAL**, 43 E. 19th St., New York NY 10003. (212)254-4996. Fax: (212)995-0911. E-mail: info@si-i.com. Website: www.si-i.com. Commercial illustration representative. Estab. 1983. Member of SPAR, Graphic Artists Guild. Represents 50 illustrators. Specializes in license characters, educational publishing and children's illustration, digital art and design, mass market paperbacks. Markets include design firms; publishing/books; sales/promotion firms; licensing firms; digital art and design firms.
Handles: Illustration. Looking for artists "who have the ability to do children's illustration and to do license characters either digitally or reflexively."
Terms: Rep receives 25-30% commission. Advertising costs are split: 70% paid by talent; 30% paid by representative. "Contact agency for details. Must have mailer." Advertises in *Picturebook*.
How to Contact: For first contact, send query letter, tearsheets. Reports in 3 weeks. After initial contact, write for appointment to show portfolio of tearsheets, slides.

N: LIZ SANDERS AGENCY, 16 Phaedra, Laguna Niguel CA 92677. (949)495-3664. Fax: (949)495-0229. E-mail: liz@lizsanders.com. Website: www.lizsanders.com. Commercial illustration representative. Estab. 1985. Represents 15 illustrators. 20% ("and growing!") of artwork handled is children's book illustration. Currently open to illustrators seeking representation. Open to both new and established illustrators.
Handles: Illustration.
Recent Sales: Represents Amy Ning, Tom Pansini, Chris Lensch, Barbara Johansen-Newman.
Terms: Receives 30% commission. Offers written contract. Advertises in *Picturebook*, American Showcase, *Workbook, Directory of Illustration*.
How to Contact: For first contact, send tearsheets, direct mail flier/brochure—non-returnables. Reports back. After initial contact, drop off or mail portfolio. Portfolio should include tearsheets, photocopies. Obtains new talent through recommendations from others, conferences and queries/solicitations.

Clubs & Organizations

Contacts made through organizations such as the ones listed in this section can be quite beneficial for children's writers and illustrators. Professional organizations provide numerous educational, business and legal services in the form of newsletters, workshops or seminars. Organizations can provide tips about how to be a more successful writer or artist, as well as what types of business records to keep, health and life insurance coverage to carry and competitions to consider.

An added benefit of belonging to an organization is the opportunity to network with those who have similar interests, creating a support system. As in any business, knowing the right people can often help your career, and important contacts can be made through your peers. Membership in a writer's or artist's organization also shows publishers you're serious about your craft. This provides no guarantee your work will be published, but it gives you an added dimension of credibility and professionalism.

Some of the organizations listed here welcome anyone with an interest, while others are only open to published writers and professional artists. Organizations such as the Society of Children's Book Writers and Illustrators (SCBWI) have varying levels of membership. SCBWI offers associate membership to those with no publishing credits, and full membership to those who have had work for children published. Many national organizations such as SCBWI also have regional chapters throughout the country. Write or call for more information regarding any group that sounds interesting, or check the websites of the many organizations that list them. Be sure to get information about local chapters, membership qualifications and services offered.

Information on organizations listed in the previous edition but not included in this edition of *Children's Writer's & Illustrator's Market* may be found in the General Index.

AMERICAN ALLIANCE FOR THEATRE & EDUCATION, Theatre Department, Arizona State University, Box 872002, Tempe AZ 85287-2002. (480)965-6064. Fax: (480)965-5351. E-mail: aate.info@asu.edu. Website: www.aate.com. Administrative Director: Christy M. Taylor. Purpose of organization: to promote standards of excellence in theatre and drama education by providing the artist and educator with a network of resources and support, a base for advocacy, and access to programs and projects that focus on the importance of drama in the human experience. Membership cost: $100 annually for individual in US and Canada, $130 annually for organization, $65 annually for students, $65 annually for retired people; add $20 outside Canada and US. Annual conference. Newsletter published quarterly (on website only). Contests held for unpublished play reading project and annual awards for best play. Awards plaque and stickers for published playbooks. Publishes list of unpublished plays deemed worthy of performance in newsletter and press release and staged readings at conference.

✔ **AMERICAN SCREENWRITERS ASSOCIATION**, (formerly Writers Connection), P.O. Box 12860, Cincinnati OH 45212. Phone/fax: (513)731-9212. Sponsors annual Selling to Hollywood scriptwriting conference in the Los Angeles area each August.

✔ **ARIZONA AUTHORS ASSOCIATION**, P.O. Box 87857, Phoenix AZ 85080-7857. Fax: (623)780-0468. Website: home.rmci.net/vijayaschartz/azauthors.htm. President: Vijaya Schartz. Purpose of organization: to offer professional, educational and social opportunities to writers and authors, and serve as a network. Members must be authors, writers working toward publication, agents, publishers, publicists, printers, illustrations, etc. Membership cost: $45/year writers; $30/year students; $60/year other professionals in publishing industry. Holds regular workshops and meetings. Publishes bimonthly newsletter and Arizona Literary Magazine. Sponsors Annual Literary Contest in poetry, essays, short stories, novels, with cash prizes and awards bestowed at a public banquet in Phoenix. Winning entries are also published in the Arizona Literary Magazine. Send SASE for guidelines.

ASSITEJ/USA, % Steve Bianchi, 724 Second Ave. S., Nashville TN 37210. (615)254-5719. Fax: (615)254-3255. E-mail: usassitej@aol.com. Website: www.assitej-usa.org. Purpose of organization: to promote theater for children and young people by linking professional theaters and artists together; sponsoring national, international and regional conferences and providing publications and information. Also serves as US Center for International Association of Theatre for Children and Young People. Different levels of membership include: organizations, individuals, students, retirees, libraries. *TYA Today* includes original articles, reviews and works of criticism and theory, all of interest to theater practitioners (included with membership). Publishes journal that focuses on information on field in US and abroad.

THE AUTHORS GUILD, 29th Floor, 330 W. 42nd St., New York NY 10036-6902. (212)563-5904. Fax: (212)564-8363. E-mail: staff@authorsguild.org. Website: www.authorsguild.org. Executive Director: Paul Aiken. Purpose of organization: to offer services and materials intended to help authors with the business and legal aspects of their work, including contract problems, copyright matters, freedom of expression and taxation. Guild has 7,000 members. Qualifications for membership: Must be book author published by an established American publisher within 7 years or any author who has had 3 works (fiction or nonfiction) published by a magazine or magazines of general circulation in the last 18 months. Associate membership also available. Annual dues: $90. Different levels of membership include: associate membership with all rights except voting available to an author who has a firm contract offer or is currently negotiating a royalty contract from an established American publisher. "The Guild offers free contract reviews to its members. The Guild conducts several symposia each year at which experts provide information, offer advice and answer questions on subjects of interest and concern to authors. Typical subjects have been the rights of privacy and publicity, libel, wills and estates, taxation, copyright, editors and editing, the art of interviewing, standards of criticism and book reviewing. Transcripts of these symposia are published and circulated to members. The *Authors Guild Bulletin*, a quarterly journal, contains articles on matters of interest to writers, reports of Guild activities, contract surveys, advice on problem clauses in contracts, transcripts of Guild and League symposia and information on a variety of professional topics. Subscription included in the cost of the annual dues."

█N█ ☑ CANADIAN SOCIETY OF CHILDREN'S AUTHORS, ILLUSTRATORS AND PERFORMERS, (CANSCAIP), Northern District Library, Lower Level, 40 Orchard View Blvd., Toronto, Ontario M4R 1B9 Canada. (416)515-1559. Fax: (416)515-7022. E-mail: office@canscaip.org. Website: www.canscaip.org. Office Manager: Nancy Prasad. Purpose of organization: development of Canadian children's culture and support for authors, illustrators and performers working in this field. Qualifications for membership: Members—professionals who have been published (not self-published) or have paid public performances/records/tapes to their credit. Friends—share interest in field of children's culture. Membership cost: $60 (members dues), $25 (friends dues), $30 (institution dues). Sponsors workshops/conferences. Publishes newsletter: includes profiles of members; news round-up of members' activities countrywide; market news; news on awards, grants, etc; columns related to professional concerns.

☑ THE CHILDREN'S BOOK COUNCIL, INC., 12 W. 37th St., 2nd Floor, New York NY 10018. (212)966-1990. Fax: (212)966-2073. E-mail: joanncbc@aol.com. Website: www.cbcbooks.org. Purpose of organization: "A nonprofit trade association of children's and young adult publishers and packagers, CBC promotes the enjoyment of books for children and young adults and works with national and international organizations to that end. The CBC has sponsored National Children's Book Week since 1945 and Young People's Poetry Week since 1999." Qualifications for membership: US trade publishers and packagers of children's and young adult books and related literary materials are eligible for membership. Membership cost: $60. Publishers wishing to join should contact the CBC for dues information." Sponsors workshops and seminars. Publishes a newsletter with articles about children's books and publishing and listings of free or inexpensive materials available from member publishers. Individuals wishing to receive mailings from the CBC (our semi-annual newsletter *CBC Features*—and our materials brochures) may be placed on our mailing list for a one-time-only fee. Sells reading encouragement graphics and informational materials suitable for libraries, teachers, booksellers, parents, and others working with children.

FLORIDA FREELANCE WRITERS ASSOCIATION, Cassell Network of Writers, P.O. Box A, North Stratford NH 03590. (603)922-8338. Fax: (603)922-8339. E-mail: danakcnw@ncia.net. Website: www.writers-editors.com. Executive Director: Dana K. Cassell. Purpose of organization: To act as a link between Florida writers and buyers of the written word; to help writers run more effective communications businesses. Qualifications for membership: "None—we provide a variety of services and information, some for beginners and some for established pros." Membership cost: $90/year. Publishes a newsletter focusing on market news, business news, how-to tips for the serious writer. Non-member subscription: $39—does not include Florida section—includes national edition only. Annual *Directory of Florida Markets* included in FFWA newsletter section. Publishes annual *Guide to CNW/Florida Writers*, which is distributed to editors around the country. Sponsors contest: annual deadline March 15. Guidelines available fall of each year and on website. Categories: juvenile, adult nonfiction, adult fiction and poetry. Awards include cash for top prizes, certificate for others. Contest open to non-members.

GRAPHIC ARTISTS GUILD, 90 John St., Suite 403, New York NY 10038. (212)791-3400. Fax: (212)791-0333. E-mail: execdir@gag.org. Website: www.gag.org/. Executive Director: Paul Basista, CAE. Purpose of organization: "to promote and protect the economic interests of member artists. It is committed to improving conditions for all creators of graphic arts and raising standards for the entire industry." Qualification for full membership: 50% of income derived from artwork. Associate members include those in allied fields, students and retirees. Initiation fee: $25. Full memberships $120, $165, $215, $270; student membership $55/year. Associate membership $115/year. Publishes *Graphic Artists Guild Handbook, Pricing and Ethical Guidelines* and bimonthly *Guild News* (free to members, $12 to non-members). "The Guild UAW Local 3030 is a national union that embraces all creators of graphic arts intended for presentation as originals or reproductions at all levels of skill and expertise. The long-range goals of the Guild are: to educate graphic artists and their clients about ethical and fair business practices; to educate graphic artists about emerging trends and technologies impacting the industry; to offer programs and services that anticipate and respond to the needs of our members, helping them prosper and enhancing their health and security, to advocate for the interests of our members in the legislative, judicial and regulatory arenas; to assure that our members are recognized financially and professionally for the value they provide; to be responsible stewards for our members by building an organization that works efficiently on their behalf."

N. HORROR WRITERS ASSOCIATION, P.O. Box 50577, Palo Alto CA 94303. E-mail: hwa@horror.org. Website: www.horror.org. Office Manager: Nancy Etchemendy. Purpose of organization: To encourage pubic interest in horror and dark fantasy and to provide networking and career tools for members. Qualifications for membership: Anyone who can demonstrate a serious interest in horror may join as an affiliate. Any non-writing professional in the horror field may join as an associate. (Booksellers, editors, agents, librarians, etc.) To qualify for full active membership, you must be a published, professional writer of horror. **Open to students** as affiliates, if unpublished in professional venues. Membership cost: $55 annually in North America; $65 annually elsewhere. Holds annual Stoker Awards Weekend and HWA Business Meeting. Publishes monthly newsletter focusing on market news, industry news, HWA business for members. Sponsors awards. We give the Bram Stoker Awards for superior achievement in horror annually. Awards include a handmade Stoker trophy designed by sculptor Stephen Kirk. Awards open to non-members.

N. INTERNATIONAL READING ASSOCIATION, 800 Barksdale Rd., Newark DE 19714-8139. (302)731-1600 ext. 293. Fax: (302)731-1057. E-mail: jbutler@reading.org. Website: www.reading.org. . Public Information Associate: Janet Butler. Purpose of organization: "Formed in 1956, the International Reading Association seeks to promote high levels of literacy for all by improving the quality of reading instruction through studying the reading process and teaching techniques; serving as a clearinghouse for the dissemination of reading research through conferences, journals, and other publications; and actively encouraging the lifetime reading habit. Its goals include professional development; enhance and improve professional development, advocacy, partnerships, research and global literacy development. **Open to students.** Basic membership: $30. Sponsors annual convention. Publishes a newsletter called "Reading Today." Sponsors a number of awards and fellowships. Visit the IRA website for more information on membership, conventions and awards. (this contact name will only be included if it's different from the one given in #1).

N. LITERARY MANAGERS AND DRAMATURGS OF THE AMERICAS, Box 355, CASTA, CUNY Grad Center, 33 W. 42nd St., New York NY 10036. (212)642-2657. Fax: (212)642-1977. E-mail: hbc3@columbia. edu. LMDA is a not-for-profit service organization for the professions of literary management and dramaturgy. Student Membership: $20/year. Open to students in dramaturgy, performing arts and literature programs, or related disciplines. Proof of student status required. Includes national conference, New Dramaturg activities, local symposia, job phone and select membership meetings. Active Membership: $45/year. Open to full-time and part-time professionals working in the fields of literary management and dramaturgy. All privileges and services including voting rights and eligibility for office. Associate Membership: $35/year. Open to all performing arts professionals and academics, as well as others interested in the field. Includes national conference, local symposia and select membership meetings. Institutional Membership: $100/year. Open to theaters, universities, and other organizations. Includes all privileges and services except voting rights and eligibility for office. Publishes a newsletter featuring articles on literary management, dramaturgy, LMDA program updates and other articles of interest.

✓ NATIONAL WRITERS UNION, 113 University Place, 6th Floor, New York NY 10003. (212)254-0279. Website: www.nwu.org. **Open to students.** Purpose of organization: Advocacy for freelance writers. Qualifications for membership: "Membership in the NWU is open to all qualified writers, and no one shall be barred or in any manner prejudiced within the Union on account of race, age, sex, sexual orientation, disability, national origin, religion or ideology. You are eligible for membership if you have published a book, a play, three articles,

TO RECEIVE REGULAR TIPS AND UPDATES about writing and Writer's Digest publications via e-mail, send an e-mail with "SUBSCRIBE NEWSLETTER" in the body of the message to newsletter-request@writersdigest.com

five poems, one short story or an equivalent amount of newsletter, publicity, technical, commercial, government or institutional copy. You are also eligible for membership if you have written an equal amount of unpublished material and you are actively writing and attempting to publish your work." Membership cost: annual writing income under $5,000—$90/year; annual writing income $5,000-25,000—$145/year; annual writing income over $25,000—$195/year. Holds workshops throughout the country. Offers national union newsletter quarterly, *American Writer*, issues related to freelance writing and to union organization for members. Offers contract and grievance advice.

PEN AMERICAN CENTER, 568 Broadway, New York NY 10012. (212)334-1660. Fax: (212)334-2181. E-mail: jm@pen.org. Purpose of organization: "To foster understanding among men and women of letters in all countries. International PEN is the only worldwide organization of writers and the chief voice of the literary community. Members of PEN work for freedom of expression wherever it has been endangered." Qualifications for membership: "The standard qualification for a writer to join PEN is that he or she must have published, in the United States, two or more books of a literary character, or one book generally acclaimed to be of exceptional distinction. Editors who have demonstrated commitment to excellence in their profession (generally construed as five years' service in book editing), translators who have published at least two book-length literary translations, and playwrights whose works have been professionally produced, are eligible for membership." An application form is available upon request from PEN Headquarters in New York. Candidates for membership should be nominated by 2 current members of PEN. Inquiries about membership should be directed to the PEN Membership Committee. Friends of PEN is also open to writers who may not yet meet the general PEN membership requirements. PEN sponsors public events at PEN Headquarters in New York, and at the branch offices in Boston, Chicago, New Orleans, San Francisco and Portland, Oregon. They include tributes by contemporary writers to classic American writers, dialogues with visiting foreign writers, symposia that bring public attention to problems of censorship and that address current issues of writing in the United States, and readings that introduce beginning writers to the public. PEN's wide variety of literary programming reflects current literary interests and provides informal occasions for writers to meet each other and to welcome those with an interest in literature. Events are all open to the public and are usually free of charge. The Children's Book Authors' Committee sponsors biannual public events focusing on the art of writing for children and young adults and on the diversity of literature for juvenile readers. The PEN/Norma Klein Award was established in 1991 to honor an emerging children's book author. Pamphlets and brochures all free upon request. Sponsors several competitions per year. Monetary awards range from $2,000-20,000.

🇳 PLAYMARKET, P.O. Box 9767, Te Aro Wellington New Zealand. Phone/fax: 0064(4)3828461. Director: Dilys Grant. Administrator: Laura Hill. Script Advisor: Susan Wilson. Purpose of organization: funded by the Arts Council of New Zealand, Playmarket serves as New Zealand's script advisory service and playwrights agency. Playmarket offers script assessment, development and agency services to help New Zealand playwrights secure professional production for their plays. Playmarket also assists with negotiations for film and television, radio and publishing. Holds workshops/conferences. Publishes *Playmarket Directory of New Zealand Plays and Playwrights*. Nonmember subscription $10/year. Assists with the Bruce Mason Award: "*Sunday Star Times* Bruce Mason Award for Playwright at Beginning of Career." Award includes $5,000 annually. Contest open to nonmembers, who must be residents of New Zealand.

🔳 PUPPETEERS OF AMERICA, INC., P.O. Box 29417, Parma OH 44129-0417. (888)568-6235. Fax: (440)843-7867. E-mail: pofajoin@aol.com. Website: www.puppeteers.org. Membership Officer: Gayle Schluter. Purpose of organization: to promote the art of puppetry as a means of communications and as a performing art. Qualifications for membership: interest in the art form. Membership cost: single adult, $40; youth member, $25; retiree, $25 (65 years of age); family, $60; couple, $50. Membership includes a bimonthly newsletter. Sponsors workshops/conferences. Publishes newsletter. *The Puppetry Journal* provides news about puppeteers, puppet theaters, exhibitions, touring companies, technical tips, new products, new books, films, television, and events sponsored by the Chartered Guilds in each of the 8 P of A regions. Subscription: $35 (libraries only).

SOCIETY OF CHILDREN'S BOOK WRITERS AND ILLUSTRATORS, 8271 Beverly Blvd., Los Angeles CA 90048. (323)782-1010. E-mail: info@scbwi.org (autoresponse). Website: www.scbwi.org. President: Stephen Mooser. Executive Director: Lin Oliver. Chairperson, Board of Directors: Sue Alexander. Purpose of organization: to assist writers and illustrators working or interested in the field. Qualifications for membership: an interest in children's literature and illustration. Membership cost: $50/year. Plus one time $10 initiation fee. Different levels of membership include: full membership—published authors/illustrators; associate membership—unpublished writers/illustrators. Holds 100 events (workshops/conferences) around the country each year. Open to nonmembers. Publishes a newsletter focusing on writing and illustrating children's books. Sponsors grants for writers and illustrators who are members.

SOCIETY OF ILLUSTRATORS, 128 E. 63rd St., New York NY 10021-7303. (212)838-2560. Fax: (212)838-2561. Website: www.societyillustrators.org. Director: Terrence Brown. Purpose of organization: to promote interest in the art of illustration for working professional illustrators and those in associated fields. Membership cost: Initiation fee—$250. Annual dues for non-resident members (those living more than 125 air miles from SI's headquarters) are $287. Dues for Resident Artist Members are $475 per year; Resident Associate Members $552. Different levels of membership: *Artist Members* "shall include those who make illustration their profession" and through which they earn at least 60% of their income. *Associate Members* are "those who earn their living in the arts or who have made a substantial contribution to the art of illustration." This includes art directors, art buyers, creative supervisors, instructors, publishers and like categories. The candidate must complete and sign the application form which requires a brief biography, a listing of schools attended, other training and a résumé of his or her professional career." Candidates for *Artist* membership, in addition to the above requirements, must submit examples of their work. Sponsors "The Annual of American Illustration." Awards include gold and silver medals. Open to nonmembers. Deadline: October 1. Sponsors "The Original Art: The Best of Children's Book Illustration." Deadline: mid-August. Call for details.

N: TEXT AND ACADEMIC AUTHORS ASSOCIATION, University of South Florida, St. Petersburg FL 33701. (813)553-1195. E-mail: taa@bayflash.stpt.usf.edu. Website: http://taa.winona.msus.edu/taa. Executive Director: Ronald Pynn. Purpose of organization: to address the professional concerns of text and academic authors, to protect the interests of creators of intellectual property at all levels, and support efforts to enforce copyright protection. Qualifications for membership: all authors and prospective authors are welcome. Membership cost: $30 first year; $60 per year following years. Workshops/conferences: June each year. Newsletter focuses on all areas of interest to text authors.

✓ WESTERN WRITERS OF AMERICA, INC., 1012 Fair St., Franklin TN 37064-2718. (615)791-1444. Fax: (615)791-1444. E-mail: candywwa@aol.com or tncrutch@aol.com. Website: www.westernwriters.org. Secretary/Treasurer: James A. Crutchfield. **Open to students.** Purpose of organization: to further all types of literature that pertains to the American West. Membership requirements: must be a *published* author of Western material. Membership cost: $75/year ($90 foreign). Different levels of membership include: Active and Associate—the two vary upon number of books published. Holds annual conference. The 2001 conference will be held in Idaho Falls, ID. Publishes bimonthly magazine focusing on market trends, book reviews, news of members, etc. Nonmembers may subscribe for $30 ($50 foreign). Sponsors contests. Spur awards given annually for a variety of types of writing. Awards include plaque, certificate, publicity. Contest open to nonmembers.

✓ ⚜ WRITERS GUILD OF ALBERTA, 11759 Groat Rd., Percy Page Centre, Edmonton, Alberta T5M 3K6 Canada. (780)422-8174. Fax: (780)422-2663. E-mail: wga@oanet.com. Website: www.writersguild.ab.ca. Executive Director: Mr. Miki Andrejevic. Purpose of organization: to provide meeting ground and collective voice for the writers in Alberta. Membership cost: $60/year; $20 for seniors/students. Holds workshops/conferences. Publishes a newsletter focusing on markets, competitions, contemporary issues related to the literary arts (writing, publishing, censorship, royalties etc.). Nonmembers may subscribe to newsletter. Subscription cost: $60/year. Sponsors annual literary awards program in 7 categories (novel, nonfiction, short fiction, children's literature, poetry, drama, best first book). Awards include $500, leather-bound book, promotion and publicity. Open to nonmembers.

N: WRITERS OF KERN, P.O. Box 6694, Bakersfield CA 93386-6694. (661)664-7947. Open to published writers and any person interested in writing. Dues: $35/year, $20 for students. Types of memberships: professional, writers with published work; associate—writers working toward publication, affiliate—beginners and students. Monthly meetings held on the third Saturday of every month. Bi- or tri-annual writers' workshops, with speakers who are authors, agents, etc., on topics pertaining to writing; critique groups for several fiction genres, nonfiction, journalism and screenwriting which meet bimonthly. Members receive a monthly newsletter with marketing tips, conferences and contests; access to club library; discount to annual CWC conference.

Conferences & Workshops

Writers and illustrators eager to expand their knowledge of the children's publishing industry should consider attending one of the many conferences and workshops held each year. Whether you're a novice or seasoned professional, conferences and workshops are great places to pick up information on a variety of topics and network with experts in the publishing industry, as well as your peers.

Listings in this section provide details about what conference and workshop courses are offered, where and when they are held, and the costs. Some of the national writing and art organizations also offer regional workshops throughout the year. Write or call for information.

Writers can find listings of more than 750 conferences (searchable by type, location and date) at The Writer's Digest/Shaw Guides Directory to Writers' Conferences, Seminars and Workshops—www.writersdigest.com/conferences.

Members of the Society of Children's Book Writers and Illustrators can find information on conferences in national and local SCBWI newsletters. Nonmembers may attend SCBWI events as well. SCBWI conferences are listed in the beginning of this section under a separate subheading. For information on SCBWI's annual national conferences, contact them at (323)782-1010 or check their website for a complete calendar of national and regional events (www.scbwi.org).

Information on conferences listed in the previous edition but not this edition of *Children's Writer's & Illustrator's Market* may be found in the General Index.

Helpful Distinctions in Terminology

Although terminology can vary widely, these are the various types of meetings available to writers and illustrators:

Conference: A one- or two-day group of sessions in which a variety of speakers present on a balanced group of topics. This is a good place to find out where you are deficient in a skill and where you might find help. It's a great place for networking. Rarely will you have time to actually work on something during a conference. Novels are the hardest things to get help with here.

Workshop: An intensive look at one aspect of writing or illustrating. This can be as short as a couple hours or as long as a couple of days. Presentations are not usually meant to be balanced, but to focus on a single topic. Usually there is time to work on specific exercises provided.

Retreat: A longer meeting, usually extending over several days, where time is provided for you to work on your own writing. Speakers may provide instruction and specific exercises, but you have more control over what you work on during the writing times. If you want help with a novel, this is the best place to look for programs that fit your needs.

—Darcy Pattison

Note: Turn to Great Expectations: Conferences Can Make a Difference on page 67 for more tips on getting the most from conferences and workshops.

SCBWI Conferences

The Society of Children's Book Writers and Illustrators (SCBWI) is an international organization with about 12,000 members. SCBWI offers an array of regional events that can be attended by both members and nonmembers. Listings of regional events follow. For more information, contact the conference coordinators listed or visit SCBWI's website, www.scbwi.org for a complete calendar of events. SCBWI members will also find event information listed in the bimonthly SCBWI *Bulletin*, free with membership. In addition to the regional events, SCBWI offers two national conferences—one in August in Los Angeles, the other in February in New York City. For information about conferences or membership in SCBWI, check www.scbwi.org or contact the SCBWI offices: 8271 Beverly Blvd., Los Angeles CA 90048, (323)782-1010.

☑ SCBWI—ARIZONA; ANNUAL EDITORS DAY, 735 W. Pine St., Tucson AZ 85704. (520)544-2650. E-mail: desertmorn@aol.com. Regional Advisor: Dawn Dixon. **Open to Students.** Editors are invited to speak to book and illustration needs. Usually includes 2-3 book publishers, Q&A sessions included. Usually has 75-85 participants. No limit on registration. Cost of workshop: $80-90. Information available on SCBWI website; registration begins in January.

☑ SCBWI—ARIZONA; RETREAT, P.O. Box 11834, Prescott AZ 86304. (520)443-5481. Fax: (520)717-2426. E-mail: karylmoore@juno.com. Regional Advisor: Karyl Moore. Writer workshops geared toward intermediate, advanced and professional levels. **Open to Students.** Offers hands-on critique sessions of mss in progress (art as well as text). Annual workshop. Workshop held the end of September or early October. Registration limited to 35. The facility is a camp—very basic. Cost of workshop: $230; includes 2 nights lodging and 4 meals. Deposits are accepted to reserve a space beginning in March.

⟦N⟧ SCBWI—ARIZONA; WORKING WRITERS RETREAT, 735 W. Pine St., Tucson AZ. (520)544-2650. E-mail: desertmorn@aol.com. Regional Advisor: Dawn Dixon. **Open to students.** Annual fall hands-on workshop for writers with works-in-progress. Presenters include 2-3 editors. Q&A sessions included. Registration limited to 25. Cost of workshop: $225-265. Information available on SCBWI website; registration begins in August.

⟦N⟧ SCBWI—CANADA; ANNUAL CONFERENCE, 130 Wren St., Dunrobin, Ontario K0A 1T0 Canada. E-mail: lflatt@muskoka.com. Contact: Lizanne Flatt or Noreen Violetta. Writer and illustrator conference geared toward all levels. Offers spearkers forums, book sale, portfolio displays, one-on-one critiques and a silent auction. Annual conference held in May. Write above address for brochure or e-mail for more information.

☑ SCBWI—CAROLINAS; ANNUAL FALL CONFERENCE. Contact: Frances A. Davis, Regional Advisor at (919)967-2452. E-mail: Earl-frandavis@prodigy.net. Conference will be held in September or October 2001, and geared toward picture books, writing for middle grade, and young adults. Speakers vary, including published writers, illustrators, an editor, and additional professionals of interest to writers and illustrators. Fee: $60 for SCBWI members, $65 for NCWN and SCWN members, and $70 for nonmembers. Critiques for writers, illustration portfolios displayed. Conference open to adult students.

SCBWI—FLORIDA CONFERENCE, 2158 Portland Ave., Wellington FL 33414. (561)798-4824. E-mail: barcafer@aol.com. Florida Regional Advisor: Barbara Casey. Writer and illustrator workshops geared toward beginner, intermediate, advanced and professional levels. Subjects to be announced. Annual workshop. Workshop dates and location to be announced. Registration limited to 100/class. Cost of workshop: $60 for members, $65 for non-members. Special rates are offered through the West Palm Beach Airport Hilton Hotel for those attending the conference who wish to spend the night. Write for more information.

☑ SCBWI—HOUSTON CONFERENCE, 23111 Berry Pine Dr., Spring TX 77313. (281)651-8955. Fax: (281)618-7103. E-mail: Charles.Trevino@NHMCCD.edu. Regional Advisor: Charles Trevino. Writer and illustrator workshops geared toward all levels. **Open to students.** Annual conference. Conference covers picture books, text and illustration, middle grade novels and nonfiction. Editors' Open House held February 10, 2001. Conference held November 3, 2001. Cost of workshop: $85; includes lunch; critiques $25 extra. Contact Mary Wade for more information.

⟦N⟧ SCBWI—ILLINOIS; SPRING RETREAT—THE WRITE CONNECTION: 3 ACQUIRING EDITORS, 2408 Elmwood, Wilmette IL 60091. E-mail: esthersh@aol.com. Regional Advisor, SCBWI-Illinois: Esther Hershenhorn.
• The workshop is held in Woodstock, Illinois. Next scheduled retreat April 2002.
Writer workshops geared toward intermediate, advanced and professional levels. Offers teaching sessions; open mike; ms critiques; panel discussions; editor presentations. Biannual workshop.

N: SCBWI—INDIANA; SPRING & FALL WRITERS' AND ILLUSTRATORS' CONFERENCE, 934 Fayette St., Indianapolis IN 46202. E-mail: s_murray@iquest.net. Conference Director: Sara Murray-Plumer. Writer and illustrator workshops geared toward all levels. Two conferences held annually in April and October. Length of each session: 45 minutes to 1½ hours. Cost of workshop includes meal and workshops. Write or e-mail for more information.

✓ SCBWI—IOWA CONFERENCE, 1462 Olde Freeport Place, Bettendorf IA 52722-7001. (319)359-0337. Iowa SCBWI Regional Advisor: Connie Heckert. Writer workshops geared toward all levels. "Usually speakers include one to two acquiring book editors who discuss the needs of their publishing house and manuscripts that caught their attention. Also, we usually have several published Iowa authors discussing specific genres and/or topics like promotion, marketing, school visits, etc." Annual conference. Iowa has 1 or 2 conferences a year, usually in May and September or October. Cost of conference includes lunch and refreshments: usually about $60-75; less for SCSWI members. Individual critique costs $30 extra. Work must be submitted in advance.

N: SCBWI—LOS ANGELES COUNTY (CALIFORNIA); ILLUSTRATOR'S DAY, P.O. Box 1728, Pacific Palisades CA 90272. (310)573-7318. Co-regional Advisors: Claudia Harrington (claudiascbwi@att.net) and Collyn Justus (collynscbwi@aol.com). A one-day conference for children's book illustrators, usually includes a featured editor, presentations by published illustrators, workshops, a general portfolio display, and optional paid portfolio review. This is an annual event held late September/early October. Conference fee $70-85, includes entire day of speakers and lunch. Individual portfolio review fee $10-15.

N: SCBWI—LOS ANGELES COUNTY (CALIFORNIA); WORKING WRITER'S RETREAT, P.O. Box 1728, Pacific Palisades CA 90272. (310)573-7318. Co-regional Advisors: Claudia Harrington (claudiascbwi @att.net) and Collyn Justus (collynscbwi@aol.com). A three-day, two-night retreat in Encino, California, usually featuring a children's book editor, presentations by published authors, creativity workshops, and numerous critiquing sessions facilitated by staff. This is an annual event held mid to late October. Attendance is limited. Event fees $275-325; covers all events lodgings and meals.

N: SCBWI—LOS ANGELES COUNTY (CALIFORNIA); WRITER'S DAY, P.O. Box 1728, Pacific Palisades CA 90272. (310)573-7318. Co-regional Advisors: Claudia Harrington (claudiascbwi@att.net) and Collyn Justus (collynscbwi@aol.com). A one-day conference for children's book writers geared toward all levels. Emphasizes fiction and nonfiction writing for children from picture books through young adult. Conference includes presentations by a children's book editor and children's book authors. Annual conference, next held April 21, 2001. Cost of conference: $70-85; includes entire day of speakers, lunch and a Writer's Day Contest.

✓ SCBWI—MICHIGAN; ANNUAL WORKING WRITER'S RETREAT, 446 Kensington Rd., East Lansing MI 48823. E-mail: celenzaa@msu.edu. Retreat Chair: Anna Celenza. Writer and illustrator workshops geared toward intermediate and advanced levels. Program focus: the craft of writing. Features peer facilitated critique groups, creativity, motivation and professional issues. Featured speakers: Jean Gralley and Kathryn O. Galbraith. Retreat held October 6-8, 2000 in Gull Lake (near Battle Creek and Kalamazoo). Registration limited. Cost of retreat: $199 for members, $219 for nonmembers; includes meals, lodging, linens and tuition. Write or e-mail for additional information.

✓ SCBWI—MICHIGAN; FOCUS ON PICTURE BOOKS, JUNE 2001, 1152 Stellma Ln., Rochester Hills MI 48309. Fax: (248)651-6489. E-mail: bsz@flash.net. Event Chairs: Brenda Yee, Buffy Silverman and Harry Levine. Location TBA. One-day workshop for writers and illustrators interested in the genre of picture books. Speakers will include an editor from a major publishing house, published authors, and illustrators. Registration fee TBA, but approximately $75, including lunch.

SCBWI—MIDSOUTH CONFERENCE, 2802 Acklen Ave., Nashville TN 37212. (615)297-6785. E-mail: scbwi.midsouth@juno.com. Regional Advisor: Tracy Barrett. Writer workshops geared toward all levels. Illustrator workshops geared toward beginner and intermediate levels. **Open to Students.** Previous workshop topics have included Promoting Yourself, A Beginner's Guide to Getting Published, Writing for the Older Child, Stone Soup: The Making of a Picture Book, Introduction to Magazine Illustration. There are also opportunities for ms and portfolio critiques and critique groups can be formed at the conference. Conference held April 21, 2001. Speakers include Marion Dane Bauer, Paul Brett Johnson, and others. Cost of conference: $60 SCBWI members; $65 nonmembers; ms critiques extra. Manuscripts for critique must be typed, double-spaced, and submitted in advance with payment. Portfolios are brought to the conference, but reservations for critique time and payment must be made in advance.

N: SCBWI—NATIONAL CONFERENCE ON WRITING AND ILLUSTRATING FOR CHILDREN, 8271 Beverly Blvd., Los Angeles CA 90048. (323)782-1010. Fax: (323)782-1892. E-mail: scbwi@scbwi.org. Website: www.scbwi.org. Conference Director: Lin Oliver. Writer and illustrator workshops geared toward all levels. **Open to students.** Covers all aspects of children's book and magazine publishing—the novel, illustration techniques, marketing, etc. Annual conference held in August each year. Cost of conference: approximately $350; includes all 4 days and one banquet meal. Write for more information or visit our website. SCBWI also holds a Midwinter National Conference in New York City. Dates for 2001 are February 17-18.

 SCBWI—NEW YORK; CONFERENCE FOR CHILDREN'S BOOK ILLUSTRATORS & AUTHOR/ILLUSTRATORS, Society of Illustrators, 128 E. 63rd St., New York 10021. (845)356-7273. Conference Chair: Frieda Gates. Held May 7, 2001. Registration limited to 80 portfolios shown out of 125 conferees. Portfolios are not judged—first come—first served. Cost of conference: with portfolio—$95, members, $100 others; without portfolio—$60 members, $70 others; $50 additional for 30-minute portfolio evaluation; $25 additional for 15-minute book dummy evaluation. Call Frieda Gates (845)356-7273 to receive a flier. "In addition to an exciting program of speakers, this conference provides a unique opportunity for illustrators and author/illustrators to have their portfolios reviewed by scores of art buyers and agents from the publishing and allied industries. Art buyers admitted free. Our reputation for exhibiting high-quality work of both new and established children's book illustrators, plus the ease of examining such an abundance of portfolios, has resulted in a large number of productive contacts between buyers and illustrators."

N: SCBWI—NEW YORK STATE, NORTH COUNTRY (WATERTOWN); SPRING INTO ACTION, P.O. Box 710, Black River NY 13612. (315)773-5847. E-mail: hmarston@imcnet.net. Contact: Hope Irvin Marston. Writer and illustrator workshops geared toward all levels. Key note speaker: Bruce Coville. Additional presenters include literary agents Ginny Knowlton and Scott Triemel; art agent Christina Tageau; book editor Laura Tillotson; illustrator Kathy Coville and magazine editor Marileta Robinson. Breakout sessions will be conducted by local published authors and illustrators. Annual workshop held April 21, 2001. Cost of workshop: $55 for members; $60 for nonmembers; includes coffee, lunch and conference packet. Limited number of individual critique sessions with the agents are available for an additional fee of $35. Send SASE for registration form after February 1, 2001.

SCBWI—NORCAL; RETREAT AT ASILOMAR. Registration forms and current information at www.scbwi Norca.org. Regional Advisor: JoAnne Stewart Wetzel. While we welcome "not-yet-published" writers and illustrators, lectures and workshops are geared toward professionals and those striving to become professional. Program topics cover aspects of writing or illustrating picture books to young adult novels. Past speakers include editors, art directors, published authors and illustrators. Annual conference, generally held last weekend in February; Friday evening through Sunday lunch. Registration limited to 70. Most rooms shared with one other person. Additional charge for single when available. Desks available in most rooms. All rooms have private baths. Conference center is set in wooded campus on Asilomar Beach in Pacific Grove CA. Cost of $250 for SCBWI members, $280 for nonmembers, includes shared room, 6 meals, ice breaker party and all conference activities. Vegetarian meals available. One full scholarship is available to SCBWI members. Registration opens at the end of September and the conference sells out very quickly. A waiting list is formed. "Coming together for shared meals and activities builds a strong feeling of community among the speakers and conferees."

 SCBWI—NORTH CENTRAL CALIFORNIA; MARCH IN MODESTO, 8931 Montezuma Rd., Jamestown CA 95327. (209)984-5556. Fax: (209)984-0636. E-mail: trigar@mlode.com. SCBWI North Central CA Regional Advisor: Teckla White. Conference Coordinator: Tricia Gardella. Writer and illustrator workshops geared toward all levels. **Open to students.** Offers talks on different genres, illustration evaluations and afternoon question breakout sessions. Annual conference. Conference held March 2001. Cost of conference: $55; $60 for nonmembers. Write for more information.

SCBWI—OREGON CONFERENCE, P.O. Box 336, Noti OR 97461. E-mail: robink@rio.com. Regional Advisor: Robin Koontz. Writer and illustrator workshops and presentations geared toward all levels. "We invite editors, agents, authors, illustrators and others in the business of writing and illustrating for children. They present lectures, workshops and critiques." Annual retreat and conference. Two events per year: Working Writers and Illustrators Retreat: Retreat held in September (3-5 days). Cost of retreat: $200-350 (depending on length); includes double occupancy and all meals; Spring Conference: Held in Tualatin, Oregon (1-day event); cost: about $60, includes continental breakfast and lunch. Registration limited to 100 for the conference and 50 for the retreat.

FOR EXPLANATIONS OF THESE SYMBOLS,
SEE THE INSIDE FRONT AND BACK COVERS OF THIS BOOK

N: SCBWI—POCONO MOUNTAINS WRITERS' RETREAT, 708 Pine St., Moscow PA 18444. Conference Director: Susan Campbell Bartoletti. Workshop held third or fourth weekend in April, depending upon Easter and Passover. Registration limited to 75. Cost of workshop: about $350; includes tuition, room and board. Send SASE in December or January for more information.

N: SCBWI—SAN FRANCISCO SOUTH; KITTREDGE RETREAT AT ASILOMAR, Registration forms and current information available at www.scbwiNorCa.org. Regional Advisor: JoAnne Stewart Wetzel. "No formal meetings! No speakers! No workshops! Just time for ourselves, our work, our creativity. A private meeting room is set up for work, pre-dinner get-togethers, and evening gatherings with informal attendee-led discussions about writing, illustrating, etc., and we have our own tables in the dining hall." Annual retreat, generally held in early October, Sunday evening through Wednesday lunch. Registration limited to 25. Most rooms shared with 1 other person. Additional charge for single when available. Desks are available in most rooms. All rooms have private baths. Conference center is set in wooded campus on Asilomar Beach in Pacific Grove, CA. Cost is $246 for SCBWI members, $276 for nonmembers; includes shared room, 9 meals, refreshments and all conference activities. Vegetarian meals available. Registration closes two months before the conference date.

N: SCBWI—SOUTHERN BREEZE; SPRINGMINGLE '01, P.O. Box 26282, Birmingham AL 35260. E-mail: joanbroerman@home.com. Website: members.home.net/southernbreeze. Regional Advisor: Joan Broerman. Writer and illustrator workshops geared toward intermediate, advanced and professional levels. **Open to college students.** All sessions pertain specifically to the production and support of quality children's literature. Annual conference held in one of the three states comprising the Southern Breeze region. Registration limited to 60. Cost of conference: $100 for members; $110 for nonmembers; includes Saturday lunch and Saturday banquet. Breakfast is complimentary for hotel guests. Pre-registration is necessary. Write to Southern Breeze, P.O. Box 26282, Birmingham AL 35260 for more information or visit our website: members.home.net/southernbreeze. "Springmingle will be held in Jackson Mississippi from February 23-25, 2001. Speakers are Richard Peck, an award winning author; Patricia Lee Gauch, Editorial Director, Philomel Books; and writer/illustrator Nina Laden."

SCBWI—SOUTHERN BREEZE; WRITING AND ILLUSTRATING FOR KIDS, P.O. Box 26282, Birmingham AL 35260. E-mail: joanbroerman@home.com. Website: members.home.net/southernbreeze/. Regional Advisor: Joan Broerman. Writer and illustrator workshops geared toward all levels. **Open to college students.** All sessions pertain specifically to the production and support of quality children's literature. This one-day conference offers 30 workshops on craft and the business of writing. Picture books, chapter books, novels covered. Entry and professional level topics addressed by published writers and illustrators, editors and agents. Annual conference. Fall conference is held in October. All workshops are limited to 20 or fewer people. Pre-registration is necessary. Some workshops fill quickly. This is a metropolitan area with many museums in a short driving distance. Also—universities and colleges. Cost of conference: $60 for members, $75 for nonmembers; includes program—key note and luncheon speaker, wrap-up panel, 4 workshops (selected from 30). Does not include lunch (about $6 or registrant can brown bag) or individual consultations (mss must be sent early). Registration is by mail ahead of time. Manuscript and portfolio reviews must be pre-paid and scheduled. Write to: Southern Breeze, P.O. Box 26282, Birmingham AL 35260 or visit webpage: members.home.net/southernbreeze/. "Fall conference is always held in Birmingham, AL. Room block at a hotel near conference site (usually a school) is by individual reservation and offers a conference rate."

☑ SCBWI—UTAH/IDAHO; SPRING INTO ACTION, 1194 E. 11000 S., Sandy UT 84094. (801)523-6311. E-mail: kimorchid@aol.com or utidscbwi@aol.com. Utah/Idaho SCBWI Regional Advisor: Kim Williams-Justesen. Writer workshops geared toward all levels. Illustrator workshops geared toward beginners and intermediate. **Open to students.** Topics for children's writing and illustration "A Day in the Life of an Illustrator;" "Getting Your Feet Wet;" "Understanding Your Audience;" Local editor's panel; plot and character; effective dialogue. Annual conference. Conference held April 27-28, 2001. Cost of conference: $65 SCBWI members; $75 nonmembers; includes workshops, registration packet, artist's portfolio display, door prize drawing, information materials. Write or e-mail for more information.

N: SCBWI—VENTURA/SANTA BARBARA; FALL CONFERENCE, P.O. Box 941389, Simi Valley CA 93094-1389. (805)581-1906. E-mail: alexisinca@aol.com. Regional Advisor: Alexis O'Neill. Writers conference geared toward all levels. "We invite editors, authors and author/illustrators and agents. We have had speakers on the picture book, middle grade, YA, magazine and photo essay books. Both fiction and nonfiction are covered." Conference held in October from 9:00 a.m.-4 p.m. on Saturdays. Cost of conference $65; includes all sessions and lunch. Write for more information.

☑ SCBWI—WASHINGTON STATE CONFERENCE, 14816 205th Ave., SE, Renton WA 98059-8926. (425)235-0566. Regional Advisor: S. Ford. Writer workshops geared toward all levels. **Open to students.** All aspects of writing and illustrating children's books are covered from picture books to YA novels, from contracts to promotion. Editors, an art director, an agent and published authors and illustrators serve as conference faculty.

Annual conference and workshop. Conference held April 7, 2001. Registration limited to about 250. Cost of conference: $60-90; includes registration, morning snack and lunch. The conference is a one-day event held at Seattle Pacific University. Hour sessions run back-to-back so attendees have 4 or 5 choices. "In this way we can meet the needs of both entry-level and those more advanced."

N **SCBWI—WISCONSIN; FALL RETREAT FOR WORKING WRITERS**, 51243 Redtail Rd., Gays Mills WI 54631. (608)735-4707. Fax: (608)735-4700. E-mail: pfitsch@mwt.net Co-Regional Advisor: Patricia C. Pfitsch. Writer and illustrator conference geared toward all levels. All our sessions pertain to children's writing/illustration. Faculty addresses writing/illustrating/publishing. Annual conference held October 12-14, 2001 in Racine WI. Registration limited to 55. Bedrooms have desks/conference center has small rooms—can be used to draw/write. Program has free time scheduled in. Cost of conference: $230; includes program, meals, lodging. Write for more information. "We usually offer individual critique of manuscripts with faculty—$35 extra."

Other Conferences

Many conferences and workshops included here focus on children's writing or illustrating and related business issues. Others appeal to a broader base of writers or artists, but still provide information that can be useful in creating material for children. Illustrators may be interested in painting and drawing workshops, for example, while writers can learn about techniques and meet editors and agents at general writing conferences. For more information visit the websites listed or contact conference coordinator.

AMERICAN CHRISTIAN WRITERS CONFERENCE, P.O. Box 110390, Nashville TN 37222-0390. 1(800)21-WRITE or (615)834-0450. Fax: (615)834-7736. E-mail: regaforder@aol.com. Website: www.ecpa.org/acw. Director: Reg Forder. Writer and illustrator workshops geared toward beginner, intermediate and advanced levels. Classes offered include: fiction, nonfiction, poetry, photography, music, etc. Workshops held in 3 dozen US cities. Call or write for a complete schedule of conferences. 75 minutes. Maximum class size: 30 (approximate). Cost of conference: $99, 1-day session; $169, 2-day session (discount given if paid 30 days in advance) includes tuition only.

N **ANNUAL MIDWEST POETS AND WRITERS CONFERENCE**, P.O. Box 23100, Detroit MI 48223. (313)897-2551. Fax: (248)557-2606. E-mail: daysdawn@prodigy.net. Website: www.blackarts-literature.org. Director: Heather Buchanan. Writer and illustrator workshops geared toward beginner, intermediate and advanced levels. **Open to students.** Includes sessions on writing for children and writing for young adults. Annual conference. Conference held August 31-September 2, 2000. [2001 date?] Cost of workshop: $125 (early registration); $150 (late registration); includes admission to opening reception, admission to all workshops, closing ceremony. Write for more information. "Individual manuscript critiques available for additional fee; manuscript must be submitted prior to conference."

N **ANNUAL SPRING POETRY FESTIVAL**, City College, 138th St. at Convent Ave., New York NY 10031. (212)650-6343. E-mail: barrywal23@aol.com. Director, Poetry Outreach Center: Barry Wallenstein. Writer workshops geared to all levels. **Open to students.** The 29th Annual Spring Poetry Festival will be held on Wednesday, May 16th, 2001. Registration limited to 325. Cost of workshop: free. Write for more information.

ARKANSAS WRITERS' CONFERENCE, 6817 Gingerbread Lane, Little Rock AR 72204. (501)565-8889. Fax: (501)565-7220. Counselor: Peggy Vining. Writer workshops geared toward beginner, intermediate and advanced levels. **Open to students.** Annual conference. Conference always held the first full weekend in June. Cost of conference: $7.50/day; includes registration and workshops. Contest fees, lodging and food are not included. Send SASE for brochure after March 1. Offers 34 different awards for various types of writing, poetry and essay.

AUSTIN WRITERS' LEAGUE CONFERENCE WORKSHOP SERIES, 1501 W. Fifth St., Suite E-2, Austin TX 78703. (512)499-8914. Fax: (512)499-0441. E-mail: writersleague.org. Executive Director: Jim Bob McMillan. Writer and illustrator workshops and conferences geared toward all levels for children and adults. Annual conferences. Classes are held during the week, and workshops are held on Saturdays during March, April, May, September, October and November. Annual Teddy Children's Book Award of $1,000 presented each spring to book published in previous year. Write for more information. The Austin Writers' League has available audiotapes of past workshop programs.

☑ **AUTUMN AUTHORS' AFFAIR . . . A WRITER'S RENDEZVOUS**, 1507 Burnham Ave., Calumet City IL 60409. (708)862-9797. President: Nancy McCann. Writer workshops geared toward beginner, intermediate, advanced levels. **Open to students.** Sessions include children/teen/young adult writing, mysteries, romantic suspense, romance, nonfiction, etc. Annual workshop. Workshops held in October. Cost of workshop: $75 for 1 day, $120 for weekend, includes meals Friday night, Saturday morning, and Saturday afternoon, Saturday night, and breakfast/brunch Sunday morning. Write for more information.

N: THE BAY AREA WRITERS LEAGUE 13TH ANNUAL CONFERENCE, P.O. Box 728, Seabrook TX 77586. (281)268-7500. Fax: E-mail: bawlconference@aol.com. Website: www.angelfire.com/tx2/bawl. Writer and illustrator workshops geared toward beginner level. **Open to students.** "We had one session on children's writing at our 2000 conference. We had several sessions on publishing and marketing that were appropriate for all writers." Annual workshop. Workshop held May 2001. Cost of workshop: $100 for both days; $50 for one day; $35 for students; includes lunch, Friday reception, all materials. Write for more information. There is a contest associated with this conference. It does not include a specific children's category.

BE THE WRITER YOU WANT TO BE—MANUSCRIPT CLINIC, Villa 30, 23350 Sereno Court, Cupertino CA 95014-6507. (415)691-0300. Fax: (650)903-5920. Contact: Louise Purwin Zobel. Writer workshops geared toward beginner, intermediate and advanced levels. **Open to students.** Annual workshop. "Participants may turn in manuscripts at any stage of development to receive help with structure and style, as well as marketing advice. Manuscripts receive some written criticism and an oral critique from the instructor, as well as class discussion." Annual workshop. Usually held in the spring. Registration limited to 20-25. Cost of workshop: $45-65/day, depending on the campus; includes an extensive handout. SASE for more information.

N: BLUE RIDGE WRITERS CONFERENCE, Continuing Education Center, Virginia Tech, Blacksburg VA 24061. E-mail: agoethe@usit.net. Website: www.conted.vt.edu/brw.htm. President: Ann Goethe. Writer and illustrator workshops geared toward intermediate level. **Open to students.** Annual conference. Conference held in the autum. Cost of workshop: $60; includes conference, breakfast, lunch, reception. Write for more information.

BUTLER UNIVERSITY CHILDREN'S LITERATURE CONFERENCE, 4600 Sunset Drive, Indianapolis IN 46208. (317)940-9861. Fax: (317)940-9644. E-mail: sdaniell@butler.edu. Contact: Shirley Daniell. Writer and illustrator conference geared toward intermediate level. Open to college students. Annual conference held January 27, 2001. Includes sessions such as The Joy of Writing Nonfiction, Creating the Children's Picture Book, and Nuts and Bolts for Beginning Writers. Registration limited to 300. Cost of conference: $80; includes meals, registration, 3 plenary addresses, 2 workshops, book signing, reception and conference bookstore. Write for more information. "The conference is geared toward three groups: teachers, librarians and writers/illustrators."

✓ CAPE COD WRITER'S CONFERENCE, Cape Cod Writer's Center, P.O. Box 186, Barnstable MA 02630. (508)362-2718. Fax: (508)362-2718. E-mail: ccwc@capecod.net. Website: www.capecod.net/writers. Writer conference and workshops geared toward beginner, intermediate and professional levels. **Open to students.** "We hold a young writer's workshop at our annual conference each summer (2 sessions per day with youngsters ages 12-16)." 39th annual conference held third week in August. Cost of conference includes $60 to register; $85 per course (we offer 9); manuscript evaluation, $75; personal conference, $50. Write for more information.

✓ CAT WRITERS ASSOCIATION ANNUAL WRITERS CONFERENCE, 22841 Orchid Creek Lane, Lake Forest CA 92630. (949)454-1368. Fax: (949)454-0134. E-mail: kthornton@home.com. Website: www.catwr iters.org. President: Amy D. Shojai. Writer workshops geared toward beginner, intermediate, advanced and professional levels. Illustrator workshops geared toward intermediate, advanced and professional levels. **Open to students.** Annual workshop. Workshop held in November. Cost of workshop: approximately $90; includes 9-10 seminars, 2 receptions, 1 banquet, 1 breakfast, press pass to other events, interviews with editors and book signing/art sale event. Conference information becomes available in June/July prior to event, and is posted on the website (including registration material). Seminars held/co-sponsored with the Dog Writers Association (We often receive queries from publishers seeking illustrators or writers for particular book/article projects—these are passed on to CWA members).

CELEBRATION OF CHILDREN'S LITERATURE, Montgomery College, 51 Mannakee St., Office of Continuing Education, Room 220, Rockville MD 20850. (301)251-7914. Fax: (301)251-7937. E-mail: ssonner@mc.c c.md.us. Senior Program Director: Sandra Sonner. Writer and illustrator workshops geared toward all levels. **Open to students.** Past topics included The Publisher's Perspective, Successful Picture Book Design, The Oral Tradition in Children's Literature, The Best and Worst Children's Books, Websites for Children, The Pleasures of Nonfiction and The Book as Art. Annual workshop. Will be held April 21, 2001. Registration limited to 200. Writing/art facilities, continuing education classrooms and large auditorium. Cost of workshop: approximately $75; includes workshops, box lunch and coffee. Contact Montgomery College for more information.

N: CHATTANOOGA CONFERENCE ON SOUTHERN LITERATURE, P.O. Box 4203, Chattanooga TN 37405-0203. (423)267-1218. Fax: (423)267-1018. E-mail: srobinson@artsedcouncil.org. Website: www.artse dcouncil.org. Executive Director: Susan Robinson. **Open to students.** Conference is geared toward readers. No workshops are held. Biennial conference. Conference held April 19-21, 2001. Registration limited to first 1,000 people. Cost of conference: $50. Write for more information. "The Chattanooga Conference on Southern Literature is a conference that celebrates literature of the South. Panel discussions, readings, music, food and art are featured."

N: CHILDREN'S BOOK ILLUSTRATION WITH DEBORAH NOURSE LATTIMORE, 108 Civic Plaza Dr., Taos NM 87571. (505)758-2793. E-mail: tia@taosnet.com. Website: www.tiataos.com. Curriculum Director: Susan Miholic. Illustrator workshop geared toward beginner, intermediate and advanced levels. **Open to students over 18.** Workshops take place March-October 2001—check website for dates. Registration limited to 15. All classroom needs are accommodated, but students buy/bring materials, computers, etc. Cost: $355 plus $40 registration fee.

N: CHILDREN'S BOOK WRITING WITH DONNA W. GUTHRIE, 108 Civic Plaza Dr., Taos NM 87571. (505)758-2793. E-mail: tia@taosnet.com. Website: www.tiataos.com. Curriculum Director: Susan Miholic. Writer workshop geared toward beginner, intermediate and advanced levels. **Open to students over 18.** Workshops take place March-October 2001—check website for dates. Registration limited to 12. All classroom needs are accommodated, but students buy/bring materials, computers, etc. Cost: $340 plus $40 registration fee.

✓ CHILDREN'S LITERATURE CONFERENCE, 250 Hofstra University, U.C.C.E., Hempstead NY 11549. (516)463-5016. Fax: (516)463-4833. E-mail: uccelibarts@hofstra.edu. Website: continuinglearners@www.hofstra.edw. Writers/Illustrators Contact: Kenneth Henwood, director, Liberal Arts Studies. Writer and illustrator workshops geared toward all levels. Emphasizes: fiction, nonfiction, poetry, submission procedures, picture books. Workshops will be held April 21, 2001. Length of each session: 1 hour. Registration limited to 35/class. Cost of workshop: approximately $75; includes 2 workshops, reception, lunch, 2 general sessions, and panel discussion with guest speakers and/or critiquing. Write for more information. Co-sponsored by Society of Children's Book Writers & Illustrators.

✓ CHILDREN'S WRITER'S CONFERENCE, St. Charles County Community College, P.O. Box 76975, 103 CEAC, St. Peters MO 63376-0975. (314)213-8000 ext. 4108. E-mail: suebe@inlink.com. Website: http://communities.postnet.com/stlouis/scbwimo. SCBWI MO Regional Advisor: Sue Bradford Edwards. Writer and illustrator conference geared toward all levels. **Open to students.** Speakers include editors, writers and other professionals, mainly from the Midwest. Topics vary from year to year, but each conference offers sessions for both writers and illustrators as well as for newcomers and published writers. Previous topics included: "What Happens When Your Manuscript is Accepted" by Dawn Weinstock, editor; "Writing—Hobby or Vocation?" by Chris Kelleher; "Mother Time Gives Advice: Perspectives from a 25 Year Veteran" by Judith Mathews, editor; "Don't Be a Starving Writer" by Vicki Berger Erwin, author; and "Words & Pictures: History in the Making," by author-illustrator Cheryl Harness. Annual conference held in early November. For exact date and planned sessions, see events page of the Missouri SCBWI website: http://communities.postnet.com/stlouis/scbwimo. Registration limited to 50-70. Cost of conference: $50-70; includes one day workshop (8:00 a.m. to 5:00 p.m.) plus lunch. Write for more information.

N: CHRISTIAN WRITERS' CONFERENCE, P.O. Box 42429, Santa Barbara CA 93140. (805)647-9162. Coordinator: Opal Dailey. Writer conference geared toward beginner, intermediate and advanced levels. **Open to students.** Sessions at 2000 conference included one with Ellen Kelly—"Writing for Children: How to make your story garden grow." (writing and marketing). We always have children writing instruction. Annual conference. Conference held October 6, 2001. Registration limited to 100. Cost of conference: approximately $59; includes lunch and refreshment breaks. Write for more information.

✓ CLEVELAND HEIGHTS/UNIVERSITY HEIGHTS WRITER'S MINI-CONFERENCE, 34200 Ridge Rd., #201, Willoughby OH 44094-2954. (440)943-3047. E-mail: lealoldham@aol.com. Coordinator: Lea Leever Oldham. Writer workshops geared toward all levels. **Open to students.** Conference will cover children's writing, young adult fiction, nonfiction, poetry, marketing, query letters, tax and bookkeeping, copyright protection and other topics of interest to the beginning or advanced writer. Annual conference. Conference held annually in October at Taylor Academy in Cleveland Heights, OH. Cost of conference: $39; includes sessions by published authors and refreshments.

✓ COLLEGE OF NEW JERSEY WRITERS CONFERENCE, Dept. of English, The College of New Jersey, P.O. Box 7718, Ewing NJ 08628-0718. (609)771-3254. Fax: (609)637-5112. E-mail: write@tcnj.edu. Director: Jean Hollander. Writer and illustrator workshop geared toward all levels. **Open to students.** Sessions at 2000 workshop included "Literature for the Young," taught by Nancy Hinkel, assistant editor, Knopf and Crown Books for Young Readers. Annual conference held in April. Cost: $40-70 ($20 and up for students); includes admission to all talks, panels and readings. Workshops are $10 each.

N CONFERENCE FOR WRITERS & ILLUSTRATORS OF CHILDREN'S BOOKS, 51 Tamal Vista Blvd., Corte Madera CA 94925. (415)927-0960, ext. 229. Fax: (415)927-3069. E-mail: conferences@bookpassage.com. Website: www.bookpassage.com. Conference Coordinator: Sarah Wingfield. Writer and illustrator conference geared toward beginner, intermediate and advanced levels. Sessions cover such topics as the nuts and bolts of writing and illustrating, publisher's spotlight, market trends, developing characters/finding voice in your writing. Conference held annually in October. Registration limited to 100. Cost: mid-$400 range, includes 3 lunches and a gala opening reception and dinner.

N A CRITIQUE RETREAT FOR WRITING WOMEN, P.O. Box 14282, Pittsburgh PA 15239. (724)325-4964. Fax: (724)387-1438. Website: www.geocities.com/jmjwriter/index.html. Co-director: MaryJo Rulnick. Writer workshop geared toward beginner, intermediate and advanced levels. The weekend includes five critiquing sessions for attendees. Group leaders include published authors, screenplay writers and freelance writers, editors and columnists. Networking and advice discussions. Annual workshop held twice a year. Annual workshop held June and fall. Registration limited to under 100. Attendees have their own rooms which is included in the price along with meals. Cost of workshop: $225; includes five critiquing sessions, five meals, two nights' accommodations and writer's information packet. Write for more information. The retreat is held at St. Joseph's Center in Greensburg, PA (30 minutes outside Pittsburgh).

PETER DAVIDSON'S HOW TO WRITE A CHILDREN'S PICTURE BOOK SEMINAR, 982 S. Emerald Hills Dr., P.O. Box 497, Arnolds Park IA 51331-0497. Fax: (712)362-8363. Seminar Presenter: Peter Davidson. "This seminar is for anyone interested in writing and/or illustrating children's picture books. Beginners and experienced writers alike are welcome. **Open to students.** If participants have a manuscript in progress, or have an idea, they are welcome to bring it along to discuss with the seminar presenter." *How to Write a Children's Picture Book* is a one-day seminar devoted to principles and techniques of writing and illustrating children's picture books. Topics include Definition of a Picture Book, Picture Book Sizes, Developing an Idea, Plotting the Book, Writing the Book, Illustrating the Book, Typing the Manuscript, Copyrighting Your Work, Marketing Your Manuscript and Contract Terms. Seminars are presented year-round at community colleges. Even-numbered years, presents seminars in Minnesota, Iowa, Nebraska, Kansas, Colorado and Wyoming. Odd-numbered years, presents seminars in Illinois, Minnesota, Iowa, South Dakota, Missouri, Arkansas and Tennessee (write for a schedule). One day, 9 a.m.-4 p.m. Cost of workshop: varies from $40-59, depending on location; includes approximately 35 pages of handouts. Write for more information.

FEMINIST WOMEN'S WRITING WORKSHOPS, P.O. Box 6583, Ithaca NY 14850. Co-director: Kit Wainer. Writer's workshop geared toward beginner, intermediate, advanced and professional levels. **Open to students.** Annual workshop. Workshop held July, 2001. Registration limited to 45 women. Writing facilities available: 4-6 one day workshops; 4-5 four day work groups. Cost: $550; includes tuition, private room, 3 meals for 8 days. 3-10 page writing sample required for new participants. Write for more information. "We don't have 'writing for children' workshops every year. A brochure available in late February will specify."

N FIRST COAST WRITERS' FESTIVAL, 101 W. State St., Jacksonville FL 32202. (904)633-8327. Fax: (904)633-8435. E-mail: kclower@fccj.org. Website: www.fccj.org/wf. Media Production Manager: Kathleen Clower. Writer workshops geared to all levels. Illustrators workshops geared to beginner level. **Open to students.** "For our 2000 Festival, children's author John Cech presented a three-hour preconference workshop 'Writing for Children.' During the festival he presented a shorter workshop on fiction writing for children and met with individuals in one-on-one sessions as well. Several workshops dealt with publishing and marketing. Annual workshop held May of each year, typically the weekend after Mothers' Day; May 17-19, 2001. Cost of workshop: 1-day festival (with lunch) $75 (early bird); 2-day festival (with lunch) $150 (early bird); Preconference workshop $30 (early bird). "Children's writing/illustration is one of many offerings at the festival. Other presentations include freelancing, writing memoirs, poetry, humorous essay, nonfiction, working with an editor, getting published."

FISHTRAP, INC., P.O. Box 38, Enterprise OR 97828-0038. (541)426-3623. Fax: (541)426-3324. E-mail: rich@fishtrap. Website: www.fishtrap.org. Director: Rich Wandschneider. Writer workshops geared toward beginner, intermediate, advanced and professional levels. **Open to students.** Not specifically writing for children, although we have offered occasional workshops in the field. A series of eight writing workshops (enrollment 12/workshop) and a writers' gathering is held each July; a winter gathering concerning writing and issues of public concern held in February. Dates for the winter gathering are February 25-27, 2001 (2001 theme: "humor"); and for the summer gathering July 8-15, 2001 (2001 theme: "Legacy of Vietnam"). During the school year Fishtrap brings writers into local schools and offers occasional workshops for teachers and writers of children's and young adult books. Also brings in "Writers in Residence" (10 weeks). Cost of workshops: $100-240 for 1-4 days; includes workshop only. Food and lodging can be arranged. College credit is available. Please contact for more information.

☑ **FLORIDA CHRISTIAN WRITERS CONFERENCE**, 2344 Armour Ct., Titusville FL 32780. (321)269-5831. Fax: (321)264-7424. E-mail: bwilson@digital.net. Website: www.Kipertek.com/writer. Conference Director: Billie Wilson. Writer workshops geared toward all levels. **Open to students.** "We offer 48 one-hour workshops and 7 five-hour classes. Approximately 24 of these are for the children's genre: Seeing Through the Eyes of an Artist; Characters . . . Inside and Out; Seeing Through the Eyes of a Child; Picture Book Toolbox; and CD-ROM & Interactive Books for Children. Annual workshop held each January. We have 30 publishers and publications represented by editors teaching workshops and reading manuscripts from the conferees. The conference is limited to 200 people. Usually workshops are limited to 25-30. Advanced or professional workshops are by invitation only via submitted application." Cost of workshop: $400; includes food, lodging, tuition and manuscript critiques and editor review of your manuscript. Write for more information.

[N] **GLORIETA CHRISTIAN WRITERS' CONFERENCE**, P.O. Box 8, Glorieta NM 87535-0008. ((800)797-4222. Fax: (505)757-6161. E-mail: mona@sedona.net. Website: www.desertcritters.com. Writer conference geared toward all levels. **Open to students.** Sessions include children's writing, screenwriting, poetry, public speaking, novel, magazine writing, drama, nonfiction books, . . . etc. Annual conference held October 16-20, 2001. Lines for modems in all hotel rooms and classrooms. Cost of conference: $460-510; includes tuition, double or single hotel room for 4 nights, 12 all you can eat meals. Write for more information. Check out the website (www.desertcritters.com) for additional information.

☑ **GREEN RIVERS WRITERS NOVELS-IN-PROGRESS WORKSHOP**, 11906 Locust Rd., Middletown KY 40243-1413. (502)245-4902. E-mail: mary_odell@ntr.net. President: Mary O'Dell. Writer workshops geared toward intermediate and advanced levels. Workshops emphasize novel writing. New retreat format will not feature any certain topics or class structure; activity will be self-generated. Workshop held March 11-18, 2001. Registration limited to 49. Participants will need to bring own computers, typewriters, etc. Private rooms are available for sleeping, working. No art facilities. Cost of workshop: not set as yet, but will be under $400, including grad dorm housing. Writers must supply 40-60 pages of manuscript with outline, synopsis or treatment. Write for more information. Conference held on Shelby Campus at University of Louisville; private rooms with bath between each 2 rooms. Linens furnished. $22 per night.

[N] **HAYSTACK PROGRAM/PORTLAND STATE UNIVERSITY**, P.O. Box 1491, Portland OR 97207-1491. (503)725-3484. Fax: (503)725-4840. E-mail: shayj@pdx.edu. Website: www.haystack.pdx.edu. Program Assistant: Jennifer Shay. Writer workshops geared toward beginner and intermediate levels. Illustrator workshops geared toward intermediate level. **Open to students.** Sessions include easy to read, hard to write; writing the perfect picture book; how to succeed in the business of illustrating picture books by trying very hard; the passionate picture book: nonfiction for the young; Holden Caulfield revisited: writing contemporary fiction; etc. This is year two for Children's Book Festival, the 32nd year of the Haystack Program. Annual workshop held July 17-21, 2000. [2001 date?] Cost of workshop: $400, noncredit; $25, credit. Write for more information. "Please visit our website for complete information or call to have a Haystack brochure mailed to you. If you still have questions, please e-mail shayj@pdx.edu or call Jennifer Shay at (503)725-3484.

☑ **HIGHLAND SUMMER CONFERENCE**, Box 7014 Radford University, Radford VA 24142-7014. (540)831-5366. Fax: (540)831-5004. E-mail: jasbury@radford.edu. Website: www.radford.edu/~arsc. Director: Grace Toney Edwards. Assistant to the Director: Jo Ann Asbury. **Open to students.** Writer workshops geared toward beginner, intermediate and advanced levels. Emphasizes Appalachian literature, culture and heritage. Annual workshop. Workshop held (last 2 weeks in June annually). Registration limited to 20. Writing facilities available: computer center. Cost of workshop: Regular tuition (housing/meals extra). Must be registered student or special status student. E-mail, fax or call for more information. Past visiting authors include: Wilma Dykeman, Sue Ellen Bridgers, George Ella Lyon, Lou Kassem.

[N] **HIGHLIGHTS FOUNDATION WRITERS WORKSHOP AT CHAUTAUQUA**, Dept. CWL, 814 Court St., Honesdale PA 18431. (570)253-1192. Fax: (570)253-0179. Conference Director: Ken Brown. Writer workshops geared toward those interested in writing for children; beginner, intermediate and advanced levels. Classes offered include: Children's Interests; Writing Dialogue; Beginnings and Endings; Rights; Contracts; Copyrights; Science Writing. Annual workshop. Workshops held July 14-21, 2001, at Chautauqua Institution, Chautauqua, NY. Registration limited to 100/class. Cost of workshop: $1,485; includes tuition, meals, conference supplies. Cost does not include housing. Call for availability and pricing. Scholarships are available for first-time attendees. Write for more information.

☑ **HOFSTRA UNIVERSITY SUMMER WRITERS' CONFERENCE**, 250 Hofstra University, UCCE, Hempstead NY 11549. (516)463-5016. Fax: (516)463-4833. E-mail: uccelibarts@hofstra.edu. Director, Liberal Arts Studies: Kenneth Henwood. Writer workshops geared toward all levels. Classes offered include fiction, nonfiction, poetry, children's literature, stage/screenwriting and other genres. Children's writing faculty has included Pam Conrad, Johanna Hurwitz, Tor Seidler and Jane Zalben, with Maurice Sendak once appearing as guest speaker. Annual workshop. Workshops held for 2 weeks July 9-20, 2001. Each workshop meets for 2½ hours daily for a total of 25 hours. Students can register for 2 workshops, schedule an individual conference with the writer/instructor and submit a short ms (less than 10 pages) for critique. Enrollees may register as certificate students or credit students. Cost of workshop: certificate students enrollment fee is approximately $425; 2-credit student enrollment fee is approximately $1,000/workshop undergraduate and graduate (2 credits); $2,000 undergraduate and graduate (4-credits). On-campus accommodations for the sessions are available for approximately $350/person for the 2-week conference. Students may attend any of the ancillary activities, a private conference, special programs and social events.

☑ **HUDSON WRITERS MINI CONFERENCE**, 34200 Ridge Rd., #201, Willoughby OH 44094. (440)943-3047. E-mail: lealoldham@aol.com. Coordinator: Lea Leever Oldham. Writer workshops geared toward all levels. **Open to students.** Covers children's writing, young adult, fiction, nonfiction, poetry, marketing, query letters, fax and bookkeeping, copyright protection and other topics of interest. Annual conference. Conference held annually at Hudson High School in Hudson, OH, in May. Cost of conference: $39; includes half-day and refreshments.

☑ **INSPIRATIONAL WRITERS ALIVE!**, 6038 Greenmont, Houston TX 77092. (713)686-7209. E-mail: mroger353@aol.com. Annual conference held 1st Saturday in August. **Open to students** and adults. Registration usually 60-75 conferees. Writing/art facilities available: First Baptist Church, Christian Life Center, Houston TX. Cost of conference: member $65; nonmember $75; seniors $60; at the door: members $85; nonmembers $100. Write for more information. "Annual IWA Contest presented. Manuscripts critiqued along with one-on-one 15 minute sessions with speaker(s). (Extra ms. if there is room.)" For more information send for brochure: Attn: Martha Rogers, Board President, 6038 Greenmont, Houston TX 77092, (713)686-7209 or Maxine Holder, (903)795-3986 or Pat Vance, (713)477-4968.

Ⓝ INSTITUTE FOR READERS THEATRE, P.O. Box 17193, San Diego CA 92177. (619)276-1948. Fax: (858)576-7369. E-mail: RTInst@aol.com. Website: www.readerstheatre.net. . Director: Dr. William Adams. Writer workshops geared toward beginner, intermediate and advanced levels. **Open to students.** Topics include oral interpretation; script writing (converting literary material into performable scripts); journal writing (for credit participants). Annual workshop held July 15-27, 2001. Registration limited to 50. Cost of workshop: $1,395; includes 2 weeks room and breakfast Wellington Hall—London, England airfare and university credit (optional) are extra. Write for more information.

☑ **INTERNATIONAL READERS THEATRE WORKSHOP**, P.O. Box 17193, San Diego CA 92177. (858)276-1948. Fax: (858)576-7369. E-mail: RTInst@aol.com. Website: www.readerstheatre.net. Director: Dr. Bill Adams. Writer workshops geared toward all levels. **Open to Students.** Program includes scriptmaking, direction, performance, storytelling, theater seminar and more. Annual workshop. Workshop held July 15-28, 2001. Registration limited to 70. Full conference facilities, Wellington Hall, King's College, London. Cost of workshop: $1,395; includes room, large English breakfast, refreshments, workshop fees. Write for more information.

Ⓝ INTERNATIONAL CREATIVE WRITING CAMP, 1725 11th St. S.W., Minot ND 58701. (701)838-8472. Fax: (701)838-8472. E-mail: imc@minot.com. Camp Director: Joseph T. Alme. Writer and illustrator workshops geared toward beginner, intermediate and advanced levels. **Open to students.** Sessions offered include those covering poems, plays, mystery stories, essays. Annual workshop held the last week in July of each summer. Registration limited to 20. The summer camp location at the International Peace Garden on the Border between Manitoba and North Dakota is an ideal site for generating creative thinking. Excellent food, housing and recreation facilities are available. Cost of workshop: $195. Write for more information.

I'VE ALWAYS WANTED TO WRITE BUT—BEGINNERS' CLASS, Villa 30, 23350 Sereno Ct., Cupertino CA 95014. (415)691-0300. Contact: Louise Purwin Zobel. Writer workshops geared toward beginner and intermediate levels. "This seminar/workshop starts at the beginning, although the intermediate writer will benefit, too. There is discussion of children's magazine and book literature today, how to write it and how to market it. Also, there is discussion of other types of writing and the basics of writing for publication." Annual workshops. "Usually held several times a year; fall, winter and spring." Sessions last 1-2 days. Cost of workshop: $45-65/day, depending on the campus; includes extensive handout. Write with SASE for more information.

Ⓝ KENTUCKY WOMEN WRITERS CONFERENCE, 251 W. Second St., Lexington KY 40507. (859)254-4175. Fax: (859)281-1151. E-mail: kywwc@hotmail.com. Website: www.carnegieliteracy.org. Contact: Jan Isenhour. Writer workshops geared toward beginner, intermediate and advanced levels. **Open to students.** Past sessions have included "writing for young adults" with Gloria Velasquez, author of *Tommy Stands Alone*; a variety of workshops with children's writer George Ella Lyons, Anne Shelby and other women writers such as Maya Angelou, Alice Walker, Joy Harjo, Barbara Kingsolver, Lee Smith and a host of others. Annual conference. Cost of conference: $80-150; includes all conference registration, some meals, some performances. Write for more information.

LAKEWOOD MINI CONFERENCE, (formerly Lorain County Community College Writer's Mini-Conference), 34200 Ridge Rd., #201, Willoughby OH 44094-2954. (440)943-3047. E-mail: lealoldham@aol.com. Coordinator: Lea Leever Oldham. Writer workshops geared toward all levels. **Open to students.** Offers sessions on children's writing, poetry, self-publishing, fiction, nonfiction, articles and other topics of interest to the beginning or advanced writer. Conference held in November at Lakewood High School. Cost of conference: $39.

N LIFEWAY WORKSHOP, 127 Ninth Ave. N., Nashville TN 37234-0148. (615)251-2756. Fax: (615)251-5067. E-mail: mfink@lifeway.com. Workshop Director: Michael Fink. Writer workshops geared toward beginner and intermediate levels. **Open to students.** Bible study curriculum, devotional materials, leisure-reading materials, magazine articles for parents and leaders. Annual workshop held July 30-August 2, 2001. Registration limited to 100. Cost of workshop: $90 (early bird) or $110; includes participation in all workshop presentations and conferences, folio of workshop materials and handouts, banquet, breaks with editors, free evaluation of a writing sample. Write for more information.

☑ LIGONIER VALLEY WRITERS CONFERENCE, P.O. Box B, Ligonier PA 15658-1602. (724)537-3341. Fax: (724)537-0482. Contact: Sally Shirey. Writer programs geared toward all levels. Annual conference features fiction, nonfiction, poetry and other genres. Conference held July 13-15, 2001. Write or call for more information.

MANHATTANVILLE WRITERS' WEEK, Manhattanville College, 2900 Purchase St., Purchase NY 10577-2103. (914)694-3425. Fax: (914)694-3488. E-mail: rdowd@mville.edu. Dean, School of Graduate & Professional Studies: Ruth Dowd. Writer workshops geared toward beginner, intermediate and advanced levels. **Open to students.** Writers' week offers a special workshop for writers interested in children's/young adult writing. We have featured such workshop leaders as: Patricia Gauch, Richard Peck, Elizabeth Winthrop and Lore Segal. Annual workshop held last week in June. Length of each session: one week. Cost of workshop: $560 (non-credit); includes a full week of writing activities, 5-day workshop on children's literature, lectures, readings, sessions with editors and agents, etc. Workshop may be taken for 2 graduate credits. Write for more information.

☑ MAPLE WOODS COMMUNITY COLLEGE WRITERS' CONFERENCE, 2601 NE Barry Rd., Kansas City MO 64156. (816)437-3011. Fax: (816)437-3484. E-mail: schumacp@maplewoods.cc.mo.us. Director Community Education: Paula Schumacher. Contact: Paula Schumacher. Writing conference geared toward advanced and aspiring writers. Various writing topics and genres covered. Covers where do you get your ideas for children's books; how to write children's books and get published; panels comprised of children's book authors, librarians and book sellers. Conference held September 2000. Registration limited to 500. Cost of workshop: $155; includes continental breakfast, refreshments and two networking sessions.

MARITIME WRITERS' WORKSHOP, Department Extension & Summer Session, P.O. Box 4400, University of New Brunswick, Fredericton, New Brunswick E3B 5A3 Canada. Phone/fax: (506)474-1144. E-mail: k4jc@unb.ca. Website: www.unb.ca/web/coned/writers/marritrs.html. Coordinator: Rhona Sawlor. Week-long workshop on writing for children, general approach, dealing with submitted material, geared to all levels and held in July. Annual workshop. 3 hours/day. Group workshop plus individual conferences, public readings, etc. Registration limited to 10/class. Cost of workshop: $350 tuition; meals and accommodations extra. Room and board on campus is approximately $280 for meals and a single room for the week. 10-20 ms pages due before conference (deadline announced). Scholarships available.

MENDOCINO COAST WRITERS CONFERENCE, College of the Redwoods, 1211 Del Mar Dr., Ft. Bragg CA 95437. (707)961-6248. E-mail: mcwc@jps.net. Website: www.mcwcwritewhale.com. Registrar: Jan Boyd. Writing workshops geared toward beginner, intermediate and advanced levels. Annual conference in its 12th year. This year's conference will take place June 7-9, 2001. Registration limited to 99. Conference is held on the campus of College of Redwoods. Cost of conference (early registration): $250-300, includes Friday and Saturday lecture sessions, 2 social events; 2 lunches; 2 breakfasts; 1 dinner; editor/agent panels. $300 includes all of the above plus Thursday intensive workshops (choice of one) in poetry, fiction, nonfiction, screen and YA/children's. After April 2000 price increases to $300/350. "What we offer for children's writers varies from year to year."

☑ MIDLAND WRITERS CONFERENCE, Grace A. Dow Memorial Library, 1710 W. St. Andrews, Midland MI 48640-2698. (517)837-3435. Fax: (517)837-3468. E-mail: ajarvis@midland-mi.org. Website: www.grace dowlibrary.org. Conference Chair: Ann Jarvis. **Open to students.** Writer and illustrator workshops geared toward all levels. "Each year, we offer a topic of interest to writers of children's literature. Last year, Pete Hautman spoke on the differences and similitarities between young adult fiction and adult fiction." Classes offered include: how to write poetry, writing for youth, your literary agent/what to expect. Annual workshop. Workshops held usually second Saturday in June. Length of each session: concurrently, 4 1-hour sessions repeated in the afternoon. Maximum class size: 50. "We are a public library." Cost of workshop: $60; $50 seniors and students; includes choice of workshops and the keynote speech given by a prominent author (last year Artur Golden). Write for more information.

N: MIDWEST WRITERS' CONFERENCE, 6000 Frank Ave. NW, Canton OH 44720-7599. Fax: (330)244-3535. E-mail: wshoemaker@stark.kent.edu. Assistant Director: Willetta Shoemaker. Writer workshops geared toward beginner, intermediate and advanced levels. Topics include: Fiction, Nonfiction, Juvenile Literature and Poetry. Juvenile literature presenter Dandi Daley Mackall has written over 200 titles. She will present "Writing for Children and Teens." Annual conference. Conference dates: October 6-7, 2000. Length of each session: 1 hour. Registration limited to 400 total people. Cost of workshop: $125; includes Friday afternoon workshops, keynote address, Saturday workshops, buffet luncheon roundtables. Additional fees: critique service, $40; keynote speakers dinner, $25. Write for more information.

N: MIDWEST WRITERS WORKSHOP, Department of Journalism, Ball State University, Muncie IN 47306. (765)285-5587. Fax: (765)285-7997. Director: Earl L. Conn. Writer workshops geared toward intermediate level. Topics include fiction and nonfiction writing. Past workshop presenters include Joyce Carol Oates, James Alexander Thom, Bill Brashler and Richard Lederer. Workshop also includes ms evaluation and a writing contest. Annual workshop. Workshop will be held July 26-28, 2001. Registration tentatively limited to 125. Cost of workshop: $195; includes everything but room and meals. Offers scholarships. Write for more information.

MISSISSIPPI VALLEY WRITERS CONFERENCE, 3403 45th St., Moline IL 61265. E-mail: kimseuss@aol.com. Conference Director: David R. Collins. Writer workshops geared toward all levels. Conference open to adults. Weeklong workshops in Basics for Beginners, Poetry, Juvenile Writing, Nonfiction, Basics of the Novel, Novel Manuscript Seminar, Short Story, Photography, Writing to Sell. Annual workshop. Workshops held June 4-9, 2001; usually it is the second week in June each year. Length of each session: Monday-Friday, 1 hour each day. Registration limited to 20 participants/workshop. Writing facilities available: college library. Cost of workshop: $25 registration; $50 to participate in 1 workshop, $90 in 2, $40 for each additional; $25 to audit a workshop. Write for more information.

MONTROSE CHRISTIAN WRITER'S CONFERENCE, 5 Locust St., Montrose PA 18801-1112. (570)278-1001. Fax: (570)278-3061. E-mail: mbc@montrosebible.org. Website: www.montrosebible.org. Executive Director: Jim Fahringer. **Open to adults and students.** Writer workshops geared toward beginner, intermediate and advanced levels. Annual workshop. Workshop held in July. Cost of workshop: $110; includes tuition. Write for more information.

N: MOONDANCE INTERNATIONAL FILM FESTIVAL, P.O. Box 3348, Boulder CO 80302-3348. (303)545-0202. E-mail: moondanceff@aol.com. Website: www.moondancefilmfestival.com. Executive Director: Elizabeth English. Writer and illustrator workshops geared toward all levels. **Open to students.** Sessions include screenwriting, playwriting, short stories, film making (feature, documentary, short, animation), TV and video filmmaking, writing for TV (MOW, sitcoms, drama), writing for animation, adaptation to screenplays (novels and short stories). Annual workshop held January 19-21, 2001. Cost of workshop: $100 registration plus a la carte workshops at $25 each, seminars, panel, pitch session at $50 each. $100 registration fee is for festival attendence only. All else is a la carte. Check website for more information and registration forms. "The competition is for women only, but the festival is for all. International participants are encourated to attend."

☑ MOUNT HERMON CHRISTIAN WRITERS CONFERENCE, Mount Hermon Christian Conference Center, P.O. Box 413, Mount Hermon CA 95041-0413. (831)335-4466. Fax: (831)335-9413. E-mail: talbott@mhcamps.org. Website: www.mounthermon.org. Director of Specialized Programs: David R. Talbott. Writer workshops geared toward all levels. Open to students over 16 years. Emphasizes religious writing for children via books, articles; Sunday school curriculum; marketing. Classes offered include: Suitable Style for Children; Everything You Need to Know to Write and Market Your Children's Book; Take-Home Papers for Children. Workshops held annually over Palm Sunday weekend: April 6-10, 2001. Length of each session: 5-day residential conferences held annually. Registration limited 45/class, but most are 10-15. Conference center with hotel-style accommodations. Cost of workshop: $565-800 variable; includes tuition, resource notebook, refreshment breaks, full room and board for 13 meals and 4 nights. Write for more information.

THE NATIONAL WRITERS ASSOCIATION CONFERENCE, 3140 S. Peoria #295, Aurora CO 80014. (303)841-0246. Executive Director: Sandy Whelchel. Writer workshops geared toward all levels. Classes offered include marketing, agenting, "What's Hot in the Market." Annual workshop. In 2001 the workshop will be held in Denver, Colorado, June 8-10. Write for more information or check our website: www.nationalwriters.com.

☑ NORTH CAROLINA WRITERS' NETWORK FALL CONFERENCE, P.O. Box 954, Carrboro NC 27510-0954. (919)967-9540. Fax: (919)929-0535. E-mail: mail@ncwriters.org. Website: www.ncwriters.org. Program and Services Director: Joe Newberry. Writer workshops geared toward beginner, intermediate, advanced and professional levels. **Open to students.** "We offer workshops and critique sessions in a variety of genres: fiction, poetry, children's. Past young adult and children's writing classes included: 'Everybody's Got a Story to Tell—or Write!' with Eleanora Tate; 'Writing Young Adult Fiction' with Sarah Dessen and 'Writing for Children' with Carole Boston Weatherford." Annual conference. Conference held November 10-12, 2000 in Raleigh, NC. Lee Smith and Jill McCorkel joint keynote and readings done by Ellen Gilchrist and Afaa Michael Weaver. Cost of workshop: approximately $175/NCWN members, $200/nonmembers; includes workshops, panel discussions, round table discussions, social activities and 2 meals. "Cost does not include fee for critique sessions or accommodations."

☑ **OAKLAND UNIVERSITY WRITER'S CONFERENCE**, 221 Varner Hall, Oakland University, Rochester MI 48309-4401. (248)370-3125. Fax: (248)370-4280. E-mail: gjboddy@oakland.edu. Website: www.oakland.edu/contin-ed/writersconf. Program Director: Gloria J. Boddy. Writer and illustrator conference geared toward beginner, intermediate, advanced and professional levels. **Open to Students**. Offers sessions in Children's Poetry, Marketing a Children's Book Manuscript, Writing Nonfiction for Teens. Annual conference. Conference held October, 2000. Limited to 10 per workshop. Cost of conference: $85; includes attendance at a choice of 40 presentations; $48; includes hands on workshops, chance to read work and receive feedback. Write or call for more information.

OF DARK AND STORMY NIGHTS, P.O. Box 1944, Muncie IN 47308-1944. (765)288-7402. E-mail: spurge onmwa@juno.com. Director: W.W. Spurgeon. Writer workshops geared toward beginner, intermediate, advanced and professional. **Open to adults and students**. Topics include mystery and true crime writing for all ages. Annual workshop. Location: Rolling Meadows, IL (suburban Chicago). Workshop held June 9, 2001. Registration limited to 175. "This is a concentrated one-day program with panels and speakers." Cost of workshop: $150; includes all sessions, continental breakfast and full luncheon. Mss critiques available for an extra charge. Write for more information.

OHIO KENTUCKY INDIANA CHILDREN'S LITERATURE CONFERENCE, % Greater Cincinnati Library Consortium (GCLC), 2181 Victory Parkway, Suite 214, Cincinnati OH 45206-2855. (513)751-4422. Fax: (513)751-0463. E-mail: gclc@gclc-lib.org. Website: www.gclc-lib.org. Staff Development Coordinator: Judy Malone. Writer and illustrator conference geared toward all levels. **Open to students.** Annual conference. Emphasizes multicultural literature for children and young adults. Next conference November 4, 2000. Contact GCLC for more information. Registration limited to 250. Cost of conference: $40; includes registration/attendance at all workshop sessions, continental breakfast, lunch, author/illustrator signings. Write for more information.

☑ **OKLAHOMA ARTS INSTITUTE**, (formerly Quartz Mountain), 105 N. Hudson, Suite 101, Oklahoma City OK 73154. (405)319-9019. Fax: (405)319-9099. E-mail: okarts@telepath.org. Website: www.okartinst.org. Artistic and Managing Director: Lee Warren. Writing workshops geared toward intermediate, advanced and professional levels. Writing topics include children's writing, fiction, nonfiction, poetry, and the art of teaching writing. Other arts workshops include instruction in the visual arts, photography, and music and performing arts. The four-day weekend workshops are held at Quartz Mountain Arts and Conference Center in Southwest Oklahoma. Registration is limited to 20 participants per workshop; 5 workshops each weekend. Cost of workshop: $450; includes tuition, double-occupancy room and board. Write for more information. "Catalogs are available. Each workshop is taught by a professional artist of national reputation."

☑ **OUTDOOR WRITERS ASSOCIATION OF AMERICA ANNUAL CONFERENCE**, 158 Lower Georges Valley Rd., Spring Mills PA 16875. (814)364-9557. Fax: (814)364-9558. E-mail: eking4owaa@cs.com. Meeting Planner: Eileen King. Writer workshops geared toward all levels. Annual workshop. Workshop held in June. Cost of workshop: $140; includes attendance at all workshops and most meals. Attendees must have prior approval from Executive Director before attendance is permitted. Write for more information.

OZARK CREATIVE WRITERS, INC. CONFERENCE, 6817 Gingerbread Lane, Little Rock AR 72204. (501)565-8889. Fax: (510)565-7220. E-mail: pvining@aristotle.net. Counselor: Peggy Vining. **Open to students.** Writer's workshops geared to all levels. "All forms of the creative process dealing with the literary arts. We sometimes include songwriting. We invite excellent speakers who are selling authors. We also promote writing by providing competitions in all genres." Always the second full weekend in October at Inn of the Ozarks in Eureka Springs AR (a resort town). Morning sessions are given to main attraction author . . . six 1-hour satellite speakers during each of the 2 afternoons. Two banquets. "Approximately 200 attend the conference yearly . . . many others enter the creative writing competition." Cost of registration/contest entry fee approximately $50-60. Includes entrance to all sessions, contest entry fees. "This does not include meals or lodging. We block off 70 rooms prior to August 15 for OCW guests." Send #10 SASE for brochure by May 1st to Peggy Vining, 6817 Gingerbread Ln., Little Rock, AR 72204. "Reserve early."

☑ **PERSPECTIVES IN CHILDREN'S LITERATURE CONFERENCE**, School of Education, 226 Furcolo Hall, University of Massachusetts, Amherst MA 01003-3035. (413)545-4325 or (413)545-1116. Fax: (413)545-2879. E-mail: childlit@educ.umass.edu. Website: www.unix.oit.umass.edu/~childlit. Coordinator of Conference: Jane Kelley Pierce. Writer and illustrator workshops geared to all levels. Conference 2001 will feature Gail Carson Levine and Julius Lester as keynote speakers. Additional presenters include Barry Moser, Jane Dyer, Liza Ketchum, Jane Yolen, Patricia MacLachlan and Rich Michelson and Enchanted Circle Theater.

Presenters talk about what inspires them, how they bring their stories to life and what their visions are for the future. Next conference will be held on Saturday, March 31, 2001, at the University of Massachusetts. For more information contact Jane Kelley Pierce by phone, fax or e-mail."

PHOTOGRAPHY: A DIVERSE FOCUS, 895 W. Oak St., Zionsville IN 46077-1220. Phone/fax: (317)873-0738. Director: Charlene Faris. Writer and illustrator workshops geared to beginners. "Conferences focus primarily on children's photography; also literature and illustration. Annual conferences are held very often throughout year." Registration is not limited, but "sessions are generally small." Cost of conference: $165 (2 days), $85 (1 day). "Inquiries with a SASE only will receive information on seminars."

GARY PROVOST'S WRITERS RETREAT WORKSHOP, % Write It/Sell It, 2507 S. Boston Place, Tulsa OK 74114. (800)642-2494 (for brochure). Fax: (918)583-1471. E-mail: wrwwisi@aol.com. Website: www.channe l1.com/wisi. Director: Gail Provost Stockwell. Contact: Lance Stockwell, assistant director. Writer workshops geared toward beginner, intermediate and advanced levels. Workshops are appropriate for writers of full length novels for children/YA. Also, for writers of all novels or narrative nonfiction. Annual workshop. Workshops held May-June 3, 2001. Registration limited to small groups: beginners and advanced. Writing facilities available: private rooms with desks. Cost of workshop: $1,635; includes tuition, food and lodging for nine nights, daily classes, writing space, time and assignments, consultation and instruction. Requirements: short synopsis required to determine appropriateness of novel for our nuts and bolts approach to getting the work in shape for publication. Write for more information. For complete details, call 800 number.

ROBERT QUACKENBUSH'S CHILDREN'S BOOK WRITING AND ILLUSTRATING WORK-SHOP, 460 E. 79th St., New York NY 10021-1443. Phone/fax: (212)861-2761. E-mail: rqstudios@aol.com. (E-mail inquirers please include mailing address). Website: www.rquackenbush.com. Contact: Robert Quackenbush. Writer and illustrator workshops geared toward all levels. **Open to students.** Five-day extensive workshop on writing and illustrating books for children, emphasizes picture books from start to finish. Also covered is writing fiction and nonfiction for middle grades and young adults, if that is the attendees' interest. Current trends in illustration are also covered. This July workshop is a full 5-day (9 a.m.-4 p.m) extensive course. Next workshop July 9-16, 2001. Registration limited to 10/class. Writing and/or art facilities available; work on the premises; art supply store nearby. Cost of workshop: $650 for instruction. Cost of workshop includes instruction in preparation of a ms and/or book dummy ready to submit to publishers. Class limited to 10 members. Attendees are responsible for arranging their own hotel and meals, although suggestions are given on request for places to stay and eat. "This unique workshop, held annually since 1982, provides the opportunity to work with Robert Quackenbush, a prolific author and illustrator of children's books with more than 170 fiction and nonfiction books for young readers to his credit, including mysteries, biographies and song-books. The workshop attracts both professional and beginning writers and artists of different ages from all over the world." Recommended by Foder's *Great American Learning Vacations*.

N! SAGE HILL WRITING EXPERIENCE, Writing Children's & Young Adult Fiction Workshop, Box 1731, Saskatoon, Saskatchewan S7K 3S1 Canada. Phone/fax: (306)652-7395. E-mail: sage.hill@sk.sympatic o.ca Website: www.lights.com/sagehill. . Executive Director: Steven Ross Smith. Writer conference geared toward intermediate level. **Open to students.** Conference occurs every 2 or 3 years. Conference held July 25-August 5. Registration limited to 6 participants. Cost of conference: $595; includes instruction, meals, accommodation. Require ms samples prior to registration. Write for more information.

SAN DIEGO STATE UNIVERSITY WRITERS' CONFERENCE, The College of Extended Studies, San Diego CA 92182-1920. (619)594-2517. Fax: (619)594-8566. E-mail: ppierce@mail.sdsu.edu. Website: www.ces. sdsu.edu. Conference Facilitator: Paula Pierce. Writer workshops geared toward beginner, intermediate and advanced levels. Emphasizes nonfiction, fiction, screenwriting, advanced novel writing; includes sessions specific to writing and illustrating for children. Workshops offered by children's editors, agents and writers. Workshops held third weekend in January each year. Registration limited. Cost of workshop: approximately $225. Write for more information or see our home page at the above website.

N! SANDHILLS WRITERS CONFERENCE, Augusta State University, 2500 Walton Way, Augusta GA 30904. (706)737-1500. Fax: (706)667-4770. E-mail: akellman@aug.edu. Website: www.aug.edu//Langlitcom/ sand_hills_conference. Conference Director: Anthony Kellman. Writer and illustrator workshops geared toward beginner and intermediate levels. **Open to students.** "Each year we have a children's literature author on our

---

MARKET CONDITIONS are constantly changing! If you're still using this book and it is 2002 or later, buy the newest edition of *Children's Writer's & Illustrator's Market* at your favorite bookstore or order directly from Writer's Digest Books.

staff who speaks on various aspects of the craft of this genre." Annual conference held March 22-24, 2001. Registration limited to 150. "We have free word processing and Internet access through our Reese Library and our Writing Center." Cost of conference: $156; includes 1 ms consultation, 2 luncheons, attendence at all events, one ms submission. Participants should submit mms samples usually by the second week of February. The professional staffer critiques these prior to registration and meets with the authors of the scripts in one-on-one conferences during the conference.

THE WILLIAM SAROYAN WRITER'S CONFERENCE, P.O. Box 5331, Fresno CA 93755-5331. Phone/fax: (559)224-2516. E-mail: law@pacbell.net. President: Linda West. Writer and illustrator workshops geared toward advanced level. **Open to Students.** Past sessions have featured Barbara Kuroff, editor of Writer's Digest Books and Andrea Brown, agent for children's book authors and illustrators. Annual conference. Conference held April, 2001 at Piccadilly Inn-airport. Registration limited to 275. Cost of conference: $285. Friday noon to Sunday noon workshops (35 to choose from) most meals, critique groups, one-on-ones with agents, editors. Write for more information. "We try to cover a wide variety of writing. Children's books would be one topic of many."

SEATTLE CHRISTIAN WRITERS CONFERENCE, sponsored by Writers Information Network, P.O. Box 11337, Bainbridge Island WA 98110. (206)842-9103. Fax: (206)842-0536. Director: Elaine Wright Colvin. Writer workshops geared toward all levels. Conference open to students. Past conferences have featured subjects such as 'Making It to the Top as a Children's Book Author,' featuring Debbie Trafton O'Neal. Quarterly workshop (4 times/year). Workshop dates to be announced. Cost of workshop: $25. Write for more information and to be added to mailing list.

SELF PUBLISHING YOUR OWN BOOK, 34200 Ridge Rd., #201, Willoughby OH 44094. (440)943-3047. E-mail: lealoldham@aol.com. Coordinator: Lea Leever Oldham. **Open to students.** Covers options for publishing, ISBN, copyright, fair use, pricing, bar codes, size and binding and other topics of interest to the potential self publisher. Workshop will be offered one on one by appointment. Cost of workshop $25/person.

⟨N⟩ SKYLINE WRITERS' CONFERENCE, P.O. Box 33343, N. Royalton OH 44133. (440)234-0763. Annual conference held the first Saturday in August. Conference Director: Lilie Kilburn. Workshops geared toward all levels. **Open to students.** Conference writing topics include writing and marketing children's literature. Literary contest with cash prizes for first, second, and third place winners; mss critiqued by a professional. Cost of conference: $50; includes conference fee, continental breakfast, lunch, door prizes. Write for more information or visit our website: www.delphi.com/skylinewriters.

⟨N⟩ SOCIETY OF SOUTHWESTERN AUTHORS' WRANGLING WITH WRITING, P.O. Box 30355, Tucson AZ 85751-0355. (520)546-9382. Fax: (520)296-0409. E-mail: wporter202@aol.com. Website: www.azstarnet.com/nonprofit/ssa. Conference Director: Penny Porter. Writer workshops geared toward all levels. "Limited scholarships available." Sessions include Writing and Publishing the Young Adult Novel, What Agents Want to See in a Children's Book, Writing Books for Young Children. "We always have several children's book editors and agents interested in meeting with children's writers." Annual workshop held January 19-20, 2001; January 18-19, 2002; January 17-18, 2003 (usually MLK weekend). Registration limited to 500—usually 220-300 people attend. Hotel rooms have dataports for internet access. Tucson has many art galleries. Tentative cost: $250 non-members, $200 for SSA members; includes 3 meals and 2 continental breakfasts, all workshop sessions—individual appointments with agents and editors are extra. Hotel accommodations are not included. Some editors and agents like to see mss prior to the conference; information about requirements is in the brochure. If you want a portfolio of artwork critiqued, please contact us directly, and we'll try to accommodate you. Write for more information. SSA has put on this conference for over 25 years now. It's hands-on, it's friendly, and every year writers sell their manuscripts.

☑ SOUTHWEST WRITERS, 8200 Mountain Rd., NE, Suite 106, Albuquerque NM 87110-7835. (505)265-9485. Fax: (505)265-9483. E-mail: swriters@aol.com. Website: www.southwestwriters.org. Contact: Stephanie Dooley. **Open to adults and students.** Writer workshops geared toward all genres at all levels of writing. Various aspects of writing covered including children's. Examples from conferences: Preconference workshops on the juvenile/young adult/novel taught by Penny Durant; SCBWI Panel, Preconference session on generating ideas by Elsie Karr Kreischer, conference lectures on characterization by Kreischer, lecture by Kelly White of *Girl's Life* magazine. We emphasize everything from idea generating to selling to editors. There will be a few sessions on children's writing. Annual conference. Conference held September 21-24, 2001 at the Alburquerque Marriott Hotel. Length of sessions varies. Cost of workshop: $210 for members and $270 for nonmembers by August 25; after this date $240 for members and $300 for nonmembers; includes all sessions, 2 meals and one ten-minute session with an editor or agent. Also offers critique groups (for $60/year, offers 2 monthly meetings, monthly newsletter, annual writing contest and occasional workshops). Write for more information.

☑ SPLIT ROCK ARTS PROGRAM, University of Minnesota, 360 Coffey Hall, 1420 Eckles Ave., St. Paul MN 55108-6084. (612)625-8100. Fax: (612)624-6210. E-mail: srap@cce.umn.edu. Website: www.cce.umn. edu/splitrockarts. Writing workshops including poetry, stories, memoirs, novels and personal essays geared toward intermediate, advanced and professional levels. Workshops begin in July for 5 weeks. Optional college credits available. Registration limited to 16 per workshop. Workshops held on the University of Minnesota-Duluth campus. Cost of workshop: $480; includes tuition and fees. On-campus apartments and residence hall housing available. Complete catalogs available in March. Call or e-mail anytime to be put on mailing list or check out website for complete workshop offerings. Some workshops fill very early.

☑ **STATE OF MAINE WRITERS' CONFERENCE**, 18 Hill Rd., Belmont MA 02478. (617)489-1548. Chairs: June Knowles and Mary Pitts. Writers' workshops geared toward beginner, intermediate, advanced levels. **Open to students and adults.** Emphasizes poetry, prose, mysteries, editors, publishers, etc. August 2001 conference dates to be determined. Cost of workshop: $100; includes all sessions and supper, snacks, poetry booklet. Send SASE for more information.

STEAMBOAT SPRINGS WRITERS CONFERENCE, P.O. Box 774284, Steamboat Springs CO 80477. (970)879-8079. E-mail: freiberger@compuserve.com. Conference Director: Harriet Freiberger. Writers' workshops geared toward intermediate levels. **Open to students.** Some years offer topics specific to children's writing. Annual conference since 1982. Workshops held July 22, 2000. 2001 Conference will be July 14. Registration limited to 25-30. Cost of workshop: $45; includes 4 seminars and luncheon. Write or e-mail for more information.

SUNSHINE COAST FESTIVAL OF THE WRITTEN ARTS, P.O. Box 2299, Sechelt, British Columbia V0N-3A0 Canada. (604)885-9631, 1-800-565-9631. Fax: (604)885-3967. E-mail: written_arts@sunshine.net. Website: www.sunshine.net/rockwood. Festival Producer: Gail Bull. Writer and illustrator workshops geared toward professional level. **Open to Students.** Annual literary festival held August 10-13, 2000. Writers-in-residence workshops. Pavilion seating 500 per event. Festival pass $150; individual events $12. Writer's workshops are 3 days. Fee schedule available upon request.

Ⓝ TAOS SUMMER WRITERS' CONFERENCE, University of New Mexico, Humanities 255, Albuquerque NM 87121. (505)277.6248. Fax: (505)277-5573. E-mail: swarner@unm.edu. Website: www.unm.edu/~taosconf. Director: Sharon Oard Warner. Writer workshops geared toward all levels. **Open to students.** Must be 18 years old. "Our conference offers both week-long and week-end conferences, not only in children's writing, but also adult fiction (novel, short story), creative nonfiction, poetry and screenwriting." Annual conference held July 14-July 20, 2001—(usually 3rd week of July). Maximum of 12 people per workshop. Usually 3 or 4 weekend workshops and 8- or 10-week-long workshops. "We provide an on-site computer room." Cost of conference: approximately $475/weeklong; $200/weekend; includes tuition, opening and closing night dinner, all the readings by instructors, Wednesday night entertainment. Lodging and meals extra but we offer a reduced rate at the Sagebrush Inn in Taos. Write for more information.

☑ **TO WRITE, WRITERS' GUILD OF ACADIANA**, P.O. Box 51532, Lafayette LA 70505-1532. Contact: Marilyn Continé (337)981-5153 or Ro Foley (337)234-8694. Fax: (337)367-6860. E-mail: mmcontine@aol.com. Next conference to be held in 2002.

TUSCAN CASTLE ART'S RETREAT, GREAT TRAVELS, INC., 5506 Connecticut Ave., NW, Suite 23, Washington DC 20015. (800)411-3728. Fax: (209)966-6972. E-mail: gtravels@erols.com. Website: www.great-travels.com. Writer and illustrator retreat geared toward all levels. **Open to Students.** Retreat held each September or October. Registration limited to 18 writers, 12 artists. Cost of retreat: $1,759 double occupancy plus $350-550 for single occupancy; includes transfers, accommodations in the castle, 6 gourmet dinners served with mineral water or wine, welcome reception, Florence walking tour. Send writing sample for writers. "You will reside in the heart of Tuscany, birthplace of Dante, Boccaccio, Leonardo da Vinci and Michelangelo. Your home and studio is the medieval fortress, Castello di Montegufoni built in the 11th century, later refined by the Renaissance. Montegufoni stands on a peaceful country road, the same Via Volterrana once followed by Charlemagne to Rome. In World War II the *Birth of Venus* and the *Primavera*, paintings by Botticelli, were hidden in the cellars of Montegufoni. Our retreat brings artists and writers to this special place once again."

Ⓝ THE 21ST CENTURY WRITER'S GET-A-WAY, 625 Schuring, Suite B, Portage MI 49024-5106. (616)232-2100. Fax: (509)694-1153. E-mail: ishaeefaw@aol.com. Website: justfriendspublishing.com. Public Relations Manager: John Williams. Writer and illustrator workshops geared toward all levels. Sessions offered include "Marketing Strategies For The 21st Century." **Open to students.** In this workshop our workshop facilitator brings the latest information on software for graphic arts design and/or recommended art workshops. Workshop held twice a year, April 20-22 and August 10-12, 2001. This event will be held at Michigan State University Kellogg Biological Station. All workshops include writing, and one workshop will demo structure book cover designs. Cost of workshop: $200. $150 covers 5 meals, notebook and materials plus registration fee. $50 covers lodging. Write for more information.

Ⓝ UMKC/WRITERS PLACE WRITERS WORKSHOPS, University of Missouri—Kansas City, 5100 Rockhill Rd., 215 55B, Kansas City MO 64110-2499. (816)235-2736. Fax: (816)235-5279. E-mail: mckinleym@

umkc.edu. Continuing Education Manager: Mary Ann McKinley. Writer workshops geared toward intermediate, advanced and professional levels. Workshops open to students and community. Semi-annual workshops. Workshops held in fall and spring. Cost of workshop: $45. Write for more information.

WESLEYAN WRITERS CONFERENCE, Wesleyan University, Middletown CT 06459. (860)685-3604. Fax: (860)685-2441. E-mail: agreene@wesleyan.edu. Website: www.wesleyan.edu/writing/conferen.html. Director: Anne Greene. Writer workshops geared toward all levels. "This conference is useful for writers interested in how to structure a story, poem or nonfiction piece. Although we don't always offer classes in writing for children, the advice about structuring a piece is useful for writers of any sort, no matter who their audience is." Classes in the novel, short story, fiction techniques, poetry, journalism and literary nonfiction. Guest speakers and panels offer discussion of fiction, poetry, reviewing, editing and publishing. Individual ms consultations available. Conference held annually the last week in June. Length of each session: 6 days. "Usually, there are 100 participants at the Conference." Classrooms, meals, lodging and word processing facilities available on campus. Cost of workshop: tuition—$500, room—$105, meals (required of all participants)—$190. "Anyone may register; people who want financial aid must submit their work and be selected by scholarship judges." Call for a brochure or look on the web at address above.

☑ **WESTERN RESERVE WRITERS AND FREELANCE CONFERENCE**, Lakeland Community College, 7700 Clocktower Dr., Kirtland OH 44094. (440)943-3047. E-mail: lealoldham@aol.com. Coordinator: Lea Leever Oldham. Writer workshops geared toward all levels. **Open to students.** Emphasizes fiction, nonfiction, articles, children's writing, poetry, marketing, tax for freelancers, copyright issues and other topics of interest to the beginning or advanced writer. All-day conference held annually in mid-September. Cost of workshop: $59 includes lunch and all day sessions by published authors and other experts. Held at Lakeland Community College, Kirtland, OH.

☑ **WESTERN RESERVE WRITERS MINI CONFERENCE**, 34200 Ridge Rd. #201, Willoughby OH 44094. E-mail: lealoldham@aol.com. Coordinator: Lea Leever Oldham. Writer workshops geared toward beginner, intermediate and advanced levels. **Open to students.** Topics include children's writing, fiction, nonfiction, poetry, articles, marketing and other topics of interest to the beginning or advanced writer. Annual conference end of March. Held at Lakeland Community College, Kirtland OH. Cost of conference: $39. Write for more information.

☑ **WHIDBEY ISLAND WRITERS' CONFERENCE**, 5456 Pleasant View Ln., Freeland WA 98249. (360)331-6714. E-mail: writers@whidbey.com. Website: www.whidbey.com/writers. Director: Celeste Mergens. Writer and illustrator workshops geared toward beginner, intermediate and advanced levels. **Open to students.** Topics include "Writing for Children," "Writing in a Bunny Eat Bunny World," "The Art of Revision." Annual conference. Registration limited to 275. Cost of conference: $258; includes all workshops and events, 2 receptions, activities and daily luncheons. "For writing consultations participants pay $35 for 20 minutes to submit the first five pages of a chapter book, youth novel or entire picture book idea with a written 1-page synopsis." Write, e-mail or check website for more information. "This is a uniquely personable weekend that is designed to be highly interactive."

WILLAMETTE WRITERS ANNUAL WRITERS CONFERENCE, 9045 SW Barbur Blvd., Suite 5A, Portland OR 97219. (503)452-1592. Fax: (503)452-0372. E-mail: wilwrite@teleport.com. Office Manager: Bill Johnson. Writer workshops geared toward all levels. Emphasizes all areas of writing, including children's and young adult. Opportunities to meet one-on-one with leading literary agents and editors. Workshops held in August. Cost of conference: $246; includes membership.

N WISCONSIN REGIONAL WRITER'S ASSOCIATION, INC., 510 W. Sunset Ave., Appleton WI 54911-1139. (920)734-3724. E-mail: wrwalakefield.net. Website: www.inkwells.net/wrwa. President: Patricia Dunson Boverhuis. Writer workshops geared toward all levels. **Open to students.** "Our conference topics/speakers vary with each event." Semiannual conference held May 6, 2000, September 23-24, 2000 [2002 dates?] Cost of conference: $35-50; includes conference attendence only. The higher cost is for the 2-day conference in the fall. Write for more information.

☑ **WRITE ON THE SOUND WRITERS CONFERENCE**, 700 Main St., Edmonds WA 98020-3032. (425)771-0228. Fax: (425)771-0253. E-mail: wots@ci.edmonds.wa.us. Website: www.ci.edmonds.wa.us. Cultural Resources Coordinator: Frances Chapin. Writer workshops geared toward beginner, intermediate, advanced and professional levels with some sessions on writing for children. Annual conference held the first weekend in October with 2 full days of a variety of lectures and workshops. Registration limited to 200. Cost of workshop: approximately $50/day, or $85 for the weekend, includes 4 workshops daily plus one ticket to keynote lecture. Brochures are mailed in August. Attendees must preregister. Write, e-mail or call for brochure.

WRITERS' FORUM, 1570 E. Colorado Blvd., Pasadena CA 91106-2003. (626)585-7608. Coordinator of Forum: Meredith Brucker. Writer workshops geared toward all levels. Workshops held March 17, 2001. Length of sessions: 1 hour and 15 minutes including Q & A time. Cost of day: $100; includes lunch. Write for more information to Extended Learning, Pasadena City College, 1570 E. Colorado Blvd., Pasadena CA 91106-2003.

WRITE-TO-PUBLISH CONFERENCE, 9731 N. Fox Glen Dr., #6F, Niles IL 60714-4222. (847)296-3964. Fax: (847)296-0754. E-mail: linjohnson@compuserve.com. Website: www.writetopub.com. Director: Lin Johnson. Writer workshops geared toward all levels. **Open to students.** Conference is focused for the Christian market and includes a class on writing for children. Annual conference held 6-9, 2001. Cost of conference: $325; includes conference and banquet. For information, call (847)299-4755 or e-mail linjohnson@compuserve.com. Conference takes place at Wheaton College in the Chicago area.

WRITING CHILDREN'S FICTION, Rice University, Houston TX 77005. (713)527-4803. Fax: (713)285-5213. E-mail: scs@rice.edu. Website: www.scs.rice.edu. Contact: School of Continuing Studies. Children's writing courses and workshops geared toward all levels. Topics include issues in children's publishing, censorship, multiculturalism, dealing with sensitive subjects, submissions/formatting, the journal as resource, the markets—finding your niche, working with an editor, the agent/author connection, the role of research, and contract negotiation. Annual week-long workshop held every July. Weekly evening courses held year-round. Contact Rice Continuing Studies for current information on course offerings.

WRITING TODAY, Birmingham-Southern College, Box 549003, Birmingham AL 35254. (205)226-4921. Fax: (205)226-3072. E-mail: dcwilson@bsc.com. Director of Special Events: Martha Ross. Writer's workshop geared toward all levels. **Open to students.** "The Writing Today Conference brings together writers, editors, publishers, playwrights, poets and other literary professionals from around the country for two days of workshops and lectures on the literary arts, as well as practical information necessary to the craft of writing. Programs explore poetry, playwriting, children's books, novels, short stories, etc." Major speakers for the 2000 conference include Ernest Gaines, Grandmaster, Sena Jeter Naslund, Ishmael Reed, Claudia Johnson, Aileen Kilgore Henderson and William Cobb. Annual Conference. Conference held April 7-8, 2000. Registration limited to 500. Cost of Conference: $120; includes all workshop sessions, continental breakfast and lunch both days and a Friday and Saturday reception. Individual mss critiques available for an additional fee. Write for more information.

Contests & Awards

Publication is not the only way to get your work recognized. Contests can also be viable vehicles to gain recognition in the industry. Placing in a contest or winning an award validates the time spent writing and illustrating. Even for those who don't place, many competitions offer the chance to obtain valuable feedback from judges and other established writers or artists.

When considering contests, be sure to study guidelines and requirements. Regard entry deadlines as gospel and note whether manuscripts and artwork should be previously published or unpublished. Also, be aware that awards vary. While one contest may award a significant amount of money or publication, another may award a certificate or medal instead.

Note that some contests require nominations. For published authors and illustrators, competitions provide an excellent way to promote your work. Your publisher may not be aware of local competitions such as state-sponsored awards—if your book is eligible, have the appropriate person at your publishing company nominate or enter your work for consideration.

To select potential contests for your work, read through the listings that interest you, then send for more information about the types of written or illustrated material considered and other important details, such as who retains the rights to prize-winning material. A number of contests offer such information through websites given in their listings. If you are interested in knowing who has received certain awards in the past, check your local library or bookstores or consult *Children's Books: Awards & Prizes*, compiled and edited by the Children's Book Council (www.c bcbooks.org). Many bookstores have special sections for books that are Caldecott and Newbery Medal winners. Visit these websites for more information on award-winning children's books: The Caldecott—www.ala.org/alsc/caldecott.html; The Newbery—www.ala.org/alsc/newbery.html; The Coretta Scott King Award—www.ala.org/srrt/csking; The Michael L. Printz Award— www.ala.org/yalsa/printz; The Boston Globe-Horn Book Award—www.hbook.com/bghb.html; The Golden Kite Award—www.scbwi.org/goldkite.htm.

Information on contests listed in the previous edition but not included in this edition of *Children's Writer's & Illustrator's Market* **may be found in the General Index.**

AIM Magazine Short Story Contest, P.O. Box 1174, Maywood IL 60153-8174. (773)874-6184. Contest Directors: Ruth Apilado, Mark Boone. Annual contest. **Open to students.** Estab. 1983. Purpose of contest: "We solicit stories with social significance. Youngsters can be made aware of social problems through the written word, and hopefully they will try solving them." Unpublished submissions only. Deadline for entries: August 15. SASE for contest rules and entry forms. SASE for return of work. No entry fee. Awards $100. Judging by editors. Contest open to everyone. Winning entry published in fall issue of *AIM*. Subscription rate $12/year. Single copy $4.50.

✓ 🍁 **ALCUIN CITATION AWARD**, The Alcuin Society, P.O. Box 3216, Vancouver, British Columbia V6B 3X8 Canada. (604)888-9049. Fax: (604)888-9052. E-mail: deedy@attglobal.net. Website: www.slais.ubc.ca/ users/Alcuin. Secretary: Doreen E. Eddy. Annual award. Estab. 1983. **Open to students.** Purpose of contest: Alcuin Citations are awarded annually for excellence in Canadian book design. Previously published submissions only, "in the year prior to the Awards Invitation to enter; i.e., 1996 awards went to books published in 1995." Submissions made by the author, publishers and designers. Deadline for entries: March 15. SASE. Entry fee is $10 per book. Awards certificate. Judging by professionals and those experienced in the field of book design. Requirements for entrants: Winners are selected from books designed and published in Canada. Awards are presented annually at the Annual General Meeting of the Alcuin Society held in late May or early June each year.

✓ **AMHA MORGAN ART CONTEST**, American Morgan Horse Association, Box 960, Shelburne VT 05482. (802)985-4944. Fax: (802)985-8897. E-mail: info@morganhorse.com. Website: www.morganhorse.com.

Membership Recognition Coordinator: Sara Luneau. Annual contest. **Open to students.** The art contest consists of two categories: Morgan art (pencil sketches, oils, water colors, paintbrush), Morgan specialty pieces (sculptures, carvings). Unpublished submissions only. Deadline for entries: October 1. Contest rules and entry forms available for SASE. Entries not returned. Entry fee is $5. Awards $50 first prize in 2 divisions (for adults) and AMHA gift certificates to top 6 places (for children). Judging by *The Morgan Horse* magazine staff. "All work submitted becomes property of The American Morgan Horse Association. Selected works may be used for promotional purposes by the AMHA." Requirements for entrants: "We consider all work submitted." Works displayed at the annual convention and the AMHA headquarters; published in *AMAHA News* and *Morgan Sales Network* and in color in the *Morgan Horse Magazine* (TMHA). The contest divisions consist of Junior (to age 17), Senior (18 and over) and Professional (commercial artists). Each art piece must have its own application form and its own entry fee. Matting is optional.

☑ AMERICA & ME ESSAY CONTEST, Farm Bureau Insurance, Box 30400, 7373 W. Saginaw, Lansing MI 48909-7900. (517)323-7000. Fax: (517)323-6615. E-mail: lfedewa@fbinsmi.com. Website: farmbureauinsurance-mi.co. Contest Coordinator: Lisa Fedewa. Annual contest. **Open to students.** Estab. 1968. Purpose of the contest: to give Michigan 8th graders the opportunity to express their thoughts/feelings on America and their roles in America. Unpublished submissions only. Deadline for entries: mid-November. SASE for contest rules and entry forms. "We have a school mailing list. Any school located in Michigan is eligible to participate." Entries not returned. No entry fee. Awards savings bonds and plaques for state top ten ($500-1,000), certificates and plaques for top 3 winners from each school. Each school may submit up to 10 essays for judging. Judging by home office employee volunteers. Requirements for entrants: "Participants must work through their schools or our agents' sponsoring schools. No individual submissions will be accepted. Top ten essays and excerpts from other essays are published in booklet form following the contest. State capitol/schools receive copies."

Ⓝ AMERICAN ASSOCIATION OF UNIVERSITY WOMEN, NORTH CAROLINA DIVISION, AWARD IN JUVENILE LITERATURE, North Carolina Literary and Historical Association, 4610 CMS Center, Raleigh NC 27699-4610. (919)733-9375. Fax: (919)733-8807. Award Coordinator: Dr. Jerry C. Cashion. Annual award. Purpose of award: to reward the creative activity involved in writing juvenile literature and to stimulate in North Carolina an interest in worthwhile literature written on the juvenile level. Book must be published during the year ending June 30 of the year of publication. Submissions made by author, author's agent or publisher. Deadline for entries: July 15. SASE for contest rules. Awards a cup to the winner and winner's name inscribed on a plaque displayed within the North Carolina Division of Archives and History. Judging by Board of Award selected by sponsoring organization. Requirements for entrants: Author must have maintained either legal residence or actual physical residence, or a combination of both, in the State of North Carolina for three years immediately preceding the close of the contest period.

Ⓝ AMERICAS AWARD, Consortium of Latin American Studies Programs (CLASP), CLASP Committee on Teaching and Outreach, % Center for Latin America and Caribbean Studies, University of Wisconsin-Milwaukee, P.O. Box 413, Milwaukee WI 53201. (414)229-5986. Fax: (414)229-2879. E-mail: jkline@uwm.edu. Website: www.uwm.edu/Dept/CLA/outreach_americas.html. Coordinator: Julie Kline. Annual award. Estab. 1993. Purpose of contest: "Up to two awards are given each spring in recognition of U.S. published works (from the previous year) of fiction, poetry, folklore or selected nonfiction (from picture books to works for young adults) in English or Spanish which authentically and engagingly relate to Latin America, the Caribbean, or to Latinos in the United States. By combining both and linking the "Americas," the intent is to reach beyond geographic borders, as well as multicultural-international boundaries, focusing instead upon cultural heritages within the hemisphere." Previously published submissions only. Submissions open to anyone with an interest in the theme of the award. Deadline for entries: December 1. SASE for contest rules and any committee changes. Awards $200 cash prize, plaque and a formal presentation at the Library of Congress, Washington DC. Judging by a review committee consisting of individuals in teaching, library work, outreach and children's literature specialists.

☑ AMHA LITERARY CONTEST, American Morgan Horse Association Youth, P.O. Box 960, Shelburne VT 05482. (802)985-4944. E-mail: info@morganhorse.com. Website: www.morganhorse.com. Contest Director: Sara Luneau. Annual contest. Open to students under 21. Purpose of contest: "to award youth creativity." The contest includes categories for both poetry and essays. Unpublished submissions only. Submissions made by author. Deadline for entries: October 1. SASE for contest rules and entry forms. No entry fee. Awards $25 cash and ribbons to up to 5th place. "Winning entry will be published in *AMHA News and Morgan Sales Network*, a monthly publication."

Ⓝ ARTS RECOGNITION AND TALENT SEARCH (ARTS), National Foundation for Advancement in the Arts, 800 Brickell Ave., Suite 500, Miami FL 33131. (305)377-1147. Fax: (305)377-1149. E-mail: nfaa@nfaa. org. Website: www.ARTSaward.org. Contact: Myriam Crespo. **Open to students/high school seniors or 17- and 18-year-olds.** Annual award. Estab. 1981. "Created to recognize and reward outstanding accomplishment in dance, music, jazz, theater, photography, film and video, visual arts and/or writing. Arts Recognition and Talent Search (ARTS) is an innovative national program of the National Foundation for Advancement in the Arts (NFAA). Established in 1981, ARTS touches the lives of gifted young people across the country, providing financial support, scholarships and goal-oriented artistic, educational and career opportunities. Each year, from a pool of more than 8,000 applicants, an average of 400 ARTS awardees are chosen for NFAA support by panels of distinguished artists and educators. Deadline for entries: June 1 and October 1. Entry fee is $25/35. Fee waivers available based on need. Awards $100-3,000—unrestricted cash grants. Judging by a panel of authors and educators recognized in the field. Rights to submitted/winning material: NFAA/ARTS retains the right to duplicate work in an anthology or in Foundation literature unless otherwise specified by the artist. Requirements for entrants: Artists must be high school seniors or, if not enrolled in high school, must be 17 or 18 years old. Applicants must be US citizens or residents, unless applying in jazz. Works will be published in an anthology distributed during ARTS Week, the final adjudication phase which takes place in Miami. NFAA will invite a total of 125 artists to participate in "ARTS Week 2001," in January in Miami-Dade County, Florida. ARTS Week is a once-in-a-lifetime experience consisting of performances, master classes, workshops, readings, exhibits, and enrichment activities with renowned artists and arts educators. All expenses are paid by NFAA, including airfare, hotel, meals and ground transportation.

✓ 🍁 ATLANTIC WRITING COMPETITION, Writer's Federation of Nova Scotia, 1113 Marginal Rd., Halifax, Nova Scotia B3H 4P7 Canada. (902)423-8116. Fax: (902)422-0881. E-mail: talk@writers.ns.ca. Website: www.writers.ns.ca. **Open to students.** Annual contest. Estab. 1970s. Purpose is to encourage new and emerging writers and encourages all writers in Atlantic Canada to explore their talents by sending in new, untried work to any of five categories: novel, short story, poetry, writing for children or magazine article. Unpublished submissions only. Submissions made by author. Deadline for entries: July 31, 2000. SASE for contest rules and entry forms. Entry fee is $15 (Canadian). Judging by a writer, bookseller and publisher. Only open to residents of Atlantic Canada who are unpublished in category they enter. Judges return comments to all entrants.

BAKER'S PLAYS HIGH SCHOOL PLAYWRITING CONTEST, Baker's Plays, P.O. Box 6992222, Quincy MA 02269-9222. Fax: (617)745-9891. E-mail: info@bakersplays.com. Website: www.bakersplays.com. Contest Director: Raymond Pape. Annual contest. Estab. 1990. Purpose of the contest: to acknowledge playwrights at the high school level and to insure the future of American theater. Unpublished submissions only. Postmark deadline: January 30, 2001. Notification: May. SASE for contest rules and entry forms. No entry fee. Awards $500 to the first place playwright and Baker's Plays will publish the play; $250 to the second place playwright with an honorable mention; and $100 to the third place playwright with an honorable mention in the series. Judged anonymously. **Open to any high school student.** Plays must be accompanied by the signature of a sponsoring high school drama or English teacher, and it is recommended that the play receive a production or a public reading prior to the submission. "Please include a SASE." Teachers must not submit student's work. The first place playwright will have their play published in an acting edition the September following the contest. The work will be described in the Baker's Plays Catalogue, which is distributed to 50,000 prospective producing organizations.

Ｎ BAY AREA BOOK REVIEWER'S ASSOCIATION (BABRA), %*Poetry Flash*, 1450 Fourth St., #4, Berkeley CA 94710. (510)525-5476. Fax: (510)525-6752. E-mail: babra@poetryflash.org. Website: www.poetryflash.org. Contact: Joyce Jenkins. Annual award for outstanding book in children's literature, open to books published in the current calendar year by Northern California authors. Annual award. Estab. 1981. "BABRA presents annual awards to Bay Area (northern California) authors annually in fiction, nonfiction, poetry and children's literature. Purpose is to encourage writers and stimulate interest in books and reading." Previously published books only. Must be published the calendar year prior to spring awards ceremony. Submissions nominated by publishers; author or agent could also nominate published work. Deadline for entries: December. No entry forms. Send 3 copies of the book to attention: Babra. No entry fee. Awards $100 honorarium and award certificate. Judging by voting members of the Bay Area Book Reviewer's Association. Books that reach the "finals" (usually 3-5 per category) displayed at annual award ceremonies (spring). Nominated books are displayed and sold at BABRA's annual awards ceremonies in the spring of each year; the winner is asked to read at the San Francisco Public Library's Main Branch.

Ｎ JOHN AND PATRICIA BEATTY AWARD, California Library Association, 717 K. Street Suite 300, Sacramento CA 95814. (916)447-8541. Fax: (916)447-8394. E-mail: info@cla-net.org. Website: www.cla-net.org. Executive Director: Susan Negreen. Annual award. Estab. 1987. Purpose of award: "The purpose of the John and Patricia Beatty Award is to encourage the writing of quality children's books highlighting California, its

FOR EXPLANATIONS OF THESE SYMBOLS,
SEE THE INSIDE FRONT AND BACK COVERS OF THIS BOOK

culture, heritage and/or future." Previously published submissions only. Submissions made by the author, author's agent or review copies sent by publisher. The award is given to the author of a children's book published the preceding year. Deadline for entries: Submissions may be made January-December. Contact CLA Executive Director who will liaison with Beatty Award Committee. Awards cash prize of $500 and an engraved plaque. Judging by a 5-member selection committee appointed by the president of the California Library Association. Requirements for entrants: "Any children's or young adult book set in California and published in the U.S. during the calendar year preceding the presentation of the award is eligible for consideration. This includes works of fiction as well as nonfiction for children and young people of all ages. Reprints and compilations are not eligible. The California setting must be depicted authentically and must serve as an integral focus for the book." Winning selection is announced through press release during National Library Week in April. Author is presented with award at annual California Library Association Conference in November.

☑ **THE IRMA S. AND JAMES H. BLACK BOOK AWARD**, Bank Street College of Education, 610 W. 112th St., New York NY 10025-1898. (212)875-4450. Fax: (212)875-4558. E-mail: lindag@bnkst.edu. Website: http://streetcat.bnkst.edu/html/isb.html. Contact: Linda Greengrass. Annual award. Estab. 1972. Purpose of award: "The award is given each spring for a book for young children, published in the previous year, for excellence of both text and illustrations." Entries must have been published during the previous calendar year (between January '01 and December '01 for 2001 award). Deadline for entries: January 1. "Publishers submit books to us by sending them here to me at the Bank Street library. Authors may ask their publishers to submit their books. Out of these, three to five books are chosen by a committee of older children and children's literature professionals. These books are then presented to children in selected second, third and fourth grade classes here and at a few other cooperating schools on the East Coast. These children are the final judges who pick the actual award. A scroll (one each for the author and illustrator, if they're different) with the recipient's name and a gold seal designed by Maurice Sendak are awarded in May."

WALDO M. AND GRACE C. BONDERMAN/IUPUI NATIONAL YOUTH THEATRE PLAYWRITING COMPETITION AND DEVELOPMENT WORKSHOP AND SYMPOSIUM, Indiana University-Purdue University at Indianapolis, 425 University Blvd. #309, Indianapolis IN 46202-5140. (317)274-2095. Fax: (317)278-1025. E-mail: dwebb@.iupui.edu. Website: www.iupui.edu/~comstudy/playsym/symwork.html. Director: Dorothy Webb. **Open to students.** Entries should be submitted to W. Mark McCreary, Literary Manager at IUPUI, 525 N. Blackford St., #117, Indianapolis IN 46202. Contest every two years; next competition will be 2002. Estab. 1983. Purpose of the contest: "to encourage writers to create artistic scripts for young audiences. It provides a forum through which each playwright receives constructive criticism of his/her work and, where selected, writers participate in script development with the help of professional dramaturgs, directors and actors." Unpublished submissions only. Submissions made by author. Deadline for entries: September 1, 2002. SASE for contest rules and entry forms. No entry fee. "Awards will be presented to the top ten finalists. Four cash awards of $1,000 each will be received by the top four playwrights whose scripts will be given developmental work culminating in polished readings showcased at the symposium held on the IUPUI campus. This symposium is always held opposite years of the competition. Major publishers of scripts for young audiences, directors, producers, critics and teachers attend this symposium and provide useful reactions to the plays. If a winner is unable to be involved in preparation of the reading and to attend the showcase of his/her work, the prize will not be awarded. Remaining finalists will receive certificates." Judging by professional directors, dramaturgs, publishers, university professors. Write for guidelines and entry form.

☑ **BOOK OF THE YEAR FOR CHILDREN**, Canadian Library Association, 328 Frank St., Ottawa, Ontario K2P 0X8 Canada. (613)232-9625. Fax: (613)563-9895. Contact: Chairperson, Canadian Association of Children's Librarians. Annual award. Estab. 1947. "The main purpose of the award is to encourage writing and publishing in Canada of good books for children up to and including age 14. If, in any year, no book is deemed to be of award calibre, the award shall not be made that year. To merit consideration, the book must have been published in Canada and its author must be a Canadian citizen or a permanent resident of Canada." Previously published submissions only; must be published between January 1 and December 1 of the previous year. Deadline for entries: January 1. SASE for award rules. Entries not returned. No entry fee. Awards a medal. Judging by committee of members of the Canadian Association of Children's Librarians. Requirements for entrants: Contest open only to Canadian authors or residents of Canada. Winning books are on display at CLA headquarters.

BOOK PUBLISHERS OF TEXAS, Children's/Young People's Award, The Texas Institute of Letters, % Center for the Study of the Southwest, P.O. Box 298300, Ft. Worth TX 76129. (512)245-2232. Fax: (512)245-7462. E-mail: mbl3@swt.edu. Website: www.English.swt.edu/css/TIL/rules.htm. Contact: Mark Busby. Send SASE to above address for list of judges to whom entries should be submitted. Annual award. Purpose of the award: "to recognize notable achievement by a Texas writer of books for children or young people or by a writer whose work deals with a Texas subject. The award goes to the author of the winning book, a work published during the calendar year before the award is given. Judges list available each July. Submissions go directly to judges, so current list of judges is necessary. Write to above address. Deadline is first postally operative day of

January." Previously published submissions only. SASE for award rules and entry forms. No entry fee. Awards $250. Judging by a panel of 3 judges selected by the TIL Council. Requirements for entrants: The writer must have lived in Texas for 2 consecutive years at some time, or the work must have a Texas theme.

✓ **THE BOSTON GLOBE-HORN BOOK AWARDS**, The Boston Globe & The Horn Book, Inc., The Horn Book, 56 Roland St., Suite 200, Boston MA 02129. (617)628-0225. Fax: (617)628-0882. E-mail: info@hboo k.com. Website: www.hbook.com/. Award Directors: Stephanie Loer and Roger Sutton. Writing Contact: Stephanie Loer, children's book editor for *The Boston Globe*, 298 North St., Medfield MA 02052. Annual award. Estab. 1967. Purpose of award: "to reward literary excellence in children's and young adult books. Awards are for picture books, nonfiction and fiction. Up to two honor books may be chosen for each category." Books must be published between June 1, 2000 and May 31, 2001. Deadline for entries: May 15. "Publishers usually submit books. Award winners receive $500 and silver engraved bowl, honor book winners receive a silver plate." Judging by 3 judges involved in children's book field who are chosen by Roger Sutton, editor-in-chief for The Horn Book, Inc. (*The Horn Book Magazine* and *The Horn Book Guide*) and Stephanie Loer, children's book editor for *The Boston Globe*. "*The Horn Book Magazine* publishes speeches given at awards ceremonies. The book must have been published in the U.S. The awards are given at the fall conference of the New England Library Association."

✓ **ANN ARLYS BOWLER POETRY CONTEST**, *Read* Magazine, 200 First Stamford Place, P.O. Box 120023, Stamford CT 06912-0023. (203)705-3406. Fax: (203)705-1661. E-mail: jkroll@weeklyreader.com. Website: www.weeklyreader.com/read.html. Contest Director: Jennifer Kroll. Annual contest. Estab. 1988. **Open to students.** Purpose of the contest: to reward young-adult poets (grades 6-12). Unpublished submissions only. Submissions made by the author or nominated by a person or group of people. Entry form must include signature of teacher, parent or guardian, and student verifying originality. Maximum number of submissions per student: three poems. Deadline for entries: January 1. SASE for contest rules and entry forms. No entry fee. Awards 6 winners $100 each, medal of honor and publication in *Read*. Semifinalists receive $50 each. Judging by *Read* and *Weekly Reader* editors and teachers. Requirements for entrants: the material must be original. Winning entries will be published in a spring issue of *Read*.

✓ **BUCKEYE CHILDREN'S BOOK AWARD**, State Library of Ohio, 65 S. Front St., Columbus OH 43215-4163. (614)644-7061. Fax: (614)728-2788. E-mail: rmetcalf@slomu.state.oh.us. Website: www.wpl.lib.oh.us/ buckeyebook/. Chairperson: Nancy Smith. Correspondence should be sent to Ruth A. Metcalf at the above address. **Open to students.** Award offered every two years. Estab. 1981. Purpose of the award: "The Buckeye Children's Book Award Program was designed to encourage children to read literature critically, to promote teacher and librarian involvement in children's literature programs, and to commend authors of such literature, as well as to promote the use of libraries. Awards are presented in the following three categories: grades K-2, grades 3-5 and grades 6-8." Previously published submissions only. Deadline for entries: February 1. "The nominees are submitted by this date during the even year and the votes are submitted by this date during the odd year. This award is nominated and voted upon by children in Ohio. It is based upon criteria established in our bylaws. The winning authors are awarded a special plaque honoring them at a banquet given by one of the sponsoring organizations. The BCBA Board oversees the tallying of the votes and announces the winners in March of the voting year in a special news release and in a number of national journals. The book must have been written by an author, a citizen of the United States and originally copyrighted in the U.S. within the last three years preceding the nomination year. The award-winning books are displayed in a historical display housed at the Columbus Metropolitan Library in Columbus, Ohio."

✓ **BYLINE MAGAZINE CONTESTS**, P.O. Box 130596, Edmond OK 73013-0001. E-mail: mpreston@byli nemag.com. Website: www.bylinemag.com. Contest Director: Marcia Preston. **Open to adults.** Purpose of contest: *ByLine* runs 4 contests a month on many topics to encourage and motivate writers. Past topics include first chapter of a novel, children's fiction, children's poem, nonfiction for children, personal essay, general short stories, valentine or love poem, etc. Send SASE for contest flier with topic list. Unpublished submissions only. Submissions made by the author. "We do not publish the contests' winning entries, just the names of the winners." SASE for contest rules. Entry fee is $3-4. Awards cash prizes for first, second and third place. Amounts vary. Judging by qualified writers or editors. List of winners will appear in magazine.

BYLINE MAGAZINE STUDENT PAGE, P.O. Box 130596, Edmond OK 73013. (405)348-5591. Website: www.bylinemag.com. Contest Director: Marcia Preston, publisher. Estab. 1981. **Open to students.** "We offer writing contests for students in grades 1-12 on a monthly basis, September through May, with cash prizes and publication of top entries." Previously unpublished submissions only. "This is not a market for illustration." Deadline for entries varies. "Entry fee usually $1." Awards cash and publication. Judging by qualified editors and writers. "We publish top entries in student contests. Winners' list published in magazine dated 2 months past deadline." Send SASE for details.

✓ **RANDOLPH CALDECOTT MEDAL**, Association for Library Service to Children, Division of the American Library Association, 50 E. Huron, Chicago IL 60611. (312)280-2163. Website: www.ala.org/alsc/

caldecott.html. Interim Executive Director: Stephanie Anton. Annual award. Estab. 1938. Purpose of the award: to honor the artist of the most distinguished picture book for children published in the US (Illustrator must be US citizen or resident.) Must be published year preceding award. Deadline for entries: December. SASE for award rules. Entries not returned. No entry fee. "Medal given at ALA Annual Conference during the Newbery/Caldecott Banquet."

✓ **CALIFORNIA YOUNG PLAYWRIGHTS CONTEST**, Playwrights Project, 450 B St., Suite 1020, San Diego CA 92101. (619)239-8222. Fax: (619)239-8225. E-mail: write@playwrightsproject.com. Website: www.playwrightsproject.com. Director: Deborah Salzer. **Open to Californians under age 19.** Annual contest. Estab. 1985. "Our organization and the contest is designed to nurture promising young writers. We hope to develop playwrights and audiences for live theater. We also teach playwriting." Submissions required to be unpublished and not produced professionally. Submissions made by the author. Deadline for entries: April 1. SASE for contest rules and entry form. No entry fee. Award is professional productions of 3-5 short plays each year, participation of the writers in the entire production process, with a royalty award of $250 per play. Judging by professionals in the theater community, a committee of 5-7; changes somewhat each year. Works performed in San Diego at the Cassius Carter Centre Stage of the Old Globe Theatre. Writers submitting scripts of 10 or more pages receive a detailed script evaluation letter.

CALLIOPE FICTION CONTEST, Writers' Specialized Interest Group (SIG) of American Mensa, Ltd., P.O. Box 466, Moraga CA 94556-0466. E-mail: cynthia@theriver.com. Fiction Editor: Sandy Raschke. Submit entries to Sandy Raschke, fiction editor. **Open to students.** Annual contest. Estab. 1991. Purpose of contest: To promote good writing and opportunities for getting published. To give our member/subscribers and others an entertaining and fun exercise in writing. Unpublished submissions only (all genres, no violence, profanity or extreme horror). Submissions made by author. Deadline for entries: changes annually but usually around September 15. Entry fee is $2 for non-subscribers; subscribers get first entry fee. Awards small amount of cash (up to $25 for 1st place, to $5 for 3rd), certificates, full or mini-subscriptions to *Calliope* and various premiums and books, depending on donations. All winners are published in subsequent issues of *Calliope*. Judging by fiction editor, with concurrence of other editors, if needed. Requirements for entrants: one-time rights. Open to all writers. No special considerations—other than following the guidelines. Contest theme, due dates and sometimes entry fees change annually. Always send SASE for complete rules; available after April 15 each year.

✓ ⚑ **CANADA COUNCIL GOVERNOR GENERAL'S LITERARY AWARDS**, 350 Albert St., P.O. Box 1047, Ottawa, Ontario K1P 5V8 Canada. (613)566-4410, ext. 5576. Fax: (613)566-4410. E-mail: josiane.polidori@canadacouncil.ca.or. Officer, Writing and Publishing Section Officer: Josiane Polidori. Annual award. Estab. 1937. Purpose of award: given to the best English-language and the best French-language work in each of the seven categories of Fiction, Literary Nonfiction, Poetry, Drama, Children's Literature (text), Children's Literature (illustration) and Translation. Books must be first-edition trade books that have been written, translated or illustrted by Canadian citizens or permanent residents of Canada. In the case of Translation, the original work written in English or French, must also be a Canadian-authored title. English titles must be published between September 1, 2000 and September 30, 2001. Books must be submitted by publishers. Books published in English between September 1, 2000 and February 28, 2001 must reach the Canada Council For the Arts no later than April 15, 2000. For books and bound proofs published between March 1, 2001 and September 30, 2001, the deadline is August 15, 2001. The deadlines are final; no bound proofs or books that miss the applicable deadlines will be given to the peer assessment committees. The awards ceremony is scheduled mid-November. Amount of award to be announced in late September 2000.

Ⓝ REBECCA CAUDILL YOUNG READERS' BOOK AWARD, Illinois Reading Council, Illinois School Library Media Association, Illinois Association of Teachers of English, P.O. Box 6536, Naperville IL 60567-6536. (630)420-6378. Fax: (630)420-3241. Award Director Bonita Slovinski. Annual award. Estab. 1988. Purpose of contest: to award the Children's Choice Award for grades 4-8 in Illinois. Submissions nominated by students. Must be published within the last 5 years. Awards honorarium, plaque. Judging by children, grades 4-8.

Ⓝ CHILDREN'S BOOK AWARD, Federation of Children's Book Groups. The Old Malt House, Aldbourne Marlborough, Wiltshire SN8 2DW England. 01672 540629. Fax: 01672 541280. E-mail: marianneadey@cs.com. Coordinator: Marianne Adey. Purpose of the award: "The C.B.A. is an annual prize for the best children's book of the year judged by the children themselves." Categories: (I) picture books, (II) short novels, (III) longer novels. Estab. 1980. Previously unpublished submissions only. Deadline for entries: December 31. SASE for rules and entry forms. Entries not returned. Awards "a magnificent silver and oak trophy worth over $6,000 and a portfolio of children's work." Silver dishes to each category winner. Judging by children. Requirements for entrants: Work must be fiction and published in the UK during the current year (poetry is ineligible). Work will be published in current "Pick of the Year" publication.

CHILDREN'S WRITERS FICTION CONTEST, Stepping Stones, P.O. Box 8863, Springfield MO 65801-8863. (417)863-7670 or (417)866-0744. Fax: (417)864-4745. E-mail: wilyams4@vista-business.zzn.com. Coordinator: V.R. Williams. Annual contest. Estab. 1994. Purpose of contest: to promote writing for children, by giving children's writers an opportunity to submit work in competition. Unpublished submissions only. Submissions made by the author. Deadline for entries: July 31. SASE for contest rules and entry forms. Entry fee is $5. Awards cash prize, certificate and publication in chapbook; certificates for Honorable Mention. Judging by Goodin, Williams and Goodwin. First rights to winning material acquired or purchased. Requirements for entrants: Work must be suitable for children and no longer than 1,000 words. "Send SASE for list of winners."

☑ **THE CHRISTOPHER AWARD**, The Christophers, 12 E. 48th St., New York NY 10017. (212)759-4050. E-mail: awards-coordinator@christophers.org, Website: www.christophers.org. Christopher Awards Program Manager: Judith Trojan. Children's Book Coordinator: Virginia Armstrong. Annual award. Estab. 1969 (for young people; books for adults honored since 1949). "Christopher Awards are presented annually to films, TV broadcast and cable network programs, books for adults and books for children that affirm the highest values of the human spirit. Christopher Award winners remind readers (in this case), of any faith and no particular faith, of their worth, individuality and power to make a difference and positively impact and shape our world. In a nutshell, Christopher Award winners celebrate the humanity of people in a positive way." Previously published submissions only; must be published between January 1 and December 31. Two calls for entry deadlines: June 1 and November 1 per year, but books may be submitted throughout year of release/publication.. Two copies should be sent to Judith Trojan, 12 E. 48th St., New York NY 10017 and two copies to Virginia Armstrong, 22 Forest Ave., Old Tappan NJ 07675." Also send promo materials with the books (press releases, press kits and/or catalog copy with books to both individuals above). Entries not returned. No entry fee. Awards a bronze medallion. Books are judged by both reading specialists and young people. Requirements for entrants: "only published works are eligible and must be submitted during the calendar year in which they are first published."

🅽 **COLORADO BOOK AWARDS**, Colorado Center for the Book, 2123 Downing St., Denver CO 80205. (303)839-8320. Fax: (303)839-8319. E-mail: ccftb@compuserve.com. Website: www.coloradobook.org. Award Director: Christiane Citron. Award open to adults. Annual award. Estab. 1993. Previously published submissions only. Submissions are made by the author, author's agent, nominated by a person or group of people. Requires Colorado residency by authors. Deadline for entries: January 15, 2001. SASE for contest rules and entry forms. Entry fee is $30. Awards $500 and plaque. Judging by a panel of literary agents, booksellers and librarians. Please note, we *also* have an annual competition for illustrators to design a poster and associated graphics for our summer reading program. The date varies. Inquiries are welcomed. Call us at (303)839-8320.

CHRISTOPHER COLUMBUS SCREENPLAY DISCOVERY AWARDS, Christopher Columbus Society of the Creative Arts, #600, 433 N. Camden Dr., Beverly Hills CA 90210. (310)288-1988. Fax: (310)288-0257. E-mail: awards@hollywoodawards.com. Website: screenwriters.com. Award Director: Mr. Carlos Abreu. Annual and monthly awards. Estab. 1990. Purpose of award: to discover new screenplay writers. Unpublished submissions only. Submissions are made by the author or author's agent. Deadline for entries: August 1st and monthly (last day of month). Entry fee is $55. Awards: (1) Feedback—development process with industry experts. (2) Financial rewards—option moneys up to $10,000. (3) Access to key decision makers. Judging by entertainment industry experts, producers and executives.

☑ **THE COMMONWEALTH CLUB'S BOOK AWARDS CONTEST**, The Commonwealth Club of California, 595 Market St., San Francisco CA 94105. (415)597-6700. Fax: (415)597-6729. E-mail: cwc@sirius.com. Website: www.commonwealthclub.org/bookawards. Attn: James Wilson. Chief Executive Officer: Gloria Duffy. Annual contest. Estab. 1932. Purpose of contest: the encouragement and production of literature in California. Juvenile category included. Previously published submission; must be published from January 1 to December 31, previous to contest year. Deadline for entries: January 31. SASE for contest rules and entry forms. No entry fee. Awards gold and silver medals. Judging by the Book Awards Jury. The contest is only open to California writers/illustrators (must have been resident of California when ms was accepted for publication). "The award winners will be honored at the Annual Book Awards Program." Winning entries are displayed at awards program and advertised in newsletter.

CRICKET LEAGUE, *Cricket Magazine*, P.O. Box 300, 315 Fifth St., Peru IL 61354. (815)224-6633. Website: www.cricketmag.com. Address entries to: Cricket League. Monthly. Estab. 1973. **Open to students.** "The purpose of Cricket League contests is to encourage creativity and give young people an opportunity to express themselves in writing, drawing, painting or photography. There is a contest each month. Possible categories include story, poetry, art or photography. Each contest relates to a *specific theme* described on each *Cricket* issue's Cricket League page. Signature verifying originality, age and address of entrant required. Entries which do not relate to the current month's theme cannot be considered." Unpublished submissions only. Deadline for entries: the 25th of each month. Cricket League rules, contest theme, and submission deadline information can be found in the current issue of *Cricket*. "We prefer that children who enter the contests subscribe to the magazine or that they read *Cricket* in their school or library." No entry fee. Awards certificate suitable for framing and children's books or art/writing supplies. Judging by *Cricket* editors. Obtains right to print prizewinning entries in magazine. Refer to contest rules in current *Cricket* issue. Winning entries are published on the Cricket League pages in the *Cricket* magazine 3 months subsequent to the issue in which the contest was announced. Current theme, rules, and prizewinning entries also posted on the website.

CUNNINGHAM PRIZE FOR PLAYWRITING, The Theatre School, DePaul University, 2135 N. Kenmore Ave., Chicago IL 60614-4111. Submit entries to: Cunningham Prize Selection Committee. Annual award. Estab. 1990. Purpose of award: to recognize and encourage the writing of dramatic works which affirm the centrality of religion, broadly defined and the human quest for meaning, truth and community. It is the intent of the endowment to consider submissions of new dramatic writing in all genres, including works for children and young people. Submissions made by the author. Playwrights who have won the award within the last five years are not eligible. Candidates must be writers whose residence is in the Chicago area, defined as within 100 miles of the Loop. Deadline for entries: December 1. SASE for return of materials. Awards $5,000. Judging by The Selection Committee, composed of distinguished citizens including members of DePaul University, representatives of the Cunnningham Prize Advisory Committee, critics, and others from the theatre professions and is chaired by the dean of The Theatre School.

☑ **MARGUERITE DE ANGELI PRIZE**, Delacorte Press, Random House Books for Young Readers, 1540 Broadway, New York NY 10036. Estab. 1992. Fax: (212)782-9452 (note re: Marguerite De Angeli Prize). Website: www.randomhouse.com. Annual award. Purpose of the award: to encourage the writing of fiction for children aged 7-10, either contemporary or historical; to encourage unpublished writers in the field of middle grade fiction. Unpublished submissions only. No simultaneous submissions. Length: between 40-144 pages. Submissions made by author or author's agent. Entries should be postmarked between April 1st and June 30th. SASE for award rules. No entry fee. Awards a $1,500 cash prize plus a hardcover and paperback book contract with a $3,500 advance against a royalty to be negotiated. Judging by Delacorte Press editorial staff. Open to US and Canadian writers who have not previously published a novel for middle-grade readers (ages 7-10). Works published in an upcoming Bantam Doubleday Dell Books for Young Readers list.

☑ **DELACORTE PRESS PRIZE FOR A FIRST YOUNG ADULT NOVEL**, Delacorte Press, Books for Young Readers Department, 1540 Broadway, New York NY 10036. (212)354-6500. Fax: (212)782-9452. Website: www.randomhouse.com/kids/submit. Annual award. Estab. 1982. Purpose of award: to encourage the writing of contemporary young adult fiction. Previously unpublished submissions only. Mss sent to Delacorte Press may not be submitted to other publishers while under consideration for the prize. "Entries must be submitted between October 1 and New Year's Day. The real deadline is a December 31 postmark. Early entries are appreciated." SASE for award rules. No entry fee. Awards a $1,500 cash prize and a $6,000 advance against royalties for world rights on a hardcover and paperback book contract. Works published in an upcoming Delacorte Press, an imprint of Random House, Inc., Books for Young Readers list. Judged by the editors of the Books for Young Readers Department of Delacorte Press. Requirements for entrants: The writer must be American or Canadian and must *not* have previously published a young adult novel but may have published anything else. Foreign-language mss and translations and mss submitted to a previous Delacorte Press are not eligible. Send SASE for new guidelines. Guidelines are also available on our website: www.randomhouse.com/kids/submit.

MARGARET A. EDWARDS AWARDS, American Library Association, 50 East Huron St., Chicago IL 60611-2795. (312)944-6780 or (800)545-2433. Fax: (312)664-7459. E-mail: yalsa@ala.org. Website: www.ala.org/yalsa. Annual award administered by the Young Adult Library Services Association (YALSA) of the American Library Association (ALA) and sponsored by *School Library Journal* magazine. Purpose of award: "ALA's Young Adult Library Services Association (YALSA), on behalf of librarians who work with young adults in all types of libraries, will give recognition to those authors whose book or books have provided young adults with a window through which they can view their world and which will help them to grow and to understand themselves and their role in relationships, society and the world." Previously published submissions only. Submissions are nominated by young adult librarians and teenagers. Must be published five years before date of award. SASE for award rules and entry forms. No entry fee. Judging by members of the Young Adult Library Services Association. Deadline for entry: June 1. "The award will be given annually to an author whose book or books, over a period of time, have been accepted by young adults as an authentic voice that continues to illuminate their experiences and emotions, giving insight into their lives. The book or books should enable them to understand themselves, the world in which they live, and their relationship with others and with society. The book or books must be in print at the time of the nomination."

☑ **ARTHUR ELLIS AWARD**, Crime Writers of Canada, 3007 Kingston Rd., Box 113, Scarborough, Ontario M1M 1P1 Canada. (416)461-9826. Fax: (416)461-4489. E-mail: ap113@torfree.net.on.ca. Submit entries to: Secretary/Treasurer. Annual contest. Estab. 1984. Purpose of contest: to honor the best juvenile writing with a theme of crime, detective, espionage, mystery, suspense and thriller, fictional or factual accounts of criminal doings. Includes novels with a criminous theme. Previously published submissions only. Submissions made by author or by author's agent or publisher. Must be published during year previous to award. Deadline for entries: January 31. SASE for contest rules and entry forms. Awards a statuette of a hanged man—with jumping jack limbs. Judging by 2 nonmembers and one member per category. Can be any publication, regardless of language, by a writer, regardless of nationality, resident in Canada or a Canadian writer resident abroad.

ⓝ DOROTHY CANFIELD FISHER CHILDREN'S BOOK AWARD, Vermont Department of Libraries, % Northeast Regional Library, 23 Tilton Rd., St. Johnsbury VT 05819. (802)828-3261. Fax: (802)828-2199. E-mail: ggreene@dol.state.vt.us. Website: www.dol.state.vt.us. Chairman: Joanna Rudge Long. Annual award. Estab. 1957. Purpose of the award: to encourage Vermont children to become enthusiastic and discriminating readers by providing them with books of good quality by living American authors published in the current year. Deadline for entries: December of year book was published. SASE for award rules and entry forms. No entry fee. Awards a scroll presented to the winning author at an award ceremony. Judging is by the children grades 4-8. They vote for their favorite book. Requirements for entrants: "Titles must be original work, published in the United States, and be appropriate to children in grades 4 through 8. The book must be copyrighted in the current year. It must be written by an American author living in the U.S."

N: FLICKER TALE CHILDREN'S BOOK AWARD, Flicker Tale Award Committee, North Dakota Library Association, Hazen Public Library, Hazen ND 58545. (701)748-2977. Fax: (701)748-2559. Award Director: Konnie Wightman. Estab. 1979. Purpose of award: to give children across the state of North Dakota a chance to vote for their book of choice from a nominated list of 10: 5 in the picture book category; 5 in the juvenile category. Also, to promote awareness of quality literature for children. Previously published submissions only. Submissions nominated by a person or group of people. Awards a plaque from North Dakota Library Association and banquet dinner. Judging by children in North Dakota. Entry deadline in July.

FLORIDA STATE WRITING COMPETITION, Florida Freelance Writers Association, P.O. Box A, North Stratford NH 03590. (603)922-8338. Fax: (603)922-8339. E-mail: danakcnw@ncia.net. Website: www.writers-editors.com. Executive Director: Dana K. Cassell. Annual contest. Estab. 1984. Categories include children's literature (length appropriate to age category). Entry fee is $5 (members), $10 (nonmembers). Awards $100 first prize, $75 second prize, $50 third prize, certificates for honorable mentions. Judging by teachers, editors and published authors. Judging criteria: interest and readability within age group, writing style and mechanics, originality, salability. Deadline: March 15. For copy of official entry form, send #10 SASE or go to www.writers-editors.com. List of 1999 and 2000 winners on website.

FOR A GOOD TIME THEATRE COMPANY'S ANNUAL SCRIPT CONTEST, For A Good Time Theatre Company, P.O. Box 5421, Saginaw MI 48603-0421. (517)753-7891. Fax: (517)753-5890. E-mail: theatre co@aol.com. Contest Director: Lee-Perry Belleau, artistic director. Annual contest. Estab. 1997. Purpose of contest: To award top-notch playwrights in theater for young audiences with a production by a critically acclaimed regional theater company. Unpublished submissions only. Submissions made by author or by author's agent. Deadline for entries: May 1 (postmark). SASE for contest rules and entry forms. Entry fee is $10. Awards production of the winning script; cash award of $1,000 and a videotape of the produced script. Judging by For A Good Time Theatre's staff dramaturg (prescreening). Screening is then done by the producer. Final judging is done by the artistic director. Acquires regional production rights for the year of the contest. Plays must be 50 minutes long; must be a musical (composed music is not necessary, just song lyrics); written for multiple characters played by three actors, with roles for men and women. Other criteria, such as subject matter, varies from year to year. Send SASE for details.

DON FREEMAN MEMORIAL GRANT-IN-AID, Society of Children's Book Writers and Illustrators, 8271 Beverly Blvd., Los Angeles CA 90048. E-mail: scbwi@scbwi.org. Website: www.scbwi.org. Estab. 1974. Purpose of award: to "enable picture book artists to further their understanding, training and work in the picture book genre." Applications and prepared materials will be accepted between January 15 and February 15. Grant awarded and announced on June 15. SASE for award rules and entry forms. SASE for return of entries. No entry fee. Annually awards one grant of $1,500 and one runner-up grant of $500. "The grant-in-aid is available to both full and associate members of the SCBWI who, as artists, seriously intend to make picture books their chief contribution to the field of children's literature."

AMELIA FRANCES HOWARD GIBBON AWARD FOR ILLUSTRATION, Canadian Library Association, 328 Frank St., Ottawa, Ontario K2P 0X8 Canada. (613)232-9625. Contact: Chairperson, Canadian Association of Children's Librarians. Annual award. Estab. 1971. Purpose of the award: "to honor excellence in the illustration of children's book(s) in Canada. To merit consideration the book must have been published in Canada and its illustrator must be a Canadian citizen or a permanent resident of Canada." Previously published submissions only; must be published between January 1 and December 31 of the previous year. Deadline for entries: January 1. SASE for award rules. Entries not returned. No entry fee. Awards a medal. Judging by selection committee of members of Canadian Association of Children's Librarians. Requirements for entrants: illustrator must be Canadian or Canadian resident. Winning books are on display at CLA Headquarters.

GOLD MEDALLION BOOK AWARDS, Evangelical Christian Publishers Association, 1969 East Broadway Rd., Suite Two, Tempe AZ 85282. (480)966-3998. Fax: (480)966-1944. E-mail: jmeegan@ecpa.org. Website: www.ecpa.org. President: Doug Ross. Annual award. Estab. 1978. Categories include Preschool Children's Books, Elementary Children's Books, Youth Books. "All entries must be evangelical in nature and cannot be contrary to ECPA's Statement of Faith (stated in official rules)." Deadlines for entries: December 1. SASE for award rules and entry form. "The work must be submitted by the publisher." Entry fee is $300 for nonmembers. Awards a Gold Medallion plaque.

☑ **GOLDEN KITE AWARDS**, Society of Children's Book Writers and Illustrators, 8271 Beverly Blvd., Los Angeles CA 90048. (323)782-1010. E-mail: scbwi@scbwi.org. Website: www.scbwi.org. Coordinators: Ruby Guerrero and Mercedes Coats. Annual award. Estab. 1973. "The works chosen will be those that the judges feel exhibit excellence in writing, and in the case of the picture-illustrated books—in illustration, and genuinely appeal to the interests and concerns of children. For the fiction and nonfiction awards, original works and single-author collections of stories or poems of which at least half are new and never before published in book form are eligible—anthologies and translations are not. For the picture-illustration awards, the art or photographs must be original works (the texts—which may be fiction or nonfiction—may be original, public domain or previously published). Deadline for entries: December 15. SASE for award rules. No entry fee. Awards statuettes and plaques. The panel of judges will consist of professional authors, illustrators, editors or agents." Requirements for entrants: "must be a member of SCBWI." Winning books will be displayed at national conference in August. Books to be entered, as well as further inquiries, should be submitted to: The Society of Children's Book Writers and Illustrators, above address.

AURAND HARRIS MEMORIAL PLAYWRITING AWARD, The New England Theatre Conference, Northeastern University, 360 Huntington Ave., Boston MA 02115. Annual award. Estab. 1997. Unpublished submissions only. Submissions by author. Deadline for entries: May 1. Handling fee is $20; no fee to current members of New England Theatre Conference. Awards 2 cash prizes: First prize of $1,000 and second prize of $500. Judging by a panel of judges named by the NETC Executive Board. Playwrights living outside of New England may participate by joining NETC. No scripts will be returned. Winners notified by mail.

☑ **HIGHLIGHTS FOR CHILDREN FICTION CONTEST**, 803 Church St., Honesdale PA 18431-2030. (570)253-1080. Fax: (570)253-7847. E-mail: highlights@ezaccess.net. Mss should be addressed to Fiction Contest. Editor: Kent L. Brown Jr. Annual contest. Estab. 1980. Purpose of the contest: to stimulate interest in writing for children and reward and recognize excellence. Unpublished submissions only. Deadline for entries: February 28; entries accepted after January 1 only. SASE for contest rules and return of entries. No entry fee. Awards 3 prizes of $1,000 each in cash and a pewter bowl (or, at the winner's election, attendance at the Highlights Foundation Writers Workshop at Chautauqua). Judging by *Highlights* editors. Winning pieces are purchased for the cash prize of $1,000 and published in *Highlights*; other entries are considered for purchase. Requirements for entrants: open to any writer. Winners announced in June. Length up to 900 words. Stories for beginning readers should not exceed 500 words. Stories should be consistent with *Highlights* editorial requirements. No violence, crime or derogatory humor. Send SASE for guidelines and contract theme.

N: HRC'S ANNUAL PLAYWRITING CONTEST, Hudson River Classics, Inc., P.O. Box 940, Hudson NY 12534. (518)851-6840. Fax: (518)851-2631. President: Jan M. Grice. Annual contest. Estab. 1992. Hudson River Classics is a not-for-profit professional theater company dedicated to the advancement of performing in the Hudson River Valley area through reading of plays and providing opportunities for new playwrights. Unpublished submissions only. Submissions made by author and by the author's agent. Deadlines for entries: May 1st. SASE for contest rules and entry forms. Entry fee is $5. Awards $500 cash plus concert reading by professional actors. Judging by panel selected by Board of Directors. Requirements for entrants: Entrants must live in the northeastern US.

☒ **INFORMATION BOOK AWARD**, Children's Literature Roundtables of Canada, Dept. of Language Education, University of British Columbia, 2125 Main Mall, Vancouver, British Columbia V6T 1Z4 Canada. (604)822-5788. Fax: (604)922-1666. E-mail: aprilg@direct.ca. Website: www.library.ubc.ca/edlib/rdtable.html. Award Directors: April Gill and Dr. Ron Jobe. Annual contest. Estab. 1987. Purpose of contest: The Information Book Award recognizes excellence in the writing of information books for young people from 5 to 15 years. It is awarded to the book that arouses interest, stimulates curiosity, captures the imagination, and fosters concern for the world around us. The award's aim is to recognize excellence in Canadian publishing of nonfiction for children. Previously published submissions only. Submissions nominated by a person or group of people. Work must have been published the calendar year previous to the award being given. Send SASE for contest rules. Certificates are awarded to the author and illustrator, and they share a cash prize of $500 (Canadian). Judging by members of the children's literature roundtables of Canada. In consultation with children's bookstores across Canada, a national committee based in Vancouver sends out a selective list of over 20 titles representing the best of the information books from the preceding year. The Roundtables consider this preliminary list and send back their recommendations, resulting in 5-7 finalists. The Roundtables make time at their Fall meetings to discuss the finalists and vote on their choices, which are collated into one vote per Roundtable (the winner is announced in November for Canada's Book Week). The award is granted at the Serendipity Children's Literature Conference held in February in Vancouver British Columbia.

INSPIRATIONAL WRITERS ALIVE! OPEN WRITERS COMPETITION, Texas Christian Writer's Forum, 6038 Greenmont, Houston TX 77092-2332. Fax: (713)686-7209. E-mail: mrogers353@aol.com or patav@a ol.com. Contact: Contest Director. Annual contest. Estab. 1990. Purpose of contest: to help aspiring writers in the inspirational/religion markets and to encourage writers in their efforts to write for possible future publication. Our critique sheets give valuable information to our participants. Unpublished submissions only. Submissions made by author. Deadline: May 1. SASE for contest rules. Entry fee is $10 (devotional, short story or article); $10 (3 poems). Awards certificate of merit for 1st, 2nd and 3rd place; plus a small monetary award of $25 1st, $15 2nd, $10 3rd. Requirements for entrants: Cannot enter published material. "We want to aid especially new and aspiring writers." Contest has 5 categories—to include short story (adult), short story (for children and teens) article, daily devotions, and poetry and book proposal. Request complete guidelines from M. Rogers. Entry forms and info available after January 1, 2001. "*Must* include a cover sheet with every category."

☑ JOSEPH HENRY JACKSON AND JAMES D. PHELAN LITERARY AWARDS, The San Francisco Foundation, 446 Valencia St., San Francisco CA 94103. (415)626-2787. Fax: (415)626-1636. E-mail: jacksonphel an@theintersection.org. Submit entries to Awards Coordinator. **Open to Students**. Annual award. Estab. 1937. Purpose of award: to encourage young writers for and unpublished manuscript-in-progress. Submissions must be unpublished. Submissions made by author. Deadline for entry: January 31. SASE for contest rules and entry forms. Judging by established peers. All applicants must be 20-35 years of age. Applicants for the Henry Jackson Award must be residents of northern California or Nevada for 3 consecutive years immediately prior to the January 31, deadline. Applicants for the James D. Phelan awards must have been born in California but need not be current residents.

☑ THE EZRA JACK KEATS NEW WRITER AWARD, Ezra Jack Keats Foundation/Administered by the New York Public Library Early Childhood Resource and Information Center, 66 Leroy St., New York NY 10014. (212)929-0815. Fax: (212)242-8242. E-mail: rpayne@nypl.org. Program Coordinator: Rachel Payne. **Open to students.** Annual award. Purpose of the award: "The award will be given to a promising new writer of picture books for children. Selection criteria include books for children (ages nine and under) that reflect the tradition of Ezra Jack Keats. These books portray: the universal qualities of childhood, strong and supportive family and adult relationships, the multicultural nature of our world." Submissions made by the author, by the author's agent or nominated by a person or group of people. Must be published in the preceding year. Deadline for entries: December 15, 2000. SASE for contest rules and entry forms. No entry fee. Awards $1,000 coupled with Ezra Jack Keats Silver Medal. Judging by a panel of experts. "The author should have published no more than five books. Entries are judged on the outstanding features of the text, complemented by illustrations. Candidates need not be both author and illustrator. Entries should carry a 2000 copyright (for the 2001 award)." Winning books and authors to be presented at reception at The New York Public Library.

N: EZRA JACK KEATS/KERLAN COLLECTION MEMORIAL FELLOWSHIP, University of Minne-sota, 113 Elmer L. Andersen Library, 222 21st Ave. S., Minneapolis MN 55455. (612)624-4576. Fax: (612)625-5525. E-mail: clrc@tc.umn.edu. Website: http://special.lib.umn.edu/clrc/. Competition open to adults. Offered annually. Deadline for entries: April 27, 2001. Send request with SASE, including 52¢ postage. The Ezra Jack Keats/Kerlan Collection Memorial Fellowship from the Ezra Jack Keats Foundation will provide $1,500 to a "talented writer and/or illustrator of children's books who wishes to use the Kerlan Collection for the furtherance of his or her artistic development. Special consideration will be given to someone who would find it difficult to finance the visit to the Kerlan Collection." The fellowship winner will receive transportation and per diem. Judging by the Kerlan Award Committee—3 representatives from the University of Minnesota faculty, one from the Kerlan Friends, and one from the Minnesota Library Association.

N: KENTUCKY BLUEGRASS AWARD, Northern Kentucky University & Kentucky Reading Association, % Jennifer Smith, Steely Library, Northern Kentucky University, Highland Heights KY 41099. (859)572-6620. Fax: (859)572-5390. E-mail: smithjen@nku.edu. Award Directors: Jennifer Smith. Submit entries to: Jennifer Smith. Annual award. Estab. 1983. Purpose of award: to promote readership among young children and young adolescents. Also to recognize exceptional creative efforts of authors and illustrators. Previously published sub-missions only. Submissions made by author, made by author's agent, nominated by teachers or librarians. Must be published between 1997 and 2000. Deadline for entries: March 15. SASE for contest rules and entry forms. No entry fee. Awards a framed certificate and invitation to be recognized at the annual luncheon of the Kentucky Bluegrass Award. Judging by children who participate through their schools or libraries. "Books are reviewed by a panel of teachers and librarians before they are placed on a Master List for the year. These books must have been published within a three year period prior to the review. Winners are chosen from this list of pre-selected books. Books are divided into four divisions, K-2, 3-5, 6-8, 9-12 grades. Winners are chosen by children who either read the books or have the books read to them. Children from the entire state of Kentucky are involved in the selection of the annual winners for each of the divisions."

☑ KERLAN AWARD, University of Minnesota, 113 Elmer L. Andersen Library, 222-21st Ave. S, Minneapo-lis MN 55455. (612)624-4576. Website: http://special.lib.umn.edu/clrc. Curator: Karen Nelson Hoyle. Annual award. Estab. 1975. "Given in recognition of singular attainments in the creation of children's literature and in appreciation for generous donation of unique resources to the Kerlan Collection." Previously published submis-sions only. Deadline for entries: October 16. Anyone can send nominations for the award, directed to the Kerlan Collection. No materials are submitted other than the person's name. Requirements for entrants: open to all who are nominated. "For serious consideration, entrant must be a published author and/or illustrator of children's books (including young adult fiction) and have donated original materials to the Kerlan Collection."

CORETTA SCOTT KING AWARD, Coretta Scott King Task Force, Social Responsibility Round Table, American Library Association, 50 E. Huron St., Chicago IL 60611. Website: www.ala.org/srrt/csking. "The Coretta Scott King Award is an annual award for a book (1 for text and 1 for illustration) that conveys the spirit of brotherhood espoused by M.L. King, Jr.—and also speaks to the Black experience—for young people. There is an award jury that judges the books—reviewing over the year—and making a decision in January. A copy of an entry must be sent to each juror. Acquire jury list from SRRT office in Chicago."

☑ **ANNE SPENCER LINDBERGH PRIZE IN CHILDREN'S LITERATURE**, The Charles A. and Anne Morrow Lindbergh Foundation, 2150 Third Ave., Suite 310, Anoka MN 55303. (763)576-1596. Fax: (763)576-1664. E-mail: lindbergh@isd.net. Website: www.lindberghfoundation.org. Competition open to adults. Contest is offered every 2 years. Estab. 1996. Purpose of contest: To recognize the children's fantasy novel judged to be the best published in the English language during the 2-year period. Prize program honors Anne Spencer Lindbergh, author of a number of acclaimed juvenile fantasies, who died in late 1993 at the age of 53. Previously published submissions only. Submissions made by author, author's agent or publishers. Must be published between January 1 of odd numbered years and December 31 of even numbered years. Deadline for entries: November 1 of even numbered years. Entry fee is $25. Awards $5,000 to author of winning book. Judging by panel drawn from writers, editors, librarians and teachers prominent in the field of children's literature. Requirements for entrants: Open to all authors of children's fantasy novels published during the 2-year period. Entries must include 4 copies of books submitted. Winner announced in January.

☑ **LONGMEADOW JOURNAL LITERARY COMPETITION**, % Rita and Robert Morton, 6750 N. Longmeadow, Lincolnwood IL 60712. (312)726-9789. Fax: (312)726-9772. Contest Director: Rita and Robert Morton. Competition open to students (anyone age 10-19). Held annually and published every year. Estab. 1986. Purpose of contest: to encourage the young to write. Submissions are made by the author, made by the author's agent, nominated by a person or group of people, by teachers, librarians or parents. Deadline for entries: June 30. SASE. No entry fee. Awards first place, $175; second place, $100; and five prizes of $50. Judging by Rita Morton and Robert Morton. Works are published every year and are distributed to teachers and librarians and interested parties at no charge.

MAGAZINE MERIT AWARDS, Society of Children's Book Writers and Illustrators, 8271 Beverly Blvd., Los Angeles CA 90048. Fax: (323)782-1010. E-mail: scbwi@scbwi.org. Website: www.scbwi.org. Award Coordinator: Dorothy Leon. Annual award. Estab. 1988. Purpose of the award: "to recognize outstanding original magazine work for young people published during that year and having been written or illustrated by members of SCBWI." Previously published submissions only. Entries must be submitted between January 31 and December 15 of the year of publication. For brochure (rules) write Award Coordinator. No entry fee. Must be a SCBWI member. Awards plaques and honor certificates for each of the 3 categories (fiction, nonfiction, illustration). Judging by a magazine editor and two "full" SCBWI members. "All magazine work for young people by an SCBWI member—writer, artist or photographer—is eligible during the year of original publication. In the case of co-authored work, both authors must be SCBWI members. Members must submit their own work." Requirements for entrants: 4 copies each of the published work and proof of publication (may be contents page) showing the name of the magazine and the date of issue. The SCBWI is a professional organization of writers and illustrators and others interested in children's literature. Membership is open to the general public at large.

☑ **MILKWEED PRIZE FOR CHILDREN'S LITERATURE**, Milkweed Editions, 1011 Washington Ave. S., Suite 300, Minneapolis MN 55415-1246. (612)332-3192. Fax: (612)215-2550. E-mail: editor@milkweed.org. Website: www.milkweed.org. Award Director: Emilie Buchwald, publisher/editor. Annual award. Estab. 1993. Purpose of the award: to find an outstanding literary novel for readers ages 8-13 and encourage writers to turn their attention to readers in this age group. Unpublished submissions only "in book form." Must send SASE for award guidelines. The prize is awarded to the best work for children ages 8-13 that Milkweed agrees to publish in a calendar year by a writer not previously published by Milkweed. The Prize consists of a $10,000 advance against royalties agreed to at the time of acceptance. Submissions must follow our usual children's guidelines.

☑ **N.C. WRITERS' NETWORK INTERNATIONAL LITERARY PRIZES**, N.C. Writers' Network, 3501 Hwy. 54 W, Studio C, Chapel Hill NC 27516. (919)967-9540. Fax: (919)929-0535. E-mail: mail@ncwriters.org. Website: www.ncwriters.org. Program Coordinator: Whitney Vaughn. **Open to students.** Annual contest. *Thomas Wolfe Fiction Prize* (TWFP), est. 1994, awards $1,000 prize for best piece of fiction (short story or novel excerpt not to exceed 12 pp.), winning entry will be considered for publication in Carolina quarterly; *Paul Green*

Playwrights Prize (PGPP), est. 1995, awards $500 prize for best play, any length, no musicals, winning entry will be considered for production by a consortium of North Carolina theaters. *Randall Jarrell Poetry Prize* (RJPP), est. 1990, awards $1,000 prize, publication and reading/reception for best poem, winning poem published in Parnassus: Poetry in Review. Unpublished submissions only. Submissions made by the author. Deadline for entries: TWFP—Aug. 31; PGPP—Sept. 30; RJPP—Nov. 1. SASE for award rules and entry forms. Entry fees for contests are: $10 for NCWN members, $12 for nonmembers. Judging by published writers or editors. Previous judges have included: Anne Tyler, Barbara Kingsolver, Donald Hall, Lucille Clifton, Romulus Linney.

THE NATIONAL CHAPTER OF CANADA IODE VIOLET DOWNEY BOOK AWARD, Suite 254, 40 Orchard View Blvd., Toronto, Ontario M5R 1B9 Canada. (416)487-4416. Award Director: Sandra Connery. Annual award. Estab. 1985. Purpose of the award: to honor the best children's English language book by a Canadian, published in Canada for ages 5-13, over 500 words. Fairy tales, anthologies and books adapted from another source are not eligible. Previously published submissions only. Books must have been published in Canada in previous calendar year. Submissions made by author, author's agent; anyone may submit. Three copies of each entry are required. Must have been published during previous calendar year. Deadline for entries: December 31, 2000. SASE for award rules and entry forms. No entry fee. Awards $3,000 for the year 2001 for books published in 2000. Judging by a panel of 6, 4 IODE members and 2 professionals.

NATIONAL CHILDREN'S THEATRE FESTIVAL, Actor's Playhouse at the Miracle Theatre, 280 Miracle Mile, Coral Gables FL 33134. (305)444-9293. Fax: (305)444-4181. Website: www.actorsplayhouse.org. Director: Earl Maulding. **Open to Students**. Annual contest. Estab. 1994. Purpose of contest: to encourage new, top quality musicals for young audiences. Submissions must be unpublished. Submissions are made by author or author's agent. Deadline for entries: August 1, 2001. SASE for contest rules and entry forms or online at www.actorsplayhouse.org. Entry fee is $10. Awards: first prize of $500 plus production. Final judges are of national reputation. Past judges include Joseph Robinette, Moses Goldberg and Luis Santeiro.

NATIONAL PEACE ESSAY CONTEST, United States Institute of Peace, 1200 17th St. NW, Washington DC 20036. (202)429-3854. Fax: (202)429-6063. E-mail: usip_requests@usip.org. Website: www.usip.org. Contest Director: Heather Kerr-Stewart. Annual contest. Estab. 1987. "The contest gives students the opportunity to do valuable research, writing and thinking on a topic of importance to international peace and conflict resolution. Teaching guides available for teachers to use the contest as a classroom assignment." Deadline for entries is January 24, 2001. "Interested students, teachers and others may write or call to receive free contest kits. Please do not include SASE." No entry fee. State Level Awards are college scholarships in the following amounts: first place $1,000. National winners are selected from among the 1st place state winners. National winners receive scholarships in the following amounts: first place $10,000; second $5,000; third $2,500. Judging is conducted by education professionals from across the country and by the Board of Directors of the United States Institute of Peace. "All submissions become property of the U.S. Institute of Peace to use at its discretion and without royalty or any limitation. Students grades 9-12 in the U.S., its territories and overseas schools may submit essays for review by completing the application process. U.S. citizenship required for students attending overseas schools. National winning essays for each competition will be published by the U.S. Institute of Peace for public consumption."

THE NENE AWARD, Hawaii State Library, 478 S. King St., Honolulu HI 96813. (808)586-3510. Fax: (808)586-3584. E-mail: hslear@netra.lib.state.hi.us. Estab. 1964. "The Nene Award was designed to help the children of Hawaii become acquainted with the best contemporary writers of fiction, become aware of the qualities that make a good book and choose the best rather than the mediocre." Previously published submissions only. Books must have been copyrighted not more than 6 years prior to presentation of award. Work is nominated. Ballots are usually due around the beginning of March. Awards Koa plaque. Judging by the children of Hawaii in grades 4-6. Requirements for entrants: books must be fiction, written by a living author, copyrighted not more than 6 years ago and suitable for children in grades 4, 5 and 6. Current and past winners are displayed in all participating school and public libraries. The award winner is announced in April.

NEW ENGLAND BOOK AWARDS, New England Booksellers Association, 847 Massachusetts Ave., Cambridge MA 02139. (617)576-3070. Fax: (617)576-3091. E-mail: neba@neba.org. Website: newenglandbooks.org. Award Director: Nan Sorensen. Annual award. Estab. 1990. Purpose of award: "to promote New England authors who have produced a body of work that stands as a significant contribution to New England's culture and is deserving of wider recognition." Previously published submissions only. Submissions made by New England booksellers; publishers. "Award given to authors 'body of work' not a specific book." Entries must be still in print and available. Deadline for entries: October 31. SASE for contest rules and entry forms. No entry fee. Judging by NEBA membership. Requirements for entrants: Author/illustrator must live in New England. Submit written nominations only; actual books should not be sent. Member bookstores receive materials to display winners' books.

NEW VOICES AWARD, Lee & Low Books, 95 Madison Ave., New York NY 10016. (212)779-4400. Fax: (212)683-1894. E-mail: info@leeandlow.com. Website: www.leeandlow.com. Editor: Laura Atkins. **Open**

to students. Annual award. Estab. 2000. Purpose of contest: Lee & Low Books is one of the few publishing companies owned by people of color. We have published over fifty first-time writers and illustrators. Titles include *In Daddy's Arms I Am Tall: African Americans Celebrating Fathers*, winner of the 1998 Coretta Scott King Illustrator Award; *Passage to Freedom: The Sugihara Story*, an American Library Association Notable Book; and *Under the Lemon Moon*, a *Smithsonian* magazine 'Notable Children's Books'' selection. Submissions made by author. Deadline for entries: September 30, 2001. SASE for contest rules and entry forms. No entry fee. Awards New Voices Award—$1,000 prize and a publication contract along with an advance on royalties; New Voices Honor Award—$500 prize. Judging by Lee & Low editors. Restrictions of media for illustrators: The author must be a writer of color who is a resident of the US and who has not previously published a children's picture book. For additional information, send SASE or call for entries or visit Lee & Low's website.

☑ **JOHN NEWBERY MEDAL AWARD**, Association for Library Service to Children, Division of the American Library Association, 50 E. Huron, Chicago IL 60611. Website: www.ala.org/alsc/newbery.html. (312)280-2163. Executive Director, ALSC: vacant. Annual award. Estab. 1922. Purpose of award: to recognize the most distinguished contribution to American children's literature published in the US. Previously published submissions only; must be published prior to year award is given. Deadline for entries: December. SASE for award rules. Entries not returned. No entry fee. Medal awarded at Caldecott/Newbery banquet during annual conference. Judging by Newbery Committee.

☑ **NORTH AMERICAN INTERNATIONAL AUTO SHOW SHORT STORY AND HIGH SCHOOL POSTER CONTEST**, Detroit Auto Dealers Association, 1900 W. Big Beaver Rd., Troy MI 48084-3531. (248)643-0250. Fax: (248)637-0734. E-mail: aprice@dada.org. Website: naias.com. Director of Communications: Sharon Kelsey. **Open to students.** Annual contest. Submissions made by the author and illustrator. Deadline to be determined for 2001. Contact DADA for contest rules and entry forms. No entry fee. Five winners of the short story contest will each receive $500. Entries will be judged by an independent panel comprised of knowledgeable persons engaged in the literary field in some capacity. Entrants must be Michigan residents, including high school students enrolled in grades 9-12. Junior high school students in 9th grade are also eligible. Awards in the High School Poster Contest are as follows: Best Theme, Best Use of Color, Best Use of Graphics & Most Creative. A winner will be chosen in each category from grades 9, 10, 11 and 12. Each winner in each grade from each category will win $250. The winner of the Chairman's Award will receive $1,000. Entries will be judged by an independent panel of recognized representatives of the art community. Entrants must be Michigan high school students enrolled in grades 9-12. Junior high students in 9th grade are also eligible. Winners will be announced during the North American International Auto Show in January and may be published in the *Auto Show Program* at the sole discretion of the D.A.D.A.

THE SCOTT O'DELL AWARD FOR HISTORICAL FICTION, 1700 E. 56th St., Suite 3907, Chicago IL 60637-1936. Award Director: Mrs. Zena Sutherland. Annual award. Estab. 1981. Purpose of the award: "To promote the writing of historical fiction of good quality for children and young adults." Previously published submissions only; must be published between January 1 and December 31 previous to deadline. Deadline for entries: December 31. "Publishers send books, although occasionally a writer sends a note or a book." SASE for award rules. No entry fee. There is only 1 book chosen each year. Award: $5,000. Judging by a committee of 3. Requirements for entrants: "Must be published by a U.S. publisher in the preceding year; must be written by an American citizen; must be set in North or South America; must be historical fiction."

OHIOANA BOOK AWARDS, Ohioana Library Association, 65 S. Front St., Suite 1105, Columbus OH 43215. (614)466-3831. Fax: (614)728-6974. E-mail: ohioana@winslo.state.oh.us. Website: www.oplin.lib.oh.us/OHIOANA/. Director: Linda R. Hengst. Annual award. "The Ohioana Book Awards are given to books of outstanding literary quality. Purpose of contest: to provide recognition and encouragement to Ohio writers and to promote the work of Ohio writers. Up to six are given each year. Awards may be given in the following categories: fiction, nonfiction, children's literature, poetry and books about Ohio or an Ohioan. Books must be received by the Ohioana Library during the calendar year prior to the year the award is given and must have a copyright date within the last two calendar years." Deadline for entries: December 31. SASE for award rules and entry forms. No entry fee. Winners receive citation and glass sculpture. "Any book that has been written or edited by a person born in Ohio or who has lived in Ohio for at least five years" is eligible. The Ohioana Library Association also awards the "Ohioana Book Award in the category of juvenile books." Send SASE for more information.

OKLAHOMA BOOK AWARDS, Oklahoma Center for the Book, 200 NE 18th, Oklahoma City OK 73105. (405)521-2502. Fax: (405)525-7804. E-mail: gcarlile@oltn.odl.state.ok.us. Website: www.odl.state.ok.us/ocb. Annual award. **Open to students.** Estab. 1989. Purpose of award: "to honor Oklahoma writers and books about our state." Previously published submissions only. Submissions made by the author, author's agent, or entered by a person or group of people, including the publisher. Must be published during the calendar year preceding the award. Awards are presented to best books in fiction, nonfiction, children's, design and illustration, and poetry books about Oklahoma or books written by an author who was born, is living or has lived in Oklahoma. Deadline for entries: early January. SASE for award rules and entry forms. No entry fee. Awards a medal—no cash prize.

Judging by a panel of 5 people for each category—a librarian, a working writer in the genre, booksellers, editors, etc. Requirements for entrants: author must be an Oklahoma native, resident, former resident or have written a book with Oklahoma theme. Winner will be announced at banquet in Oklahoma City. The Arrell Gibson Lifetime Achievement Award is also presented each year to an Oklahoma author for a body of work.

N: ONCE UPON A WORLD BOOK AWARD, Simon Wiesenthal Center's Museum of Tolerance, 1399 S. Roxbury Dr., Los Angeles CA 90035-4709. (310)772-7605. Fax: (310)277-6568. E-mail: library@wiesenthal. net or aklein@wiesenthal.net. Award Director: Adaire J. Klein. Submit entries to: Adaire J. Klein, Director of Library and Archival Services. Annual award. Estab. 1996. Submissions made by publishers, author or by author's agent. Must be published January-December of previous year. Deadline for entries: March 31, 2001. SASE for contest rules and entry forms. Awards $1,000 and plaque. Judging by 3 independent judges familiar with children's literature. Award open to any writer with work in English language on subject of tolerance, diversity, and social justice for children 6-10 years old. Award is presented in October. Book Seal available from the Library. 2000 winner: Ruby Bridges, *Through My Eyes* (NY: Scholastic Press, 1999).

N: THE ORIGINAL ART, Society of Illustrators, 128 E. 63rd St., New York NY 10021-7303. (212)838-2560. Fax: (212)838-2561. E-mail: si1901@aol.com. Website: www.societyillustrators.org. Annual contest. Estab. 1981. Purpose of contest: to celebrate the fine art of children's book illustration. Previously published submissions only. Deadline for entries: August 20. Request "call for entries" to receive contest rules and entry forms. Entry fee is $20/book. Judging by seven professional artists and editors. Works will be displayed at the Society of Illustrators Museum of American Illustration in New York City October-November annually. Medals awarded.

☑ HELEN KEATING OTT AWARD FOR OUTSTANDING CONTRIBUTION TO CHILDREN'S LITERATURE, Church and Synagogue Library Association, P.O. Box 19357, Portland OR 97280-0357. (503)244-6919. Fax: (503)977-3734. E-mail: csla@worldaccessnet.com. Website: www.worldaccessnet.com/~cs la. Chair of Committee: Dean Debolt. Annual award. Estab. 1980. "This award is given to a person or organization that has made a significant contribution to promoting high moral and ethical values through children's literature." Deadline for entries: April 1. "Recipient is honored in July during the conference." Awards certificate of recognition and a conference package consisting of all meals, day of awards banquet, two nights' housing and a complimentary 1 year membership. "A nomination for an award may be made by anyone. It should include the name, address and telephone number of the nominee, plus the church or synagogue relationship where appropriate. Nominations of an organization should include the name of a contact person. A detailed description of the reasons for the nomination should be given, accompanied by documentary evidence of accomplishment. The person(s) making the nomination should give his/her name, address and telephone number and a brief explanation of his/ her knowledge of the nominee's accomplishments. Elements of creativity and innovation will be given high priority by the judges."

☑ ☑ OWL MAGAZINE CONTESTS, Writing Contest, Photo Contest, Poetry Contest, *OWL Magazine*, 179 John St., Suite 500, Toronto, Ontario M5T 3G5 Canada. (416)340-2700. Fax: (416)340-9769. E-mail: owl@owlkids.com. Website: www.owlkids.com. Contact: Hoot Editor. Annual contests. Purpose of contests: "to encourage children to contribute and participate in the magazine." Unpublished submissions only. Deadlines change yearly. Prizes/awards "change every year. Often we give books as prizes." Winning entries published in the magazine. Judging by art and editorial staff. Entries become the property of Bayard Press. "The contests and awards are open to children up to 14 years of age. Check the Hoot section of *OWL* for information and updates. Contests have specific themes, so children should not send unsolicited poetry and fiction until they have checked contest details."

PATERSON PRIZE FOR BOOKS FOR YOUNG PEOPLE, Poetry Center at Passaic County Community College, One College Blvd., Paterson NJ 07505-1179. (973)684-6555. Fax: (973)684-5843. E-mail: mgillan@pcc c.cc.nj.us. Website: www.pccc.cc.nj.us/poetry. Director: Maria Mazziotti Gillan. **Open to students.** Estab. 1996. Poetry Center's mission is "to recognize excellence in books for young people." Previously published submissions only. Submissions made by author, author's agent or publisher. Must be published between January 1, 1999-December 31, 2000. Deadline for entries: March 15, 2001. SASE for contest rules and entry forms or visit website. Awards $500 for the author in either of 3 categories: PreK-Grade 3; Grades 4-6, Grades 7-12. Judging by a professional writer selected by the Poetry Center. Contest is open to any writer/illustrator.

N: PEN/NORMA KLEIN AWARD FOR CHILDREN'S FICTION, PEN American Center, 568 Broadway, New York NY 10012. (212)334-1660. Awarded in odd-numbered years. Estab. 1990. "In memory of the late PEN member and distinguished children's book author Norma Klein, the award honors new authors whose books demonstrate the adventuresome and innovative spirit that characterizes the best children's literature and Norma Klein's own work." Previously published submissions only. "Candidates may not nominate themselves. We welcome all nominations from authors and editors of children's books." Deadline for entries: December. Awards $3,000 which will be given in May. Judging by a panel of 3 distinguished children's book authors. Nominations open to authors of books for elementary school to young adult readers. "It is strongly recommended that the nominator describe in some detail the literary character of the candidate's work and how it promises to enrich American literature for children."

☑ **PENNSYLVANIA YOUNG READER'S CHOICE AWARDS PROGRAM**, Pennsylvania School Librarians Association, 148 S. Bethelehem Pike, Ambler PA 19002-5822. (215)643-5048. Fax: (215)628-8441. E-mail: bellavance@erols.com. Coordinator: Jean B. Bellavance. Annual award. Estab. 1991. Submissions nominated by a person or group. Must be published within 5 years of the award—for example, for 2001-2002 books published 1997 to present. Deadline for entries: September 15. SASE for contest rules and entry forms. No entry fee. Framed certificate to winning authors. Judging by children of Pennsylvania (they vote). Requirements for entrants: currently living in North America. Reader's Choice Award is to promote reading of quality books by young people in the Commonwealth of Pennsylvania, to promote teacher and librarian involvement in children's literature, and to honor authors whose work has been recognized by the children of Pennsylvania. Three awards are given, one for each of the following grade level divisions: K-3, 3-6, 6-8.

☑ **PLEASE TOUCH MUSEUM® BOOK AWARD**, Please Touch Museum, 210 N. 21st St., Philadelphia PA 19103-1001. (215)963-0667. Fax: (215)963-0667. E-mail: marketing@pleasetouchmuseum.org. Website: www.pleasetouchmuseum.org. **Open to students.** Annual award. Estab. 1985. Purpose of the award: "to recognize and encourage the publication of books for young children by American authors that are of the highest quality and will aid them in enjoying the process of learning through books. Awarded to two picture books that are particularly imaginative and effective in exploring a concept or concepts, one for children age three and younger, and one for children ages four-seven. To be eligible for consideration a book must: (1) Explore and clarify an idea for young children. This could include the concept of numbers, colors, shapes, sizes, senses, feelings, etc. There is no limitation as to format. (2) Be distinguished in both text and illustration. (3) Be published within the last year by an American publisher. (4) Be by an American author and/or illustrator." Deadline for entries: (submissions may be made throughout the year). SASE for award rules and entry forms. No entry fee. Judging by selected jury of children's literature experts, librarians and early childhood educators. Education store purchases books for selling at Book Award Celebration Day and throughout the year. Receptions and autographing sessions held in bookstores, Please Touch Museum, and throughout the city.

🔃 **POCKETS MAGAZINE FICTION CONTEST**, The Upper Room, P.O. Box 340004, Nashville TN 37203-0004. (615)340-7333. Fax: (615)340-7006. E-mail: pockets@upperroom.org. Website: www.upperroom.org/pockets. Associate Editor: Lynn Gilliam. **Open to students.** Annual contest. Estab. 1990. Purpose of contest: "to discover new freelance writers for our magazine and to encourage freelance writers to become familiar with the needs of our magazine." Unpublished submissions only. Submissions made by the author. Deadline for entries: August 15. SASE for contest rules and entry forms. No entry fee. Awards $1,000 and publication. Judging by *Pockets'* editors and 3 other editors of other Upper Room publications. Winner published in the magazine.

🔃 **MICHAEL L. PRINTZ AWARD**, Young Adult Library Services Association, Division of the American Library Association, 50 E. Huron, Chicago IL 60611. Website: www.ala.org/yalsa/printz. The Michael L. Printz Award is an award for a book that exemplifies literary excellence in young adult literature. It is named for a Topeka, Kansas school librarian who was a long-time active member of the Young Adult Library Services Association. It will be selected annually by an award committee that can also name as many as four honor books. The award-winning book can be fiction, non-fiction, poetry or an anthology, and can be a work of joint authorship or editorship. The books must be published between January 1 and December 31 of the preceding year and be designated by its publisher as being either a young adult book or one published for the age range that YALSA defines as young adult, e.g. ages 12 through 18. The deadline for both committee and field nominations will be December 1.

☑ **PRIX ALVINE-BELISLE**, Association pour l'avancement des sciences et des techniques de la documentation (ASTED) Inc., 3414 Avenue Du Parc, Bureau 202, Montreal, Québec H2X 2H5 Canada. (514)281-5012. Fax: (514)281-8219. E-mail: info@asted.org. Award President: Micheline Patton. Award open to children's book editors. Annual award. Estab. 1974. Purpose of contest: To recognize the best children's book published in French in Canada. Previously published submissions only. Submissions made by publishing house. Must be published the year before award. Deadline for entries: June 1. Awards $500. Judging by librarians jury.

QUILL AND SCROLL INTERNATIONAL WRITING/PHOTO CONTEST, *Quill and Scroll*, School of Journalism, University of Iowa, Iowa City IA 52242-1528. (319)335-5795. Fax: (319)335-5210. E-mail: quill-scroll@uiowa.edu. Website: www.uiowa.edu/~quill-sc. Contest Director: Richard Johns. **Open to students.** Annual contest. Previously published submissions only. Submissions made by the author or school newspaper adviser. Must be published February 6, 2000 to February 4, 2001. Deadline for entries: February 5. SASE for contest rules and entry forms. Entry fee is $2/entry. Awards engraved plaque to junior high level sweepstakes winners. Judging by various judges. *Quill and Scroll* acquires the right to publish submitted material in the magazine if it is chosen as a winning entry. Requirements for entrants: must be students in grades 9-12 for high school division.

THE ERIN PATRICK RABORG POETRY AWARD, *AMELIA Magazine*, 329 E St., Bakersfield CA 93304-2031. (805)823-4064. Fax: (805)323-5326. E-mail: amelia@lightspeed.net. Submit entries to: Frederick A. Raborg, Jr., editor. **Open to students.** Estab. 1992. Purpose of contest: To draw attention to childhood lifestyles and consequences. Also, to explore the humor as well as the pathos of childhood. Unpublished submissions only. Submissions made by author. Deadline for entries: December 1 annually. SASE for contest rules. Entry fee is $3 each entry. Award consists of $50 and publication in *AMELIA*. Judging is done in-house. Rights to winning material acquired: first North American serial only. "Be consistent within the form chosen." Sample copy $10.95.

N RIP VAN WINKLE AWARD, School Library Media Specialists of Southeastern NY. (845)486-4840, ext. 3061. Award Director: Maxine Kamin. Annual award. Purpose of award: given to reward an author, illustator or author/illustrator residing in the seven county SLMSSENY region (Dutchess, Putnam, Orange, Rockland, Sullivan, Ulster and Westchester Counties, NY) for his/her outstanding contributions in the field of children's/young adult literature. Previously published submissions only. Submissions nominated by a person or group. Judging by Executive Board of Organization.

✔ ☺ SASKATCHEWAN BOOK AWARDS: CHILDREN'S LITERATURE, Saskatchewan Book Awards, Box 1921, Regina, Saskatchewan S4P 3E1 Canada. (306)569-1585. Fax: (306)569-4187. E-mail: sk.book awards@dlewest.com. Website: www.bookawards.sk.ca. Award Director: Joyce Wells. **Open to Saskatchewan authors.** Annual award. Estab. 1995. Purpose of contest: to celebrate Saskatchewan books and authors and to promote their work. Previously published submissions only. Submissions made by author, author's agent or publisher by September 30. SASE for contest rules and entry forms. Entry fee is $15 (Canadian). Awards $1,000 (Canadian). Judging by two children's literature authors outside of Saskatchewan. Requirements for entrants: Must be Saskatchewan resident; book must have ISBN number; book must have been published within the last year. Award winning book will appear on TV talk shows and be pictured on book marks distributed to libraries, schools and bookstores in Saskatchewan.

✔ SHUBERT FENDRICH MEMORIAL PLAYWRITING CONTEST, Pioneer Drama Service, Inc., P.O. Box 4267, Englewood CO 80155-4267. Fax: (303)774-4315. E-mail: editors@pioneerdrama.com. Website: www.pioneerdrama.com. Director: Beth Somers. Annual contest. **Open to students.** Estab. 1990. Purpose of the contest: "to encourage the development of quality theatrical material for educational and family theater." Previously unpublished submissions only. Deadline for entries: March 1. SASE for contest rules and guidelines. No entry fee. Cover letter must accompany all submissions. Awards $1,000 royalty advance and publication. Upon receipt of signed contracts, plays will be published and made available in our next catalog. Judging by editors. All rights acquired with acceptance of contract for publication. Restrictions for entrants: Any writers currently published by Pioneer Drama Service are not eligible.

✔ SKIPPING STONES YOUTH HONOR AWARDS, *Skipping Stones*, P.O. Box 3939, Eugene OR 97403-0939. (541)342-4956. E-mail: skipping@efn.org. Website: www.efn.org/~skipping. Annual award. Purpose of contest: "to recognize youth, 7 to 17, for their contributions to multicultural awareness, nature and ecology, social issues, peace and nonviolence. Also to promote creativity, self-esteem and writing skills and to recognize important work being done by youth organizations." Submissions made by the author. The theme is "Multicultural and Nature Awareness." Deadline for entries: June 20. SASE for contest rules. Entries must include certificate of originality by a parent and/or teacher and background information on the author written by the author. Entry fee is $3. Judging by *Skipping Stones*' staff. "Up to ten awards are given in three categories: (1) Compositions—(essays, poems, short stories, songs, travelogues, etc.) should be typed (double-spaced) or neatly handwritten. Fiction or nonfiction should be limited to 750 words; poems to 30 lines. Non-English writings are also welcome. (2) Artwork—(drawings, cartoons, paintings or photo essays with captions) should have the artist's name, age and address on the back of each page. Send the originals with SASE. Black & white photos are especially welcome. Limit: 8 pieces. (3) Youth Organizations—Tell us how your club or group works to: (a) preserve the nature and ecology in your area, (b) enhance the quality of life for low-income, minority or disabled or (c) improve racial or cultural harmony in your school or community. Use the same format as for compositions." The winners are published in the September-October issue of *Skipping Stones*. The winners also receive "Honor certificates, five books and a subscription. Everyone who enters the contest receives the Sept.-Oct. issue featuring Youth Awards.

✔ KAY SNOW WRITERS' CONTEST, Williamette Writers, 9045 SW Barbur Blvd. #5A, Portland OR 97219-4027. (503)452-1592. Fax: (503)452-0372. E-mail: wilwrite@teleport.com. Website: www.teleport.com/~wilwrite/. Contest Director: Liam Callen. Annual contest. **Open to students.** Purpose of contest: "to encourage beginning and established writers to continue the craft." Unpublished, original submissions only. Submissions made by the author or author's agent. Deadline for entries: May 15. SASE for contest rules and entry forms. Entry fee is $10, Williamette Writers' members; $15, nonmembers; free for student writers 6-18. Awards cash prize of $300 per category (fiction, nonfiction, juvenile, poetry, script writing), $50 for students in three divisions: 1-5, 6-8, 9-12. "Judges are anonymous."

☑ **SOCIETY OF MIDLAND AUTHORS AWARDS**, Society of Midland Authors, P.O. Box 10419, Chicago IL 60610-0419. E-mail: writercc@aol.com. Website: www.midlandauthors.com. **Open to students.** Annual award. Estab. 1915. Purpose of award: "to stimulate creative literary effort, one of the goals of the Society. There are six categories, including children's fiction, children's nonfiction, adult fiction and nonfiction, biography and poetry." Previously published submissions only. Submissions made by the author or publisher. Must be published during calendar year previous to deadline. Deadline for entries: March 1. SASE for award rules and entry forms or check website. No entry fee. Awards plaque given at annual dinner, cash (minimum $300). Judging by panel (reviewers, university faculty, writers, librarians) of 3 per category. Author must be currently residing in the Midlands, i.e., Illinois, Indiana, Iowa, Kansas, Michigan, Minnesota, Missouri, Nebraska, North Dakota, South Dakota, Ohio or Wisconsin.

SPUR AWARDS, Western Writers of America, 60 Sandpiper Court, Conway AR 72032. (501)450-0086. Award Director: W.C. Jameson. Annual award. Estab. 1953. Previously published submissions only. Submissions made by author, author's agent or publisher. Must be published the year previous to the award. SASE for contest rules and entry forms. Awards plaque. Judging by panel of 3 published writers. Awards given in June 2001 at Idaho Falls, Idaho.

THE STANLEY DRAMA AWARD, Stanley-Tomolat Foundation, Wagner College, One Campus Rd., Staten Island NY 10301. (718)390-3325. Fax: (718)390-3323. E-mail: tsweetwagner.edu. Award Director: Tanya Sweet. **Open to students.** Annual award. Estab. 1957. Purpose of contest: to support new works and playwrights. Unpublished submissions only. Submissions made by author. Deadline for entries: October 1. SASE for contest rules and entry forms. Entry fee is $20. Awards $2,000. Judging by committee. Award is to a full-length play or musical, previously unpublished and/or produced. One-act plays must be a full evening of theater; accepts series of one-acts related to one theme. "We will consider only one submission per playwright."

☑ **SUGARMAN FAMILY AWARD FOR JEWISH CHILDREN'S LITERATURE**, District of Columbia Jewish Community Center, 1529 16th St. N.W., Washington DC 20036. (202)518-9400. Fax: (202)518-9420. E-mail: kate@dcjcc.org. Award director: Kate Kline. **Open to students.** Biannual award. Estab. 1994. Purpose of contest: to enrich all children's appreciation of Jewish culture and to inspire writers and illustrators for children. Newly published submissions only. Submissions are made by the author, made by the author's agent. Must be published January-December of year previous to award year. Deadline: June 30, 2001. SASE for entry deadlines, award rules and entry forms. Entry fee is $25. Award at least $750. Judging by a panel of three judges—a librarian, a children's bookstore owner and a reviewer of books. Requirements for entrants: must live in the United States. Work displayed at the D.C. Jewish Community Center Library. Presentation of awards—October 2001.

☑ **SWW ANNUAL CONTEST**, SouthWest Writers, 8200 Mountain Rd. NE, Suite 106, Albuquerque NM 87110. (505)265-9485. Fax: (505)265-9483. E-mail: SWriters@aol.com. Website: www.southwestwriters.org. Submit entries to: Contest Chair. Annual contest. Estab. 1982. Purpose of contest: to encourage writers of all genres. Previously unpublished submissions only. Submissions made by author. Deadline for entries: May 1, 2001. SASE for contest rules and entry forms. Entry fee. Award consists of cash prizes in each of over 15 categories. Judging by national editors and agents. Official entry form is required.

☒ **TOMÁS RIVERA MEXICAN AMERICAN CHILDREN'S BOOK AWARD**, Southwest Texas State University, EDU, 601 University Dr., San Marcos TX 78666-4613. (512)245-2357. Fax: (512)245-7911. E-mail: jb23@academia.swt.edu. Award Director: Dr. Jennifer Battle. Competition open to adults. Annual contest. Estab. 1995. Purpose of award: "To encourage authors, illustrators and publishers to produce books that authentically reflect the lives of Mexican American children and young adults in the United States." Previously published submissions only. Submissions made by "any interested individual or publishing company." Must be published during the year of consideration. Deadline for entries: February 1 post publication year. Contact Dr. Jennifer Battle for nomination forms, or send copy of book. No entry fee. Awards $3,000 per book. Judging of nominations by a regional committee, national committee judges finalists. Annual ceremony honoring the book and author/illustrator is held during Hispanic Heritage Month at Southwest Texas State University.

☑ **TREASURE STATE AWARD**, Missoula Public Library, Missoula County Schools, Montana Library Assoc., 301 E. Main, Missoula MT 59802. (406)721-2005. Fax: (406)728-5900. E-mail: bammon@missoula.lib.mt.us. Website: www.missoula.lib.mt.us. Award Directors: Bette Ammon and Carole Monlux. Annual award. Estab. 1990. Purpose of the award: Children in grades K-3 read or listen to a ballot of 5 picture books and vote on their favorite. Previously published submissions only. Submissions made by author, nominated by a person or group of people—children, librarians, teachers. Must be published in previous 5 years to voting year. Deadline for entries: March 20. SASE for contest rules and entry forms. No entry fee. Awards a plaque or sculpture. Judging by popular vote by Montana children grades K-3.

VEGETARIAN ESSAY CONTEST, The Vegetarian Resource Group, P.O. Box 1463, Baltimore MD 21203. (410)366-VEGE. Fax: (410)366-8804. E-mail: vrg@vrg.org. Website: www.vrg.org. Address to Vegetarian Essay

Contest. Annual contest. Estab. 1985. Purpose of contest: to promote vegetarianism in young people. Unpublished submissions only. Deadline for entries: May 1 of each year. SASE for contest rules and entry forms. No entry fee. Awards $50 savings bond. Judging by awards committee. Acquires right for The Vegetarian Resource Group to reprint essays. Requirements for entrants: age 18 and under. Winning works may be published in *Vegetarian Journal*, instructional materials for students. "Submit 2-3 page essay on any aspect of vegetarianism, which is the abstinence of meat, fish and fowl. Entrants can base paper on interviewing, research or personal opinion. Need not be vegetarian to enter."

VFW VOICE OF DEMOCRACY, Veterans of Foreign Wars of the U.S., 406 W. 34th St., Kansas City MO 64111. (816)968-1117. Fax: (816)968-1149. Website: www.vfw.org. **Open to students.** Annual contest. Estab. 1960. Purpose of contest: to give high school students the opportunity to voice their opinions about their responsibility to our country and to convey those opinions via the broadcast media to all of America. Deadline for entries: November 1st. No entry fee. Winners receive awards ranging from $1,000-25,000. Requirements for entrants: "Ninth-twelfth grade students in public, parochial, private and home schools are eligible to compete. Former first place state winners are not eligible to compete again. Contact your participating high school teacher, counselor or your local VFW Post to enter."

N VOLUNTEER STATE BOOK AWARD, Tennessee Library Association, P.O. Box 158417, Nashville TN 37215-8417. (615)297-8316. Award Co-Chairs: Kathy Patten, Patty Williams. Competition open to adults only. Annual award. Estab. 1978. Purpose of award: to promote awareness, interest, and enjoyment of good new children's and young adult literature and to promote literacy and life-long reading habits by encouraging students to read quality contemporary literature which broadens understanding of the human experience and provides accurate, factual information. Previously published submissions only. Submissions made by author, by the author's agent and nominated by a person or group of people. Must be published in 5 years prior to year of voting. SASE for contest rules and entry forms. No entry fee. Awards plaque. Judging by children. Any public or private school in Tennessee is eligible to participate. It is not required that the entire school be involved. Each participating school must have a minimum of twelve of the twenty titles per division available.

N VSA (VERY SPECIAL ARTS) PLAYWRIGHT DISCOVERY PROGRAM, VSA, 1300 Connecticut Ave., NW, Suite 700, Washington DC 20036. (202)628-2800 or 1-800-933-8721. TTY: (202)737-0645. Fax: (202)737-0725. E-mail: playwright@vsarts.org. Website: www.vsarts.org. Program Manager: Barbara Witten. Annual contest. Estab. 1984. "All scripts must document the experience of living with a disability." Unpublished submissions only. Deadline for entries: April 30, 2001. Write to Playwright Discovery Program Manager for contest rules and entry forms. No entries returned. No entry fee. Judging by Artists Selection Committee. Entrants must be people with disabilities. "Script will be selected for production at The John F. Kennedy Center for the Performing Arts, Washington DC. The winning play(s) is presented each fall."

THE STELLA WADE CHILDREN'S STORY AWARD, *Amelia* Magazine, 329 E St., Bakersfield CA 93304. (805)323-4064. Editor: Frederick A. Raborg, Jr. Annual award. Estab. 1988. Purpose of award: "With decrease in the number of religious and secular magazines for young people, the juvenile story and poetry must be preserved and enhanced." Unpublished submissions only. Deadline for entries: August 15. SASE for award rules. Entry fee is $7.50 per adult entry; there is no fee for entries submitted by young people under the age of 17, but such entry must be signed by parent, guardian or teacher to verify originality. Awards $125 plus publication. Judging by editorial staff. Previous winners include Maxine Kumin and Sharon E. Martin. "We use First North American serial rights only for the winning manuscript." Contest is open to all interested. If illustrator wishes to enter only an illustration without a story, the entry fee remains the same. Illustrations will also be considered for cover publication. Restrictions of mediums for illustrators: Submitted photos should be no smaller than 5 × 7; illustrations (drawn) may be in any medium. "Winning entry will be published in the most appropriate issue of either *Amelia, Cicada* or *SPSM&H*—subject matter would determine such. Submit clean, accurate copy." Sample issue: $10.95.

☑ WASHINGTON CHILDREN'S CHOICE PICTURE BOOK AWARD, Washington Library Media Association, P.O. Box 16084, Seattle WA 98116. E-mail: galantek@edmonds.wednet.edu. Award Director: Kristin Galante. Submit entries to: Kristin Galante, chairman. Annual award. Estab. 1982. Previously published submissions only. Submissions nominated by a person or group. Must be published within 2-3 years prior to year of award. Deadline for entries: March 1. SASE for contest rules and entry forms. Awards pewter plate, recognition. Judging by WCCPBA committee.

☑ WASHINGTON POST/CHILDREN'S BOOK GUILD AWARD FOR NONFICTION, % Kathleen Karr, President of the Children's Book Guild of Washington, D.C., 1916 Bitmore St. NW, Washington DC 20009. Fax: (202)387-3009. E-mail: karr@bellatlantic.net. Website: www.childrensbookguild.org. **Open to students.** Annual award. Estab. 1977. Purpose of award: "to encourage nonfiction writing for children of literary quality. Purpose of contest: "to call attention to an outstanding nonfiction author of several works, judged on the author's total output, to encourage authors to write nonfiction." Awarded for the body of work of a leading American nonfiction author." Awards being negotiated and an engraved crystal paperweight. Judging by a jury of Children's Book Guild librarians and authors and a *Washington Post* book critic. "One doesn't enter. One is selected. Authors and publishers mistakenly send us books. Our jury annually selects one author for the award."

WE ARE WRITERS, TOO!, Creative With Words Publications, P.O. Box 223226, Carmel CA 93922. Fax: (831)655-8627. E-mail: cwwpub@usa.net. Website: members.tripod.com/CreativeWithWords. Contest Director: Brigitta Geltrich. Four times a year (April, May, June, September). Estab. 1975. Purpose of award: to further creative writing in children. Unpublished submissions only. Can submit year round on any topic. Deadlines for entries: year round. SASE for contest rules and entry forms. SASE for return of entries "if not on accepted entry." No entry fee. Awards publication in an anthology, on website if winning poem, and a free copy for "Best of the Month." Judging by selected guest editors and educators. Contest open to children only (up to and including 19 years old). Writer should request contest rules. SASE with all correspondence. Age of child and home address must be stated and manuscript must be verified of its authenticity. Each story or poem must have a title. Creative with Words Publications publishes the top 100-120 manuscripts submitted to the contest and also publishes anthologies on various themes throughout the year to which young writers may submit. Request theme list, include SASE, or visit our website. "Website offers special contests to young writers with prizes."

N. WESTERN HERITAGE AWARDS, National Cowboy Hall of Fame, 1700 NE 63rd St., Oklahoma City OK 73111-7997. (405)478-2250. Fax: (405)478-4714. E-mail: nchf@aol.com. Website: www.cowboyhalloffame. com. Director of Public Relations: Lynda Haller. Annual award. Estab. 1961. Purpose of award: The WHA are presented annually to encourage the accurate and artistic telling of great stories of the West through 15 categories of western literature, television and film, including fiction, nonfiction, children's books and poetry. Previously published submissions only; must be published the calendar year before the awards are presented. Deadline for literary entries: November 30. Deadline for film, music and television entries: December 31. SASE for award rules and entry forms. Entries not returned. Entry fee is $35. Awards a Wrangler bronze sculpture designed by famed western artist, John Free. Judging by a panel of judges selected each year with distinction in various fields of western art and heritage. Requirements for entrants: The material must pertain to the development or preservation of the West, either from a historical or contemporary viewpoint. Literary entries must have been published between December 1 and November 30 of calendar year. Film, music or television entries must have been released or aired between January 1 and December 31 of calendar year of entry. Works recognized during special awards ceremonies held annually at the museum. There is an autograph party preceding the awards. Film clips of award winner are shown during the awards presentation. Awards ceremonies are sometimes broadcast.

WESTERN WRITERS OF AMERICA AWARD, Western Writers of America, Inc., 60 Sandpiper, Conway AR 72032. (501)450-0086. E-mail: carlj@mail.uca.edu. Website: www.imt.net/~gedison/wwahome.html. Award Director: W.C. Jameson. **Open to students.** Submit entries to: W.C. Jameson. Annual award. Purpose of award: to recognize the best western writing. Western material is defined by the WWA, Inc. as that which is set in the territory west of the Mississippi River or on the early frontier. Previously published submissions only. Submissions made by author. Must be published in the previous year. Deadline for entries: December 31. SASE for contest rules and entry forms. No entry fee. Awards include the Spur Awards, the Medicine Pipe Bearer Award for Best First Novel and the Storyteller Award for the Best Children's Picture Book of the West.

JACKIE WHITE MEMORIAL NATIONAL CHILDREN'S PLAY WRITING CONTEST, Columbia Entertainment Company, 309 Parkade Blvd., Columbia MO 65202-1447. (573)874-5628. Contest Director: Betsy Phillips. Annual contest. Estab. 1988. Purpose of contest: to find good plays for 30-45 theater school students, grades 6-9, to perform in CEC's theater school and to encourage writing production of large cast scripts suitable for production in theater schools. Previously unpublished submissions only. Submissions made by author. Deadline for entries: June 1. SASE for contest rules and entry forms. Entry fee is $10. Awards $250, production of play, travel expenses to come see production. Judging by board members of CEC and at least one theater school parent. Play is performed during the following season. 2000 winner to be presented during CEC's 2000-01 season. We reserve the right to award 1st place and prize monies without a production.

LAURA INGALLS WILDER AWARD, Association for Library Service to Children, Division of the American Library Association, 50 E. Huron, Chicago IL 60611. (312)280-2163. Website: www.ala.org/alsc. Interim Executive Director, ALSC: Stephanie Anton. Award offered every 3 years. Purpose of the award: to recognize an author or illustrator whose books, published in the US, have over a period of years made a substantial and lasting contribution to children's literature. Awards a medal presented at banquet during annual conference. Judging by Wilder Committee.

VISIT THE WRITER'S DIGEST WEBSITE at www.writersdigest.com for hot new markets, daily market updates, writers' guidelines and much more.

⟦N⟧ PAUL A. WITTY OUTSTANDING LITERATURE AWARD, International Reading Association, Special Interest Group, Reading for Gifted and Creative Learning, School of Education, P.O. Box 297900, Fort Worth TX 76129. (817)921-7660. Award Director: Dr. Cathy Collins Block. Annual award. Estab. 1979. Categories of entries: poetry/prose at elementary, junior high and senior high levels. Unpublished submissions only. Deadline for entries: February 1. SASE for award rules and entry forms. SASE for return of entries. No entry fee. Awards $25 and plaque, also certificates of merit. Judging by 2 committees for screening and awarding. Works will be published in International Reading Association publications. "The elementary students' entries must be legible and may not exceed 1,000 words. Secondary students' prose entries should be typed and may exceed 1,000 words if necessary. At both elementary and secondary levels, if poetry is entered, a set of five poems must be submitted. All entries and requests for applications must include a self-addressed, stamped envelope."

✓ PAUL A. WITTY SHORT STORY AWARD, International Reading Association, P.O. Box 8139, 800 Barksdale Rd., Newark DE 19714-8139. (302)731-1600. E-mail: exec@reading.org. or jbutler@reading.org. Website: www.reading.org. The entry must be an original short story appearing in a young children's periodical for the first time during 2000. The short story should serve as a literary standard that encourages young readers to read periodicals. Deadline for entries: The entry must have been published for the first time in the eligibility year; the short story must be submitted during the calendar year of publication. Anyone wishing to nominate a short story should send it to the designated Paul A. Witty Short Award Subcommittee Chair by December 1. Send SASE for guidelines. Award is $1,000 and recognition at the annual IRA Convention.

WOMEN IN THE ARTS ANNUAL CONTESTS, Women In The Arts, P.O. Box 2907, Decatur IL 62524-2907. (217)872-0811. Submit entries to Vice President. **Open to students.** Annual contest. Estab. 1995. Purpose of contest: to encourage beginning writers, as well as published professionals, by offering a contest for well-written material in fiction, essay and poetry. Submissions made by author. Deadline for entries: November 1 annually. SASE for contest rules and entry forms. Entry fee is $2/item. Prize consists of $30 1st place; $25 2nd place; $15 3rd place. Send SASE for complete rules.

ALICE LOUISE WOOD OHIOANA AWARD FOR CHILDREN'S LITERATURE, Ohioana Library Association, 65 S. Front St., Suite 1105, Columbus OH 43215. (614)466-3831. Fax: (614)728-6974. E-mail: ohioana@winslo.state.oh.us. Website: www.oplin.lib.oh.us/OHIOANA/. Director: Linda R. Hengst. Annual award. Estab. 1991. Purpose of award: "to recognize an Ohio author whose body of work has made, and continues to make a significant contribution to literature for children or young adults." SASE for award rules and entry forms. Award: $1,000. Requirements for entrants: "must have been born in Ohio, or lived in Ohio for a minimum of five years; established a distinguished publishing record of books for children and young people; body of work has made, and continues to make, a significant contribution to the literature for young people; through whose work as a writer, teacher, administrator, or through community service, interest in children's literature has been encouraged and children have become involved with reading."

⟦N⟧ CARTER G. WOODSON BOOK AWARD, National Council for the Social Studies, 3501 Newark St. NW, Washington DC 20016-3167. (202)966-7840. Fax: (202)966-2061. E-mail: excellence@ncss.org. Website: www.ncss.org. Contact: Manager of Recognition Programs. Annual award, named after Carter G. Woodson (1875-1950, a distinguished African-American historian, educator and social activist. Purpose of contest: to recognize books relating to ethnic minorities and authors of such books. NCSS established the Carter G. Woodson Book Awards for the most distinguished social science books appropriate for young readers which depict ethnicity in the United States. This award is intended to "encourage the writing, publishing, and dissemination of outstanding social studies books for young readers which treat topics related to ethnic minorities and race relations sensitively and accurately." Submissions must be previously published and are made by publishers because copies of the book must be supplied to each member of the committee and NCSS headquarters. Eligible books must be published in the year preceding the year in which award is given, i.e., 1997 for 1998 award. Books must be received by members of the committee by February 1. Rules, criteria and requirements are available at www.ncss.org/awards and are mailed to various publishers in December. Publishers that would like to be added to this mailing list should e-mail or mail their request to the contact information listed above, attention: Carter G. Woodson. No entry fee. Award consists of: a commemorative gift, annual conference presentation, and an announcement published in NCSS periodicals and forwarded to national and Council affiliated media. The publisher, author and illustrator receive written notification of the committee decision. Reviews of award-winning books and "honor books" are published in the NCSS official journal, *Social Education*. The award is presented at the NCSS Annual Conference in November. Judging by committee of social studies educators (teachers, curriculum supervisors and specialists, college/university professors, teacher educators—with a specific interest in multicultural education and the use of literature in social studies instruction) appointed from the NCSS membership at large.

WORK-IN-PROGRESS GRANTS, Society of Children's Book Writers and Illustrators, 8271 Beverly Blvd., Los Angeles CA 90048. Fax: (323)782-1892. E-mail: scbwi@scbwi.org. Website: www.scbwi.org. Annual award. "The SCBWI Work-in-Progress Grants have been established to assist children's book writers in the completion of a specific project." Five categories: (1) General Work-in-Progress Grant. (2) Grant for a Contemporary Novel for Young People. (3) Nonfiction Research Grant. (4) Grant for a Work Whose Author Has Never Had a Book Published. (5) Grant for a Picture Book Writer. Requests for applications may be made beginning October 1. Completed applications accepted February 1-May 1 of each year. SASE for applications for grants. In any year, an applicant may apply for any of the grants except the one awarded for a work whose author has never had a book published. (The recipient of this grant will be chosen from entries in all categories.) Five grants of $1,500 will be awarded annually. Runner-up grants of $500 (one in each category) will also be awarded. "The grants are available to both full and associate members of the SCBWI. They are not available for projects on which there are already contracts." Previous recipients not eligible to apply.

WRITER'S BLOCK LITERARY CONTEST, *Writer's Block* Magazine, #32, 9944-33 Ave., Edmonton, Alberta T6N 1E8 Canada. Contest Director: Shaun Donnelly. Submit entries to: Shaun Donnelly, editor. **Open to students.** Biannual contest. Estab. 1994. Purpose of contest: to discover outstanding fiction/poetry by new writers for inclusion in *Writer's Block* magazine. Unpublished submissions only. Submissions made by author. Deadline for entries: March 30 and September 30. SASE for contest rules and entry forms. Entry fee is $5. Prize consists of publication, $100-150 cash, hardcover books in author's genre. Judging by independent judges (usually writers).

WRITER'S EXCHANGE POETRY CONTEST, 616 Eagle Bend Rd., Clinton TN 37716. E-mail: eboone@aol.com. Website: members.aol.com/WriterNet or members.aol.com/WEBBASE1. Contest Director: Gene Boone. Quarterly contest. **Open to students.** Estab. 1985. Purpose of the contest: to promote friendly competition among poets of all ages and backgrounds, giving these poets a chance to be published and win an award. Submissions are made by the author. Continuous deadline; entries are placed in the contest closest to date received. SASE for contest rules and entry forms. Entry fee is $2 first poem, $1 each additional poem. Awards 50% of contest proceeds, usually $35-100 varying slightly in each quarterly contest due to changes in response. Judging by Gene Boone or a guest judge such as a widely published poet or another small press editor. "From the entries received, we reserve the right to publish the winning poems in an issue of *Writer's Exchange*, a literary newsletter. The contest is open to any poet. Poems on any subject/theme, any style, to 30 lines, may be entered. Poems should be typed, single-spaced, with the poet's name in the upper left corner."

WRITER'S INT'L FORUM CONTESTS, Bristol Services Int'l., P.O. Box 2109, Sequim MA 98382. Website: www.bristolservicesintl.com. Estab. 1997. Purpose to inspire excellence in the traditional short story format and for tightly focused essays. "In fiction we like identifiable characters, strong storylines, and crisp, fresh endings. Open to all ages." SASE or see website to determine if a contest is currently open. Only send a manuscript if an open contest is listed at website. Read past winning manuscripts online. Judging by Bristol Services Int'l. staff.

WRITING CONFERENCE WRITING CONTESTS, The Writing Conference, Inc., P.O. Box 27288, Overland Park KS 66225-7288. Phone/fax: (913)681-8894. E-mail: jbushman@writingconference.com. Website: www.writingconference.com. Contest Director: John H. Bushman. **Open to students.** Annual contest. Estab. 1988. Purpose of contest: to further writing by students with awards for narration, exposition and poetry at the elementary, middle school and high school levels. Unpublished submissions only. Submissions made by the author or teacher. Deadline for entries: January 8. SASE for contest rules and entry form or consult website. No entry fee. Awards plaque and publication of winning entry in *The Writers' Slate*, March issue. Judging by a panel of teachers. Requirements for entrants: must be enrolled in school—K-12th grade.

YEARBOOK EXCELLENCE CONTEST, *Quill and Scroll*, School of Journalism, University of Iowa, Iowa City IA 52242-1528. (319)335-5795. Fax: (319)335-5210. E-mail: quill-scroll@uiowa.edu. Website: www.uiowa.edu/~quill-sc. Executive Director: Richard Johns. **Open to students.** Annual contest. Estab. 1987. Purpose of contest: to recognize and reward student journalists for their work in yearbooks and to provide student winners an opportunity to apply for a scholarship to be used freshman year in college for students planning to major in journalism. Previously published submissions only. Submissions made by the author or school yearbook adviser. Must be published between November 1, 1999 and November 1, 2000. Deadline for entries: November 1. SASE for contest rules and entry form. Entry fee is $2 per entry. Awards National Gold Key; sweepstakes winners receive plaque; seniors eligible for scholarships. Judging by various judges. Winning entries may be published in *Quill and Scroll* magazine.

YOUNG ADULT CANADIAN BOOK AWARD, The Canadian Library Association, 328 Frank St., Ottawa, Ontario K2P 0X8 Canada. (613)232-9625. Fax: (613)563-9895. Contact: Committee Chair. Annual award. Estab. 1981. Purpose of award: "to recognize the author of an outstanding English-language Canadian book which appeals to young adults between the ages of 13 and 18 that was published the preceding calendar year. Information is available for anyone requesting. We approach publishers, also send news releases to various journals, i.e., *Quill & Quire*." Entries are not returned. No entry fee. Awards a leather-bound book. Requirement for entrants: must be a work of fiction (novel or short stories), the title must be a Canadian publication in either hardcover or paperback, and the author must be a Canadian citizen or landed immigrant. Award given at the Canadian Library Association Conference.

YOUNG READER'S CHOICE AWARD, Pacific Northwest Library Association, Box 352930, University of Washington, Graduate School of Library and Information Science, Seattle WA 98195-2930. (206)543-1897. Award Director: Carole Monlux, chair YRCA. Annual award for published authors. Estab. 1940. Purpose of award: "to promote reading as an enjoyable activity and to provide children an opportunity to endorse a book they consider an excellent story." No unsolicited mss or published novels are accepted. Deadline for entries: February 1. SASE for award rules and entry forms. No entry fee. Awards a silver medal, struck in Idaho silver. "Children vote for their favorite books from a list of titles nominated by librarians, teachers, students and other interested persons." Contact Carole Monlux at Paxson Elementary School Library, 101 Evans, Missoula MT 59801; (406)542-4055; fax: (406)543-5358; e-mail: monlux@montana.com.

THE ANNA ZORNIO MEMORIAL CHILDREN'S THEATRE PLAYWRITING AWARD, University of New Hampshire Theatre in Education Program, Department of Theatre and Dance, Paul Creative Arts Center, 30 College Rd., University of New Hampshire, Durham NH 03824-3538. (603)862-2291. Fax: (603)862-0298. E-mail: jbrinker@cis.unix.unh.edu. Website: www.unh.edu/theatre-dance. Contact: Julie Brinker. Contest every 4 years; next contest is 2001. Estab. 1979. Purpose of the award: "to honor the late Anna Zornio, an alumna of The University of New Hampshire, for dedication to and inspiration of children's theater playwriting. Open to playwrights who are residents of the U.S. and Canada. Production should run about 45 minutes." Unpublished submissions only. Submissions made by the author. Deadline for entries: September 1, 2001. SASE for award rules and entry forms. No entry fee. Awards $1,000 plus guaranteed production. Judging by faculty committee. Acquires rights to campus production. Write for details.

Helpful Books & Publications

The editor of *Children's Writer's & Illustrator's Market* suggests the following books and periodicals to keep you informed on writing and illustrating techniques, trends in the field, business issues, industry news and changes, and additional markets.

BOOKS

☑ **AN AUTHOR'S GUIDE TO CHILDREN'S BOOK PROMOTION**, by Susan Salzman Raab, 345 Millwood Rd., Chappaqua NY 10514. (914)241-2117. E-mail: info@raabassociates.com. Website: www.raabassociates.com/authors.htm.

CHILDREN'S WRITER GUIDE, (annual), The Institute of Children's Literature, 95 Long Ridge Rd., West Redding CT 55104. (800)443-6078.

CHILDREN'S WRITER'S REFERENCE, by Berthe Amoss and Eric Suben, Writer's Digest Books, 1507 Dana Ave., Cincinnati OH 45207. (800)289-0963. Website: www.writersdigest.com.

CHILDREN'S WRITER'S WORD BOOK, by Alijandra Mogilner, Writer's Digest Books, 1507 Dana Ave., Cincinnati OH 45207. (800)289-0963. Website: www.writersdigest.com.

🆕 **CREATING CHARACTERS KIDS WILL LOVE**, by Elaine Marie Alphin, Writer's Digest Books, 1507 Dana Ave., Cincinnati OH 45207. (800)289-0963. Website: www.writersdigest.com.

GETTING STARTED AS A FREELANCE ILLUSTRATOR OR DESIGNER, by Michael Fleischman, North Light Books, 1507 Dana Ave., Cincinnati OH 45207. (800)289-0963. Website: www.writersdigest.com.

GUIDE TO LITERARY AGENTS, (annual) edited by Donya Dickerson, Writer's Digest Books, 1507 Dana Ave., Cincinnati OH 45207. (800)289-0963. Website: www.writersdigest.com.

HOW TO PROMOTE YOUR CHILDREN'S BOOK: A SURVIVAL GUIDE, by Evelyn Gallardo, Primate Production, P.O. Box 3038, Manhattan Beach CA 90266, Website: www.evegallardo.com/promote.html.

HOW TO SELL YOUR PHOTOGRAPHS & ILLUSTRATIONS, by Elliot & Barbara Gordon, North Light Books, 1507 Dana Ave., Cincinnati OH 45207. (800)289-0963.

HOW TO WRITE A CHILDREN'S BOOK & GET IT PUBLISHED, by Barbara Seuling, Charles Scribner's Sons, 1230 Avenue of the Americas, New York NY 10020. (212)702-2000.

HOW TO WRITE AND ILLUSTRATE CHILDREN'S BOOKS AND GET THEM PUBLISHED, edited by Treld Pelkey Bicknell and Felicity Trottman, Writer's Digest Books, 1507 Dana Ave., Cincinnati OH 45207. (800)289-0963. Website: www.writersdigest.com.

HOW TO WRITE AND SELL CHILDREN'S PICTURE BOOKS, by Jean E. Karl, Writer's Digest Books, 1507 Dana Ave., Cincinnati OH 45207. (800)289-0963. Website: www.writersdigest.com.

HOW TO WRITE ATTENTION-GRABBING QUERY & COVER LETTERS, by John Wood, Writer's Digest Books, 1507 Dana Ave., Cincinnati OH 45207. (800)289-0963. Website: www.writersdigest.com.

HOW TO WRITE, ILLUSTRATE, AND DESIGN CHILDREN'S BOOKS, by Frieda Gates, Lloyd-Simone Publishing Company, distributed by Library Research Associates, Inc., Dunderberg Rd. RD 6, Box 41, Monroe NY 10950. (914)783-1144.

LEGAL GUIDE FOR THE VISUAL ARTIST, 4th edition, by Tad Crawford, North Light Books, 1507 Dana Ave., Cincinnati OH 45207. (800)289-0963.

MARKET GUIDE FOR YOUNG WRITERS, Fifth Edition, by Kathy Henderson, Writer's Digest Books, 1507 Dana Ave., Cincinnati OH 45207. (800)289-0963. Website: www.writersdigest.com.

N STORY SPARKERS: A CREATIVITY GUIDE FOR CHILDREN'S WRITERS, by Marcia Thornton Jones and Debbie Dadey, Writer's Digest Books, 1507 Dana Ave., Cincinnati OH 45207. (800)289-0963. Website: www.writersdigest.com.

A TEEN'S GUIDE TO GETTING PUBLISHED, by Danielle Dunn & Jessica Dunn, Prufrock Press, P.O. Box 8813, Waco TX 76714-8813. (800)998-2208.

TEN STEPS TO PUBLISHING CHILDREN'S BOOKS, by Berthe Amoss & Eric Suben, Writer's Digest Books, 1507 Dana Ave., Cincinnati OH 45207. (800)289-0963. Website: www.writersdigest.com.

THE ULTIMATE PORTFOLIO, by Martha Metzdorf, North Light Books, 1507 Dana Ave., Cincinnati OH 45207. (800)289-0963.

THE WRITER'S DIGEST GUIDE TO MANUSCRIPT FORMATS, by Dian Dincin Buchman & Seli Groves, Writer's Digest Books, 1507 Dana Ave., Cincinnati OH 45207. (800)289-0963. Website: www.writersdigest.com.

THE WRITER'S ESSENTIAL DESK REFERENCE, Second Edition, Writer's Digest Books, 1507 Dana Ave., Cincinnati OH 45207. (800)289-0963. Website: www.writersdigest.com.

WRITING AND ILLUSTRATING CHILDREN'S BOOKS FOR PUBLICATION: TWO PERSPEC-TIVES, by Berthe Amoss and Eric Suben, Writer's Digest Books, 1507 Dana Ave., Cincinnati OH 45207. (800)289-0963. Website: www.writersdigest.com.

WRITING BOOKS FOR YOUNG PEOPLE, Second Edition, by James Cross Giblin, The Writer, Inc., 120 Boylston St., Boston MA 02116-4615. (617)423-3157.

WRITING FOR CHILDREN & TEENAGERS, Third Edition, by Lee Wyndham and Arnold Madison, Writer's Digest Books, 1507 Dana Ave., Cincinnati OH 45207. (800)289-0963. Website: www.writersdigest.com.

WRITING FOR YOUNG ADULTS, by Sherry Garland, Writer's Digest Books, 1507 Dana Ave., Cincinnati OH 45207. (800)289-0963. Website: www.writersdigest.com.

WRITING WITH PICTURES: HOW TO WRITE AND ILLUSTRATE CHILDREN'S BOOKS, by Uri Shulevitz, Watson-Guptill Publications, 1515 Broadway, New York NY 10036. (212)764-7300.

YOU CAN WRITE CHILDREN'S BOOKS, by Tracey E. Dils, Writer's Digest Books, 1507 Dana Ave., Cincinnati OH 45207. (800)289-0963. Website: www.writersdigest.com.

PUBLICATIONS

☑ BOOK LINKS: Connecting Books, Libraries and Classrooms, editor Judith O'Malley, American Library Association, 50 E. Huron St., Chicago IL 60611. (800)545-2433. Website: www.ala.org/BookLinks. *Magazine published 6 times a year (September-July) for the purpose of connecting books, libraries and classrooms. Features articles on specific topics followed by bibliographies recommending books for further information. Subscription: $25.95/year.*

☑ CHILDREN'S BOOK INSIDER, editor Laura Backes, 901 Columbia Rd., Ft. Collins CO 80525-1838. (970)495-0056 or (800)807-1916. E-mail: mail@write4kids.com. Website: www.write4kids.com. *Monthly newsletter covering markets, techniques and trends in children's publishing. Subscription: $29.95/year. Official update source for* Children's Writer's & Illustrator's Market, *featuring quarterly lists of changes and updates to listings in CWIM.*

☑ CHILDREN'S WRITER, editor Susan Tierney, The Institute of Children's Literature, 95 Long Ridge Rd., West Redding CT 06896-0811. (800)443-6078. Website: www.childrenswriter.com. *Monthly newsletter of writing and publishing trends in the children's field. Subscription: $26/year; special introductory rate: $15.*

☑ THE FIVE OWLS, editor Dr. Mark West, 2004 Sheridan Ave. S., Minneapolis MN 55405. (612)377-2004. Website: www.fiveowls.com. *Bimonthly newsletter for readers personally and professionally involved in children's literature. Subscription: $35/year.*

☑ **THE HORN BOOK MAGAZINE**, editor-in-chief Robert Sutton, The Horn Book Inc., 56 Roland St., Suite 200, Boston MA 02129. (800)325-1170. E-mail: info@hbook.com. Website: www.hbook.com. *Bimonthly guide to the children's book world including views on the industry and reviews of the latest books. Subscription: special introductory rate: $29.95.*

☑ **THE LION AND THE UNICORN: A CRITICAL JOURNAL OF CHILDREN'S LITERATURE**, editors Jack Zipes and Louisa Smith, The Johns Hopkins University Press, P.O. Box 19966, Baltimore MD 21211-0966. (800)548-1784 or (410)516-6987. Website: www.press.jhu.edu/press/journals/uni/uni.html. *Magazine published 3 times a year serving as a forum for discussion of children's literature featuring interviews with authors, editors and experts in the field. Subscription: $26.50/year.*

ONCE UPON A TIME, editor Audrey Baird, 553 Winston Court, St. Paul MN 55118. (651)457-6223. Fax: (651)457-9565. Website: http://members.aol.com/OUATMAG/. *Quarterly support magazine for children's writers and illustrators and those interested in children's literature. Subscription: $24.25/year.*

☑ **PUBLISHERS WEEKLY**, editor-in-chief Nora Rawlinson, Bowker Magazine Group, Cahners Publishing Co., 249 W. 17th St., New York NY 10011. (800)278-2991. Website: www.publishersweekly.com. *Weekly trade publication covering all aspects of the publishing industry; includes coverage of the children's field and spring and fall issues devoted solely to children's books. Subscription: $189/year. Available on newsstands for $4/issue. (Special issues are higher in price.)*

☑ **RIVERBANK REVIEW of books for young readers**, editor Martha Davis Beck, University of St. Thomas, 1000 LaSalle Ave., MOH-217, Minneapolis MN 55403-2009. (615)962-4372. E-mail: riverbank@sttho mas.edu. Website: http://department.stthomas.edu/RBR/. *Quarterly publication exploring the world of children's literature including book reviews, articles and essays. Subscription: $20/year.*

SOCIETY OF CHILDREN'S BOOK WRITERS AND ILLUSTRATORS BULLETIN, editors Stephen Mooser and Lin Oliver, SCBWI, 8271 Beverly Blvd., Los Angeles CA 90048. (323)782-1010. Website: www.scb wi.org/bulletin.htm. *Bimonthly newsletter of SCBWI covering news of interest to members. Subscription with $50/year membership.*

Get Your Children's Stories Published
with Help from These Writer's Digest Books!

2001 Guide to Literary Agents
Agents can open doors for you in the publishing industry. You can team up with an agent using this invaluable directory (now in its 9th year). Over 500 listings of literary and script agents, plus inside information on the industry will help you choose the right agent to represent you.
#10684/$21.99/368p/pb

Creating Characters Kids Will Love
The key to creating engaging stories for kids is developing vivid characters. Veteran children's author Elaine Alphin gives you concrete tips for bringing your characters to life.
#10669/$16.99/208p/pb

NEW!

Story Sparkers: A Creativity Guide for Children's Writers
Using exercises, worksheets and guidelines, this book shows you how to generate, assess, and apply ideas for fiction as well as nonfiction, in your children's stories.
#10700/$16.99/208p/pb

NEW!

How to Write and Illustrate Children's Books and Get Them Published
Consulting editors Treld Pelkey Bicknell and Felicity Trotman have brought together some of the finest talents in children's publishing to provide insightful and inspired instruction for writing and illustrating children's books. *New in paperback!*
#10694/$19.99/144p/pb

You Can Write Children's Books
Writer and editor Tracey Dils gives you the essential writing and submission guidelines you need to get your work in print. She reveals the hot trends in children's publishing, how to maintain a structured format, ways to target the right age group, how to produce a professional package, and more.
#10547/$12.99/128p/pb

Children's Writer's Word Book
This fast-reference guide will help to ensure your writing speaks to your young audience. Complete with word lists, thesaurus of synonyms, and tips on word usage and sentence length.
#10649/$16.99/352p/pb

Books are available at your local bookstore, or directly from the publisher using the order card on the reverse.

Useful Online Resources

The editor of *Children's Writer's & Illustrator's Market* suggests the following websites to keep you informed on writing and illustrating techniques, trends in the field, business issues, industry news and changes, and additional markets.

AMAZON.COM: www.amazon.com
Calling itself "A bookstore too big for the physical world," Amazon.com has more than 3 million books available on their website at discounted prices, plus a personal notification service of new releases, reader reviews, bestseller and suggested book information. Be sure to check out Amazon.com Kids.

ASSOCIATION FOR LIBRARY SERVICE TO CHILDREN: www.ala.org/alsc/awards.html
This site provides links to information about Newbery, Caldecott, Coretta Scott King and Michael L. Printz Awards as well as a host of other awards for notable children's books.

AUTHORS AND ILLUSTRATORS FOR CHILDREN WEBRING: www.webring.org/cgi-bin/webring?ring=aicwebring;list
Here you'll find a list of link of sites of interest to children's writers and illustrators or created by them.

THE AUTHORS GUILD ONLINE: www.authorsguild.org/
The website of The Authors Guild offers articles and columns dealing with contract issues, copyright, electronic rights and other legal issues of concern to writers.

☑ **BARNES & NOBLE ONLINE:** www.bn.com
The world's largest bookstore chain's website contains 600,000 in-stock titles at discount prices as well as personalized recommendations, online events with authors and book forum access for members.

BOOKWIRE: www.bookwire.com
A gateway to finding information about publishers, booksellers, libraries, authors, reviews and awards. Also offers frequently asked publishing questions and answers, a calendar of events, a mailing list and other helpful resources.

CANADIAN CHILDREN'S BOOK CENTRE: www3.sympatico.ca/ccbc/
The site for the CCBC includes profiles of illustrators and authors, information on recent books, a calendar of upcoming events, information on CCBC publications, and tips from Canadian children's authors.

THE CHILDREN'S BOOK COUNCIL: www.cbcbooks.org/
This site includes a complete list of CBC members with addresses, names and descriptions of what each publishes, and links to publishers' websites. Also offers previews of upcoming titles from members; articles from CBC Features, *the Council's newsletter; and their catalog.*

CHILDREN'S LITERATURE WEB GUIDE: www.ucalgary.ca/~dkbrown/index.html
This site includes stories, poetry, resource lists, lists of conferences, links to book reviews, lists of awards (international), and information on books from classic to contemporary.

☑ **CHILDREN'S PUBLISHERS' SUBMISSION GUIDELINES:** www.signaleader.com/childrens-writers/
This site features links to websites of children's publishers and magazines and includes information on which publishers offer submission guidelines online.

☑ **CHILDREN'S WRITER'S AND ILLUSTRATOR'S RESOURCE LIST:** www.pfdstudio.com/cwrl.html
Maintained by Peter Davis, this site includes lists of books on writing and illustrating, books on the business of illustration, organizations and periodicals and Internet resources.

☑ **CHILDREN'S WRITING SUPERSITE:** www.write4kids.com
This site (formerly Children's Writers Resource Center) includes highlights from the newsletter Children's Book Insider; *definitions of publishing terms; answers to frequently asked questions; information on trends; information on small presses; a research center for Web information; and a catalog of material available from CBI.*

THE DRAWING BOARD: http://members.aol.com/thedrawing
This site for illustrators features articles, interviews, links and resources for illustrators from all fields.

EDITOR & PUBLISHER: www.mediainfo.com
The Internet source for Editor & Publisher, *this site provides up-to-date industry news, with other opportunities such as a research area and bookstore, a calendar of events and classifieds.*

INKSPOT: www.inkspot.com
An elaborate site that provides information about workshops, how-to information, copyright, quotations, writing tips, resources, contests, market information (including children's writers marketplace), publishers, booksellers, associations, mailing lists, newsletters, conferences and more.

N INTERNATIONAL READING ASSOCIATION: www.reading.org
This website includes articles; book lists; event, conference and convention information; and an online bookstore.

KEYSTROKES: www.writelinks.com/keystrokes/
This online monthly newsletter for writers features articles on an array of topics, including topics related to writing for children. The site offers a years' worth of the newsletter.

ONCE UPON A TIME: http://members.aol.com/OUATMAG
This companion site to Once Upon A Time *magazine offers excerpts from recent articles, notes for prospective contributors, and information about OUAT's 11 regular columnists.*

N PICTUREBOOK: www.picture-book.com
This site brought to you by Picturebook *sourcebook offers tons of links for illustrators, portfolio searching, and news, and offers a listserv, bulletin board and chatroom.*

PUBLISHERS' CATALOGUES HOME PAGE: www.lights.com/publisher/index.html
A mammoth link collection of more than 6,000 publishers around the world arranged geographically. This site is one of the most comprehensive directories of publishers on the Internet.

N PUBLISHERS WEEKLY CHILDREN'S FEATURES: www.publishersweekly.com/childrensindex.asp
This is a direct link to Publishers Weekly *articles relating to children's publishing and authors.*

☑ THE PURPLE CRAYON: www.underdown.org
Editor Harold Underdown's site includes articles on trends, business, and cover letters and queries as well as interviews with editors and answers to frequently asked questions. He also includes links to a number of other sites helpful to writers.

SLANTVILLE: www.slantville.com/
An online artists community, this site includes a yellow pages for artists, frequently asked questions and a library offering information on a number of issues of interest to illustrators. This is a great site to visit to view artists' portfolios.

SOCIETY OF CHILDREN'S BOOK WRITERS AND ILLUSTRATORS: www.scbwi.org
This site includes information on awards and grants available to SCBWI members, a calendar of events listed by date and region, a list of publications available to members, and a site map for easy navigation. Balan welcomes suggestions for the site from visitors.

UNITED STATES POSTAL SERVICE: www.usps.gov/welcome.htm
Offers domestic and International postage rate calculator, stamp ordering, zip code look up, express mail tracking and more.

☑ VERLA KAY'S WEBSITE: www.verlakay.com
Author Verla Kay's website features writer's tips, articles, a schedules of online workshops (with transcripts of past workshops), a good news board and helpful links.

WRITERSDIGEST.COM: www.writersdigest.com
Brought to you by Writer's Digest *magazine and* Writer's Market, *this site features a hot list, conference listings, markets of the day, and a searchable database of more than 1,500 writer's guidelines.*

N WRITERSMARKET.COM: www.writersmarket.com
This gateway to the Writer's Market *online edition offers market news, FAQs, tips, featured markets and web resources, a free newsletter, and more.*

Glossary

AAR. Association of Authors' Representatives.

ABA. American Booksellers Association.

ABC. Association of Booksellers for Children.

Advance. A sum of money a publisher pays a writer or illustrator prior to the publication of a book. It is usually paid in installments, such as one half on signing the contract; one half on delivery of a complete and satisfactory manuscript. The advance is paid against the royalty money that will be earned by the book.

ALA. American Library Association.

All rights. The rights contracted to a publisher permitting the use of material anywhere and in any form, including movie and book club sales, without additional payment to the creator. (See The Business of Writing & Illustrating.)

Anthology. A collection of selected writings by various authors or gatherings of works by one author.

Anthropomorphization. The act of attributing human form and personality to things not human (such as animals).

ASAP. As soon as possible.

Assignment. An editor or art director asks a writer, illustrator or photographer to produce a specific piece for an agreed-upon fee.

B&W. Black and white.

Backlist. A publisher's list of books not published during the current season but still in print.

Biennially. Occurring once every 2 years.

Bimonthly. Occurring once every 2 months.

Biweekly. Occurring once every 2 weeks.

Book packager. A company that draws all elements of a book together, from the initial concept to writing and marketing strategies, then sells the book package to a book publisher and/or movie producer. Also known as book producer or book developer.

Book proposal. Package submitted to a publisher for consideration usually consisting of a synopsis, outline and sample chapters. (See Before Your First Sale.)

Business-size envelope. Also known as a #10 envelope. The standard size used in sending business correspondence.

Camera-ready. Refers to art that is completely prepared for copy camera platemaking.

Caption. A description of the subject matter of an illustration or photograph; photo captions include persons' names where appropriate. Also called cutline.

Clean-copy. A manuscript free of errors and needing no editing; it is ready for typesetting.

Clips. Samples, usually from newspapers or magazines, of a writer's published work.

Concept books. Books that deal with ideas, concepts and large-scale problems, promoting an understanding of what's happening in a child's world. Most prevalent are alphabet and counting books, but also includes books dealing with specific concerns facing young people (such as divorce, birth of a sibling, friendship or moving).

Contract. A written agreement stating the rights to be purchased by an editor, art director or producer and the amount of payment the writer, illustrator or photographer will receive for that sale. (See The Business of Writing & Illustrating.)

Contributor's copies. The magazine issues sent to an author, illustrator or photographer in which her work appears.

Co-op publisher. A publisher that shares production costs with an author, but, unlike subsidy publishers, handles all marketing and distribution. An author receives a high percentage of royalties until her initial investment is recouped, then standard royalties.

Copy. The actual written material of a manuscript.

Copyediting. Editing a manuscript for grammar usage, spelling, punctuation and general style.

Copyright. A means to legally protect an author's/illustrator's/photographer's work. This can be shown by writing ©, the creator's name, and year of work's creation. (See The Business of Writing & Illustrating.)

Cover letter. A brief letter, accompanying a complete manuscript, especially useful if responding to an editor's request for a manuscript. May also accompany a book proposal. (See Before Your First Sale.)

Cutline. See caption.

Disk. A round, flat magnetic plate on which computer data may be stored.

Division. An unincorporated branch of a company.

Dummy. A loose mock-up of a book showing placement of text and artwork.

Electronic submission. A submission of material by modem or on computer disk.

E-mail. Electronic mail. Messages sent from one computer to another via a modem or computer network.

Final draft. The last version of a polished manuscript ready for submission to an editor.

First North American serial rights. The right to publish material in a periodical for the first time, in the United States or Canada. (See The Business of Writing & Illustrating.)

Flat fee. A one-time payment.

Galleys. The first typeset version of a manuscript that has not yet been divided into pages.

Genre. A formulaic type of fiction, such as horror, mystery, romance, science fiction or western.

Glossy. A photograph with a shiny surface as opposed to one with a non-shiny matte finish.

Gouache. Opaque watercolor with an appreciable film thickness and an actual paint layer.

Halftone. Reproduction of a continuous tone illustration with the image formed by dots produced by a camera lens screen.

Hard copy. The printed copy of a computer's output.

Hardware. All the mechanically-integrated components of a computer that are not software—circuit boards, transistors and the machines that are the actual computer.

Hi-Lo. High interest, low reading level.

Home page. The first page of a website.

Imprint. Name applied to a publisher's specific line of books.

Internet. A worldwide network of computers that offers access to a wide variety of electronic resources.

IRA. International Reading Association.

IRC. International Reply Coupon. Sold at the post office to enclose with text or artwork sent to a foreign buyer to cover postage costs when replying or returning work.

Keyline. Identification, through signs and symbols, of the positions of illustrations and copy for the printer.

Layout. Arrangement of illustrations, photographs, text and headlines for printed material.

Line drawing. Illustration done with pencil or ink using no wash or other shading.

Mass market books. Paperback books directed toward an extremely large audience sold in supermarkets, drugstores, airports, newsstands and bookstores.

Mechanicals. Paste-up or preparation of work for printing.

Middle grade. See middle reader.

Middle reader. The general classification of books written for readers approximately ages 9-11. Also called middle grade.

Modem. A small electrical box that plugs into the serial card of a computer, used to transmit data from one computer to another, usually via telephone lines.

Ms (mss). Manuscript(s).

NCTE. National Council of Teachers of English.

One-time rights. Permission to publish a story in periodical or book form one time only. (See The Business of Writing & Illustrating.)

Outline. A summary of a book's contents in 5-15 double-spaced pages; often in the form of chapter headings with a descriptive sentence or two under each heading to show the scope of the book.

Package sale. The sale of a manuscript and illustrations/photos as a "package" paid for with one check.

Payment on acceptance. The writer, artist or photographer is paid for her work at the time the editor or art director decides to buy it.

Payment on publication. The writer, artist or photographer is paid for her work when it is published.

Photostat. Black and white copies produced by an inexpensive photographic process using paper negatives; only line values are held with accuracy. Also called stat.

Picture book. A type of book aimed at preschoolers to 8-year-olds that tells a story using a combination of text and artwork.

Print. An impression pulled from an original plate, stone, block, screen or negative; also a positive made from a photographic negative.

Proofreading. Reading a typescript to correct typographical errors.

Query. A letter to an editor designed to capture interest in an article or book you have written or propose to write. (See Before Your First Sale.)

Reading fee. Money charged by some agents and publishers to read a submitted manuscript.

Reprint rights. Permission to print an already published work whose first rights have been sold to another magazine or book publisher. (See The Business of Writing & Illustrating.)

Response time. The average length of time it takes an editor or art director to accept or reject a query or submission and inform the creator of the decision.

Rights. The bundle of permissions offered to an editor or art director in exchange for printing a manuscript, artwork or photographs. (See The Business of Writing & Illustrating.)

Rough draft. A manuscript that has not been checked for errors in grammar, punctuation, spelling or content.

Roughs. Preliminary sketches or drawings.

Royalty. An agreed percentage paid by a publisher to a writer, illustrator or photographer for each copy of her work sold.

SAE. Self-addressed envelope.

SASE. Self-addressed, stamped envelope.

SCBWI. The Society of Children's Book Writers and Illustrators. (See listing in Clubs & Organizations section.)

Second serial rights. Permission for the reprinting of a work in another periodical after its first publication in book or magazine form. (See The Business of Writing & Illustrating.)

Semiannual. Occurring every 6 months or twice a year.

Semimonthly. Occurring twice a month.

Semiweekly. Occurring twice a week.

Serial rights. The rights given by an author to a publisher to print a piece in one or more periodicals. (See The Business of Writing & Illustrating.)

Simultaneous submissions. Queries or proposals sent to several publishers at the same time. (See Before Your First Sale.)

Slant. The approach to a story or piece of artwork that will appeal to readers of a particular publication.

Slush pile. Editors' term for their collections of unsolicited manuscripts.

Software. Programs and related documentation for use with a computer.

Solicited manuscript. Material that an editor has asked for or agreed to consider before being sent by a writer.

SPAR. Society of Photographers and Artists Representatives.

Speculation (spec). Creating a piece with no assurance from an editor or art director that it will be purchased or any reimbursements for material or labor paid.

Stat. See photostat.

Subsidiary rights. All rights other than book publishing rights included in a book contract, such as paperback, book club and movie rights. (See The Business of Writing & Illustrating.)

Subsidy publisher. A book publisher that charges the author for the cost of typesetting, printing and promoting a book. Also called a vanity publisher.

Synopsis. A brief summary of a story or novel. Usually a page to a page and a half, single-spaced, if part of a book proposal.

Tabloid. Publication printed on an ordinary newspaper page turned sideways and folded in half.

Tearsheet. Page from a magazine or newspaper containing your printed art, story, article, poem or photo.

Thumbnail. A rough layout in miniature.

Trade books. Books sold strictly in bookstores, aimed at a smaller audience than mass market books, and printed in smaller quantities by publishers.

Transparencies. Positive color slides; not color prints.

Unsolicited manuscript. Material sent without an editor's or art director's request.

Vanity publisher. See subsidy publisher.

Word processor. A computer that produces typewritten copy via automated text-editing, storage and transmission capabilities.

World Wide Web. An Internet resource that utilizes hypertext to access information. It also supports formatted text, illustrations and sounds, depending on the user's computer capabilities.

Work-for-hire. An arrangement between a writer, illustrator or photographer and a company under which the company retains complete control of the work's copyright. (See The Business of Writing & Illustrating.)

YA. See young adult.

Young adult. The general classification of books written for readers approximately ages 12-18. Often referred to as YA.

Young reader. The general classification of books written for readers approximately ages 5-8.

Age-Level Index

This index lists book and magazine publishers by the age-groups for which they publish. Use it to locate appropriate markets for your work, then carefully read the listings and follow the guidelines of each publisher. Use this index in conjunction with the Subject Index to further narrow your list of markets. **Picture Books** and **Picture-Oriented Material** are for preschoolers to 8-year-olds; **Young Readers** are for 5- to 8-year-olds; **Middle Readers** are for 9- to 11-year-olds; and **Young Adults** are for ages 12 and up.

BOOK PUBLISHERS

Middle Readers

MAGAZINES

Picture-Oriented Material

Young Readers

Middle Readers

Subject Index

This index lists book and magazine publishers by the fiction and nonfiction subject area in which they publish. Use it to locate appropriate markets for your work, then carefully read the listings and follow the guidelines of each—publisher. Use this index in conjunction with the Age-Level Index to further narrow your list of markets.

BOOK PUBLISHERS: FICTION

BOOK PUBLISHERS: NONFICTION

Social Issues

Special Needs

Sports

MAGAZINES: FICTION

MAGAZINES: NONFICTION

Live Wire 238
National Geographic World 239
Spider 248
Turtle Magazine 250

Health
American Cheerleader 212
Blabber Mouth 213
Boys' Life 214
Careers & Colleges 216
Child Life 218
Children's Digest 218
Children's Playmate 218
College Bound Magazine 220
CosmoGIRL! 221
Discovery 222
DynaMath 225
Encounter 225
For Seniors Only 227
Girls' Life 228
Highlights for Children 229
Holidays & Seasonal Celebrations 230
Humpty Dumpty's Magazine 231
I.D. 232
Insight 232
Kids' Wall Street News 237
Listen 238
Live Wire 238
National Geographic World 239
On the Line 242
Seventeen Magazine 246
Today's Christian Teen 249
Touch 250
Turtle Magazine 250
U*S* Kids 250
What! A Magazine 251
Winner 252
YES Mag 253
Young & Alive 253
ZILLIONS 254

History
Advocate, PKA's Publication 211
Archaeology's Dig 213
Blabber Mouth 213
Boys' Life 214
Boys' Quest 214
Calliope 215
Children's Digest 218
Children's Playmate 218
Cobblestone 219
Cricket Magazine 221
Discoveries 222
Discovery 222

DynaMath 225
Faces 225
Footsteps 227
Friend Magazine, The 228
Guideposts for Kids 228
Highlights for Children 229
Holidays & Seasonal Celebrations 230
I.D. 232
Jack and Jill 232
Kids' Wall Street News 237
Live Wire 238
Muse 239
National Geographic World 239
New Moon 240
On the Line 242
Power and Light 243
READ 244
Skipping Stones 247
Spider 248
U*S* Kids 250
Young & Alive 253

Hobbies
Advocate, PKA's Publication 211
Blabber Mouth 213
Children's Digest 218
Cricket Magazine 221
Crusader 221
Discovery 222
DynaMath 225
Encounter 225
Focus on the Family Clubhouse; Focus on the Family Clubhouse Jr. 226
Fox Kids Magazine 227
Girls' Life 228
Highlights for Children 229
Hopscotch 230
Jump 237
Listen 238
National Geographic World 239
New Moon 240
Nick Jr. Magazine 240
On Course 242
On the Line 242
Seventeen Magazine 246
Touch 250
U*S* Kids 250
What! A Magazine 251
Winner 252
ZILLIONS 254

How-to
Advocate, PKA's Publication 211
American Cheerleader 212

Blabber Mouth 213
Boys' Quest 214
Career World 216
Careers & Colleges 216
Children's Digest 218
Children's Playmate 218
Chirp 218
Class Act 219
College Bound Magazine 220
CosmoGIRL! 221
Cricket Magazine 221
Crusader 221
Crystal Ball, The 222
Discovery 222
Discovery Trails 223
Dramatics 224
DynaMath 225
Encounter 225
Faces 225
Focus on the Family Clubhouse; Focus on the Family Clubhouse Jr. 226
For Seniors Only 227
Fox Kids Magazine 227
Friend Magazine, The 228
Guideposts for Kids 228
Guideposts for Teens 229
Highlights for Children 229
Hopscotch 230
Humpty Dumpty's Magazine 231
I.D. 232
Inteen 232
Jack and Jill 232
Listen 238
Live Wire 238
Nature Friend Magazine 239
Nick Jr. Magazine 240
On the Line 242
Power and Light 243
Seventeen Magazine 246
Touch 250
U*S* Kids 250
What! A Magazine 251
Winner 252
With 252
Young Salvationist 254
ZILLIONS 254

Humor
Advocate, PKA's Publication 211
Blabber Mouth 213
Boys' Quest 214
Careers & Colleges 216
Chickadee 217
Child Life 218

Poetry Index

This index lists markets that are open to poetry submissions and is divided into book publishers and magazines. It's important to carefully read the listings and follow the guidelines of each publisher to which you submit.

Photography Index

This index lists markets that buy photos from freelancers, and is divided inbo book publishers, magazines and greeting cards. It's important to carefully read the listings and follow the guidelines of each publisher to which you submit.

General Index

Market listings that appeared in the 2000 edition of *Children's Writer's & Illustrator's Market* but do not appear in this edition are identified with a two-letter code explaining why the listing was omitted: **(NR)**—No (or late) Response to Listing Request; **(NS)**—Not Currently Accepting Submissions; **(RP)**—Business Restructured or Purchased; **(RR)**—Removed by Request; **(OB)**—Out of Business; **(UC)**—Unable to Contact; **(UF)**—Uncertain Future.